THE PROVISIONAL AUSTRIAN
REGIME IN LOMBARDY-VENETIA, 1814–1815

THE
PROVISIONAL
AUSTRIAN REGIME
IN LOMBARDY-VENETIA
1814–1815

R. JOHN RATH

UNIVERSITY OF TEXAS PRESS

AUSTIN & LONDON

Standard Book Number 292–78385–X
Library of Congress Catalog Card No. 69–18808
Copyright © 1969 R. John Rath

Type set by G&S Typesetters, Austin
Printed by Von Boeckmann-Jones Company, Austin
Bound by Universal Bookbindery, Inc., San Antonio

To Isabel Swain
and
Isabel Ferguson

PREFACE

After five days of bitter fighting between March 18 and March 23, 1848, the Habsburg troops under the command of Field Marshal Joseph Wenzel Radetzky were forced to withdraw from Milan to the fortresses of the Quadrilateral. On March 22 Venetian liberals occupied the arsenal without encountering any resistance. From Milan and Venice the revolt spread throughout Lombardy and Venetia. Although the revolution collapsed in Lombardy when Radetzky's troops re-entered Milan on August 8, the flames of rebellion were not extinguished in Venice before August 25, 1849.

As elsewhere in Europe, the 1848–1849 revolutionary movement in Lombardy and Venetia had a strong nationalist and liberal coloration. The revolutionists were ardently pro-Italian and violently anti-Austrian. They fought for a constitutional government with the usual guarantees of individual rights demanded by the liberals of that time.

The spread of the revolutionary movement to Lombardy and Venetia made it clear that the prevailing European nationalist and liberal ideologies had by then made a deep imprint on the politically conscious intelligentsia and bourgeoisie as well as on other groups in the two provinces. It also became obvious that by 1848 a large number of Lombards and Venetians were permeated by a deep distrust, intense dislike, and even bitter hatred of their Austrian governors. Why? Was it that the forces of nationalism and liberalism had become so irrepressible that an alien monarch who had not allowed his powers to be limited by a "liberal" constitution, no matter how just, benevolent, or enlightened his rule, could contain them only with naked military force? Or was it that the policies and practices of the Austrians were so arbitrary, shortsighted, and oppressive that they drove to revolt a populace which had during the Napoleonic era looked back with fond remembrances to the benign regime of Maria Theresa? Or was it a combination of both these factors that explains the ever increasing alienation of the political elite from the Habsburg government?

Some of the answers to such questions can be found, at least in part, by a detailed analysis of the shifts of public opinion and the political, administrative, economic, and cultural policies and practices pursued in Lombardy-Venetia by the Austrians during the first two years of their occupation—a period when the permanent political, administrative, and economic system which was later to be adopted in the area was still in the process of formation. Many of the basic principles which were later to serve as guidelines for Habsburg policies and practices until 1848, or even 1859, were formulated during the first two years of provisional administration. Moreover, many of the attitudes adopted by the newly re-acquired Italian subjects of the monarchy towards their Austrian rulers were based on what they saw or thought they saw of Austrian rule during the first two critical years following the return of the Habsburgs to the area.

In evaluating Habsburg rule in Italy between 1813 and 1815, as well as later, one must make a sharp distinction between Lombardy and Venetia, for both the political opinions of the inhabitants and the practices of the Austrians were very different in the two areas, especially during the period covered by this study. Such a differentiation has heretofore not been adequately taken into account. All too frequently writers have led readers to believe that the attitude of the Venetians towards the Habsburgs was basically the same as that of the Lombard middle class.

In the past too much stress has been put on political history, the "liberal" and "patriotic" views of anti-Austrian Lombard intellectuals and bourgeoisie, and the machinations of the secret societies. Moreover, at least a few of the conjectures of the past half century about the widespread discontent with Habsburg rule in 1814–1815 and the role played by secret societies in various liberal plots have been based at least partly on evidence that is open to question. Then, too, with the notable exception of some of the works of such men as Alessandro Luzio and Domenico Spadoni, much that has been written by the older generation of Italian historians has been colored by their strong liberal and nationalist predilections. Furthermore, thus far very little attention has been paid to economic conditions or to Austrian economic policies and practices, which played a significant role in determining the initial reaction of many elements of the population to the newly restored Habsburg administration.

Essential as a study of the Austrian provisional regime in Lombardy-Venetia is to an understanding of Austro-Italian relations during the first half of the nineteenth century, nothing has been written that presents the reader with a comprehensive view of the whole subject since Joseph Alexander von Helfert published his *Ausgang der französischen Herrschaft in Ober-Italien und Brescia-Miländer Militär-Verschwörung* in 1890 and his *Kaiser Franz I. von Österreich und die Stiftung des Lombardo-Venetianischen Königreichs* in 1901. Helfert wrote little about economic matters and devoted the major part of his account to Lombardy. In his *La restaurazione austriaca a Milano nel 1814* Francesco Lemmi concentrated his attention almost exclusively on Lombardy and wrote little about most aspects of the subject discussed in the present volume. Augusto Sandonà's classic *Il Regno Lombardo Veneto 1814–1859* (1912) is mainly concerned with Habsburg administrative affairs during a later period. Domenico Spadoni's monumental three-volume *Milano e la congiura militare nel 1814 per l'indipendenza italiana* (1936–1937) deals exclusively with the liberal movement in Lombardy, the Brescian-Milanese conspiracy, and the trial of its ringleaders. Such twentieth century scholars as Alessandro Luzio, Angelo Ottolini, Oreste Dito, Pietro Pedrotti, Ilario Rinieri, Renato Soriga, Armando Saitta, and Carlo Francovich for the most part have written about the liberal and nationalist movement and secret societies.

The present writer has attempted to deal with all facets of Lombard and Venetian history between October, 1813, when Habsburg troops first set foot on Italian soil, and the spring of 1815, when Joachim Murat's efforts to establish an independent Italy under his domination ended in failure and when the outlines of the permanent government which the Austrians intended to establish in Lombardy-Venetia were clearly spelled out in the imperial patent of April 7, 1815. Much of his study is based on archival materials in Vienna, Milan, and Venice. Some of the most important documents dealing with the Austrian administration in Lombardy-Venetia were either totally ruined or else seriously damaged when the Austrian ministry of justice palace was set on fire during the July 15, 1927, riots. Fortunately, summaries of many pertinent records stored in this building could be found in the *Staats-Rath Akten* and the *Conferenz Akten*, both of which were housed in the *Haus-, Hof-, und Staatsarchiv*. Unfortunately the part of both of these collections that deals with the first half of the nineteenth century, which was transported to what was believed to be a safe hiding place in Upper Austria, was entirely destroyed during the last days of fighting between German and United States troops in the spring of 1945. While he was in Vienna as a pre-doctoral Social Science Research Council Fellow shortly before the second World War broke out, the present writer managed to take detailed notes on all documents in both collections pertaining to Lombardy-Venetia during the period discussed in this book.

The writer was not so fortunate with valuable documents in the *Archivio di Stato* of Milan destroyed during the last war. He managed to take only fragmentary notes for 1814 from just part of them. Among the invaluable collections that were ruined were the *Commissione Plenipotenziaria presieduta dal Conte di Bellegarde* and the trial records of the Brescian-Milanese conspirators, which Domenico Spadoni found after many years of careful search. Some of the documents that survived the ravages of World War II, especially those designated as "*Atti secreti*" or "*Atti secretissimi*," need to be scrutinized with great care, for they consist of reports of secret informers or agents who were often highly inaccurate in the information which they supplied to their superior officials. Be that as it may, the *Atti secreti* of the *Presidenza di governo*, which are very significant for this study, are intact, as are the papers in the *Uffici e Tribunali Regi* collection. Of equal importance for this study, thirty years ago Spadoni published detailed and careful summaries of all the protocols of the trial of the Brescian-Milanese conspirators. Then, too, the rich documentary collections dealing with the period that are in the *Archivio di Stato* in Venice are wholly intact. In this archive are many documents that apply to Lombardy, if only indirectly, as well as to Venetia.

The writer is deeply indebted to numerous persons and institutions for the assistance which they so kindly gave him in pursuing his study. In the first place, he wishes to thank the directors of the *Haus-, Hof-, und Staatsarchiv*, the *Kriegs-Archiv*, the *Hofkammer Archiv*, and the *Verwaltungsarchiv*, in Vienna; the *Archivio di Stato* of Milan; and the *Archivio di Stato* of Venice for their help in providing him with the appropriate documents in their custody. He also wishes to express his appreciation to the directors of the *Österreichische Nationalbibliothek*; the *Biblioteca di San Marco* and the *Museo del Risorgimento italiano*, of Venice; the *Biblioteca Ambrosiana*, the *Biblioteca Braidense*, and the *Museo del Risorgimento*, of Milan; the Widener Library, of Harvard University; and The University of

Texas Library for the helpful manner in which their personnel put material at his disposal.

As has already been mentioned, a pre-doctoral Social Science Research Council Fellowship made it possible for the author to examine the documents used in this study that were later destroyed during World War II. All the archival sources and other manuscripts as well as many books examined since the war were studied by him while he was a Guggenheim Fellow in Italy. This writer wishes to express his deep appreciation to the Guggenheim Memorial Foundation for making it possible for him to devote his attention for most of a year to Austrian policies and practices in Lombardy-Venetia between 1814 and 1821. He also wishes to thank The University of Texas Committee on Research and Creative Writing for a grant allowing him to devote a semester to research on this topic. In addition, he wants to acknowledge his debt to Rice University for a substantial grant for the publication of this book.

The manuscript was typed by Kathlyn Knobloch, formerly of the editorial staff of the *Austrian History Yearbook*. The index was prepared by Mrs. Stephanie Lowe. The maps were drawn by Clifford Woerner, of The University of Texas. The author's wife spent countless hours in proofreading and other assistance. He wishes to thank her for invaluable advice and encouragement that were so valuable for the completion of the work.

R. John Rath
Houston, Texas

CONTENTS

LIST OF MAPS

THE PROVISIONAL AUSTRIAN
REGIME IN LOMBARDY-VENETIA, 1814–1815

Chapter 1

THE PROVISIONAL GOVERNMENT IN VENETIA

On August 12, 1813, the Habsburg emperor declared war on Napoleon. In September an Austrian corps under the supreme command of General Johann von Hiller[1] crossed the Drava and, aided by an insurrection of the Dalmatians and Croatians, quickly ousted the French from Illyria. By October 5 Austrian troops were in possession of Laibach, the Illyrian capital. Then, pushing westward, Habsburg troops crossed the Isonzo on October 24, forcing Prince Eugene,[2] Napoleon's viceroy in the Kingdom of Italy, to withdraw to Udine and then, on November 4, to Verona, on the Adige. At the same time, General Peter Marchall occupied Mestre to blockade Venice, with the help of British naval detachments. Moving further southward, contingents led by General Anton Gundaker Starhemberg occupied Rovigo on December 9. By the middle of December most of Venetia was under Austrian control.

In the meantime, the king of Bavaria's abandonment of his alliance with Napoleon on October 8 freed troops stationed in Western Austria to cross the Alps and advance down the Adige to threaten the

[1] Baron Johann von Hiller (1754–1819), the son of a colonel in the Habsburg army, spent his whole life in the army. Advancing through the ranks from cadet (to which rank he was appointed in 1769) to colonel (in 1793), he was appointed major general in 1794 and lieutenant field marshal in 1799. From 1801 to 1805 he was commandant in Innsbruck. From 1805 to 1809 he was commanding general in the Tyrol and Vorarlberg; from 1809 to 1811, in Croatia; and from 1811 to 1813, in Slavonia. In 1813 he was appointed commander of the Inner Austrian army. The next year he became commanding general in Transylvania. Later he served in the same capacity in Galicia. He died at Lemberg.

[2] Prince Eugène de Beauharnais (1781–1824), the son of Napoleon's first wife and General Alexandre de Beauharnais, was Napoleon's viceroy in the Kingdom of Italy from 1805 to 1814. He retired to Bavaria in 1814. In 1817 he acquired the titles of duke of Leuchtenberg and prince of Eichstätt.

French-Italian army from the north, while Joachim Murat's[3] desertion of his brother-in-law on January 11, 1814, and his subsequent occupation of Ferrara and Bologna on January 18 brought new dangers to Eugene's forces from the south. In order to shorten his lines, Prince Eugene abandoned the Adige on February 4 to take up a defensive position behind the Mincio River. Four days later General Heinrich Joseph Bellegarde,[4] who had on December 15, 1813, succeeded General Hiller as commander-in-chief of the Austrian army in Italy, made a vain attempt to cross the Mincio to attack him.

Early in March a third power entered the theater of combat in Italy. On March 7, English, Sicilian, and German forces under the command of Lord William Bentinck[5] disembarked at Leghorn, from which they departed to capture Genoa. On April 13 Murat crossed the Taro. Two days later his forces drove the French out of Piacenza, on the Po. Meanwhile, the Austrian army on the Mincio was steadily winning ground. By the middle of April the viceroy's position was utterly hopeless. Upon hearing that his stepfather had, on April 11, renounced his rights to the throne in the Treaty of Fontainebleau, Prince Eugene formally gave up the struggle on April 16 by signing

[3] Joachim Murat (1767–1815), one of Napoleon's marshals and the husband of his sister Caroline, was chosen in 1808 to succeed Napoleon's brother Joseph as king of Naples. In March, 1815, he deserted his new allies to again join forces with Napoleon. After his defeat at Tolentino in May, 1815, he fled to Corsica. In the fall of 1815 he attempted to regain Naples but was arrested and executed.

[4] Count Heinrich Joseph Johann Bellegarde (1756–1845), the son of a Saxon infantry general, entered the Habsburg military service as a second lieutenant in 1772. He won rapid promotions in the Austrian army. In 1789 he became a colonel, and three years later he was promoted to the rank of major general. In 1799 he was made commander of the Army of the Tyrol. After the battle of Marengo he was called to the command of the Italian army. In 1809 he was named a field marshal. The next year he was appointed president of the aulic war council. In 1814 he became imperial commissioner for the newly re-acquired Italian provinces. The next year he was made grand master of the Habsburg court in Italy. In 1820 he was called for a second time to the presidency of the aulic war council. He retired from active service in 1825.

[5] Lord William C. Bentinck (1774–1839), after commanding one of the divisions of Sir Arthur Wellesley's army, served as governor of Madras (1803–1807). In 1811 he was named ambassador to Sicily and commander-in-chief of the British troops stationed on that island. There he interfered much in political affairs and deprived the Bourbon monarch, Ferdinand IV, of most of his powers. After the 1814 campaign Bentinck returned to Palermo, from which city he was driven by the king in July, 1814. Now in disgrace, Bentinck was appointed to only one other government post: that of governor general of Bengal (1828–1836).

the Convention of Schiarino-Rizzino. In accord with the stipulations of this agreement, Austrian contingents entered the fortresses of Legnago, Palmanova, Osoppo, and Venice on April 20. After still another convention was signed at Mantua on the 23rd, Peschiera was handed over to the Allies on April 24 and Mantua on May 1. The remaining fortresses and towns surrendered to the first Austrian troops that arrived.[6]

The territory in northern Italy conquered by the Austrian army and assigned to the Habsburgs by the Allied Powers in 1814 was a rich prize. Of the twenty-four departments of the former Kingdom of Italy, one (Alto Adige) was incorporated in the Tyrol and part of another (Passariano) was united with the Küstenland. Thirteen of the twenty-four became parts of the provinces of Lombardy and Venetia. The department of Adda, comprising the Valtelline, Chiavenna, and Bormio, which the Swiss Confederation insisted should be incorporated into Swiss territory, was placed under Austrian military occupation in 1814 and added to Lombardy the next year. The rest of the areas of the former Kingdom of Italy went to the Papal States, Modena, and Sardinia.[7]

Lombardy and Venetia together had an area of 787.30 German, or 17,509 English, square miles and, in 1813, a population of 4,125,941.

[6] For more detailed discussions of the 1813–1814 Italian campaign, see especially my *The Fall of the Napoleonic Kingdom of Italy (1814)* (No. 484 of *Studies in History, Economics and Public Law*), pp. 45–61; Italy. Ministero della guerra, commando del corpo di stato maggiore—ufficio storico, *Gli Italiani in Illiria e nella Venezia (1813–1814)*, pp. 75–131; Ludwig von Welden, *Der Krieg der Österreicher in Italien gegen die Franzosen in den Jahren 1813 und 1814*; Georg von Holtz, *Die innerösterreichische Armee 1813 und 1814* (Vol. IV of Alois Veltzé [ed.], *1813–1815: Österreich in den Befreiungskriegen*); *Précis historique des opérations militaires de l'armée d'Italie, en 1813 et 1814, par le chef de l'état-major-général de cette armée; Journal historique sur la campagne du Prince Eugène, en Italie, pendant les années 1813 et 1814, par L. D****, capitaine attaché à l'état-major du Prince, et chevalier de la légion d'honneur*; and *Dernière campagne de l'armée franco-italienne, sous les ordres d'Eugène-Beauharnais, en 1813 et 1814, suivie de mémoires secrets sur la révolution de Milan, du 20 avril 1814, et les deux conjurations du 25 avril 1815; la campagne des Autrichiens contre Murat; sa mort tragique, et la situation politique actuelle des divers états d'Italie, par le chevalier S. J***, témoin oculaire*.

[7] Kübeck report to the aulic central organization commission on the organization of the re-acquired Upper-Italian provinces, Vienna, December 8, 1814, Joseph Alexander Helfert, *Zur Geschichte des Lombardo-Venezianischen Königreichs* (Vol. XCVIII of *Archiv für österreichische Geschichte*), Appendix I, pp. 261–263.

The departments east of the Mincio River, which comprised Venetia after 1814, had a combined area of 458.48 German, or 10,196 English, square miles and 2,021,502 inhabitants; Lombardy had 2,104,439 people and a territorial extent of 328.82 German, or 7,313 English, square miles.[8] Included in Lombardy were the eighteenth century duchies of Milan and Mantua and the regions of the former Venetian Republic which lay west of the Mincio (Brescia, Bergamo, and Crema). With the exception of a few former Venetian territories which were incorporated into the Küstenland, Austrian Venetia was made up of the former Venetian lands east of the Mincio.

In both Lombardy and Venetia the landscape was varied. The northernmost part of Lombardy, bordering on the crest of the Western Alps, was mainly a grazing area, with extensive cattle and sheep pastures, valuable tracts of timber, and small plots of arable land, either in tiny mountain valleys or on small terraces clinging to mountain slopes, on which grapevines, cereals, and hay were raised. Landholdings were small, but they were generally owned by the persons who actually farmed them. Below this region was the hill country, dominated by the beautiful Lombard lakes—Maggiore, Lugano, Como, Iseo, and Garda—and the upper reaches of the main rivers —the Olona, the Adda, and the Oglio. It was an area rich in orchards, mulberries, grapes, wheat, maize, and vegetables. Most of the land was tilled by sharecroppers rather than by peasant proprietors. The southern and, agriculturally speaking, by far the richest part of Lombardy, was the large, flat plain north of the Po, east of the Ticino, west of the Mincio, and south of a line passing from a little above Milan to a few miles below Brescia. This area was mostly a vast, irrigated plain through which flowed the water from the northern lakes and the mountain rivers to the Po. It was a land of rich rice fields and irrigated pastures, with mulberries and cereals raised in large quantities. It was a region of large estates, which required large capital investments for development. On the average, there was one farm for approximately every hundred agricultural workers.[9]

---

[8] Bellegarde report on the Austrian-Italian provinces, October 25, 1814, Joseph Alexander Helfert, *Kaiser Franz I. von Österreich und die Stiftung des Lombardo-Venetianischen Königreichs. Im Zusammenhang mit den gleichzeitigen allgemeinen Ereignissen und Zuständen Italiens* (Vol. VII of *Quellen und Forschungen zur Geschichte, Litteratur und Sprache Österreichs und seiner Kronländer*), Appendix I, pp. 521–522.

[9] Kent Roberts Greenfield, *Economics and Liberalism in the Risorgimento: A*

The capital and largest city, Milan, had a population of 134,528 in 1800. Other important towns were Mantua, Pavia, Brescia, Bergamo, Como, Cremona, and Lodi.

Although the geographic features of Venetia were as diverse as those in Lombardy, the land was less fertile and the inhabitants were less prosperous. In many mountainous areas, where lumbering, cattle raising, and sheepherding were the only profitable occupations, many a father or elder son, living on the barest level of existence even during the good years, had to supplement his meager income by working for several months of the year as an agricultural laborer in the adjacent plain or as an unskilled workman in Venice or some other town. The intermediate hill country, dominated by the Alpine valleys of the Adige, Brenta, Piave, Bacchiglione, and Tagliamento, was more flourishing though hardly opulent. Here grapes, mulberries, cattle, sheep, and cereals were the main products. Although the area along the Adriatic north of Venice was infertile, arid, and poorly cultivated, the rest of the Venetian plain constituted the backbone of the Venetian agricultural economy. The most productive and prosperous areas were the Polesine of Rovigo, which was the granary of Venetia, and the flat country centering around Padua and Vicenza, where the climate was excellent, the soil was rich, and there was an abundance of water for irrigation. Cereal crops, cattle, horses, sheep, and grapes abounded in this region, but frequent floods in many of these low-lying areas, crisscrossed by rivers and canals, made farming somewhat hazardous.[10] The capital, Venice, the population of which was somewhat smaller than that of Milan, was an important maritime center and noted for its manufacture of crystals, woollen and cotton goods, and clothing. Other important towns in Venetia were Padua, Verona, Vicenza, Treviso, and Udine.

Except for Brescia, Bergamo, and Crema (the provinces of the former Venetian Republic west of the Mincio), all Lombardo-Venetian territories acquired by the Habsburgs in 1814 had previously been under Austrian rule. In pre-revolutionary Lombardy, compris-

Study of Nationalism in Lombardy, 1814–1848, pp. 1–35; Matteo Bianchi, *Geografia politica dell'Italia*, pp. 702–708; Filippo de Boni, *Lo straniero in Lombardia*, pp. 113–115; Mario Romani, *L'agricoltura in Lombardia dal periodo delle riforme al 1859: struttura, organizzazione sociale e tecnica*, pp. 11–111.

[10] Observations on Venetia drawn up for Governor Goëss' personal use, March, 1815, *Archivio di Stato* (Venice) (hereafter cited as "A. S. [Venice]"), Presidio di governo, 1815, No. 85/v.b.p.; Bianchi, *Geografia dell'Italia*, pp. 791–798.

ing the duchies of Milan and Mantua—which the Habsburgs had acquired in 1713–1714—the administration was relatively simple and, for the most part, was in the hands of the Lombards themselves. During the reign of Maria Theresa the Lombard government was, after 1760, under the superintendence of the Italian department of the aulic chancellery in Vienna. In Milan the highest political authority was the governing conference, which was composed of the governor, a minister plenipotentiary, a state secretary, and two advisers. Under it, the financial magistracy oversaw the financial affairs of Lombardy, supervised the royal delegates in the provinces, and approved or disallowed the enactments of the state congregation, which was made up of deputies from each province and from the city of Milan and which administered the economic affairs of Lombardy and looked after the apportionment and collection of taxes. In each of the provinces was a royal delegate, assisted by a patrimonial congregation, which managed the property and economic affairs of the province. In addition, there was a general congregation, to which representatives were sent by the communes. It selected most of the members of the patrimonial congregations, examined their accounts, and advised them on the affairs of the province. Each province was divided into districts, in each of which a tax officer, the so-called *cancelliere del censo*, kept the tax register, supervised the collection of taxes, and executed the laws and decrees handed down to him by superior authorities in the communes which made up his district. Under his supervision, the communal governments—the lowest political units—administered the property of the communes and looked after all local matters. Under the chairmanship of the *cancelliere del censo*, a general communal assembly, attended by all taxpaying landowners, as well as by representatives chosen by persons who paid poll and trade and handicraft taxes, met twice a year to choose the communal officials (the syndic and the taxpayers' deputies), to check the accounts of the communal government, and to look after the most important communal affairs.

This uncomplicated administrative scheme, which left much power in the hands of the provincial and communal authorities and in which representatives of the people wielded considerable influence, did not, however, suit the absolutist and centralist ideas of Joseph II. In 1786 Joseph abolished the whole system, with the exception of the patrimonial congregations (whose powers he sharply limited), the *cancellieri del censo*, and the communal administrations. He re-

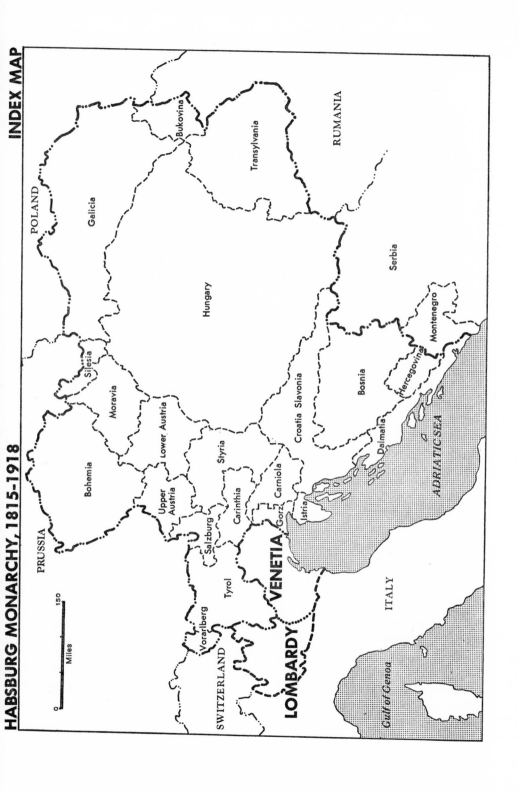

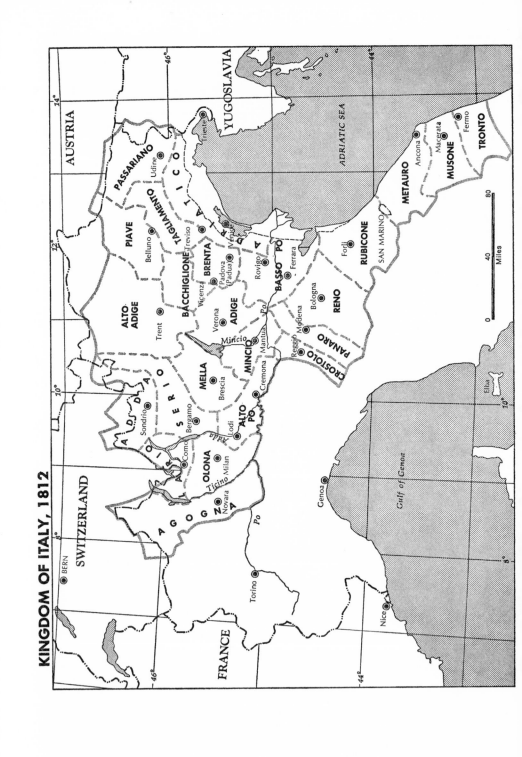

KINGDOM OF ITALY, 1812

LOMBARDY — VENETIA

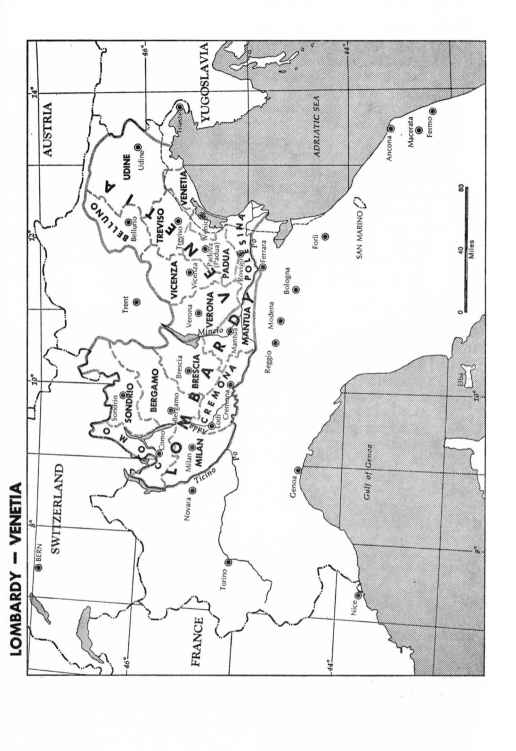

placed them with a more centralized government in Milan, presided over by a minister plenipotentiary; and with political intendants in the provinces, which had attributes similar to those of the district officials in the German provinces of the monarchy. In this way the new emperor created a hierarchy of officials who formed a regular chain of command through which orders could rapidly be transmitted from the top. Joseph's administrative system, however, lasted only until 1791, when Leopold II, yielding to the remonstrances of the Lombards over the privileges which they had lost, restored the old Maria Theresian system, with a few modifications of little real importance.[11]

Venetia did not go to Austria until 1798. For centuries the patrician families of the city of Venice had exercised their sovereignty over the *terra ferma* and over the transmarine possessions of the Venetian Republic in Istria, on various islands, and on the Dalmatian coast. Nowhere did the middle or lower classes have a voice in the government. Even the territorial nobility were excluded from citizenship. Nominal sovereignty was vested in the grand council, which the approximately one thousand patricians of the city who were at least twenty-five years old could attend. The grand council elected the members of the senate, which was the real center of political power. The *signoria* executed the measures enacted by the grand council and the senate. The council of ten was vested with police powers and investigated violations of good customs and morals, while a council of inquisitors protected the Republic against conspiracies and treason. At the head of the whole oligarchic edifice was an ornamental doge, with few actual powers but much pomp and dignity.[12]

---

[11] Bellegarde report on the Austrian-Italian provinces, October 25, 1814, Helfert, *Kaiser Franz und die Stiftung des Lombardo-Venetianischen Königreichs*, Appendix I, pp. 535–541; Kübeck report to the aulic central organization commission on the organization of the re-acquired Upper-Italian provinces, Vienna, December 8, 1814, Helfert, *Zur Geschichte des Lombardo-Venezianischen Königreichs*, Appendix I, pp. 263–270. See also Augusto Sandonà, *Il Regno Lombardo Veneto 1814–1859, la costituzione e l'amministrazione. Studi di storia e di diritto; con la scorta degli atti ufficiali dei dicasteri centrali di Vienna*, pp. 8–12; Ludwig von Simonyi, *Geschichte des Lombardisch Venezianischen Königreich: Charakteristisch-Artistisch-Topographisch-Statistisch- und Historisch*, Vol. II, pp. 399–408; and Carlo Tivaroni, *L'Italia prima della rivoluzione francese (1735–1789)* (Vol. I of his *Storia critica del Risorgimento italiano*), pp. 98–135.

[12] Tivaroni, *L'Italia prima della rivoluzione francese*, pp. 1–31; Kübeck report

When the Austrians took possession of the parts of Venetia east of the Mincio[13] they introduced a government that was almost like that in the German states. Under the supervision of the aulic chancellery and the aulic exchequer, a general government, located at Venice and headed by an imperial commissioner, looked after the political and financial affairs of the city of Venice and the *terra ferma*, while a police director superintended police and censorship activities. In addition, accounting and fiscal offices and a public works directory were attached to the general government. The special offices for customs, lottery, tobacco, the stamp tax, and domains, however, were directly dependent upon the exchequer in Vienna. The land was divided into seven captaincies or districts, each with a royal captainship, which had the same personnel and duties as the district governments of the old Austrian provinces. The organization of the local administrations had still not been completed when the Habsburgs had to surrender Venetia to the French in December, 1805.[14]

When the French assumed control of Lombardy in 1796 they created a Cisalpine Republic, which was comprised of Lombardy, the Venetian lands west of the Mincio, Modena, and the Papal Legations. In 1802 the Cisalpine Republic was transformed into the Italian Republic and then, in 1805, into the Kingdom of Italy. Venetia was incorporated into the latter in January, 1806. Later the Papal Marches and Duchies and the South Tyrol were also added to it.

Napoleon welded all these disparate regions together, like the other territories under his dominion, into a highly centralized political unit, nominally under the control of his viceroy, Eugene Beauharnais, but in reality under his own close personal supervision. The most important authority in the kingdom, next to the king and his

---

to the aulic central organization commission on the organization of the re-acquired Upper-Italian provinces, Vienna, December 8, 1814, Helfert, *Zur Geschichte des Lombardo-Venezianischen Königreichs*, Appendix I, pp. 270–271.

[13] The areas of the Venetian Republic west of the Mincio River had been taken over by France in 1796.

[14] Kübeck report to the aulic central organization commission on the organization of the re-acquired upper-Italian provinces, Vienna, December 8, 1814, Helfert, *Zur Geschichte des Lombardo-Venezianischen Königreichs*, Appendix I, p. 271; Joseph Kropatschek, *Oestreichs Staatsverfassung vereinbart mit den zusammengezogenen bestehenden Gesetzen, zum Gebrauche der Staatsbeamten, Advokaten, Oekonomen, Obrigkeiten, Magistraten, Geistlichen, Bürger und Bauern, zum Unterrichte, für angehende Geschäftsmänner*, Supplement, pp. 297–299.

viceroy, was the senate, the members of which were chosen by Napoleon himself. To it were presented proposed statutes and laws; treaties of peace, alliance, and commerce; declarations of war; conventions providing for the cession of territories; and the accounts of the various ministers. It decided the punishments which were to be meted out for excesses or abuses in ecclesiastical jurisdiction and for conspiracies against civil liberty. Above the senate were the electoral colleges, divided into the three separate bodies of landed proprietors, tradespeople, and "intellectuals," to which was assigned the duty of deciding whether or not the decisions of the senate were constitutional, whether or not any officials had misused public funds, and whether or not malfeasant public servants should be suspended from office.

The senate and electoral colleges were to represent the will of the people. Still other bodies were directly subject to the king. One of these was the council of state, presided over by Napoleon himself, which had the duty of advising the government on judicial, religious, financial, administrative, military, and naval matters. There were also seven ministers of state, each of whom owed his appointment to the king: a minister of justice, a minister of foreign affairs, a minister of interior, a minister of finance, a minister of war and marine, a minister of the treasury, and a minister of religion.

To facilitate provincial and local administration, the kingdom was divided into twenty-four departments, each presided over by a prefect, who represented the central government in his department. The prefect was assisted by both a prefectural and a general council. Every department was divided into several districts, in each of which, except the one where the prefect resided, was a vice-prefect to represent his superior in that district and to carry out and enforce all laws and ordinances. He was aided by a district council of eleven members. Every district was divided into cantons, each with a justice of peace and most with, in addition, a *cancelliere del censo* to apportion and levy all taxes. The cantons were divided into communes, the smallest of the administrative subdivisions, in each of which were a municipal representative, to represent the central authority, and a communal council, the members of which were named by Napoleon in the first and second class communes, and by the prefect in those of the third class.

Parallel with the political administration were a financial and a judicial hierarchy. At the head of the financial organization of the kingdom were the ministries of the treasury and of finance. The first of these ministries controlled the spending of the revenues brought to it by the second. In the finance ministry were special directories for the direct taxes and for each of the indirect taxes, as well as for the royal domains and forests, the mint, and the postal service. The liquidation of the public debt was the special charge of the Monte Napoleone, which was under the control of the ministry. In each department there was an intendancy of finance, composed of from five to seven members, which, acting under the direct orders of the ministry of finance, supervised all financial concerns in the department except those which appertained to the royal domains—those being handled by a separate administration. Local financial matters were handled by the *cancellieri del censo* in the cantons and by the communal governments in the communes.

The administration of the judicial system of the kingdom was the special province of the ministry of justice. At the top of the judicial hierarchy were a court of cassation and five courts of appeals, located in Milan, Venice, Brescia, Bologna, and Ancona. In each departmental capital were a civil and criminal court and a separate first instance court. The latter handled civil cases which involved relatively small sums of money and criminal cases of a minor nature. In each canton was a justice of the peace, who acted as a mediator, judged civil processes involving sums of less than 100 Italian lire, and carried out whatever criminal investigations he was directed to make by higher authorities.[15]

After occupying the Kingdom of Italy, the Austrians temporarily retained much of the existing administrative machinery. When the Habsburg armies advanced into Venetia, all communications were

[15] The above analysis of the administrative organization of the Kingdom of Italy has been largely drawn from the following sources: Reuss-Plauen to Ugarte, Udine, February 11, 1814, *Haus-, Hof-, und Staatsarchiv* (Vienna) (hereafter cited as "St. A. [Vienna]"), Kaiser Franz Akten, Fasz. XXVII, Kon. 1, Fos. 20–23; Bellegarde report on the Austrian-Italian provinces, October 25, 1814, Helfert, *Kaiser Franz und die Stiftung des Lombardo-Venetianischen Königreichs*, Appendix I, pp. 525–535; Cesare Cantù, *Della indipendenza italiana cronistoria*, Vol. I, pp. 410–423; *Storia di Milano*, Vol. XIII: *L'età napoleonica (1796–1814)*, pp. 221–232; Giovanni Natali, *L'Italia durante il regime napoleonico: Lezioni tenuti alla Facoltà di Lettere dell'Università di Bologna durante l'Anno Accademico 1954–55*, p. 101; and Melchiorre Roberti, *Milano capitale napoleonica: la formazione di uno stato moderno 1796–1814*, Vol. II, pp. 157–190, 206–247, 272–321, and 344–355.

cut off between the areas under their occupation and the capital at
Milan; consequently, the commanding general of the invading armies needed to devise makeshift arrangements to fill the gap at the
top. However, he could, and did, retain most of the existing offices
and personnel which he found behind the lines of combat in the provincial, district, cantonal, and communal administrations.

On November 8, 1813—two weeks after his arrival in Trent—General Hiller issued an order announcing that in the areas to be occupied by the Habsburg army all employees of the former Kingdom of
Italy who had remained at their posts were provisionally to continue
serving under the Austrians. Beginning on the day when they took
an oath of loyalty to their new sovereign, they were to be paid the
same salary which they had received from the French. Likewise, the
existing departmental, district, and communal councils were to be
preserved. The prefects were still left in charge of the government
of the departments, but they were to receive their orders from and
send their reports directly to the commanding general. Furthermore,
General Hiller expressly stipulated that all their official actions had to
be approved by the departmental prefectural council, which, in addition to its regular membership under the former regime, was to include representatives from the general council of the department
and from the so-called "college of learned men." The intendants of
finance, who had previously reported directly to the central government in Milan, were also to be members of the prefectural council
and were to be placed under its supervision. All taxes collected in the
department were to be kept in a departmental bank, which was to
be established immediately. A special committee was to be created
in each department to provide the Habsburg army with food, lodging, transport, and other necessities. All existing courts were confirmed. Since no court of appeals was located in the areas which the
Habsburgs expected to occupy in the near future, the first instance
courts were ordered carefully to preserve an exact record of all processes that might later be appealed to higher judicial authorities.[16]

On November 9 General Hiller ordered Baron Antonio Marenzi,
his chief army commissioner, to go to the capitals of all the occupied
departments to put the stipulations of this proclamation into effect

---

[16] Hiller order, Trent, November 8, 1813, *Collezione di leggi e regolamenti
pubblicati dall'imp. regio governo delle provincie venete*, 1813–1814, Vol. I, pp.
3–16 (hereafter cited as *Collezione di leggi venete*).

as soon as possible.[17] Even before Marenzi left Trent to carry out these instructions news arrived at army headquarters that Emperor Francis had, on October 25, appointed Prince Heinrich Reuss-Plauen[18] military governor of all areas in Italy under the control of the Austrian army.[19] To superintend the Venetian government during the intervening period, until the new governor could assume his duties, Hiller designated Count Johann Thurn[20] as temporary military governor[21] and ordered all the officials in Venetia, whether Austrian or Italian, to submit to him all decrees and regulations which concerned administrative, judicial, police, or financial matters before putting them into effect. During his brief period in office Thurn made no innovations in the existing political and administrative set-up, and, except for appointing a very limited number of employees, on a provisional basis, to fill a few indispensable positions that had been vacated when their incumbents departed with the retreating French armies, he retained all the former French-Italian officials.[22]

Reuss-Plauen arrived at army headquarters in Vicenza on December 18 to take over his new post.[23] He came with instructions from

[17] Hiller to Marenzi, Trent, November 9, 1813, A. S. (Venice), Governo veneto, 1813, Atti Hiller, No. 1.

[18] Prince Heinrich Reuss-Plauen (1751–1825) began service in the Habsburg army in 1763. In 1788 he was promoted to the rank of colonel, and in 1793 to that of general. In 1797 he became a field marshal and was appointed a division commander in Archduke Charles' army. He fought in all the Austrian wars against Napoleon. He served as provisional governor of Venetia until 1815, when he returned for the time being to private life. In 1819 he was appointed commanding general of Galicia—a post which he held until 1824.

[19] Emperor Francis to Reuss-Plauen, Jena, October 25, 1813, A. S. (Venice), Governo veneto, 1813, Organizzazione, Fasc. IV–V, No. 16/F (enclosure).

[20] Count Johann B. Thurn-Hofer und Valsassina was a counselor in the government of Lower Austria before he came to Venetia.

[21] Marenzi to Thurn, Vicenza, November 21, 1813, A. S. (Venice), Governo veneto, 1813, Atti Hiller, no number given.

[22] Reuss-Plauen to Ugarte, Udine, February 11, 1814, St. A. (Vienna), Kaiser Franz Akten, Fasz. XXVII, Kon. 1, Fo. 18; Lelio Ottolenghi, *Padova e il Dipartimento del Brenta dal 1813 al 1815*, pp. 102–103; Lenguazza to general and military government in Udine, Padua, January 5, 1814, Ottolenghi, *Padova e il Dipartimento del Brenta*, Doc. XIV, pp. 393–394.

[23] Thurn to Prefect of Bacchiglione, Vicenza, December 18, 1813, A. S. (Venice), Governo veneto, 1814, Organizzazione, Rub. A, No. 936; Huegel diary, December 18, 1813, Francesco Lemmi (ed.), *La restaurazione in Italia nel 1814 nel diario del barone von Huegel (9 decembre 1813–25 mai 1814)*, p. 4 (hereafter cited as "Lemmi, *Diario del Huegel*").

the emperor to regard all territories under his jurisdiction as lands under military occupation. He was ordered to tamper with the existing French-Italian administrative apparatus only in case of real urgency. Furthermore, he was to leave at their posts all French-Italian employees except those who had perpetrated some crime or misdemeanor or who were known to be ardent supporters of the French. Immediately after his arrival in Italy he was to take possession of all state property in the emperor's name and to make arrangements to insure that all the existing taxes would be collected. He was to secure provisions for the Austrian military forces in the peninsula and to make detailed reports on the conditions of the land and its inhabitants. Above all, he was to do everything in his power to insure that Italian public opinion would continue to be favorable to Austria.[24] About all matters of importance he was to write to and receive his instructions from the emperor himself. Concerning less urgent affairs, however, he was to correspond directly with the appropriate aulic offices in Vienna.[25]

To aid him in governing the occupied Italian areas, the emperor assigned Count Thurn as his general and principal assistant.[26] Appointed to supervise civil affairs in the occupied territories under the

[24] Emperor Francis to Reuss-Plauen, Frankfurt, November 9, 1813, St. A. (Vienna), Conferenz Akten, Ser. b, 1813, No. 789. Professor Arthur G. Haas also found an imperial resolution dated November 28, 1813, in the *Hofkanzlei Akten* which dealt with Austrian policy in both the conquered Italian and the conquered Illyrian areas. In this resolution the emperor instructed his military governors to exert themselves "to care for the winning of public sentiment and to ascertain popular wishes." Although no mention was made about it in his instructions to Reuss-Plauen, in the imperial resolution of November 28 Emperor Francis also charged both military governors with arranging the administrative offices and practices in these areas in such a manner that they would conform as much as possible with those in the German areas of the monarchy. See Arthur G. Haas, *Metternich, Reorganization and Nationality 1813–1818: A Story of Foresight and Frustration in the Rebuilding of the Austrian Empire*, pp. 37–38 and 200–201, n. 80.

[25] Emperor Francis to Reuss-Plauen, Frankfurt, November 14, 1813, St. A (Vienna), Conferenz Akten, Ser. b, 1813, No. 789; Ugarte to Reuss-Plauen, Vienna, December 11, 1813, A. S. (Venice), Governo veneto, 1813, Organizzazione, Fasc. IV–V, No. 16/F (enclosure).

[26] The emperor made this appointment on October 25 (Emperor Francis to Zichy, Jena, October 25, 1813, St. A. [Vienna], Conferenz Akten, Ser. b, 1813, No. 650).

new governor were, first, Baron Bernhard Rosetti von Rosenegg,[27] and then, after he was ordered to army headquarters as Field Marshal Bellegarde's general intendant, Baron Bernhard Hingenau.[28] In January a third experienced Austrian official, Karl Ronner, was sent to Reuss-Plauen to take charge of all military matters that fell within the province of the central government.[29]

A small group of Italian administrators was assigned to aid this handful of Habsburg officials in conducting the affairs of the civil government in the occupied areas. During the early weeks of 1814 Marquis Luigi Paulucci was named secretary of the government and placed in charge of all "presidential" affairs. Claudio Marlianici was selected to take care of matters which appertained to the judiciary, religion, education, and public welfare; Andrea Fattori was chosen to superintend the sanitation, tax, agricultural, and waterways, highways, and bridges administrations; and Guido Anzidei was entrusted with the financial administration.[30] Two of these men had previously been in Austrian service. The other two had held positions of trust in the preceding French-Italian regime. Thus, during the first few months of Austrian rule in Venetia the central government was run by only eight experienced officials, four of them Austrian and four of them Italian, plus five assistants, a couple of dozen clerks, and a few other minor employees.[31]

Of these officials Count Thurn was by far the most active and influential.[32] Under Reuss-Plauen he worked with tireless energy to coordinate all branches of the administration into a unified body. He read the reports of most of the administrative departments and offices and advised the governor about how they should be dealt with.

27 *Ibid.*; Emperor Francis to Reuss-Plauen, Frankfurt, November 9, 1813, *ibid.*, No. 789.

28 Emperor Francis to Zichy, Freyburg, December 21, 1813, *ibid.*, No. 925; Reuss-Plauen to Zichy, January 26, 1814, *ibid.*, 1814, No. 354.

29 Reuss-Plauen to Ugarte, Udine, February 11, 1814, St. A (Vienna), Kaiser Franz Akten, Fasz. XXVII, Kon. 1, Fo. 29.

30 *Ibid.*; Ugarte report, Vienna, May 7, 1814, *Verwaltungsarchiv* (Vienna), Hofkanzlei, Lombardei-Venedig, Fasz. III, A, 4, No. 445 ex Mai 1814.

31 Ugarte report, Vienna, May 7, 1814, *Verwaltungsarchiv* (Vienna), Hofkanzlei, Lombardei-Venedig, Fasz. III, A, 4, No. 445 ex Mai 1814.

32 Entry of August 12, 1814, *Museo del Risorgimento italiano* (Venice), "Il diario di Emanuele Cicogna," p. 2027 (hereafter cited as *Museo* [Venice], "Diario di Cicogna").

In addition, he served as the chief liaison official between the governor's office and the Austrian armies operating in the field.[33] Thurn's influence was so great, in fact, that some Venetians felt that he, rather than Prince Reuss-Plauen, was the actual governor.[34]

At the outset the offices of the Venetian central government were often moved. For a brief interval Reuss-Plauen and his staff were located at Udine. Then they operated as best they could from army headquarters first at Vicenza and subsequently at Verona. A few weeks later the governor and his staff established offices in Padua.[35] Finally, after protracted and involved preparations,[36] during the course of which the governor was bombarded with insistent demands by the emperor that he move the capital from Padua as quickly as possible,[37] the seat of the government was transferred, on September 14, to the royal palace on San Marco Square in Venice.[38]

These frequent moves help in part to explain why the Venetian government operated so inefficiently during the first few months after its establishment. More important, the vicissitudes of warfare would have made it impossible for almost anyone, even an administrator much more capable than Reuss-Plauen, to fashion a smoothly functioning apparatus before the enemy was defeated. Taking care of urgent contingencies as they arose, often unexpectedly, maintaining order and security in an area that had just changed masters, and providing the Habsburg armies with provisions, transport, and supplies consumed most of the energies of the governor and his small

[33] St. A. (Vienna), Kaiser Franz Akten, Fasz. XXVII, Kon. 1, Fo. 28.

[34] Francesco Cavazzocca diary, May 29, 1814, as quoted in Giuseppe Biadego, *La dominazione austriaca e il sentimento pubblico a Verona dal 1814 al 1847*, p. 15.

[35] Hingenau's letter to Zichy on February 24, 1814, indicates that at that time the capital had already been moved to Padua (St. A. [Vienna], Conferenz Akten, Ser. b, 1814, No. 507).

[36] See Lederer to Reuss-Plauen, Padua, July 20, 1814, A. S. (Venice), Presidio di governo, 1814, No. 641; Reuss-Plauen to aulic central organization commission, Padua, August 24, 1814, *ibid.*, No. 927.

[37] Imperial cabinet writing, Gutenbrun, August 9, 1814, St. A. (Vienna), Conferenz Akten, Ser. b, 1814, No. 1393; Lazanzky to Reuss-Plauen, Vienna, August 11, 1814, A. S. (Venice), Presidio di governo, 1814, No. 927.

[38] Venetian central government to aulic central organization commission, Padua, September 10, 1814, A. S. (Venice), Presidio di governo, 1814, No. 1166; entry of September 14, 1814, *Museo* (Venice), "Diario di Cicogna," p. 2047; *Giornale di Venezia*, No. 129 (September 15, 1814), p. 3.

staff during the initial stages of the occupation. They had neither the time nor the stamina to select the additional competent personnel which was badly needed for the care of many important matters left unattended or to establish efficient, orderly methods of procedure.[39]

Furthermore, it must not be forgotten that the new governor had to start from scratch in creating a provisional central government. He could and did make use of existing provincial and local administrative organs and their personnel. However, because of the severance of communications with the capital of the former Kingdom of Italy, nothing even vaguely resembling a central administration was at hand for him to take over and utilize or fashion for his own purposes —a situation which was bound to create great difficulties in an area as highly centralized as the Kingdom of Italy, with its many echelons of the provincial and local administrative machinery directly dependent upon the ministries and central directories in Milan. Since the Austrians had to devise stopgap measures, hurriedly and haphazardly as the situation demanded, the inefficiency of the central government during the first few months was appalling.[40] In the resultant confusion, much of it due to circumstances beyond the governor's control, important directives and letters were lost, decrees providing for emergency situations were issued weeks late, and ordinary routine affairs were handled months behind schedule.[41]

Perhaps nothing even resembling an efficiently functioning central government can be expected in an area in which a military campaign is being waged. After the fighting was over, however, Prince Reuss-Plauen never succeeded in turning his provisional government into anything approximating an effective or efficient organization. Although he cut down the number of collegiate meetings with his counselors from two to one per week, initiated a few short cuts in the ever-mounting paper work,[42] and permitted his counselors on

[39] Reuss-Plauen to Ugarte, Udine, February 11, 1814, St. A. (Vienna), Kaiser Franz Akten, Fasz. XXVII, Kon. 1, Fo. 28.

[40] Galvagna report, Venice, March 1, 1820, A. S. (Venice), Presidio di governo, 1815–1819, Finanza, Fasc. IV, ad No. 2431/P.P. del 1819.

[41] Secret report to Hager, Padua, June 20, 1814, A. S. (Venice), Presidio di governo, 1814, No. 790; entry of August 13, 1814, *Museo* (Venice), "Diario di Cicogna," p. 2028.

[42] Presidential notice, Venice, December 1, 1814, A. S. (Venice), Presidio di governo, 1814, No. 2111.

their own authority to choose a number of their subordinate employees on a provisional basis,[43] the Venetian government continued to be inexcusably inefficient and slow in transacting its work[44] long after the government had moved to Venice. In fact, in the fall of 1814, several months after the end of the military campaign, the central administration still discharged its duties in such an inept and disorganized manner that the director of the Austrian police in Venetia lamented that no single "province in the Austrian monarchy is more badly administered than Venetia."[45]

One reason for the serious deficiencies in the functioning of the Venetian central government was the continued shortage of competent officials and other high-ranking administrative personnel. Another was Reuss-Plauen himself. Like many another army officer temporarily assigned to political duty, he was sadly lacking in experience and in administrative talent.[46] Wanting to do everything himself, he refused to delegate even the most insignificant matters to subordinate officials.[47]

The main guilt, however, lay in the very nature of the Habsburg political and administrative system. Little could be decided in Venice. Inconsequential minutiae had to be referred to Vienna for action. Although the numerous reforms which had been wrought by Maria Theresa and Joseph II had enormously multiplied the administrative burdens of the imperial government in Vienna, Emperor Francis still insisted on personally tending to all but the tiniest details in the same manner as his absolutist predecessors had before 1740.[48] Infinitesimal minutiae took up so much of his time that essential work was frequently delayed for months while the emperor dug out another

[43] Reuss-Plauen to his counselors and reporters, Venice, December 9, 1814, A. S. (Venice), Governo veneto, 1814, Organizzazione, Fasc. I, B, No. 44,684/5588.

[44] Hager report, May 23, 1814, St. A (Vienna), Kabinets-Akten, 1814, No. 1583; Kallinich report, April 2, 1814, St. A. (Vienna), Conferenz Akten, Ser. b, 1814, No. 910.

[45] Hager report, October 10, 1814, St. A. (Vienna), Kabinets-Akten, 1814, No. 766.

[46] Staats-Kabinet report, May 23, 1814, *ibid.*, No. 1583.

[47] Hager report, October 10, 1814, *ibid.*, No. 766.

[48] See Friedrich Walter, *Die Zeit Franz' II. (I.) und Ferdinands I. (1792–1848)* (Vol. I of *Die österreichische Zentralverwaltung*, Pt. II: *Von der Vereinigung der österreichischen und böhmischen Hofkanzlei bis zur Einrichtung der Ministerialverfassung [1749–1848]*), pp. 26–33.

unimportant little report and wrote another one of his innumerable sovereign resolutions.

When the Austrians first took over Venetia they asked all police employees of the former kingdom who had remained at their posts to continue working. They instructed them to enforce the existing French-Italian laws and police regulations, which were provisionally confirmed, and to discharge their duties in cooperation with the Austrian military commandants, to whom they were to turn over all military personnel who had run afoul of the law. They were to protect the lives and property of the inhabitants and to keep a sharp eye on dangerous French sympathizers who circulated subversive writings, engaged in espionage, corresponded with the enemy, or sought to incite disorders.[49]

For the first few weeks after the Habsburgs occupied Venetia the police remained under the control and supervision of the prefects of the particular departments to which they were assigned, as had been the case in the Kingdom of Italy.[50] As can be expected, the aulic police directory in Vienna was highly displeased with the arrangement and insisted that the Italian security forces be made directly responsible to well-trained Austrian officers selected by the emperor himself. Emperor Francis was in complete accord with Police President Franz von Hager's [51] views and ordered Anton von Raab[52] to go to Venetia to institute a central Venetian police directory which was to superintend all police activities in the occupied Italian provinces. The emperor also appointed Barons von Maurizio, Ehrenheim, Stocca, and Emberg police commissioners to assist Raab in carrying out his new assignment.[53]

[49] Police instructions, November 24, 1813, *Collezione di leggi venete,* 1813–1814, Vol. I, pp. 19–26.

[50] Reuss-Plauen to Ugarte, Udine, February 11, 1814, St. A. (Vienna), Kaiser Franz Akten, Fasz. XXVII, Kon. 1, Fos. 19 and 25.

[51] Baron Franz von Hager von Allentsteig (1750–1816), after serving in the Austrian district administration service since 1786, was, in 1803, made aulic counselor in the Austrian police and censorship in Vienna. In 1806 he was appointed vice-president, and in 1813 president, of that office.

[52] Before going to Venetia Raab was police director at Linz. In April, 1815, Emperor Francis made him a knight of the Leopold order. In September, 1816, he became police director of Lombardy.

[53] Staats-Conferenz to president of the aulic police department, December 2, 1813, St. A. (Vienna), Conferenz Akten, Ser. b, 1813, No. 766; Hager to Reuss-Plauen, Vienna, January 16, 1814, A. S. (Venice), Governo veneto, 1814, Organizzazione, Rub. B, No. 3116.

Raab arrived in Italy late in January or early in February, 1814. He immediately instructed several of the Austrian commissioners who had accompanied him to take direct charge of the police activities in various departments. In conformity with the administrative procedures of the Kingdom of Italy, which were still in force, the commissioners were placed under the control of the prefect to whose administrative jurisdiction they were assigned. They were told to correspond directly with the central police director or with the governor in urgent or special cases.[54] In accord with the administrative practices of the French-Italian regime, all regular police reports were to be sent to the central government by the prefects.[55]

Since the Austrian commissioners in charge of departmental police affairs were hand-picked in Vienna, Police President von Hager had no reservations about their ability to discharge their duties faithfully, loyally, and efficiently, even though they momentarily had to function under the superintendence of the departmental prefects. However, he did have serious misgivings about a number of Italian police officials who had been retained by the Austrians and particularly about a number of employees of the provisional Venetian police directory and about the police chief of the city of Venice.[56] His uneasiness about them was augmented by various anonymous denunciations which were sent in about them.[57] His suspicions fell, above all, on Sormani, the secretary, and Contarini and Vitalini, two of the section chiefs of the central police directory; Lancetti, another official of the central directory; and Baron Antonio Mulazzani,[58] the chief of police of the city of Venice.[59]

No one took up the cudgel to defend Vitalini. Even the Venetians

[54] Reuss-Plauen to Ugarte, February 11, 1814, St. A. (Vienna), Kaiser Franz Akten, Fasz. XXVII, Kon. 1, Fos. 20 and 25.

[55] Venetian central government, circular to the provisional prefects of Udine, Treviso, Belluno, Vicenza, Padua, Verona, Ferrara, and Venice, Padua, April 28, 1814, A. S. (Venice), Presidio di governo, 1814, ad No. 22.

[56] See especially Hager to Reuss-Plauen, Vienna, May 12, 1814, *ibid.*, ad No. 599.

[57] For example, see secret police report to Hager, Venice, June 22, 1814, *ibid.*, No. 790.

[58] Baron Antonio Mulazzani became a district police commissioner for the French in 1796. Later he served as a police employee in the Cisalpine Republic and the Kingdom of Italy. His last position was that of general police director of Venice.

[59] Protocol of the presidency of the Venetian government, May 12, 1814, A. S. (Venice), Presidio di governo, 1814, ad No. 599; Hager to Reuss-Plauen,

recognized that he was a scoundrel of the first order.[60] In the summer of 1814 he was peremptorily replaced as head of the criminal investigation section by another Italian, Police Commissioner Giavarina, of Padua. As the denunciations against Sormani were not substantiated, he was transferred to the police administration in Milan, where he was discharged in October for giving false information about a long leave.[61] His position as secretary of the Venetian central police directory was taken over by a German. Even though he had been a fanatical supporter of the French, Contarini was allowed to continue at his post until November, when he was replaced by Stocca and assigned to a minor post in the central government. Lancetti was retained in office. When the police of the city of Venice were put under the immediate control of the central police directory, Mulazzani lost his position. However, since he was highly esteemed as a capable official, Governor Reuss-Plauen bombarded Hager's office with such flattering descriptions of Mulazzani's unusual talents that he was appointed to the position of counselor in the Venetian central government.[62] Eventually he was to become one of the most trusted secret police officials in Venetia.

Mulazzani turned over his office as police chief of Venice to Raab on August 16.[63] Two months later, on October 10, the emperor declared Raab's appointment as provisional director of the Venetian central police directory to be permanent. Raab was to have the rank of government counselor and a salary of 3,000 florins per annum, in addition to a free dwelling and wood.[64] Until the Venetian police

---

July 12, 1814, *ibid.*, No. 635; Torresani to Raab, Padua, August 12, 1814, *ibid.*, No. 685.

[60] See especially entries of September 2, 1814, and January 30, 1815, *Museo* (Venice), "Diario di Cicogna," pp. 2040–2041 and 2092–2093.

[61] Reuss-Plauen to Bellegarde, Venice, October 20, 1814, *Archivio di Stato* (Milan) (hereafter cited as "A. S. [Milan]"), Commissione Plenipotenziaria presieduta dal Conte di Bellegarde, Busta unica, No. 9842.

[62] Hager to Reuss-Plauen, Vienna, May 12, June 11, 17, and 29, July 12, and November 30, 1814, A. S. (Venice), Presidio di governo, 1814, ad No. 599, and Nos. 132, 445, 635, and 2222; Reuss-Plauen to Hager, Padua, July 27, 1814, *ibid.*, No. 635; Reuss-Plauen to Raab, Padua, August 12, 1814, *ibid.*, No. 635; Raab to Reuss-Plauen, Padua, August 16, 1814, *ibid.*, No. 867.

[63] Raab to Reuss-Plauen, Padua, August 16, 1814, *ibid.*, No. 867.

[64] Imperial resolution, October 10, 1814, St. A. (Vienna), Kabinets-Akten, 1814, No. 754; Hager to Reuss-Plauen, Vienna, October 13, 1814, A. S. (Venice), Presidio di governo, 1814, No. 1722.

administration could be organized along the same lines as the police administration in the German provinces of Austria, he was instructed to enforce the existing French-Italian laws and regulations in the same "spirit of moderation which the Austrian administration always follows." However, he was to take advantage of every opportunity gradually to introduce Austrian policies and practices into the organization of which he was in charge. As soon as possible he was to submit a detailed plan for the permanent organization of the Venetian police to the aulic offices in Vienna.[65]

By the fall of 1814 the Habsburgs had thus made substantial progress in putting the Venetian police *administration* on a regular footing. However, they were still far from having an adequate and well-drilled police *force* to cope with the many petty crimes and disturbances which plagued the Venetians during the uneasy months following the overthrow of the French regime. On account of the privations and breakdowns stemming from the war and the resultant political changes, robbery and theft were rampant in Venetia.[66] To provide for the maintenance of order and security in the country districts, the Austrians, immediately after entering Venetia, resurrected the old Venetian constabulary, the so-called *satellizio*, which the French had supplanted with gendarme companies. The constabulary, which were headed in each department by an inspector appointed by the prefect and responsible to him, were always to be ready to repress disorders and insurrections and were, in addition, to execute the orders given to them by the courts of justice, justices of the peace, mayors, and police commissioners in each department.[67] By the early summer of 1814 constabulary detachments were stationed in all the Venetian provinces; however, in numerous places their number was insufficient to enable them to serve as an efficient deterrent force.[68]

[65] Reuss-Plauen to Raab, Padua, August 12, 1814, A. S. (Venice), Presidio di governo, 1814, No. 685.

[66] Reuss-Plauen to Raab, Padua, July 9, 1814, *ibid.*, No. 538/360 P.R.; Hager to Reuss-Plauen, Vienna, July 13, 1814, *ibid.*, No. 636; Reuss-Plauen to Hager, Padua, July 26, 1814, *ibid.*

[67] Provisional regulation for the constabulary guard, December 14, 1813, *Collezione di leggi venete*, 1813–1814, Vol. I, pp. 27–37.

[68] See especially protocol of the Venetian government, May 25 and 28, 1814, A. S. (Venice), Presidio di governo, 1814, No. 118; Hager to Reuss-Plauen, Vienna, July 8, 1814, *ibid.*, No. 538; Reuss-Plauen to Hager, Padua, July 26, 1814, *ibid.*, No. 636; Venetian general government to president of the aulic po-

In the fall of 1814 the special police guard detachments established to enforce the peace in the cities were in no better position to maintain law and order than the constabulary forces in the country districts. The systematization of these units was delayed so long that they could not begin functioning on the *terra ferma* before September 1.[69] In the interim, the patrolling of city streets was performed by persons recruited from the former French guard,[70] by other soldiers,[71] and by special citizens' details.[72] In the city of Venice the police guard detachments were not instituted before the last days of 1814. Their organization was delayed, first of all, by the dilatoriness of the Venetian police directory in submitting plans to Hager's office and then by the emperor's slowness in approving them. When Emperor Francis finally did give his consent on November 19 to the establishment of a police guard in Venice, he stipulated that the force was to be made up of two companies, each of 150 men, selected from volunteers who had previously seen military service.[73]

The *satellizio* and police guards which the Austrians finally succeeded in organizing, however, proved to be utterly incapable of giving adequate protection to the life and property of the Venetian populace. Even though Baron von Hager sincerely believed that these newly instituted police forces would be an excellent substitute for the former French gendarmes and national guard and would be well fitted "to the genius of the Venetian nation,"[74] in practice they did not live up to his expectations. This was particularly true with the *satellizio*. Since the old constabulary had been dismissed when the French took over Venetia, they were now badly out of practice. Most of the rank and file were recruited from the poorer classes and sympathized with them. Because the pay was wretched, some of

---

lice, Padua, July 26, 1814, *ibid.*, No. 682; protocol of the Venetian central government, September 6, 1814, A. S. (Venice), Governo veneto, 1814, Polizia, Fasc. VI, B, No. 29,489/445; and Mulazzani to inspector of the *satellizio*, July 16, 1814, *Carte segrete ed atti ufficiali della polizia austriaca in Italia dal 4 giugno 1814 al 22 marzo 1848*, Vol. I, p. 226.

[69] Reuss-Plauen to Hager, Venice, September 16, 1814, A. S. (Venice), Presidio di governo, 1814, No. 1143.

[70] Bellegarde to Marchal, Milan, June 26, 1814, *ibid.*, No. 383.

[71] Marchal to Reuss-Plauen, Venice, August 19, 1814, *ibid.*, No. 920.

[72] Reuss-Plauen to Hager, Venice, November 26, 1814, *ibid.*, No. 2011 e 2024.

[73] Hager to Reuss-Plauen, Vienna, December 22, 1814, *ibid.*, No. 2483.

[74] Hager to Reuss-Plauen, Vienna, July 8, 1814, *ibid.*, No. 538.

them not only engaged in petty graft but even themselves broke into houses and robbed people on the roads and streets.[75] The police guards were little better. Needless to say, the constabulary and police guards did not succeed in appreciably checking the numerous petty crimes which sorely afflicted the Venetian populace!

The Habsburgs were as tardy in establishing an efficient censorship administration in Venetia as they were in creating a reliable police force. When they first arrived in Italy the Austrians provisionally retained the existing French censorship regulations and invited the officials who had tended to censorship duties under the previous regime temporarily to remain in office. The only change they made in the prevailing practices was to instruct the press and book inspectors in the departments to address their correspondence directly to the Austrian civil commissioner rather than to the censorship directory in Milan.[76] A few months later, the Austrians, finding the French regulations—which permitted local authorities to pass on all notices and circulars of fewer than five pages[77]—too lax for their taste, ordered all printers to submit everything they wished to print, whether one-page advertisements or large books, to the departmental prefectures for prior approval or revision.[78] The results were not too fortunate. Since every little bit of trivia now had to be submitted to the departmental capital for censorship, the already overworked prefectural offices were swamped with reams of inconsequential minutiae, while loud complaints were voiced about the ruinous effects on the printing business caused by the long delays resulting from this complicated system.[79] Heeding these objections, the Habsburgs final-

[75] Helfert, *Kaiser Franz und die Stiftung des Lombardo-Venetianischen Königreichs*, p. 24.

[76] Decree of November 29, 1813, *Collezione di leggi venete*, 1813–1814, Vol. I, p. 26; instructions to the police, Padua, November 29, 1813, A. S. (Venice), Governo veneto, 1813–1814, Polizia, Fasc. VI, A, No. 183.

[77] Prefecture of Treviso to Venetian central government, Treviso, May 12, 1814, A. S. (Venice), Governo veneto, 1814, Polizia, Fasc. VI, D, Rub.: Stampa e censura, No. 9452/5043; prefecture of Brenta to Venetian central government, Padua, August 4, 1814, *ibid.*, Fasc. VI, B, No. 515 P.S.

[78] Venetian central government to prefectures in Udine, Padua, Treviso, Ferrara, Belluno, Vicenza, and Verona, Padua, March 12, 1814, *ibid.*, Fasc. VI, A, C, F, No. 6074.

[79] Prefecture of Treviso to Venetian central government, Treviso, May 12, 1814, *ibid.*, Fasc. VI, D, Rub.: Stampa e censura, No. 9452/5043; prefecture of Brenta to Venetian central government, Padua, August 4, 1814, *ibid.*, Fasc. VI, B, No. 515 P.S.

ly gave the vice-prefects permission in September to censor single sheets printed in their districts, if the sheets dealt strictly with private matters or with religious affairs.[80]

The censorship of only relatively inconsequential matters was left to the district and less-important departmental offices. Newspapers were too vital to be controlled by subordinate prefectural employees who had been taken over almost as a body from the French. Since most of the departmental police commissioners had actually been selected in Vienna, in the summer of 1814 Governor Reuss-Plauen turned the censoring of newspapers directly over to them.[81] In addition, the prefect's personal approval was required before articles describing public functions or ceremonies could be published. [82] Certainly this obligation did not inflict an onerous burden on these offices. At the most, each commissioner and prefect had only one journal to watch, for in the Kingdom of Italy only a single newspaper was allowed in each department. Even Venice had only a single gazette: the *Giornale di Venezia*.[83] To gain even tighter control over newspapers, the government announced in September that on January 1, 1815, all licenses that had previously been granted to newspaper publishers would be invalid. After January 1 new permits went only to reliable publishers to print such gazettes as the Habsburg authorities deemed advisable to have in circulation.[84] Later in 1814 a decree was issued stipulating that only foreign papers approved for circulation in the monarchy by the supreme censorship office in Vienna could be sold in Venetia.[85]

[80] Torresani to provisional prefectures of Belluno, Padua, Vicenza, Verona, Treviso, and Udine, Venice, September 19, 1814, A. S. (Venice), Presidio di governo, 1814, No. 1150.

[81] Reuss-Plauen to Hager, Padua, July 20, 1814, *ibid.*, No. 516.

[82] Torresani to provisional prefectures of Padua, Vicenza, Verona, Belluno, and Udine, Venice, October 8, 1814, *ibid.*, No. 1476.

[83] Hager to Goëss, Vienna, April 3, 1815, *ibid.*, 1815, No. 197/v.b.p. In the spring of 1814 the Austrians had given official permission for a new newspaper, the *Nuovo osservatore*, to be founded. However, its license was suspended later in the same year. For 1815 the government approved the publication of two journals in the capital: the *Giornale di Venezia* and the *Notizie del mondo* (*ibid.*).

[84] Protocol of the Venetian central government, September 27, 1814, A. S. (Venice), Governo veneto, 1814, Polizia, Fasc. VI, D, No. 32,540/511, 34,145/573, 34,096/587.

[85] Hager to Reuss-Plauen, Vienna, November 28, 1814, A. S. (Venice), Presidio di governo, 1814, No. 2225.

Since Emperor Francis was so perturbed about the dangers of subversive literature and since he had established tight censorship con-
trols over the monarchy long before 1814, it is perhaps singular that
no over-all censorship bureau was created in Venetia for more than
a year after the Austrian occupation. Police President von Hager had
actually empowered Reuss-Plauen in August, 1814, to create a provisional office in Venice to censor such manuscripts as were submitted to it for publication.[86] Overburdened, understaffed, and lacking
in energy and administrative talent as he was, however, the Venetian
governor somehow never found or took the time to set up such a
bureau.[87] As a consequence, nothing resembling a real censorship
office was organized for Venetia before a permanent censorship administration was activated on June 15, 1815.[88] Until that time most
of the actual censoring of books was performed by largely untrained
subordinate personnel on the departmental level, usually on the basis
of lists of prohibited and tolerated books which were regularly supplied to them by the central government in Vienna.[89] Only manuscripts dealing with recent political events or with the policies of the
Habsburg government had to be submitted to the Venetian central
government for approval before they could be printed or circulated.[90]

The Venetian provisional government, the police force, and the
censorship administration were thus in 1814 and 1815 everything but
the model of efficiency which the French had accustomed the Italians to expect of their governing officials. Seeing confusion rather
than orderliness, inexplicable delays rather than hasty decisions, and
vacillation and hesitation rather than decisiveness or even arbitrariness, some Venetians began to grumble loudly soon after the Habsburgs took over their government about the lumbering gait of the
administrative process, the stupidity and incapability of Austrian officials, and the abuses allegedly perpetrated by incompetent or

---

[86] Hager to Reuss-Plauen, Vienna, A. S. (Venice), Governo veneto, 1814,
Polizia, Fasc. VI, D, ad No. 32,219/499.

[87] Reuss-Plauen to Hager, Venice, December 22, 1814, *ibid.*, No. 47,324/1202.

[88] Notification, Venetian government, June 1, 1815, *Collezione di leggi venete*,
1815, Vol. I, p. 241.

[89] See, for example, Torresani to provincial prefects of Padua, Vicenza, Verona,
Treviso, Udine, Belluno, and Venice, Venice, November 14 and December 12,
1814, A. S. (Venice), Presidio di governo, 1814, Nos. 2005 and 2190.

[90] Ottolenghi, *Padova e il Dipartimento del Brenta*, p. 154.

haughty administrators.[91] One opponent vented his spleen over the government's inability to work effectively by posting this notice on the main door of the government building in Padua: "This is the government that is always writing but never produces anything."[92] Other Venetians expressed their dislike for the Habsburgs by voicing a distrust of all Austrian officials in general[93] or by singling out particular individuals as objects for animadversion.

Among these was no less a figure than the governor himself. Although Prince Reuss-Plauen was well liked by a large majority of the populace, he had numerous critics who complained that he was too weak, inexperienced, incompetent, and vacillating, and too easily influenced by others to be a forceful executive.[94] One satirist dubbed him "Prince Southwesterly Sofia-Wind," for he "is of brief duration and does not change the weather, inasmuch as," like the "Sofia-Wind," "he leaves everything the way he finds it."[95] Another lampooner wrote of the governor:

> "He came from Istrian territory
> As Caesar's minister plenipotentiary,
> With full and ample authority
> To accomplish an impressive nihility."[96]

Since the governor seemed ill-qualified to carry out his duties, some Venetians actually believed the gossip that he did only what his alter ego and principal assistant, Count Thurn, and his presidential secretary, Marquis Paulucci, told him to do.[97] Hardly any old

[91] Kallinich report, April 2, 1814, St. A. (Vienna), Conferenz Akten, Ser. b, 1814, No. 910; Hager report, July 8, 1814, *ibid.*, No. 1346.

[92] Cicogna diary, August 13, 1814, A. Pilot, "Venezia nel blocco del 1813–14. Da noterelle inedite del Cicogna," *Nuovo Archivio Veneto,* Vol. XIV (1914), p. 226.

[93] Entry of May 5, 1815, *Museo* (Venice), "Diario di Cicogna," p. 3018.

[94] Staats-Kabinet report, April 5, 1814, St. A. (Vienna), Kabinets-Akten, 1814, No. 1371; Hager report, October 10, 1814, *ibid.*, No. 766.

[95] Mulazzani to Reuss-Plauen, Venice, May 28, 1814, A. S. (Venice), Presidio di governo, 1814, ad No. 135.

[96] As quoted in Vittorio Malamani, *L'Austria e i Bonapartisti (1815–1848). Studi fatti negli archivi del governo austriaco nel Lombardo-Veneto* (estratto della *Rivista Storica Italiana,* Vol. VII, Fasc. 2, [1890]), p. 4.

[97] Hager reports, April 5, May 11, and May 23, 1814, St. A. (Vienna), Kabinets-Akten, 1814, Nos. 1371, 1551, and 1583.

wives' tale could have been more damaging to the governor's reputation, since both of these individuals were highly unpopular. Thurn
was intensely disliked on account of his inordinate pride and haugh-
tiness and was charged with having stolen money from the government coffers in Udine. Paulucci was branded as a venal double-dealer
and as a dangerous person who had strong pro-French sympathies.
He was even denounced as a French spy.[98]

For a brief moment during the summer of 1814 it appeared that
the critics of the governor's immediate circle would be stilled. After
receiving insistent reports that Thurn was universally hated, Emperor Francis dismissed him from his post in July [99] and recalled him
to Vienna.[100] Paulucci was also removed from his post as secretary
on the pretext that he did not know enough German to handle his
job.[101]

Thurn's recall and Paulucci's dismissal, however, did not quiet for
long the defamers of the provisional government. Now they concentrated their ire on Baron Hingenau, charging that he had used his
daughter to win Reuss-Plauen's favor and to gain an inordinate influence over him.[102] They also vented their spleen on various officials
in the Venetian central adminstration who had been taken over from
the former French regime and whom they accused of working hard to
maintain all the tyrannical and oppressive policies of the Napoleonic
rule.[103] For them the chief villains of the piece were Marlianici, who
was accused of being a great admirer of the former government and
an influential Freemason; Del Rio and Renier, who were dubbed
worthless incompetents;[104] Mulazzani, the police chief of Venice,
who was branded as a Freemason and an enemy of Austria; Galvag-

---

[98] Hager reports, May 11 and 23, 1814, *ibid.*, Nos. 1551 and 1583; protocol,
Staats-Conferenz, June 14, 1814, St. A. (Vienna), Conferenz Akten, Ser. b,
1814, No. 1102; Ugarte report, July 1, 1814, *ibid.*, No. 1312.

[99] Imperial resolution, Baden, July 17, 1814, St. A. (Vienna), Conferenz
Akten, Ser. b, 1814, No. 1312.

[100] Reuss-Plauen report, August 10, 1814, *ibid.*, No. 1616.

[101] Aichelburg to Reuss-Plauen, Vienna, July 22, 1814, *ibid.*, ad No. 1699.

[102] Hager report, October 10, 1814, St. A. (Vienna), Kabinets-Akten, 1814,
No. 766.

[103] Staats-Conferenz report, June 14, 1814, St. A. (Vienna), Conferenz Akten,
Ser. b, 1814, No. 1102.

[104] Hager report, October 10, 1814, St. A. (Vienna), Kabinets-Akten, 1814,
No. 766.

na, who was described as a heartless man;[105] and Barbò and Toni, who were denounced as scoundrels.[106] Certainly no one could lament that the Venetians were departing from their accustomed grumbling after the Austrians replaced the French as their masters!

The Venetian central government, hastily organized from scratch as the Habsburg armies fought their way across Northern Italy, was such an amorphous, badly functioning body that it perhaps deserved many of the aspersions cast upon it by the more caustic Venetians. The departmental administrative offices, however, deserved more respect, although even here all was not well. On the departmental level the Austrians could and did adapt for their purposes an administrative apparatus that had been operating successfully for a number of years. As has already been pointed out,[107] immediately after he came to Italy General Hiller confirmed the existing French departmental system, with a few indispensable modifications, and invited all the employees of the Kingdom of Italy who had not deserted their posts to remain temporarily in office. Those departmental offices which under the French-Italian regime had been under the direct control of the ministries in Milan were for the time being to be under the immediate supervision of the departmental prefects.[108]

Yet, even though the Austrians took over practically all the departmental administrative machinery and personnel of the former Kingdom of Italy they found upon their arrival, the transfer from French to Austrian rule did not proceed smoothly. The French-Italian government had directed all the prefects and their subordinate personnel to vacate their offices as soon as Austrian troops approached, and a number of prefects complied with this order. The Habsburgs found it rather difficult to fill some of the vacated posts as long as the outcome of the war was still in doubt, and in numerous instances only second-rate opportunists who had nothing to fear from a change in regime could be induced to apply for the positions that were open.[109]

---

[105] Hager report, July 8, 1814, St. A. (Vienna), Conferenz Akten, Ser. b, 1814, No. 1346.

[106] Hager report, August 13, 1814, *ibid.*, No. 1590.

[107] See *ante*, p. 16.

[108] *Oesterreichisch-Kaiserliche privilegirte Wiener Zeitung nebst Amtsblatt*, February 22, 1814, p. 215 (hereafter cited as *Wiener Zeitung*).

[109] Reuss-Plauen to Lazanzky, Venice, December 6, 1814, A. S. (Venice), Presidio di governo, 1814, No. 2110.

The Austrians filled in the gaps as best they could. To replace the prefect of Tagliamento, they appointed Count Antonio Porcia, who had formerly been in Austrian service. Count Cornieri, an intelligent, hard-working civil servant, who had been persecuted by the French, was named provisional prefect of Bacchiglione. Rizzardo Lenguazza, a competent, trustworthy administrator, was made prefect of Brenta. Savorgnani, who had served Austria in 1789 and again in 1805, was chosen for the same post in Passariano department; and Onego was selected for the prefectureship in Piave. Then, after these key replacements, the Habsburgs, as time and energy permitted, filled the vacancies in subordinate positions with personnel which they hoped would be both trustworthy and popular.[110]

On the whole, only the absolute minimum of indispensable changes were made in the departmental prefectural offices. In the district and communal administrations the Habsburgs made a few more innovations than they had in that of the departments, but here, too, much that was French was retained. The vice-prefects of the districts still continued to discharge the same duties which they had discharged in the past. Although the separate administrative divisions of cantons and communes were abolished on March 1, 1814, and all the communes in a former canton were grouped together in a single unit now called the commune, the *cancellieri del censo* and the justices of the peace—the only cantonal officials in the previous regime—went on with their work as they had before.

The French division of communes into three classes, each with a different set of governing officials,[111] was discarded. Each commune,

[110] Reuss-Plauen to Ugarte, Udine, February 11, 1814, St. A. (Vienna), Kaiser Franz Akten, Fasz. XXVII, Kon. 1, Fos. 18–19; Hager to Emperor Francis, March 26, 1815, A. S. (Venice), Presidio di governo, 1815, No. 764.

[111] In the Kingdom of Italy the membership of the communal municipality and of the communal council varied according to the rank of the commune. The municipality was composed of a mayor and six "learned men" in the communes of the first class; a mayor and four "learned men," in those of the second class; and a syndic and two "seniors," in those of the third class. A commune of the first class had a communal council of forty members; one of the second class, a council of thirty members; and one of the third class, a council of fifteen members (Bellegarde report on the Austrian-Italian provinces, October 25, 1815, Helfert, *Kaiser Franz und die Stiftung des Lombardo-Venetianischen Königreichs*, Appendix I, pp. 529 and 531; Kübeck report to the aulic central organization commission on the organization of the re-acquired Upper-Italian provinces, Vienna, December 8, 1814, Helfert, *Zur Geschichte des Lombardo-Venezianischen Königreichs*, Appendix I, pp. 273–275.

however, still continued to be administered by a municipality and a communal council, as it had been before the Habsburg army invaded Italy. Regardless of the size of the commune, the municipality now consisted of a mayor, nominated by the communal council and selected for a three-year term by the central government, and six so-called "learned men," elected by secret ballot by the communal council. Appointed by and dependent on the municipality were a communal agent, a bailiff, a secretary, and a number of clerks to deal with routine matters. The municipality was charged, as it had been by the French, with administering municipal affairs and executing the orders of the prefect in the commune. The communal council, composed of forty of the highest taxpayers of the commune who were nominated by the council itself and chosen by the central government, examined the accounts of the municipality, appointed the municipal officials, approved the budget, and determined the taxes which were to be levied in the commune. All its enactments had to be submitted to the prefect for approval.[112]

Acting upon the instructions of the emperor,[113] the Habsburg officials in Italy thus made few alterations in the existing departmental and local administrative apparatus. Following the same policy, they made only such modifications in the financial and judicial administrations as were necessary to plug up the holes left by the change in government.

Early in November, 1813, General Hiller invited all the departmental collectors of direct taxes who had not departed with the retreating French to continue to discharge their duties as they had in the past. Also retained in office were the departmental intendants of finance, who supervised, as they had previously, the levying and collecting of indirect taxes, and now, in addition, looked after all state property located in the department.[114] Instead of reporting to the ministry of finance, as they formerly had done, the intendants were now to receive their orders from and send their communications directly to the governor's office.[115]

[112] Proclamation of February 19, 1814, *Collezione di leggi venete,* 1813–1814, Vol. I, pp. 94–111.

[113] See especially Emperor Francis to Reuss-Plauen, Frankfurt, November 9, 1813, St. A. (Vienna), Conferenz Akten, Ser. b, 1813, No. 789.

[114] Hiller order, Trent, November 8, 1813, *Collezione di leggi venete,* 1813–1814, Vol. I, pp. 13–14.

[115] A directive to all intendants of finance from the Venetian government in

Since many of the tax collectors and intendants had deserted the capital, along with the prefects, just ahead of the advancing Habsburg army, the same confusion which beset the departmental prefectural offices during the first few months of Habsburg rule also exerted a deleterious effect on the financial administration. As was the case with the prefectural offices, the Habsburgs found it difficult to find satisfactory substitutes for the French-Italian financial employees who had fled. Ardent champions of the Napoleonic regime were naturally reluctant to expose themselves to French vengeance in case the enemy might return to power. As a consequence, all too many inexperienced incompetents crept into positions of influence,[116] while the former French-Italian employees who remained in office were thoroughly despised by the populace as symbols of the vexatious exactions which the French had levied upon them during the last days of the Kingdom of Italy.[117]

The inefficiency on the departmental level reflected itself in even greater deficiencies at the top. In the Kingdom of Italy all important decisions had been made either by the ministries of finance and of the treasury in Milan or else by the directories attached to them.[118] As a consequence, the finance offices in the departments were relatively small in size. Now that all lines of communication with Milan were severed the departmental staffs were entirely too undermanned to cope with the large volume of business which suddenly inundated them at a time when the Habsburgs, whose main efforts were concentrated on winning the war, still had not found the time to piece together anything resembling a central financial administration to deal with even the most urgent and pressing emergencies.

The main burden of devising some kind of central organization to restore order to the chaotic and deplorable financial jumble in Venetia

---

Padua, dated April 18, 1814, specified what their regular reports to the central government were to include. See A. S. (Venice), Governo veneto, 1814, Organizzazione, Fasc. I, A, B, No. 8409/241.

[116] Reuss-Plauen to Lazanzky, Venice, December 6, 1814, A. S. (Venice), Presidio di governo, 1814, No. 2110.

[117] See especially Torresani to Raab, Venice, October 17, 1814, ibid., No. 1530; and the anonymous letter sent to the presidency of the Venetian government on November 5, 1814, ibid., No. 1760.

[118] For a good analysis of the financial administration of the Kingdom of Italy, see Galvagna report, Venice, March 1, 1820, ibid., 1815–1819, Finanza, Fasc. IV, ad No. 2431/P.P. del 1819.

at first fell upon the shoulders of Tax Commissioner Romani,[119] a competent, honest man, who was, however, an ineffectual leader of men and too old to cope with the crushing burdens of his office; and the financial counselor of the central government, Anzidei, who had been intendant of finance of the department of Piave before the Austrians had selected him for his present position. Both officials were unable to make much headway in regularizing the finances, not because they were incompetent, as the Habsburg government in Vienna believed, but rather because such a pitifully inadequate staff was allotted to them that not even a financial wizard could have accomplished the job. As a consequence, instead of being able to concentrate on top level planning, Romani and Anzidei had to fritter away their energies in checking thousands of petty tax accounts and in disposing of other minutiae that are usually better taken care of by subordinate clerks.[120]

Unfortunately, Governor Reuss-Plauen was not provided with an experienced, top-level financial administrator to assist him with systematizing the financial administration until the summer of 1814,[121] when Emperor Francis sent Imperial Counselor Joseph Mayer von Gravenegg[122] to Venetia to advise the governor on all financial matters.[123] Mayer von Gravenegg was to supervise and bring order to the Venetian financial administration, to make provision to insure that all existing taxes were punctually and faithfully collected, and to give advice on how the financial administration could be improved. Except in cases of extreme urgency, however, he was to inaugurate no changes in the existing setup before obtaining the emperor's express approval.[124]

[119] Romani was sent to Venetia from Görz early in February, 1814 (Ugarte to Reuss-Plauen, February 6, 1814, A. S. [Venice], Presidio di governo, 1814, ad No. 2099).

[120] Reuss-Plauen to Lazanzky, Venice, December 6, 1814, *ibid.*, No. 2110; Lazanzky to Reuss-Plauen, Vienna, November 14, 1814, *ibid.;* Galvagna report, Venice, March 1, 1820, *ibid.*, 1815–1819, Finanza, Fasc. IV, ad No. 2431/P.P. del 1819.

[121] Lazanzky to Reuss-Plauen, Vienna, September 12, 1814, A. S. (Venice), Presidio di governo, 1814, No. 1482 R.R.

[122] Mayer von Gravenegg was an official of the Hofkammer in Vienna. In 1815 he returned to his former position in the Habsburg capital.

[123] Emperor Francis to Ugarte, June 7, 1814, St. A. (Vienna), Conferenz Akten, Ser. b, 1814, No. 1098; Ugarte note, Vienna, July 8, 1814, *Verwaltungsarchiv* (Vienna), Hofräte, Lombardei-Venedig, Fasz. III, A, 4, No. 15,577/1009.

[124] Imperial resolution, Schönbrunn, September 9, 1814, *Hofkammer Archiv*

Upon arriving in Venice, Mayer von Gravenegg concentrated his attention first on making an attempt to improve the efficiency of the central accounting office. Immediately after Austrian troops had occupied the Venetian provinces, the Habsburgs had established a central accounting bureau to examine all tax records and other financial papers that had previously been dispatched to Milan for auditing and to keep track of all government expenditures. With a typical Habsburg penchant for economy, however, the Austrians assigned only nineteen employees to the office—at a time when a veritable avalanche of records was pouring into the office for examination! As a consequence, the accounting office fell so far behind in its work that no one had anything approximating an exact idea about what the actual monthly receipts and expenditures were or even about what revenues the Habsburgs could expect to collect in the occupied Italian provinces. Even in August when, presumably on Mayer von Gravenegg's recommendation, the personnel was increased to fifty-eight, the central accounting office was still unable to catch up with the huge backlog of work, let alone organize regular procedures for the orderly transaction of the government's financial business. In October Mayer von Gravenegg estimated that an office force of at least one hundred was urgently needed to handle the routine affairs of the central accounting office.[125]

After trying, in vain, to turn the central accounting office into something at least resembling an efficient operation, Mayer von Gravenegg devoted himself to reforming the offices concerned with the collection of indirect taxes, which were under the supervision of Tax Commissioner Romani. Since Romani's incapacity for leadership was obvious, Mayer decided to ease him out of his job and replace him with Baron von Waldstätten, the deputy director of the Venetian tobacco administration, who he thought was an intelligent and ener-

---

(Vienna), Central-Organisirungs-Hof-Commission Akten, Rinna, 1814, No. 1025/125; Rinna to Bellegarde and Reuss-Plauen, Vienna, September 12, 1814, *ibid.*; Lazanzky to Reuss-Plauen, Vienna, September 12, 1814, A. S. (Venice), Presidio di governo, 1814, No. 1482 R.R.; instructions to Mayer von Gravenegg proposed by the Hofkammer and the aulic central organization commission, n.d., *Hofkammer Archiv* (Vienna), Kredit Akten, Fasz. XIVB1, No. 8045 ex X 1814.

[125] Reuss-Plauen to Stadion, Venice, October 19, 1814, A. S. (Venice), Presidio di governo, 1814, No. 1557; presidential reports of the Venetian central government to the aulic central organization commission, Venice, September 19 and October 23, 1814, *ibid.*, Nos. 1262 and 1678.

getic young administrator.[126] For this purpose, he established a special office to superintend the collection of all indirect taxes—customs, salt, consumption, stamp, roads, powder, saltpeter, navigation, and tobacco—and named Waldstätten as its director. Romani was assigned to him as chief assistant.[127]

Hardly any decision which Mayer von Gravenegg might have made could have ended in more unfortunate consequences for the Venetian tax administration. Shortly after the new office, which was activated on November 1, had begun its operations a serious misunderstanding arose between Romani and Waldstätten, as a consequence of which the former went off in a huff on a four weeks' vacation to Görz,[128] which he later extended another six weeks.[129] Worse still, the government at Vienna, rightly as it turned out, looked askance at the appointment to such an important post of a man with as little actual experience as Waldstätten and allowed him to remain at his post only until a better qualified administrator could be sent to Venice.[130] Early in 1815 Frauel von Weissenthurm replaced him, and Waldstätten returned to his previous position in the tobacco administration.[131] It was high time! Too incompetent for such an important post, yet anxious to change everything at once, Waldstätten during his few weeks in office had succeeded only in greatly augmenting the confusion and disorder which had beset the Austrian tax administration in Venetia from the very beginning.[132]

Thus the provisional Habsburg financial administration in Venetia

[126] Presidential report of the Venetian central government to the aulic central organization commission, Venice, November 16, 1814, *ibid.*, No. 1912; Reuss-Plauen to Lazanzky, Venice, December 7, 1814, *ibid.*, No. 2188.

[127] Lazanzky to Reuss-Plauen, Vienna, October 10, 1814, *ibid.*, No. 1912; Reuss-Plauen to Waldstätten, Venice, October 18, 1814, *ibid.*, No. 1537; Reuss-Plauen to Romani, Venice, October 24, 1814, *ibid.*, No. 1627; Reuss-Plauen to aulic central organization commission, Venice, November 7, 1814, *ibid.*, No. 1814.

[128] Lazanzky to Reuss-Plauen, Vienna, November 22, 1814, *ibid.*, No. 2188 P.R.

[129] Reuss-Plauen to aulic central organization commission, Venice, December 1, 1814, *ibid.*, No. 2099.

[130] Lazanzky to Reuss-Plauen, Vienna, November 22, 1814, *ibid.*, No. 2188 P.R.

[131] Heberstein Moltke to Reuss-Plauen, Vienna, January 18, 1815, *ibid.*, 1815–1819, Finanza, Fasc. IV 4/4, No. 774/148,458/P.P.

[132] Galvagna report, Venice, March 1, 1820, *ibid.*, Fasc. IV, ad No. 2431/P.P. del 1819.

was anything but a model of efficiency and competence. Fortunately, the change-over from the French to the Habsburg system of judicial administration proceeded much more smoothly. In the Kingdom of Italy there had been a court of cassation and five courts of appeals. The court of appeals for the departments situated between the Isonzo and Adige Rivers was located in Venice. In each department capital there had been a civil and criminal court and a tribunal of first instance to handle civil and criminal cases. In each canton there had been a justice of the peace. Special courts had handled cases not provided for by the ordinary courts.[133]

Immediately after their troops arrived in Italy the Austrians issued a circular announcing that all the French courts except the court of cassation, the courts of appeals, and the special courts were provisionally to be retained and that all the existing criminal, civil, and commercial laws of the Kingdom of Italy, as well as all decrees and special regulations passed by the previous government, were to continue in force.[134] Until a permanent judicial organization was created all cases previously handled by the court of cassation in Milan were to be disposed of by the supreme court in Vienna.[135] For the trying of cases of appeal, it was first provided that, beginning on February 1, 1814, the departmental courts of justice were to judge them. Cases appealed from the court in Treviso were to be tried by the departmental court of justice at Udine. Those appealed from Udine and Belluno were to be handled at Treviso; those from Padua, at Vicenza; and those from Vicenza, at Padua.[136] After the capture of the city of Venice on April 20 this function of the departmental courts was suspended, and the court of appeals in that city was again made the court of appeals for all Venetia,[137] as it had been when Venetia was

133 Reuss-Plauen to Ugarte, Udine, February 11, 1814, St. A. (Vienna), Kaiser Franz Akten, Fasz. XVII, Kon. 1, Fo. 22.

134 Hiller order, Trent, November 8, 1813, *Collezione di leggi venete*, 1813–1814, Vol. I, pp. 10–12; proclamation of January 9, 1814, *ibid.*, pp. 66–67; proclamation, Count Porcia, Padua, November 8, 1813, A. S. (Venice), Governo veneto, 1813-1814, Polizia, Fasc. V, A, No. 1138.

135 See the circulars dated July 21 and August 26, 1814, *Collezione di leggi venete*, 1813–1814, Vol. II, pp. 10–11 and 36–44.

136 Decree of January 21, 1814, *ibid.*, Vol. I, pp. 78–80. See also Ottolenghi, *Padova e il Dipartimento del Brenta*, pp. 122–123.

137 Proclamation of May 5, 1814, *Collezione di leggi venete*, 1813–1814, Vol. I, pp. 232–234; Staats-Conferenz to Reuss-Plauen, Vienna, May 7, 1814, St. A. (Vienna), Conferenz Akten, Ser. b, 1814, No. 932.

under French-Italian domination. During the month of May still another modification was made in the French judicial system as provisionally taken over by the Habsburgs. In order to reduce the cost of trying cases involving petty sums of money or minor infractions of the law, the office of justice of the peace was abolished. Bailiffs were appointed to replace the justices of the peace in the towns where they had had their office.[138]

With these changes, the main gaps in the Venetian judiciary, as inherited from the French, were filled. Having set up what appeared to be an adequate provisional structure, the Habsburgs now busied themselves with devising a permanent judicial administration for the occupied provinces. To pave the way, Emperor Francis instructed Baron von Hager, in April, 1814, to provide the supreme court in Vienna with reports on the talents, character, political opinions, and experience of all judicial officials in the occupied provinces.[139] In May he issued orders that the Austrian civil code was to be translated into Italian.[140] Then, after consulting the state conference,[141] the emperor decided in June, 1814, to send Imperial Counselor Leopold von Plenciz,[142] the aulic justice regulation commissioner in Illyria, to Venetia to head a commission charged with making recommendations on how the Venetian judicial system could be integrated into that of the Habsburg monarchy.[143] The next month Counselor of Appeals, and later Imperial Counselor, Johann Franz Fratnich, Imperial Secretary von Beine, and two subordinate clerks, Hyronimus Ruberti[144] and Micaele Chiarini,[145] were sent to Venice to assist Plenciz in this work.

Perhaps in part because Emperor Francis felt so strongly that an

---

[138] Circular dated May 10, 1814, *Collezione di leggi venete*, 1813-1814, Vol. I, pp. 234–236.

[139] Staats-Conferenz to Hager, Vienna, April 13, 1814, St. A. (Vienna), Conferenz Akten, Ser. b, 1814, No. 762.

[140] Emperor Francis to Zichy, Paris, May 14, 1814, *ibid.*, No. 996.

[141] Imperial resolution, Chaumont, March 15, 1814, *ibid.*, No. 629.

[142] In 1815 Plenciz was given the additional assignment of president of the court of appeals in Venice. The next year he was appointed second vice-president of the supreme court of justice in Vienna. In addition, he was made president of the Italian senate of the supreme court in Verona.

[143] Öttingen to Reuss-Plauen, Vienna, June 7, 1814, A. S. (Venice), Governo veneto, 1814, Organizzazione, Fasc. I, A, B, No. 18,845/4030.

[144] Ugarte to Reuss-Plauen, Vienna, July 26, 1814, *ibid.*, No. 25,804/2119.

[145] Plenciz to Venetian central government, Venice, July 28, 1814, *ibid.*, Fasc. I, B, No. 1/6, 814.

effective and impartial judiciary was the necessary foundation for a successful government, the judicial organization which the Habsburgs hastily devised on a provisional basis functioned better than any of their other makeshift administrations in Venetia. The emperor was also adamant in insisting that all the administrative offices in Venetia were to be staffed with able, reliable, and loyal employees.

When their armies first entered Italy, the Austrians adopted the policy of retaining in office all employees of the former Kingdom of Italy who had remained at their posts, if they were not hated by the populace, if they were not known to be fanatical supporters of the French, and if they would take oaths of allegiance to the Habsburg emperor.[146] Count Thurn and Prince Reuss-Plauen faithfully followed this policy during the first few months of the Austrian occupation.[147]

Convenient or even necessary as this policy may have been in making it possible for the Habsburgs to find enough manpower for their administrative offices, this retention en masse of servants of a former government had grave shortcomings. Knowing on which side their bread was now buttered, some of the former French-Italian officials injured the Austrian cause by protesting their continued loyalty to the Habsburgs in too servile and fawning a manner, thereby earning for themselves the contempt of both the populace and their new masters. Others were suspected of unfaithfulness and of deliberately adopting unpopular administrative practices and tactics for the express purpose of stirring up those with whom they dealt against the Austrians. Still others behaved in such an arbitrary and officious manner that they exasperated the inhabitants.[148]

When Emperor Francis learned of the objectionable conduct of some of his newly appointed Italian officials he gave strict orders that all Italian employees in Venetia be carefully screened. Those who had lost public confidence, who were immoral or untalented, or

---

[146] Emperor Francis to Reuss-Plauen, Frankfurt, November 9, 1813, St. A. (Vienna), Conferenz Akten, Ser. b, 1813, No. 789; Hiller order, Trent, November 8, 1813, *Collezione di leggi venete*, 1813–1814, Vol. I, p. 5.

[147] Reuss-Plauen to Ugarte, Udine, February 11, 1814, St. A. (Vienna), Kaiser Franz Akten, Fasz. XXVII, Kon. 1, Fo. 18; Giacomo Jacotti to Venetian central government, n.p., n.d., A. S. (Venice), Governo veneto, 1814, Organizzazione, Fasc. I, B, No. 1/921.

[148] Hager report, January 11, 1814, St. A. (Vienna), Conferenz Akten, Ser. b, 1814, No. 38; Hingenau to Zichy, Padua, February 24, 1814, *ibid.*, No. 507; Staats-Kabinet reports of February 6 and March 1, 1814, St. A. (Vienna), Kabinets-Akten, 1814, Nos. 1077 and 1193.

whose loyalty to the Austrian monarch was questionable were to be dismissed.[149] The emperor was especially frightened over the capacity for mischief of officials who were Masons or members of other secret societies. Having already ordered the abolition of all secret societies in his monarchy on April 23, 1801,[150] he readily believed the admonitions of Police President von Hager that the Freemasons were an almost universally hated sect of avowed enemies of Austria.[151] Disturbed over the reports that many of the former officials of the Kingdom of Italy who were provisionally retained in office still continued their membership in Masonic lodges,[152] he ordered that all employees who belonged to secret societies were to be allowed to continue in their positions only if they immediately withdrew from any sect with which they might be connected and promised under oath that they would never again join one.[153] In order to insure that proficient, upright, hard-working employees devoted to the Habsburg cause were appointed to replace those who were dismissed for belonging to dangerous sects or for other reasons, the emperor ordered his officials to make reliable reports about the capabilities, religious beliefs, moral behavior, and political views of all employees of the Venetian government between 1798 and 1805,[154] when Vene-

[149] Emperor Francis to Zichy, Basel, January 12, 1814, St. A. (Vienna), Conferenz Akten, Ser. b, 1814, No. 131; protocol of the Staats-Conferenz, February 15, 1814, *ibid.*, No. 147; Emperor Francis to Zichy, Paris, April 25, 1814, *ibid.*, No. 893; imperial resolution, Chaumont, March 9, 1814, St. A. (Vienna), Kabinets-Akten, 1814, No. 1262; Staats-Kabinet report, January 17, 1814, *ibid.*, No. 957.

[150] Ignaz Beidtel, *Geschichte der österreichischen Staatsverwaltung, 1740–1848*, Vol. II, p. 96.

[151] See Staats-Conferenz report, January 11, 1814, St. A. (Vienna), Conferenz Akten, Ser. b, 1814, No. 51.

[152] Hager to Staats-Conferenz, January 5, 1814, *ibid.*

[153] Staats-Conferenz report, March 15, 1814, *ibid.*, No. 587; Staats-Conferenz to Öttingen, Vienna, March 29, 1814, *ibid.*, No. 655; Hager to Baron von Lattermann, Prince Reuss-Plauen, and General von Tomassich, Vienna, March 20, 1814, Joseph Alexander Helfert, *La caduta della dominazione francese nell'alta Italia e la congiura bresciano-milanese nel 1814*, Appendix I, pp. 233–234. A copy of the oath which all employees took is included in Reuss-Plauen to Ugarte, Padua, April 11, 1814, St. A. (Vienna), Conferenz Akten, Ser. b, 1814, No. 952.

[154] Zichy to Lazanzky, February 24, 1814, *Verwaltungsarchiv* (Vienna), Hofkanzlei, Lombardei-Venedig, Fasz. III, A, 4, ex Februar 1814; Ugarte to Reuss-Plauen, Vienna, June 25, 1814, A. S. (Venice), Presidio di governo, 1814, No. 443.

tia had previously been under Austrian rule, as well as of all persons employed in 1814.[155]

The emperor no doubt sincerely hoped that the investigations of the past and present employees would be carried out in a discreet and unbiased manner. However, at a time when political tensions were high and when many hotheads were inclined to hold former French officials personally responsible for oppressions which they had suffered during the Napoleonic regime, it was too much to think that such an inquiry could be impartial. As was to be expected under the circumstances, various persons, many with axes to grind, secretly fed the Austrian police with the wildest and most incredible denunciations of French-Italian officials who now held positions of trust in the Habsburg government.[156]

The accusations of these anonymous "patriots" might have opened the door to an orgy of "witch hunts" had not the responsible officials in Venetia shown intelligence and circumspection in evaluating many a clandestine denunciation that reached their offices. The police director, Raab, a tolerant, fair-minded, and prudent man, acted on the principle that a government employee was not necessarily untrustworthy just because he had faithfully served the Napoleonic regime. In his opinion, the very fact that a lesser official had demonstrated his loyalty to the previous regime might give proof that he would also honestly serve the Austrians. Furthermore, Raab admonished, one should not be too much influenced by reports that officials were unpopular with the inhabitants, since frequently the most able and reliable administrators were in bad repute only because they had conscientiously fulfilled their obligations with undeviating honesty.[157] Governor Reuss-Plauen also frequently defended officials who had been accused by vindictive calumniators. At times, rather than fire a man who proved to be unsuitable in one spot, he recommended his transfer to another post where he could give better service. However, the governor could not defend everyone in a government post, since

[155] Hager to Reuss-Plauen, Vienna, May 12, 1814, A. S. (Venice), Presidio di governo, 1814, ad No. 599; protocol, presidency of the Venetian central government, May 1, 1814, *ibid.*, ad No. 779; Reuss-Plauen to Hager, Venice, December 12, 1814, *ibid.*, No. 1903, 2026, 2028, 2049.

[156] For examples, see the secret reports dated Padua, June 20, and Venice, June 22, 1814, *ibid.*, No. 790; and Torresani to Hager, Venice, March 21, 1815, *ibid.*, 1815, No. 198/v.b.p.

[157] Raab report, Padua, June 5, 1814, *ibid.*, 1814, No. 443.

his authority over appointments was limited to minor jobs. The naming of all personnel which in the Kingdom of Italy had been reserved to Napoleon—a long list, indeed![158]—was the special prerogative of the aulic government in Vienna.[159]

Emperor Francis was thus insistent that all government officials in Venetia were to be able and efficient and loyal to the Habsburgs. He was equally determined that all pensions due them were to be paid. Shortly after Habsburg troops entered Italy he ordered the employees of former Austrian Lombardy to be compensated for all pensions still coming to them and asked his officials to prepare reliable lists of persons entitled to such payments.[160] He also agreed that the pensions due former employees of the Kingdom of Italy[161] and of the previous Austrian government in Venetia were to be charged to the Habsburg treasury, and in June he asked his officials to draw up workable plans to discharge this obligation.[162] It was high time. By the summer of 1814 a large number of pensioners, having received only one small payment since September, 1813, were reduced to dire straits and were grumbling loudly about the inexcusable slowness of the Austrians in meeting their obligations.[163] Yet, even though the Austrians were fully aware that many former government employees were almost in a state of desperation, the wheels of their bureaucratic

[158] In the Kingdom of Italy the king, in addition to selecting the personnel for all important posts in the central government, appointed the prefects, vice-prefects, prefectural counselors, general secretaries, members of the departmental councils, tax officers, and counselors of the first and second class communes (Bellegarde report on the Austrian-Italian provinces, October 25, 1814, Helfert, *Kaiser Franz und die Stiftung des Lombardo-Venetianischen Königreichs*, Appendix I, pp. 531–532).

[159] Protocol of the Venetian central government, August 12 and 16, 1814, A. S. (Venice), Governo veneto, 1814, Organizzazione, Fasc. I, B, No. 2192/118.

[160] Emperor Francis to Zichy, Vendeuvre, February 24, 1814, St. A. (Vienna), Conferenz Akten, Ser. b, 1814, No. 486.

[161] According to the Treaty of Paris of May 30, 1814, the French were not obligated to pay pensions due after January 1, 1814, to persons living in territories that were taken away from them.

[162] Emperor Francis to Ugarte, June 14, 1814, St. A. (Vienna), Conferenz Akten, Ser. b, 1814, No. 1057.

[163] Staats-Conferenz report, June 15, 1814, *ibid.*, No. 1101; Hager to Staats-Conferenz, June 17, 1814, *ibid.*, No. 1174; Hager report, July 8, 1814, *ibid.*, No. 1346; secret report to Hager, Padua, June 20, 1814, A. S. (Venice), Presidio di governo, 1814, No. 790; Mulazzani to Reuss-Plauen, Venice, May 28, 1814, *ibid.*, No. 132.

machine ground so slowly that they were not in a position to make
the first payment to the needy pensioners before September, 1814.[164]

The Austrian emperor was personally concerned about the loyalty
and well-being of all officials in his service. However, of all persons
who made the public welfare their business no group received more
attention from him than the clergy. Having a great interest in the
moral and religious training of all his subjects, he believed that it was
especially important to make an all-out effort to restore the clergy
to their former position of influence in the re-acquired Italian lands,
if only because the French had so badly neglected the religious and
moral training of the youth.[165]

As was true in other lands under Napoleonic rule, the Italian
church had suffered much during the revolutionary and Napoleonic
eras. The French had suppressed all but a handful of eight hundred
monasteries and convents which had existed in Lombardy and Venetia before 1796 and had appropriated the income from the benefices
which supported them and other religious pursuits. Except for those
who proved useful in furthering French interests, the clergy endured
a host of petty indignities during the period of Napoleonic domination.[166]

When the Habsburgs returned to Italy it was made plain to the
clergy that the Austrian monarch would support their efforts to instill
in the populace a deep reverence for Christian religious and moral
principles.[167] To restore religion to its former uncorrupted position,
the emperor prescribed the substitution of the Austrian for the old
Bossuet catechism which the French had introduced into Italy.[168] To
make it clear that he would tolerate only churchmen who merited
the respect of the Venetian populace, he ordered all bawdy and li-
centious clergymen to be disciplined.[169]

[164] Galvagna notice, Venice, September 3, 1814, *Giornale di Venezia*, No. 125
(September 6, 1814), p. 4.
[165] See especially Hager to Staats-Conferenz, April 16, 1814, St. A. (Vienna),
Conferenz Akten, Ser. b, 1814, No. 917.
[166] Helfert, *Kaiser Franz und die Stiftung des Lombardo-Venetianischen Königreichs*, pp. 38–39.
[167] Lazanzky to Reuss-Plauen, Vienna, August 25, 1814, A. S. (Venice), Presidio di governo, 1814, ad No. 1117; Lazanzky to Venetian provisional government, Vienna, October 24, 1814, *ibid.*, No. 2008 P.R.
[168] Circular of August 18, 1814, *Collezione di leggi venete*, 1813–1814, Vol.
II, p. 33.
[169] Hager to Reuss-Plauen, Vienna, September 7, 1814, A. S. (Venice), Pre-

The emperor also issued instructions that arrangements were to be made to take care of the monks and nuns whose houses had been dissolved by the French. He directed his governor in Venetia to make a detailed report about all former monasteries that had been suppressed and all monastic properties that had been confiscated. Reuss-Plauen was to advise him in regard to how many and which of these cloisters it would be useful and desirable to restore.[170] Until such time as the emperor came to a definite decision about which monasteries were to be reinstated the monks and nuns who had been dismissed by the French were to be paid the same pensions that they had received from the previous government.[171] He stressed the fact, however, that not all of them would be permitted to return to their former houses. Emperor Francis was still too much under the influence of his uncle, Joseph II, to be willing to allow more regular clergy to come back to Venetia than were needed to render necessary and useful services. Furthermore, although he issued orders to prevent further confiscations,[172] he fully recognized that it was both inadvisable and impossible to return to the clergy the rich church properties which the French had sold to private persons.

Josephinist that he was, Emperor Francis zealously protected the sovereign rights which he claimed that he had in regard to the temporal affairs of the church. From the outset he insisted that no pastoral letter, proclamation, or decree could be issued or published in Austria and that, with the exception of those originating in the Roman penitentiary or dealing strictly with spiritual matters, no bull, constitution, or other instruction coming from abroad could be enforced in the monarchy unless the government had given previous consent.[173] Before any mandate issued by the papacy was accorded

sidio di governo, 1814, No. 1190; Raab to Venetian central government, Venice, December 4, 1814, *ibid.*, ad No. 2181.

[170] Lazanzky to Reuss-Plauen, Vienna, August 25, 1814, *ibid.*, ad No. 1117.

[171] Helfert, *Kaiser Franz und die Stiftung des Lombardo-Venetianischen Königreichs*, p. 139.

[172] Aulic central organization commission report, January 30, 1815, St. A. (Vienna), Staats-Rath Akten, 1815, No. 1048; imperial resolution, Vienna, February 26, 1815, *ibid.*

[173] Lazanzky to Reuss-Plauen, Vienna, August 25 and September 5, 1814, A. S. (Venice), Presidio di governo, 1814, ad No. 1117 and No. 1204; Ottolenghi, *Padova e il Dipartimento del Brenta*, pp. 178–181. See also Ferdinand Maass, *Der Josephinismus. Quellen zu seiner Geschichte in Österreich 1760–1850. Amtliche Dokumente aus dem Haus-, Hof- und Staatsarchiv und dem Allgemeinen*

such approval it was always first to be legitimized by the Habsburg agent in Rome, Carlo von Andreoli.[174]

In the summer of 1814 the emperor's determination to assert the temporal rights of the Habsburg sovereign collided head-on with Pius VII's equal resolve to maintain his own authority over the Catholic church. The issue arose over the appointment of a new patriarch for Venice. In 1811 Napoleon had chosen Bishop Stefano Bonsignore of Faenza for the position. A willing tool of the French ruler, Bonsignore assumed the post notwithstanding the fact that the pope refused to confirm the appointment. A few days after the Austrians occupied Venice in April, 1814, the patriarch's cathedral chapter, asserting that Bonsignore's appointment had been made in violation of well established principles of canon law, refused to give him its obedience any longer, and the Venetian populace, irritated because of the patriarch's fawning devotion to Napoleon, warned him to leave the city within twenty-four hours. Bonsignore left.[175]

After the former bishop of Faenza's inglorious departure from Venice the cathedral chapter of canons elected Archdeacon Luciano Luciani general capitular vicar of the patriarchate. Just as the government in Vienna was at the point of asking Reuss-Plauen whether the new vicar had suitable administrative abilities and the proper political views to take over the office, it learned, to its consternation, that, to repress serious disorders in the diocese, the pope had designated the bishop of Chioggia, Giuseppe Maria Peruzzi, as temporal and spiritual administrator of the patriarchate. In making the appointment, Pius VII expressed the opinion that, by electing and supporting Bonsignore, the cathedral chapter had lost every right to elect a vicar.[176]

Verwaltungsarchiv in Wien, Vol. IV: *Der Spätjosephinismus 1790-1820*, pp. 99-102.

[174] Lazanzky to Reuss-Plauen, Vienna, October 3, 1814, A. S. (Venice), Presidio di governo, 1814, No. 1725; decree sent to all provincial offices, dated July 21, 1814, Maass, *Der Josephinismus*, Vol. IV, p. 478.

[175] Ugarte report, July 16, 1814, St. A. (Vienna), Staats-Rath Akten, 1814, No. 1812; Teresa Confalonieri Casati to Federico Confalonieri, Milan, May 21, 1814, Giuseppe Gallavresi (ed.), *Carteggio del conte Federico Confalonieri ed altri documenti spettanti alla sua biografia; con annotazioni storiche*, Vol. I, p. 144.

[176] Lebzeltern to Metternich, Rome, June 15, 1814, St. A. (Vienna), Staatskanzlei Akten, 1814, No. 15D; Ugarte to Staats-Rath, July 16, 1814, St. A. (Vienna), Staats-Rath Akten, 1814, No. 1812; aulic central organization commission

Pius VII's actions were in direct violation of what the Austrians claimed were their long established sovereign rights. Reuss-Plauen was instructed to inform Peruzzi that the emperor refused to grant him the necessary *placetum regium* to exercise the duties of his office. At the same time, the Habsburg embassy in Rome was advised to notify the pope that Emperor Francis was withholding his approval of Peruzzi's appointment because "the administration of the temporalities of the church can be disposed of only by the sovereign" and not by the pope. Furthermore, "the spiritual administration can be taken care of only by persons who were either appointed or confirmed by the sovereign."[177] Then, in order to have a suitable candidate on hand, the emperor instructed the Venetian governor in November and again in December to submit to him the names of able persons from whom he himself could choose a new patriarch.[178]

In the meantime, Prince Klemens Wenzel Metternich, fearing that an open quarrel between the Habsburg government and the papacy might adversely affect public opinion, and believing that the growing disorders among the Venetian clergy would continue as long as the Venetian church had no recognized head, urged his monarch on October 29 and again on January 4 to choose a patriarch as quickly as possible. His own nominee for the post was Peruzzi, whose appointment Cardinal Ettore Consalvi and the papal nuncio at Vienna, Count Gabriele Severoli, had strongly recommended and who, in Governor Reuss-Plauen's opinion, was fully qualified for the job.[179]

Metternich might have won his point had not the religious counselor of the government in Vienna, Martin Lorenz, a strong Josephinist and a bitter enemy of the ultramontanists, vigorously opposed

report, August 8, 1814, St. A. (Vienna), Conferenz Akten, Ser. b, 1814, No. 1529; papal nuncio to Metternich, Vienna, August 28, 1814, St. A. (Vienna), Staatskanzlei, Bello Severoli, ex 28 August 1814.

[177] Emperor Francis to Metternich, Vienna, September 6, 1814, St. A. (Vienna), Staats-Rath Akten, 1814, No. 1812. See also Ugarte to Staats-Rath, July 16, 1814, *ibid.*; imperial resolution, Vienna, September 6, 1814, *ibid.*; and Metternich to Severoli, Baden, September 4, 1814, Maass, *Der Josephinismus*, Vol. IV, pp. 81–82.

[178] Lazanzky to Reuss-Plauen, Vienna, November 8, 1814, A. S. (Venice), Presidio di governo, 1814, No. 1953 P.R.

[179] Metternich report, January 4, 1815, St. A. (Vienna), Staats-Rath Akten, 1815, No. 98; Metternich to Emperor Francis, Vienna, January 4, 1815, St. A. (Vienna), Staatskanzlei, Vorträge, 1815, No. 98. A copy of the last letter can also be found in Maass, *Der Josephinismus*, Vol. IV, pp. 489–490.

such a course of action. Lorenz insisted that by appointing a temporal and spiritual administrator for the Venetian patriarchate without previously consulting the emperor the pope had obviously hurled defiance at well established Austrian rights in such an unjustifiable manner that the most deleterious consequences would ensue if his pretensions were left unchallenged. Furthermore, Lorenz maintained, the pope had deliberately chosen Peruzzi for the position, not because of his talents and knowledge, which were limited, but only because of his strong championship of papal rights. Through Peruzzi the pope hoped to wield a powerful influence over the Venetian populace.[180]

Very probably because Lorenz expressed opinions very similar to his own, Emperor Francis sided with his religious counselor and refused again to countenance Peruzzi's appointment. He promised, however, to appoint someone immediately after suitable recommendations were sent him by his officials, and expressed the hope that the pope would not delay in confirming the person he chose for the office.[181] On April 10, 1815, the emperor selected the bishop of Concordia, Augusto Bressa, as patriarch.[182] Since Bressa refused to accept the appointment, it was not until December 8, 1815, when the emperor named Francesco Milesi, the bishop of Vigevano, to the post that the Venetian patriarchate acquired a head. The pope raised no objections to his selection, and Milesi was formally installed in the office on February 5, 1816.[183]

Emperor Francis was determined that the Venetian clergy should remain under his control and influence. He also insisted that as soon as possible school reforms should be made in Venetia which would insure that the Venetian youngsters would be given the same kind of citizenship training that the school children in the German regions of his monarchy received.[184] On July 11, 1814, he informed his

180 Votum of state counselor Lorenz, January 11, 1815, Helfert, *Kaiser Franz und die Stiftung des Lombardo-Venetianischen Königreichs*, Appendix III, pp. 548–549.

181 Imperial resolution, Vienna, January 26, 1815, St. A. (Vienna), Staats-Rath Akten, 1815, No. 98. Another copy can be found in St. A. (Vienna), Staatskanzlei, Vorträge, 1815, No. 98.

182 Imperial resolution, Vienna, April 10, 1815, St. A. (Vienna), Staats-Rath Akten, 1815, No. 1943.

183 Helfert, *Kaiser Franz und die Stiftung des Lombardo-Venetianischen Königreichs*, pp. 111 and 437–438.

184 For a discussion of Emperor Francis' views on citizenship training in the

state and conference minister Count Alois Ugarte[185] that the Venetian educational system was to be organized on the same basis as the one in the German provinces of the empire.[186] Four days later he directed Governor Reuss-Plauen to draw up a detailed report on the state of Venetian education which the emperor could use in reorganizing the Venetian schools. The governor was also asked to keep an eagle eye on the University of Padua, where studies were reportedly being badly neglected,[187] and to make a thorough investigation of all teachers and professors accused of being ardent French sympathizers,[188] especially those at the University of Padua (where five professors had left with the departing French army and where five others were accused of having strong anti-Austrian predilections).[189] Those who had abandoned their posts were under no circumstances to be permitted to return to Austrian territory without the emperor's special permission.[190]

In 1814 and 1815, however, the Habsburgs failed to make any permanent innovations in the Venetian educational system. The same was true in the political sphere. On all levels the government was operated on a provisional basis throughout 1814, during most of 1815, and in most instances for several years longer.[191] The Austrian

---

Habsburg monarchy, see my article on "Training for Citizenship in the Austrian Elementary Schools during the Reign of Francis I," *Journal of Central European Affairs*, Vol. IV, No. 2 (July, 1944), pp. 147–164.

[185] Count Ugarte (1749–1817), after serving in various capacities in the Habsburg service in Bohemia, Galicia, and Moravia, was appointed chancellor of the united aulic chancellery in 1802. In 1813 he was made a state and conference minister and chief chancellor. He was one of Emperor Francis' most trusted advisors for internal affairs.

[186] Emperor Francis to Ugarte, Baden, July 11, 1814, *Unterrichtsarchiv* (Vienna), Studienhofcommission Akten, No. 56 ex August 1814.

[187] Studienhofkommission to Reuss-Plauen, Vienna, July 15, 1814, *ibid.*, ad No. 94 ex August 1814.

[188] Emperor Francis to Ruess-Plauen, Paris, May 7, 1814, St. A. (Vienna), Kabinets-Akten, 1814, No. 103; Emperor Francis to Reuss-Plauen, Baden, July 11, 1814, St. A. (Vienna), Conferenz Akten, Ser. b, 1814, No. 1164.

[189] Hager report, April 24, 1814, St. A. (Vienna), Kabinets-Akten, 1814, No. 103.

[190] Emperor Francis to Reuss-Plauen, Paris, May 7, 1814, *ibid.* A copy can also be found in A. S. (Venice), Presidio di governo, 1814, No. 113.

[191] See my "The Austrian Provisional Government in Lombardy-Venetia, 1814–1815," *Journal of Central European Affairs*, Vol. II, No. 3 (October, 1942), pp. 263–266.

provisional government was probably neither more nor less efficient than those in the many other areas subjected to provisional military administration. The hastily patched together local, provincial, and judicial administrations functioned reasonably well—perhaps as well as could be expected under the existing circumstances. The financial administration, however, bordered on chaos, while the central government operated so inefficiently that, in spite of repeated injunctions from Vienna, work progressed at a snail's pace and highly important reports were held up for months.

Judging from the lack of complaints in the pertinent documents in the Venetian and Austrian state archives, one can conclude that, except for those made about the incompetence of the central government and the virtual paralysis of the financial administration, the chief criticisms of the populace about their new provisional regime were voiced not because of the innovations which the Habsburgs had made but rather because there were so few. Thoroughly disgusted with the French, the Venetians wanted the overthrow of all vestiges of the hated French rule. They found it difficult to understand why the Habsburgs did not emulate the Sardinian, Tuscan, and Papal governments in making haste to throw out all trappings of the former French regime and restoring the old pre-revolutionary order.[192] The Venetians were so disconsolate over the fact that the Habsburgs had not immediately rid them of the whole French system, lock, stock, and barrel, that the Austrian police reported the preservation of the French administrative system to be one of the main causes for complaint and dissatisfaction in Venetia.[193] Just as irritating to the Italians was the retention of practically all the employees of the Kingdom of Italy who had not fled with the retreating French army. Many of them were able and conscientious officials, who performed the duties of their offices as well for the Austrians as they had for the French. But as servants of the former French regime they were personally held responsible for all the vexatious grievances which the inhabitants had endured. When the Habsburgs arrived, the Venetians

[192] Hager report, July 15, 1814, St. A. (Vienna), Conferenz Akten, Ser. b, 1814, No. 1393.

[193] See especially Staats-Kabinet reports, January 17 and March 1 and 25, 1814, St. A. (Vienna), Kabinets-Akten, 1814, Nos. 957, 1193, and 1320; Hager report, April 16, 1814, St. A. (Vienna), Conferenz Akten, Ser. b, 1814, No. 917; and political report of the department of Adriatico for October, 1814, dated Venice, November 2, 1814, A. S. (Venice), Presidio di governo, 1814, ad No. 1749.

expected them immediately to dismiss all the French officials. Instead, the Austrians allowed nearly all of them to continue to discharge their duties as they had before.[194] Thus many Venetians became disillusioned with the Habsburgs within a few months after their arrival in the country, not because the Austrians tried overnight to inflict a German system of government upon them, but, instead, because in not doing so they allowed them to remain under a French system which they thoroughly scorned and hated.

[194] See especially Hager reports, January 1 and May 23, 1814, St. A. (Vienna), Kabinets-Akten, 1814, Nos. 957 and 1583; Hager reports, April 16 and June 17, 1814, St. A. (Vienna), Conferenz Akten, Ser. b, 1814, Nos. 917 and 1174; and Staats-Kabinet reports, February 6 and March 1, 1814, St. A. (Vienna), Kabinets-Akten, 1814, Nos. 1077 and 1193.

Chapter 2

THE LOMBARD PROVISIONAL GOVERNMENT

The Habsburgs were able to establish a provisional administration with much less difficulty in Lombardy than in Venetia, and their government in Lombardy functioned with considerably more dispatch and efficiency than in the territory of the former Republic of San Marco. In Venetia they had been faced, not only with the problem of organizing suitable provincial, local, financial, and judicial administrations, but also with the necessity of hastily devising an entirely new governing apparatus for the area as a whole at a time when nearly all their efforts were of necessity devoted to fighting a war to a successful conclusion. In Lombardy, where they could make use of many of the central administrative offices of the highly centralized Kingdom of Italy that were located in Milan, they were confronted with a revolution—the Milanese revolution of April 20.[1] Napoleon had already abdicated his position as king of Italy at Fontainebleau on April 11, and, through his resignation, his all-embracing dictatorial powers in the Kingdom of Italy had fallen upon the shoulders of his viceroy, Prince Eugene Beauharnais. On April 20—a few days before Austrian troops arrived in the Lombard capital—revolutionists in Milan ousted the viceroy from the government; forced the senate, which, next to the king and the viceroy, was the highest political authority in the kingdom, to declare itself abolished; and suppressed the council of state. It is true that the whole local and provincial administrative systems were still intact, but all that was left of the central government after the smoke of revolution had been cleared away was the electoral colleges (a democratic window-dressing with no real powers), the seven ministries of state, and the lesser directories

[1] For a detailed account of this revolution, see my *Fall of the Napoleonic Kingdom of Italy*, pp. 81–126.

and divisions subordinated to these ministries. Although the administrative bureaus were still in existence, the central directing bodies were gone.

To assume the powers left vacant by the expulsion from the kingdom of the king and the viceroy and the abolition of the senate and the council of state, the communal council of the city of Milan appointed, on the evening of April 20, a provisional regency, with Carlo Verri as president, Giuseppe Pallavicini as secretary, and Giorgio Giulini, Alberto Litta, Giberto Borromeo, Giacomo Mellerio, Domenico Pino, and Giovanni Bazetta as its other members.[2] At a meeting hastily called for April 22 the electoral colleges confirmed this regency and enlarged it by adding to it Giacomo Muggiasca to represent the department of Lario; Giovanni Batista Vertova, for the department of Serio; Matteo Sommariva, for Alto Po; Lucrezio Longo, for Mella; Luigi Tonni, for Mincio; Giovanni Batista Tarsis, for Agogna; and Francesco Peregalli, for Adda.[3]

To soothe the bitter discontent of the populace and to insure that some semblance of political stability would be maintained, the provisional regency abolished certain enactments of the previous regime which were especially opprobrious. It ordered that, although the Kingdom of Italy was to continue as a separate political unit, henceforth all official pronouncements were to bear the notation, "during the provisional regency."[4] It abolished or reduced a number of taxes that were particularly abominated[5] and declared that all persons who had been imprisoned for evading the conscription laws, for failing to comply with the financial regulations, or for expressing opinions inimical to the French were to be immediately freed, provided that they had not engaged in violence or any other crime.[6] Only sons and supporters of families were exempted from military service,[7] and the

[2] Protocol of the Milan communal council, Milan, April 21, 1814, *Museo del Risorgimento italiano* (Milan), "Carte del Giacomo Beccaria," Busta I, Carte 8, Fasc. I, Pezza 6, B (hereafter cited as *Museo* (Milan), "Carte Beccaria").

[3] Decree, electoral colleges, Milan, April 24, 1814, *Raccolta degli atti del governo e delle disposizioni generali emanate dalle diverse autorità in oggetti sì amministrativi che giudiziarj,* 1814, p. 14 (hereafter cited as *Atti del governo lombardo*).

[4] Decree, provisional regency, Milan, April 22, 1814, *ibid.,* p. 7.

[5] See *post,* pp. 105–106.

[6] Decree, provisional regency, Milan, April 23, 1814, *Atti del governo lombardo,* 1814, pp. 12–13.

[7] Decree, provisional regency, Milan, April 25, 1814, *ibid.,* p. 16.

use of the pillory was abolished as a means of punishment for women who had committed merely minor offenses.[8] The deduction of a fifth of the pay of all Italian troops which had been stipulated by a decree of January 7, 1814, was discontinued.[9] With the exception that the portfolio of minister of interior was given to Paolo de Capitani[10] and that of the ministry of finance, which was vacant, to Francesco Barbò,[11] all judicial and administrative authorities in the kingdom were provisionally retained in their posts, although the regency reserved for itself the right to make such changes in personnel as it might deem necessary.[12]

On their part, the electoral colleges officially decreed the abolition of the senate and the council of state, named General Pino commander-in-chief of the army, granted full amnesty to all deserters and to persons who had evaded military conscription, declared that the Roman Catholic religion was the religion of the state, announced that the continental system was null and void, and abrogated hunting rights.[13]

Thus when Lieutenant Field Marshal Marquis Annibale Sommariva[14] and Count Julius Joseph Strassoldo[15] arrived in Milan on April 26 to take charge of Lombardy in the name of the Allied Powers, they had to deal with a provisional central government which had sud-

---

[8] Decree, provisional regency, Milan, April 26, 1814, *ibid.*, pp. 19–20.

[9] Decree, provisional regency, Milan, April 25, 1814, *ibid.*, p. 15.

[10] Decree, provisional regency, Milan, April 24, 1814, *ibid.*, p. 14.

[11] Decree, provisional regency, Milan, April 21, 1814, *ibid.*, p. 6.

[12] Decree, provisional regency, Milan, April 21, 1814, *ibid.*, p. 6; proclamation, provisional regency, Milan, April 23, 1814, *ibid.*, pp. 8–9.

[13] Report from Milan, April 25, 1814, *Wiener Zeitung*, May 14, 1814, p. 537; proclamation, electoral colleges, Milan, April 22, 1814, *Oesterreichischer Beobachter*, No. 130 (May 10, 1814), p. 709; *Giornale italiano*, No. 117 (April 27, 1814), p. 474.

[14] Marquis Sommariva (1755–1829), a member of an old noble Lombard family, began his military career in 1771. Gradually rising through the commissioned ranks, he was made a lieutenant field marshal in 1807, an inspector general of troops in 1811, and a commanding general in 1820. He participated in the Italian campaign in 1813–1814. In 1825 he was appointed commander of the guard at the Hofburg palace in Vienna.

[15] Count Strassoldo (1773–1830) left Milan for Parma on May 16 in the capacity of imperial commissioner to take over the government in the name of Maria Louisa. Later he installed a provisional administration in the Papal Legations. In 1816 he was appointed police director of Lombardy. Two years later he was made president of the government of Lombardy. He held this post until he died.

enly come into being as the consequence of a revolution and which had already decreed a number of important reforms during the first few days of its existence. Since the fate of Lombardy, unlike that of Venetia, had not yet been decided,[16] Field Marshal Bellegarde, who had commissioned them to go to the Lombard capital, had instructed Sommariva and Strassoldo to look upon the Austrian occupation of Lombardy as merely a temporary military one. They were to make no changes in the government without the field marshal's personal consent. All the political and administrative authorities who had remained at their posts were for the present to be confirmed in their positions, but they were to be under the supervision of the Habsburg military commander. To prevent the spread of partisanship and intrigue, the two commissioners were to take direct control of the police. Furthermore, they were to take care that the interests of the Allied Powers would in no way be impaired.[17]

Acting in accord with these instructions, Sommariva, immediately after arriving in Milan, handed the communal council a letter from Bellegarde informing its members that he had been sent to take possession of Lombardy in the name of the Allied Powers and that he had been instructed "to contribute by all possible means to the reestablishment of public order and tranquillity."[18] At the same time, he notified the president of the provisional regency that, although it was to be under the superintendence of the Habsburg military commander,[19] the regency was provisionally to continue to exercise the functions[20] which had been assigned to it by the communal council and the electoral colleges. On the same day Sommariva issued a

[16] It was apparently decided in late April or early May, 1814. See my *Fall of the Napoleonic Kingdom of Italy,* pp. 180–191; and Haas, *Metternich, Reorganization and Nationality,* p. 198, n. 31.

[17] Bellegarde to Emperor Francis, Verona, May 4, 1814, St. A. (Vienna), Kaiser Franz Akten, Fasz. XXVII, Kon. 2, Fos. 32–37; Bellegarde to Strassoldo, n.d. (enclosed with the above letter), *ibid.,* Fo. 33; Bellegarde to Sommariva, Verona, April 29, 1814, *ibid.,* Fos. 38–39; Bellegarde to Sommariva, Verona, May 2, 1814, *ibid.,* Fos. 56–57.

[18] Bellegarde to communal council, Verona, April 26, 1814, Francesco Lemmi, *La restaurazione austriaca a Milano nel 1814 (con appendice di documenti tratti dagli archivi di Vienna, Londra, Milano, ecc.),* Appendix XI, p. 408.

[19] Bellegarde to Emperor Francis, Verona, May 4, 1814, St. A. (Vienna), Kaiser Franz Akten, Fasz. XXVII, Kon. 1, Fo. 44.

[20] Sommariva to president of the provisional regency, Milan, April 26, 1814, *Museo* (Milan), "Carte Beccaria," Busta I, Carte 8, Fasc. I, Pezza 1.

proclamation to the Italian people informing them that he was assuming control of the government in the name of the Allies and beseeching them to await peacefully the decision which the Allied Powers would make about their future destiny.[21]

Sommariva asked the president of the provisional regency to designate someone in the ministry of war to answer all inquiries of the Austrian commissioner about the Italian military forces. Another official was to be made available to answer any questions which Strassoldo might wish to ask about the public administration or the public economy.[22] The regency was to exercise its authority over all Lombardy. It was to handle strictly administrative matters in any way it saw fit but was to keep the Habsburg commissioners informed about everything it did. It was, however, to make no innovations and to issue no decrees abolishing or modifying existing laws or regulations before obtaining Sommariva's personal approval.[23] Sommariva himself assumed supreme command of the Lombard police.

In conformity with their orders, Sommariva and Strassoldo thus adopted a posture of preserving the *status quo ante* when they first arrived on the scene in Milan. They departed from this policy of noninterference in internal affairs, however, in matters which involved the maintenance of public tranquillity. To prevent the circulation of material which might inflame the passions of the populace, Strassoldo carefully censored the newspapers and all the public proclamations of the provisional regency and other public officials. Since they suspected that the electoral colleges might attempt to make further innovations in existing laws and institutions and since they feared that because the electoral colleges constituted a kind of popular representation their very existence might encourage malcontents to make demands for liberal reforms, the Austrian commissioners in Milan seriously considered abolishing them before the electoral colleges themselves suspended their sessions on May 2.[24]

[21] Proclamation, Sommariva, Milan, April 26, 1814, *Atti del governo lombardo*, 1814, p. 18.

[22] Sommariva to president of the provisional regency, Milan, April 26, 1814, *Museo* (Milan), "Carte Beccaria," Busta I, Carte 8, Fasc. I, Pezza 1.

[23] Sommariva to Verri, Milan, May 3, 1814, St. A. (Vienna), Kaiser Franz Akten, Fasz. XXVII, Kon. 1, Fos. 67–68; Strassoldo to Rosetti, Milan, May 3, 1814, *ibid.*, Fo. 66; Bellegarde to Emperor Francis, Verona, May 4, 1814, *ibid.*, Fo. 44.

[24] Bellegarde to Emperor Francis, Verona, May 4, 1814, *ibid.*, Fos. 43–44; Strassoldo to Bellegarde, Milan, April 26, 1814, *ibid.*, Fos. 35–36; Strassoldo to Bellegarde, Milan, April 30, 1814, *ibid.*, Fos. 53–55.

Sommariva and Strassoldo were soon joined in the Lombard capital by other Habsburg officials. On April 28 Lieutenant Field Marshal Albert Adam Neipperg[25] entered Milan with fourteen thousand soldiers under his command. On the same day Lieutenant Field Marshal Anton Mayer von Heldenfeld arrived in Mantua and Lieutenant Field Marshal Franz Fenner von Fennenberg occupied Brescia. Ten days later Bellegarde left his army headquarters at Verona to proceed to Milan, which he reached on May 8 at the head of twelve thousand troops.[26] The commander-in-chief was accompanied by Baron von Rosetti, whom the emperor had assigned to him as general intendant during the past December.[27]

Aside from replacing General Giuseppe Fontanelli as minister of war with General Bianchi d'Adda,[28] at the request of the provisional regency, Bellegarde followed the same policy of preserving the *status quo* which Sommariva and Strassoldo had pursued until he received further orders from the emperor later in May. He reassured the regency that it was the only governing body which he would recognize before the fate of the kingdom was decided by the Allied Powers and instructed it to make no innovations and "to take only those measures which are necessary to avoid trouble and disorders."[29] During the first few weeks of his stay in Milan nearly all Bellegarde's efforts were directed towards lessening the existing spirit of partisanship and assuaging the fears and passions which the April 20 revolution had aroused.[30]

The fate of the Kingdom of Italy was soon decided. Venetia had already been promised to Austria by the Allies in the summer of 1813

25 Count Neipperg (1775–1829) was a dashing officer who distinguished himself in numerous campaigns and rapidly rose to the rank of lieutenant field marshal. After leaving Milan he escorted Maria Louisa from France to Parma. Remaining in that duchy, he became Maria Louisa's lover and the virtual ruler of the country.

26 See my *Fall of the Napoleonic Kingdom of Italy*, pp. 144 and 146.

27 Emperor Francis to Zichy, Freyburg, December 21, 1813, St. A. (Vienna), Conferenz Akten, Ser. b, 1813, No. 925.

28 Decree, provisional government, Milan, May 10, 1814, *Atti del governo lombardo*, 1814, p. 37.

29 Bellegarde to Verri, Milan, May 11, 1814, *Museo* (Milan), "Carte Beccaria," Busta I, Carte 8, Fasc. I, No. 40.

30 Pietro Dolce report, Milan, June 30, 1816, A. S. (Milan), Commissario Plenipotenziario I. R. Lomb. Veneto. Presidenza di governo. Atti secreti (hereafter cited as A. S. [Milan], Presidenza di governo. Atti secreti), 1816, Cart. XI, Rub. 669/geh. (Reisenden Dolce), Pezza 224.

as part of an offer made to Emperor Francis to induce him to join the war against Napoleon. Lombardy was apparently not assigned to the Habsburgs before late April or early May, 1814. A deputation sent to the Allied Powers in Paris by the Lombard provisional regency was informed about this decision on May 6.[31] The rest of the territories of the kingdom were returned to the Papal States, Modena, and Sardinia.

Now that Lombardy was his, Emperor Francis wrote Marshal Bellegarde from Paris on May 14 to outline the policies which he was henceforth to follow in Lombardy. In addition to retaining command of the Austrian army in Italy, Bellegarde was, as commissioner plenipotentiary, to supervise the political administration in Lombardy and in the former Venetian territories west of the Mincio River. For the time being, he was to allow the Milanese provisional regency to continue to supervise the government of Lombardy, but he himself was to assume the presidency of this body. Only the provisional regency or Bellegarde himself was to give orders in the name of the government. "Since the land has been conquered," Emperor Francis continued, "there can be no talk of a constitution, nor of a senate or other similar bodies, nor of representation." For this reason, the electoral colleges were to be abolished if they were still in existence. Bellegarde was to take measures which would insure that the administration of justice would be prompt and just, that all government business would be transacted quickly and efficiently, and that peace and order would always be maintained. With the exception that he was to have the electoral colleges dissolved, Emperor Francis' commissioner plenipotentiary was to make only urgently needed changes in the existing governmental structure and then only if he was convinced that they were in full accord with the emperor's instructions. He was to report directly to the emperor on the conditions of the country, especially on the state of public opinion and the sentiments of the Italian army. Bellegarde was to issue a proclamation notifying the populace that, since Lombardy was now part of the Habsburg monarchy, the commissioner plenipotentiary would from now on act, not in the name of the Allied Powers, but only in that of the Habsburg emperor.[32]

[31] See my *Fall of the Napoleonic Kingdom of Italy*, pp. 182–192.

[32] Emperor Francis to Bellegarde, Paris, May 14, 1814, St. A. (Vienna), Conferenz Akten, Ser. b, 1814, No. 996.

Perhaps to give Bellegarde supplementary instructions, Metternich wrote him the next day to express his anxiety over the existence in the Apennine peninsula of "the so-called *Italian* spirit." To counteract this Italian spirit, he suggested that it would be well "to revive the *Lombard* spirit." It was precisely for this reason that the emperor "decided to add to his other titles that of *King of Lombardy*," to include the Lombard crown of iron in the imperial coat of arms, and to conserve the order of the iron crown. The commissioner plenipotentiary was to announce this decision of their new sovereign to the Lombards when he took over control of their government.[33]

Bellegarde received the emperor's instructions on May 22.[34] Three days later, on May 25, he notified the populace of his appointment as commissioner plenipotentiary. He gave notice that while the provisional regency, the ministries, and other authorities were to continue to exist, the senate, council of state, and electoral colleges, as well as all other associations and congresses which could not be justified, were suppressed.[35] The next day, May 26, Bellegarde formally took over the presidency of the Lombard provisional government.[36]

On June 2 Metternich instructed Bellegarde, on behalf of his monarch, to proclaim Austrian sovereignty over all parts of Lombardy, to require all state employees to take an oath of allegiance to the Habsburg emperor, and to announce to the populace that as soon as their new emperor returned to Vienna he would busy himself with devising the permanent political, administrative, and legal institutions which were to be established in their country.[37] The commissioner plenipotentiary carried out the chancellor's orders on June 12 and 13. In a special proclamation on the 12th he informed the inhabitants about the "happy destiny" that awaited them now that they were "united and equally protected under the scepter of the august

[33] Metternich to Bellegarde, Paris, May 15, 1814, St. A. (Vienna) Staatskanzlei, Provinzen, Lombardei-Venedig, Fasz. III, Kon. 2, Fos. 50–53.

[34] Entry of May 23, 1814, *Biblioteca Ambrosiana* (Milan), Luigi Mantovani, "Diario politico-ecclesiastico di Milano" (hereafter cited as *Biblioteca Ambrosiana* [Milan], Mantovani, "Diario di Milano"), Vol. V, p. 269.

[35] Proclamation, Bellegarde, Milan, May 25, 1814, *Atti del governo lombardo*, 1814, pp. 52–53.

[36] *Wiener Zeitung*, June 11, 1814, p. 642; *Giornale italiano*, No. 148 (May 28, 1814), p. 604; Teresa Confalonieri Casati to Confalonieri, Milan, May 27, 1814, Gallavresi, *Carteggio del conte Federico Confalonieri*, Vol. I, p. 158.

[37] Metternich to Bellegarde, Paris, June 2, 1814, St. A. (Vienna), Staatskanzlei, Provinzen, Lombardei-Venedig, Fasz. III, Kon. 2, Fo. 58.

emperor and king," Francis I.[38] To celebrate this "joyous occasion" as well as the peace that had been signed at Paris on May 30, a special *Te Deum* was sung on the same day in all churches in Milan.[39] The next day, the 13th, a decree of the provisional regency was posted to announce that all emblems and coats-of-arms of the preceding government were to be removed from all public places. The formula, "during the reign of His Majesty, Francis I, Emperor and King," was to be substituted in official documents for the expression, "during the provisional regency." Also, the special cockade which had been introduced by the Milan commune and approved by the regency immediately after the April 20 revolution was no longer to be worn.[40]

Thus, by the middle of June, 1814, Bellegarde was the real master of Lombardy. Nonetheless, the whole administrative system under his control was still the same as it had been at the moment when the Austrians came to Milan. Under the commissioner plenipotentiary's presidency, the provisional regency continued to direct the government of Lombardy and, for a time, to give instructions to the seven ministers of the former Kingdom of Italy:[41] the minister of foreign affairs, the minister of interior, the minister of justice, the minister of finance, the minister of the treasury, the minister of religion, and the minister of war and of the navy.[42]

Not before the end of July did the Habsburgs make any significant change in the administrative setup in Lombardy and then only because the existence of separate ministries was obviously irreconcilable with Austrian interests in Italy. Since ministries are attributes of independent states and not of dependent provinces, permitting them to continue to function would have been tantamount to recognizing Lombardy as an independent political entity. For this reason,

[38] Proclamation, Bellegarde, Milan, June 12, 1814, *Atti del governo lombardo,* 1814, pp. 60–61.

[39] Entry of June 12, 1814, *Biblioteca Ambrosiana* (Milan), Mantovani, "Diario di Milano," Vol. V, pp. 278–279; *Giornale italiano,* No. 164 (June 13, 1814), p. 670.

[40] Decree, imperial provisional regency, June 13, 1814, *Atti del governo lombardo,* 1814, pp. 62–64.

[41] Bellegarde report, May 31, 1814, St. A. (Vienna), Conferenz Akten, Ser. b, 1814, No. 1249.

[42] For a good description of the duties of the various ministers of the Kingdom of Italy and of the various directories and departments subordinated to them, see Bellegarde's report on the Austrian-Italian provinces, October 25, 1814, Helfert, *Kaiser Franz und die Stiftung des Lombardo-Venetianischen Königreichs,* Appendix I, pp. 526–528 and 532–535.

Emperor Francis, who could hardly have done otherwise, ordered Bellegarde, on July 11, to dissolve them.[43]

In line with these instructions, the Habsburg commissioner plenipotentiary announced, on July 27, that the ministries of foreign affairs, of the treasury, of finance, of interior, and of justice were to cease functioning on July 31. The few duties which had been performed by the ministry of foreign affairs after the demise of the Kingdom of Italy were to be disposed of in Vienna.[44] The functions formerly discharged by the ministry of the treasury were to be assumed by the provisional regency.[45] In place of the ministry of finance, a general intendancy of finance, similar to the one which had existed in Lombardy before 1796, was created and charged with the administration of the lottery, of customs, of monopolies, and of various indirect taxes. The direct tax, mint, and post offices were placed immediately under the provisional regency.[46] According to the practices in other Austrian territories, part of the duties of the ministry of justice were assigned to the Lombard tribunals of first instance, the courts of appeals, and the court of cassation; the rest were provisionally to be discharged by the regency.[47] The work done by the ministry of religion, which was abolished on August 1, was also assumed by the regency.[48] All matters which had been transacted in the ministry of interior except those which concerned the police, the press, and libraries were now concentrated in the regency. The police, press, and library directories, however, were made directly responsible to the commissioner plenipotentiary.[49] The marine division

---

[43] Protocol, Staats-Conferenz, August 23, 1814, St. A. (Vienna), Conferenz Akten, Ser. b, 1814, No. 1570; Bellegarde to Emperor Francis, Milan, August 5, 1814, *Hofkammer Archiv* (Vienna), Kredit Akten, Fasz. IIC/4, No. 7973 ex Oktober 1814.

[44] Bellegarde to Emperor Francis, Milan, August 5, 1814, *Hofkammer Archiv* (Vienna), Kredit Akten, Fasz. IIC/4, No. 7973 ex Oktober 1814.

[45] Decree, Bellegarde, Milan, July 29, 1814, *Atti del governo lombardo*, 1814, pp. 110–111.

[46] Decree, Bellegarde, Milan, July 27, 1814, *ibid.*, pp .100–101; Bellegarde to Emperor Francis, Milan, August 5, 1814, *Hofkammer Archiv* (Vienna), Kredit Akten, Fasz. IIC/4, No. 7973 ex Oktober 1814.

[47] Decree, Bellegarde, Milan, July 27, 1814, *Atti del governo lombardo*, 1814, pp. 92–97; Bellegarde to Emperor Francis, Milan, August 5, 1814, *Hofkammer Archiv* (Vienna), Kredit Akten, Fasz. IIC/4, No. 7973 ex Oktober 1814.

[48] Decree, Bellegarde, Milan, July 27, 1814, *Atti del governo lombardo*, 1814, p. 102.

[49] Decree, Bellegarde, Milan, July 27, 1814, *ibid.*, pp. 98–99.

of the ministry of war and the navy, which was dissolved on August 18, was transferred to Venice.[50] An extraordinary commission, headed by Lieutenant Field Marshal Sommariva, was created to liquidate all matters previously taken care of by the war division. When the commission completed its work, it was dissolved on October 31.[51]

The abolition of the ministries resulted in the dismissal of a considerable number of superfluous French-Italian government employees. A relatively large army of government workers had manned the numerous offices and bureaus in Milan of the highly centralized administration of the Kingdom of Italy. Many of them were quite well paid. Now that Lombardy, which constituted only one-third of the territory of the former kingdom, was a mere province of the Habsburg monarchy, it was obvious that the retention of only a relatively small fraction of the multitude of employees which the Austrians had inherited from the former kingdom could be justified, particularly considering the embarrassing financial situation of the Habsburg monarchy in 1814.[52] Then, too, it is but to be expected that, since the first loyalty of many French-Italian officials was to the French, their fidelity to the Habsburg sovereign was open to serious question. To this picture one must add only Emperor Francis' extreme suspicion of "radicals" to understand why to Bellegarde, as well as to the government in Vienna, the problem of getting rid of supernumerary Italian officials seemed urgent.[53]

As early as May 13 Baron von Rosetti had attempted to impress upon the provisional regency the necessity for decreasing the number of employees.[54] A few days later the various ministries were instructed to make a serious effort to reduce their subalterns by one-third and to cut the pay of those who remained by the same

---

[50] Teresa Confalonieri Casati to Confalonieri, Milan, July 23, 1814, Gallavresi, *Carteggio del conte Federico Confalonieri*, Vol. I, p. 222.

[51] Decrees, Bellegarde, Milan, August 16 and October 20, 1814, *Atti del governo lombardo*, 1814, pp. 118–120 and 143–144; Bellegarde report on the Austrian-Italian provinces, October 25, 1814, Helfert, *Kaiser Franz und die Stiftung des Lombardo-Venetianischen Königreichs*, Appendix I, pp. 534–535.

[52] See *post*, pp. 91–93.

[53] See Bellegarde report, May 31, 1814, St. A. (Vienna), Conferenz Akten, Ser. b, 1814, No. 1249; and Bellegarde to Metternich, Milan, June 4, 1814, Lemmi, *La restaurazione austriaca a Milano*, Appendix XXI, pp. 424–425.

[54] Verri to deputation in Paris, Milan, May 13, 1814, *Museo* (Milan), "Carte Beccaria," Busta I, Carte 8, Fasc. 1, No. 36.

amount.[55] The maximum pay for officials was limited to 18,000 lire per annum and that of ministers to 12,000.[56] Furthermore, the provisional regency suspended the filling of all vacant posts and ordered the dismissal of all employees residing in territories not under Austrian control.[57]

To mitigate the hardship and deprivations that would result from the carrying out of the above decrees, Bellegarde proposed that Austrian citizenship be granted to some of the officials who were not allowed to return to their native lands and granted a month's extra pay and pensions to those who were removed from their jobs.[58] Furthermore, kind-hearted and affable as he was, Bellegarde dismissed no more persons than he absolutely had to. When Baron von Rosetti, who was much harsher than the field marshal, asserted, at a meeting of the provisional regency, that half of the clerks now in the government offices were enough to do the work, the commissioner plenipotentiary rejoined: "Yes, half would be enough for His Majesty's service, but His Majesty is necessary for the other half."[59] As long as he could prevent it, Bellegarde refused to make beggars out of hundreds of persons who had faithfully served the preceding government.[60]

[55] Teresa Confalonieri Casati to Confalonieri, Milan, May 27, 1814, Gallavresi, *Carteggio del conte Federico Confalonieri*, Vol. I, p. 158; Adolf von Wiedemann-Warnhelm, *Die Wiederherstellung der österreichischen Vorherrschaft in Italien (1813–1815)*, p. 53.

[56] Decree, provisional regency, Milan, June 8, 1814, A. S. (Milan), Uffici e Tribunali Regi. Parte Moderne, Cart. LVI–LVII–LVIII, Governo, Registro Generale del Regno d'Italia e della Reggenza Austriaca, 2 gennaio al 31 luglio 1814, No. 1933.

[57] Provisional regency to minister of interior, June 2, 1814, *ibid.*, No. 1605; Helfert, *La caduta della dominazione francese*, p. 159; Lemmi, *La restaurazione austriaca a Milano*, p. 301.

[58] Rasini to Confalonieri, Milan, June 8, 1814, Gallavresi, *Carteggio del conte Federico Confalonieri*, Vol. I, p. 182; anonymous letter to Hager, June 9, 1814, A. S. (Milan), Presidenza di governo. Atti secreti, 1814, Cart. I, No. 89/P.R.; provisional regency to minister of interior, June 2, 1814, A. S. (Milan) Uffici e Tribunali Regi. Parte Moderne, Cart. LVI–LVII–LVIII, Governo, Registro Generale, 2 gennaio al 31 luglio 1814, No. 1605.

[59] Teresa Confalonieri Casati to Confalonieri, Milan, July 23, 1814, Gallavresi, *Carteggio del conte Federico Confalonieri*, Vol. I, p. 222. The same expression, worded differently, can also be found in the entry of July 22, 1814, *Biblioteca Ambrosiana* (Milan), Mantovani, "Diario di Milano," Vol. V, p. 294.

[60] Francesco Cusani, *Storia di Milano dall'origine ai nostri giorni e cenni storico-statistici sulle città e province lombarde*, Vol. VII, p. 248.

When the ministries were dissolved, however, hundreds of their employees were, of necessity, discharged, and a thousand families would have been threatened with dire poverty at a single stroke of the pen had not Bellegarde taken steps to mitigate their hardship. Many of them were absorbed by the provisional regency or by the other agencies which took over the work of the abolished ministries. Others were temporarily employed on special projects which were devised for the express purpose of giving them something useful to do.[61] Those without jobs were assured that they would receive favorable consideration if they applied for positions in the permanent administrative offices which the Habsburgs would soon establish in their country.[62] Subaltern officials who lost their jobs because the positions in which they had served were abolished were paid a substantial part of their salaries for a period of two months after their employment ended.[63] In September Bellegarde extended the time during which discharged employees could draw unemployment benefits until they received their first regular pension checks. Dismissed employees who had received salaries of less than 1,000 lire per annum were to be paid three-fourths of their former salary. Those with salaries between 1,001 and 3,000 were to receive two-thirds; those between 3,001 and 4,000 lire, one-half; and those between 4,001 and 6,000, one-third.[64]

Notwithstanding the measures taken by the Austrians to ease the transfer of discharged public servants to private life, the dismissal of so many officials was bound to make an unfavorable impression on the Milanese. Many ousted clerks became open critics of their former

[61] Entry of August 3, 1814, *Biblioteca Ambrosiana* (Milan), Mantovani, "Diario di Milano," Vol. V, p. 298.

[62] See, for example, Bellegarde to the secretary of state of the former Kingdom of Italy, Milan, July 19, 1814, A. S. (Milan), Uffici e Tribunali Regi. Parte Moderne, Cart. LII (Governo Reggenza. Impiegati, 1814-1815), ad No. 4400; and Bellegarde to minister of interior, Milan, July 27, 1814, *ibid.*, Cart. LVI–LVII–LVIII, Governo, Registro Generale, 2 gennaio al 31 luglio 1814, No. 1064.

[63] De Capitani to Alberto Alemagna, Milan, July 30, 1814, A. S. (Milan), Uffici e Tribunali Regi. Parte Moderne, Cart. LI (Tribunali, Governo Reggenza, Provvid. gener. 1814–1815), No. 8516; Hager report, August 5, 1814, St. A. (Vienna), Kabinets-Akten, 1814, No. 1783; protocol, provisional regency, September 16, 1814, *Biblioteca di Brera* (Milan), "Protocolli originali della reggenza provvisoria del Regno d'Italia nel 1814."

[64] Imperial resolution, Vienna, December 23, 1814, *Hofkammer Archiv* (Vienna), Central-Organisirungs-Hof-Commission Akten, Rinna, 1814, No. 5601/576.

colleagues and accused them of incompetence and even of various malfeasances, while those who were still in office became cautious and timid out of fear of compromising themselves. The families of thousands of men who had lost their positions or who feared they might became terrified at the prospect of joining the ranks of the breadless. Other persons grumbled about unworthy dolts who were still on the government payroll or bemoaned the taxes they would have to pay to support a horde of undeserving pensioners.[65]

A much larger number of Milanese, however, complained because as the summer went on persons ousted from government service and retired French-Italian and former Austrian officials were still not receiving the pension payments to which they were entitled. Beginning in 1806 a sum of 800,000 livres had been set aside yearly for pensions in the Monte Napoleone, the state bank. All state employees contributed 2 per cent of their salaries to the Monte for this purpose. They were entitled to pensions after fifteen years of service or even earlier if they had to retire because of some physical disability or the abolition of their jobs.[66] That dismissed and retired employees had a right to collect the pensions to which they had contributed was fully recognized by Marshal Bellegarde,[67] Baron von Rosetti, and the provisional regency.[68] However, they found it utterly impossible to pay them before 1815. The Habsburg treasury was extremely hard pressed for ready money, the bureaucracy was stultified by its own paper work, and the pension fund in the Monte Napoleone existed only on paper. Furthermore, the portion of the fund which Modena, Parma, Sardinia, and the Papal States were obligated to contribute still had to be settled at the Congress of Vienna.[69] As a consequence, the Austrians were unable to provide even the back pension payments of

[65] See especially anonymous report, Milan, May 31, 1814, A. S. (Milan), Presidenza di governo. Atti secreti, 1814, Cart. I, No. 20/P.R.; and Hager reports, August 13 and September 2, 1814, St. A. (Vienna), Conferenz Akten, Ser. b, 1814, Nos. 1590 and 1651.

[66] Bellegarde report, Milan, July 19, 1814, St. A. (Vienna), Conferenz Akten, Ser. b, 1814, No. 1452. See also Roberti, *Milano capitale napoleonica*, Vol. II, pp. 200–205.

[67] Bellegarde report, Milan, July 19, 1814, St. A. (Vienna), Conference Akten, Ser. b, 1814, No. 1452.

[68] Protocols, provisional regency, May 23 and October 13, 1814, *Biblioteca di Brera* (Milan), "Protocolli originali della reggenza provvisoria."

[69] Wiedemann-Warnhelm, *Die Wiederherstellung der österreichischen Vorherrschaft in Italien*, p. 55.

former nuns and monks before October, 1814.[70] The pension payments for dismissed and retired civil servants were not systematized before February, 1815.[71]

Besides occupying himself with reducing the size of the surplus administrative personnel, looking after the welfare of dismissed officials, and worrying about how to find funds to pay the arrears in pensions, Bellegarde was faced with the problem of deciding what to do with able officials who were known admirers of Napoleon and the revolutionary system. He might easily have succumbed to the temptation of throwing them out of office, as some other governments did after Napoleon's overthrow. Plenty of pressure was put on him to do so by Lombard reactionaries, secret denunciators, and some of his superiors in Vienna.[72] Yet, even though he was fully aware that the French-Italian officials and the middle class from which most of them came were the principal enemies of Habsburg rule in Italy, the field marshal resisted the exhortations of the ultraconservatives and the pusillanimous to purge the public offices of all liberals and steadfastly insisted that "the past conduct of these people can not be grounds for investigation or criminal procedure." For the commissioner plenipotentiary the only thing that mattered was whether the French-Italian officials retained in office would *now* serve the Habsburgs faithfully, efficiently, and loyally.[73]

What makes Bellegarde's attitude all the more remarkable is that he had at his side a mere handful of top-level Austrian assistants— the only kind of person whose loyalty to the Habsburg sovereign was absolutely unquestioned by conservatives in unsettled times like those in 1814. One of the two commissioners whom the field marshal had sent to Milan late in April to take control of the government in the name of the Allied Powers, Strassoldo, left Milan on May 16 to

[70] Entry of October 6, 1814, *Biblioteca Ambrosiana* (Milan), Mantovani, "Diario di Milano," Vol. V, p. 315.

[71] See proclamation, Bellegarde, Milan, February 17, 1815, *Atti del governo lombardo*, 1815, Vol. I, pp. 11–15.

[72] For examples, see Torresani to Bellegarde, Padua, July 26, 1814, A. S. (Venice), Presidio di governo, 1814, No. 599; and Hager to Bellegarde, Vienna, July 14, 15, 16, 17, and 29, August 11 and 19, and September 3, 1814, A. S. (Milan), Presidenza di governo. Atti secreti, 1814, Cart. I, Nos. 89/P.R., 92/P.R., 94/P.R., 124/P.R., 183/P.R., 205/P.R., 247/P.R., and 330/P.R.

[73] Bellegarde to Hager, Milan, July 27, 1814, A. S. (Milan), Presidenza di governo. Atti secreti, 1814, Cart. I, No. 87 fino al 97/R.; Hager to Bellegarde, Vienna, August 8, 1814, *ibid.*, Cart. II, No. 195/P.R.

accompany Maria Louisa to Parma[74] and then to install a provisional administration in the Papal Legations.[75] The other, Sommariva, gave up his post on May 25.[76] That the commissioner plenipotentiary urgently needed the assistance of experienced Austrian administrators, particularly after the departure of Strassoldo and Sommariva, was fully recognized by both Emperor Francis[77] and the state conference.[78] To provide him with such help, Emperor Francis in July assigned Bellegarde's former general army intendant, Baron von Rosetti, to him as special counselor in civil and financial matters[79] and transferred Imperial Secretary Franz Hauer von Spech to Milan to take over the presidential affairs of the government.[80] During the same month Imperial Bookkeeper Ignaz von Schäffer and Imperial Counselor Peregrin von Menz were sent to assist the field marshal in directing the accounting and financial administrations.[81] Menz was also to make recommendations to the emperor on how to improve the Lombard taxation and financial systems.[82] Two months later Count

[74] Entry of May 17, 1814, *Biblioteca Ambrosiana* (Milan), Mantovani "Diario di Milano," Vol. V, p. 264.

[75] Bellegarde report, May 21, 1814, St. A. (Vienna), Conferenz Akten, Ser. b, 1814, No. 1228.

[76] Domenico Spadoni, *Milano e la congiura militare nel 1814 per l'indipendenza italiana: Il moto del 20 aprile e l'occupazione austriaca*, p. 174 (hereafter cited as Spadoni, *Il moto del 20 aprile*).

[77] Emperor Francis to Bellegarde, Paris, May 14, 1814, St. A. (Vienna), Conferenz Akten, Ser. b, 1814, No. 996.

[78] Staats-Conferenz report, May 29, 1814, *ibid.*

[79] Emperor Francis to Ugarte, July 8, 1814, St. A. (Vienna), Staats-Rath Akten, 1814, No. 2224.

[80] Emperor Francis to Ugarte, Vienna, July 7, 1814, *Verwaltungsarchiv* (Vienna), Hofkanzlei, Lombardei-Venedig, Fasz. III, A, 4, No. 786 ex Juli 1814; Emperor Francis to Bellegarde, Vienna, July 7, 1814, St. A. (Vienna), Conferenz Akten, Ser. b, 1814, No. 1170; Bellegarde to provisional regency, July 30, 1814, A. S. (Milan), Commissione Plenipotenziaria, Busta unica, No. 1082.

[81] Ugarte note, Vienna, July 8, 1814, *Verwaltungsarchiv* (Vienna), Hofräte, Lombardei-Venedig, Fasz. III, A, 4, No. 15,577/1009 ex Juli 1814; Ugarte to Bellegarde, Vienna, July 8, 1814, A. S. (Milan), Commissione Plenipotenziaria, Busta unica, No. 957/P.R.; Bellegarde to Saurau, Milan, August 9, 1814, *ibid.*, No. 1409.

[82] Emperor Francis to Bellegarde, Schönbrunn, July 12, 1814, St. A. (Vienna), Conferenz Akten, Ser. b, 1814, No. 1249; imperial resolution, Schönbrunn, September 9, 1814, *Hofkammer Archiv* (Vienna), Kredit Akten, Fasz. XIVB1, No. 8045 ex Oktober 1814; Rinna to Bellegarde, Vienna, September 12, 1814, *Hofkammer Archiv* (Vienna), Central-Organisirungs-Hof-Commission Akten, Rinna, 1814, No. 1025/125.

Karl Ronner, a bank examiner, was dispatched to Lombardy to supervise matters dealing with banks and banking.[83] Even after these functionaries arrived in Milan the number of Habsburg officials in Lombardy was still utterly inadequate. Including Bellegarde himself, in the late summer of 1814 there were still only six top-level Austrian administrators to handle the multitude of difficult problems involved in governing a newly re-acquired area of 7,313 square miles with a population of 2,104,439 during a period when the political, economic, and social structure of the country was badly shaken by the sudden overthrow of a regime which had effectively ruled the region for over fifteen years!

Given this shortage of Austrian personnel, it is fortunate that Bellegarde sought to conserve the Lombard provisional regency as long as possible. After its members took an oath of allegiance to the emperor and promised faithfully to carry out his orders as transmitted to them through his commissioner plenipotentiary[84] the Habsburg field marshal allowed them, with only a few exceptions, to continue to supervise the administration of the country in much the same manner as they had before he came to Milan. At first the orders and decrees of the regency went directly to the different ministries for execution.[85] Then after the latter were abolished they were sent to the various bureaus that took over their duties.

Shortly after the ministries were liquidated the former minister of interior, De Capitani, was made a member of the regency. About the same time Count Antonio Strigelli was appointed general secretary of the same body, and Gaudenzio de Pagave was employed as special secretary to write up the protocols of its sessions.[86] Pino, Borromeo, and Litta must have resigned during the course of the summer, for in the fall of 1814 their names were no longer included in the protocols; otherwise the membership remained the same as it was when

[83] Bellegarde to Lazanzky, Milan, September 8, 1814, A. S. (Milan), Commissione Plenipotenziaria, Busta unica, No. 2406; Lazanzky to Bellegarde, Vienna, September 26, 1814, ibid., No. 9571.

[84] For a copy of the oath which the members of the provisional regency took, see Helfert, La caduta della dominazione francese, Appendix II, pp. 234–235.

[85] Bellegarde report, May 31, 1814, St. A. (Vienna), Conferenz Akten, Ser. b, 1814, No. 1249.

[86] Entry of August 3, 1814, Biblioteca Ambrosiana (Milan), Mantovani, "Diario di Milano," Vol. V, pp. 298–299; list of employees added to the provisional regency, n.d., A. S. (Milan), Uffici e Tribunali Regi. Parte Moderne, Cart. LII (Impiegati), No. 1393.

the provisional regency was first organized. With the exception of Verri, whose strong liberalism made him a thorn in the side of the Austrians,[87] Bellegarde regarded all the members of the regency as honest, hard-working, well-disposed, and intelligent men who rendered excellent service to the new masters of the country.[88]

At the outset the organizational structure of the provisional regency was relatively simple and its personnel was comparatively small. In June it was subdivided into three sections. To handle the routine work of the section, a secretary was provided for each; also two had one subordinate clerk apiece, and one had two clerks. In addition, seven secretaries were assigned to the regency as a whole. There were three employees in the protocol section, twelve clerks and copyists in the mailing and shipping division, five persons in the archival branch, one accountant, and one economist.[89]

After much of the work of the abolished ministries devolved upon it, however, the regency became a much more complex body. By the fall of 1814 the three sections into which it had been divided in June had grown into eleven full-fledged departments, each with one or two regency members in charge and each with its own subordinate personnel. Late in July Giulini and De Capitani were placed in charge of the department of interior. Bazetta and Peregalli superintended the affairs of the department of justice. Tonni headed the department of religion; Verri, the department of education; Mellerio, the department of the treasury and royal domains; Muggiasca, the department of mining; Borromeo, the department of public welfare; and Longo, the department of finance.[90] The names of the regents who directed the affairs of the other three departments are unknown to this writer. Nine of the departments were supplied with a secretary and a clerk apiece. Another department employed two secretaries

[87] Saurau to Sedlnitzky, February 8, 1817, A. S. (Milan), Presidenza di governo. Atti secreti, 1816–1817, Cart. XIII, No. 43.

[88] Bellegarde report, May 31, 1814, St. A. (Vienna), Conferenz Akten, Ser. b, 1814, No. 1249; Bellegarde to Emperor Francis, Milan, March 25, 1816, St. A. (Vienna), Kaiser Franz Akten, Fasz. XV, Kon. 2, Fos. 118–119.

[89] List of employees of the provisional regency approved by Bellegarde on June 14, 1814, A. S. (Milan), Uffici e Tribunali Regi. Parte Moderne, Cart. LII (Impiegati), No. 2378.

[90] Teresa Confalonieri Casati to Confalonieri, Milan, July 31, 1814, Gallavresi, *Carteggio del conte Federico Confalonieri*, Vol. I, pp. 227–229; entry of August 3, 1814, *Biblioteca Ambrosiana* (Milan), Mantovani, "Diario di Milano," Vol. V, pp. 298–299.

and one clerk; and the other, one secretary, one clerk, and two copyists. For the regency as a whole there were now two general secretaries and one subordinate clerk. Fifteen persons were employed in
the protocol section; thirty-three, in the mailing and shipping division; and twelve, in the registrar's office (the former archival
branch).[91]

For administrative purposes, the work of the provisional regency
was separated into the following categories: (1) routine matters,
which were taken care of by the particular department in whose
province they fell; and (2) affairs which were considered important
enough to be acted upon by the regency as a whole. Concerns which
involved nothing more important than the execution of clearly understood, well established regulations fell under the first heading. All
other business belonged in the second category. The protocol office
sent to each of the eleven departments of the regency all papers dealing with affairs that fell within its competence. The particular member or members of the regency in charge of the department then decided whether the business brought before it fell into the category
which was to be disposed of by his own section. If it did, the matter
was taken care of immediately and passed on to the president of the
regency for revision and execution. Concerns which were deemed
important enough to be decided by the whole body were acted upon
in collegiate sessions after the head of the appropriate department
gave the regency his own recommendations on how the matter
should be dealt with. Urgent or secret business was taken care of by
the president himself.[92]

Transacting its business in the above manner, the provisional regency rendered excellent service to the Austrians—a fact which Bellegarde well recognized.[93] Not only did it serve as a useful buffer between the Austrians and the populace, but also it proved to be an
efficient and effective governing body. A substantial part of the credit
for the fact that the central government of Lombardy functioned so
much more efficiently than that of Venetia must be given to the excellent work performed by the Milanese provisional regency.

91 List of employees of the provisional regency, n.d., A. S. (Milan), Uffici e
Tribunali Regi. Parte Moderne, Cart. LII (Impiegati), No. 1393.

92 Instructions to the members and secretaries of the provisional regency, 1814,
ibid., Cart. LI, no number given.

93 Bellegarde to Emperor Francis, Milan, March 25, 1816, St. A. (Vienna),
Kaiser Franz Akten, Fasz. XV, Kon. 2, Fos. 118–119.

The provisional regency supervised all branches of the central political administration of Lombardy except the police and censorship offices, which were under the immediate supervision of the commissioner plenipotentiary himself. In the Kingdom of Italy the police had been under the immediate control of a general police director in the ministry of interior, who, however, had the right to communicate directly with the viceroy. In his office there were a general secretary, five section chiefs, and a number of subordinate employees. In all departments except Olona, where there was a separate police prefecture, and Adriatico, which had its own police commissariat, the general police director sent his orders to and received reports directly from the prefect. Under the prefect's supervision, a special section of the prefecture supervised the police administration of the department and directed the police activities of the vice-prefects in the various districts into which each department was subdivided. Each commune with a population of more than five thousand and every city with at least ten thousand inhabitants had its own police commissioner. In the smaller communes the mayor or syndic himself handled police affairs. A separate gendarmerie created in 1802, aided by the few constables (the *sbirri*) who were still retained and the rural guards, created in 1811, executed the orders of the police.[94]

When the Austrians came to Milan late in April, 1814, they found the general police director of the former Kingdom of Italy, Giacomo Luini, a former president of the civil and criminal court, still in office. He was an able, honest, and experienced administrator, but he was an ardent French partisan; hence, the Austrian commissioners Sommariva and Strassoldo, fearing that such a zealous supporter of the former regime was potentially dangerous in such a sensitive post, transferred him to the court of cassation[95] and placed the police administration directly under the control of the minister of interior, De Capitani, in whom they had complete confidence.[96] At the same time,

[94] Bellegarde to Hager, Milan, July 13, 1814, A. S. (Milan), Presidenza di governo. Atti secreti, 1814, Cart. I, No. 25; Strassoldo's proposals for the organization of the Lombard police, December 13, 1815, *ibid.*, 1815, Cart. IX, ad No. 60/P 1815.

[95] Teresa Confalonieri Casati to Confalonieri, Milan, May 8, 1814, Gallravresi, *Carteggio del conte Federico Confalonieri*, Vol. I, p. 109; Bellegarde to Hager, Milan, July 13, 1814, A. S. (Milan), Presidenza di governo. Atti secreti, 1814, Cart. I, No. 25.

[96] Strassoldo to Rosetti, Milan, May 3, 1814, St. A. (Vienna), Kaiser Franz

Carlo Sormani was appointed De Capitani's assistant to supervise police matters.[97] In Milan, where the police prefect, Carlo Villa, had been dismissed by the provisional regency after the April 20 revolution, the police direction was provisionally entrusted to the former secretary of the police prefecture, Giulio Pagani.[98]

After Bellegarde arrived at the Lombard capital he took the supervision of the police in his own hands and instructed Sormani to send his reports directly to him.[99] Then, in accord with orders, which he had received directly from Police President von Hager, to make certain that the key police officials were honorable, fair-minded men, familiar with both Austrian administrative procedures and the character of the Italian people,[100] he dismissed three ecclesiastics and several foreigners from the general police directory.[101] However, except for making these changes in personnel and except for the fact that, of necessity, he cooperated closely with a few Austrian police officials like Feuerle who were dispatched to Lombardy on special missions,[102] throughout 1814 and the early part of 1815 the commissioner plenipotentiary preserved practically all of the organizational structure and personnel of the former French police administration which he found on his arrival in Milan. The only really significant changes which he made were (1) to assume direct control of the central police directory rather than leave it under the superintendence of the minister of interior, as it had been during the French regime; and (2)

Akten, Fasz. XXVII, Kon. 1, Fo. 63; Bellegarde to Emperor Francis, Milan, May 9, 1814, *ibid.*, Fo. 61.

97 Bellegarde to Emperor Francis, Milan, May 9, 1814, *ibid.*; Strassoldo to Rosetti, Milan, May 6, 1814, *ibid.*, Fo. 74; decree, provisional regency, Milan, May 5, 1814, *Atti del governo lombardo*, 1814, p. 33.

98 Bellegarde to Hager, Milan, July 13, 1814, A. S. (Milan), Presidenza di governo. Atti secreti, 1814, Cart. I, No. 25.

99 Bellegarde to officials of the ministry of interior, Milan, July 11, 1814, *ibid.*, No. 14; Bellegarde report, May 21, 1814, St. A. (Vienna), Conferenz Akten, Ser. b, 1814, No. 1248; provisional regency to minister of interior, Milan, July 11, 1814, St. A. (Milan), Uffici e Tribunali Regi. Parte Moderne, Cart. LVI–LVII–LVIII, Governo, Registro Generale, 2 gennaio al 31 luglio 1814, No. 14.

100 Hager to Bellegarde, Vienna, June 30, 1814, A. S. (Milan), Presidenza di governo. Atti secreti, 1814, Cart. I, No. 44/P.R.

101 Bellegarde to police director in Milan, July 9, 1814, *ibid.*, No. 13; Bellegarde to Hager, Milan, July 13, 1814, *ibid.*, No. 25.

102 Hager to Bellegarde, Vienna, August 1 and November 7, 1814, *ibid.*, Cart. II, No. 180, and Cart. III, No. 757/P.R.

to place the police forces of the departments into which Lombardy was divided under the direction of a special police commissioner who was under the immediate supervision of the general police directory in Milan rather than under that of a special section of the departmental prefecture, as had been the case in the Kingdom of Italy.[103] The gendarmerie, which had been established by the French, was also provisionally retained by the Habsburgs.[104]

Not until late in 1814 did the Austrians get around to supplying the Lombard police organization with an Austrian director and then only after there were numerous complaints about Sormani on account of his old age, lack of vigor, and inefficiency.[105] In December, 1814, Emperor Francis transferred Count Strassoldo, one of the two commissioners who had taken control of Lombardy in the name of the Allied Powers late in April, from Bologna to Milan in the capacity of police director of Lombardy.[106] At the same time, Pagani's temporary appointment as director of the Milan police became permanent.[107]

Thus in 1814 the Habsburgs made only a minimum number of changes in the French-Italian police administration which they found on their arrival in Lombardy. It was the same story with the censorship. A few days after Sommariva came to Milan he was instructed to put the press under his own personal supervision.[108] However, for several weeks after the overthrow of the Napoleonic regime the censoring of other written material was still handled by the press and library section of the police directory in the ministry of interior, as

[103] Bellegarde to Hager, Milan, August 25, 1814, *ibid.*, Cart. II, No. 220 ½ / P.R.

[104] Provisional police director to Bellegarde, Milan, July 22, 1814, *ibid.*, Cart. I, No. 75/P.R.; Hager report, August 13, 1814, St. A. (Vienna), Conferenz Akten, Ser. b, 1814, No. 1590; *Giornale di Venezia*, No. 115 (August 13, 1814), p. 3; Teresa Confalonieri Casati to Confalonieri, Milan, August 6, 1814, Gallavresi, *Carteggio del conte Federico Confalonieri*, Vol. I, p. 230.

[105] Bellegarde to Hager, Milan, July 19, 1814, A. S. (Milan), Presidenza di governo. Atti secreti, 1814, Cart. I, No. 49/P.R.; Hager report, September 14, 1814, St. A. (Vienna), Conferenz Akten, Ser. b, 1814, No. 1690.

[106] Imperial resolution, December 2, 1814, St. A. (Vienna), Kabinets-Akten, 1814, No. 892; Hager to Bellegarde, Vienna, December 4, 1816, A. S. (Milan), Commissione Plenipotenziaria, Busta unica, No. 11,050; Bellegarde to Strassoldo, Milan, December 20, 1814, *ibid.*

[107] Bellegarde to Pagani, December 28 and 30, 1814, A. S. (Milan), Presidenza di governo. Atti secreti, 1814, Cart. VII, Nos. 1001/P.R. and 985/P.R.

[108] Bellegarde to Sommariva, Verona, May 2, 1814, St. A. (Vienna), Kaiser Franz Akten, Fasz. XXVII, Kon. 1, Fo. 56.

it had been under the French.[109] Only in late July, when the abolition of the ministry of interior made it imperative for the Austrians to make arrangements to take care of the duties formerly discharged by that ministry, did Bellegarde place the censorship office under his direct personal control.[110] At the same time, in compliance with instructions from Baron von Hager,[111] he appointed a special committee, with Marquis Filippo Ghisilieri, a devoted Austrian partisan,[112] as its chairman, to compile a special index of all Italian books that should either be absolutely prohibited or else allowed to have only a limited circulation. The other members of the committee were the provisional press and library director, Count Scopoli; Dr. Gaetano Bugatti, of the Ambrosian Library; and Abbé Giovanni Palamede Carpani, of the Brera Library.[113]

In line with the practices followed by the Austrian censorship, the committee divided the books which were not to be freely circulated in public into three classes: (1) those which attacked religious beliefs, sound moral precepts, or worthy political principles were to be absolutely prohibited; (2) useful books, even though they were objectionable in content, could be read by persons who had been granted special clearance by the censorship; and (3) certain works could be freely sold but not displayed or advertised.[114] The committee completed its work in September.[115] Two months later Ghisilieri was appointed head of a newly created provisional censorship office,[116]

109 De Capitani to Bellegarde, Milan, July 13, 1814, A. S. (Milan), Presidenza di governo. Atti secreti, 1814, Cart. I, No. 37/P.R.

110 Decree, Bellegarde, Milan, July 27, 1814, *Atti del governo lombardo,* 1814, p. 99; announcement, Bellegarde, Milan, July 28, 1814, A. S. (Milan), Uffici e Tribunali Regi. Parte Moderne, Cart. LVI–LVII–LVIII, Governo, Registro Generale, 2 gennaio al 31 luglio 1814, No. 1068.

111 Hager to Bellegarde, Vienna, July 24, 1814, A. S. (Milan), Presidenza di governo. Atti secreti, 1814, Cart. II, No. 139/P.R.

112 Bellegarde to Metternich, Verona, April 28, 1814, M[aurice] H[enri] Weil, *Joachim Murat, roi de Naples. La dernière année de règne (mai 1814–mai 1815),* Vol. I, pp. 530–531.

113 Bellegarde to Hager, Milan, August 7, 1814, A. S. (Milan), Presidenza di governo. Atti secreti, 1814, Cart. II, No. 139; Bellegarde to provisional censorship director, Milan, August 7, 1814, *ibid.,* No. 158.

114 Protocol of the first session of the committee to compile an index of prohibited Italian books, August 16, 1814, *ibid.,* Cart. VI, No. 764/P.R.

115 Committee to compile an index of prohibited Italian books to Bellegarde, Milan, September 16, 1814, *ibid.*

116 Bellegarde to Ghisilieri, Milan, November 10, 1814, A. S. (Milan), Com-

and the former press and library directory headed by Count Scopoli, which had been provisionally retained, was incorporated in it. Immediately after his appointment Ghisilieri instructed the prefects to order all printers and book dealers in their department to send him lists of every book they had in stock so that the Milanese censorship could inform them about whether any of these books were to be prohibited or sold only on a restricted basis.[117] Bellegarde's reluctance to make hasty changes in the police and censorship administrations reflected his policy of dealing with the Lombards in general. Tolerant, courteous, and considerate as he was,[118] the commissioner plenipotentiary followed a policy of circumspection, patience, and forbearance intended to win the respect and love of the Italians for the Habsburgs.[119] Although reactionaries, both in Lombardy and elsewhere in the empire, put pressure on him to eradicate all liberal trappings overnight and as rapidly as possible to make the administration of Lombardy similar to that in the hereditary German states, in order to spare the sensibilities of the populace, the field marshal did not budge from his moderate course. Carrying out the wishes of his sovereign[120] as he interpreted them, he made only such changes in the political system which he inherited as were absolutely indispensable for Habsburg interests.[121]

---

missione Plenipotenziaria, Busta unica, No. 1455; Bellegarde to Lazanzky, Milan, December 21, 1814, A. S. (Milan), Presidenza di governo. Atti secreti, 1814, Cart. VII, No. 977.

[117] Ghisilieri to all Lombard prefects, Milan, December 3, 1814, A. S. (Milan), Presidenza di governo. Atti secreti, 1814, Cart. VII, No. 1017/P.R.

[118] Hager report, September 5, 1814, St. A. (Vienna), Kabinets-Akten, 1814, No. 220; entry of June 1, 1815, *Biblioteca Ambrosiana* (Milan), Mantovani, "Diario di Milano," Vol. V, p. 365.

[119] See especially Pietro Dolce report, Milan, June 30, 1816, A. S. (Milan), Presidenza di governo. Atti secreti, 1816, Cart. XI, Rub. 669/geh. (Reisenden Dolce), Pezza 224; and Freddi to Hager, Vienna, December 26, 1814, M[aurice] H[enri] Weil, *Les dessous de Congrès de Vienne, d'après les documents originaux des archives du ministère impérial et royal de l'intérieur à Vienne,* Vol. I, p. 745.

[120] See especially Emperor Francis to Bellegarde, Schönbrunn, July 12, 1814, St. A. (Vienna), Conferenz Akten, Ser. b, 1814, No. 1249; Emperor Francis to Bellegarde, Laxenberg, July 16, 1814, *ibid.,* No. 1322; and imperial resolution, Vienna, January 10, 1815, St. A. (Vienna), Staats-Rath Akten, 1814, No. 4439.

[121] Bellegarde report, May 31, 1814, St. A. (Vienna), Conferenz Akten, Ser. b, 1814, No. 1249; Bellegarde to Emperor Francis, Milan, March 25, 1816, St. A. (Vienna), Kaiser Franz Akten, Fasz. XV, Kon. 2, Fo. 117.

Although Bellegarde was esteemed for the above qualities,[122] he was by no means universally loved and respected by the populace. In fact, the very desirable qualities which should have made him well liked gave rise to criticism by the Lombards. The public muttered that his affable, forbearing, and easygoing nature was nothing but a cover for his inertia and lack of energy, and they dubbed him a timid, vacillating, inert old army officer who was incapable of governing.[123]

Part of the reason for the discontent of various Italians with the field marshal's supposed weakness and inability lay in the considerable amount of work which he delegated to Baron von Rosetti. Not only was Rosetti Bellegarde's deputy in charge of the general management of the whole administration, but also, as vice-president of the provisional regency, he attended all its sessions and presided over them[124] during the numerous occasions when his superior was absent. A reader of the protocols of the regency can not help getting the impression that Rosetti wielded tremendous influence on that body. A resolute, intelligent, sometimes harsh and strict, but always competent and hard-working, bureaucrat, he was a singularly unlovable man and an ardent reactionary. Unfortunately, he was looked upon, and also feared, by at least some Milanese as the real ruler in Milan.[125]

Another cause for grumbling, this time particularly among the pro-

---

[122] Hager report, August 2, 1814, St. A. (Vienna), Conferenz Akten, Ser. b, 1814, No. 1506; Hager report, September 5, 1814, St. A. (Vienna) Kabinets-Akten, 1814, No. 220; entry of June 1, 1815, *Biblioteca Ambrosiana* (Milan), Mantovani, "Diario di Milano," Vol. V, p. 365.

[123] Entries of June 30 and July 7, 1814, *Biblioteca Ambrosiana* (Milan), Mantovani, "Diario di Milano," Vol. V, pp. 286 and 288; Hager report, September 5, 1814, St. A. (Vienna), Kabinets-Akten, 1814, No. 220; Giovanni de Castro, "I ricordi autobiografici inediti del marchese Benigno Bossi," *Archivio storico lombardo*, Vol. XVII (1890), p. 911.

[124] Bellegarde to provisional regency, Milan, July 17, 1814, St. A. (Milan), Commissione Plenipotenziaria, Busta unica, ad No. 779.

[125] Teresa Confalonieri Casati to Confalonieri, Milan, July 23 and August 6, 1814, Gallavresi, *Carteggio del conte Federico Confalonieri*, Vol. I, pp. 222 and 230; Hager report, September 2, 1814, St. A. (Vienna), Conferenz Akten, Ser. b, 1814, No. 1651; confidential report from Milan, July 20, 1814, St. A. (Vienna), Kabinets-Akten, 1814, No. 220; entry of September 10, 1814, *Biblioteca Ambrosiana* (Milan), Mantovani, "Diario di Milano," Vol. V, p. 309; Giovanni de Castro, "La restaurazione austriaca in Milano (1814–1817). Notizie desunte da diarj e testimonianze contemporanee," *Archivio storico lombardo*, Vol. XV (1888), p. 631.

Austrian and other conservative groups, was the fact that Bellegarde retained in key posts numerous officials of the former Kingdom of Italy, many of whom they suspected of being immoral opportunists or dangerous Jacobins or Freemasons[126] on whose loyalty the Habsburgs could hardly count.[127] More important, numerous Lombards were unhappy because during all of 1814 and most of 1815 the Austrians left intact many of the central administrative offices and practices of the hated French regime which had just been overthrown.[128] As was true in Venetia, the French had a mere handful of supporters in Lombardy in 1814.[129] Embittered as the overwhelming majority of Lombards, both conservatives and liberals, were by the vexatious and oppressive practices of the Napoleonic officials, they were most unhappy because the Austrians failed to destroy all vestiges of the opprobrious French regime immediately after arriving on the scene in Italy.

As has been noted, except for abolishing the ministries, the Habsburgs preserved for almost two years nearly all the organs of the central government and much of the former French-Italian personnel which they found when they came to Lombardy. It was the same story with the departmental, district, cantonal, communal, financial, and judicial administrations. For two years after the demise of Prince Eugene's kingdom the departments continued to be governed by their prefects and their prefectural and general councils, as they had been under Napoleon. The only change which the Habsburgs made in the French system was that after the ministries were abolished the prefects corresponded with and received their orders directly from the provisional regency rather than from the appropriate ministries. The districts were still under the supervision of the vice-prefects and

[126] See especially confidential reports from Milan, June 9 and 23, 1814, A. S. (Milan), Presidenza di governo. Atti secreti, 1814, Cart. I, No. 89/P.R.; Hager to Bellegarde, Vienna, July 17, 1814, *ibid.*, Cart. II, No. 124/P.R.; and Hager reports, June 25 and 29, 1814, St. A. (Vienna), Conferenz Akten, Ser. b, 1814, Nos. 1262 and 1276.

[127] Bellegarde to Emperor Francis, Milan, November 11, 1814, *Kriegs-Archiv* (Vienna), Feld Akten (Italien), 1814, Fasz. XI, No. 14 ½; Pirelli di Varena to Bellegarde, Varena, July 15, 1814, A. S. (Milan), Presidenza di governo. Atti secreti, 1814, Cart. I, No. 57/P.R.

[128] See especially entries of August 1, 1814, and June 27, 1815, *Biblioteca Ambrosiana* (Milan), Mantovani, "Diario di Milano," Vol. V, pp. 296–297 and 370.

[129] See *post*, p. 147.

the district councils, and there was still a justice of peace in each canton and a *cancelliere del censo* in most of them. The French communal system was also provisionally preserved.[130] Also, to the indignation of at least some of the inhabitants, the Austrians still kept at their posts the large majority of employees who had occupied them under the French, notwithstanding the fact that some of them were known to have been ardent partisans of Napoleon.[131]

Even though the Austrians placed primary emphasis on establishing a sound financial administration in Lombardy as quickly as possible,[132] during the first two years of their occupation they made only a few more changes in the prevailing French setup than they did in the previously existing departmental and local governments. In the Kingdom of Italy the financial administration had been superintended by two offices: the ministry of the treasury and the ministry of finance. The former, which was divided into three divisions, not only took care of the collecting, safeguarding, and disbursing of state revenues, but also supervised the various accounting and bookkeeping offices in the kingdom. The ministry of finance, which was composed of five departments, collected all the direct and indirect taxes, looked after the forests and domains, managed the postal service, controlled the coinage and mint, and handled all credit matters. Attached to the finance ministry were special directories for (1) land and direct taxes; (2) customs and tolls; (3) salt, tobacco, powder, saltpeter, and consumption taxes; (4) the domains and forests; (5) the mint and coinage; (6) the postal service; and (7) the lottery. In addition, the prefecture of the Monte Napoleone (the state bank) and the exchequer board were under the direction of the minister of finance. In every department there was an intendancy of finance to carry out the orders of the ministry of finance in regard to all financial matters except those which concerned the administration of the domains.[133]

130 Bellegarde report on the Austrian-Italian provinces, October 25, 1814, Helfert, *Kaiser Franz und die Stiftung des Lombardo-Venetianischen Königreichs*, Appendix I, pp. 528–532.

131 See, for example, anonymous to Bellegarde, Mantua, received by Bellegarde on July 16, 1814, A. S. (Milan), Presidenza di governo. Atti secreti, 1814, Cart. I, No. 40 R; and Hager report, August 2, 1814, St. A. (Vienna), Conferenz Akten, Ser. b, 1814, No. 1506.

132 See especially Staats-Conferenz report, May 29, 1814, St. A. (Vienna), Conferenz Akten, Ser. b, 1814, No. 996.

133 Bellegarde report on the Austrian-Italian provinces, October 25, 1814, Hel-

Immediately after the Austrians arrived in Milan, Bellegarde inaugurated steps intended to insure the regular collection of the existing taxes,[134] but he made no changes in the prevailing French-Italian financial administrative system. When the ministries were abolished late in July, the duties previously performed by the ministry of the treasury were assumed by the banking and general accounting departments of the provisional government. A general intendancy of finance, similar to the one which had existed in Lombardy before 1796, was hastily instituted to take over the administration of indirect taxes. To prevent confusion, although their names were now changed to "administrations," all the directories of the former ministry of finance except the one for domains were still left in operation. The work formerly performed by the directory for domains was divided between the salt, tobacco, and consumption tax administration and a newly established finance office. The supervision of all matters dealing with loans and credit, the land tax and other direct taxes, the postal service, and coinage and the mint was the direct responsibility of the provisional regency. In accord with the practices prevailing in the hereditary German areas of the Habsburg monarchy, the exchequer board of the former ministry of finance and the bookkeeping section of the ministry of the treasury were combined to form a newly organized general accounting department.[135] These were the only significant changes made in the Lombard financial administration before the permanent Austrian financial system was inaugurated between 1816 and 1820.

One of the special charges that fell upon the Habsburg financial administration in Lombardy-Venetia was the liquidation of the obligations of the former French state bank in the Kingdom of Italy, the Monte Napoleone, in which the state debt, clerical, civil, and military pensions, and various other state liabilities had been consolidated. It was estimated that the outstanding indebtment of the Monte Napoleone amounted to 23,984,484 francs in the spring of 1814. In both the Treaty of Fontainebleau of April 11 and the Treaty of Paris

fert, *Kaiser Franz und die Stiftung des Lombardo-Venetianischen Königreichs*, Appendix I, pp. 533–534.

[134] Bellegarde report, May 21, 1814, St. A. (Vienna), Conferenz Akten, Ser. b, 1814, No. 1248; Hager to Staats-Conferenz, June 8, 1814, *ibid.*, No. 1153.

[135] Bellegarde report on the Austrian-Italian provinces, October 25, 1814, Helfert, *Kaiser Franz und die Stiftung des Lombardo-Venetianischen Königreichs*, Appendix I, p. 534.

of May 30 the Allied Powers promised to take over these obligations. It was agreed that a proportionate amount of the charge was to fall on all the territories which had previously constituted the Kingdom of Italy. Although the exact amount was to be determined at the Congress of Vienna by negotiations between the powers concerned, Austrian officials calculated in May, 1814, that the amount of the debt which Austria was to bear would be 9,025,511 francs.[136] Until the whole matter was finally settled by common agreement in Vienna, Bellegarde was ordered to suspend all payments of the Monte.[137]

In the judicial administration, too, the Habsburgs temporarily left nearly all the French system intact. Aside from abolishing the special courts which the French had created,[138] Emperor Francis provisionally confirmed all the existing French law courts. He merely enjoined Bellegarde to make certain that justice would be fairly and well administered and that court proceedings would not be in arrears.[139] When the ministries were abolished, the first instance courts were placed under the supervision of the courts of appeals and the courts of appeals under that of the court of cassation, in accordance with practices in the other Habsburg provinces. The other duties of the abolished ministry of justice, including the hiring and firing of judicial personnel, the granting of immunities, and the commutation of sentences, were for the time being assigned to the provisional regency.[140] When the court of cassation was abolished on December 28, 1814, the work previously performed by that court was transferred to the supreme court in Vienna.[141]

[136] Report on the Monte Napoleone sent from Paris on May 29, 1814, St. A. (Vienna), Kaiser Franz Akten, Fasz. XVIII, Kon. 5, Fos. 34–36; Bellegarde to Strassoldo, Verona, May 3, 1814, ibid., Fasz. XXVII, Kon. 1, Fo. 46; Bellegarde to Emperor Francis, Verona, May 4, 1814, ibid., Fos. 44–47.

[137] Emperor Francis to Bellegarde, Schönbrunn, July 12, 1814, St. A. (Vienna), Conferenz Akten, Ser. b, 1814, No. 1249.

[138] Decree, provisional regency, Milan, May 6, 1814, Giornale italiano, No. 127 (May 8, 1814), p. 518.

[139] Emperor Francis to Bellegarde, Paris, May 14, 1814, St. A. (Vienna), Conferenz Akten, Ser. b, 1814, No. 996.

[140] Bellegarde report on the Austrian-Italian provinces, October 25, 1814, Helfert, Kaiser Franz und die Stiftung des Lombardo-Venetianischen Königreichs, Appendix I, p. 526; decree, Bellegarde, July 27, 1814, Atti del governo lombardo, 1814, pp. 92–97.

[141] Helfert, Kaiser Franz und die Stiftung des Lombardo-Venetianischen Königreichs, p. 31; entry of January 24, 1815, Biblioteca Ambrosiana (Milan), Mantovani, "Diario di Milano," Vol. V, p. 336.

With a few exceptions, the Habsburgs also retained the French civil and criminal codes until such time as they could introduce the Austrian legal code. A few French practices, however, differed too radically from the fundamental spirit of Habsburg legislation to make it seem advisable to permit them to continue. In order as quickly as possible to bring the laws dealing with marriages in harmony with what the Austrians believed were proper Catholic religious and moral principles, the Habsburgs, on June 13, 1814, abolished those parts of the French civil code which permitted divorce and instructed their officials in Lombardy to allow no divorced person to remarry.[142] A couple of months later the commissioner plenipotentiary was instructed to suppress gambling.[143] A few modifications were also made in the French code to mitigate some of the rigorous penalties which they prescribed. In November, 1814, for example, Emperor Francis asked Bellegarde to place severe limitations on the use of branding,[144] and the following spring he ordered the abolition of the use of the pillory in Lombardy.[145]

The above measures, however, were only stopgaps to fill in the most obvious loopholes until the judicial system could be assimilated to that of the other parts of the empire. To prepare the way for this, in the summer of 1814, at the same time that Von Plenciz was sent to Venetia as head of a special justice regulation commission, the emperor commissioned Francesco de Patroni, who was then in Milan, to act in a similar capacity in Lombardy.[146] The president of the Inner Austrian court of appeals, Franz von Enzenberg, and Counselor of Appeals Franz Xaver von Brenner were named as the other members of the commission.[147] They were to make a careful study of the Lombard judiciary and as quickly as possible to send recommenda-

---

[142] Bellegarde report, May 21, 1814, St. A. (Vienna), Conferenz Akten, Ser. b, 1814, No. 1248; decree, provisional regency, Milan, June 13, 1814, *Atti del governo lombardo*, 1814, pp. 65–67.

[143] Hager to Bellegarde, Vienna, August 16, 1814, A. S. (Milan), Presidenza di governo. Atti secreti, 1814, Cart. II, No. 246/P.R.

[144] Helfert, *Kaiser Franz und die Stiftung des Lombardo-Venetianischen Königreichs*, pp. 29–30.

[145] *Ibid.*, p. 30; protocol, provisional regency, June 3, 1815, *Biblioteca di Brera* (Milan), "Protocolli originali della reggenza provvisoria."

[146] Imperial resolution, Baden, June 30, 1814, St. A. (Vienna), Conferenz Akten, Set. b, 1814, No. 1286.

[147] Imperial resolution, Baden, July 18, 1814, *ibid.*, No. 1313.

tions to Vienna on how a permanent judicial system similar to that in the hereditary German states could be instituted in Lombardy.[148]

The Habsburgs took pains to conserve most of the French-Italian political, financial, and judicial setup in Lombardy in the same state in which they found it until they could cautiously and gradually introduce a new system that was identical with or similar to that in the hereditary German provinces. However, Emperor Francis looked upon the changes which the French had made in church affairs as too contrary to sound religious principles for him to follow a correspondingly wary and circumspect policy in religious matters. Just as they had done in Venetia, shortly after they arrived in Lombardy the Austrians took hurried steps to correct some of the worst abuses in the Catholic church. Immoral clergy were dismissed; ecclesiastical pensions were regularized (although not before early 1815);[149] the Austrian catechism was re-introduced;[150] ecclesiastical patronage by private families was abolished;[151] and provision was made for the orderly re-establishment of such monasteries and convents as the Habsburgs wished to have re-instituted.[152]

Strongly under Josephinist influence particularly when it came to religious matters, the Habsburg monarch was insistent, as he had been in Venetia, that the Lombard clergy not impair his own privileges and powers in regard to the Catholic church. The government in Milan was to approve all appeals and letters of Lombard bishops to Rome for dispensations or other matters, and its assent was required before any bulls, papal briefs, bestowals of benefices, or any other communications from Rome could be circulated in Lombardy. Likewise, the special consent of the government had to be procured before Lombard bishops or capitulary vicars could publish any pastoral letter or other message to the faithful.[153] Emperor Francis was

148 Supreme court report, July 22, 1814, *ibid.*, No. 1418; imperial resolution, n.d., *ibid.*

149 Entry of February 19, 1815, *Biblioteca Ambrosiana* (Milan), Mantovani, "Diario di Milano," Vol. V, p. 341.

150 Bellegarde to Hager, Milan, August 30, 1814, A. S. (Milan), Presidenza di governo. Atti secreti, 1814, Cart. II, No. 212/P.R.

151 Decree, provisional regency, Milan, July 16, 1814, *Atti del governo lombardo*, 1814, pp. 86–88; entry of July 24, 1814, *Biblioteca Ambrosiana* (Milan), Mantovani, "Diario di Milano, "Vol. V, p. 294.

152 Decree, provisional regency, Milan, April 10, 1815, *Atti del governo lombardo*, 1815, Vol. I, pp. 30–40.

153 Protocols of the provisional regency, September 10 and 17, 1814, *Biblio-*

as emphatic about asserting his rights over the Lombard clergy as over those in Venetia and elsewhere in the empire.

No less than his interest in a strong but subordinate church was the emperor's concern about having the Lombard educational system organized as soon as possible in the same way as in his German states.[154] Shortly after Lombardy was assigned to Austria he asked Bellegarde to draft a detailed report about the Lombard educational setup and make recommendations to the aulic education commission which it could draw upon in devising a permanent school system for Lombardy.[155] To aid him in outlining these proposals, the commissioner plenipotentiary appointed a special committee presided over by the vice-president of the provisional government, Baron von Rosetti. Its other members were Giulini, of the provisional regency; Ghisilieri, chairman of the committee to compile an index of prohibited books; Scopoli, then provisional director of public education; Schimmelfenning, of the presidency of the Lombard government; De Pagave, secretary of the provisional regency; Vittadini, rector of the Milan seminary; and Professors Carminati, Gaetano Giudici, Raccogni, and Londinio. This committee, which met between September 3 and October 31, 1814, discussed in detail how the existing system of public instruction in Lombardy, from the elementary schools to the university, could be merged into that in the Habsburg monarchy. It pointed out some of the difficulties involved in introducing the Habsburg system into Italy, since the minimum school attendance requirements, the teacher training methods, school supervision and examination procedures, and the courses taught in the elementary and secondary schools differed considerably from those in the German provinces.[156] In accord with specific instructions from the emperor, the committee also made a careful investigation of the moral conduct and other qualifications of all Lombard teachers and pro-

---

teca di Brera (Milan), "Protocolli originali della reggenza provvisoria"; Bellegarde to Lombard bishops, Milan, November 22, 1814, Maass, *Der Josephinismus*, Vol. IV, pp. 487–488.

154 Emperor Francis to Bellegarde, Baden, July 11, 1814, St. A. (Vienna), Kabinets-Akten, 1814, No. 130.

155 Studienhofcommission to Bellegarde, August 22, 1814, *Unterrichtsarchiv* (Vienna), Studienhofcommission Akten, No. 94 ex August 1814.

156 See protocols of the committee to establish a system of public instruction in Lombardy, September 3 and October 10 and 31, 1814, *Biblioteca di Brera* (Milan), "Protocolli originali della reggenza provvisoria."

fessors and busied itself with readying the University of Pavia to open its doors to students as quickly as possible.[157] The work of the committee progressed rapidly enough so that the University of Pavia could formally open the fall session on November 12.[158]

It is obvious that the provisional government functioned more efficiently in Lombardy than in Venetia. Even though the complaints which the Lombards voiced about their commissioner plenipotentiary bore a strong resemblance to those which the Venetians made about their provisional governor, Bellegarde was a more able administrator than Reuss-Plauen. Of greater importance, Bellegarde was fortunate in having more capable top-level assistants than Reuss-Plauen. The Venetian central government was plagued by a continual shortage of competent high-ranking administrative personnel, and several of the governor's key officials had to be dismissed during the summer of 1814. Bellegarde's administrators were able and efficient. He profited from the fact that he fell heir to a highly competent provisional regency which had sprung into existence as a result of the Milanese revolution of April 20 and that he was astute enough to allow this regency, under his supervision, to act as the real ruler of Lombardy.

However, the difference between the way the two provisional governments conducted the administration must be ascribed more than anything else to accident. The Venetian government was organized while a military campaign was being fought on Venetian territory. Handling emergencies in connection with the war and maintaining order and security in the areas immediately behind the battle zone took up so much of Reuss-Plauen's time that he had little energy left to devote to creating a central government in Venetia. As a result, all too many administrative offices and measures were haphazardously devised as stopgap measures. Bellegarde was harassed by none of these problems—problems which would have made it extremely difficult for almost anyone to fashion a smoothly functioning governing

[157] Protocols of the committee to establish a system of public instruction in Lombardy, October 11 and 31, 1814, *ibid.*; protocol, provisional regency, October 21, 1814, *ibid.*; protocols, presidency of the government, November 13, 1814, A. S. (Milan), Presidenza di governo. Atti secreti, 1814, Cart. V, Nos. 727/P.R. and 728/P.R.

[158] Provisional Olona department police prefecture report, Milan, November 16, 1814, A. S. (Milan), Presidenza di governo. Atti secreti, 1814, Cart. VI, No. 776/P.R.

apparatus. The war ended before the Habsburgs took control of Lombardy. Then, too, the governor of Venetia had nothing even vaguely resembling a central administrative organization to adapt to his purposes. All the central administrative offices of the Kingdom of Italy were located at Milan, and all communications were cut off between Venetia and Milan during the course of the Italian campaign. Bellegarde, on the other hand, was able to make use of the entire top governing apparatus of an efficiently administered kingdom, as well as a ready-made highly competent provisional regency.

Bellegarde and Reuss-Plauen both followed the same general policies in governing the areas of which they were in charge. To the consternation of many Venetians and Lombards, both governors retained most of the administrative machinery and most of the personnel of the former Kingdom of Italy until well into 1815 and 1816. Perhaps the most significant change made in either area during the period of the provisional Habsburg administration came in the spring of 1815. This was the addition to Lombardy in the spring of 1815 of a part of the former Kingdom of Italy which the Italians had expected to lose to Switzerland: Bormio, Chiavenna, and the Valtelline.[159]

[159] In May, 1814, while the fate of the area was still undecided, three thousand Grison troops invaded the area, carrying with them a proclamation of the Grison government, dated May 3, 1814 (St. A. [Vienna], Staatskanzlei, Provinzen, Lombardei-Venedig, Fasz. III, Kon. 3, Fo. 199), advising the inhabitants that they were occupying their territory to facilitate its incorporation into Grison territory. The inhabitants of the region were almost unanimously opposed to falling under the rule of the Grisons, and at the Congress of Vienna they presented several petitions beseeching the Allied Powers to permit them to remain united with Lombardy and to pass under Austrian sovereignty. The Grisons were just as insistent that the territory be given to them. The Habsburgs were perfectly willing to return the Valtelline to the Swiss on condition that its residents enjoy the same civil liberties and independence as the people living in the other cantons of Switzerland. The populace of the Valtelline, Chiavenna, and Bormio, however, absolutely refused to return to Swiss domination under any conditions. In the end the Allied Powers decided, in March, 1815, to annex these territories to Lombardy. For the protocols of the various sittings of the committee on Swiss affairs at the Congress of Vienna at which the fate of the Valtelline, Chiavenna, and Bormio was discussed, see Johann Ludwig Klüber, *Acten des Wiener Congresses in den Jahren 1814 und 1815*, Vol. V, pp. 117–328.

Chapter 3

AUSTRIAN ECONOMIC POLICIES AND PRACTICES IN LOMBARDY-VENETIA, 1814–1815

Lombardy, where the Austrians were able to avail themselves of much of the machinery of the central government of the former Kingdom of Italy, was much more efficiently governed in 1814–1815 than Venetia. The Lombards also suffered much less from the vicissitudes of warfare and from repressive economic measures than the Venetians.

It is true that both areas were sorely afflicted by the vexatious and oppressive economic policies of their French masters during the last years of the Kingdom of Italy. In spite of the introduction of the French civil and commercial codes, the systematic and efficacious repression of brigandage, and the construction of roads, bridges, canals, and irrigation works, all of which stimulated commerce and industry, Lombard and Venetian business and industry fell victim to many annoying handicaps during the period of French domination. The incessant conscription took many workers away from farm and factory. The arbitrary confiscation of merchandise and the frequent checks and hindrances placed upon commerce tended to create a sense of insecurity which was prejudicial to business expansion. Irritating customs regulations discouraged trade with the countries on the continent of Europe, and the continental blockade ruined, not only the maritime trade, but also such industries as the manufacture of silk products, the prosperity of which was dependent upon the British market. Other businesses were damaged by Napoleon's policy of favoring native French industry by all possible means and of making Italy only an economic colony of his empire to be exploited for the benefit of French enterprises.[1] Agriculture fared somewhat better, since the French emperor tried to make Italy a vast granary for the French industrial population. Various encouragements offered to Italian agriculturists, the abolition of entailment, and the selling of ecclesiastical properties resulted in the expansion and improvement of many landholdings and an increase in food production. Yet these benefits were offset by the high duties and other obstructions placed on the exportation of agricultural products to countries other than France, the fixing of maximum food prices at levels favorable to the urban working classes, and the levying of crippling land taxes.[2]

Expenditures and taxes in the Kingdom of Italy increased sharply during the years preceding 1814. In 1805 the total annual expenditures had amounted to 103,282,143 lire. By 1809 they had risen to 136,000,000; by 1811, to 142,444,870; and by 1812, to 144,000,000. Of the 144,000,000 spent in 1812, 46,000,000 lire went to the army and navy; 22,000,000 lire were allocated towards the servicing of the public debt, of which a large amount had been charged to the treasury of the Kingdom of Italy; and 30,000,000 were turned over directly to the imperial treasury in Paris.[3] By the same year the public debt of the kingdom had risen to 298,000,000 lire.[4]

This increase in expenditures naturally brought about a substantial augmentation in taxes. During the last year of the existence of the Kingdom of Italy, for example, the inhabitants of the provinces which had constituted Austrian Venetia between 1798 and 1805 paid 40,-000,000 lire in land taxes alone, as compared with 7,000,000 gulden,

[1]See Eugène Tarlé, *Le Blocus continental et le Royaume d'Italie. La Situation économique de l'Italie sous Napoléon Ier d'après des documents inédits*, pp. 364–371; *Storia di Milano*, Vol. XIII: *L'età napoleonica*, pp. 374–387; Carlo Tivaroni, *L'Italia durante il dominio francese (1789–1815)*, Vol. I: *L'Italia settentrionale*, pp. 310–311; and Roberti, *Milano capitale napoleonica*, Vol. III, pp. 482–491.

[2] See *Storia di Milano*, Vol. XIII: *L'età napoleonica*, pp. 373–380; Tivaroni, *L'Italia durante il dominio francese*, Vol. I, pp. 309–310; Tarlé, *Le Blocus continental et le Royaume d'Italie*, pp. 90–114; A. de Maddalena, "I prezzi dei generi commestibili e dei prodotti agricoli sul mercato di Milano dal 1800 al 1890," *Archivio economico dell'unificazione italiana*, Vol. V, Fasc. 3 (1957), p. 4; Roberto Cessi, "Il Veneto nel Risorgimento," *Rassegna storica del Risorgimento*, Vol. XLIV, Fasc. 4 (October–December, 1957), pp. 574–575; and Roberti, *Milano capitale napoleonica*, Vol. III, pp. 436–447.

[3] Tarlé, *Le Blocus continental et le Royaume d'Italie*, pp. 29–31; Roberti, *Milano capitale napoleonica*, Vol. II, p. 366.

[4] Sandonà, *Il Regno Lombardo Veneto*, p. 60.

or 18,101,300 Italian lire,[5] annually when they were under Austrian occupation.[6] By 1812 the land tax in Venetia had risen to 66 denari for every scudo of assessed value. In addition, there were a number of surtaxes levied on real estate. It has been estimated that the total amount of the taxes paid by Venetian landowners ran close to one-half of the income from the land.[7] In the provinces which comprised pre-revolutionary Lombardy the total land tax came to 21,299,134.20 Italian lire in 1814. In 1795 the same territory had paid only 8,235,769.98. In Lombardy the land tax absorbed 25 per cent of the income from the land in 1812 and 29 per cent in 1813.[8] Over and above the land tax were a large number of other direct and indirect taxes, including the poll tax (5.80 lire per person), business taxes, the tax on artisans and professional people, the stamp tax, the registration tax, the consumption tax, and more than a dozen other special taxes.

As the spring of 1814 approached taxes climbed steadily upward. To meet the expenses of the wars fought in 1812 and 1813, Napoleon, in August, 1813, levied a surcharge of 1½ centesimi for every scudo of assessed value on landed property.[9] In October Prince Eugene ordered an advance payment of the personal tax. The next month he levied a forced loan of 3,000,000 lire on the city of Milan.[10] In January, 1814, he added another surcharge of 1 centesimo to the land tax and imposed a special tax of 1 per cent on all capital.[11] At the same time, Napoleon authorized his viceroy to levy any contributions and taxes which he deemed necessary to pay the expenses of the French army.[12]

As the result of the harsh exploitation of the Kingdom of Italy by

---

[5] The value of the Austrian gulden or florin in Italian lire has been computed here and subsequently in this chapter on the basis of one florin or gulden to 2.5859 lire. This was the comparative value assigned to the two moneys in 1814 by the Austrian central accounting office in Venetia. See Mayer von Gravenegg to Wurmser, Venice, December 20, 1814, A. S. (Venice), Presidio di governo, 1814, No. 2312.

[6] Report from Paris, May 29, 1814, St. A. (Vienna), Kaiser Franz Akten, Fasz. XVIII, Kon. 5, Fo. 31.

[7] Sandonà, Il Regno Lombardo Veneto, p. 67.

[8] Ibid., p. 60.

[9] Ottolenghi, Padova e il Dipartimento del Brenta, p. 53.

[10] Tivaroni, L'Italia durante il dominio francese, Vol. I, p. 311.

[11] Decree, Prince Eugene, Verona, January 24, 1814, Bollettino delle leggi della Repubblica Italiana e del Regno d'Italia, 1814, pp. 17–20.

[12] Decree, Napoleon, Tuileries, January 23, 1814, ibid., pp. 15–16.

the French, the ever-increasing tax burden, and the vicissitudes of warfare came an avalanche of business failures as the Napoleonic era drew to a close. In May, 1813, the Bignami house, one of the largest financial institutions in Milan, crashed.[13] By June, 1813, nineteen other large business houses had failed in the cities of Milan and Venice alone.[14] A succession of bankruptcies and the disastrous war of the fall of 1813 brought misery to the country. By October, 1813, the royal treasury was bankrupt,[15] and commerce and industry were almost at a standstill.

To add to the miserable lot of the inhabitants, the 1813 harvest was unusually poor, especially in the mountain valleys of Venetia, where a plague seriously decimated the herds of cattle. Repeated hail storms in the Alpine areas had destroyed most of the crops, and early snows had buried the few remaining sprouts of late maturation. In the Alpine areas indescribable squalor and suffering abounded. Many unhappy wretches had no bread, and quite a few inhabitants were suffering from pellagra. The landowners, overburdened with heavy taxes and requisitions and exhausted from several years of heavy losses, were too impoverished to render more than a modicum of assistance to the needy.[16]

To give succor and hope to the miserable populace and thereby win their gratitude and affection, the Habsburg army should have come to Venetia well provided with food and money. Unfortunately, Habsburg finances, which had been on an unsound foundation from the beginning of the revolutionary wars, were in too desperate and chaotic a condition to make this possible. Ever since 1792 the increased expenses necessitated by the war had been met only by col-

---

[13] Lemmi, *La restaurazione austriaca a Milano*, p. 45.

[14] Tarlé, *Le Blocus continental et le Royaume d'Italie*, p. 238.

[15] *Ibid.*, p. 31; Cusani, *Storia di Milano*, Vol. VII, pp. 22–25.

[16] See especially prefect of Passariano to Marenzi, Udine, December 10, 1813, A.S. (Venice), Governo veneto, 1813, Pubblico politico, Busta VIII–IX, Rub. 14, No. 820; prefect of Bacchiglione to Thurn, Vicenza, December 10, 1813, *ibid.*, No. 27,798; Bellegarde to Reuss-Plauen, n.d., *ibid.*, Busta VI–VII, Rub. 3, No. 1068; prefect of Tagliamento to Reuss-Plauen, Treviso, December 30, 1813, A. S. (Venice), Governo veneto, 1814, Imposta, Busta XXXII, Fasc. 23, No. 22,634; districts of Brenta to Reuss-Plauen, March, 1814, *ibid.*, Fasc. 76, No. 3139; prefect of Tagliamento to presidency of the Venetian government, Treviso, May 18, 1814, A. S. (Venice), Presidio di governo, 1814, ad No. 669; and police delegate of Treviso to Venetian general government, Treviso, June 16, 1814, *ibid.*, No. 240.

lecting subsidies from England, levying higher taxes, increasing the public debt, exacting compulsory loans, and increasing the number of bank notes.[17] Long before 1813 the paper money in circulation was hopelessly out of proportion to the gold and silver available to redeem it. As a consequence, its value fell to such a low point that in 1810 one florin in gold was worth 12.40 florins in bank notes.[18]

In an attempt to stave off bankruptcy, a new paper currency, the so-called "redemption notes" (*Einlösungs-Scheine*), was substituted in 1811 for the old bank notes. The new money was to have the same value as gold and silver coins of similar denominations, and the older bills were to be exchanged for them up to December 31, 1811, at the rate of five to one. It was expressly stipulated that after that date the redemption notes were to be the only paper money in circulation in the empire and that the total amount was never to exceed 212,159,750 florins.[19]

Austria's financial troubles did not end with the substitution of the redemption notes for the old bank bills. Like the former bank notes, the redemption certificates lacked sufficient gold and silver coverage and quickly depreciated in value. Also, since military exigencies necessitated the spending of large sums by the treasury, which could not be paid with redemption notes because the emperor had promised in 1811 never to increase the number in circulation, the government, on April 16, 1813, began issuing so-called "anticipation notes" (*Anticipations-Scheine*), which were to be backed by the future proceeds of the land tax. They were to be limited in amount to 45,000,000 florins, and beginning in 1814, 3,750,000 florins of them were to be withdrawn from circulation each year.[20] This sum, however, proved to be insufficient to meet Austria's desperate financial needs. As a consequence, in spite of the emperor's promise in April, before the

[17] Beidtel, *Geschichte der österreichischen Staatsverwaltung*, Vol. II, pp. 173–177.

[18] *Ibid.*, p. 190; Moriz Bermann, *Oesterreich-Ungarn im neunzehnten Jahrhundert. Mit besonderer Berücksichtigung aller wichtigen Vorfälle in der Geschichte, Wissenschaft, Kunst, Industrie und dem Volksleben*, p. 230.

[19] Decree, Emperor Francis, Vienna, June 20, 1811, Francis II (I), *Politische Gesetze und Verordnungen für die Oesterreichischen, Böhmischen und Galizischen Erbländer. Auf allerhöchsten Befehl, und unter Aufsicht der Directorii herausgegeben*, Vol. XXXVI (1811), pp. 195–207; Beidtel, *Geschichte der österreichischen Staatsverwaltung*, Vol. II, pp. 192–193.

[20] Decree, Emperor Francis, Vienna, April 16, 1813, Francis II (I), *Politische Gesetze und Verordnungen*, Vol. XL (1813), pp. 77–81.

end of 1813, 100,000,000 florins more were put into circulation. In 1814 this amount was increased by 150,000,000 and in 1815 by 155,000,000 florins.[21] Naturally, since the anticipation notes did not have the proper backing, they soon circulated below their par value. By November, 1813, one gold florin was worth 1.69 in anticipation notes; and in April, 1814, 2.38.[22]

When Habsburg troops arrived in Venetia in the fall of 1813 three different kinds of money thus circulated in Austria: gold and silver, redeemable at par; and redemption and anticipation notes, the value of which fluctuated considerably but was always much below par.

Since the Austrian government was hard pressed for money, the Habsburg troops, instead of coming to Italy with large funds of gold and silver to relieve the indescribable misery of the inhabitants of the mountain valleys, brought the depreciated paper money with which they were paid—to the consternation of the inhabitants on whom they tried to foist it. Instead of arriving with wagon trains laden with food, the Austrians came with sheaves of requisition orders to commandeer for the support of their army large quantities of foodstuffs and other necessities that would otherwise have been available for public consumption.

When Habsburg soldiers first appeared in Venetia their commander-in-chief, General Hiller, posted a proclamation ordering the Italians to accept the depreciated redemption and anticipation bills at their full nominal value: one kreuzer in Austrian money in exchange for three centesimi in Italian. The Venetians, however, were not allowed to use Austrian currency to pay their first installment of direct taxes, although General Hiller promised them that Austrian redemption and anticipation notes would be accepted in partial payment for subsequent tax bills. They were also permitted to buy salt and tobacco with the paper money, at its full value.[23]

Had they deliberately tried to exasperate the Venetians, the Austrians could hardly have done more to exacerbate them than by

[21] Adolf Beer, *Die Finanzen Österreichs im XIX. Jahrhundert. Nach archivalischen Quellen*, pp. 84–85. See also Alois Brusatti, "Graf Philipp Stadion als Finanzminister," in *Österreich und Europa: Festgabe für Hugo Hantsch zum 70. Geburtstag*, pp. 282–283; and Hellmuth Rössler, *Graf Johann Philipp Stadion, Napoleons deutscher Gegenspieler*, Vol. II, p. 158.

[22] Beidtel, *Geschichte der österreichischen Staatsverwaltung*, Vol. II, p. 197.

[23] Hiller proclamation, Vicenza, November 17, 1813, A. S. (Venice), Governo veneto, 1813, Atti Hiller, no number given.

coercing them to accept the depreciated Habsburg currency. The police reports were unanimous in agreeing that the compulsory circulation of Austrian currency was one of the most bitter grievances of the populace during the first few months of the Habsburg occupation.[24] Austrian soldiers used all possible means to compel the inhabitants to exchange the depreciated paper money with which they were paid for gold and silver coin. Since the tax authorities would not accept the Austrian notes, wild rumors spread that the Habsburg government was planning to decrease the value of the currency even more, and soldiers who did not use intimidation or naked force received very little for their money.[25] Fearing that the continued circulation of Austrian paper money in the Apennine peninsula would lead to its further devaluation, Governor Reuss-Plauen and Marshal Bellegarde both exhorted their government to put an end to the compulsory acceptance of the redemption and anticipation notes in Italy.[26]

When his attention was called to the situation, Emperor Francis lost no time in repairing as quickly as possible the mischief done in Italy by General Hiller's unfortunate order. On January 2, 1814, he instructed Bellegarde to take strong measures to repress all attempts by Austrian soldiers to dragoon the Venetians into accepting paper money.[27] Four days later he made arrangements to send 500,000 florins each month to Bellegarde and Reuss-Plauen to pay the troops in coin and to defray other military expenses.[28] Still further, 285,000 florins were immediately sent to Italy from Klagenfurt and 115,000 more from Vienna.[29]

Emperor Francis' injunction prohibiting his soldiers from com-

---

[24] Staats-Kabinet report, January 17, 1814, St. A. (Vienna), Kabinets-Akten, 1814, No. 957.

[25] Reuss-Plauen to Ugarte, Udine, January 9, 1814, St. A. (Vienna), Kaiser Franz Akten, Fasz. XXVII, Kon. I, Fos. 8–9; Wiedemann-Warnhelm, *Die Wiederherstellung der österreichischen Vorherrschaft in Italien*, pp. 14–15.

[26] Reuss-Plauen to Emperor Francis, Udine, January 9, 1814, St. A. (Vienna), Kaiser Franz Akten, Fasz. XXVII, Kon. 1, Fo. 7; Reuss-Plauen to Ugarte, Udine, January 9, 1814, *ibid.*, Fos. 8–9; Bellegarde to Metternich, Vicenza, December 18 and 21, 1813, and January 3, 1814, St. A. (Vienna), Staatskanzlei, Provinzen, Lombardei-Venedig, Fasz. III, Kon. 3, Fos. 1–3, 4–7, and 11–12.

[27] Emperor Francis to Bellegarde, Freiburg, January 2, 1814, St. A. (Vienna), Conferenz Akten, Ser. b, 1814, No. 104.

[28] Imperial resolution, Freiburg, January 6, 1814, *ibid.*, No. 857.

[29] Protocol, Kriegs-Ministerium, January 16, 1814, *Kriegs-Archiv* (Vienna), Kriegs-Ministerium Akten, 1814, Fasz. I, No. 75.

pelling the Venetians to accept depreciated Austrian currency at its full value was announced to the inhabitants of the occupied areas on January 29, 1814. They were notified that beginning on February 1 the Habsburg troops in Italy would be paid in hard money and all redemption and anticipation notes would be withdrawn from circulation in Venetia. Since all military provisions would likewise be purchased in the same denomination, tobacco and salt would also be sold to the public only for coin.[30] Likewise, all taxes were to be paid for only in hard money.[31] The next day the Habsburg troops were informed that enlisted men would be given half and officers and civilian employees of the army two-thirds of their pay in sound money. Strict orders were issued to them never again to attempt to exchange their paper bills for gold and silver.[32]

By February an extremely vexatious grievance of the Venetian people was thus repaired but it was replaced by another one that exasperated them still more. Since Austria's own finances were tottering on the brink of disaster, the commanding general of the Habsburg army in Italy was enjoined to procure as much food and as many other purveyances for his military forces as he possibly could through requisitions on the Italian populace.[33] To assist him in doing so, General Hiller appointed a special committee in each department to provide lodging, comestibles, and supplies for the troops at the expense of the inhabitants.[34]

A few examples will illustrate the onerousness of some of the burdens which the Austrians imposed. On November 7, 1813—the very day on which the first contingent of troops arrived there—the mayor of Padua was commanded to furnish the Habsburg military with approximately 500 yards of cloth. A few days later he was told that all soldiers around Padua were to be fed and clothed at the expense of the city. In addition, the Padua authorities were immediately to

30 Proclamation, Reuss-Plauen, Udine, January 29, 1814, St. A. (Vienna), Staatskanzlei, Provinzen, Lombardei-Venedig, Fasz. XVIII, Kon. 1, Fo. 2; *Wiener Zeitung*, February 22, 1814, p. 215.

31 Ugarte to Reuss-Plauen, Vienna, January 21, 1814, St. A. (Vienna), Conferenz Akten, Ser. b, 1814, No. 283.

32 Army order, Vicenza, February 1, 1814, *Kriegs-Archiv* (Vienna), Feld Akten (Italien), 1814, Fasz. II, No. 1.

33 Emperor Francis to Reuss-Plauen, Frankfurt, November 9, 1813, St. A. (Vienna), Conferenz Akten, Ser. b, 1813, No. 789.

34 Hiller order, Trent, November 8, 1813, *Collezione di leggi venete*, 1813–1814, Vol. I, pp. 9–10.

deliver to the army 8,000 pairs of trousers, 2,000 shoes, 1,500 boots, 1,200 rations of wine for one battalion, a quart of wine for each soldier in two other battalions, and 15,634 hundredths of hay.[35] In the department of Tagliamento, which, among other things, had to provide subsistence for an average of 5,000 to 6,000 soldiers and 2,000 to 4,000 horses,[36] military requisitions were so oppressive that by the end of January, 1814, they amounted to as much as the heavy land taxes of the department for a whole year.[37] In the department of Bacchiglione, where General Hiller had requisitioned enough cloth to make 8,000 overcoats and 1,000 pairs of trousers immediately after coming to Vicenza, by the middle of December, 1813, the inhabitants already furnished 5,000,000 lire for provisioning the Austrian army.[38] In February 2,000,000 florins, half in supplies and half in money, were demanded from the city of Verona.[39] Other areas had to render similar requisitions. By the end of March, 1814, the seven occupied Venetian provinces had delivered a total of 30,000,000 Italian lire worth of supplies to the Austrian army.[40] By the end of June this amount had risen to 38,500,701.[41]

These onerous requisitions, which bore down particularly heavily on the areas immediately east of the Mincio River and west of the city of Venice, where the bulk of the Habsburg troops were stationed for several months,[42] gave cause for universal complaint. In commune after commune people wrung their hands over the harshness and unfairness of the assessments imposed upon them and remonstrated

[35] Ottolenghi, *Padova e il Dipartimento del Brenta*, pp. 95–99.

[36] Prefect of Tagliamento to presidency of the Venetian government, Treviso, May 18, 1814, A. S. (Venice), Presidio di governo, 1814, No. 9983.

[37] Porcia to Reuss-Plauen, Treviso, January 30, 1814, A. S. (Venice), Governo veneto, 1814, Imposta, Busta XXXII, Fasc. 64, No. 1693.

[38] Prefect of Bacchiglione to Reuss-Plauen, Vicenza, December 19, 1813, A. S. (Venice), Governo veneto, 1813, Pubblico politico, Busta VI–VII, No. 28,611. 28,611.

[39] Huegel diary, March 1, 1814, Lemmi, *Diario del Huegel*, p. 44.

[40] Reuss-Plauen to Stadion, Venice, November 23, 1814, A. S. (Venice), Presidio di governo, 1814, No. 2040; Reuss-Plauen to Lazanzky, Venice, December 2, 1814, *ibid.*, No. 1207.

[41] Statement on direct taxes in Venetia, 1814–1815, St. A. (Vienna), Kaiser Franz Akten, Fasz. XVIII, Kon. 5, Fo. 195.

[42] Staats-Kabinet report, March 25, 1814, St. A. (Vienna), Kabinets-Akten, 1814, No. 1320; Hager to Staats-Conferenz, April 16, 1814, St. A. (Vienna), Conferenz Akten, Ser. b, 1814, No. 917; Cicogna diary, June 3, 1814, Pilot, "Venezia nel blocco del 1813–1814," p. 221.

bitterly that they had nothing left with which to pay their taxes after the military requisitioners had left their doors.[43]

Again, as was the case when he heard about the lamentable consequences of the compulsory circulation of paper money in Italy, Emperor Francis, immediately after learning about the deleterious effects of military requisitions upon the Venetian economy, inaugurated steps to mitigate the worst burdens. He urged his authorities in Italy forthwith to cease all unnecessary and unjust requisitions and to abolish the most hated ones[44] and authorized Governor Reuss-Plauen and Marshal Bellegarde to pay cash for military deliveries whenever they believed that the circumstances justified it.[45] There was universal rejoicing among the Venetians when they learned that they were now freed from the most onerous military requisitions.[46] However, as had been the case with the use of paper money, much damage had already been done and numerous potential friends had been turned into enemies before the Habsburgs gave up their Draconian practices of requiring the inhabitants to provision the invading army.

Then, too, the fact that some of the money now used to buy military supplies and to pay the army in gold and silver had to be procured through forced loans on the inhabitants nullified at least some of the good will won by the Habsburgs' cessation of the most oppressive military requisitions. Since financial resources were so desperately short in Austria, Emperor Francis, early in December, 1813,

[43] Reuss-Plauen to Ugarte, Udine, February 11, 1814, St. A. (Vienna), Kaiser Franz Akten, Fasz. XXVII, Kon. 1, Fo. 24; Staats-Kabinet report, February 6, 1814, St. A. (Vienna), Kabinets-Akten, 1814, No. 1077; Bombardini to Hiller, Bassano, November 11, 1813, A. S. (Venice), Governo veneto, 1813, Atti Hiller, No. 28; prefect of Brenta to Thurn, Padua, November 29, 1813, A. S. (Venice), Governo veneto, 1813, Pubblico politico, Busta VI–VII, Rub. 3, No. 26,737; prefect of Piave to Reuss-Plauen, Belluno, January 5, 1814, A. S. (Venice), Governo veneto, 1814, Polizia, Busta XXXIX, Fasc. 23, No. 163; intendant of Padua to Reuss-Plauen, Padua, January 10, 1814, A. S. (Venice), Governo veneto, 1814, Dazi consumo, Busta XIX–XX, Rub. 1, No. 2507; prefect of Adige to Venetian central government, Verona, March 24, 1814, A. S. (Venice), Governo veneto, 1814, Imposta, Busta XXXII, Fasc. 176, No. 2660.

[44] Emperor Francis to Zichy, Dijon, April 6, 1814, St. A. (Vienna), Conferenz Akten, Ser. b, 1814, No. 778.

[45] Staats-Kabinet report, March 26, 1814, St. A. (Vienna), Kabinets-Akten, 1814, No. 1331.

[46] Secret report to Hager, Padua, June 20, 1814, A. S. (Venice), Presidio di governo, 1814, No. 790.

authorized the Venetian governor to contract short-term loans in the Italian provinces.[47] Even before these instructions arrived in Italy individual commanders had resorted to compulsory loans to help them out of pressing financial difficulties. For instance, as early as November 7, 1813, a loan of 200,000 lire was exacted from "men of wealth" in the department of Brenta.[48] During the same month a loan of 50,000 lire was imposed on the department of Tagliamento.[49] The next month the commercial classes in the department of Passariano were called upon to contribute 100,000 lire.[50] These were only some of the loans assessed against various groups to procure funds to defray urgent expenses.

Not until the Austrians resolved to put an end to the circulation of paper money in Italy and to pay their troops in gold and silver, however, did the governor of Venetia himself impose a compulsory loan on all the occupied provinces. The 400,000 florins sent to Italy from the German provinces in January were wholly insufficient to cover the expenses involved in establishing a sound currency. To acquire the necessary supplements to inaugurate the reform, Reuss-Plauen called representatives of various Venetian moneyed interests to meet with him in Udine between January 18 and 22 to secure their approval for a non-interest bearing loan of 2,000,000 florins (approximately 5,200,000 Italian lire) in gold and silver, which was to be repaid within six or eight months. The government pledged 2,000,000 florins in redemption and anticipation notes as security for its repayment. The deputies could come to no agreement with the governor on the terms of the loan;[51] hence Reuss-Plauen felt obliged to turn

[47] Imperial resolution, Frankfurt, December 9, 1813, St. A. (Vienna), Conferenz Akten, Ser. b, 1813, No. 856.

[48] Ottolenghi, *Padova e il Dipartimento del Brenta*, p. 97; Lenguazza to general and military government in Udine, Padua, January 5, 1814, *ibid.*, Appendix XIV, p. 392.

[49] Prefecture of Tagliamento to Thurn, Treviso, November 12, 1813, A. S. (Venice), Governo veneto, 1813, Atti Hiller, No. 20,205.

[50] Prefecture of Passariano to Marenzi, Udine, December 10, 1813, A. S. (Venice), Governo veneto, 1813, Pubblico politico, Busta VIII–IX, Rub. 14, No. 820.

[51] Ugarte to Reuss-Plauen, Vienna, January 21, 1814, St. A. (Vienna), Conferenz Akten, Ser. b, 1814, No. 283; Porcia to Reuss-Plauen, Treviso, January 30, 1814, A. S. (Venice), Governo veneto, 1814, Imposta, Busta XXXII, Fasc. 64, No. 1693; Staats-Kabinet report, February 13, 1814, St. A. (Vienna), Kabinets-Akten, 1814, No. 1109; imperial resolutions, Troyes, February 14, 1814, and Chaumont, February 28, 1814, *ibid.*, Nos. 1109 and 1204; Ottolenghi, *Padova e il Dipartimento del Brenta*, pp. 134–136.

to a forced loan to procure funds to stave off inflation in Venetia. In March he decreed a compulsory loan of 1,200,000 florins (about 3,120,000 lire), carrying 5 per cent interest; 800,000 of this sum was to be imposed on businessmen and 400,000 on the landowners in the departments then under Austrian occupation. Reuss-Plauen was empowered to compel the property and money-holding groups to subscribe to this loan if they did not do so voluntarily.[52]

The very fact that the loan was compulsory made it highly unpopular,[53] and there was widespread resistance to it. By the end of October, 1814, 1,349,912 of the approximately 3,120,000 lire called for by the loan had still not been subscribed,[54] in spite of the pressures put on recalcitrants by the government. In the end, the entire amount of the loan was repaid by the Austrians with full interest but not before late in 1815.[55] However, even though the lenders eventually got their money back the long delay of the Austrians in returning it gave rise to mutterings about the bad faith of the Habsburgs in honoring their promises.

Besides the paper money, the forced loans, and the military requisitions, another source of irritation for the natives was the conduct of Austrian soldiers, some of whom all too frequently participated in riotous drinking and brawls and insulted and even attacked and manhandled the inhabitants.[56] So crude were some of the offenses that the enraged populace vociferously clamored for strong meas-

---

[52] Imperial resolution, Chaumont, February 28, 1814, St. A. (Vienna), Kabinets-Akten, 1814, No. 1204; Staats-Kabinet report, March 26, 1814, *ibid.*, No. 1331; Ottolenghi, *Padova e il Dipartimento del Brenta*, p. 136.

[53] Hager to Staats-Conferenz, April 16, 1814, St. A. (Vienna), Conferenz Akten, Ser. b, 1814, No. 917.

[54] Reuss-Plauen to Stadion, Venice, November 23, 1814, A. S. (Venice), Presidio di governo, 1814, No. 2040.

[55] Heberstein Malik to Hingenau, Vienna, March 17, 1815, *ibid.*, 1815–1819, Censo, Fasc. VIII 3/13, No. 1170/P.P.; Stadion to Goëss, Vienna, December 15, 1815, *ibid.*, Fasc. VIII 3/15, No. 7596/P.P.; notification, October 11, 1815, *Collezione di leggi venete*, 1815, Vol. II, pp. 112–114.

[56] For examples, see prefectural council of Piave to Porcia, Belluno, November 16, 1813, A.S. (Venice), Governo veneto, 1813, Atti Hiller, No. 11; prefectural council of Passariano to Thurn, Udine, November 28, 1813, A. S. (Venice), Governo veneto, 1813, Finanza, Busta I, Rub. 5, No. 97; Sardegna to Emperor Francis, Verona, April 2, 1814, *Kriegs-Archiv* (Vienna), Feld Akten (Italien), 1814, Fasz. IV, No. 23 2/4; Hager report, May 23, 1814, St. A. (Vienna), Kabinets-Akten, 1814, No. 1583; and Mulazzani to Reuss-Plauen, Venice, May 28, 1814, A. S. (Venice), Presidio di governo, 1814, No. 132.

ures to repress the outrages perpetrated by the military.[57] When the protests of the Venetians finally reached his ears, Emperor Francis commanded Bellegarde and the imperial war council to punish severely all soldiers who insulted or abused the inhabitants and to stop at no measures necessary to restore discipline.[58] Nonetheless, even though eventually discipline was more or less restored in the Habsburg army, the memory of the shocking behavior of drunken and boorish troops still rankled.

Irritating as were the compulsory circulation of depreciated Austrian currency, the forced loans, the military requisitions, and the conduct of certain soldiers, the Habsburg tax policies were even more maddening to a populace which had been almost totally exhausted from the oppressive obligations imposed by the French. Unfortunately, by 1814 the Habsburgs were in almost as desperate need of revenue as the French. The tax burden had been heavy in the German provinces of the monarchy for several years. On top of the existing taxes, in the summer of 1812 the emperor levied an extra tax of 4,000,000 florins on the landowners, and in addition to the regular capitation tax, a surtax of one florin per person on every inhabitant of the German provinces.[59] He also increased the taxes on trade and commerce by 90 per cent.[60] The Habsburg government was thus too desperately in need of tax income willingly to forego the 11,616,190 florins which it estimated that the taxes in the five occupied Venetian departments would bring in during 1814, especially since the estimated expenses of maintaining the army in Italy and of taking care of the civil administration in Venetia amounted to 3,459,873 florins more than the total receipts from the Venetian provinces.[61]

For these reasons, Emperor Francis urged his governor in Venetia to reduce the costs of the civil administration to the lowest possible

[57] Staats-Conferenz report, June 14, 1814, St. A. (Vienna), Conferenz Akten, Ser. b, 1814, No. 1102.

[58] Imperial resolution, Freiburg, January 2, 1814, *ibid.*, No. 104; imperial resolutions, March 27 and April 6, 1814, St. A. (Vienna), Kabinets-Akten, 1814, Nos. 1320 and 1371.

[59] Hofkanzlei decree, July 24, 1812, Francis II (I), *Politische Gesetze und Verordnungen*, Vol. XXXIX (1812), pp. 17–19.

[60] Hofkammer decree, October 10, 1813, *ibid.*, Vol. XLI (1813), pp. 195–196.

[61] Reuss-Plauen to Ugarte, Udine, January 9, 1814, St. A. (Vienna), Kaiser Franz Akten, Fasz. XXVII, Kon. 1, Fos. 9–14.

level[62] and to collect all existing taxes and imposts and to utilize them to the best advantage of the state.[63] He was to take strong measures to insure that all taxes due the government were paid.[64] They could be lowered only in most unusual cases and then only when complainants produced incontrovertible evidence that a gross injustice had been perpetrated.[65] Only after repeated reports came to him that desperate inhabitants were openly resisting tax collectors and that many tax payments were long in arrears did the emperor authorize his officials in Venetia to abolish a few of the most hated and oppressive taxes and to reduce others enough to prevent the economy from collapsing.[66]

It was high time! The Venetian archives are replete with entreaties from local officials imploring the Austrians to lower taxes, denouncing the harshness and cruelty of tax collectors,[67] and complaining about the unfairness of compelling the Venetians to pay their taxes in gold and silver while at the same time coercing them to accept depreciated Austrian paper money.[68] Some landowners insisted that during the first three months under Habsburg rule the amount they had given to the Austrians in requisitions alone equalled their taxes to the French for the whole previous year.[69] Others stated that during the first five months of 1814 they paid more taxes than their whole income for 1813.[70] Many Venetians were so infuriated over

[62] Ugarte to Reuss-Plauen, Vienna, January 21, 1814, St. A. (Vienna), Conferenz Akten, Ser. b, 1814, No. 283.

[63] Imperial resolution, Frankfurt, December 9, 1813, *ibid.*, 1813, No. 856; Emperor Francis to Reuss-Plauen, Frankfurt, November 9, 1813, *ibid.*, No. 789.

[64] Zichy to Reuss-Plauen, Vienna, December 16, 1813, A. S. (Venice), Governo veneto, 1813, Finanza, Busta I–II, Rub. 1, No. 1164.

[65] Ugarte to Reuss-Plauen, Vienna, December 11, 1813, A. S. (Venice), Governo veneto, 1813, Organizzazione, Fasc. IV–V, enclosed in No. 16/F.

[66] Emperor Francis to Zichy, Dijon, April 6, 1814, St. A. (Vienna), Conferenz Akten, Ser. b, 1814, No. 778; imperial resolution, Basel, January 21, 1814, St. A. (Vienna), Kabinets-Akten, 1814, No. 1006.

[67] See A. S. (Venice), Governo veneto, 1813, Atti Hiller, *passim*; A. S. (Venice), Governo veneto, 1814, Imposta, Busta XXXIX, *passim*; and A. S. (Venice), Governo veneto, 1814, Polizia, Busta XXXIX, *passim*.

[68] Staats-Kabinet report, January 20, 1814, St. A. (Vienna), Kabinets-Akten, 1814, No. 1006.

[69] Porcia to Reuss-Plauen, Treviso, January 30, 1814, A. S. (Venice), Governo veneto, 1814, Imposta, Busta XXXII, Fasc. 64, No. 1693.

[70] Hager to Staats-Conferenz, June 7, 1814, St. A. (Vienna), Conferenz Akten, Ser. b, 1814, No. 1163.

the exorbitant taxes that Austrian officials warned Vienna that military contingents must be put at the disposal of the departmental tax collectors if they were expected to continue collecting.[71]

In some areas actual revolts broke out against the tax collectors. At Dezra, Igne, Bragherezza, Pozzale, and Forzenighe armed mobs of women, accompanied by a few men, forcibly prevented the communal authorities from sequestering the belongings of villagers owing taxes to the government.[72] In the communes of Cavasso and Castegnamoro the enraged citizens attacked the tax collectors while they were holding proceedings against tax delinquents and compelled them to flee.[73] At Cadore riots during the whole month of February prevented the tax collector from impounding goods for back taxes.[74]

In various communes in the mountain valleys the chief object for opprobrium was the collector of the hated consumption tax, which was levied upon such necessities as food and fuel. At Gemona, near Udine; in the district of Asiago; in several villages in the district of Schio; and in the communes of Posina and Valdagno open revolts were staged against consumption tax collectors, which were put down only with difficulty after several days of tumult and disorder.[75] In the district of Cadore the inhabitants absolutely refused to pay

[71] Staats-Kabinet report, January 1, 1814, St. A. (Vienna), Kabinets-Akten, 1814, No. 1006; Novari to Venetian central government, Vicenza, March 25, 1814, A. S. (Venice), Governo veneto, 1814, Imposta, Busta XXXII, Fasc. 216, No. 3723.

[72] Prefect of Piave to Reuss-Plauen, Belluno, January 15, 1814, A. S. (Venice), Governo veneto, 1814, Polizia, Busta XXXIX, Fasc. 55, No. 73/74; prefect of Piave to Venetian central government, Udine, January 26, 1814, ibid., Fasc. 68, No. 3067.

[73] Prefect of Bacchiglione to Venetian central government, Vicenza, February 1, 1814, A. S. (Venice), Governo veneto, 1814, Imposta, Busta XXXII, Fasc. 53, No. 1983.

[74] Prefect of Piave to Venetian central government, Belluno, March 14, 1814, ibid., Fasc. 190, No. 240b.

[75] Prefectural council of Passariano to Marenzi, Udine, November 20, 1813, A. S. (Venice), Governo veneto, 1813, Finanza, Busta I–II, Rub. 5, No. 18,714; prefect of Bacchiglione report, Vicenza, January 10, 1814, A. S. (Venice), Governo veneto, 1814, Polizia, Busta XXXIX, Fasc. 11, No. 451; prefect of Bacchiglione to Reuss-Plauen, Vicenza, February 28, 1814, A. S. (Venice), Governo veneto, 1814, Imposta, Busta XXXII, Fasc. 47, No. 4249.

the tax.[76] The inhabitants of the commune of Castelfranco were so sullen that the intendant of finance of the department of Bacchiglione warned that no one should risk going there to try to collect the consumption tax.[77]

In the winter of 1813–1814 and spring of 1814 the Habsburgs were unfortunately confronted with other problems besides the isolated revolts against tax collectors. They had to fight a crime wave which for a time threatened to get entirely out of hand. The collapse of the French regime and the tenuousness of the new one, the bitterness engendered by the excessive military requisitions and the oppressive taxes, and the dire poverty of tens of thousands of miserable wretches, accompanied as they were by the undermining of traditional loyalties and the seeming breakdown of an economic, social, and political order to which the Venetians were accustomed, had a debilitating effect upon the moral fiber of many inhabitants and beckoned many a man down the road to crime who might under normal circumstances have led a useful life. The escape from the French-Italian army of soldiers recruited from prisons and houses of correction added to the prevailing insecurity. So did the large horde of deserters from the Napoleonic army and the comparatively small number from the Austrian military, who, joined by draft evaders, collected together in bands and traveled through the countryside plundering and robbing. In many places the roads were so perilous that few persons dared to brave them without escort. In the country landowners were forced to hire armed men to protect their property. Even the streets of the towns and cities were far from safe.[78]

To stop the depredations of the deserters from the French-Italian army, the Habsburgs named two battalions of the Austrian army "Battalions of Italian Volunteers" and invited Italian soldiers who wished to fight against their former French masters to join them.[79]

[76] Prefect of Piave to Reuss-Plauen, Belluno, January 5, 1814, A. S. (Venice), Governo veneto, 1814, Dazi consumo, Busta XIX–XX, Rub. 1, No. 2126.

[77] In a letter to the Venetian central government, Vicenza, March 6, 1814, *ibid.*, No. 1422.

[78] *Oesterreichischer Beobachter*, No. 32 (February 1, 1814), p. 185; Hager to Staats-Conferenz, June 17, 1814, St. A. (Vienna), Conferenz Akten, Ser. b, 1814, No. 1174; Raab to Venetian central government, Padua, June 4, 1814, A. S. (Venice), Governo veneto, 1814, Polizia, Fasc. VI, B, No. 781; Ottolenghi, *Padova e il Dipartimento del Brenta*, p. 199.

[79] Proclamation, Reuss-Plauen, Udine, January 8, 1814, St. A. (Vienna), Conferenz Akten, Ser. b, 1814, No. 357.

In an attempt to check crimes and misdemeanors, the Austrians organized civic patrols, to which all men between eighteen and fifty
were subject, to keep an eye on country roads and city streets. They
also established a constabulary force and commissioned military detachments to go through the countryside looking for miscreants.[80]
Through these efforts they managed, by the summer of 1814, appreciably to reduce the number of misdeeds,[81] although crimes were
still far too frequent and widespread to give the Venetians a real
feeling of security.

Thus, on the whole, the situation of the Venetians was extremely
unfortunate and depressing during the course of the Italian campaign, and, with a few exceptions, the Austrians did little to alleviate
it while the fighting was going on. In the emperor's opinion, the job
to concentrate on for the moment was winning the war, and everything else had to be subordinated to it. Since Austria's finances were
on the brink of disaster, all possible sources of income, in Italy as
elsewhere, had to be tapped to support the monarchy's military efforts. The inhabitants of the non-Italian provinces of the monarchy,
who were extremely heavily taxed, were making tremendous sacrifices; therefore, the emperor deemed that it would be extremely unjust to tax them even more in order to reduce the burden in Italy—an
area where the populace had previously paid just as onerous contributions to the French as they were now being asked to render to
the Habsburgs.[82] For this reason, all substantial reductions in taxes
had to be avoided in Venetia until the war was won.[83]

In spite of Emperor Francis' insistence that the Italians were not
to be spared until peace was restored, military reasons impelled the
Austrians to enact an economic measure that was roundly applauded
by the Venetians several weeks before the campaign was over. On
March 24 Governor Reuss-Plauen posted a circular announcing the
abolition of Napoleon's continental system in the Italian provinces.
Substituted for the prohibitive customs duties that had been levied
to enforce it was the former Austrian tariff which had been in effect

[80] Hager to Staats-Conferenz, June 17, 1814, *ibid.*, No. 1174; Hager report,
July 8, 1814, *ibid.*, No. 1355; Ottolenghi, *Padova e il Dipartimento del Brenta*,
p. 202.

[81] Hager report, July 15, 1814, St. A. (Vienna), Conferenz Akten, Ser. b,
1814, No. 1393.

[82] Ugarte to Reuss-Plauen, Vienna, January 29, 1814, *ibid.*, No. 291.

[83] Ugarte to Reuss-Plauen, Vienna, January 21, 1814, *ibid.*, No. 283.

in Venetia in 1805, with such modifications as the existing circumstances required.[84]

Furthermore, at the end of the war the governor, without waiting for superior approval from Vienna, announced the postponement of the due date for the May installment of the land tax until July, when the harvest would be over and when a new and more equitable land tax rate would be put into effect.[85] Reuss-Plauen's bold step was subsequently approved by the emperor.[86] The suspension of the collection of the land tax until after the harvest had a favorable effect upon Venetian public opinion,[87] although the effect was lessened by the Venetians' knowledge of the substantial tax reductions that had already been made in Lombardy.[88]

The truth of the matter is that the Lombards suffered much less at the hands of the Habsburgs than did the Venetians. Since the war in Italy was fought wholly on Venetian territory, the Lombards naturally did not have to endure the ravages of warfare or deliver military requisitions to the Austrians. Neither did they have to submit to the compulsory circulation of Austrian paper money[89] and to the forced loans to which the Venetians were subjected. Of course, the Lombards had to bear the full weight of equally oppressive exactions which the French inflicted upon them, but that in itself should have made the Lombards inclined to look more favorably upon the Habsburgs than the Venetians did.

More important, immediately after the fighting ended the Lombards enjoyed a number of tax reductions which the Venetians never received. The day after the April 20 revolution in Milan the Milanese communal council cut the prices of salt and tobacco into half and also reduced the consumption tax to 50 per cent of its former

[84] For copies of this decree, see *Giornale di Venezia*, No. 39 (May 2, 1814), pp. 3–4; and *Collezione di leggi venete*, 1813–1814, Vol. I, pp. 132–133.

[85] Circular, May 25, 1814, *Collezione di leggi venete*, 1813–1814, Vol. I, pp. 240–241; Reuss-Plauen to aulic police president, Padua, May 27, 1814, A. S. (Venice), Presidio di governo, 1814, ad No. 669; Hager to Staats-Conferenz, June 7, 1814, St. A. (Vienna), Conferenz Akten, Ser. b, 1814, No. 1163.

[86] Emperor Francis to Zichy, June 6, 1814, St. A. (Vienna), Conferenz Akten, Ser. b, 1814, No. 1116.

[87] Hager report, July 16, 1814, *ibid.*, No. 1407.

[88] Reuss-Plauen to aulic police president, Padua, May 27, 1814, A. S. (Venice), Presidio di governo, 1814, ad No. 669.

[89] Decree, provisional regency, Milan, April 28, 1814, St. A. (Vienna), Kaiser Franz Akten, Fasz. XXVII, Kon. 1, Fos. 51–52.

rate.[90] On the same day the provisional regency abolished the hated registration tax.[91] On April 22 it lowered the tariff on colonial wares to one-third of its former rate.[92] The next day it extended to all Lombardy the decreases which the communal council had ordered in salt and tobacco prices and in the consumption tax.[93] On the 26th it repealed the tax on artisans and businessmen[94] and brought down the postal rates on letters by one-half.[95]

The Austrian commissioner Sommariva, who arrived in Milan on April 26 to take control of Lombardy in the name of the Allied Powers, approved these tax abatements, and on April 30 he allowed the provisional regency either to abrogate or to decrease a number of vexatious judicial taxes.[96] When the Habsburgs assumed authority in their own name, Bellegarde, wisely realizing that any effort to re-institute the taxes which had been abrogated might incite the public to renewed disorders,[97] retained all the reductions except those in the prices of salt and tobacco and abolished a few other unpopular taxes. Declaring that the 50 per cent cut in the salt and tobacco prices lowered the sale price to less than the actual cost of production, he decreed that henceforth these products would be sold at the same price which had been charged for them in 1796.[98] Nevertheless, the public had little justified cause for complaint, since these prices were substantially below those which had been asked before April 20.[99] On June 16 the commissioner plenipotentiary abolished the distasteful tax of 1 per cent on capital assets which Prince Eugene had collected as a special war levy.[100] A month later he

90 Notification, Barbò, Milan, April 21, 1814, *Kriegs-Archiv* (Vienna), Feld Akten (Italien), 1814, Fasz. XIII, No. 83.

91 Decree, provisional regency, Milan, April 21, 1814, *Atti del governo lombardo*, 1814, p. 5.

92 Decree, Barbò, Milan, April 23, 1814, *ibid.*, p. 11.

93 Decree, Barbò, Milan, April 23, 1814, *ibid.*, p. 10.

94 Decree, provisional regency, Milan, April 26, 1814, *ibid.*, p. 17.

95 Decree, provisional regency, Milan, April 26, 1814, *ibid.*, p. 21.

96 See decree, provisional regency, Milan, April 30, 1814, *ibid.*, pp. 28–30.

97 Bellegarde report, May 31, 1814, St. A. (Vienna), Conferenz Akten, Ser. b, 1814, No. 1249.

98 See the two decrees of the provisional government dated Milan, May 24, 1814, *Atti del governo lombardo*, 1814, pp. 40 and 49.

99 *Wiener Zeitung*, June 11, 1814, p. 642.

100 Decree, provisional regency, Milan, June 16, 1814, *Atti del governo lombardo*, 1814, p. 71.

abrogated the 50 per cent tax on the importation of books in Italian and Latin which the French had imposed.[101] Finally, in November the government did away with the burdensome special war levy which the French had assessed on all state employees.[102]

Thus, in the spring and summer of 1814 numerous taxes which were still collected in Venetia were repealed in Lombardy. The real estate taxes which the Lombards paid to the Austrians were also substantially lower than those in Venetia. Although the land tax was never so high in Lombardy as in Venetia, during the period of the French occupation it had risen from 17 to 48 denari (or 15.4 centesimi) for every scudo of assessed value.[103] Over and above the tax itself there were still additional levies to defray the expenditures of the provincial and communal governments.[104] As his financial needs became more pressing, particularly during the last few months of the War of Liberation, Prince Eugene collected more and more each month in land taxes. For the six months between January 1 and June 30, 1814, the French assessed on Lombard landowners a tax burden of 48 denari, or as much as was paid during the whole year in 1812.[105] It is no wonder that there were universal complaints about the severity of the land tax.[106]

The high land tax rate which the French, on April 6, had prescribed for the month of June was allowed to stand.[107] Without waiting for the emperor's approval, however, Bellegarde announced on June 14 that the tax for July would be limited to just 1 centesimo for

[101] Decree, provisional regency, Milan, July 24, 1814, *Giornale italiano*, No. 206 (July 25, 1814), p. 838; *Oesterreichischer Beobachter*, No. 325 (August 13, 1814), p. 1201.

[102] Protocol, provisional regency, November 25, 1814, *Biblioteca di Brera* (Milan), "Protocolli originali della reggenza provvisoria"; entry of November 30, 1814, *Biblioteca Ambrosiana* (Milan), Mantovani, "Diario di Milano," Vol. V, p. 326.

[103] Bellegarde report, May 31, 1814, St. A. (Vienna), Conferenz Akten, Ser. b, 1814, No. 1249.

[104] Sandonà, *Il Regno Lombardo Veneto*, p. 67.

[105] Bellegarde report, May 21, 1814, St. A. (Vienna), Conferenz Akten, Ser. b, 1814, No. 1248.

[106] Bellegarde report, May 31, 1814, *ibid.*, No. 1249.

[107] Protocol, provisional regency, May 23, 1814, *Biblioteca di Brera* (Milan), "Protocolli originali della reggenza provvisoria"; decree, provisional regency, Milan, May 23, 1814, *Atti del governo lombardo*, 1814, p. 39.

every scudo of assessed valuation.[108] This amounted to a reduction of 22 per cent in the regular land tax rate which the French had collected in 1812 and 44 per cent in that which they had assessed for the period from January 1 to June 30, 1814. The rate for August was again set at 1 centesimo.[109]

Emperor Francis severely reprimanded the field marshal for lightening the burdens of the Lombard landlords without first consulting the government in Vienna. He commanded Bellegarde to send a detailed explanation of why he had diminished the land taxes at a time when it was obvious that the Habsburg treasury needed to collect all possible revenues[110] and he further expressly ordered that no further tax reductions be made without his personal consent.[111] Thus Bellegarde's efforts sharply to reduce land taxes in Lombardy were abruptly checked. For October, 1814, the tax rate was set at 1.3 centesimi.[112] For November and again for December it was fixed at 1.25.[113] This meant that during the last three months of 1814 the Austrians established approximately the same land tax rate which the French had levied in 1812 and half of what they had prescribed for the first six months of 1814. For the year 1815 the Austrian emperor ordered his commissioner plenipotentiary to fix the land tax quota at three-fourths of what the French-Italian government had set it at the beginning of 1814.[114] In line with these instructions, Bellegarde established the tax rate for January, 1815, at 1.28 centesimi per month.[115] The unusual expenses incurred in fighting Napoleon and Murat in the spring of 1815 necessitated increasing the land tax levy slightly to 1.30 centesimi for the spring and summer

---

[108] Decree, provisional regency, June 14, 1814, *Atti del governo lombardo,* 1814, p. 68; entry of June 16, 1814, *Biblioteca Ambrosiana* (Milan), Mantovani, "Diario di Milano," Vol. V, p. 281.

[109] Gallavresi, *Carteggio del conte Federico Confalonieri,* Vol. I, p. 221 n.

[110] Emperor Francis to Bellegarde, Schönbrunn, July 12, 1814, St. A. (Vienna), Conferenz Akten, Ser. b, 1814, No. 1249.

[111] Emperor Francis to Bellegarde, August 5, 1814, *ibid.,* No. 1399.

[112] Decree, provisional regency, October 7, 1814, *Atti del governo lombardo,* 1814, p. 137.

[113] Decree, provisional regency, November 12, 1814, *ibid.,* pp. 158–159.

[114] Imperial resolution, Vienna, November 15, 1814, St. A. (Vienna), Staats-Rath Akten, 1814, No. 3079.

[115] Decree, provisional regency, Milan, December 30, 1814, *Atti del governo lombardo,* 1814, pp. 173–174.

months,[116] but from September to December, 1815, the rate was again fixed at 1.28 per month.[117]

In 1815 the total land taxes obtained in Lombardy amounted to 5,442,479 florins (approximately 14,096,000 lire). In 1795, just before Lombardy came under French control, the taxes added up to only 1,798,487 florins (approximately 4,658,000 lire). Aside from the numerous surtaxes which they wrung from the Lombards, during the last years of the Kingdom of Italy the French secured 19,133,697.34 lire per annum in regular land taxes alone. The sum total of all taxes collected in 1815 amounted to 12,046,402 florins (approximately 30,220,180 lire); in 1795, to 6,073,925 florins (approximately 15,731,465 lire); and in 1812, to 51,973,641.94 lire.[118] Thus, the land taxes received by the Austrians in 1815 amounted to slightly more than three times those which they had levied in 1795 but were approximately 36 per cent less than the regular land taxes (not including the various surtaxes imposed on top of them) extracted by the French during the last years of the Napoleonic regime. As for the sum total of all taxes paid, although those imposed in 1815 were almost double those in 1795, they were 38 per cent less than those which the French had collected in 1812. They were also substantially less than those which the Venetians were paying in 1814.[119]

The Lombards complained loudly about the high taxes which the Habsburgs imposed on them in 1814–1815;[120] however, their anger

[116] See decree, provisional regency, Milan, July 11, 1815, *ibid.*, 1815, Vol. I, pp. 131–132.

[117] Decrees, provisional regency, Milan, August 16 and October 13, 1815, *ibid.*, Vol. I, p. 152, and Vol. II, p. 696.

[118] See budget estimates for Lombardy in 1795 and 1815 in Sandonà, *Il Regno Lombardo Veneto*, p. 384; and the "comparison" handed to the British government by the Austrians at the Congress of Verona in 1822, in *ibid.*, pp. 400 and 401–402.

[119] In October, 1814, for instance, when the land tax rate in Lombardy amounted to 1.30 centesimi per scudo of assessed valuation, the rate in Venetia was more than 2 centesimi (Hager report, November 13, 1814, St. A. [Vienna], Kabinets-Akten, 1814, No. 850).

[120] For examples, see Hager report, August 2, 1814, St. A. (Vienna), Conferenz Akten, Ser. b, 1814, No. 1506; Hager to Bellegarde, Vienna, July 17, 1814, A. S. (Milan), Presidenza di governo. Atti secreti, 1814, Cart. II, No. 124; general police directory bulletins, Milan, August 24 and October 5, 1814, *ibid.*, Cart. II, No. 227/P.R., and Cart. IV, No. 442/P.R.; and Castro, "I ricordi autobiografici di Bossi," p. 914.

over the taxes which they had to pay was comparatively mild in contrast to their exasperation over the onerous burdens which they had to endure in providing for the large contingents of Habsburg troops stationed in Lombardy in the spring and summer of 1814. The French had quartered nearly all their troops in barracks. Only those in transit were lodged in private homes.[121] However, since nearly all the regular army quarters were still occupied by the French-Italian troops, Sommariva issued orders, immediately after coming to Milan, that the Austrian military forces were to stay in private residences.[122] After the next land tax installment was paid, those who furnished rooms were to be remunerated.[123]

The Austrians originally intended to quarter only officers in Italian homes;[124] however, so few barracks were available for enlisted men that an estimated 6,000 common soldiers in or around Milan were also housed with Lombard families.[125] In addition, the local inhabitants had to find quarters for an estimated 800 to 900 officers, together with their large retinues of servants and horses.[126]

Taking care of the officers frequently resulted in considerable hardship for the host family. For example, General Neipperg, who was quartered with the Serbellonis, had with him 117 horses and a corresponding number of servants, all sheltered and fed at the Serbellonis' expense;[127] 4 officers, with 12 servants and 35 horses, were taken care of by the Santa family.[128] Teresa Confalonieri Casati's mother had an officer, with 3 servants and 3 horses, staying at her home. At their house at Valmadrera the Federico Confalonieris took

121 Albert Pingaud, "La Lombardie en 1814," *Revue d'histoire diplomatique*, Vol. XLI (1927), p. 459.

122 Provisional regency to deputation in Paris, Milan, April 27, 1814, *Museo* (Milan), "Carte Beccaria," Busta I, Carte 8, Fasc. I, No. 3.

123 Teresa Confalonieri Casati to Federico Confalonieri, Milan, May 2, 1814, Gallavresi, *Carteggio del conte Federico Confalonieri*, Vol. I, p. 94.

124 *Wiener Zeitung*, May 14, 1814, p. 538.

125 Entry of May 11, 1814, *Biblioteca Ambrosiana* (Milan), Mantovani, "Diario di Milano," Vol. V, p. 262.

126 Teresa Confalonieri Casati to Federico Confalonieri, Milan, May 8, 1814, Gallavresi, *Carteggio del conte Federico Confalonieri*, Vol. I, p. 109; provisional regency to deputation at Paris, Milan, May 9, 1815, *Museo* (Milan), "Carte Beccaria," Busta I, Carte 8, Fasc. I, No. 27.

127 Teresa Confalonieri Casati to Federico Confalonieri, Milan, April 29, 1814, Gallavresi, *Carteggio del conte Federico Confalonieri*, Vol. I, p. 85.

128 Teresa Confalonieri Casati to Federico Confalonieri, Milan, May 6, 1814, *ibid.*, p. 194.

care of 3 officers and 300 soldiers. In addition, they expected to have an officer, with 2 servants and 4 horses, living with them in Milan.[129]

The expenses of maintaining this large retinue of officers and enlisted men ran to a considerable sum. In May the city of Milan distributed 9,000 rations of fodder and 15,000 rations of food each day.[130] Luigi Mantovani estimated that the cost of provisioning the Habsburg army amounted to more than 90,000 lire daily for the city of Milan alone.[131] The provisional government complained that the expenses were so heavy that they were actually a "war contribution,"[132] and its president argued that the burden was so onerous that the Lombards were unable to bear it.[133]

Not only officials of the Milanese and Lombard governments but ordinary citizens cried out against the unfairness of requiring them to quarter and provision the Habsburg military forces. Many were exasperated over the way military lodgings were assigned. Country dwellers asserted that the soldiers were destroying the crops and crowding them out of their homes, while town and city dwellers insisted that the soldiers should be kept in the country. The inhabitants of the areas where most of the troops were stationed wailed loudly that the burden of maintaining them should fall on the whole populace.[134]

Obviously there was considerable justification for the bitter complaints voiced by the inhabitants, and the Habsburg officials bestirred themselves to do what they could to remedy the worst abuses in the housing and provisioning system. On April 28 they empowered the communes to sign contracts for military supplies with private

[129] Teresa Confalonieri Casati to Federico Confalonieri, Milan, May 8 and 11, 1814, *ibid.,* pp. 109 and 114.

[130] C. G. Londonio to Beccaria, Milan, May 14, 1814, Giuseppe Gallavresi, "Per una futura biografia di F. Confalonieri," *Archivio storico lombardo,* Vol. XXXIV (1907), p. 449.

[131] Entry of May 11, 1814, *Biblioteca Ambrosiana* (Milan), Mantovani, "Diario di Milano," Vol. V, p. 262.

[132] Provisional regency to deputation at Paris, Milan, May 9, 1814, *Museo* (Milan), "Carte Beccaria," Busta I, Carte 8, Fasc. I, No. 27.

[133] Provisional regency to deputation at Paris, Milan, May 9, 1814, *ibid.,* No. 26.

[134] See especially anonymous report, Milan, May 31, 1814, A. S. (Milan), Presidenza di governo. Atti secreti, 1814, Cart. I, No. 20/P.R.; daily report, Milan police prefecture, June 20, 1814, *ibid.,* No. 18/P.R.; and Pallavicini to Confalonieri, Milan, May 7, 1814, Gallavresi, *Carteggio del conte Federico Confalonieri,* Vol. I, p. 107.

persons and allowed them to make arrangements to pay for such deliveries with money collected from land taxes or even with funds
from the public treasury in case the tax receipts were insufficient.[135]
The provisional regency, on its part, allotted 600,000 florins (about
1,554,000 lire) to the communes to help them defray the costs of provisioning the army.[136] More important, late in May Bellegarde received orders to send back home all but the seventy thousand troops
which the emperor thought were still necessary to maintain peace in
the Apennine peninsula.[137] A few weeks later Emperor Francis instructed Bellegarde to abolish the practice of quartering troops in
private homes[138] and notified the Lombards that, beginning on July
1, the cost of maintaining the Austrian army was no longer to be
charged to them.[139] Furthermore, to provide funds to reimburse the
communes and all private individuals for their expenses in quartering and provisioning the Austrian army, a special tax was levied
which bore equally on all inhabitants of Lombardy and not just on
those unfortunate persons located in the areas where the troops were
concentrated.[140]

There was universal rejoicing in Lombardy when the Habsburgs
abolished the practice of quartering officers and soldiers in private
homes.[141] The jubilation of the populace, however, was soon mingled
with sadness and even bitterness, since the inhabitants still had to
endure various annoyances and insults from Austrian troops. When
the Habsburgs first arrived in Lombardy their soldiers gave the appearance of being well disciplined, and the conduct of the officers

[135] Decree, provisional regency, Milan, April 28, 1814, *Atti del governo lombardo,* 1814, p. 25; protocol, provisional regency, May 23, 1814, *Biblioteca di
Brera* (Milan), "Protocolli originali della reggenza provvisoria."

[136] Protocol, provisional regency, May 20, 1814, *Biblioteca di Brera* (Milan),
"Protocolli originali della reggenza provvisoria."

[137] Emperor Francis to Bellegarde, Paris, May 26, 1814, *Kriegs-Archiv* (Vienna), Feld Akten (Italien), 1814, Fasz. V, No. 118¼.

[138] Emperor Francis to Ugarte, June 14, 1814, St. A. (Vienna), Conferenz
Akten, Ser. b, 1814, No. 1097.

[139] *Wiener Zeitung,* July 16, 1814, p. 783.

[140] Protocol, provisional regency, July 7, 1814, A. S. (Milan), Uffici e Tribunali Regi. Parte Moderne, Cart. LIII (Appuntamenti 1814), no number given;
decree, provisional regency, Milan, July 15, 1814, *Atti del governo lombardo,*
1814, pp. 81–84.

[141] General police directory bulletin, Milan, July 6, 1814, A. S. (Milan),
Presidenza di governo. Atti secreti, 1814, Cart. I, Fasc. 24/P.R., No. 9.

seemed exemplary.[142] Nevertheless, as long as Austrian officers and enlisted men were living in private homes quarrels naturally broke out between them and their "hosts" over the quality and quantity of food, lodgings, and personal services provided to the soldiers and over real or alleged damage to private property by various officers and enlisted men. Then, too, some of the Austrians were ill-mannered and indiscreet, while others assumed an arrogant, overbearing attitude that was infuriating to the Italians.[143] More galling, as the rigors of the battlefield faded into the past, the discipline of the troops relaxed considerably, and shocking breaches of good conduct became all too frequent. Intoxicated Austrian soldiers cast aspersions on the courage, character, and political opinions of the Italians, crudely insulted the virtue of the Italian women, forced tavern owners and shopkeepers to give them liquor or goods for depreciated paper money or for nothing at all, plundered private shops, engaged in riotous brawls, and every now and then beat up persons who were guilty of momentarily arousing their displeasure.[144]

During the summer and fall of 1814 the conduct of the Habsburg troops stationed in Venetia, however, was just as bad as that of those in Lombardy. While the behavior of many enlisted men and officers was commendable,[145] others were as poorly disciplined and as ill-

[142] Pallavicini to Confalonieri, Milan, May 7, 1814, Gallavresi, *Carteggio del conte Federico Confalonieri,* Vol. I, p. 107; Castro, "I ricordi autobiografici di Bossi," p. 912; Wiedemann-Warnhelm, *Die Wiederherstellung der österreichischen Vorherrschaft in Italien,* p. 43.

[143] Pagani report, Milan, May 28, 1814, A. S. (Milan), Presidenza di governo. Atti secreti, 1814, Cart. I, No. 8717; Teresa Confalonieri Casati to Federico Confalonieri, Milan, May 6, 1814, Gallavresi, *Carteggio del conte Federico Confalonieri,* Vol. I, p. 104; Pingaud, "La Lombardie en 1814," pp. 459–460; Lemmi, *La restaurazione austriaca a Milano,* pp. 249–250; Wiedemann-Warnhelm, *Die Wiederherstellung der österreichischen Vorherrschaft in Italien,* pp. 41–42.

[144] For examples, see daily police prefecture reports, Milan, June 20 and July 13, 1814, A. S. (Milan), Presidenza di governo. Atti secreti, 1814, Cart. I, Nos. 10,093 and 11,876; Pagani reports, Milan, June 2, August 22, and December 1 and 7, 1814, *ibid.,* Cart. III, No. 14,927, Cart. IV, No. 24,229, and Cart. VI, No. 24,649; general police directory bulletins, Milan, July 30, August 3 and 24, and December 7 and 10, 1814, *ibid.,* Cart. II, Nos. 108/P.R., 160/P.R., and 227/P.R., and Cart VII, Nos. 873/P.R. and 874/P.R.; and Francesco Filos, *Autobiografia. Memorie e confessioni di me stesso. Con note a cura di Bruno Emmert,* p. 100.

[145] Brenta department, political reports for September, October, and December, 1814, Ottolenghi, *Padova e il Dipartimento del Brenta,* Appendices XXV,

mannered as those in Lombardy,[146] in spite of the efforts of the authorities to restrain them.[147]

Then, too, for some time after the Italian campaign was over and after the policy had apparently been discontinued in Lombardy, the Venetians had to make special payments or render extraordinary services to support the Habsburg army. It is true that in May the emperor had assured the Venetians that they would no longer be required to provision troops in transit; however, the practice was not actually abandoned until July. Although Emperor Francis issued orders on July 7 that military requisitioning was to be abandoned entirely,[148] until October the Venetians had to deliver free of charge foodstuffs, wood, and straw to the Habsburg barracks and field hospitals. In December they were still furnishing military transport for Austrian troops.[149] As late as November the Venetians had still not been repaid for the estimated 12,000,000 florins[150] (31,030,800 Italian lire) worth of goods in military requisitions which were levied on

XXVII, and XXIX, pp. 419, 436, and 455; prefecture of Tagliamento, political report for September, 1814, A. S. (Venice), Presidio di governo, 1814, ad No. 2234; Raab to presidency of the Venetian central government, Venice, December 27, 1814, ibid., No. 2477.

[146] For examples, see Raab to Reuss-Plauen, Padua, June 23, 1814, A. S. (Venice), Presidio di governo, 1814, ad No. 845–846; Reuss-Plauen to Hager, Padua, July 20, October 6, and November 8, 1814, ibid., Nos. 499, 1425, and 1783; Torresani to Venetian central government, Venice, December 23, 1814, ibid., No. 2391; prefecture of Tagliamento, political reports for July and September, 1814, ibid., ad Nos. 1483 and 2234; Raab to Venetian central government, Venice, November 10, 1814, A. S. (Venice), Governo veneto, 1814, Oggetti di polizia, Fasc. VI, B, No. 14,542; and Reuss-Plauen report, Venice, November 5, 1814, Kriegs-Archiv (Vienna), Hof Kriegs-Rath–Präsidial Akten, Italien, 1814, Fasz. XII, No. 6.

[147] See Bellegarde to Reuss-Plauen, Milan, July 10 and August 2, 1814, A. S. (Venice), Presidio di governo, 1814, ad No. 845–846 and No. 846; Hager to Reuss-Plauen, Vienna, September 15, 1814, ibid., No. 1317; Lazanzky to Reuss-Plauen, Vienna, September 29, 1814, ibid., No. 1487; Reuss-Plauen to Lazanzky, Venice, October 24, 1814, ibid., No. 1613; and Venetian central government to Hager, Padua, July 26, 1814, ibid., No. 682.

[148] Imperial resolution, Vienna, July 7, 1814, St. A. (Vienna), Conferenz Akten, Ser. b, 1814, No. 1146.

[149] Reuss-Plauen to Lazanzky, Venice, December 2, 1814, A. S. (Venice), Presidio di governo, 1814, No. 1207.

[150] Central-Organisirungs-Hof-Commission report, January 20, 1815, St. A. (Vienna), Staats-Rath Akten, 1815, No. 848.

them during and shortly after the Italian campaign.[151] In the fall of 1814, the winter of 1814–1815, and spring of 1815 the Venetian central government still had to make substantial payments to Habsburg military and naval authorities in Italy. For the months of October, November, and December, 1814, these payments amounted to a total of 2,034,093 florins[152] (5,259,961 Italian lire). Between January 19 and May 29, 1815, they added up to 3,071,282 florins[153] (7,942,028 lire).

Thus it is apparent that, although the Lombards had many justifiable reasons for complaining about the onerous burden of quartering and provisioning Austrian troops and about the reprehensible behavior of some of the soldiers, the Venetians had even more cause to be unhappy on both counts. In one respect, however, the Lombards and the Venetians probably suffered equally in 1814 and early 1815. The crime rate appears to have been correspondingly high in both provinces. From all parts of Lombardy reports poured in about the lamentable insecurity of the public highways and the less frequented village and city streets. Robbery was an almost daily occurrence and murders were frequent. Very little was spared by the individual thieves, the gangs of deserters, and the robber bands who infested the area. Private persons, country and town homes, shops, farms, and churches were indiscriminately robbed. Even the palace in which Bellegarde was living was visited by thieves.[154] Since the usual police methods were insufficient to halt the large number of crimes, the government resorted more and more to general searches in its efforts to apprehend the large number of thieves and other criminals who were hardly ever discovered by the police.[155]

[151] Central-Organisirungs-Hof-Commission report, November 29, 1814, *ibid.*, 1814, No. 4117.

[152] Reuss-Plauen to Stadion, Venice, December 24, 1814, A. S. (Venice), Presidio di governo, 1814, No. 2411.

[153] Table of payments to the military, Venice, June 2, 1815, *ibid.*, 1815–1819, Censo, Fasc. VIII 1/1, ad No. 1778/P.P.

[154] See especially Hager to Bellegarde, Vienna, August 26 and September 30, 1814, A. S. (Milan), Presidenza di governo. Atti secreti, 1814, Cart. III, No. 292/P.R., and Cart. IV, No. 493/P.R.; Bellegarde to Hager, Milan, September 6 and 14 and October 11, 1814, *ibid.*, Cart. III, Nos. 264/P.R. and 292/P.R., and Cart. IV, No. 493/P.R.; general police directory bulletin, Milan, September 14, 1814, *ibid.*, Cart. III, No. 339/P.R.; and entries of October 25 and 31, November 4 and 7, 1814, and January 10, 1815, *Biblioteca Ambrosiana* (Milan), Mantovani, "Diario di Milano," Vol. V, pp. 317, 320–322, and 335.

[155] General police directory bulletins, September 24, October 5, 19, 22, and

In Venetia the crime rate was just as high during the summer and fall of 1814 and winter of 1814–1815. Unemployed workers and peasants, deserters, vagabonds, and released prisoners, in addition to the usual professional swindlers and thieves, roamed the countryside almost at will. The city of Venice resembled a den of robbers. There people could not travel down even well frequented streets without running the risk of being robbed. The same conditions prevailed in much of the *terra ferma*, where the unusually large number of murders, waylaying of travelers on lonely roads and streets, and thefts in churches, stores, and private homes gave both the local populace and the Austrians no little concern.[156]

As in Lombardy, the government drew up elaborate plans for a general search. Such a dragnet was executed between November 1 and 8 in all Venetia and in the neighboring areas of Lombardy, Illyria, the Tyrol, and the Papal Legations as well.[157] A considerable number of suspicious persons were apprehended.[158] As a consequence of

29, and November 3, 9, and 26, 1814, A. S. (Milan), Presidenza di governo. Atti secreti, 1814, Cart. IV, Nos. 423/P.R., 442/P.R., 545/P.R., and 578/P.R., Cart. V, Nos. 695/P.R., 688/P.R., and 719/P.R., and Cart. VI, No. 823/P.R.

[156] See especially entry of November 23, 1814, *Museo* (Venice), "Diario di Cicogna," p. 2077; Central-Organisirungs-Hof-Commission report, November 29, 1814, St. A. (Vienna), Staats-Rath Akten, 1814, No. 4117; Raab to Venetian central government, Venice, November 10, 1814, A. S. (Venice), Governo veneto, 1814, Oggetti di polizia, Fasc. VI, B, No. 14,542; Reuss-Plauen to Hager, Venice, October 6 and 12 and November 6 and 26, 1814, A. S. (Venice), Presidio di governo, 1814, Nos. 1425, 1462, 1743, and 2047; prefect of Bacchiglione to Venetian central government, Vicenza, August 31, 1814, *ibid.*, No. 1083; and Ottolenghi, *Padova e il Dipartimento del Brenta*, pp. 204–205, 236–238, and 301–306.

[157] Raab to Venetian central government, Venice, September 3, 1814, A. S. (Venice), Governo veneto, 1814, Polizia, Fasc. VI, B, No. 11,069; protocol, Venetian central government, September 9, 1814, *ibid.*; Bellegarde to Venetian central government, Milan, September 26, 1814, *ibid.*, Fasc. VI, A, C, F, No. 5803/511; Reuss-Plauen to Hager, Venice, November 26, 1814, A. S. (Venice), Presidio di governo, 1814, No. 2047.

[158] By November 7, 350 rogues and malefactors had been arrested in the department of Bacchiglione alone (Provisional prefect of Bacchiglione to Venetian central government, A. S. [Venice], Governo veneto, 1814, Polizia, Fasc. VI, B, No. 370 P.R.). In the department of Adriatico 250 were caught (Raab to Venetian central government, Venice, November 14, 1814, *ibid.*, Fasc. VI, A, C, F, No. 14,508). In the department of Brenta the number of arrests totaled 351 (Brenta department, political report for November 1814, Ottolenghi, *Padova e il Dipartimento del Brenta*, Appendix XXVIII, p. 444).

this energetic measure the number of aggressions dropped appreciably for a brief interval, but unfortunately only for a few weeks. During the last days of November the crime rate returned to its usual pattern, and the Venetian government warned the Habsburg court that court martial procedures must be inaugurated to deal with the increasing lawlessness.[159] In February, 1815, the special courts created by the French in March, 1808, and ordered abolished by General Hiller on November 8, 1813, were re-established to help cope with the alarming number of crimes and disorders.[160]

Even though the Lombards underwent a serious crime wave and endured insults from Habsburg soldiers, the burdens from which they suffered and the inequities to which they were subjected by the Habsburgs were relatively light compared to those of the Venetians. The Lombards were spared entirely the heavy wartime military requisitions, the forced loans, the compulsory circulation of paper money, and the destruction of property which the Venetians had to put up with during the winter of 1813–1814 and the spring of 1814. Economic conditions were also relatively prosperous in Lombardy in comparison with those in Venetia. It is true that the heavy exactions of the French, the April 20 revolution, and the change in government brought in their train distressing economic dislocations and an appreciable increase in unemployment.[161] The dismissal of government employees and the failure of the Austrians to pay the arrears in pensions during the summer of 1814[162] increased the misery of a large number of Milanese, and as the summer went on the Austrians began to worry about the large number of beggars in the streets.[163]

Nonetheless, this writer has been able to find no documents in the Viennese and Milanese archives which mention actual famine condi-

[159] Protocol, presidency of the Venetian government, [November 25, 1814], A. S. (Venice), Presidio di governo, 1814, ad No. 2011 e 2024.

[160] Reuss-Plauen order, Venice, February 4, 1815, *Notizie del mondo,* March 13, 1815, p. 1.

[161] Wilson diary, Milan, April 30, 1814, Robert Wilson, *Private Diary of Travels, Personal Services, and Public Events, during Mission and Employment with the European Armies in the Campaigns of 1812, 1813, 1814,* Vol. II, p. 383.

[162] See *ante,* pp. 64–68.

[163] Lazanzky to Bellegarde, Vienna, September 10, 1814, A. S. (Milan), Commissario Plenipotenziaria, Busta XXVI, Polizia, No. 3112. This document and a few others in this series which have been cited by the author were destroyed during World War II.

tions in Lombardy. It is true that a large number of records dealing with social and economic conditions were destroyed in Milan during the second World War. However, in the Viennese archives and in the few documents dealing with economic and social concerns which he examined in the *Archivio di Stato* in Milan in the summer of 1938 the author found no evidence of actual starvation. In contrast, he has run across a document in the Venetian archives which expressly points out that conditions were much better at least in the agricultural regions of Lombardy than they were in Venetia. On November 23, 1814, Governor Reuss-Plauen wrote Count Johann Philipp Stadion, the Habsburg minister of finance, that, whereas the 1814 harvest was "a complete failure" in Venetia, "it can not be counted among the bad ones" in Lombardy.[164]

In Lombardy the loud complaints (and there were plenty of them) voiced about economic matters were largely directed against the high price of foodstuffs and the usuriousness of various grain speculators, grocers, and bakers.[165] There was also much grumbling about unemployment, and there is evidence that the gravity of the situation prompted the Austrians to inaugurate a few public works projects in Lombardy in 1814 and 1815 for the express purpose of providing jobs for the unemployed.[166] They also made serious, though usually futile, attempts to hold down the cost of living by prohibiting the export of grain and other food products and by establishing and enforcing maximum prices for foodstuffs.[167]

In contrast to the total absence of documents alluding to famine conditions in Lombardy, the Venetian and Viennese archives are filled with hundreds of reports describing abject misery and actual

---

[164] See A. S. (Venice), Presidio di governo, 1814, No. 2040.

[165] See especially police report, Milan, December 1, 1814, *Kriegs-Archiv* (Vienna), Feld Akten (Italien), 1814, Fasz. XII, No. 3; decree, provisional regency, Milan, July 2, 1815, *Atti del governo lombardo,* 1815, Vol. I, p. 130; Giovanni de Castro, *Milano e le cospirazioni lombarde (1814–1820) giusta le poesie, le caricature, i diari e altre testimonianze dei tempi,* pp. 225–226; and report, prefect of Cremona, Cremona, May 13, 1815, A. S. (Milan), Commissario Plenipotenziaria, Busta XXVI, Polizia, No. 233. The original copy of the last document cited was destroyed during the war.

[166] See protocol, provisional regency, November 26, 1814, *Biblioteca di Brera* (Milan), "Protocolli originali della reggenza provvisoria."

[167] Protocols, provisional regency, November 18, 1814, and June 9, 1815, *ibid.*; decree, provisional regency, December 13, 1814, *Atti del governo lombardo,* 1814, pp. 163–164.

starvation in large areas in Venetia. As we have already seen,[168] the 1813 harvest had been unusually poor in Venetia. There was no appreciable improvement in 1814. The wine yield, which was the chief source of cash income in several departments, was just as scanty as during the previous year. The maize and grain crops, which were the chief source of nourishment for the great mass of agricultural population, was practically a complete failure. The sugar beet and rice harvests were almost a total loss, and the olive and mulberry yields were extremely low.[169] In 1815 the early crops were even poorer than those of the preceding year.[170] The same unfavorable weather which existed in most of the other provinces of the Austrian monarchy destroyed the early summer wheat crop.[171] Fortunately, the maize, millet, and rice crops, which were harvested later, were fairly good.[172]

As a consequence of the economic stagnation and crop failures, the situation of many impoverished Venetians became desperate in the winter of 1814–1815. In the mountain areas in the departments of Bacchiglione, Passariano, Tagliamento, and Piave thousands of miserable wretches were living in a pitiful state of hunger.[173] The inhabitants were sometimes reduced to subsisting on the most revolting kind of nourishment: in some localities the populace kept alive by eating bean husks and wild berries;[174] in others they fared on a bread made of the leaves of bean plants.[175] A few ate hay and other food

[168] See *ante*, p. 91.
[169] Reuss-Plauen to Lazanzky, Venice, December 2, 1814, A. S. (Venice), Presidio di governo, 1814, No. 1207.
[170] Hager report, July 15, 1815, St. A. (Vienna), Kabinets-Akten, 1815, No. 756; Brenta department political report for April, 1815, Ottolenghi, *Padova e il Dipartimento del Brenta*, Appendix XXXVIII, p. 501.
[171] Protocol, Staats-Conferenz, September 17, 1815, St. A. (Vienna), Staats-Rath Akten, 1815, No. 6284.
[172] Lazanzky report, November 8, 1815, St. A. (Vienna), Kaiser Franz Akten, Fasz. XVIII, Kon. 1, Fo. 43.
[173] Hager report, February 4, 1815, St. A. (Vienna), Kabinets-Akten, 1815, No. 427; Central-Organisirungs-Hof-Commission report, February 12, 1815, St. A. (Vienna), Staats-Rath Akten, 1815, No. 965.
[174] Report of the military supply administrator, Udine, February 11, 1815, St. A. (Vienna), Kabinets-Akten, 1815, ad No. 427.
[175] Hager report, March 15, 1815, *ibid.*, ad No. 361; Central-Organisirungs-Hof-Commission report, March 15, 1815, St. A. (Vienna), Staats-Rath Akten, 1815, No. 1773.

fit only for, and sometimes refused by, animals.[176] Numerous reports to the government bear witness to the fact that hundreds of people were suffering from pellagra[177] and that in various places people actually starved to death.[178]

Although the squalor and wretchedness in the city of Venice were by no means comparable to that in the mountain areas of Venetia, commerce and industry there were in a sad state of neglect and decay. The 274 boats which entered the harbor between May 1 and May 28, 1814,[179] had increased in September to only 352, of which 159 were filled only with firewood;[180] in October the number fell to 245, nearly all of them laden with foodstuffs and wood.[181] Hundreds of boats were rotting away at the docks, while thousands of sailors were condemned to a life of abject misery. Trade was nearly at a standstill, while the merchants of the once proud city were watching

[176] Venetian central government to Central-Organisirungs-Hof-Commission, Venice, February 7, 1815, *Hofkammer Archiv* (Vienna), Kredit Akten, Fasz. XVIB1/13, No. 7534 ex Juli 1815.

[177] Hager report, February 6, 1815, St. A. (Vienna), Kabinets-Akten, 1815, No. 289; Venetian central government to Central-Organisirungs-Hof-Commission, February 7, 1815, *Hofkammer Archiv* (Vienna), Kredit Akten, Fasz. XVIB1/13, No. 7534 ex Juli 1815; Central-Organisirungs-Hof-Commission report, March 30, 1815, St. A. (Vienna), Staats-Rath Akten, 1815, No. 2292; Lazanzky report, May 16, 1815, *ibid.*, No. 3460.

[178] For instance, it was reported that in the mountain areas of Germonia, Faedis, and San Pietro de Schiavoni, in the department of Passariano, sixty-eight persons had actually starved to death (police report, April 10, 1815, St. A. [Vienna], Kabinets-Akten, 1815, ad No. 427). According to another report, three people had starved to death in the parish of Recoaro, in the department of Bacchiglione; and two persons had died at Schio (also in Bacchiglione) because they had eaten nothing but hay (Venetian central government to Central-Organisirungs-Hof-Commission, Venice, February 7, 1815, *Hofkammer Archiv* [Vienna], Kredit Akten, Fasz. XVIB1/13, No. 7534 ex Juli 1815). It was also reported that seven persons had died from starvation in San Pietro de Schiavoni, in the department of Passariano (Central-Organisirungs-Hof-Commission report, March 15, 1815, St. A. [Vienna], Staats-Rath Akten, 1815, No. 1773). See also Hager report, February 4, 1815, St. A. (Vienna), Kabinets-Akten, 1815, No. 427; report of the military supply administrator, Udine, February 11, 1815, *ibid.*, ad No. 427; Lazanzky report, May 16, 1815, St. A. (Vienna), Staats-Rath Akten, 1815, No. 3460; and Central-Organisirungs-Hof-Commission reports of February 12 and March 30, 1815, *ibid.*, Nos. 965 and 2292.

[179] Mulazzani to Reuss-Plauen, Venice, May 28, 1814, A. S. (Venice), Presidio di governo, 1814, No. 132.

[180] Reuss-Plauen to Hager, Venice, October 12, 1814, *ibid.*, No. 1462.

[181] Raab to Reuss-Plauen, Venice, November 2, 1814, *ibid.*, No. 1749.

their meager resources dwindling away. The factories and workshops could sell little which they manufactured and had to dismiss many of their workers to join the ranks of the unemployed.[182] Venice was too impoverished any longer to serve as an outlet for the surplus population of the mountain hinterland. In a desperate search for subsistence for their families, a large number of Venetian mountain folk wandered to Rome, Trieste, Istria, Hungary, and Germany in search of jobs.[183]

Yet, notwithstanding the fact that the plight of the Venetians was desperate while the Lombards were fairly well off in comparison, the Habsburgs taxed the Venetians much more heavily in 1814 and early 1815 than they did the Lombards. As we have seen,[184] shortly after the demise of the French regime a number of vexatious taxes were either abolished or substantially reduced in Lombardy. The Venetians expected the Austrians to make similar reductions for them.[185] In fact, Governor Reuss-Plauen admonished the central government in Vienna on May 27 that substantial decreases needed to be made immediately to prevent a revolt from breaking out.[186] Prompted by such urgings, the authorities in the Austrian capital gave the governor permission to lower some taxes, although not as much as in Lombardy. In accord with the June 5 instructions from the emperor,[187] Governor Reuss-Plauen on July 1 reduced the price of refined salt to 68 lire per metric quintal. The price of other kinds of salt was similarly cut.[188] After these changes in rate became effective the Venetians actually paid 5 to 10 per cent less for salt than the Lombards.[189]

---

[182] Secret report to Hager, Padua, June 20, 1814, *ibid.*, No. 790; department of Adriatico political report for October, 1814, *ibid.*, ad No. 1749.

[183] Prefecture of Udine, political report for September, 1814, *ibid.*, ad No. 2234; department of Adriatico, political report for October, 1814, *ibid.*, ad No. 1749; Reuss-Plauen to Hager, Venice, November 6, 1814, *ibid.*, No. 1743.

[184] See *ante*, pp. 105–107.

[185] Secret report to Hager, Padua, June 20, 1814, A. S. (Venice), Presidio di governo, 1814, No. 790.

[186] Staats-Conferenz report, June 21, 1814, St. A. (Vienna), Conferenz Akten, Ser. b, 1814, No. 1143. See also Hager report, May 17, 1814, *ibid.*, No. 1102.

[187] Central-Organisirungs-Hof-Commission report, November 29, 1814, St. A. (Vienna), Staats-Rath Akten, 1814, No. 4117.

[188] Notification, July 1, 1814, *Collezione di leggi venete*, 1813–1814, Vol. II, pp. 3–4.

[189] On May 24, 1814, the price of refined salt was set at 75 centesimi per

The price of tobacco, however, was not lowered at all, although it was in Lombardy. On July 7, Reuss-Plauen was authorized to decrease the registration, poll, and consumption taxes,[190] and on August 4 he posted three notices announcing such reductions. The inhabitants were informed that the registration tax was to be diminished by two-thirds. The consumption tax was to be lowered to stipulated percentages of the tariff which the French had established on August 16, 1813. Beginning on October 1 the poll tax was to drop from 5.80 to 4.00 lire per annum. One-fourth of the revenue from the last tax was to be turned over to the communes.[191]

The Venetians were happy over these decreases in taxes,[192] even though the reductions made in their province were appreciably less than those enjoyed by the Lombards. The consumption tax was cut in Lombardy as well as in Venetia. Whereas the registration tax was only diminished by two-thirds in Venetia, it was entirely abolished in Lombardy. Furthermore, in 1814 the following reductions were made in Lombardy which were not enacted in Venetia: a substantial cut in tobacco prices, a two-thirds decrease in the tariff on colonial wares, the lowering of postal rates on letters by one-half, a decrease in judicial taxes, and the abolition of the taxes on artisans and businessmen, on capital assets, and on the importation of books, as well as the war contribution levied on state employees. To offset these advantages for the Lombards were only the slightly lower price of salt and the reduction of the poll tax in Venetia, and the latter was again raised from 4.00 lire to 5.80 in the summer of 1815.[193]

The most crushing tax burden, the land tax, was considerably higher in Venetia than in Lombardy. For taxation purposes the French had raised the assessed value of Venetian land to a point sub-

---

metric pound or kilogram in Lombardy (decree, provisional regency, Milan, May 24, 1814, *Atti del governo lombardo*, 1814, p. 40).

[190] Imperial resolution, Vienna, July 7, 1815, St. A. (Vienna), Conferenz Akten, Ser. b, 1814, No. 1146.

[191] See the three notices dated August 4, 1814, in *Collezione di leggi venete*, 1813–1814, Vol. II, pp. 19–24. Also in *Giornale di Venezia*, No. 113 (August 9, 1814), pp. 3–4.

[192] Reuss-Plauen to Hager, Venice, September 16, 1814, A. S. (Venice), Presidio di governo, 1814, No. 1143.

[193] Central-Organisirungs-Hof-Commission report, May 15, 1815, St. A. (Vienna), Staats-Rath Akten, 1815, No. 3624; imperial resolution, Heldenberg, June 8, 1815, *ibid.*; notification, July 10, 1815, *Collezione di leggi venete*, 1815, Vol. II, pp. 3–4.

stantially higher than its real value and had increased the land tax rate from 24 to between 48 and 53 denari per scudo (from 10 to 20–22 per cent) of its exaggerated assessed valuation. To alleviate the desperate plight of the impoverished landowners, Reuss-Plauen in May, 1814, took away from the prefects the privilege of imposing surtaxes on top of the regular taxes, reduced the land tax rate to 10 denari for the next two-month payment period (the equivalent of 3.20 centesimi or 1.60 *per month* in Italian lire),[194] and postponed the time when taxes had to be paid until after the harvest in July.[195] Then on June 26 he reduced the total assessed valuation of Venetian landed property by 17,288,464 scudi[196] (79,526,894 Italian lire), or by approximately 18 per cent. The land valuation still remained the same as before in the more prosperous departments of Adige and Adriatico, but it was drastically cut (from 17,866,050 to 11,189,659 scudi) in the impoverished department of Passariano and substantially lowered in the departments of Bacchiglione, Brenta, Piave, and Tagliamento.[197] On the same day (June 26) the governor again fixed the land tax rate for the two-month period ending in August at 10 denari, or the equivalent of 1.60 centesimi *per month* in Italian money, but this time it was assessed on the rectified valuation which he had approved on the same day.[198] This tax was 60 per cent higher per scudo of assessed value than the land tax prescribed in Lombardy for the same period.

Unfortunately, Reuss-Plauen announced these decreases in land valuation and in the tax rate before consulting the emperor, and, without knowing it, he made promises which were contrary to his monarch's intentions. What Emperor Francis actually had in mind was made clear in a letter which he wrote the Venetian governor on July 7, before he learned what Reuss-Plauen had done. In it he ad-

---

194 In several Austrian documents which the writer has examined the value of 1 denaro was given as 0.32 centesimi in Italian lire.

195 Protocol, Staats-Conferenz in regard to the June 2, 1814, proposals of the Vereinigte Hofkanzlei, June 21, 1814, St. A. (Vienna), Conferenz Akten, Ser. b, 1814, No. 1120; protocol, Staats-Conferenz in regard to the Geheime Credits-Commission report of May 11, 1814, June 21, 1814, *ibid.*, No. 1146.

196 Central-Organisirungs-Hof-Commission report, January 20, 1815, St. A. (Vienna), Staats-Rath Akten, 1815, No. 848; Sandonà, *Il Regno Lombardo Veneto,* p. 62.

197 See table in Sandonà, *Il Regno Lombardo Veneto,* p. 62.

198 Notification, June 26, 1814, *Collezione di leggi venete,* 1813–1814, Vol. I, pp. 255–256.

vised his governor not to reduce land taxes[199] before a careful investigation was made of the whole Venetian land tax system. For the purpose of making such a study and recommending necessary modifications in the Venetian land tax system, he was sending Count Christian Wurmser, president of the Austrian land tax regulation commission, to Venetia immediately after his reorganization of the Illyrian tax structure.[200] When, to his dismay, he learned of the decrees which the Venetian governor had issued on June 26, the emperor was forced temporarily to modify his plans. To prevent confusion, he approved, but only on a temporary basis, the changes in land evaluation which Reuss-Plauen had put through and also allowed the August tax rate to stand. On September 20, however, he stipulated that the tax installment that fell due on October 15 was to be paid on the basis of 13 denari[201] (or 4.2 centesimi) in taxes for every scudo of assessed value. In other words, the September-October land tax rate was to be 62 per cent higher in Venetia than the one which Bellegarde had set for the month of October in Lombardy.

The governor received the emperor's orders just as he was at the point of fixing the September-October rate at 7 denari (2.24 centesimi, or 1.2 centesimi for a single month)—a rate which was close to the one which Bellegarde had prescribed for Lombardy. He was deeply perturbed over his sovereign's decision. The terrible havoc wrought by the Italian campaign, the total crop failure during the summer, the devastating cattle epidemic, and the fact that special city and town levies and the poll and inheritance taxes all fell due in October convinced him that it was foolhardy to attempt to collect an exorbitant 13 denari rate at this time,[202] especially since the Venetians were already complaining bitterly because their taxes were so much higher than those in Lombardy. Furthermore, there were large tax arrears, the property of many impoverished or recalcitrant taxpayers had already been sequestrated, and the government was having considerable difficulty in collecting the consumption and poll

---

[199] Imperial resolution, Vienna, July 7, 1814, St. A. (Vienna), Conferenz Akten, Ser. b, 1814, No. 1146.

[200] Emperor Francis to Wurmser, Vienna, July 7, 1814, ibid., No. 1120. Another copy can be found in A. S. (Venice), Presidio di governo, 1814, No. 1863.

[206] Central-Organisirungs-Hof-Commission report, January 20, 1915, St. A. (Vienna), Staats-Rath Akten, 1815, No. 848.

[202] Reuss-Plauen to Lazanzky, Venice, December 2, 1814, A. S. (Venice), Presidio di governo, 1814, No. 1207.

taxes.[203] For these reasons the governor, after consulting his advisers in Venice, decided to disobey his monarch's orders and to leave the September–October land tax rate at 7 denari rather than fix it at 13 denari, as the emperor had instructed him to do.[204]

For his foolhardiness in daring to act in the interests of the province of which he was in charge rather than subserviently enforcing his sovereign's orders, Reuss-Plauen was severely reprimanded by the aulic central organization commission and by the emperor himself. In strong and no uncertain terms he was commanded to set the rate at 13 denari (2.1 centesimi per month, or 60 per cent more than the land tax rate in Lombardy for the same months) for the November-December period and to collect before December 31 the total of 36 denari in land taxes[205] which had been fixed by the emperor for the last half of 1814. This meant that, in addition to all the officially announced land taxes, he had to levy an extra 6 denari to make up the difference between the 7 denari rate which he had fixed on his own authority and the 13 denari which had been prescribed by the emperor for September and October.[206]

Having no choice but to comply, Reuss-Plauen announced to the Venetians on November 28 that the land tax rate for the last two months of 1814 was to be increased to 13 denari[207] (4.2 centesimi)— a rate that was 6 denari (1.92 centesimi) higher than for the previous two-month period. At the same time he wrote the authorities in Vienna entreating them not to insist on exacting the full 36 denari (11.52 centesimi) for the half year and admonishing them that if they persisted in collecting more than 30 denari (9.60 centesimi), or

[203] Brenta department, political reports for October and November, 1814, Ottolenghi, *Padova e il Dipartimento del Brenta*, Appendices XXVII and XXVIII, pp. 438 and 446–447; Adriatico department, political report for October, 1814, A. S. (Venice), Presidio di governo, 1814, ad No. 1749; Reuss-Plauen to Hager, Venice, November 6 and December 27, 1814, *ibid.*, Nos. 1743 and 2441; Hager report, November 13, 1814, St. A. (Vienna), Kabinets-Akten, 1814, No. 850.

[204] Notification, October 8, 1814, *Collezione di leggi venete*, 1813–1814, Vol. II, pp. 58–59; Reuss-Plauen to Lazanzky, Venice, December 2, 1814, A. S. (Venice), Presidio di governo, 1814, No. 1207.

[205] Lazanzky to Reuss-Plauen, Vienna, November 8 and 23, 1814, A. S. (Venice), Presidio di governo, 1814, Nos. 1207 and 2213.

[206] Central-Organisirungs-Hof-Commission report, January 20, 1815, St. A. (Vienna), Staats-Rath Akten, 1815, No. 848.

[207] Advice, November 28, 1814, *Collezione di leggi venete*, 1813–1814, Vol. II, pp. 77–78.

the sum total of taxes that had now been officially prescribed for the last half of the year, they would inflict the most flagrant injustice upon the Venetian landlords and tax them far beyond their capacity to pay.[208]

Fortunately for the poverty-stricken Venetian landowners, their governor managed to win over the aulic credit and central organization commissions to his point of view. Upon their recommendation,[209] Emperor Francis agreed to limit the total amount of land taxes for July-December to 30 denari. In addition, he gave his officials in Venetia authority to defer tax payments until after the next harvest and even to forego them entirely in special cases of urgent need.[210] The aulic central organization commission predicted that by allowing the half-year rate to stand at 30 denari for every scudo of estimated value the Austrians would collect a total of 4,350,000 florins (11,248,665 Italian lire) and Reuss-Plauen estimated that they would receive 4,939,000 florins (14,717,601 lire) in land taxes during 1814. This sum would still be substantially more than three times the average sum of 1,382,152 florins (3,565,107 Italian lire) per year which the Venetian departments had paid between 1798 and 1805 and more than three-fourths of the 5,800,000 florins (14,998,220 lire) which the French had collected during recent years.[211]

Emperor Francis hoped that Count Wurmser could finish his study of the Venetian tax structure in time to introduce the pre-revolutionary Lombard land tax assessment and tax systems there in January, 1815.[212] Wurmser's report, however, was far from completed at the end of 1814; consequently the government in Venice, apparently with the approval of the authorities at the Habsburg capital, decided to establish the same tax rate in Venetia for January and February, 1815, as was in effect in Lombardy: 8 denari, or 2.60 centesimi for

[208] Reuss-Plauen to Lazanzky, Venice, December 2, 1814, A. S. (Venice), Presidio di governo, 1814, No. 1207.

[209] Central-Organisirungs-Hof-Commission report, January 20, 1815, St. A. (Vienna), Staats-Rath Akten, 1815, No. 848.

[210] Imperial resolution, Vienna, February 17, 1815, ibid.; Guicciardi to Venetian central government, Vienna, February 19, 1815, A. S. (Venice), Presidio di governo, 1815–1819, Censo, Fasc. VIII 3/11, No. 795/P.P.

[211] Central-Organisirungs-Hof-Commission report, January 20, 1815, St. A. (Vienna), Staats-Rath Akten, 1815, No. 848.

[212] Central-Organisirungs-Hof-Commission report, January 17, 1815, ibid., No. 996.

every scudo of assessed value.[213] The government in Vienna sent instructions to Reuss-Plauen to levy the same 8 denari rate again in March and April. Before these orders arrived the Venetian governor, still not having learned the previous fall that it was highly indiscreet to enact important changes without the prior approval of the superior authorities in Vienna, concluded that, on account of the widespread famine and the landowners' need for all possible cash to finance the next crop, taxes should be considerably lowered for March and April. Consequently, after consulting Count Wurmser, who heartily agreed with him, he decided to reduce the second two-month rate for 1815 to the equivalent of 6 denari[214] (1.92 centesimi), or three-fourths the tax rate effective in Lombardy during the same period. Acting on Wurmser's advice,[215] he did not officially stipulate that each landowner was to pay a certain percentage of the assessed value of his landholdings. Instead, he merely announced that for March and April the Venetian landowners were to pay a total sum of 1,358,626.62 Italian lire[216] (525,379 florins). Of this amount, the property holders of the department of Adige were to pay 180,049.60 lire; those of Brenta, 316,783.83; those of Tagliamento, 247,739.54; those of Passariano, 142,352.91; those of Bacchiglione, 248,316.49; those of Adriatico, 180,503.49; and those of Piave, 42,879.76.[217]

Since this was the third time in less than a year that the Venetian governor either deliberately violated his instructions or else made an important decision without previously consulting his superior authorities, there was an angry explosion in the Austrian capital when the government learned what he had done. In strong, unequivocal language, the aulic central organization commission informed Reuss-Plauen that the 8 denari assessment was never again to be reduced without the express permission of the emperor. Peremptorily it ordered the governor immediately to impose a large enough supple-

213 Notification, January 20, 1815, *Collezione di leggi venete*, 1815, Vol. I, pp. 6–7.

214 Venetian central government to Central-Organisirungs-Hof-Commission, Venice, April 24, 1815, A. S. (Venice), Presidio di governo, 1815–1819, Censo, Fasc. VIII 1/1, No. 1678/P.P.

215 Wurmser to Hingenau, Venice, March 21, 1815, *ibid.*, No. 1058/P.P.

216 Notification, March 25, 1815, *Collezione di leggi venete*, 1815, Vol. I, pp. 66–68.

217 See table attached to Galvagna to Wurmser, Venice, March 25, 1815, A. S. (Venice), Presidio di governo, 1815–1819, Censo, Fasc. VIII 1/1, ad No. 1058/P.P.

mentary levy to cover the difference between the 1,358,626.62 lire that the 6 denari tax was expected to bring in and the 2,122,416.22 which an 8 denari levy would have yielded.[218]

After this painful reminder that the authorities in Vienna frowned on any efforts by local authorities to make significant changes in tax rates without prior authorization, the Venetian government punctiliously observed its instructions not to reduce the 8 denari rate before receiving direct orders from the emperor to do so. The third land tax payment (for May and June) was fixed at 2,206,930.83 Italian lire[219] —a sum which required a levy of 8 denari to collect. The total sum prescribed for each of the fourth and fifth payment periods (July–October) was 2,122,421.88.[220] To procure this, the government set approximately the same land tax levy (8 denari, or 2.56 centesimi, per scudo of assessed valuation for each bi-monthly interval) as the one imposed in Lombardy (1.30 centesimi per month, or 2.60 for each bi-monthly period, during the spring and summer months and 1.28 centesimi per month, or 2.56 for every two months, for September-December). On September 20 the emperor took a significant step to reduce the burden of the land taxes in Venetia by decreeing that no landowner was to pay more than one-fifth of his net income in taxes and by stipulating, in addition, that the total sum of land taxes during 1815 was not to exceed 11,000,000.00 Italian lire.[221]

In actual fact only a gross total of 10,667,827 or a net amount of 10,386,006 lire was actually assessed upon Venetian landowners during 1815. Of this sum only 8,098,693 lire were actually collected in land taxes by the end of the year. In 1814 a gross sum of 7,833,572 lire or a net sum of 7,263,101 had actually been levied by the Austrians (both the aulic central organization commission's and Reuss-Plauen's estimates proved to be greatly exaggerated[222]), of which only 5,512,890 were collected by December 31, 1814. To this should be added the special levies amounting to 38,500,701 lire which the

[218] Lazanzky to presidency of the Venetian government, Vienna, April 14, 1815, A. S. (Venice), Presidio di governo, 1815, No. 248/v.b.p.

[219] Advice, May 4, 1815, *Collezione di leggi venete*, 1815, Vol. I, pp. 165–166.

[220] Notifications dated June 23 and August 28, 1815, *ibid.*, Vol. I, pp. 297–299, and Vol. II, pp. 42–43.

[221] Decree, Goëss, Venice, October 28, 1815, *Notizie del mondo*, 1815, No. 295 (October 31, 1815), p. 4; entry of November 4, 1815, *Biblioteca Ambrosiana* (Milan), Mantovani, "Diario di Milano," Vol. V, p. 411.

[222] See *ante*, p. 126.

Venetians paid to support the Austrians troops between November, 1813, and July, 1814, and a supplementary assessment of 489,785 lire imposed in 1815 to cover the cost of providing military transport during the "hundred days." During the last years of the Kingdom of Italy the French had collected 14,998,220 lire per annum, or more than twice the net total assessed by the Austrians in 1814 and over 44 per cent more than the net total in 1815 in regular land taxes in Venetia. In addition, they received various surtaxes from the land-owners. The sum total of all direct taxes (land, poll, artisan and business taxes, and special military levies) collected by the Austrians amounted to 47,267,009 lire in 1814 and to 12,503,024 in 1815.[223] The total net income from all indirect taxes was 13,755,978.20 in 1814 and 17,688,625.13 in 1815.[224] The total sum of all taxes, both direct and indirect, which were actually *collected* in Venetia amounted to 61,022,987.20 lire in 1814 and to 30,191,649.13 in 1815.

In 1814 Venetian landowners paid approximately 60 per cent higher taxes for every scudo of assessed valuation than those in Lombardy. In 1815 the land tax rates were approximately the same in both areas. Nevertheless, even during the latter year the tax burden was much more onerous in Venetia than in Lombardy, since the Venetian landlords had still not recovered from the vicissitudes of warfare and the inordinately high military levies in 1814, while the complete crop failure in 1814 and the almost total failure in 1815 ruined the Venetian agricultural economy to the point where many landowners had lost all hope of ever again becoming solvent. On both scores the Lombards suffered very little by comparison. Lacking all ready cash, the great majority of Venetian property holders were unable to pay back their creditors, let alone pay their taxes.[225] As a consequence, tax payments were far in arrears. In spite of the concerted efforts made by the government to collect them, by the end of June, 1815, 2,748,376 lire, or 38 per cent, of the land taxes due in 1814

---

[223] Statement on direct taxes in Venetia in 1814 and 1815, St. A. (Vienna), Kaiser Franz Akten, Fasz. XVIII, Kon. 5, Fos. 195–196.

[224] Statement on indirect taxes in Venetia in 1813, 1814, and 1815, *ibid.*, Fos. 200 and 214. The total income from all indirect taxes was 19,008,531.52 lire in 1813 (*ibid.*).

[225] Goëss to Lazanzky, Belluno, April 26, 1815, *Hofkammer Archiv* (Vienna), Central-Organisirungs-Hof-Commission Akten, Rinna, 1815, No. 10,719/1137; Goëss to Lazanzky, Belluno, April 28, 1815, A. S. (Venice), Presidio di governo, 1815, No. 192/v.b.p.

were still in default.[226] Nearly all the 1814 taxes due from the department of Adige, seventh-eighths of those from the department of Passariano, and over one-half of those from the department of Tagliamento still remained uncollected in the spring of 1815.[227] Of the land taxes in 1815, 2,287,312 lire, or 21 per cent, were in arrears at the end of the year. It was the same story with other taxes. For example, of the total sum of 1,258,823 lire due in poll taxes in 1814, 623,175, or 52 per cent, were still unpaid on December 31, 1814. Of the total of 1,199,847 lire due the following year, 467,651, or 39 per cent, had still not been paid by the end of December. As for the tax on crafts, businesses, and professions, 104,942 (35 per cent) of the 302,582 lire due in 1814 were still unpaid on the last day of December, 1814. Of the 474,249 lire collectible in 1815, 112,381 (24 per cent) were in arrears at the end of that year.[228]

This delinquency was certainly not because the Habsburgs were negligent in their efforts to collect the taxes. With a few minor modifications instituted in the spring of 1815, the Austrians still used the harsh methods of collecting land taxes which the French had introduced in the Kingdom of Italy. Taxes were not levied on individuals but on departments and then on communes. In each commune the tax collector, who had purchased the privilege, turned in the whole quota, less 3 per cent, on a stipulated day, whether or not he had actually collected it. He had the right to sequester the property of delinquent taxpayers and to sell it at public auction to recover the sums owed him. If he failed to procure the sums due him by this method, he could hold the highest taxpayers of the commune responsible for his losses. In that case, a supplementary tax was imposed on them, and the property owners thus taxed could then sequester the property of the delinquents and either sell it or administer it as communal property.[229]

With the general impoverishment and terrible want in Venetia, the system came close to breaking down in 1814–1815. Tax collectors became so thoroughly despised and so bitterly hated in many areas

[226] Protocol, aulic credit commission, September 1, 1815, *Hofkammer Archiv* (Vienna), Kredit Akten, Fasz. XIII/2, No. 9687 ex September 1815.

[227] Lazanzky to presidency of the Venetian government, Vienna, April 14, 1815, A. S. (Venice), Presidio di governo, 1815, No. 248/v.b.p.

[228] Statement on direct taxes in Venetia in 1814 and 1815, St. A. (Vienna), Kaiser Franz Akten, Fasz. XVIII, Kon. 5, Fos. 195–196.

[229] Sandonà, *Il Regno Lombardo Veneto*, pp. 57–59.

that people no longer submitted bids for the job, and the government was forced to draft prosperous landowners to act in such capacities. Since a property holder thus designated ran the double risk of having his own belongings sold to make up for the delinquent taxes of others and of earning the lasting opprobrium of the populace as well, in commune after commune landowners positively refused to accept the burden under any condition. In April, 1815, the Habsburgs were forced to abandon the practice and employ military detachments to intimidate the most recalcitrant taxpayers into paying, in the hope of thereby influencing the others to do so, too.[230] At the same time, a decree was issued exempting farm animals, agricultural implements, artisans' tools, furniture, and necessary clothing from sequestration for delinquent taxes.[231]

In place after place mutinies broke out against tax collectors. In the summer of 1814 the district of Cadore, in the department of Piave, which had been the focal point of considerable trouble in December, 1813, became a center of commotion. At Valisella and Arronzo, in this district, the finance guards were chased out of town.[232] At Caorle, in Adriatico department, the populace assumed such a threatening attitude towards the finance guards that for a time the government stood ready to send troops there at any minute.[233] The worst disorders, however, took place in the badly impoverished department of Passariano. There a mutiny broke out at Gemona, which was rigorously repressed by a special military detachment just as the trouble was at the point of spreading to the surrounding communes.[234] At Ronchis and Tolmezzo mutinies erupted when the tax collectors tried to sequester the property of delin-

---

[230] *Ibid.*, pp. 236–238.

[231] Notification, March 26, 1815, *Collezione di leggi venete*, 1815, Vol. I, pp. 76–77.

[232] Prefect of Piave to Venetian central government, Belluno, August 4, 1814, A. S. (Venice), Governo veneto, 1814, Polizia, Fasc. VI, B, No. 361 P.S.; protocol, Venetian central government, August 12, 1814, *ibid.*, No. 26,090/6628; imperial procurator of the department of Piave to Venetian central government, Belluno, August 31, 1814, *ibid.*, No. 2506; Reuss-Plauen to Hager, Padua, September 3, 1814, A. S. (Venice), Presidio di governo, 1814, No. 1005.

[233] Raab to Venetian central government, Venice, August 24, 1814, Governo veneto, 1814, Polizia, Fasc. VI, B, No. 10,434/10,484.

[234] Prefecture of Udine to presidency of the Venetian central government, Udine, July 14, 1814, A. S. (Venice), Presidio di governo, 1814, No. 558.

quent taxpayers.[235] The government had to send troops to Caporetto to check repeated disturbances.[236] A popular revolt also took place at Marano.[237] By the fall of 1814, apparently, quiet was still not restored in the department of Passariano. At least in October troops were sent to Tomba to aid the collector in confiscating the property of recalcitrant taxpayers who were supported by an infuriated populace.[238] During the same month there were again revolts in the district of Cadore, in Piave department.[239]

During the winter of 1814–1815 the Venetian authorities continued to send in reports about mutinies against tax collectors at places like Porto Gruaro, in the department of Adriatico; Cison, Vigolino,[240] and Seravalli,[241] in the department of Tagliamento; Trevignano, Turrida, and Godroipo,[242] in the department of Passariano; and Pozzonuovo, in the department of Brenta.[243] There were also riots in the Polesine, but they were directed against speculators and food hoarders rather than against tax collectors. In the canton of Lendenara the mayor was able to prevent the sacking of grain supplies only by promising to requisition foodstuffs and to suspend taxes. Mob violence was averted by similar actions at Stranghella, in the district of Este. At Praglia, in the canton of Teolo, a mob of 2,000 men and women sacked the granary of a rich merchant. From there the tumult spread to several surrounding communities, where seven

235 Prefecture of Udine to Venetian central government, Udine, August 13, 1814, A. S. (Venice), Governo veneto, 1814, Polizia, Fasc. VI, B, No. 275–278 P.R.

236 Torresani to provisional prefect of Passariano, [August 23, 1814,] *ibid.*, No. 28,350/347; provisional prefect of Passariano to Venetian central government, Udine, September 6, 1814, *ibid.*, ad No. 28,350/347.

237 Raab to Venetian central government, Venice, August 24, 1814, *ibid.*, No. 10,434/10,484.

238 Prefecture of Udine to Venetian central government, Udine, October 25, 1814, *ibid.*, No. 451 P.R.

239 Reuss-Plauen to Hager, Venice, October 13, 1814, A. S. (Venice), Presidio di governo, 1814, No. 1488.

240 Protocol, Venetian central government, February 1, 1815, *Hofkammer Archiv* (Vienna), Kredit Akten, Fasz. XVIB1/13, No. 7534 ex Juli 1815.

241 Central-Organisirungs-Hof-Commission report, March 30, 1815, St. A. (Vienna), Staats-Rath Akten, 1815, No. 2292.

242 Hager report, February 18, 1815, St. A. (Vienna), Kabinets-Akten, 1815, ad No. 427; Schwarzenberg report, February 27, 1815, *ibid.*, ad No. 361.

243 Brenta department, political report for December, 1814, Ottolenghi, *Padova e il Dipartimento del Brenta*, Appendix XXIX, p. 454.

other granaries were plundered. At Limena another granary was despoiled. Serious depredations were averted in other places only by the timely arrival of sizable military contingents.[244]

Acting upon orders from Vienna,[245] the government took strong measures against the leaders of these riots and turned a number of them over to the judicial authorities for trial and punishment. The Habsburgs, however, did not limit themselves to repressing riots and disorders, but also took a number of positive steps to alleviate the misery of the inhabitants. They made serious efforts to curb speculators and to hold food prices to prescribed tariffs.[246] Even though the landowners and commercial classes were clamoring loudly for the free exportation of agricultural products,[247] and although in November, 1814, the emperor allowed Venetian cereals freely to go to Lombardy, the Tyrol, and the other adjacent Habsburg provinces,[248] when it seemed necessary to preserve the supply to prevent prices from rising, in April, 1815, the emperor again forbade the export of cereals from Venetia until after the harvest.[249]

Acting upon the express orders of the emperor,[250] the Habsburgs also took more direct measures to alleviate the suffering and misery

[244] Brenta department, political report for January, 1815, *ibid.*, Appendix XXXI, pp. 465–467; protocol, Venetian central government, February 1, 1815, *Hofkammer Archiv* (Vienna), Kredit Akten, Fasz. XVIB1/13, No. 7534 ex Juli 1815.

[245] Hager to Reuss-Plauen, Vienna, July 5, 1814, A. S. (Venice), Presidio di governo, 1814, No. 510.

[246] See especially political report of the prefecture of Tagliamento for July, 1814, *ibid.*, ad No. 1483; Mulazzani to prefecture of the Adriatico, Venice, September 24, 1814, A. S. (Venice), Governo veneto, 1814, Polizia, Fasc. VI, F, E, G, Rub.: Vettovaglie, No. 32,670/377; Raab to Venetian central government, Venice, December 24, 1814, *ibid.*, No. 16,489; Raab to presidency of the Venetian government, Venice, March 14, 1815, A. S. (Venice), Presidio di governo, 1815–1819, Polizia, Fasc. II 10/1, No. 221 P.R.; Brenta department, political report for April, 1815, Ottolenghi, *Padova e il Dipartimento del Brenta*, Appendix XXXVIII, p. 502.

[247] Emperor Francis to Lazanzky, Gutenbrun, August 9, 1814, St. A. (Vienna), Conferenz Akten, Ser. b, 1814, No. 1393.

[248] Notification, November 9, 1814, *Collezione di leggi venete*, 1813–1814, Vol. II, pp. 69–70.

[249] Circular, April 19, 1815, *ibid.*, 1815, Vol. I, p. 101.

[250] Imperial resolution, Vienna, July 7, 1814, St. A. (Vienna), Conferenz Akten, Ser. b, 1814, No. 1146; Emperor Francis to Ugarte, July 17, 1814, St. A. (Vienna), Staats-Rath Akten, 1814, No. 2454; imperial resolution, Vienna, March 21, 1815, *ibid.*, No. 1257.

of the Venetians. In line with Emperor Francis' instructions, money and work were provided for the most poverty-stricken inhabitants. Private charity associations, patterned after the German model, were established in the chief cities of each department, and special deputations dependent upon them were appointed for the smaller cities and towns to supervise the collection and distribution of poor relief funds.[251] In response to the appeals of these organizations different groups contributed varying amounts to help the needy. Various government employees pledged 10 to 20 per cent of their salaries for this purpose. Rich landowners undertook to feed the most impoverished inhabitants of certain specified communes. The soldiers of the Ninth Ranger Battalion gave bread and Rumford soup, and those of the Saint Julien and Savoy regiments gave 1,400 loaves of bread. Private persons formed clubs to distribute Rumford soup—a very cheap but extremely nourishing comestible—to the destitute. Within a brief period the more affluent inhabitants of the department of Bacchiglione contributed 45,000 lire, 1,000 sacks of Turkish sorgho, and 1,000 pounds of potatoes, and a single anonymous benefactor gave an additional 9,300 lire to aid the neediest communes.[252] Similar funds and staples were collected from other departments.

The Austrian government itself also contributed money to feed the impoverished populace. In the summer of 1814 the Habsburg government in Venetia allocated funds to buy maize and other cereals for the poverty-stricken inhabitants of the department of Piave,[253] and Emperor Francis himself allotted 50,000 florins (129,295 Italian lire) for poor relief purposes. In December the aulic central organization commission added another 25,000 florins (64,648 lire) to this sum.[254] By January, 1815, 68,000 (175,841 lire) of these 75,000 florins

[251] Central-Organisirungs-Hof-Commission report, March 6, 1815, St. A. (Vienna), Staats-Rath Akten, 1815, No. 1709; order, prefect of Adriatico, Venice, March 21, 1815, Notizie del mondo, No. 86 (March 28, 1815), p. 4.

[252] Central-Organisirungs-Hof-Commission reports, March 30 and May 26, 1814, St. A. (Vienna), Staats-Rath Akten, 1815, Nos. 2292 and 3807; Giornale di Venezia, No. 62 (March 3, 1815), pp. 3–4, and No. 85 (March 27, 1815), p. 4.

[253] Reuss-Plauen to Hager, Padua, August 1 and September 19, 1814, A. S. (Venice), Presidio di governo, 1814, Nos. 612 and 1241; prefecture of Piave, political report for July, 1814, ibid., ad No. 1483.

[254] Helfert, Kaiser Franz und die Stiftung des Lombardo-Venetianischen Königreichs, p. 37.

had already been distributed to the famished inhabitants.[255] Early in February the Venetian government allocated 4,000 lire to buy food for the inhabitants of the department of Bacchiglione and 3,000 lire for the same purpose to each of the six other departments of Venetia.[256]

These funds were spent to provide direct relief for the Venetians. The Habsburg government also inaugurated various public works projects to help the unemployed. According to Emperor Francis, these projects were to be limited as much as possible to useful public works already begun by the French and located in the areas of greatest destitution.[257] Although this writer has found no evidence that Emperor Francis himself apportioned any substantial sums for such a scheme before November, 1815, when he assigned 200,000 lire to the Venetian government for this purpose,[258] it is evident that the authorities in Venetia had already embarked upon such a program at least eight or nine months earlier. In fact, a letter of the Venetian government to the aulic central organization commission on February 7, 1815, clearly indicates that by the beginning of 1815 the Venetian government had already arranged for the immediate resumption of various roads and waterways projects to give employment to the indigent.[259] Other documents show that several waterways projects were initiated in the department of Adriatico and other places early in 1815 to provide jobs for the destitute until field work would again be resumed.[260] In March, 1815, the aulic central organization commission allotted 37,200 lire to improve the waterways

[255] Central-Organisirungs-Hof-Commission report, February 22, 1815, St. A. (Vienna), Staats-Rath Akten, 1815, No. 1257.

[256] Venetian central government to Central-Organisirungs-Hof-Commission, Venice, February 7, 1815, *Hofkammer Archiv* (Vienna), Kredit Akten, Fasz. XVIB1/13, No. 7534 ex Juli 1815; Central-Organisirungs-Hof-Commission report, February 22, 1815, St. A. (Vienna), Staats-Rath Akten, 1815, No. 1257.

[257] Emperor Francis to Lazanzky, September 29, 1815, St. A. (Vienna), Staats-Rath Akten, 1815, ad No. 6284.

[258] Imperial resolution, November 12, 1815, St. A. (Vienna), Kaiser Franz Akten, Fasz. XVIII, Kon. 1, Fos. 47–51.

[259] Venetian central government to Central-Organisirungs-Hof-Commission, Venice, February 7, 1815, *Hofkammer Archiv* (Vienna), Kredit Akten, Fasz. XVIB1/13, No. 7534 ex Juli 1815.

[260] Central-Organisirungs-Hof-Commission report, February 22, 1815, St. A. (Vienna), Staats-Rath Akten, 1815, No. 1257; order, prefect of Adriatico, Venice, March 21, 1815, *Notizie del mondo,* 1815, No. 86 (March 28, 1815), p. 4.

leading to Friaul and Illyria.[261] About the same time public works projects were initiated in the departments of Brenta,[262] Adige, and Passariano.[263] The inauguration of these construction programs not only enabled many a hard-pressed wretch to earn bread for his family but also created a very favorable impression upon Venetian public opinion.[264]

Officials in Vienna realized that sporadic half measures like public works projects were not enough to restore prosperity in Venetia. The imperial government was fully aware that the vicissitudes of warfare, the military requisitions, the crop failures, the cattle plague, the high taxes, and the supplying of the Habsburg army in Italy mostly with goods manufactured in the German provinces of the monarchy all contributed to the existing poverty.[265] Nevertheless, the authorities in the Austrian capital had no detailed and precise information about the actual conditions in the most depressed areas in Venetia. To obtain such a report, Emperor Francis instructed Count Peter Goëss,[266] whom he had appointed to succeed Prince Reuss-Plauen as

[261] Central-Organisirungs-Hof-Commission report, March 30, 1815, St. A. (Vienna), Staats-Rath Akten, 1815, No. 2292.

[262] Central-Organisirungs-Hof-Commission report, March 23, 1815, ibid., No. 2004.

[263] Raab to presidency of the Venetian central government, March 14, 1815, A. S. (Venice), Presidio di governo, 1815–1819, Polizia, Fasc. II 10/1, No. 991 P.P.

[264] Police report, April 10, 1815, St. A. (Vienna), Kabinets-Akten, 1815, ad No. 427.

[265] Venetian central government to Central-Organisirungs-Hof-Commission, Venice, February 7, 1815, Hofkammer Archiv (Vienna), Kredit Akten, Fasc. XVIB1/13, No. 7534 ex Juli 1815; Central-Organisirungs-Hof-Commission report, February 22, 1815, St. A. (Vienna), Staats-Rath Akten, 1815, No. 1257; Goëss to Lazanzky, Belluno, April 26, 1815, Hofkammer Archiv (Vienna), Central-Organisirungs-Hof-Commission Akten, Rinna, 1815, No. 10,719/1137; Hager report, July 15, 1815, St. A. (Vienna), Kabinets-Akten, 1815, No. 756; protocol, Staats-Conferenz, September 17, 1815, St. A. (Vienna), Staats-Rath Akten, 1815, No. 6284.

[266] Goëss was born in Florence on February 8, 1774, and died in Vienna on July 11, 1846. He entered state service after studying law at the University of Vienna. In 1799 he was made an adviser in the provincial government of Carinthia. Four years later he was appointed president of the Dalmatian government. In 1806 he became vice-president of the united government of Styria and Carinthia. In 1808 he was made governor of Trieste, and in 1809, of Galicia. He was governor of Venetia from 1815 to 1819, when he was appointed chancellor of the aulic Lombardo-Venetian chancellery in Vienna.

governor of Venetia, to survey the situation in the most seriously affected districts and make recommendations on the best way to alleviate the extreme poverty and destitution.[267] The new governor of Venetia was empowered to take whatever measures he thought advisable and to distribute up to 100,000 florins (258,590 Italian lire) from the Venetian treasury to the most badly stricken districts.[268]

While on his tour of the most depressed areas of Venetia Goëss made several suggestions to the government on what it could do to improve conditions. He expressed the belief that only the revival of agriculture and industry could restore prosperity to the famished regions. This could be done only if the tax system were entirely reorganized. It was also necessary to encourage trade between Venetia and Lombardy and the adjacent hereditary German states. In order to do this, free and unhampered commerce must be permitted between the Italian and German provinces of the monarchy for such commodities as grain, hay, wine, oil, silk, wool, and flax. The free importation of flax into the Venetian provinces would be particularly helpful, since thousands of people in the mountain districts, which were the worst hit by the famine, made their living from manufacturing linen. Furthermore, it was imperative to remove many of the numerous exactions and restrictions which were impoverishing landowners to such an extent that often they no longer could find the means to pay for cultivating their estates.[269]

Until general prosperity could be attained by such measures Goëss maintained that the public works program which had already been inaugurated on a limited basis should be extended to all employable persons who were without jobs and means of subsistence. In addition, systematic procedures should be developed to give money grants to all destitute persons incapable of working.[270]

Although Governor Goëss' recommendations were warmly endorsed by the aulic central organization commission, the state confer-

[267] Zichy to Emperor Francis, Vienna, March 7, 1815, St. A. (Vienna), Conferenz Akten, Ser. a, 1815, No. 82; imperial resolution, March 8, 1815, *ibid.*; Emperor Francis to Goëss, Vienna, April 2, 1815, *ibid.*, No. 84.

[268] Emperor Francis to Goëss, Vienna, April 2, 1815, *ibid.*, No. 84. A copy of this letter can also be found in St. A. (Vienna), Staats-Rath Akten, 1815, No. 2605.

[269] Goëss to Lazanzky, Belluno, April 26, 1815, *Hofkammer Archiv* (Vienna), Central-Organisirungs-Hof-Commission Akten, Rinna, 1815, No. 10,719/1137.

[270] Central-Organisirungs-Hof-Commission report, May 26, 1815, St. A. (Vienna), Staats-Rath Akten, 1815, No. 3807.

ence,[271] and the emperor,[272] the lethargic Habsburg government took a number of years to act upon most of them. Early in 1815, however, a little progress was made towards carrying out the new governor's suggestion to permit a free exchange of goods between Venetia and Lombardy. A few weeks after Habsburg troops first entered Venetia the Austrians re-established the customs line which had existed in 1805 between Venetia and the Illyrian provinces,[273] and, with a few modifications to fit the special circumstances prevailing in 1814, they re-introduced the old 1805 tariff system in Venetia in March, 1814.[274] Immediately after assuming control of Lombardy they substituted a different tariff for the French rates in that province: the old Austrian duties which had been in force there before 1796. Since the tariffs which were instituted in Venetia and in Lombardy differed considerably from each other,[275] the Austrians established a customs line on the Mincio River, between Lombardy and Venetia, in May[276] in order to be able effectively to administer the two dissimilar tariff regulations.

The Lombards and Venetians immediately inundated the Austrian officials in Italy with loud complaints about the customs line which had just been established.[277] When these protests reached Emperor Francis' ears he instructed his commissioner plenipotentiary in Lombardy as quickly as possible to honor the promises which the emperor had made in May to the Milanese deputation at Paris[278] that goods could be freely exchanged between Lombardy and Venetia.[279]

[271] Central-Organisirungs-Hof-Commission report, February 22, 1815, ibid., No. 1257; protocol, Staats-Conferenz, September 17, 1815, ibid., ad No. 6284.

[272] Emperor Francis to Lazanzky, September 29, 1815, ibid., ad No. 6284.

[273] Imperial resolution, Freiburg, December 30, 1813, St. A. (Vienna), Conferenz Akten, Ser. b, 1814, No. 24.

[274] Circular, March 24, 1814, Collezione di leggi venete, 1813–1814, Vol. I, pp. 132–133.

[275] Bellegarde report, Milan, July 21, 1814, St. A. (Vienna), Conferenz Akten, Ser. b, 1814, No. 1454.

[276] Decree, provisional regency, Milan, May 28, 1814, Atti del governo lombardo, 1814, pp. 54–55.

[277] Protocol, Staats-Conferenz, June 28, 1814, St. A. (Vienna), Conferenz Akten, Ser. b, 1814, No. 1214; Reuss-Plauen to Lazanzky, Venice, October 3, 1814, A. S. (Venice), Presidio di governo, 1814, No. 1401.

[278] Milanese deputation to provisional regency, Paris, May 27, 1814, Museo (Milan), "Carte Beccaria," Busta I, Carte 8, Fasc. II, No. 60.

[279] Emperor Francis to Bellegarde, Baden, July 6, 1814, St. A. (Vienna),

After receiving these orders Bellegarde busied himself with finding the means to implement them. He asked the Lombard council for commerce, arts, and manufactures what kind of joint Lombardo-Venetian customs regulations it would approve.[280] He consulted Governor Reuss-Plauen as to how a mutually agreeable joint tariff could be drawn up.[281] Then he and the governor of Venetia arranged a meeting at Verona to which delegates from both provinces were called.[282] Following the recommendations of these two delegations, the two governors agreed in October, 1814, to abolish the double customs line on the Mincio River and to admit most of the products of each province duty free into the other. However, any Lombard raw silk that was not sent directly to a Venetian factory, all partially manufactured silk, and rice and cheese produced in Lombardy were still to be subject to an export duty when they passed the borders of Lombardy into Venetia. Customs duties were to be paid on foreign goods coming into either Lombardy or Venetia only when they first arrived in either province; they were not to be subject to a further duty when they passed from one province into the other.[283]

Plans were made for another joint Lombardo-Venetian commission to hold a leisurely meeting at an unspecified future date to reach an agreement on a common customs tariff for both provinces.[284] When the two governors learned, however, that Emperor Francis was highly displeased because the customs line had not already been entirely abolished in October[285] and that he wanted them to make haste to

---

Conferenz Akten, Ser. b, 1814, No. 1214; Lazanzky to Reuss-Plauen, Vienna, October 10, 1814, A. S. (Venice), Presidio di governo, 1814, No. 1912.

[280] Bellegarde to minister of interior, Milan, July 20, 1814, A. S. (Milan), Uffici e Tribunali Regi. Parte Moderne, Cart. LVI–LVII–LVIII, Governo, Registro Generale, 2 gennaio al 31 luglio 1814, No. 838.

[281] Bellegarde report, Milan, July 21, 1814, St. A. (Vienna), Conferenz Akten, Ser. b, 1814, No. 1454.

[282] Reuss-Plauen to Stadion, Venice, December 29, 1814, A. S. (Venice), Presidio di governo, 1814, No. 2444.

[283] Decree, Bellegarde, Milan, October 19, 1814, *Atti del governo lombardo,* 1814, pp. 138–142; notice, October 18, 1814, *Collezione di leggi venete,* 1813–1814, Vol. II, pp. 61–65.

[284] Reuss-Plauen to Central-Organisirungs-Hof-Commission, Venice, October 19 and November 27, 1814, A. S. (Venice), Presidio di governo, 1814, Nos. 1589 and 2054; Bellegarde to Reuss-Plauen, Milan, November 19, 1814, *ibid.,* No. 2054 P.R.

[285] Lazanzky to Reuss-Plauen, Vienna, December 12, 1814, *ibid.,* No. 2444.

come to an agreement not only on a joint tariff for Lombardy and Venetia but on one that would include the Tyrol as well,[286] they speeded up the meeting date of this commission to late January or early February, 1815.[287] The commission met in Milan. In spite of the emperor's injunctions to accelerate its deliberations, it was far from concluding its work when Napoleon's escape from Elba again plunged Europe into war.

Although the Lombard and Venetian middle classes still had reason to complain in the spring of 1815 that the emperor's promise to abolish the customs line on the Mincio River had not been entirely carried out, they had to concede that the Austrians had honored another of their sovereign's assurances to the Milanese deputation at Paris: that all national goods which had been sold by the previous regime were to remain in the hands of their present owners.[288] Although Emperor Francis advised his officials not to encourage the Italians to complete transactions to purchase ecclesiastical property which they had initiated during the last days of the former regime,[289] he felt that it was only just to regard as legal all sales of ecclesiastical or other national property which had been made by the French-Italian government. He informed Bellegarde and Reuss-Plauen that the title to such property was to be guaranteed to its purchasers if they presented proof to the Austrians that they had acquired it in a legal manner.[290] The two governors, however, were to take care that illegally procured national goods were recovered by the state. To obtain the cooperation of the populace in discovering

286 Imperial resolution, Vienna, November 25, 1814, St. A. (Vienna), Staats-Rath Akten, 1814, No. 3315.

287 Bellegarde to Reuss-Plauen, Milan, December 24, 1814, A. S. (Venice), Presidio di governo, 1814, No. 2474 P.R.; Bellegarde to Reuss-Plauen, Milan, January 10, 1815, ibid., 1815–1819, Finanza, Fasc. IV 4/3, ad No. 815/P.P.; Reuss-Plauen to Bellegarde, Venice, January 17, 1815, ibid., No. 161/P.P.

288 Milanese deputation to provisional regency, Paris, May 27, 1814, Museo (Milan), "Carte Beccaria," Busta I, Carte 8, Fasc. II, No. 60; Confalonieri to his wife, Paris, May 28, 1814, Gabrio Casati (ed.), Federico Confalonieri, Memorie e lettere (hereafter cited as Confalonieri, Memorie e lettere), Vol. II, p. 28.

289 Emperor Francis to Zichy, Baden, July 2, 1814, St. A. (Vienna), Conferenz Akten, Ser. b, 1814, No. 1273.

290 Emperor Francis to Bellegarde, June 14, 1814, ibid., No. 1111; Central-Organisirungs-Hof-Commission report, August 30, 1814, ibid., No. 1683; Emperor Francis to Bellegarde and Ugarte, Baden, July 22, 1814, ibid., No. 1273; circular, August 26, 1814, Collezione di leggi venete, 1813–1814, Vol. II, p. 34.

fraudulently acquired state goods, they were to renew the practice followed by the French of awarding one-fifth the value of all goods recovered to persons who had given information that led to their discovery.[291]

Although Emperor Francis clearly stated during the summer of 1814 that all persons who had purchased national goods were to retain full possession of them, for some reason or another Bellegarde and Reuss-Plauen did not announce his decision to the Italians before 1815. As a consequence of this delay, many alarming rumors circulated in Lombardy and Venetia to the effect that the Austrians would soon confiscate such property from its present owners. As a result, in many instances, possessors of such goods could find neither people who would buy national goods nor bankers who would accept them as collateral for loans.[292]

When the Habsburg emperor learned of what was happening, he expressed his displeasure over the fact that the governors had failed to allay the fears of the inhabitants and instructed both of them to post notices as soon as possible assuring the purchasers of national goods that their property would never be taken from them if they had fulfilled all necessary obligations to gain a legal title when they acquired these goods.[293] The requested proclamations were posted in Lombardy on May 11[294] and in Venetia on May 12, 1815.[295]

[291] Central-Organisirungs-Hof-Commission report, August 30, 1814, St. A. (Vienna), Conferenz Akten, Ser. b, 1814, No. 1683; imperial resolution, October 5, 1814, *Hofkammer Archiv* (Vienna), Kredit Akten, Fasz. X/1, No. 8236 ex December 1814; notification, November 18, 1814, *Collezione di leggi venete,* 1813–1814, Vol. II, pp. 71–73.

[292] Metternich to Bellegarde, Vienna, January 4, 1815, St. A. (Vienna), Staatskanzlei, 1815, An Bellegarde, no number given; Lazanzky to Metternich, Vienna, March 13, 1815, *ibid.,* No. 8078/1902.

[293] Emperor Francis to Central-Organisirungs-Hof-Commission, January 23, 1815, St. A. (Vienna), Staats-Rath Akten, 1815, No. 2170.

[294] Decree, provisional regency, Milan, May 11, 1815, *Atti del governo lombardo,* 1815, Vol. I, pp. 95–96.

[295] Notification, May 12, 1815, *Collezione di leggi venete,* 1815, Vol. I, pp. 177–178.

Chapter 4

PUBLIC OPINION AND LIBERAL INTRIGUES (1814)

In 1814–1815 the Lombards were better governed and more prosperous than the Venetians. The provisional government at Milan, though it had its shortcomings, was a model of efficiency in comparison with the central administration in Venetia. Because the Habsburg commissioner plenipotentiary confirmed the provisional regency which he found on his arrival at the Lombard capital and allowed it, under his personal surveillance, to direct most of the political affairs and supervise the administration of the country, the Lombards enjoyed a slight measure of self-administration which was largely denied to the Venetians. More important, the Lombards never suffered from the compulsory circulation of paper money, the forced loans, and the exorbitant military requisitions which oppressed the Venetians; and in 1814 their tax burden was substantially lighter than that of the Venetians. Moreover, although the Lombards were by no means prosperous in 1814, they were spared the crop failures, dire misery, famine, and actual starvation which so grievously plagued the Venetians. Yet, in spite of the fact that the Lombards were rather well off in comparison with the Venetians, many more Lombards than Venetians developed an intense dislike for the Austrians during the course of 1814, and what existed in the way of an independence and constitutional movement was largely confined to Lombardy.

When Austrian troops first marched into Venetia in October, 1813, they were greeted everywhere as liberators and friends. Almost to a man the inhabitants looked upon the Habsburg armies as emancipators who would chase their French oppressors from Italy, abolish the Napoleonic administrative and financial systems under which they had suffered, and inaugurate in the Apennine peninsula that era of peace, stability, and prosperity which the Italian people so fervently desired.[1] In place after place the arrival of Austrian soldiers was the occasion for triumphal celebrations. In Verona, for instance, the citizens stopped all work, and "people rushed out of the market place to the surrounding regions to be the first to bring the joyful news home."[2] The appearance of the Austrians in the city of Venice not only elicited loud "hurrahs," but also inspired some of the inhabitants to make threatening demonstrations against the French and their sympathizers.[3]

By 1814 the French were universally hated in Venetia. The union with the Kingdom of Italy had never been popular. Not only did many Venetians dislike the French for having destroyed their republic, but also they scorned and distrusted the Lombards, whom they accused of wielding the upper hand in the kingdom and of willingly cooperating with the French to reduce Venice to the status of an impoverished second-class city. Resentful of French domination, the inhabitants of several communes had responded enthusiastically to Archduke John's appeals in 1809 to rise up in open revolt against the hated Napoleon[4]—an insurrection which had been put down with harsh repressive measures. After 1809 the Venetians made no more attempts to revolt, but the ever-increasing conscription, the oppressive taxes and military requisitions, the arbitrary confiscations of merchandise, the vexatious customs regulations, and the continental

---

[1] Wiedemann-Warnhelm, *Die Wiederherstellung der österreichischen Vorherrschaft in Italien*, pp. 34–35; Sandonà, *Il Regno Lombardo Veneto*, p. 70; Giuseppe Solitro, "Maestri e scolari dell'università di Padova nell'ultima dominazione austriaca (1813–1866)," *L'Archivio Veneto-Tridentino*, Vol. I (1922), p. 112; Angela Mariutti, *Organismo ed azione delle società segrete del veneto durante la seconda dominazione austriaca (1814–1847)* (Vol. III of *Miscellanea di storia veneta*), p. 4.

[2] Report from Florence, February 10, 1814, *Wiener Zeitung*, March 5, 1814, p. 260.

[3] Cicogna diary, April 20 and 21, and May 7 and 23, 1814, Pilot, "Venezia nel blocco del 1813–1814," pp. 207–210, 215–216, and 220; Enrico Castelnuovo, *A Venezia, un secolo fa. Discorso letto nell'adunanza solenne del 25 maggio* (estratto d'*Atti del Reale Istituto Veneto di Scienze, Lettere ed Arti* [1912–1913]), pp. 7–8; Fabio Mutinelli, *Annali delle province venete dell'anno 1801 al 1840*, pp. 102–103.

[4] Wiedemann-Warnhelm, *Die Wiederherstellung der österreichischen Vorherrschaft in Italien*, p. 34; Pierre Lagarde to General Savary, Milan, June 19, 1806, and Venice, September 11, 1806, Ferdinand Boyer, "Pierre Lagarde, policier de Napoléon à Venise en 1806," *Rassegna storica del Risorgimento*, Vol. XLIV, Fasc. 1 (January–March, 1957), pp. 90 and 92–95.

144 LOMBARDY-VENETIA (1814–1815)

blockade, which practically ruined the city of Venice, drove them to the depths of despair. By 1812 and 1813 the vast majority of Venetians were bitterly discontented with the Napoleonic regime.[5]

Still, though at the outset the Venetians, grateful because they were rid of the hated French, looked upon the Austrians as liberators, as the Italian campaign progressed many of them became so disillusioned that they expressed open jubilation over the military reverses which the Habsburg army suffered on the Mincio in February, 1814.[6] Embittered as they were with the oppressions and exactions of the Napoleonic regime, they were at first amazed and then disgruntled because the French laws and judicial system and nearly all the administrative machinery and most of the officials of the previous French government were kept intact for many months after the Austrians came to Italy. Even more galling was the fact that the Habsburgs preserved the abhorred French financial system and continued to collect the excessively high taxes which the French had imposed. In addition, the deplorable conduct of some of the Habsburg soldiers irritated them, and the heavy Austrian military requisitions and the forced loans utterly exhausted the already miserable, poverty-stricken Venetians.[7]

Although some of the most onerous of these exactions were discontinued when the Italian campaign was over, most of the grievances over which the Venetians had gnashed their teeth during the course of the war continued to vex them for many months after the fighting ended. Nonetheless, even though they still had many justifiable reasons to complain, they were so jubilant over getting rid of the French that when it was made known to them that Venetia, as well as Lombardy, would definitely be incorporated into the Habsburg monarchy, the Venetians publicly demonstrated their happiness and even enthusiasm over their future prospects under their new

[5] Mulazzani to Guicciardi, Venice, November 22, 1814, St. A. (Vienna), Diego Graf Guicciardi, Geheime Correspondenz, Fasz. I, No. 21.

[6] Staats-Kabinet report, April 5, 1814, St. A. (Vienna), Kabinets-Akten, 1814, No. 1371. See also Hager report, May 26, 1814, *ibid.*, No. 1585; and entry of May 12, 1814, Lemmi, *Diario del Huegel*, p. 55.

[7] Staats-Kabinet reports, January 17, February 6, March 1 and 25, and April 5 and 6, 1814, St. A. (Vienna), Kabinets-Akten, 1814, Nos. 957, 1077, 1193, 1320, 1371, and 1385; Hager reports, April 16 and May 23, 1814, *ibid.*, Nos. 957 and 1583; Hager reports, April 16, May 17, and June 17, 1814, St. A. (Vienna), Conferenz Akten, Ser. b, 1814, Nos. 917, 1102, and 1174; Staats-Conferenz reports, January 11 and June 14, 1814, *ibid.*, Nos. 38 and 1102.

rulers.[8] During the course of the late spring and summer several measures enacted by the Austrians, like the few reductions in taxes, the abolition of the most oppressive military requisitions, the curbing of the worst excesses of the soldiers, and the dismissal of some of the most despised French officials, aroused the hopes of the inhabitants that still other much desired benefits would be accorded them.[9] Then, too, tired and impoverished from the vicissitudes of warfare and the harsh tyrannies and stringencies of the French, the Venetians were pervaded with a universal and ardent longing for peace, which they believed the mild and paternal government of the Habsburgs would guarantee them.[10]

Except for those coming from Verona[11] and Venice,[12] all reports from Venetia in the summer and fall of 1814 bear witness to the fact that, while they deplored the high taxes and certain Austrian policies, the large majority of Venetians were pro-Austrian and devoted to the Habsburg emperor.[13] It is true that shortly after the arrival of the Austrians in Venice a note was found posted in a public square calling attention to the fact that the Allied Powers had promised inde-

[8] Hager to Staats-Conferenz, June 17, 1814, St. A. (Vienna), Conferenz Akten, Ser. b, 1814, No. 1174.

[9] Hager reports, July 15 and 16, 1814, *ibid.*, Nos. 1393 and 1407; Staats-Kabinet report, June 29, 1814, St. A. (Vienna), Kabinets-Akten, 1814, No. 1583.

[10] Solitro, "Maestri e scolari dell'università di Padova," p. 112.

[11] Reuss-Plauen to Hager, Venice, November 6, 1814, A. S. (Venice), Presidio di governo, 1814, No. 1743; police directory to presidency of the Venetian central government, Venice, October 31, 1814, *Carte segrete della polizia austriaca in Italia*, Vol. I, p. 25; Cavazzocca diary, November 5, 1814, Biadego, *La dominazione austriaca a Verona*, pp. 19–20.

[12] Department of Adriatico, political report for November, 1814, A. S. (Venice), Presidio di governo, 1814, ad No. 1749; Reuss-Plauen to Hager, Venice, December 8, 1814, *ibid.*, No. 2178–2179.

[13] See especially Hager reports, May 11 and November 10, 1814, St. A. (Vienna), Kabinets-Akten, 1814, Nos. 1547 and 865; Mulazzani to Reuss-Plauen, Venice, May 28, 1814, A. S. (Venice), Presidio di governo, 1814, No. 132; Reuss-Plauen to Hager, Padua, July 10 and 26, and August 24, 1814, and Venice, September 16 and 19, and October 6 and 13, 1814, *ibid.*, Nos. 427, 682, 909, 1143, 1241, 1425, and 1488; prefecture of Piave, political report for July, 1814, *ibid.*, ad No. 1483; prefecture of Udine, political report for September, 1814, *ibid.*, ad No. 2234; and Brenta department, political reports for September, October, and November, 1814, Ottolenghi, *Padova e il Dipartimento del Brenta*, Appendix XXV, p. 418, Appendix XXVII, p. 435, and Appendix XXVIII, pp. 443–444.

pendence to the Italians.[14] Also, the Austrian police confiscated a couple of passports at Comachio which had the words "Independent Italy" written on them,[15] and a few isolated placards appeared which appealed to national independence.[16] Nevertheless, all the documents which this writer has seen in the Viennese and Venetian archives clearly show that if any trace of Italian nationalist feeling existed in Venetia in 1814 it was negligible. A few Venetians dreamt of the restoration of the old Venetian Republic. The idea of re-creating the Republic of San Marco had never been extinguished from the hearts of some of the old Venetian aristocracy, and various Englishmen who were in Venice in 1814, including the British consul, encouraged their chimerical aspirations.[17] A much larger number wished that the Habsburgs would send Archduke John or another member of the royal family to Venetia as governor or viceroy.[18] The large majority, however, wanted their country to be integrated into the Habsburg monarchy as quickly as possible.[19]

The Venetians made it perfectly clear, however, that they were willing to join some kind of administrative union with Lombardy only if Venice were made the capital of the joint political unit. If this was not done, they insisted that Venetia should remain a separate province within the Austrian empire.[20] Jealous of the Lombards

14 Mulazzani to Reuss-Plauen, Venice, May 25, 1814, A. S. (Venice), Presidio di governo, 1814, No. 122.

15 Reuss-Plauen to Bellegarde, Padua, June 20, 1814, *ibid.*, No. 230.

16 Helfert, *La caduta della dominazione francese*, pp. 143–144.

17 Hager reports, May 17, June 2, and July 8, 1814, St. A. (Vienna), Conferenz Akten, Ser. b, 1814, Nos. 1102, 1152, and 1346; Reuss-Plauen to Hager, Padua, May 7, 1814, A. S. (Venice), Presidio di governo, 1814, No. 6; Mulazzani to Reuss-Plauen, Venice, May 28, 1814, *ibid.*, No. 132; secret report to Raab, Padua, June 20, 1814, *ibid.*, No. 790; Cicogna diary, May 11, 1814, Pilot, "Venezia nel blocco del 1813–14," p. 217; P[ietro] Peverelli, *Storia di Venezia dal 1798 sino al nostri tempi*, Vol. I, p. 251.

18 Reuss-Plauen to Staats-Conferenz, Padua, May 27, 1814, St. A. (Vienna), Conferenz Akten, Ser. b, 1814, No. 1076; Hager to Staats-Conferenz, June 17, 1814, *ibid.*, No. 1174; Hager report, June 7, 1814, St. A. (Vienna), Kabinets-Akten, 1814, No. 1603; Reuss-Plauen to Hager, Venice, September 16, 1814, A. S. (Venice), Presidio di governo, 1814, No. 1143; department of Adriatico, political report for October, 1814, *ibid.*, ad No. 1749.

19 Report to Raab, Venice, July 16, 1814, *Carte segrete della polizia austriaca in Italia*, Vol. I, p. 22.

20 Staats-Conferenz report, June 14, 1814, St. A. (Vienna), Conferenz Akten, Ser. b, 1814, No. 1076; Hager report, July 15, 1814, *ibid.*, No. 1393; Hager report, June 7, 1814, St. A. (Vienna), Kabinets-Akten, 1814, No. 1603.

before the French Revolution and scornful and suspicious of them because of their dominant position in the Kingdom of Italy, the Venetians did not want to run the risk of again becoming subordinate to them in any way now that they were freed from their unwilling connection with the former Kingdom of Italy.

The Venetians were much more pro-Austrian in 1814 than the Lombards,[21] even though the great majority of Lombards probably disliked the French as intensely as the Venetians did in the spring of 1814. Napoleon had but a tiny handful of supporters left in Lombardy as well as in Venetia.

There were many Lombards, particularly among the older nobility and the clergy, but also among the petty traders and shopkeepers, the artisans, and the peasants who still had fond memories of the benign reigns of Maria Theresa and Joseph II and who looked forward to again attaining the tranquillity and security of olden times under Habsburg domination. However, to a much greater extent than in Venetia, the more politically active circles—the younger nobility, intellectuals, professional people, bankers, merchants, and businessmen—had been aroused by the stimulus of the French revolutionary and Napoleonic reforms, the anti-Napoleonic propaganda of British agents, and the writings of a handful of patriotic Italian writers to expect some kind of independent, liberal, constitutional state after the Napoleonic regime was overthrown. Many high officials and the majority of state employees of the Kingdom of Italy, the larger part of the army, and a few liberal bourgeoisie who desired to conserve the existing institutions hoped to see an independent Kingdom of Italy with Eugène de Beauharnais as its sovereign. A small faction, headed by Ugo Foscolo, Police Director Luini, and a small coterie of army officers led by General Pino, supported the pretensions of Murat to become king of a united Italy. A few "pure Italians," of whom the most important were Verri and Confalonieri, cherished vague ambitions to attain independence under an Italian king. Another group, affirming that since England was a constitutional monarchy she would always uphold the cause of freedom, wished to have the duke of Clarence, the third son of King George III of England, as their monarch. A much larger number of advo-

[21] Hager report, July 15, 1814, St. A. (Vienna), Conferenz Akten, Ser. b, 1814, No. 1393; Helfert, *La caduta della dominazione francese*, p. 143; Wiedemann-Warnhelm, *Die Wiederherstellung der österreichischen Vorherrschaft in Italien*, p. 47.

cates of an independent kingdom, however, envisioned a powerful independent kingdom under the protection of Austria and thought of an Austrian prince, perhaps Archduke Francis of Austria-Este, as its possible ruler. The lines between these parties were extremely confused and irregular, and by the spring of 1814 no group had crystallized anything more than a nebulous program. It should be noted, however, that of the parties desirous of independence only the small Muratist faction appeared to have had anything resembling a truly *Italian* nationalist program.

Attention should also be called to the fact that thus far only the politically active sections of the population have been mentioned. The masses, on the whole, took little interest in political affairs and concerned themselves only with such political policies and practices as had a direct and immediate bearing on them. Almost totally exhausted from the vicissitudes of warfare, they were, by the spring of 1814, mainly interested in one thing: peace. They worried little about what type of government would replace the French one as long as it would assure them security and tranquillity.[22]

The pro-independence and pro-Austrian factions were mainly responsible for the Milanese revolution of April 20, during the course of which the French government was overthrown in Lombardy.[23] Both of these groups, as well as many working class people and such peasants as happened to be in Milan, greeted the Habsburgs with enthusiastic demonstrations and lavish encomiums when they first arrived in the Lombard capital.[24]

[22] See my *Fall of the Napoleonic Kingdom of Italy*, pp. 81–86; Pingaud, "La Lombardie en 1814," pp. 435–452; Karl Otmar von Aretin, "Eugen Beauharnais' Königreich Italien beim Übergang zur österreichischen Herrschaft im April 1814. Aus den nachgelassenen Papieren des k. k. Feldzeugmeisters Ludwig Frhr. v. Welden," *Mitteilungen des Österreichischen Staatsarchivs*, Vol. XII (1959), pp. 263–267; Guicciardi to Metternich, Milan, June 5, 1816, St. A. (Vienna), Diego Graf Guicciardi, Geheime Correspondenz, Fasz. I, Primo protocollo degli allegati, No. C, Fos. 42–43; Helfert, *La caduta della dominazione francese*, pp. 26–36; and Lemmi, *La restaurazione austriaca a Milano*, pp. 83–122.

[23] For a detailed discussion of the revolution, see my *Fall of the Napoleonic Kingdom of Italy*, pp. 98–126.

[24] Entry of April 28, 1814, *Biblioteca Ambrosiana* (Milan), Mantovani, "Diario di Milano," Vol. V, p. 258; *Giornale italiano*, No. 119 (April 29, 1814), p. 482; Teresa Confalonieri Casati to Confalonieri, Milan, April 29, 1814, Gallavresi, *Carteggio del conte Federico Confalonieri*, Vol. I, pp. 83–84; Strassoldo to Bellegarde, Milan, April 30, 1814, St. A. (Vienna), Kaiser Franz Akten, Fasz.

Although the Allied Powers had definitely agreed in July, 1813, that Venetia was to go to Austria, the fate of Lombardy was still an open question in the latter part of April, 1814.[25] As a consequence, in their efforts to wean them from the Napoleonic regime, Austrian, as well as British and Neapolitan, officers could and did with complete honesty appeal at various times during the course of the Italian campaign to the pro-independence sentiments of the Italian people.[26] As late as the last of April, Austrian officials were still encouraging the Lombards to believe that they would be accorded an independent government under some Habsburg prince.[27] These pro-independent expressions of Habsburg generals perhaps explain in part why the liberal factions in Milan received the Austrian army with such warmhearted manifestations of joy and why they sent deputations with various demands for freedom, not only to Murat; to Lord Bentinck, the British commander-in-chief in the Mediterranean; to Lieutenant-General Robert MacFarlane, whom Bentinck sent to Milan as his agent; and to Sir Robert Wilson, the English attaché to the Austrian army in Italy; but also to Field Marshal Bellegarde and to General Laval Nugent.[28]

The encouragement which the pro-independence parties believed that they had received from both Austrian and British officials in Italy also prompted them to make various demands for territorial ad-

XXVII, Kon. 1, Fo. 49; Giacomo Lombroso, *Complicazioni promosse dall'Austria dal Congresso di Vienna sino all'esaltazione di Pio IX per conservare la Lombardia*, p. 11.

25 See my *Fall of the Napoleonic Kingdom of Italy*, pp. 180–191.

26 For the Austrian appeals, see especially Hiller proclamation, Trent, October 26, 1813, A. S. (Venice), Governo veneto, 1813–1814, Polizia, Fasc. V, A, No. 1138; Bellegarde proclamation, Soave, February 4, 1814, St. A. (Vienna), Staatskanzlei, Provinzen, Lombardei-Venedig, Fasz. III, Kon. 3, Fo. 54; Bellegarde proclamation to the Italian people, Verona, February 4, 1814, M[aurice] H[enri] Weil, *Le prince Eugène et Murat 1813–1814; opérations militaires, négociations diplomatiques*, Vol. III, pp. 647–648; and Anton Springer, *Geschichte Österreichs seit dem Wiener Frieden 1809*, Vol. I, pp. 242–243.

27 See especially Porro to provisional government, Milan, April 27, 1814, Bernardo Salvisenti, "La missione Porro presso le Alte Potenze nel 1814," *La Lombardia nel Risorgimento italiano*, Vol. I–II (June, 1914), pp. 36–40; Borda to Battista, May 10, 1814, Giuseppe Gallavresi, *Il carteggio intimo di Andrea Borda* (estratto dall'*Archivio storico lombardo*, Vol. XLVII [1920], p. 53; and provisional regency to deputation at Paris, Milan, April 27, 1814, *Museo* (Milan), "Carte Beccaria," Busta I, Carte 8, Fasc. I, No. 3.

28 See my *Fall of the Napoleonic Kingdom of Italy*, pp. 126–137 and 161–164.

ditions to the new independent Lombard state which they hoped would soon be created. Many of them had vague expectations of obtaining enough territory to assure the economic prosperity of their kingdom and land on both the Mediterranean and Adriatic coasts to facilitate the export of products from their country.[29] A few misty-eyed romanticists thought that their country should be united with Piedmont,[30] while others thought that Modena, Parma, Piacenza, and the Estenese should be added to Lombardy.[31] As soon as it became evident that these grandiose plans were unrealizable, the champions of independence followed a new tack and limited their demands to Lombardy, the lands west of the Ticino River which the Piedmontese had acquired from Lombardy in 1703, 1738, and 1743, and the territory of the former Republic of Genoa. These areas, they insisted, would be the smallest possible compensation that would be acceptable for the loss of Venetia,[32] which they all knew would not be included in the independent kingdom that they aspired to establish.

During the first couple of weeks after the April 20 revolution the liberals were by far the most articulate group in Milan. Numerous were their resolutions and loud were their entreaties for independence, a good king, and a constitution guaranteeing the separation of legislative, executive, and judicial powers, providing for some kind

[29] Giovio (president of the electoral colleges) to MacFarlane, Milan, n.d., Giuseppe Gallavresi, "La rivoluzione lombarda del 1814 e la politica inglese secondo nuovi documenti," *Archivio storico lombardo,* Vol. XXXVI (1909), p. 146; memoir of the college of commerce of Cremona, given to MacFarlane by G. P. Cadolino on April 30, 1814, *ibid.*; protocol, provisional regency, May 3, 1814, *Biblioteca di Brera* (Milan), "Protocolli originali della reggenza provvisoria."

[30] Porro Lambertenghi to Confalonieri, May 13, 1814, Gallavresi, *Carteggio del conte Federico Confalonieri,* Vol. I, p. 122; Renato Soriga, "Bagliori unitari in Lombardia avanti la restaurazione austriaca (1814)," *Bollettino della Società pavese di storia patria,* Vol. XV, Fasc. 1–2 (January–June, 1915), p. 4.

[31] Porro Lambertenghi to Confalonieri, May 13, 1814, Gallavresi, *Carteggio del conte Federico Confalonieri,* Vol. I, p. 122; protocol, provisional regency, May 3, 1814, *Biblioteca di Brera* (Milan), "Protocolli originali della reggenza provvisoria."

[32] MacFarlane to Bentinck, Milan, May 6, 1814, Gallavresi, "La rivoluzione lombardo del 1814 e la politica inglese," p. 153; MacFarlane to Castlereagh, Milan, May 4, 1814, Lemmi, *La restaurazione austriaca a Milano,* Appendix XVII, p. 421; protocol, provisional regency, May 3, 1814, *Biblioteca di Brera* (Milan), "Protocolli originali della reggenza provvisoria"; provisional regency to deputation at Paris, Milan, May 3, 1814, *Museo* (Milan), "Carte Beccaria," Busta I, Carte 8, Fasc. I, No. 359; Bellegarde report, May 31, 1814, St. A. (Vienna), Conferenz Akten, Ser. b, 1814, No. 1249.

of national representative body to make laws, approve expenditures, and apportion taxes, and insuring such freedoms as those of speech, assembly, the press, and commerce.[33]

After the overthrow of the Kingdom of Italy, however, the Lombard liberals were even more sharply divided in regard to whom they wanted for king than they had been before the Milanese revolution. Except among an extremely small handful of officials, army officers, and soldiers, Eugène de Beauharnais no longer had any supporters.[34] After April 20, Murat's champions seem to have entirely disappeared.[35] A few partisans of independence were resigned to letting the course of events determine who would be their monarch[36] or limited themselves to requesting a prince who "by his origin and qualities, may cause to be effaced the calamities which have been suffered under the government abolished."[37] Apparently after the Milanese revolution, a larger number, particularly among the commercial groups[38] and more radical intellectuals and army officers, wanted a British prince. Desiring British support for their constitutional projects and favorable commercial relations with England, they agitated for the appointment of either the duke of Cambridge

[33] See especially protocol, electoral colleges, April 23, 1814, *Giornale italiano*, No. 114 (April 24, 1814), p. 458; proclamation, provisional regency, Milan, April 29, 1814, *ibid.*, No. 119 (April 29, 1814), p. 482; Durini to Bentinck, Milan, April 20, 1814, Gallavresi, "La rivoluzione lombarda del 1814 e la politica inglese," pp. 108–109; MacFarlane to Bentinck, Milan, April 29, 1814, *ibid.*, p. 134; Sommariva to Bellegarde, Milan, April 28, 1814, *Kriegs-Archiv* (Vienna), Feld Akten (Italien), 1814, Fasz. IV, No. 226; civic guard to MacFarlane, Milan, April 30, 1814, Ugo Foscolo, "Prose politiche," in *Opere complete*, Vol. II, pp. 558–559; Alberico Felber to Confalonieri, Milan, May 2, 1814, Confalonieri, *Memorie e lettere*, Vol. II, p. 295; provisional regency to deputation at Paris, Milan, May 5, 1814, *Museo* (Milan), "Carte Beccaria," Busta I, Carte 8, Fasc. I, No. 21; and Hager report, May 23, 1814, St. A. (Vienna), Kabinets-Akten, 1814, No. 1568.

[34] Strassoldo to Bellegarde, Milan, April 30, 1814, St. A. (Vienna), Kaiser Franz Akten, Fasz. XXVII, Kon. 1, Fo. 50.

[35] Domenico Pino and a few other former Muratists now advocated a British king; the others wanted Archduke Francis of Austria-Este as ruler (Spadoni, *Il moto del 20 aprile*, pp. 91–92 and 96).

[36] Provisional regency to deputation at Paris, Milan, May 10, 1814, *Museo* (Milan), "Carte Beccaria," Busta I, Carte 8, Fasc. I, No. 28.

[37] Proclamation, provisional regency, April 23, 1814, *The Times* (London), May 9, 1814.

[38] Strassoldo to Bellegarde, Milan, April 30, 1814, St. A. (Vienna), Kaiser Franz Akten, Fasz. XXVII, Kon. 1, Fo. 50.

or the duke of Clarence as their sovereign.[39] Although Bentinck's agent MacFarlane asserted that the large majority of Milanese desired an English king,[40] the estimate of Austrian observers that the pro-British faction constituted a small minority[41] is probably closer to the truth. Nearly all except the English officials were agreed that the majority of liberals wanted a prince from the Habsburg house as ruler,[42] particularly Archduke Francis of Austria-Este. Not only was Francis an Italian by birth but also the Milanese pro-independence party believed that his candidacy would have the powerful backing of the Habsburg emperor.[43]

It is obvious that, although they were divided as to whom they wanted for their sovereign, many of the leaders of the April 20 revolution, quite a few officials of the Milanese provisional government, a large number of intellectuals and professional people, most of the officers of the Italian army, and a good sprinkling of businessmen wished to have an independent kingdom. MacFarlane and Wilson,

---

[39] MacFarlane to Bentinck, Milan, May 6, 1814, Gallavresi, "La rivoluzione lombarda del 1814 e la politica inglese," pp. 153–154; Borda to Battista, Milan, May 3, 1814, Gallavresi, *Il carteggio intimo di Andrea Borda*, pp. 47–48; Domenico Spadoni, "Federazione e Re d'Italia mancati nel 1814–15," *Nuova Rivista Storica*, Vol. XV, Fasc. 5–6 (September–December, 1931), pp. 418–419; Antonio Capograssi, *Gl'inglesi in Italia durante le campagne napoleoniche: Lord W. Bentinck*, pp. 214–215.

[40] MacFarlane to Bentinck, Milan, May 6, 1814, Gallavresi, "La rivoluzione lombarda del 1814 e la politica inglese," pp. 153–154.

[41] Strassoldo to Bellegarde, Milan, April 30, 1814, St. A. (Vienna), Kaiser Franz Akten, Fasz. XXVII, Kon. 1, Fo. 50; Bellegarde to Emperor Francis, Verona, May 4, 1814, *ibid.*, Fo. 43.

[42] Strassoldo to Bellegarde, Milan, April 30, 1814, *ibid.*, Fos. 49–50; Bellegarde to Emperor Francis, Verona, May 4, 1814, *ibid.*, Fo. 43; Bellegarde to Emperor Francis, Verona, April 28, 1814, *Kriegs-Archiv* (Vienna), Feld Akten (Italien), 1814, Fasz. IV, ad No. 229 ½; Sommariva to Bellegarde, Milan, 11:30 P.M., April 28, 1814, *ibid.*, No. 226.

[43] Provisional regency to deputation at Paris, Milan, April 27 and May 10, 1814, *Museo* (Milan), "Carte Beccaria," Busta I, Carte 8, Fasc. I, Nos. 3 and 28; protocol, provisional regency, April 29, 1814, *Biblioteca Brera* (Milan), "Protocolli originali della reggenza provvisoria"; MacFarlane to Bentinck, Milan, April 29, 1814, Lemmi, *La restaurazione austriaca a Milano*, Appendix XVI, p. 418; Borda to Battista, May 10, 1814, Gallavresi, *Il carteggio intimo di Andrea Borda*, p. 53; Bellegarde to Metternich, Verona, April 26, 1814, St. A. (Vienna), Staatskanzlei, Provinzen, Lombardei-Venedig, Fasz. III, Kon. 3, Fo. 172; Spadoni, "Federazione e Re d'Italia mancati nel 1814–15," p. 418; Castro, "La restaurazione austriaca in Milano," p. 631.

the British agents in Milan in early May, 1814, staunch liberals by conviction and antipathetic to the views of their own Tory government, reported that the Austrians were highly unpopular and that the overwhelming vote of the Milanese was for independence.[44]

The liberal members of the Milanese provisional government, too, believed that the large majority of Lombards supported their cause. Impressed with the addresses that were dispatched daily to the provisional regency from "various municipalities and other respectable bodies of the state expressing most enthusiastic votes for a liberal and beneficent constitution which will assure the dignity and independence of the Kingdom of Italy,"[45] the president of the Lombard provisional regency Verri pointed out to Bellegarde that "the public vote and the universal desire" of the populace were for independence.[46] Confalonieri's friend Giulio Padulli also insisted that the universal cry was for independence,[47] while the deputation which the Milanese provisional regency dispatched to the Allied Powers at Paris handed a memoir to Emperor Francis informing him that the electoral colleges, the only representative body in Lombardy, had passed a resolution asking the Allied Powers to grant the Lombards independence and a liberal constitution.[48]

Although they believed that the pro-independence party was smaller than the British agents in Italy and the Milanese liberals estimated it to be, the chief Austrian officials in Milan—Strassoldo, Sommariva, and Bellegarde—likewise acknowledged that there was

[44] MacFarlane to Bentinck, Milan, April 29, 1814, Lemmi, *La restaurazione austriaca a Milano*, Appendix XVI, p. 418; MacFarlane to Castlereagh, Milan, May 4, 1814, *ibid.*, Appendix XVII, p. 420; Bentinck to Castlereagh, Genoa, May 1, 1814, Gallavresi, "La rivoluzione lombarda del 1814 e la politica inglese," p. 140; Wilson to Castlereagh, Milan, May 6, 1814, *ibid.*, p. 152; entries of April 27 and May 7, 1814, Wilson, *Diary of Travels, Personal Services, and Public Events*, Vol. II, pp. 360 and 364–365.

[45] Provisional regency to deputation at Paris, Milan, May 5, 1814, *Museo* (Milan), "Carte Beccaria," Busta I, Carte 8, Fasc. I, No. 21. See also Verri to Giovio, May 4, 1814, Giuseppe Gallavresi, "Testimonianze tratte dalle carte Giovio per la storia dei fatti del 1814," *Bollettino ufficiale del primo congresso storico del Risorgimento italiano* (1906), p. 134.

[46] Protocol, provisional regency, May 9, 1814, *Biblioteca di Brera* (Milan), "Protocolli originali della reggenza provvisoria."

[47] In a letter to Confalonieri, Milan, May 21, 1814, Gallavresi, *Carteggio del conte Federico Confalonieri*, Vol. I, p. 145.

[48] Italian deputation to Emperor Francis, n.d., St. A. (Vienna), Kaiser Franz Akten, Fasz. XXVII, Kon. 1, Fo. 115.

an important faction in Lombardy which demanded independence. Strassoldo expressed the opinion that, in general, the common people and, except for a few exalted heads, the nobility, mindful of the prosperity which they had enjoyed under Maria Theresa, were well disposed towards Austria. He admitted, however, that there was another party which longed for an independent kingdom, with an Austrian archduke as its ruler, while a third group, which was small and was composed mainly of tradespeople, wanted to be under British rule.[49] Sommariva affirmed that a large number of people wanted "an independent constitutional government" with "an Austrian prince as sovereign."[50] Bellegarde conceded that, although the Milanese, on the whole, were still demonstrating their old loyalty to the Habsburg imperial house, there was an important party which wanted an independent kingdom ruled by an Austrian archduke, while "another less important group, composed mainly of tradespeople," believed that they could establish such an independent kingdom under British protection.[51] The Austrian field marshal was greatly perturbed by the spirit of partisanship in Milan. "The people desire and like us," he wrote Metternich, "but there are several factions in whom we inspire anxiety and fear."[52] These cliques, Bellegarde complained, already acted as if they thought that "the fate of the kingdom rested in their hands."[53]

Of course, because of the confused and unstable atmosphere which prevailed in Milan during the first few weeks after the overthrow of the Napoleonic regime it is difficult to disentangle honest and unselfish motives from a spirit of partisanship largely inspired by a desire for personal gain. There is evidence that the dedicated idealism of some of the political leaders may perchance have been intermingled with more ignoble considerations. According to one promi-

[49] Strassoldo to Bellegarde, Milan, April 30, 1814, *ibid.*, Fos. 49–50; Strassoldo to Rosetti, Milan, May 3, 1814, *ibid.*, Fo. 62.

[50] Sommariva to Bellegarde, Milan, April 28, 1814, *Kriegs-Archiv* (Vienna), Feld Akten (Italien), 1814, Fasz. IV, No. 226.

[51] Bellegarde to Emperor Francis, Verona, April 28, 1814, and Milan, May 9, 1814, *ibid.*, Fasz. IV, ad No. 229½, and Fasz. V, No. 35½; Bellegarde to Emperor Francis, Verona, May 4, 1814, St. A. (Vienna), Kaiser Franz Akten, Fasz. XXVII, Kon. 1, Fo. 43.

[52] Bellegarde to Metternich, Milan, May 9, 1814, Lemmi, *La restaurazione austriaca a Milano*, Appendix XIX, p. 423.

[53] Bellegarde to Emperor Francis, Milan, May 9, 1814, St. A. (Vienna), Kaiser Franz Akten, Fasz. XXVII, Kon. 1, Fo. 60.

nent Milanese observer, many of the Milanese liberals were interested mainly in "exciting new tumults and sowing seeds of dissension in order to be able in some way to assure their existence."[54] Other Italians asserted that the provisional regency—one of the key centers of liberalism in late April and May 1814—itself was permeated with intrigues and cabals. Still other prominent Milanese maintained that two of the most distinguished members of the regency, Verri, the president, and Pino, were scheming how to gain power and influence and that they exalted the idea of a powerful, independent kingdom mainly to win popular support.[55]

In all likelihood some of the liberal leaders in Milan did participate in various cabals and intrigues. It is entirely plausible to assume that many a liberal, as well as many a conservative, believing that his own personal future was intimately bound up with the kind of government which would be accorded to Lombardy, took advantage of such connections and opportunities as he may have had to strive to procure a regime that he believed would promote his own personal well-being. However, this does not belie the conclusion that must be drawn from the testimony given by various British, Italian, and Austrian observers in Milan: that a sizable party of political activists in Lombardy, particularly in Milan, wanted some kind of an independent country with a "liberal" government. Most of the members of the provisional regency, the electoral colleges, and the civic guard, nearly all the Italian army officers, and a large number of intellectuals, professional people, and tradesmen and businessmen, in short, probably the majority of the bourgeoisie, plus a small sprinkling of liberal nobles, wanted independence.

It should be emphasized, however, that the overwhelming majority of the liberals were interested only in an independent *Lombard* kingdom, with such additions of territory as they could induce the Allied Powers to grant them. When they used the terms "national liberty" and "national customs" in their various addresses to the Aus-

---

[54] Alberico Felber to Confalonieri, Milan, May 2, 1815, Confalonieri, *Memorie e lettere*, Vol. II, p. 295. Also in Gallavresi, *Carteggio del conte Federico Confalonieri*, Vol. I, pp. 94–96. Gallavresi maintains that Rasini and not Felber wrote this letter.

[55] Rasini to Confalonieri, Milan, May 11, 1814, Confalonieri, *Memorie e lettere*, Vol. II, pp. 297–298; Alberico Felber [or Rasini?] to Confalonieri, Milan, May 2, 1814, *ibid.*, p. 295; Porro Lambertenghi to Confalonieri, Milan, May 13, 1814, Gallavresi, *Carteggio del conte Federico Confalonieri*, Vol. I, p. 123.

trian and English officials in Milan and to the Lombard people, they had in mind the liberty and independence of *Lombardy* and the habits and customs of the *Lombards* rather than of the Italian people as a whole. They were Lombard patriots, *not* Italian nationalists. It is true that a handful of Lombards thought vaguely in terms of the unification and independence of the whole Apennine peninsula, but in the spring of 1814 this group was still extremely small. The few "patriots" who championed Joachim Murat's cause before April 20 may perhaps be looked upon as genuine Italian nationalists, but after the Milanese revolution this group deserted the king of Naples and advocated either a British or an Austrian king and limited their demands to a little kingdom centering around Lombardy. Most of the members of the secret societies also seem to have thought in terms of the unification of the whole Italian peninsula, but, as we shall see, this group appears to have been of little strength in Lombardy in the spring of 1814. Then, too, Foscolo[56] and possibly a few other Milanese littérateurs may perhaps be looked upon as Italian nationalists. Nonetheless, in late April and in May, 1814, the number of genuine Italian nationalists—and their influence in Lombardy was limited almost exclusively to Milan and a few provincial capitals— was so infinitesimal that their influence was very probably almost completely negligible. Although the liberal ideas of the French Revolution had made a strong impression on the Lombard bourgeoisie, the nationalist feelings aroused by the French Revolution and the Napoleonic domination seem to have left little imprint upon them.

It must also be pointed out that the intelligentsia and the bourgeoisie constituted a comparatively small element of the Lombard population in 1814. The great bulk of the nobility and the clergy were pro-Austrian. So were the working classes and the peasants, who comprised the overwhelming majority of the population. As Domenico Spadoni, the best recent Italian authority, has said of the great mass of Italians, the Lombard peasants and working classes were "tired of war and incessant tribute and of the persecution of the clergy and the venerated pope" and "desired only the return of the old peaceful and religious regimes."[57] They wanted only peace and tranquillity and were well satisfied with the prospect of being

[56] See especially Ugo Foscolo to Countess Albany, last of August, 1815, Ugo Foscolo, "Epistolario," in *Opere complete,* Vol. II, p. 198.

[57] In his "Aspirazioni unitarie d'un austriacante nel 1814," *La Lombardia nel Risorgimento italiano,* Vol. XVIII (July, 1933), p. 71.

governed by a Habsburg regime which had given them the blessings of peace, security, and relative prosperity in the eighteenth century.[58]

Even the liberals in Milan accepted the news that the Allied Powers had assigned Lombardy as well as Venetia to the Habsburgs, which they first heard on May 13,[59] with little outward show of bitterness. Like the members of the provisional government, they adopted an attitude of making "a virtue out of necessity" and concentrated their efforts on attempting to procure the best possible concessions from their Austrian masters.[60] Since independence was unattainable, they now contended that Lombardy and Venetia together should be turned into a new kingdom, with Milan as its capital and with an Austrian archduke, endowed with extensive powers, as the emperor's viceroy. The emperor was to incorporate the iron crown of Lombardy in the imperial coat of arms. An "administrative, political, and judicial organization which conforms to the customs, habits, and needs" of the people[61] and some kind of "national representation" were to be assured to them. The inviolability of all contracts, including those for national goods that had been purchased during the French regime, was to be guaranteed; Austrian paper money was never to be circulated in the kingdom; and taxes and expenditures were to be decreased. Last, but by no means least, the emperor was to consult prominent Italians before deciding what type of government was to be instituted in Lombardy.[62]

To most of these demands except the one for national representation the Austrian emperor readily acquiesced. He told the deputa-

[58] Bellegarde report, May 31, 1814, St. A. (Vienna), Conferenz Akten, Ser. b, 1814, No. 1249; Nello Quilici "Felix Austria in Lombardia," *Nuovi problemi di politica, storia ed economia*, Vol. II, Fasc. 3–4 (March–April, 1931), p. 135.

[59] Verri to deputation at Paris, Milan, May 13, 1814, *Museo* (Milan), "Carte Beccaria," Busta I, Carte 8, Fasc. I, No. 36.

[60] Rasini to Confalonieri, June 8, 1814, Gallavresi, *Carteggio del conte Federico Confalonieri*, Vol. I, p. 182.

[61] Verri to deputation at Paris, Milan, May 13, 1814, *Museo* (Milan), "Carte Beccaria," Busta I, Carte 8, Fasc. I, No. 36. See also Verri to deputation at Paris, May 24, 1814, *ibid.*, No. 71.

[62] Verri to deputation at Paris, May 24, 1814, *ibid.*, No. 71; Porro Lambertenghi to Confalonieri, May 14, 1814, Gallavresi, *Carteggio del conte Federico Confalonieri*, Vol. I, pp. 124–125; Bellegarde to Metternich, Milan, June 4, 1814, Lemmi, *La restaurazione austriaca a Milano*, Appendix XXI, p. 425; Londonio to Beccaria, Milan, May 14 and 22, 1814, Gallavresi, "Per una futura biografia di F. Confalonieri," pp. 448–449 and 454–455.

tion sent by the Milanese provisional regency to the Allied Powers in Paris that, although he could not give the Lombards either independence or a constitution, he would accept and wear the Lombard iron crown and would create out of his Italian provinces a new kingdom, with Milan as its capital and with an Austrian archduke as viceroy to govern in the emperor's name. He understood that the Italians could not be ruled by German laws and German administrative forms; therefore, he would make arrangements to insure that the Italian language, institutions, and customs would be preserved as much as possible. He assured the deputation that he would attempt, at all costs, to revive the commerce and industry of their country. Taxes would be no higher than those in the other parts of his domain. All national goods sold during the previous regime were to remain in the hands of their possessors. Most important of all, as soon as a committee was appointed to devise a permanent administration for their country, several Lombards and Venetians would be called to Vienna to assist it.[63]

These promises apparently satisfied most of the liberals for the moment. When Bellegarde took control of Lombardy in the name of the Habsburg monarch on May 25 and 26 and formally announced its annexation to Austria on June 12, except for the tearing down of the Austrian coat of arms at Brivio[64] and disorders at the Canobbiana Theater in Milan on the night of June 14 when the pro-Allied play *The Battle of Leipzig* was shown,[65] there were no visible signs of opposition. To all outward appearances, the Lombards seemed to accept their destiny either with joy or with resignation.[66]

The fact that the liberal groups did not openly oppose the new

[63] Deputation at Paris to provisional government, Paris, May 7 (2 separate letters) and 27, 1814, *Museo* (Milan), "Carte Beccaria," Busta I, Carte 8, Fasc. II, Nos. 3, 6, and 60; Confalonieri to his wife, Paris, May 8 and 28, 1814, Confalonieri, *Memorie e lettere*, Vol. II, pp. 9–11 and 26–31; Borda to Battista, June 22, 1814, Gallavresi, *Il carteggio intimo di Andrea Borda*, pp. 55–60; Ettore Verga, "La deputazione dei collegi elettorali del regno d'Italia a Parigi nel 1814," *Archivio storico lombardo*, Vol. XXXI (1904), pp. 318–320 and 327–329.

[64] Sormani to provisional regency, Milan, June 7, 1814, A. S. (Milan), Presidenza di governo. Atti secreti, 1814, Cart. I, No. 24.

[65] Castro, "La restaurazione austriaca in Milano," pp. 619–620; Helfert, *La caduta della dominazione francese*, p. 147.

[66] [Belgiojoso-Trivulzio, Principessa Cristina], *Étude sur l'histoire de la Lombardie dans les trente dernières années, ou des causes du défaut d'énergie chez les Lombards. Manuscrit d'un Italien, publié par H. Lézat de Pons*, p. 99; Cusani, *Storia di Milano*, Vol. VII, p. 202.

order in Lombardy, however, did not mean that they were satisfied with it[67] or that they found no reason to complain about it when the novelty of the change in government wore off. In fact, during the summer of 1814 many of them discovered plenty of things to grumble about.

Although the Austrian commissioner plenipotentiary Field Marshal Bellegarde was, on the whole, quite popular, malcontented persons dissected both his shortcomings[68] and those of his dictatorial chief deputy, Baron von Rosetti.[69] Some Lombards were already disheartened because a permanent government suitable to the customs and religious habits of the people had not yet been instituted.[70] Some of the pro-Austrian clergy and nobles were annoyed because their former privileges had not been immediately restored.[71] Other Habsburg partisans expressed indignation because the supporters of the previous French regime, former republicans, immoral priests, and men without religious principles had been allowed to retain their posts, while loyal pro-Austrians were not only excluded from administrative positions but also were allegedly despised and subjected to the vengeance of anti-Austrian intriguers.[72] The liberals, on the other hand, complained loudly that too many Germans were occupying positions in the Lombard government.[73]

---

[67] Bellegarde report, May 31, 1814, St. A. (Vienna), Conferenz Akten, Ser. b, 1814, No. 1249; Bellegarde to Metternich, Milan, September 22, 1814, St. A. (Vienna), Staatskanzlei, Provinzen, Lombardei-Venedig, Fasz. III, Kon. 4, Fo. 106.

[68] Freddi to Hager, December 26, 1814, Weil, *Les dessous du Congrès de Vienne*, Vol. I, p. 745; Castro, "I ricordi autobiografici di Bossi," p. 911; entries of June 30 and July 7, 1814, *Biblioteca Ambrosiana* (Milan), Mantovani, "Diario di Milano," Vol. V, pp. 286 and 288. See also *ante*, p. 78.

[69] Hager report, September 5, 1814, St. A. (Vienna), Kabinets-Akten, 1814, No. 220; Castro, "La restaurazione austriaca in Milano," p. 624; Lemmi, *La restaurazione austriaca a Milano*, p. 304.

[70] Entry of August 1, 1814, *Biblioteca Ambrosiana* (Milan), Mantovani, "Diario di Milano," Vol. V, p. 296.

[71] Ugo Foscolo to Countess Albany, Milan, June 24, 1814, Foscolo, "Epistolario," in *Opere complete*, Vol. II, p. 187.

[72] Hager reports of June 25 and 29 and July 16, 1814, St. A. (Vienna), Conferenz Akten, Ser. b, 1814, Nos. 1262, 1276, and 1407; Castro, "La restaurazione austriaca in Milano," p. 624.

[73] Teresa Confalonieri Casati to Confalonieri, Milan, July 27 and August 6, 1814, Gallavresi, *Carteggio del conte Federico Confalonieri*, Vol. I, pp. 224–225 and 229–230.

There was genuine alarm and deep concern because so many employees of the former Kingdom of Italy were being dismissed[74] and because ecclesiastical pensions were several months in arrears.[75] Lombards of all classes were vexed over the necessity of providing quarters and food for so many Austrian troops[76] and the failure of the Habsburgs to abolish the burdensome French military conscription system which had angered them for so many years.[77] The Milanese were depressed because their city, instead of being the seat of an impressive court, had sunk to the rank of a mere provincial capital.[78] The rich found fault with the fact that the high taxes which they had paid under the French regime had not been substantially reduced[79] and murmured because the Austrians had suspended the payment of interest on state bonds.[80] Commercial people were fretting because the harbor of Venice had still not been united with Lombardy,[81] while the plebeians were chafing over the high price of foodstuffs.[82]

As the summer progressed, although various confidants of the Austrian police were sending in soothing assurances about the pro-Aus-

---

[74] Daily police report, Olona department police prefecture, Milan, June 16, 1814, A. S. (Milan), Presidenza di governo. Atti secreti, 1814, Cart. I, No. 9870; Hager report, September 3, 1814, St. A. (Vienna), Conferenz Akten, Ser. b, 1814, No. 1658.

[75] Hager report, September 3, 1814, St. A. (Vienna), Conferenz Akten, Ser. b, 1814, No. 1658.

[76] See ante, pp. 111–113.

[77] Hager report, June 29, 1814, St. A. (Vienna), Conferenz Akten, Ser. b, 1814, No. 1276; Hager to Bellegarde, Vienna, July 17, 1814, A. S. (Milan), Presidenza di governo. Atti secreti, 1814, Cart. II, No. 124.

[78] Helfert, *Kaiser Franz und die Stiftung des Lombardo-Venetianischen Königreichs*, pp. 104–105; Wiedemann-Warnhelm, *Die Wiederherstellung der österreichischen Vorherrschaft in Italien*, p. 41.

[79] Hager report, June 29, 1814, St. A. (Vienna), Conferenz Akten, Ser. b, 1814, No. 1276; Hager to Bellegarde, Vienna, July 17, 1814, A. S. (Milan), Presidenza di governo. Atti secreti, 1814, Cart. II, No. 124/P.R.; Silvio Pellico to his brother Francesco, Milan, June 20, 1814, P. Ilario Rinieri, *Della Vita e delle Opere di Silvio Pellico. Da lettere e documenti inediti*, Vol. I, p. 88.

[80] Pingaud, "La Lombardie en 1814," p. 460.

[81] Hager report, June 29, 1814, St. A. (Vienna), Conferenz Akten, Ser. b, 1814, No. 1276; Hager to Bellegarde, Vienna, July 17, 1814, A. S. (Milan), Presidenza di governo. Atti secreti, 1814, Cart. II, No. 124/P.R.

[82] Ugo Foscolo to Countess Albany, Milan, June 24, 1814, Foscolo, "Epistolario," in *Opere complete*, Vol. II, p. 187.

trian sentiments of the Lombard people,[83] there were reports that a small minority of malcontents were using various opportunities to express their dislike for the Habsburg regime,[84] particularly in Milan and Brescia but also to a lesser extent in Bergamo and Pavia.[85] The suspicious Austrian police ran across a rumor that an anti-Austrian paper was secretly being published in Milan.[86] At Rivarolo,[87] Brescia,[88] and Lecco[89] they busied themselves with attempting to discover the malefactors who had torn down Austrian insignia from public places. Every now and then they occupied themselves with ferreting out the authors of seditious libels[90] or with searching for persons who had secretly posted Napoleonic coats of arms or statues in public places either to express their esteem for the past system or to vent their spleen upon the Habsburgs.[91]

Isolated and relatively insignificant as these demonstrations of anti-Austrian feeling were, they alarmed Emperor Francis enough to

[83] Pirelli di Varena to Bellegarde, Varena, July 15, 1814, A. S. (Milan), Presidenza di governo. Atti secreti, 1814, Cart. I, No. 57/P.R.; Hager report, August 2, 1814, St. A. (Vienna), Conferenz Akten, Ser. b, 1814, No. 1506; police report, Milan, August 9, 1814, *Kriegs-Archiv* (Vienna), Feld Akten (Italien) 1814, Fasz. VIII, No. 34.

[84] Hager to Bellegarde, Vienna, July 17, 1814, A. S. (Milan), Presidenza di governo. Atti secreti, 1814, Cart. II, No. 124/P.R.; Hegardt to Engestroem, Vienna, July 30, 1814, Weil, *Les dessous du Congrès de Vienne*, Vol. I, p. 35; Bellegarde to Metternich, Milan, September 22, 1814, St. A. (Vienna), Staatskanzlei, Provinzen, Lombardei-Venedig, Fasz. III, Kon. 4, Fo. 106.

[85] Hager to Staats-Conferenz, June 8, 1814, St. A. (Vienna), Conferenz Akten, Ser. b, 1814, No. 1153; Hager to Bellegarde, Vienna, July 17, 1814, A. S. (Milan), Presidenza di governo. Atti secreti, 1814, Cart. II, No. 124; Raab to Hager, Padua, June 25, 1814, Lemmi, *La restaurazione austriaca a Milano*, Appendix XXII, p. 428.

[86] Police report, Milan, August 7, 1814, *Kriegs-Archiv* (Vienna), Feld Akten (Italien), 1814, Fasz. VIII, No. 25.

[87] General police directory bulletin, Milan, July 20, 1814, A. S. (Milan), Presidenza di governo. Atti secreti, 1814, Cart. I, No. 61/P.R.

[88] General police directory bulletin, Milan, July 30, 1814, *ibid.*, Cart. II, No. 108/P.R.

[89] General police directory bulletin, Milan, July 6, 1814, *ibid.*, Cart. I, Fasc. 24/P.R., No. 9.

[90] Olona department, police prefecture report, Milan, June 18, 1814, *ibid.*, Cart. I, Fasc. 18, No. 9978; general police directory bulletin, Milan, November 26, 1814, *ibid.*, Cart. VI, No. 823/P.R.

[91] Hager to Bellegarde, Vienna, November 1, 1814, *ibid.*, Cart. V, No. 716/P.R.

prompt him to order Bellegarde, on July 16, to keep a close watch on public opinion in the Italian provinces.[92] No doubt his trepidation over the anti-Habsburg sentiments manifested by a small group of disgruntled inhabitants would have been wholly unwarranted had not the pro-independence cause been championed by powerful forces which gave strong encouragement to Austria's enemies in Lombardy-Venetia: influential officers of the Italian army, liberal British agents and travelers, the king of Elba and ex-emperor of the French, the ambitious king of Naples, and a number of secret societies. Of these groups the one that constituted the greatest immediate danger to the Austrians was the Italian army.

The attitude of the Italian army, particularly that of its officers, appeared especially ominous to the Austrians. For a long time this organization had been a hotbed of liberalism and of the minute bit of incipient nationalism that was actually developing in the Kingdom of Italy. Several of its officers strongly supported Murat's efforts to make himself king of a united Italy. Defeated and demoralized after the cause for which they had battled for eighteen years was lost, the officers of the Italian army were in an excited and turbulent mood which foreboded danger to the Austrians.[93] When they learned of the Milanese revolution of April 20, several of the officers insisted that Prince Eugene march to the Lombard capital at the head of his army and recapture it. After the viceroy refused to approve their foolhardy enterprise, Generals Giuseppe Palombini, Amilcare Paolucci, and Teodoro Lechi went to Milan in a vain attempt to induce General Pino to lead the army against the Austrians.[94]

Immediately after Prince Eugene capitulated to the Allied Powers the officers of the Italian army sent a list of demands to the Lombard provisional regency and urged it to entreat the Allied Powers to grant their petition.[95] The officers requested that the government support

[92] Hager to Bellegarde, Vienna, July 17, 1814, Lemmi, *La restaurazione austriaca a Milano*, Appendix XXV, pp. 432–433. The original copy of this letter is in A. S. (Milan), Presidenza di governo. Atti secreti, 1814, Cart. II, No. 120/ P.R.

[93] Bellegarde to Emperor Francis, Milan, March 26, 1816, St. A. (Vienna), Kaiser Franz Akten, Fasz. XV, Kon. 2, Fo. 120.

[94] Giovanni de Castro, *I congiurati lombardi del 1814. Conferenza tenuta al Circolo Filologico di Milano l'8 aprile 1894*, pp. 10–11; Helfert, *La restaurazione austriaca a Milano*, pp. 221–223; Spadoni, *Il moto del 20 aprile*, pp. 195–201.

[95] Bellegarde to Metternich, Verona, April 26, 1814, St. A. (Vienna), Staats-

their petition.[95] The officers requested that the government support invalids, veterans, and orphans, provide pensions to retired officers and soldiers, and educate the sons of military men, as the previous French regime had done. All military ranks, decorations, and pensions were to be preserved. Every prisoner of war was to be freed, and the troops were to continue receiving the same pay.[96]

Instead of assuring the Italian officers that their legitimate demands would be granted, Emperor Francis commanded Bellegarde to dissolve the Italian army.[97] The field marshal was both surprised and perturbed over his sovereign's order. Immediately he protested to Vienna that this measure was needlessly cruel to soldiers who had fought as long and as well as those in the Italian army. Arguing that these soldiers would be extremely useful to the Habsburgs, he enjoined the government to incorporate the largest possible number of Italian regiments into the Austrian army.[98] The Habsburg sovereign yielded to his commissioner plenipotentiary's entreaties and agreed to absorb the Italian troops into his own army, provided that any soldier who was not an inhabitant of Lombardy or Venetia would not be accepted in the Habsburg military forces and that permission would be freely given to anyone to leave the service who wished to do so.[99]

The emperor's assurances that the Italian soldiers would not be callously dismissed, however, did not have the beneficial effects on the morale of the Italian army for which Bellegarde had hoped. There were numerous desertions. Not only did many soldiers hate the Germans but also they feared that their wages would be less for

[95] Bellegarde to Metternich, Verona, April 26, 1814, St. A. (Vienna), Staatskanzlei, Provinzen, Lombardei-Venedig, Fasz. III, Kon. 3, Fo. 173. Also in Lemmi, *La restaurazione austriaca a Milano*, Appendix XIV, p. 414.

[96] Demands sent to the government by the generals and corps commanders of the Italian army, n.d., St. A. (Vienna), Staatskanzlei, Provinzen, Lombardei-Venedig, Fasz. III, Kon. 3, Fo. 181. Also in Lemmi, *La restaurazione austriaca a Milano*, Appendix V, pp. 402–403; and in Spadoni, *Il moto del 20 aprile*, pp. 202–203.

[97] Bellegarde to Metternich Verona, April 26, 1814, St. A. (Vienna), Staatskanzlei, Provinzen, Lombardei-Venedig, Fasz. III, Kon. 3, Fo. 173. Also in Lemmi, *La restaurazione austriaca a Milano*, Appendix XIV, p. 414.

[98] Bellegarde to Metternich, April 26, 1814, St. A. (Vienna), Staatskanzlei, Provinzen, Lombardei-Venedig, Fasz. III, Kon. 3, Fos. 173–174. Also in Lemmi, *La restaurazione austriaca a Milano*, Appendix XIV, pp. 414–415.

[99] Emperor Francis to Bellegarde, Paris, May 14, 1814, St. A. (Vienna), Conferenz Akten, Ser. b, 1814, No. 996.

serving the Austrians than the French.[100] Other bitterly discontented and disillusioned troops committed sundry excesses and hurled insults and threats against real or alleged enemies. At Cremona soldiers under General Carlo Zucchi's orders clamored for "death to all nobles, priests, and aristocrats," while some of the military forces stationed in Milan were almost as truculent in denouncing those who had aroused their ire.[101] Fights between Italian and Austrian soldiers became almost commonplace.[102] Disorders and insubordination were rampant.[103] The light infantry troops of the royal guard revolted against their officers,[104] and a number of other enlisted men made it clear that they were ready to follow this example at a moment's notice.

The spirit of the Italian army seemed so dangerous to Bellegarde that he appointed a military commission on May 20 to make inquiries into the conduct of the soldiers and to single out persons who were guilty of infractions against army discipline.[105] To remove disgruntled and trouble-making officers from Milan and other centers of discontent, he ordered all Italian officers immediately to join the corps to which they had been assigned.[106] Those temporarily without any specific command were to be quartered in two special barracks, one at Casalmaggiore and the other at Vimercate, where they could eas-

---

[100] Pallavicini to Confalonieri, Milan, May 7, 1814, Gallavresi, *Carteggio del conte Federico Confalonieri*, Vol. I, pp. 106–107; entry of May 19, 1814, Lemmi, *Diario del Huegel*, pp. 101–102.

[101] Teresa Confalonieri Casati to Confalonieri, Milan, May 6, 1814, Gallavresi, *Carteggio del conte Federico Confalonieri*, Vol. I, p. 105.

[102] Teresa Confalonieri Casati to Confalonieri, Milan, May 6, 24, and 27, 1814, *ibid.*, pp. 105, 151, and 158; entry of May 22, 1814, Lemmi, *Diario del Huegel*, p. 102; Pagani report, Milan, May 27, 1814, A. S. (Milan), Presidenza di governo. Atti secreti, 1814, Cart. I, Fasc. 17/P.R., No. 8668; Sormani to provisional government, Milan, May 31, 1814, *ibid.*, Fasc. 24, No. 4; Hager to Staats-Conferenz, June 8, 1814, St. A. (Vienna), Conferenz Akten, Ser. b, 1814, No. 1153.

[103] Entry of May 22, 1814, *Biblioteca Ambrosiana* (Milan), Mantovani, "Diario di Milano," Vol. V, p. 276.

[104] Entry of May 21, 1814, Lemmi, *Diario del Huegel*, p. 102.

[105] *Oesterreichischer Beobachter*, No. 157 (June 6, 1814), pp. 846–847; Teresa Confalonieri Casati to Confalonieri, May 21, 1814, Gallavresi, *Carteggio del conte Federico Confalonieri*, Vol. I, p. 143; entry of May 22, 1814, *Biblioteca Ambrosiana* (Milan), Mantovani, "Diario di Milano," Vol. V, pp. 267–268.

[106] Entry of May 21, 1814, Lemmi, *Diario del Huegel*, p. 102.

ily be observed. Then, in line with the emperor's instructions, the Austrian field marshal dismissed all officers who were not domiciled in Lombardy or Venetia.[107] On May 30 he published a proclamation informing the populace that enlisted men and officers of the Italian army "who had not strayed from the path of duty or honor" would be accepted for service in special regiments in the Habsburg army.[108] On June 1 the Milanese departmental guard battalion and the royal guard regiments were discharged since they did not fit into the Austrian scheme of military organization.[109] Also, a commission, composed of two Austrian and two Italian generals, was appointed to effectuate the reorganization of those Italian army corps which were to be incorporated into the Habsburg military forces.[110] Six days later dismissed Italian officers and enlisted men were prohibited from wearing military uniforms or insignia.[111] On the 13th the Italian troops were forbidden to wear the tricolor cockade.[112]

Nearly all the Italian generals and most of the other officers accepted the invitation to enlist in the Habsburg military forces in the same rank which they had attained under the French, and several of them, like Giuseppe Palombini, Filippo Severoli, Ferdinando Ceccopieri, Vacani, and Luigi Mazzuchelli, rose to high rank in the Austrian army.[113] Many enlisted men were also satisfied with the assurances given to them that they could continue their military ca-

---

[107] Cusani, *Storia di Milano*, Vol. VII, p. 238; Spadoni, *Il moto del 20 aprile*, pp. 212 and 229; Italy. Ministero della guerra, *Gli Italiani in Illiria e nella Venezia (1813–1814)*, p. 187.

[108] Bellegarde order, Milan, May 30, 1814, *Oesterreichischer Beobachter*, No. 164 (June 13, 1814), pp. 877–878.

[109] Decree, provisional regency, Milan, May 27, 1814, A. S. (Milan), Uffici e Tribunali Regi. Parte Moderne, Cart. LIII (*Appuntamenti 1814*), no number given; entry of June 1, 1814, *Biblioteca Ambrosiana* (Milan), Mantovani, "Diario di Milano," Vol. V, p. 272; Alessandro Zanoli, *Sulla milizia cisalpino-italiana. Cenni storico-statistici dal 1796 al 1814*, Vol. I, p. 36.

[110] Cusani, *Storia di Milano*, Vol. VII, p. 239; Helfert, *La caduta della dominazione francese*, p. 141; Lemmi, *La restaurazione austriaca a Milano*, p. 312.

[111] Decree, Mazzucchelli, Milan, June 6, 1814, *Giornale italiano*, No. 157 (June 6, 1814), p. 639.

[112] Decree, Bellegarde, n.d., *Giornale di Venezia*, No. 77 (June 16, 1814), pp. 3–4; Weil, *Murat*, Vol. I, p. 155.

[113] Cusani, *Storia di Milano*, Vol. VII, p. 240; Zanoli, *Sulla milizia cisalpino-italiana*, Vol. I, p. 35; entry of July 20, 1814, *Biblioteca Ambrosiana* (Milan), Mantovani, "Diario di Milano," Vol. V, p. 293.

reers.[114] A few officers, like General Pino, and some of the enlisted men, however, refused to serve under the Austrians, while both the officers and soldiers of the royal guards loudly denounced the dissolving of their regiments.[115] All told, the number of bitterly discontented Italian military prompted Bellegarde to admonish the authorities in Vienna to proceed with extreme prudence in dealing with them.[116]

As spring passed into summer, rumors circulated that the Italian army would soon be sent to the Banat or to Transylvania[117] and that the large majority of officers were to be dismissed.[118] The Italian soldiers became more dissatisfied than ever before. Vowing that they would never serve under the Habsburgs,[119] angry officers hissed at some of their former companions-in-arms who were wearing Austrian uniforms.[120] The police reported that every now and then drunken Italian soldiers were going about shouting "Long live Napoleon!" in the streets of Milan.[121] At Como Italian troopers threw cockades on the ground in disgust and spat on them, amidst cries of "Long live Napoleon!"[122] When an Austrian general inspected them, some of them even had the effrontery to shout *vivats* to the former

114 Pagani report, Milan, May 28, 1814, A. S. (Milan), Presidenza di governo. Atti secreti, 1814, Cart. I, Fasc. 17/P.R., No. 8717.

115 Department of Olona, police report, Milan, June 3, 1814, *ibid.*, Fasc. 18/P.R., No. 9100; Teresa Confalonieri Casati to Confalonieri, Milan, June 1, 1814, Gallavresi *Carteggio del conte Federico Confalonieri*, Vol. I, pp. 169–170.

116 Bellegarde to Metternich, Milan, June 4, 1814, Lemmi, *La restaurazione austriaca a Milano*, Appendix XXI, pp. 425–426.

117 Hager report, June 25, 1814, St. A. (Vienna), Conferenz Akten, Ser. b, 1814, No. 1262; Hager to Bellegarde, Vienna, July 14, 1814, A. S. (Milan), Presidenza di governo. Atti secreti, 1814, Cart. I, No. 89/P.R.

118 Helfert, *La caduta della dominazione francese*, p. 170; Lemmi, *La restaurazione austriaca a Milano*, pp. 312–313.

119 Anonymous to Hager, Milan, June 23, 1814, A. S. (Milan), Presidenza di governo. Atti secreti, 1814, Cart. I, No. 89/P.R.; Achille Monti, *Giovanni Rasori nella storia della scienza e dell'idea nazionale*. In *Corsi autunnali per Italiani e stranieri tenuti nella R. Università di Pavia. Lezione e conferenze dell'anno 1928*, p. 72.

120 Teresa Confalonieri Casati to Confalonieri, Milan, August 6, 1814, Gallavresi, *Carteggio del conte Federico Confalonieri*, Vol. I, p. 230.

121 Pagani report, Milan, June 5, 1814, A. S. (Milan), Presidenza di governo. Atti secreti, 1814, Cart. I, Fasc. 18/P.R., No. 9292; general police directory bulletin, Milan, August 6, 1814, *ibid.*, Cart. II, No. 156/P.R.

122 Teresa Confalonieri Casati to Confalonieri, Milan, July 6, 1814, Gallavresi, *Carteggio del conte Federico Confalonieri*, Vol. I, p. 212.

French emperor.[123] In Brescia on the night of June 26–27, a large number of inebriated Italian officers openly took an oath that they would never serve the Habsburgs and then broke out in loud denunciations of everything Austrian.[124] In various places Italian soldiers took advantage of every opportunity to insult the Germans, and the number of fights between them and the German men-of-arms was just as great as, if not greater than, in May.[125] A large number of troops deserted rather than become part of the Austrian army. Some of them took up service with Murat's forces, while others either returned to private life or roamed the countryside as brigands.[126] The Habsburg police directory was so alarmed by the bitter discontent and the worrisome radicalism of many Italian officers and enlisted men that it urged the emperor to remove the Italian troops from Italy to another part of the empire.[127]

During the summer of 1814 Emperor Francis still believed that it was advisable to take such a drastic step. However, he was disturbed enough by the reports of the poor morale of his Italian troops to issue instructions to his army commander in Italy to draw up plans as rapidly as possible to organize the Italian troops according to the same scheme and to put them under the same regulations as those

---

[123] Borda to Battista, July 6, 1814, Gallavresi, *Il carteggio intimo di Andrea Borda*, p. 60.

[124] Raab to Hager, Padua, July 2, 1814, *Kriegs-Archiv* (Vienna), Hof Kriegs-Rath–Präsidial Akten, Italien, 1814, Fasz. VII, No. 22; Hager report, July 13, 1814, Conferenz Akten, Ser. b, 1814, No. 1371; general police directory bulletin, Milan, July 6, 1814, A. S. (Milan), Presidenza di governo. Atti secreti, 1814, Cart. I, Fasc. 24/P.R., No. 9; Bellegarde to Hager, Milan, July 24, 1814, *ibid.*, No. 67/R.

[125] See especially entry of July 15, 1814, *Biblioteca Ambrosiana* (Milan), Mantovani, "Diario di Milano," Vol. V, pp. 290–291; Teresa Confalonieri Casati to Confalonieri, Milan, July 20, 1814, Gallavresi, *Carteggio del conte Federico Confalonieri*, Vol. I, p. 221; Pagani reports, Milan, June 3 and July 19, 1814, A. S. (Milan), Presidenza di governo. Atti secreti, 1814, Cart. I, Fasc. 18/P.R., No. 9100, and Cart. II, Fasc. 114, No. 12,393; general police directory bulletins, Milan, July 6 and 16 and August 3, 1814, *ibid.*, Cart. I, Fasc. 24/P.R., No. 9, Cart. I, No. 38/P.R., and Cart. II, No. 160/P.R.; and Hager to Bellegarde, Vienna, July 25, 1814, *ibid.*, Cart. I, No. 151/P.R.

[126] Weil, *Murat*, Vol. I, pp. 184–185; Lemmi, *La restaurazione austriaca a Milano*, pp. 308–309; Cusani, *Storia di Milano*, Vol. VII, p. 202.

[127] Hager to Staats-Conferenz, June 8, 1814, St. A. (Vienna), Conferenz Akten, Ser. b, 1814, No. 1153; Raab to Hager, Padua, June 25, 1814, Lemmi, *La restaurazione austriaca a Milano*, Appendix XXII, p. 427.

used in the German states of the empire.[128] These plans were completed early enough to be put into effect on July 31. The Italian troops were formed into infantry regiments, stationed at Como, Brescia, and Montechiari; four light infantry battalions, quartered at Bergamo, Varese, and Casalmaggiore; and one cavalry regiment. Although these units were all placed under the supreme command of Austrian officers, many Italian officers, including several who were known to be strongly anti-Austrian in sentiment, were admitted into Austrian service at the same rank which they had held in the French-Italian army. Those who could not immediately be assigned were put on half-pay and sent to quarters at Casalmaggiore, Gallarate, and Pavia.[129]

The fact that most of the Italian troops were accepted by the Habsburg army, however, did little to alleviate their discontent. Many of the officers on half-pay, looking upon their new status as humiliating, resigned their commissions and either went home or joined the Neapolitan army. Those who were dismissed inveighed loudly against a regime that dealt with them so shabbily and did all they could to stir up hatred against the Habsburgs among the populace.[130] Disgruntled Italian soldiers continued to participate in noisy quarrels, bloody fights, and duels with Austrian troops.[131] In spite of General Bellegarde's repeated invitations to deserters to resume service in the army under favorable terms, including a full amnesty,[132]

---

[128] Emperor Francis to Bellegarde, Schönbrunn, July 12, 1814, St. A. (Vienna), Conferenz Akten, Ser. b, 1814, No. 1249.

[129] Zanoli, *Sulla milizia cisalpino-italiana*, Vol. I, p. 36; Italy. Ministero della guerra, *Gli Italiani in Illiria e nella Venezia* (*1813–1814*), pp. 187–188; Lemmi, *La restaurazione austriaca a Milano*, pp. 314–315; Helfert, *La caduta della dominazione francese*, pp. 171-174.

[130] Raab to Hager, Padua, August 13, and Venice, October 6, 1814, Lemmi, *La restaurazione austriaca a Milano*, Appendices XXIX and XXXVII, pp. 436 and 445; Bellegarde to Hager, Milan, November 22, 1814, *ibid.*, Appendix XLIII, p. 454; police report, Milan, November 23, 1814, *Kriegs-Archiv* (Vienna), Feld Akten (Italien), 1814, Fasz. XI, No. 46; Hager to Bellegarde, Vienna, November 14, 1814, A. S. (Milan), Presidenza di governo. Atti secreti, 1814, Cart. VII, No. 856/P.R.

[131] General police directory bulletins, August 13 and December 10, 1814, A. S. (Milan), Presidenza di governo. Atti secreti, 1814, Cart. II, No. 202/P.R., and Cart. VII, No. 874/P.R.

[132] Bellegarde orders, Milan, July 28, August 12, 19, and 30, and October 25, 1814, *Atti del governo lombardo*, 1814, pp. 103–107, 115–117, 120–121, 125–128, and 145–149; notification, August 26, 1814, *Collezione di leggi venete*,

many Italian soldiers still left their military units illegally and roamed the countryside, plundering and stealing.[133] The report that Italian soldiers were purchasing knives and stilettos[134] again prompted the Austrians seriously to consider the advisability of transferring the Italian regiments to another part of the empire.[135]

Dissatisfied officers and enlisted men of the former Italian army contributed powerfully towards keeping a pro-independence sentiment alive in Lombardy and Venetia during the summer and fall of 1814. So did the encouragement given to the Italian liberals by various British agents and travelers. For several months the Austrians were apprehensive over the influence upon Italian malcontents of Lord William Bentinck, a liberal English Whig and British commander-in-chief in the Mediterranean during the recent wars against the French.[136] Encouraged by the foreign office in London, Bentinck had during the course of the Napoleonic wars worked hard to stir up a revolt against the French empire in Italy similar to the insurrections which the English had already assisted in provoking in Spain and Portugal. Besides overthrowing the enemy governments in the Apennine peninsula, Bentinck evidently hoped to increase British political influence there, to gain a monopoly of trade for the British in much of the peninsula, and to help make Great Britain master of the Mediterranean by, among other things, establishing an independent kingdom in northern Italy, with a liberal political system copied after the one in Great Britain.[137] To further the realization of this

---

1813–1814, Vol. II, p. 35; entries of August 6 and November 3, 1814, *Biblioteca Ambrosiana* (Milan), Mantovani, "Diario di Milano," Vol. V, pp. 300 and 321; protocol, provisional regency, October 1, 1814, *Biblioteca di Brera* (Milan), "Protocolli originali della reggenza provvisoria"; Schwarzenberg proclamation, n.d., A. S. (Milan), Presidenza di governo. Atti secreti, 1814, Cart. IV, No. 416.

[133] General police directory bulletins, August 10 and 24, October 19, and December 7, 1814, A. S. (Milan), Presidenza di governo. Atti secreti, 1814, Cart. II, Nos. 178/P.R. and 227/P.R., Cart. IV, No. 545/P.R., and Cart. VII, No. 873/P.R.

[134] Police report, September 10, 1814, *Kriegs-Archiv* (Vienna), Feld Akten (Italien), 1814, Fasz. IX, No. 39d.

[135] Raab to Hager, Padua, August 13, 1814, Lemmi, *La restaurazione austriaca a Milano*, Appendix XXIX, p. 436.

[136] Raab to Hager, Venice, October 6, 1814, *ibid.*, Appendix XXXVII, pp. 444–445; Bellegarde to Metternich, Milan, January 1, 1814, St. A. (Vienna), Staatskanzlei, Provinzen, Lombardei-Venedig, Fasz. IV, Kon. 4, Fos. 7–10.

[137] Antonio Capograssi, "L'unità d'Italia nel pensiero di Lord William Bentinck," *Rassegna storica del Risorgimento*, Vol. XXI, Fasc. 2 (March-April, 1934),

aim, he issued a proclamation at Leghorn on March 14 appealing to the Italians to assert their rights and their liberty.[138] Then, on April 26, he announced the restoration of the old Genoese Republic, together with the constitution in force in 1797, with such modifications as "the general vote" and "the general welfare" required.[139]

Since Bentinck was known to be an ardent champion of Italian independence, it was logical that after the Milanese revolution of April 20 various Lombard liberal groups sent deputations to Genoa to request Bentinck's aid for their projects for independence and constitutional government. After the British commander-in-chief sent General MacFarlane to Milan as his personal representative, "generals, statesmen, merchants, and persons from every social class" came with their liberal projects to him[140] and to Sir Robert Wilson, the British attaché to the Austrian army in Italy, who had gone to the Lombard capital from Verona. The two British officials not only promised to send their proposals to London[141] but also gave the Milanese liberals strong encouragement to believe that their desires would be sup-

---

pp. 244–245; John Rosselli, "Il progetto italiano di Lord William Bentinck, 1811–1815," *Rivista Storica Italiana*, Vol. LXXIX, Fasc. 2 (1967), pp. 355–404; Capograssi, *Gl'inglesi in Italia durante le campagne napoleoniche*, pp. 176–185; Renato Soriga, "Augusto Bozzi Granville e la Rivista 'L'Italico,'" *Bollettino della Società pavese di storia patria*, Vol. XIV (1914), p. 270; Alessandro Luzio, *La Massoneria sotto il Regno Italico e la restaurazione austriaco* (estratto dall'*Archivio storico lombardo*, Anno XLIV, Fasc. II), p. 289. The pagination of the reprint is given as pp. 241–352. A copy of the above work, which is obviously a reprint from the original article in the *Archivio storico lombardo*, Vol. XLIV (1917–1918), is in The University of Texas library. This writer has also taken notes from another edition of the same article in the Museo del Risorgimento italiano in Milan. In this edition, which was published in Milan in 1918 by L. F. Cogliati, the pages are numbered 1–116. Since the pagination in the edition published by the *Archivio storico lombardo* in 1921 is the same as that of the original article, all the author's references are to it.

138 T. C. Hansard, *The Parliamentary Debates from the Year 1803 to the Present Time*, Vol. XXIX (November 8, 1814–March 3, 1815), p. 727.

139 Bentinck proclamation, Genoa, April 26, 1814, St. A. (Vienna), Kaiser Franz Akten, Fasz. XXVII, Kon. 1, Fos. 68–69.

140 MacFarlane to Bentinck, Milan, April 29, 1814, Lemmi, *La restaurazione austriaca a Milano*, Appendix XVI, p. 418. See also Dario Biandrà Trecchi, *Milano e gli inglese nel 1814* (estratto dal *Rassegna storica del Risorgimento*, Vol. XIII [1926]), pp. 521–546.

141 Borda to Battista, July 6, 1814, Gallavresi, *Il carteggio intimo di Andrea Borda*, p. 60.

ported by the British government. They even advised them to resist the efforts of the Austrians to govern the country.[142]

The Austrians were of the opinion that the British were also attempting to exert their influence in Venice. At least the Habsburg police reported early in May that the English were trying to spread the rumor among the populace "that Venice would not remain Austrian."[143] They strongly suspected, too, that the British would have occupied the port of Venice in April had the Austrian commander not taken measures to prevent them from doing so.[144]

The Austrian officials in Italy protested loudly against the maneuvers of various British officers to incite a spirit of independence in Lombardy.[145] However, before their remonstrances prompted the Habsburg government to intercede in London, Bentinck's personal representative departed from Milan. Disgusted because Bentinck had, on his own authority, guaranteed independence to the Genoese even though his government had already agreed that Genoa was to be given to Sardinia[146] and deeply concerned over the possible mischief which the commander-in-chief might do at Milan, Lord Castlereagh instructed Bentinck early in May to recall MacFarlane from the Lombard capital and admonish him never again to "take any steps to encourage the fermentation which at present seems to prevail in Italy, on questions of government."[147]

Yet, even though the British government sided with the Austri-

[142] For a more detailed discussion of the relations between the Milanese liberals and the British officers in April and May, 1814, see my *Fall of the Napoleonic Kingdom of Italy*, pp. 159–168.

[143] Reuss-Plauen to Hager, Padua, May 7, 1814, A. S. (Venice), Presidio di governo, 1814, No. 6.

[144] Raab to Hager, Venice, October 6, 1814, Lemmi, *La restaurazione austriaca a Milano*, Appendix XXXVII, p. 444.

[145] Strassoldo to Bellegarde, Milan, April 30 and May 3, 1814, St. A. (Vienna), Kaiser Franz Akten, Fasz. XXVII, Kon. 1, Fos. 55 and 62–63; Bellegarde to Emperor Francis, Milan, May 9, 1814, *ibid.*, Fo. 60; Mier to Metternich, May 20, 1814, Weil, *Le Prince Eugène et Murat 1813–1814*, Vol. IV, p. 571; Bellegarde to Metternich, Milan, July 5, 1814, St. A. (Vienna), Staatskanzlei, Provinzen, Lombardei-Venedig, Fasz. III, Kon. 4, Fo. 1.

[146] Castlereagh to Liverpool, Paris, May 5, 1814, Charles K. Webster, *British Diplomacy, 1813–1815 (Select Documents dealing with the Reconstruction of Europe)*, pp. 180–181.

[147] Castlereagh to Bentinck, Paris, May 6, 1814, Charles Vane, Marquis of Londonderry (ed.), *Memoirs and Correspondence of Viscount Castlereagh, Second Marquess of Londonderry*, Vol. X, p. 15.

ans rather than with its own officials in Italy, Castlereagh's exhortation to Bentinck not to interfere in internal political questions in Italy actually came too late. Although the pro-English party in Lombardy really lost every legitimate reason to exist when the British foreign secretary repudiated Bentinck's interventionist policies in Italy early in May,[148] the very fact that the Lombard liberals had initially been encouraged by key officials of Great Britain in making their demands for freedom and for a constitutional government played a powerful role in stirring up their hopes that eventually they might accomplish their aims through the help of their powerful English friends—a hope which was kept alive during the summer and fall of 1814 by the encouragement unofficially given to them by various English factions who opposed the dominant Tory party in Great Britain. Bentinck's remark in Verona to Countess Marioni during the summer that he "did not know why a physically and morally strong nation like the Italian one did not think of its independence,"[149] the behavior and statements of various other English officers in Italy,[150] and the circulation in Italy of pamphlets arguing that Italian independence could be procured only by the British and the Russians[151] proved to be a source of considerable embarrassment to the Austrians, who were always afraid that the British opposition party was working to foment a liberal revolution in Italy.[152] Also, anti-Habsburg partisans believed that a powerful element in Great Britain actually did desire an independent Italy under their protection[153] and constitutional governments in the Apennine peninsula

[148] Renato Sorigo, "Ugo Foscolo e il suo amico anglo-italo Augusto Bozzi Granville," *La Lombardia nel Risorgimento italiano*, Vol. XIII (January, 1928), p. 125.

[149] Hager report, June 7, 1814, St. A. (Vienna), Kabinets-Akten, 1814, No. 1603. See also Hager report, July 5, 1814, St. A. (Vienna), Conferenz Akten, Ser. b, 1814, No. 1356; and Raab to Hager, Padua, June 25, 1814, Lemmi, *La restaurazione austriaca a Milano*, Appendix XXII, p. 428.

[150] Hager report, July 5, 1814, St. A. (Vienna), Conferenz Akten, Ser. b, 1814, No. 1356.

[151] Hager report, June 7, 1814, St. A. (Vienna), Kabinets-Akten, 1814, No. 1603.

[152] See, for example, Raab to Hager, Venice, October 6, 1814, Lemmi, *La restaurazione austriaca a Milano*, Appendix XXXVII, p. 445; Hager to Rosetti, Vienna, August 16, 1815, A. S. (Milan), Presidenza di governo. Atti secreti, 1815, Cart. IX, No. 144; and Rosetti to Strassoldo, Milan, September 4, 1815, *ibid*.

[153] Reuss-Plauen to Hudelist, Padua, July 17, 1814, St. A. (Vienna), Staatskanzlei, Provinzen, Lombardei-Venedig, Fasz. XVIII, Kon. 8, Fo. 1.

and on the whole European continent.[154] As a consequence, visionary Lombard liberals continued their agitation for an independent, constitutional state under British protection[155] long after the British commander-in-chief's policies were repudiated by his own government.

The Austrians felt certain that there was a close connection between certain Englishmen and various Italian malcontents. When Confalonieri, Litta, and Giovanni Luca Somaglia, members of the deputation sent by the Lombard provisional regency to the Allied Powers at Paris, went to London immediately after the end of the Paris peace conference in an effort to procure the support of the British government for the independence plans of the liberal factions in Milan, they were ordered to leave London at once, and after their return to the Lombard capital they were closely watched.[156] Reports that Milanese radicals were traveling to London;[157] that a society for Italian independence, composed of such renowned personages as the prince regent, Lord Wellesley, and the duke of Buckingham, existed in the British capital;[158] that the Italian independence party had its chief headquarters in England;[159] that a petition signed by six thousand British partisans in Lombardy had been forwarded to London;[160] that Italian radicals were plotting to turn Venetia into a British dependency;[161] and that the pro-British partisans in Lombardy and Venetia were wearing special insignia[162] aroused the suspicions

[154] Hager report, July 5, 1814, St. A. (Vienna), Conferenz Akten, Ser. b, 1814, No. 1356.

[155] Hager report, June 7, 1814, St. A. (Vienna), Kabinets-Akten, 1814, No. 1603.

[156] Hager to Bellegarde, Vienna, August 12, 1814, A. S. (Milan), Presidenza di governo. Atti secreti, 1814, Cart. II, No. 216; Bellegarde to Hager, Milan, September 7, 1814, *ibid.*; Hager reports, September 18 and December 11, 1814, St. A. (Vienna), Kabinets-Akten, 1814, Nos. 705 and 910.

[157] Weil, *Murat*, Vol. I, p. 368.

[158] Bellegarde to Metternich, Milan, December 5, 1814, St. A. (Vienna), Staatskanzlei, Provinzen, Lombardei-Venedig, Fasz. III, Kon. 4, Fo. 192.

[159] Hager to Reuss-Plauen, Vienna, December 21, 1814, A. S. (Venice), Presidio di governo, 1814, No. 2484.

[160] Weil, *Murat*, Vol. I, pp. 439–440.

[161] Raab to Reuss-Plauen, Venice, October 21, 1814, A. S. (Venice), Presidio di governo, 1814, ad No. 1986; Reuss-Plauen to Hager, Venice, October 26, 1814, *ibid.*; Hager to Reuss-Plauen, Vienna, November 11, 1814, *ibid.*, No. 1986.

[162] Reuss-Plauen to Bellegarde, Venice, October 19, 1814, A. S. (Milan), Presidio di governo. Atti secreti, 1814, Cart. V, No. 597.

of the Habsburgs that various English radicals were concocting machinations that were dangerous to the Austrian regime in Lombardy-Venetia. Believing that a good number of British travelers had come to Italy for the express purpose of preaching revolutionary slogans to the populace,[163] the Austrians closely supervised the actions and conversations of English officers and visitors and especially watched their associations with Italian liberals.[164] The Austrian police were particularly perturbed over the influence which the princess of Wales might exert upon disenchanted Lombards and Venetians. They faithfully reported every detail involving her activities at Como and Milan in the fall of 1814 and in Milan and Venice in May and June of 1815.[165]

Of all the British travelers in Italy, however, none worried the Habsburgs more than Augusto Bozzi Granville, a young ex-Milanese physician and a Freemason, who had been appointed translator of Italian correspondence in the British foreign office in 1813, when his good friend William Hamilton became undersecretary of state for foreign affairs.[166] At the foreign office Granville translated propaganda bulletins into Italian and edited a propaganda journal L'Italico to disseminate anti-Napoleonic propaganda among the Italian popu-

163 Humboldt memoir, Vienna, August 20, 1814, Bruno Gebhardt (ed.), Wilhelm von Humboldt's politische Denkschriften, Vol. II, p. 156; Raab to Hager, Venice, December 9, 1814, Lemmi, La restaurazione austriaca a Milano, Appendix LII, p. 469.

164 See especially Hager report, July 5, 1814, St. A. Vienna), Conferenz Akten, Ser. b, 1814, No. 1356; police reports, Milan, August 6, 8, and 9, 1814, Kriegs-Archiv (Vienna), Feld Akten (Italien), 1814, Fasz. VIII, Nos. 24, 26, and 34; Metternich to Bellegarde, Vienna, October 12, 1814, St. A. (Vienna), Staatskanzlei, Provinzen, Lombardei-Venedig, Fasz. III, Kon. 2, Fos. 84–85; and Pagani reports, Milan, June 12 and July 16 and 21, 1814, A. S. (Milan), Presidenza di governo. Atti secreti, 1814, Cart. I, Fasc. 18/P.R., No. 9651, Cart. II, Fasc. 114/P.R., No. 12,153, and Cart. I, No. 74/P.R.

165 Weil, Murat, Vol. I, p. 440; Pagani reports, Milan, October 2 and 9, 1814, A. S. (Milan), Presidenza di governo. Atti secreti, 1814, Cart. V, Nos. 19,010 and 19,793; general police directory bulletin, Milan, October 5, 1814, ibid., Cart. IV, No. 442/P.R.; entries of October 9 and 18, 1814, Biblioteca Ambrosiana (Milan), Mantovani, "Diario di Milano," Vol. V, pp. 315 and 316; Giornale di Venezia, No. 142 (October 15, 1814), p. 3; No. 146 (October 25, 1814), p. 3; No. 136 (May 18, 1815), p. 4; No. 152 (June 3, 1815), p. 4; No. 154 (June 5, 1815), p. 4; No. 164 (June 14, 1815), p. 4; and No. 170 (June 20, 1815), p. 4.

166 Alfredo Comandini, "Un Milanese per l'Italia a Londra nel 1814," Il Secolo, April 10, 1919, no pages given.

lace.[167] In the spring of 1814 he wrote an appeal to Tsar Alexander of Russia in which he beseeched the Russian sovereign to help the Italians create a united country under the rule of the king of Sardinia.[168]

In May, 1814, Granville left London for Italy, supposedly to visit his aged father in Milan. He was furnished with a confidential recommendation from Count San Martino d'Agliè, the Sardinian minister at London, to Count Antonio de Vallesa, a minister in the Sardinian government, and with various dispatches from the British foreign office. After conferring with officials in Turin about his proposal for a united Italy under Sardinian rule, Granville went to Milan, apparently to sound out various liberals about the plan. He arrived there on May 29. In Lombardy he visited his old friends and had long talks about his pro-Sardinian project with various avowed liberals like Pallavicini, Carlo Cattaneo, and Foscolo. He departed from the Lombard capital on June 7 for Parma and Bologna, from where he intended to proceed to Florence and Rome.

On the way he was warned that his movements were being carefully watched by the Austrians. Indiscreet and outspoken as he was, Granville had attracted the notice of the Austrian authorities soon after entering Lombardy. Believing that he was one of the most dangerous of all the radical intriguers, the Austrian ambassador in Rome sent a note to the Papal authorities requesting his arrest. In addition, the Habsburg police were instructed to observe all his movements closely.

The Austrians did not have to wait long before they had ample reason to seize the ex-Milanese physician. Soon after arriving in Bologna Granville chastised an Austrian officer when an unknown woman fell under the Austrian's horse during a public promenade. A lively quarrel ensued, as a consequence of which the indiscreet Italo-British pamphleteer was arrested and his papers confiscated.[169]

---

[167] Paulina B. Granville (ed.), *Autobiography of A[ugustus] B[ozzi] Granville, M.D., F.R.S.—being eighty-eight years of the life of a physician who practiced his profession in Italy, Greece, Turkey, Spain, Portugal, the West Indies, Russia, Germany, France, and England*, Vol. I, p. 335; Soriga, "Augusto Bozzi Granville e la Rivista 'L'Italico'," pp. 274–279.

[168] *Appello ad Alessandro, Imperatore e Autocrate di tutte le Russie, sul destino dell'Italia. Scritto nelle tre lingue dall'editore dell'Italico* [Bozzi Granville], pp. 25–26.

[169] Granville, *Autobiography*, Vol. I, pp. 350–452; Soriga, "Bagliori unitari in Lombardia," pp. 6–10; Bellegarde to Metternich, n.d., *ibid.*, pp. 13–14; Silvio

News of the arrest increased the concern of the government in Vienna about English intervention for Italian independence.[170] Disturbed because Granville's activities in Italy were so obviously anti-Austrian in intent, Metternich asked the Austrian ambassador in London to hand Castlereagh a confidential communiqué[171] protesting Granville's intrigues and the way British agents were seconding the efforts of various Italian Jacobins to arouse popular discontent. Metternich requested the British government to keep a close surveillance on Italian Jacobins residing in England and to recall Bentinck from Italy.[172]

In reply, Castlereagh assured Metternich that Granville was neither an employee of the British government nor a spy, although he admitted that he had gone to Italy with official dispatches and that while there he had sent confidential reports to his friend and mentor, Mr. Hamilton.[173] The British foreign secretary expressed full agreement with the Austrian chancellor about the need to repress the prevailing revolutionary spirit. For this reason, British officials in Italy, including Lord Bentinck, had been given "the most precise orders, not only to have no relations with persons who might show a tendency contrary to the spirit of the Austrian government, but also to support" the principles of the Habsburg government "by all

---

Furlani, "Augusto Bozzi Granville e l'Austria," *Rassegna storica del Risorgimento*, Vol. XXXIV, Fasc. 1–2 (January–June, 1947), pp. 65–73; Domenico Spadoni, "Carlo Comelli de Stuckenfeld e il trono de'Cesari offerto a Casa Savoja nel 1814," *Rassegna storica del Risorgimento*, Vol. XIV, Fasc. 4 (October–December, 1927), p. 622; Soriga, "Ugo Foscolo e il suo amico anglo-italo Augusto Bozzi Granville," pp. 134–137; Domenico Spadoni, "Il Foscolo cospiratore nel 1813–1814," *Studi su Ugo Foscolo, editi a cura della R. Università di Pavia nel primo centenario della morte del poeta*, pp. 584–588.

170 Anonymous report enclosed in Goëss to Archduke Rainer, Venice, May 28, 1818, St. A. (Vienna), Kabinets-Akten, 1818, ad No. 453; Bellegarde to Metternich, Milan, January 25, 1815, St. A. (Vienna), Staatskanzlei, Provinzen, Lombardei-Venedig, Fasz. IV, Kon. 4, Fos. 7–10; Weil, *Murat*, Vol. I, p. 440.

171 Metternich to Bellegarde, Vienna, October 12, 1814, St. A. (Vienna), Staatskanzlei, Provinzen, Lombardei-Venedig, Fasz. III, Kon. 2, Fos. 84–85. Other copies of this letter are in A. S. (Milan), Presidenza di governo. Atti secreti, 1814, Cart. V, No. 595/P.R.; and in Lemmi, *La restaurazione austriaca a Milano*, Appendix XXXIX, pp. 446–448.

172 Metternich to Castlereagh, Baden, August 18, 1814, Soriga, "Bagliori unitari in Lombardia," pp. 15–16.

173 Castlereagh to Metternich, Verona, October 8, 1814, *ibid.*, pp. 17–18.

means at their disposal." As far as British travelers were concerned, however, Castlereagh pointed out to the Austrian chancellor that the British government had little control of their conduct, even in England, as long as they violated none of the laws of the country, and that its power over them was infinitely less effective when they were away from home.[174]

What particularly alarmed the Habsburg government about Granville's activities in Italy was the fact that he openly championed Victor Emmanuel I of Sardinia as king of a united Italy. The circulation in Lombardy and in the Romagna, a few months after Granville's arrest, of a pamphlet advocating the unification of Italy under the king of Sardinia greatly augmented their anxiety, especially since rumors were also going around at the same time that the eastern boundary of Piedmont would soon be extended to the Mincio River.[175] The Austrians attributed the authorship or translation of this brochure first to Ugo Foscolo[176] and finally to Granville. In the end, they learned that the pamphlet was an Italian edition of Granville's appeal to Tsar Alexander, which had originally been published in England in the spring of 1814 and which had recently been printed under the false imprimatur of Novara.[177]

Not only were the Austrians greatly perturbed over propaganda advocating a united Italian state with the king of Sardinia as its ruler; they were also on guard against any possible efforts by Prince Eugene to curry favor with the Lombards and Venetians. For this reason, when the recent viceroy's secretary Nicolo Tournal arrived in Milan on a tour through Italy to sound out the opinions of Prince

[174] Metternich to Bellegarde, Vienna, October 12, 1814, St. A. (Vienna), Staatskanzlei, Provinzen, Lombardei-Venedig, Fasz. III, Kon. 2, Fos. 84–85. Other copies are in A. S. (Milan), Presidenza di governo. Atti secreti, Cart. V, No. 595/P.R.; and in Lemmi, *La restaurazione austriaca a Milano*, Appendix XXXIX, pp. 446–448.

[175] Provisional prefect of Mella to Bellegarde, Brescia, September 1, 1814, A. S. (Milan), Presidenza di governo. Atti secreti, 1814, Cart. III, No. 268/P.R.

[176] Hager to Bellegarde, Vienna, October 18, 1814, *ibid.*, Cart. IV, No. 534/P.R.; Hager report, October 28, 1814, St. A. (Vienna), Kabinets-Akten, 1815, No. 460.

[177] Bellegarde to Hager, Milan, October 22, 1814, A. S. (Milan), Presidenza di governo. Atti secreti, 1814, Cart. IV, No. 534/P.R.; Hager to Bellegarde, Vienna, November 6, 1814, *ibid.*, Cart. VI, No. 753/P.R.; Spadoni, "Carlo Comelli de Stuckenfeld," p. 622.

Eugene's former supporters, the authorities, acting on Police President von Hager's personal orders, peremptorily commanded him on July 13 to leave Austrian territory within eight days.[178]

What worried the Austrians much more than the propaganda activities of any group, whether British or Italian, was the nagging fear that Napoleon might be the center of dangerous plots to subvert the established order in the Apennine peninsula. Highly suspicious that the former French emperor had secret relations, not only with the French, but also with Murat and malcontents throughout Italy,[179] the imperial court at Vienna instructed Bellegarde carefully to watch all communications between the Italian coast and Elba.[180]

Following his directions, Bellegarde kept in close contact with numerous Austrian and Tuscan officials who devoted countless hours in attempting to find out what was going on at Elba. They seized and opened correspondence, spied on visitors to Porto Ferraio and on suspected admirers of Napoleon, and cooperated with the French and British in sneaking confidants on the island to procure first-hand knowledge of the ex-emperor's most intimate secrets. The British and French were just as vigilant as the Austrians. The main center of their intelligence activities was Leghorn, where Governor Leopold von Spannocchi, the French Consul Mariotti, and British Minister Earl Burghersh directed a large network of underground agents who checked on Napoleon.[181] Of all the spies of the Allied Powers apparently the most successful was an anonymous agent in Mariotti's employ, who went to Elba in the guise of an oil merchant, wormed

178 Hager to Bellegarde, Vienna, May 23 and July 10 and 16, 1814, A. S. (Milan), Presidenza di governo. Atti secreti, 1814, Cart. I, Nos. 1/P.R., 63/P.R., and 93/P.R.; Bellegarde to Hager, Milan, July 21, 1814, ibid., No. 63/P.R.

179 Weil, Murat, Vol. I, pp. 253–255; Lemmi, La restaurazione austriaca a Milano, pp. 334–337; secret report, n.d., ibid., Appendix XLI, pp. 450–451; Spadoni, Il moto del 20 aprile, pp. 285–286; Venetian central government to aulic police president, Padua, September 2, 1814, A. S. (Venice), Presidio di governo, 1814, No. 1076.

180 Metternich to Bellegarde, Paris, May 15, and Baden, August 28, 1814, St. A. (Vienna), Staatskanzlei, Provinzen, Lombardei-Venedig, Fasz. III, Kon. 2, Fos. 52–53 and 68; Hager to Bellegarde, Vienna, December 6, 1814, A. S. (Milan), Presidenza di governo. Atti secreti, 1814, Cart. III, ad No. 305/P.R.

181 See especially Weil, Murat, Vol. I, pp. 156–158, 220–222, 247, 289–298, and 449–466, and Vol. II, pp. 150–153 and 205–210; Marcellin Pellet, Napoléon à l'île d'Elbe—Mélanges historiques, pp. 48–52; and Spadoni, Il moto del 20 aprile, p. 286.

his way into the confidence of various Napoleonic functionaries and secret emissaries, and faithfully reported everything he had seen and heard to the French consul.[182]

Field Marshal Bellegarde himself was involved with another informant who visited Elba in the fall of 1814—a certain Domenico Ettori, a native of Lugo, an ex-monk and former French employee, who was hired in the summer of 1814 as a spy by the Milanese police. When Ettori told Bellegarde that he had excellent connections with Napoleon and proposed that he be allowed to go to Elba disguised as a merchant to report about what he might learn of the ex-emperor's designs, the Austrian commissioner plenipotentiary raised no objections, although he warned various Tuscan and Austrian officials that he suspected that the ex-monk was either a dangerous intriguer or a spy for both sides and urged them to keep an eagle eye on him.[183]

Ettori left Milan on October 4 and came to Leghorn on the 13th. After the Austrian consul there refused to give him a passport, he bribed a ship captain with 300 lire to take him clandestinely to Porto Ferraio, where he arrived on the 30th. After remaining on the island for twelve days, during the course of which he maintained that he engaged in important conversations with Napoleon, he returned to Leghorn on November 12, losing all his money on the way back.[184]

At Leghorn, Ettori told Bargello, an agent of the Tuscan government, that he had discovered at Elba that Napoleon had an intimate correspondence and close ties with Murat, with the chief marshals of France, and with the Italian Freemasons, especially those at Bologna, Venice, and Milan. He hinted that the former French emperor and these groups were plotting a revolution in the Apennine peninsula. Napoleon was to disembark at Viareggio, where he planned to incite the Lombards to rebel, while Murat was to proclaim a revolution in the rest of Italy. Fifty thousand armed men, including all

---

[182] Pellet, *Napoléon à l'île d'Elbe*, pp. 55–58; Weil, *Murat*, Vol. II, pp. 214–215 and 301–307.

[183] Bellegarde to Hager, Milan, December 14 and 22, 1814, A. S. (Milan), Presidenza di governo. Atti secreti, 1814, Cart. III, ad No. 305/P.R.; Giovanni Livi, *Napoleone all'isola d'Elba secondo le carte di un archivio segreto ed altre, edite ed inedite*, pp. 138–140.

[184] Ettori to Bellegarde, Leghorn, November 16, 1814, A. S. (Milan), Presidenza di governo. Atti secreti, 1814, Cart. III, No. 320/P.R. A copy of this letter can also be found in Livi, *Napoleone all'isola d'Elba*, Appendix X, pp. 290–292.

Napoleon's former troops, stood ready in Italy to sacrifice their lives for the French emperor the moment he gave them the signal to revolt.[185]

Since he was penniless after losing his purse on his return journey from Elba, Ettori went to Lucca in the hope of talking General Starhemberg into giving him a subsidy. He made such a bad impression on the Habsburg general that the latter denounced him to the Tuscan authorities as a dangerous intriguer. When Ettori returned to Leghorn he was arrested on November 18 and taken to Florence[186] and then to Vienna[187] for questioning.

The Habsburg police in Vienna strongly suspected that Ettori was implicated in the Brescian-Milanese conspiracy[188] and that he went to Elba with a message to Napoleon from the plotters.[189] They were probably misinformed. In their testimony in December, 1814, and early January, 1815, the conspirators themselves, although they revealed a great deal about each other,[190] gave no indication that Ettori was involved in any way in their machination.[191] Bellegarde also thought that the ex-emperor had nothing whatever to do with the Brescian-Milanese conspiracy.[192] It is very likely that much of what Ettori related to the Tuscan and Habsburg authorities was nothing but a cock-and-bull story concocted for the express purpose of wheedling substantial sums of money out of them.

Nonetheless, even though there was probably little truth in what Ettori said about Napoleon's alleged intrigues with Italian conspirators, it can not be denied that the king of Elba kept in touch with

[185] Bargello report, Leghorn, November 16, 1814, A. S. (Milan), Presidenza di governo. Atti secreti, 1814, Cart. III, No. 305/P.R.; Ettori's report on his conversations with Napoleon in November, 1814, enclosed in Fossombroni to Bellegarde, Florence, November 25, 1814, ibid., No. 320/P.R.

[186] Ettori to Bellegarde, Florence, November 24, 1814, Livi, Napoleone all'isola d'Elba, Appendix X, pp. 292–297; Weil, Murat, Vol. II, pp. 32–36.

[187] Bellegarde to General Steffanini, Milan, November 30, 1814, A. S. (Milan), Presidenza di governo. Atti secreti, 1814, Cart. III, ad No. 305/P.R.; Bellegarde to Hager, Milan, November 30, 1814, ibid.

[188] See Chapter 6.

[189] Hager to Bellegarde, Vienna, January 9, 1815, A. S. (Milan), Presidenza di governo. Atti secreti, 1814, Cart. III, No. 79/P.R.

[190] See post, pp. 275–286.

[191] Bellegarde to Hager, n.d., A. S. (Milan), Presidenza di governo. Atti secreti, 1814, Cart. III, No. 79/P.R.

[192] In an undated letter to Hager, in ibid.

and wielded at least some influence over malcontents in Italy, including those in Lombardy and Venetia. The former French emperor himself wrote that "citizens of the Kingdom of Italy, and Genoese, Piedmontese, Tuscan, and Roman soldiers who had been dismissed from the French service" frequently came to Elba.[193] It is highly probable that, in spite of the precautions taken by the Allied governments, a few Italian malcontents and other admirers of the ex-emperor may have succeeded in visiting Napoleon occasionally.[194] There is at least a little evidence that a few Lombards succeeded in getting there. Mantovani recorded in his diary that in September two Milanese citizens had just returned from Elba, where they had conversed with Napoleon,[195] and the prefect of Mincio reported to Bellegarde the following month that a certain Giovanni Ponzoni, of Mantua, had been at Elba between the 19th and 26th of October.[196] It is possible that a handful of bitterly discontented officers of the former Italian army may have managed to journey there to try to induce Napoleon to come to Italy to aid them in fighting a war of liberation against their restored sovereigns.[197]

No documents are available which indicate exactly what transpired when the above-mentioned visitors were at Elba. The pseudo-oil merchant, however, did supply Mariotti with considerable information about the conversations of Antonio Litta-Biumi, a Milanese and the brother of the well known Pompeo, who had supposedly gone there to invite Napoleon to lead an Italian insurrection against the Austrians. According to the oil merchant's account, Litta arrived at Porto Ferraio in his company on November 30.[198] The next day the governor of the island queried him about public opinion in Milan

---

[193] Napoleon I, "L'île d'Elbe et les cent-jours," *Correspondance de Napoléon Ier, publiée par ordre de l'empereur Napoléon III*, Vol. XXXI, p. 25.

[194] See Spadoni, *Il moto del 20 aprile*, pp. 292–296; Lemmi, *La restaurazione austriaca a Milano*, pp. 323–324; and Pingaud, "La Lombardie en 1814," p. 464.

[195] Entry of September 28, 1814, *Biblioteca Ambrosiana* (Milan), Mantovani, "Diario di Milano," Vol. V, pp. 312–313.

[196] In a letter dated Mantua, October 28, 1814, A. S. (Milan), Presidenza di governo. Atti secreti, 1814, Cart. III, ad No. 305/P.R. See also protocol, October 30, 1814, *ibid.*, Cart. V, No. 646/P.R.

[197] Raab to Hager, Padua, August 13, 1814, Lemmi, *La restaurazione austriaca a Milano*, Appendix XXIX, p. 436; Monti, *Rasori*, p. 75.

[198] Journal of the oil merchant, November 30, 1814, Pellet, *Napoléon à l'île d'Elbe*, Appendix VII, pp. 117–118.

and about the forces which the Austrians had at their disposal in Lombardy.[199] On December 2 Litta had a long interview with Napoleon, during the course of which, as Litta supposedly confided to the oil merchant, the former French emperor asked him searching questions about the morale of the Milanese and about the number of French-Italian troops who had agreed to serve in the Habsburg army. When Litta told him that only six thousand Italian soldiers had actually joined the Austrian military forces and that the Milanese, Venetians, Sardinians, Romagnols, Modenese, the inhabitants of the Papal Legations and Marches, and even some Ligurians and Tuscans were bitterly discontented with their present governments, Napoleon reminisced pensively about all the fine things he had dreamed of accomplishing "in Milan and in all Italy." The king of Elba questioned his visitor closely about the number of former Italian soldiers who had joined Murat's army.[200] When he learned that Litta was planning on going to Naples, he asked him to perform a special mission for him there.[201]

Since the only evidence of Litta's alleged conversations with Napoleon is a secondhand report written in dialogue form by a secret confidant, serious doubts should be raised about whether the conversations took place. That Napoleon must have been in contact with at least some Italian malcontents, including those in Lombardy and Venetia, is, however, beyond question. On numerous occasions the Austrian police voiced strong suspicions that a number of military officers who had been at Elba were attempting to stir up the populace against the government[202] and that an active, though secret, correspondence was being conducted between various Lombard and Venetian admirers of the French emperor and Porto Ferraio.[203] They

---

[199] Journal of the oil merchant, December 1, 1814, *ibid.*, p. 120.

[200] Journal of the oil merchant, December 2, 1814, *ibid.*, pp. 122–126. An identical record of Litta's interview with Napoleon, taken from the Public Record Office in London, is in Weil, *Murat*, Vol. II, Appendix XXII, pp. 564–567. Very probably Mariotti sent a copy of the oil merchant's journal to Campbell or Burghersh, who forwarded it to Castlereagh.

[201] Journal of the oil merchant, December 29, 1814, Pellet, *Napoléon à l'île d'Elbe*, Appendix VII, p. 138.

[202] Hager to Bellegarde, Vienna, August 10 and 23 and September 7, 1814, A. S. (Milan), Presidenza di governo. Atti secreti, 1814, Cart. II, Nos. 211/P.R., 274/P.R., and 332/P.R.

[203] Pagani reports, Milan, July 30 and August 11, 1814, *ibid.*, Nos. 114/P.R.

reported that some Milanese adulators of the Corsican were even selling their property to go to Elba to share his fate[204] and that Napoleon's partisans were wearing a medallion imprinted with a bee and a sleeping eagle as a secret sign of identification.[205] In September a secret informer reported to the government in Vienna that a revolutionary conspiracy had been discovered in Tuscany and Genoa which was to extend to Lombardy and Bologna. The plotters were planning to recall Bonaparte from Elba to head a revolution aimed at giving independence to the Italian people.[206]

Perhaps there might have been some connection between this plot, if it actually existed, and the machination referred to in a volume supposedly written "by a citizen of Corsica" and published in Brussels by H. Tarlier in 1825 under the title, *La vérité sur les cents jours, principalement par rapport à la renaissance projetée de l'empire romain.*[207] According to the author of this rather curious work, a group of fourteen conspirators, composed of two citizens of the former Kingdom of Italy, four Piedmontese, two Genoese, two Corsicans, and four plotters from the Papal States and the Kingdom of Two Sicilies, met in Turin in May, 1814, to discuss how Italy could be

---

and 179/P.R.; Bellegarde to Hager, Milan, November 25, 1814, *ibid.,* Cart. VI, No. 751/P.R.

[204] Hager to Staats-Conferenz, June 8, 1814, St. A. (Vienna), Conferenz Akten, Ser. b, 1814, No. 1153.

[205] Hager to Reuss-Plauen, Vienna, October 7, 1814, A. S. (Venice), Presidio di governo, 1814, No. 1566; Reuss-Plauen to Bellegarde, Venice, October 19, 1814, A. S. (Milan), Presidenza di governo. Atti secreti, 1814, Cart. V, No. 597.

[206] Copy of an anonymous report from Italy, Vienna, September 22, 1814, Lemmi, *La restaurazione austriaca a Milano,* Appendix XXXIV, p. 442. See also Hager to Bellegarde, Vienna, September 16, 1814, A. S. (Milan), Presidenza di governo. Atti secreti, 1814, Cart. V, No. 628/P.R.

[207] In the copy in the Yale University Library, which the writer used, the authorship of the above work is erroneously attributed to Melchiorre Delfico. In 1829 an Italian edition was published under the title, *Delle cause italiane nell'evasione dell'imperatore Napoleone da l'Elba.* Mazziotti maintains that the author of the volume was Cesare de Laugier (M. Mazziotti "L'offerta del trono d'Italia a Napoleone I esule all'Elba," *Rassegna storica del Risorgimento,* Vol. VII, Fasc. 1 [January–March, 1920], p. 8). Patetta, however, argues rather convincingly that the author was Count Giorgio Libri Bagnano and that De Laugier merely brought out the Italian edition (Federico Patetta, "La congiura torinese del 1814 per la rinascita dell'Impero Romano e per l'offerta del trono a Napoleone," *Atti della Reale Accademia delle Scienze di Torino,* Vol. LXXII [1936]), pp. 276–277 and 302–305).

unified. After several meetings the group came to an understanding that the government of the future united Italy which they wished to create was to be a federal constitutional monarchy. They also agreed to make an effort to enlist the king of Elba in the enterprise.

On May 19 they drafted a letter which they sent to Napoleon,[208] inviting him to head the insurrection.[209] The letter was accompanied by the draft of a constitution for a new Roman empire. As outlined in this document, the whole Apennine peninsula and the island of Elba were to be included in the new empire. Although it was expressly stipulated that sovereignty was to be vested in the Italian nation, the ruler of the country was to be Napoleon, who was to take the title of "Emperor of the Romans and King of Italy by the will of the people and the grace of God." He was to reside in Rome. Under him were to be four viceroys, who were to be chosen from princes of royal blood. However, one of them had to be Prince Eugene. These viceroys were to reside in the four most populous cities in the empire other than the capital. There was to be a bicameral legislative body, which was to hold its sittings successively in Rome, Milan, and Naples. The upper house, the senate, was to have two hundred members selected by the emperor from a triple list drawn up by the electoral colleges. They were to be at least thirty years old and were to own property with a net income of at least 30,000 francs per annum. The lower house, the house of representatives, was to be composed of three citizens for every hundred thousand inhabitants, each of whom had to be at least thirty years of age. The property requirements which they had to meet were to be fixed at the first session of the legislature, which was to be called the constituent congress and which was to fill all gaps in the constitution.[210]

The conspirators also transmitted to the former French emperor a unique, if rather impractical, plan to carry the plot to fruition. They

[208] *La vérité sur les cents jours*, pp. 4–5; Pellet, *Napoléon à l'île d'Elbe*, pp. 63–64.

[209] President and members of the constituent congress of the Roman empire to Napoleon, Turin, May 19, 1814, *La vérité sur les cents jours*, pp. 6–18. A copy of this letter can also be found in Livi, *Napoleone all'isola d'Elba*, pp. 38–41.

[210] Articles of the constitution of the new Roman empire, *La vérité sur les cents jours*, Annex A, pp. 22–52. A copy can also be found in Livi, *Napoleone all'isola d'Elba*, pp. 266–277.

proposed provoking a war between Louis XVIII and Murat. As soon as hostilities commenced, Napoleon was to leave Elba under the pretext of reconciling the two antagonists, unite the Neapolitan and French armies under his personal command, and conquer Italy.[211] Several rich Genoese capitalists promised to put 12,000,000 French francs in the hands of the revolutionary committee if Napoleon accepted their plan.[212]

Napoleon supposedly approved the proposals of the conspirators and their constitution without reservation;[213] whereupon the machinators busied themselves with preparing the ground for the realization of their complot. They dispatched agents to the principal cities of Italy and assigned two emissaries to France to incite Napoleon's supporters there to provoke Louis XVIII into declaring war on Murat.[214] All this time they were allegedly encouraged by Napoleon, who as late as October, according to the author of *La vérité sur les cents jours*, outlined to two of the leaders of the conspiracy grandiose schemes for turning the Roman empire into the most powerful nation of Europe within twenty years.[215]

Some Italian historians like Francesco Lemmi,[216] Nicomede Bianchi, Giosue Carducci, and more recently Federico Patetta[217] and M. Mazziotti[218] have accepted the veracity of the preceding account of the Turin conspiracy. Also, even though the author of *La vérité sur les cents jours* mentions only two of the plotters (Luigi Corvetto and Melchiorre Delfico) by name, various writers have embellished his account by including such patriots as Pellegrino Rossi, Giandomenico Romagnosi, Francesco Salfi, Vincenzo Cuoco, and Ugo Foscolo.[219]

Although Patetta has marshalled evidence from a detailed exami-

---

[211] Excerpt from the plan of execution to attain the rebirth of the Roman empire, dated Thursday, May 19, 1814, submitted to His Majesty, Emperor Napoleon, on the Isle of Elba by the president and members of the national constituent congress at Turin, *La vérité sur les cents jours*, Annex B, pp. 55–75.

[212] *La vérité sur les cents jours*, p. 20.

[213] *Ibid.*

[214] *Ibid.*, pp. 75–155.

[215] *Ibid.*, pp. 218–221.

[216] See his *La restaurazione austriaca a Milano*, pp. 317–323.

[217] See his "La congiura torinese del 1814."

[218] See his "L'offerta del trono d'Italia a Napoleone."

[219] Patetta, "La congiura torinese del 1814," pp. 285–288.

nation of Count Giorgio Libri Bagnano's life and activities which makes it possible to conjecture that it *might* have been possible for him to have participated in such a conspiracy,[220] the present writer is inclined to agree with authorities like M. R. Buccella,[221] P. Ilario Rinieri, and Domenico Spadoni[222] that serious doubts must be cast on the authenticity of much or all of the story. In the first place, a single anonymous work published eleven years after the conspiracy was allegedly concocted is meager evidence to support the theory of a complot which involved a fairly large number of people and which was in the planning stage for several months. It seems likely that such a formidable and extensive machination would have come to the attention of at least one of the numerous Austrian, Tuscan, or other Allied spies. Furthermore, the fact that some of the most important "documents" in the volume are in dialogue form leaves room for suspicion. Then, too, even though the author of *La vérité sur les cents jours* explained that, to prevent compromising the conspirators who were still living, he was mentioning only Corvetto and Delfico among the members of the complot, Delfico actually lived until 1835 —ten years after the work was published. Also, although the writer of the tract promised to publish other documents besides those in the book itself, none ever appeared in print. Moreover, notwithstanding the fact that it is entirely plausible that Napoleon, for opportunistic reasons, might have led Italian plotters to believe that he might possibly be interested in a project which would make him emperor of Italy, the former French emperor's ambitions always lay in recapturing France rather than in carving out an empire for himself in the Apennine peninsula. Finally, Napoleon was too calculating and clear-sighted ever to believe that an impractical, visionary scheme like that of the Turin machinators could succeed. As he wrote in his memoirs, he himself warned Italians who tried to interest him in conspiratorial projects to revolutionize Italy that they could do nothing without the powerful support of France.[223]

[220] See *ibid., passim.*

[221] See his "La congiura e l'offerta dell'impero romano a Napoleone all'isola d'Elba," *Nuova Antologia. Rivista di Lettere, Scienze ed Arti,* Anno LXV, Fasc. 1393 (April, 1930), pp. 352–362.

[222] See his *Il moto del 20 aprile,* pp. 288–289.

[223] Napoleon I, "L'île d'Elbe et les cent-jours," pp. 36–37.

Yet, although the evidence is too tenuous to support the theory that the Turin conspiracy described in Bagnano's work actually took place, there is ample testimony that Napoleon was in active contact with various Italian malcontents.[224] Napoleon himself asserted that "some Italian citizens found the means to arrive on the Isle of Elba and proposed diverse projects to stir up all Italy to revolt."[225] Even though Ettori's revelations to the Tuscan authorities that Napoleon and various of his Italian adulators were planning to disembark at Viareggio, the pseudo-oil merchant's report about Litta's trip to Elba to invite the French emperor to head an insurrection, and the confidential report to the Habsburg government of a conspiracy in Tuscany and Genoa to recall Napoleon from Elba may each be open to serious doubts, together they indicate that a few Italians at least might have entertained the idea of using Napoleon to further their conspiratorial plots and might have made vain attempts to induce him to second their efforts. Perhaps some of them may have tried to interest Napoleon in a revised version of the plan to revive a Roman empire in Italy, which the adventurous intriguer Count Carlo Francesco Comelli de Stuckenfeld attempted to sell to the British foreign office in 1813–1814 and which he revealed to the Austrian informer Esquiron de St. Agnan in the summer of 1814.[226] Whatever the actual details of their machinations may have been, it seems at least probable that various Italian groups, including a few Lombards, were attempting to procure Napoleon's support for some kind of a revolutionary conspiracy or conspiracies.[227] However, until new evidence is discovered, it is impossible to state precisely what the plot was and exactly what Napoleon's reaction to it was.

There is no doubt that at least some of these plotters were in close touch with Murat and that the king of Naples was secretly in contact with Napoleon.[228] Rightly suspicious of the attitude of the Allied

[224] See *ante,* pp. 180–181. See also Henry Houssaye, *1815: la première restauration—le retour de l'île d'Elbe—les cent jours,* p. 178.

[225] Napoleon I, "L'île d'Elbe et les cent-jours," p. 36.

[226] For the details of the proposal, see Spadoni, "Carlo Comelli de Stuckenfeld," pp. 606–629. See also *post,* pp. 246–247.

[227] See also Spadoni, *Il moto del 20 aprile,* pp. 287–298.

[228] Grégoire Orloff, *Mémoires historiques, politiques et littéraires sur le royaume de Naples,* Vol. II, p. 262; Bargello report, Leghorn, November 14,

Powers towards him, Murat was turning for help and protection to the same former French emperor[229] whom he had betrayed in January. Finding the Kingdom of Naples too small to satisfy his inordinate ambitions and yearning to make himself king of all Italy[230]— an ambition which did not remain hidden from the Austrians[231]— Murat, as early as the summer of 1814, mustered new conscripts and encouraged volunteers from all Italy to join his army, created new infantry and cavalry regiments,[232] and dispatched agents all over Italy, including Lombardy and Venetia, to stir up the fires of discontent and foster a pro-independence spirit.[233] Had he been able to count only on his own resources, the king of Naples would not have represented any real danger to the restored governments. What made him a real threat was the fact that during the summer and fall of 1814 many of the discontented liberals in all Italy, including members of various secret societies, looked to Murat for powerful support in driving the Germans out of the Apennine peninsula.[234] A war with

1814, A. S. (Milan), Presidenza di governo. Atti secreti, 1814, Cart. III, No. 305; Pellet, Napoléon à l'île d'Elbe, pp. 52 and 62; journal of the oil merchant, January 6 and February 17, 1815, ibid., Appendix VII, pp. 147 and 152; Livi, Napoleone all'isola d'Elba, p. 175; Mémoires de Marchand, premier valet de chambre et exécuteur testamentaire de l'empereur, publiés d'après le manuscrit original par Jean Bourguignon, Vol. I: L'île d'Elbe—les cents jours, pp. 86–87.

[229] Orloff, Mémoires sur le royaume de Naples, Vol. II, p. 262; Pietro Colletta, Storia del reame di Napoli dal 1734 sino al 1825, Vol. II, pp. 172 and 180.

[230] Joseph Alexander Helfert, Joachim Murat. Seine letzten Kämpfe und sein Ende. Mit Benützung von Schriftstücken des k. k. Haus-, Hof-, und Staats-Archivs, p. 12; Pingaud, "La Lombardie en 1814," p. 463.

[231] Reuss- Plauen to Hudelist, Padua, July 17, 1814, St. A. (Vienna), Staatskanzlei, Provinzen, Lombardei-Venedig, Fasz. XVIII, Kon. 8, Fo. 1; Hager report, August 13, 1814, St. A. (Vienna), Conferenz Akten, Ser. b, 1814, No. 1590.

[232] Colletta, Storia del reame di Napoli, Vol. II, pp. 175–176; Hager report, July 18, 1814, St. A. (Vienna), Conferenz Akten, Ser. b, 1814, No. 1423; excerpt from a letter from Florence to Bologna, July 28, 1814, Kriegs-Archiv (Vienna), Feld Akten (Italien), 1814, Fasz. VIII, No. 79b; Hegardt to Engeström, July 30, 1814, Weil, Les dessous du Congrès de Vienne, Vol. I, p. 35.

[233] Secret report, Venice, February 22, 1815, Helfert, Kaiser Franz und die Stiftung des Lombardo-Venetianischen Königreichs, Appendix IV, pp. 551–553; Orloff, Mémoires sur le royaume de Naples, Vol. II, pp. 262–263; Weil, Murat, Vol. I, p. 310; Vol. II, pp. 233 and 235.

[234] Hager to Bellegarde, Vienna, July 5, 1814, Lemmi, La restaurazione austriaca a Milano, Appendix XXIV, p. 431; Raab to Hager, Padua, August 13, 1814, ibid., Appendix XXIX, p. 436; Hager report, October 28, 1814, St. A.

Murat, supported by enough Italian malcontents, was a real danger to the Habsburgs in Italy, if Napoleon managed, at the same time, to escape from Elba and take supreme command of all the anti-Austrian forces in Italy.

(Vienna), Kabinets-Akten, 1814, No. 460; Hager report, July 18, 1814, St. A. (Vienna), Conferenz Akten, Ser. b, 1814, No. 1423; report from Bologna, June 30, 1814, A. S. (Milan), Presidenza di governo. Atti secreti, 1814, Cart. II, No. 118; secret report, Venice, February 22, 1815, Helfert, *Kaiser Franz und die Stiftung des Lombardo-Venetianischen Königreichs*, Appendix IV, pp. 550–551.

Chapter 5

THE SECRET WORLD

Of all the groups which fanned the embers of discontent and sustained a liberal spirit in Lombardy-Venetia in 1814, none aroused more serious apprehensions in Vienna than the secret societies. Gripped by an overpowering fear that liberal revolutionary doctrines would dangerously undermine the peace and tranquillity of his far-flung domains, Emperor Francis had from the beginning of his reign looked with trepidation upon the various secret societies which existed in Europe and which he sincerely believed had played a leading role in hurling France into a maelstrom of revolution in 1789. In January, 1795, he extended the laws applying to high treason to secret societies. Five months later he decreed that all existing Freemasonic lodges must be closed.[1] In April, 1801, he compelled all government officials, clergymen, and schoolteachers to take an oath that they belonged to no secret society or association[2]—a requirement that was extended in February, 1806, to candidates for doctoral degrees from universities.[3]

A few weeks after Austrian troops entered Venetia in the fall of 1813 the Habsburg monarch stipulated that the oath must also be subscribed to by public servants in the newly reconquered areas of the monarchy. In March, 1814, he decreed that all officials in the oc-

---

[1] Ernst Wangermann, *From Joseph II to the Jacobin Trials: Government Policy and Public Opinion in the Habsburg Dominions in the Period of the French Revolution*, pp. 170–171; Ferdinand Buquoy, "Von Kaisers Franz Logenverbot bis 1848," in *Die Freimaurerei Österreich-Ungarn. Zwölf Vorträge am 30. und 31. März und 1. April 1897 zu Wien gehalten*, pp. 250–251.

[2] Aulic Bohemian-Austrian chancellery decree, April 27, 1801, Francis II (I), *Politische Gesetze und Verordnungen*, Vol. XVI (1801), pp. 78–80.

[3] United aulic chancellery decree, February 13, 1806, *ibid.*, Vol. XXVI (1806), pp. 10–11.

cupied areas, including the Italian provinces, who had been retained at their posts were to promise under oath that they had disassociated themselves from any secret society to which they might ever have belonged and give assurance that they would never again join such an association.[4] A similar formula was included in the oath taken by the members of the Lombard provisional government in May, 1814.[5]

It was but a short step from obligating public officials to renounce membership in clandestine sects to prohibiting such organizations altogether. On June 1, 1814, Mayer von Heldenfeld, at that moment provisional military governor of Mantua, issued a proclamation announcing that all secret societies were to be strongly prohibited in the areas under his jurisdiction.[6] This proscription was soon extended to all Lombardy and Venetia. On July 14 Emperor Francis directed Bellegarde to transmit the text of any decree which he had issued or would issue banning the Freemasons in Lombardy to Governor Reuss-Plauen so that an identical edict would be proclaimed in both of Austria's Italian provinces. The two governors were instructed to order their police rigorously to enforce the provisions of the decree.[7] The requested decree was published in Milan on August 26.[8] In it the commissioner plenipotentiary announced that the Freemasons and all other similar secret societies were to be rigorously prohibited and that their property and funds were to be confiscated. Persons still belonging to such clandestine sects after the announcement of

[4] Hager to Reuss-Plauen, Vienna, March 20, 1814, A. S. (Venice), Presidio di governo, 1814, ad No. 24; Hager to Lattermann, Reuss-Plauen, and Tomassich, Vienna, March 20, 1814, Helfert, *La caduta della dominazione francese*, Appendix I, pp. 233–234.

[5] Oath formula for members of the provisional government, appended to Bellegarde to Emperor Francis, May 21, 1814, Helfert, *La caduta della dominazione francese*, Appendix II, pp. 234–235.

[6] Decree, Mayer von Heldenfeld, Mantua, June 1, 1814, *Giornale di Venezia*, No. 81 (June 21, 1814), p. 4. Also in *Wiener Zeitung*, July 4, 1814, p. 735. See also Sormani's daily report to the provisional regency, Milan, June 7, 1814, A. S. (Milan), Presidenza di governo. Atti secreti, 1814, Cart. I, Fasc. 24/P.R., No. 8.

[7] Imperial resolution, Baden, July 14, 1814, St. A. (Vienna), Conferenz Akten, Ser. b, 1814, No. 1247 (another copy of this resolution is in St. A. [Vienna], Kabinets-Akten, 1814, No. 1605); Hager to Bellegarde, Vienna, July 15, 1814, A. S. (Milan), Presidenza di governo. Atti secreti, 1814, Cart. I, No. 99/P.R.; Hager to Reuss-Plauen, A. S. (Venice), Presidio di governo, 1814, No. 687.

[8] Teresa Confalonieri Casati erroneously wrote her husband that this decree was issued on August 25. See letter dated Milan, August 26, 1814, Gallavresi, *Carteggio del conte Federico Confalonieri*, Vol. I, p. 238.

their prohibition were to be punished with prison sentences lasting from two months to one year. If they were state employees, they were also to be deprived of their jobs.[9] On August 30 Bellegarde sent two copies of this ordinance to Reuss-Plauen,[10] who had it proclaimed in identical language in Venice on September 9.[11]

The decree remained in effect only until the sections of the Austrian legal code which concerned secret societies could be introduced into Italy. After the emperor consulted his supreme justice office in regard to how this could be done,[12] a new decree was published in both Italian provinces on December 30, 1814, notifying the populace that henceforth members of clandestine sects would be punished in the manner prescribed by the Habsburg penal code. In accord with the provisions of this code, anyone founding or enrolling members in a secret society or convoking a meeting of the same was to be punished with three to six months of "harsh imprisonment" (*arresto duro*).[13] Persons attending such a gathering or corresponding with such an organization were to be placed under simple arrest[14] for a period of one week to one month. Second offenders were to serve from one to three months of "harsh imprisonment." Whoever provided or rented a house to a clandestine sect was subject to one to three months of simple arrest. However, if he actively promoted the work of such a proscribed group his one to three months' imprisonment was to be of the "harsh" variety. Officials who failed to report any information they had about secret societies to the appropriate authorities were to be subjected to the same punishment as persons who founded or enrolled members in such an organization.[15]

[9] Decree, imperial provisional regency, Milan, August 26, 1814, *Atti del governo lombardo,* 1814, pp. 123–124.

[10] Bellegarde to Reuss-Plauen, Milan, August 30, 1814, A. S. (Venice), Presidio di governo, 1814, No. 1107.

[11] Notification, September 9, 1814, *Collezione di leggi venete,* 1813–1814, Vol. II, pp. 48–50. An original copy is in A. S. (Venice), Presidio di governo, 1814, No. 1107.

[12] Emperor Francis to Ugarte, Baden, July 14, 1814, St. A. (Vienna), Staats-Rath Akten, 1814, No. 2224. Another copy is in St. A. (Vienna), Conferenz Akten, Ser. b, 1814, No. 1247.

[13] A person sentenced to *arresto duro* wore light chains on his feet, was given only water to drink, and was served only cold food once a day.

[14] They wore no chains and were allowed to eat any food which they procured for themselves or which their families sent to them.

[15] Notification, December 30, 1814, *Collezione di leggi venete,* 1813–1814,

The imperial government in Vienna called upon its officials in Italy to enforce as rigorously as possible the paragraphs in the Austrian penal code that dealt with secret societies.[16] Against the advice of both Bellegarde and Hager, who maintained that past membership in a secret society did not *ipso facto* constitute grounds for dismissal from public office,[17] lists of former Masons were drawn up, and the police made detailed investigations of the character and conduct of a large number of prominent Freemasons.[18] The Habsburgs also took energetic measures to close the Masonic lodges and to make sure that no more Masonic meetings were held.[19]

Although Bellegarde had little faith in the disturbing reports about clandestine sects which were frequently dispatched to his office,[20] the very fact that the higher authorities in the Habsburg capital were so deeply alarmed about the Freemasons and similar sects goaded on ambitious informants who believed that they could ingratiate themselves with their new masters by denouncing suspected Masons or affiliates of other undercover organizations. Minor police officials and ex-Masons sent in exaggerated reports about alleged

Vol. II, pp. 91–98; Reuss-Plauen decree, Venice, December 30, 1814, *Notizie del mondo*, No. 13 (January 13, 1815), p. 6.

[16] Hager to Reuss-Plauen, Vienna, April 24, 1814, A. S. (Venice), Presidio di governo, 1814, ad No. 24.

[17] Several ex-Masons were, in fact, given prominent positions in the Habsburg administration. See especially Mariutti, *Organismo ed azione delle società segrete del veneto*, pp. 24–25.

[18] Hager to Bellegarde, Vienna, July 5, 7, and 13, and August 8, 1814, A. S. (Milan), Presidio di governo. Atti secreti, 1814, Cart. I, Nos. 66/P.R., 87/P.R., and 88/P.R., and Cart. II, No. 195/P.R.; Reuss-Plauen to Ugarte, Padua, April 11, 1814, St. A. (Vienna), Conferenz Akten, Ser. b, 1814, No. 952; Cusani, *Storia di Milano*, Vol. VII, p. 249; Marangoni to Venetian central government, Padua, February 24, 1814, Ottolenghi, *Padova e il Dipartimento del Brenta*, Appendix XXI, pp. 410–411; Mariutti, *Organismo ed azione delle società segrete del veneto*, p. 18; Antonio Zieger, "I primi risultati delle ricerche austriache sui massoni lombardi nel 1814 e 1815," *La Lombardia nel Risorgimento italiano*, Vol. XIII (July, 1928), pp. 5–9; *Carte segrete della polizia austriaca in Italia*, Vol. I, p. 85.

[19] Bellegarde to Hager, Milan, July 20, 1814, Lemmi, *La restaurazione austriaca a Milano*, Appendix XXVI, p. 434; Bellegarde to Hager, Milan, July 27, 1814, A. S. (Milan), Presidenza di governo. Atti secreti, 1814, Cart. I, No. 87/P.R.; Hager to Bellegarde, Vienna, August 8, 1814, *ibid.*, Cart II, No. 195/P.R.; Mariutti, *Organismo ed azione delle società segrete del veneto*, pp. 19–21.

[20] Helfert, *La caduta della dominazione francese*, p. 133.

conspiracies of dangerous clubs; spies, asserting that they had inside information, furnished the police with colorful, often fanciful, tales; and anonymous accusers showered the Habsburg offices with wild accusations against suspected sectarian conspirators.[21]

Typical of the kind of baseless denunciations which were handed to Habsburg officials were those made during the summer of 1814 by Luigi Codini, a notorious swindler and self-styled economic administrator of the Bologna Masonic lodge. Codini presented the Austrian authorities in Venetia with a detailed exposé of an alleged Masonic plot to revolutionize Italy immediately after the end of the Congress of Vienna, which had supposedly been approved by Murat and the chiefs of the Masonic lodges of Ancona, Milan, Venice, and Bologna and which had, he said, already been submitted to Napoleon. The signal for revolt was to be a declaration of war by the king of Naples, after which the lodges were to deliver guns and cockades to the populace and incite them to rebel. According to Codini, 80,000 red and black cockades, 3,000,000 francs, and a quantity of arms were hidden near Bologna, in the country house of Marquis Caprara, Prince Eugene's former riding master. The meetings of the Bologna lodge, which, Codini indicated, played the leading role in the conspiracy, were held in Caprara's town house in that city.

Although the governor of Venetia was highly suspicious of Codini's account, he detailed Police Commissioner Giavarina, of Padua, to interrogate him and informed Bellegarde about his revelations.[22] The field marshal was just as skeptical about Codini's disclosures as Reuss-Plauen; nonetheless, since they were about an alleged plot that could be highly dangerous to Austria's position in Italy, he sent General Suden to Bologna to make a careful on the spot investigation.

In his inquiry the general could find no evidence that either Caprara's town or country house was used for Masonic purposes.[23]

---

[21] Ibid., pp. 191–193; Lemmi, La restaurazione austriaca a Milano, pp. 298–299; Mariutti, Organismo ed azione delle società segrete del veneto, pp. 23–24; Carte segrete della polizia austriaca in Italia, Vol. I, pp. 85–86.

[22] Reuss-Plauen to Hager, Padua, September 2, 1814, A. S. (Venice), Presidio di governo, 1814, No. 1076; Reuss-Plauen to Bellegarde, Padua, September 2, 1814, ibid.

[23] Bellegarde to Reuss-Plauen, Milan, September 15 and 19, 1814, ibid., Nos. 1281 and 1298.

Nevertheless, since, on further questioning, Codini stuck to his story and even gave Giavarina a much more detailed description of Caprara's houses than he had previously,[24] the Habsburg authorities made another careful check. Again they found nothing;[25] whereupon Giavarina was instructed to have Codini lead an Austrian police escort to the alleged Masonic cache and meeting place.[26] As expected, Codini could show them nothing.[27] He was arrested as the swindler that he obviously was and turned over to the criminal authorities for trial and punishment.[28]

In 1814 the Habsburgs were probably more worried about the Freemasons than about any of the numerous other secret societies which existed in Italy and Europe at that time. To a person living in the United States or Europe in the 1960's it is difficult to understand the Austrians' alarm over the Masons, particularly since there is good reason to believe that the Habsburg authorities had already effectively suppressed the Masonic lodges in Lombardy by the summer of 1814[29] and those in Venetia either by June, 1814,[30] or by January, 1815, at the very latest.[31]

On the surface there appeared to be little in the doctrine of Freemasonry which was dangerous to the status quo. No matter which rite they followed, the Masons were taught, in a highly symbolic language supposedly reminiscent of that used by the builders of the

[24] Torresani to Major General Suden, Venice, September 21, 1814, *ibid.*, No. 1281; Raab to Reuss-Plauen, Venice, September 21, 1814, *ibid.*, ad No. 1281; Reuss-Plauen to Hager, Venice, September 23, 1814, *ibid.*, No. 1298.

[25] Bellegarde to Reuss-Plauen, Milan, September 26, 1814, *ibid.*, No. 1374; General Eckhardt to Reuss-Plauen, Bologna, September 28, 1814, *ibid.*

[26] Reuss-Plauen to Hager, Venice, October 1, 1814, *ibid.*

[27] Torresani to General Eckhardt, Venice, October 14, 1814, *ibid.*, No. 1508.

[28] Hager to Reuss-Plauen, Vienna, October 7 and 29, 1814, *ibid.*, Nos. 1532 and 1781; Torresani to Raab, Venice, October 18 and November 13, 1814, *ibid.*, Nos. 1522.1529/P.R. and 1843.

[29] Bellegarde to Hager, Milan, July 27 and August 25, 1814, A. S. (Milan), Presidenza di governo. Atti secreti, 1814, Cart. I, No. 87/P.R., and Cart. II, No. 195 1/2/P.R.; provisional prefect of Mella to Bellegarde, Brescia, August 16, 1814, *ibid.*, Cart. II, No. 232/P.R.; Pietro Dolce to Saurau, November, 1815, Alessandro Luzio, *La Massoneria e il Risorgimento italiano. Saggio storico-critico. Con illustrazioni e molti documenti inediti,* Vol. I, Appendix VI, p. 117.

[30] Hager report, June 7, 1814, St. A. (Vienna), Kabinets-Akten, 1814, No. 1605.

[31] Mariutti, *Organismo ed azione delle società segrete del veneto,* p. 21.

temple of Solomon, to search for enlightenment, truth, and virtue. They were imbued with humanitarian ideas, philanthropic rationalism, religious toleration, and the principles of natural rights. They emphasized tolerance, uprightness, honor, peace, benevolence, and respect for law and order. In their lodges they abstained from all religious and political discussions which could lead to quarrels and dissension.[32]

After Joseph II issued his edict in 1786 tolerating the Masons various Austrian officials, including some in prominent positions in 1814, joined the lodges.[33] During the last few months of the Kingdom of Italy dissentient Freemasons had secretly collaborated with various liberal groups to overthrow the French regime in Italy.[34] In 1814 a large number of Masons, perhaps the majority, and especially those who were government employees, became almost obsequiously

[32] See especially J. G. Findel, *Geschichte der Freimaurerei von der Zeit ihres Entstehens bis auf die Gegenwart*, Vol. I, pp. 7–11; *Manuel maçonique, ou Tuileur de tous les rites de maçonnerie pratiques en France; dans lequel on trouve l'Étymologie et l'Interprétation des Mots et des Noms mystérieux de tous les Grades qui composent les différens Rites. Par un vétéran de la maçonnerie*, pp. 21–22; Carlo Francovich, "Gli Illuminati di Weishaupt et l'idea egualitaria in alcune società segrete del Risorgimento," *Movimento operaio. Rivista di storia e bibliografia*, new ser., Vol. IV (July–August, 1952), pp. 553–555 (also in Carlo Francovich, *Albori socialisti nel Risorgimento. Contributo allo studio delle società segrete [1776–1835]*, pp. 1–3, Giuseppe Leti, *Carboneria e Massoneria nel Risorgimento italiano. Saggio di critica storica*, pp. 29–30; and Pietro Dolce to Saurau, November, 1815, Luzio, *La Massoneria e il Risorgimento italiano*, Vol. I, Appendix VI, pp. 111–112.

[33] Luzio, *La Massoneria e il Risorgimento italiano*, Vol. I, pp. 60–62; Buquoy, "Von Kaisers Franz Logenverbot bis 1848," p. 253.

[34] C. Cipolla, "Un Documento austriaco sui Massoni e sui Carbonari," *La Rassegna Nazionale*, Vol. VII (1885), p. 483; Melzi to Prince Eugene, Milan, December 26, 1813, Francesco Melzi d'Eril, Duca di Lodi, *Memorie—documenti e lettere inedite di Napoleone I. e Beauharnais. Raccolte e ordinate per cura di Giovanni Melzi*, Vol. II, p. 408; Renato Soriga, "Settecento massonizzante e massonismo napoleonico nel primo risorgimento italiano," *Bollettino della Società pavese di storia patria*, Vol. XIX, Fasc. 1–4 (January–December, 1919), p. 84 (also in Soriga, *Le Società segrete, l'emigrazione politica e i primi moti per l'indipendenza. Scritti raccolti e ordinati da Silio Manfredi* [Vol. XXIX of *Collezione storica del Risorgimento italiano*], pp. 58–59); Domenico Spadoni, "Le società segrete nella rivoluzione milanese dell'aprile 1814," *Nuova Antologia. Rivista di Lettere, Scienze ed Arti*, 7th ser., Vol. CCLXV (May, 1929), p. 199; Spadoni, *Il moto del 20 aprile*, pp. 21–23.

loyal to their new masters.[35] At this time Italian Freemasonry, rent by schisms, was suffering from mass desertions.[36]

Then why did the Austrians have an almost morbid fear of the Freemasons in 1814? In the first place, one must not forget that many Austrian and other European ultraconservatives honestly believed that the French Revolution had been nothing but a diabolical Masonic plot and that Freemasonry had been used by the French as a tool to aid them in spreading the Revolution over much of Europe.[37] The rapid expansion of the sect in Italy during the recent past seemed, in their opinion, to bear this out. Although a few Masonic lodges had been established in both Lombardy and Venetia before the outbreak of the French Revolution, Masonry had relatively few adherents there before northern Italy fell under French control. After Napoleon turned the Freemasons into a political instrument of the French they spread rapidly to every part of the Apennine peninsula. By 1805 there were seven lodges in Milan, and others were established in practically all the provincial capitals of the Kingdom of Italy. Since Napoleon placed the lodges under his personal protection, showered honors and favors upon their members, and appointed some of them to the highest positions in the land, all sorts of individuals flocked into them.[38] However, when discontented Ma-

[35] Mariutti, *Organismo ed azione delle società segrete del veneto*, p. 23; Luzio, *La Massoneria e il Risorgimento italiano*, Vol. I, pp. 58–63; Pietro Dolce to Saurau, November, 1815, *ibid.*, Appendix VI, p. 117; Piero Pieri, *Le società segrete ed i moti degli anni 1820–21 e 1831. Con 159 illustrazioni e tavole fuori testo*, pp. 57–58.

[36] Luzio, *La Massoneria e il Risorgimento italiano*, Vol. I, pp. 196–197; Giuseppe Gallavresi, "La franc-maçonnerie et la formation de l'unité italienne," *Revue des questions historiques*, Vol. XCVII, No. 2 (October, 1922), pp. 419–420.

[37] See especially anonymous report, May 14, 1814, enclosed in Hager to Bellegarde, Vienna, July 7, 1814, A. S. (Milan), Presidenza di governo. Atti secreti, 1814, Cart. I, No. 88/P.R.

[38] For accounts of the Freemasons in the Kingdom of Italy, see Bianca Marcolongo, "La massoneria nel secolo XVIII," *Studi Storici*, Vol. XIX (1910), pp. 443–450; Carlo Nardi, "La vita di Francesco Saverio Salfi (1759–1832)," *Rassegna storica del Risorgimento*, Vol. VII, Fasc. 2 (April–September, 1920), pp. 225–228; Cipolla, "Un Documento austriaco sui Massoni e sui Carbonari," pp. 480–483; Renato Soriga, *Il primo Grande Oriente d'Italia* (estratto dal *Bollettino della Società pavese di storia patria*, Vol. XVII, Fasc. 1–4 [January–December, 1917]), pp. 4–18; Luzio, *La Massoneria e il Risorgimento italiano*, Vol. I, pp.

sons, tired of Napoleonic despotism and humiliated by the fawning
servility of the official lodges towards the French emperor, began
late in 1812 to agitate for autonomist reforms in their organization
that would emancipate it from French tutelage and to look with favor upon Joachim Murat's nebulous ambitions to become master of
a united Italy, the viceroy ordered the closing of all the Masonic
lodges the next year.[39] As a consequence, when Austrian troops
entered Italy they found the Freemasons virtually on the point of
dissolution and were easily able to shut down the few feeble, demoralized lodges which were still in existence.[40] Nonetheless, even
though Freemasonry was little more than a hollow specter in 1814,
various Austrian officials, particularly in Vienna, were still possessed
with an unwholesome fear about their potential dangerousness.

Another reason why many Austrian conservatives hurled anathe-
mas against the Freemasons was the conviction of the Habsburg
emperor and the conservative circles surrounding him that they
were a vehicle for the propagation of liberal ideas and were dangerous enemies of crowned sovereigns.[41] Also, rightly believing that the
Masons had been one of the chief instruments for proselytizing
Deism,[42] they feared that the society was plotting to destroy Ca-

---

30–56; Pietro Dolce to Saurau, November, 1815, *ibid.*, Appendix VI, pp. 113–
117; G[iovanni de] Castro, *Il mondo secreto*, Vol. VI, pp. 103–105; and Soriga,
"Settecento massonizzante e massonismo napoleonico," pp. 68–75.

[39] Marcolongo, "La massoneria nel secolo XVIII," pp. 450–451; Soriga, "Settecento massonizzante e massonismo napoleonico," p. 84; Cipolla, "Un Documento
austriaco sui Massoni e sui Carbonari," p. 483; Pietro Dolce to Saurau, November, 1815, Luzio, *La Massoneria e il Risorgimento italiano*, Vol. I, Appendix VI,
p. 116; Spadoni, *Il moto del 20 aprile*, pp. 21–23.

[40] Bellegarde to Hager, Milan, August 25, 1814, A. S. (Milan), Presidenza di
governo. Atti secreti, 1814, Cart. II, No. 195½/P.R.; Luzio, *La Massoneria e
il Risorgimento italiano*, Vol. I, p. 196; Lemmi, *La restaurazione austriaca a
Milano*, p. 296.

[41] Anonymous report, May 14, 1814, enclosed in Hager to Bellegarde, Vienna,
July 7, 1814, A. S. (Milan), Presidenza di governo. Atti secreti, 1814, Cart. I,
No. 88/P.R.; Ottolenghi, *Padova e il Dipartimento del Brenta*, p. 186; Franco-
vich, "Gli Illuminati di Weishaupt," p. 553 (also in his *Albori socialisti nel
Risorgimento*, p. 1).

[42] Egilberto Martire, *La massoneria italiana. A proposito di una massoneria
filo-cattolica*, pp. 11–13; Johann Michael Raich, "Freimaurerische Principien und
Logensysteme," in *Die Freimaurerei Österreich-Ungarns*, pp. 4–8 and 28–30;
August Horneffer, *Die Freimaurerei*, p. 47; Luzio, *La Massoneria e il Risorgi-*

tholicism and Christianity everywhere. Furthermore, to Emperor Francis Freemasonry was the equivalent of revolutionary Jacobinism and anarchism.[43] Then, too, the Habsburgs were apprehensive that the Masons were proselytizing the cause of Italian independence;[44] that they were seconding the campaign to unite Italy under the crown of Murat;[45] and that they were in very close contact with Napoleon at Elba.[46] Last but by no means least, disturbed by the numerous reports that the Italian Freemasons were under strong British influence, they feared that the two were exerting strenuous efforts to unite Italy into a constitutional monarchy under British hegemony.[47]

Given the pro-Austrian predilections of many Lombard and Venetian Freemasons in 1814 and the ease with which the Austrian authorities succeeded in closing the lodges, the trepidation of the Habsburg sovereign over the Masons was certainly not due to the

---

mento italiano, Vol. I, p. 10; N. Deschamps, *Les sociétés secrètes et la société ou philosophie de l'histoire contemporaine,* Vol. I, pp. lxiii, 6, and 24–39; Leti, *Carboneria e Massoneria,* p. 8.

[43] Zieger, "I primi risultati delle ricerche austriache sui massoni lombardi," p. 5.

[44] Anonymous report, May 14, 1814, enclosed in Hager to Bellegarde, Vienna, July 7, 1814, A. S. (Milan), Presidenza di governo. Atti secreti, 1814, Cart. I, No. 88/P.R.; Ottolenghi, *Padova e il Dipartimento del Brenta,* pp. 187–188.

[45] Hager to Bellegarde, Vienna, July 5, 1814, Lemmi, *La restaurazione austriaca a Milano,* Appendix XXIV, p. 431 (the original is in A. S. [Milan], Presidenza di governo. Atti secreti, 1814, Cart. I, No. 65/P.R.); Hager reports, July 5 and 18, 1814, St. A. (Vienna), Conferenz Akten, Ser. b, 1814, Nos. 1356 and 1423.

[46] Report from Bologna, June 30, 1814, A. S. (Milan), Presidenza di governo. Atti secreti, 1814, Cart. II, No. 118; Bargello report, Leghorn, November 16, 1814, *ibid.,* Cart. III, No. 305/P.R.

[47] Hager report, June 7, 1814, St. A. (Vienna), Kabinets-Akten, 1814, No. 1603; Raab to Hager, Padua, June 25, 1814, Lemmi, *La restaurazione austriaca a Milano,* Appendix XXII, pp. 426–427 (the original is in A. S. [Milan]) Presidenza di governo. Atti secreti, 1814, Cart. I, ad No. 65/P.R.); Hager report, July 5, 1814, St. A. (Vienna), Conferenz Akten, Ser. b, 1814, No. 1356; Hager to Bellegarde, Vienna, July 5, 1814, Lemmi, *La restaurazione austriaca a Milano,* Appendix XXIV, p. 431 (the original is in A. S. [Milan], Presidenza di governo. Atti secreti, 1814, Cart. I, No. 65/P.R.); Bellegarde to Metternich, Milan, July 28, 1814, A. S. (Milan), Presidenza di governo. Atti secreti, 1814, Cart. V, ad No. 595/P.R.; Reuss-Plauen to Bellegarde, Venice, October 19, 1814, *ibid.,* No. 597/P.R.; excerpts from police reports, August 31–September 3, 1814, *Kriegs-Archiv* (Vienna), Feld Akten (Italien), 1814, Fasz. IX, ad No. 10.

fact that the Freemasons actually represented a serious threat to the status quo. Much of the explanation has to be sought in the irrational anti-revolutionary hysteria which gripped many monarchs, political leaders, and clergy, as well as many among the great mass of population, not only in the Habsburg monarchy, but also in Europe as a whole. Since many ultraconservatives held the Masons at least partly responsible for the dissemination of detested revolutionary ideologies, they indiscriminately stigmatized all political and religious ideas which they abhorred as Masonic, just as their counterparts in the twentieth century have all too frequently dubbed as communistic a wide variety of leftist opinions which are anathema to them. There was all the more reason for them to hold the Masons accountable for the spread of noxious radical ideas since several early nineteenth century secret societies which actually did represent real and imminent dangers to conservative institutions and to the existing political and social order originated as offshoots of the Freemasons. Some of them were organized by Jacobin Freemasons who were disgusted because the official lodges obsequiously adulated a Napoleon who, the Jacobins believed, had betrayed the most sacred principles of the French Revolution; others were instituted by their liberal- and nationalist-minded confreres who were angry because the official organization did not protest against Napoleon's betrayal of their own particular nationalist causes. Moreover, some conspiratorial sects which probably had no official connection with the Freemasons made use of Masonic symbols and ritual either to appeal to the masses or to hide the real nature of their own organizations from the police.[48]

[48] See, for example, Pietro Dolce to Saurau, November, 1815, Luzio, *La Massoneria e il Risorgimento italiano*, Vol. I, p. 113; Angelo Ottolini, *La Carboneria dalle origini ai primi tentativi insurrezionali (1797-1817)* (Vol. XVI of *Collezione storica del Risorgimento italiano*), pp. 25–26; Galavresi, "La franc-maçonnerie et la formation de l'unité italienne," pp. 415–416 and 419–422; Leti, *Carboneria e Massoneria*, pp. 26 and 64; Deschamps, *Le sociétés secrètes*, Vol. I, pp. xxviii–xxix; Marga Barazzoni, "Le società segrete germaniche ed i loro rapporti con i cospiratori lombardi del 1821," *Rassegna storica del Risorgimento*, Vol. XIX, Fasc. 1 (January–March, 1932), pp. 91–92; Pio Ferrieri, *Dalla via del Monte di Pietà allo Spielberg*, p. 21; and Bianca Marcolongo, "Le origini della Carboneria e le Società segrete nell'Italia Meridionale dal 1810 al 1820," *Studi Storici*, Vol. XX (1812), pp. 317–318. It should be noted, however, that Alessandro Luzio (see his *La Massoneria e il Risorgimento italiano*, Vol. I, pp. 155–161 and 205–206) and Egilberto Martire (see his *La massoneria italiana*, pp.

Therefore, a detailed examination of the origins, nature, and aims of these societies is of value to a study of Lombardy and Venetia under the Austrian provisional government if only because Emperor Francis' almost morbid fear of them strongly influenced Habsburg policy and practices in Lombardy-Venetia. Such a study is all the more important because since 1917, when Alessandro Luzio published Pietro Dolce's reports to the Habsburg secret police, various Italian historians have tended to overemphasize the role which secret societies played in the liberal movement in Lombardy-Venetia in 1814. For these reasons, it is of paramount importance to make a serious effort to ascertain just what secret societies existed in Austria's Italian provinces and to find out how prominent a part they actually took in the liberal anti-Habsburg movement at that time.

Perhaps the attention of many a scholar has been drawn to the secret societies because the origins and activities of these organizations are shrouded in mystery and obscurity. To protect themselves against discovery, their officers kept few, if any, records; hence, there is little documentary evidence about them. What evidence does exist needs to be studied with the greatest care, since the conspirators occasionally fabricated records, changed codes, form, and even names, and worked through "front organizations" for the deliberate purpose of hoodwinking the police. Both their bitter Catholic and conservative opponents and various conspirators who later wrote about the secret societies frequently greatly exaggerated their size and importance. Occasional bits of "inside information" supplied by spies or other informers must be scrupulously evaluated, for some of this material was deliberately forged for the express purpose of selling it to the police.[49] Police and trial records are usually more reliable, but in many instances they are quite meager and vague.

One of the secret societies which originated as an offshoot of the Freemasons and which apparently sought to dominate and use the Masons and other sects as a tool to disseminate Jean Jacques Rousseau's egalitarian principles—principles which reflected themselves in French revolutionary Jacobinism—was the Illuminati, founded in

---

19–21) have minimized the connections between the Freemasons and the other secret societies.

[49] For an example, see my "La costituzione guelfa e i servizi segreti austriaci," *Rassegna storica del Risorgimento*, Vol. L, Fasc. 3 (July–September, 1963), pp. 343–376.

Bavaria in 1776 by Adam Weishaupt.[50] Before the order was broken up by the Bavarian government in 1785–1787 it had spread through most of Germany and had reached both Lombardy and Venetia. It is possible that Illuminati lodges were subsequently also instituted in the Kingdom of Two Sicilies, where the English may have had a hand in encouraging them.[51]

Although some authorities maintain that the Tugendbund (League of Virtue) was of Masonic origin,[52] it is entirely possible that it was a creation of the Illuminati.[53] Illuminati members probably also had a hand in founding the Philadelphia Order—a hidden organization within the official Freemasonic society, whose members secretly worked for the realization of the equalitarian aims of the old Illuminati and Jacobins by fomenting republican revolutions against the Napoleonic regime.[54] According to one tradition, they were started in Besançon in 1797. The conspirator Filippo Michele Buonarroti (1761–1837) had related that the society originated in 1799. Carlo Francovich, one of the most recent Italian authorities on secret societies, surmises that the Philadelphians were first formed in 1803 by Masonic elements in the French army and a group of Jacobins belonging to Illuminati lodges who had disguised themselves as Templars of the Masonic Scotch rite. According to other writers, the

---

[50] Francovich, "Gli Illuminati di Weishaupt," pp. 555–568 (also in his *Albori socialisti nel Risorgimento*, pp. 3–14); Elizabeth L. Eisenstein, *The First Professional Revolutionist: Filippo Michele Buonarroti (1761–1837). A Biographical Essay*, pp. 39–40; F. T. B. Clavel, *Histoire pittoresque de la franc-maçonnerie et des sociétés secrètes anciennes et modernes*, pp. 190–194; Deschamps, *Les sociétés secrètes*, Vol. II, pp. 102–105; *Philo's* [Adolf Kniegge's] *endliche Erklärung und Antwort, auf verschiedene Anforderungen und Fragen, die an ihn ergangen, seine Verbindung mit dem Orden der Illuminaten betreffend, passim.*

[51] Francovich, "Gli Illuminati di Weishaupt," pp. 570–576 (also in his *Albori socialisti nel Risorgimento*, pp. 15–18); Pietro Dolce to Saurau, November, 1815, Luzio, *La Massoneria e il Risorgimento italiano*, Vol. I, Appendix VI, pp. 115–116; Soriga, "Settecento massonizzante e massonismo napoleonico," in Soriga, *Le Società segrete*, p. 37; Eisenstein, *Buonarroti*, pp. 41–44.

[52] See, for example, Barazzoni, "Le società segrete germaniche," pp. 91–92.

[53] Clavel, *Histoire de la franc-maçonnerie*, p. 371; Francovich, "Gli Illuminati di Weishaupt," p. 585 (also in his *Albori socialisti nel Risorgimento*, p. 28).

[54] Francovich, "Gli Illuminati di Weishaupt," pp. 577–579 (also in his *Albori socialisti nel Risorgimento*, pp. 22–24). It should, however, be noted that Arturo Bersano believes that the Philadelphians were of Masonic origin. See his *L'abate Francesco Bonardi e i suoi tempi. Contributo alla storia delle società segrete*, p. 86.

organization was established in 1804. All authorities have connected Colonel Jacques Oudet (1775–1809) with the founding of the order and have maintained that its members played an important role in organizing the republican conspiracies against Napoleon in 1808 and 1812 which have usually been attributed to Claude-François de Malet. Among the leaders of the society were Buonarroti, who probably joined it in 1803 or 1804, and the Italo-French conspirator Luigi Angeloni (1758–1843).[55]

Another secret society that was even more frequently mentioned among those existing in Lombardia-Venetia in 1814 was the Adelfia.[56] The theories which have been offered in regard to the origins of the Adelfi are even more conflicting than those about the Philadelphians. The author of a report on Italian secret societies which Giuseppe Pardi found in the Tuscan archives thought that the Adelfi were of English inception.[57] Practically all other authorities are agreed, however, that the society had its beginnings in France.[58] Some believe that it began as an anti-Masonic society[59] or as a schism from or a

---

[55] See especially Francovich, "Gli Illuminati di Weishaupt," p. 577 (also in his *Albori socialisti nel Risorgimento*, p. 21); Arthur Lehning, "Buonarroti and His International Secret Societies," *International Review of Social History*, Vol. I, Pt. 1 (1956), pp. 118–120; Marcolongo, "Le origini della Carboneria," pp. 239–240; and Renato Soriga, "Le società segrete e i moti del '21 in Piemonte," in Soriga, *Le Società segrete*, p. 110; Armando Saitta, *Filippo Buonarroti. Contributi alla storia della sua vita e del suo pensiero*, Vol. I (in *Storia ed economia. Studi, testi, documenti, quaderni*), pp. 81–82.

[56] See especially Spadoni, *Il moto del 20 aprile*, p. 24; Soriga, "Le società segrete e i moti del '21 in Piemonte," pp. 110–112; and *Storia di Milano*, Vol. XIII: *L'età napoleonica*, p. 297.

[57] Collection of documents on secret societies known in Italy between 1800 and 1818, in Giuseppe Pardi, "Nuove notizie sull'origine della Carboneria e di qualche altra Società segreta," *Nuova Rivista Storica*, Vol. X, Fasc. 6 (November–December, 1926), p. 477.

[58] Pagani memoir on secret societies, 1818, Soriga, "Le società segrete e i moti del '21 in Piemonte," Appendix I, p. 124; Luzio, *La Massoneria e il Risorgimento italiano*, Vol. I, p. 196; Arturo Bersano, "Adelfi, Federati e Carbonari. Contributo alla Storia delle Società segrete," *Atti della Reale Accademia delle Scienze di Torino*, Vol. XLV (1909–1910), p. 413; P. Ilario Rinieri, "Le sette in Italia dopo la restaurazione del 1814. La congiura di Macerata (1817)," *Il Risorgimento Italiano*, Vol. XIX, Fasc. 1–2 (January–June, 1926), p. 9; Ottolini, *La Carboneria*, p. 45; Albert Falcionelli, *Les sociétés secrètes italiennes. Les Carbonari.—La Camorra. La Mafia*, p. 19.

[59] Luzio, *La Massoneria e il Risorgimento italiano*, Vol. I, p. 196.

reform of the Freemasons.[60] Others attribute its creation to left-wing Jacobins. Rinieri has suggested that the Adelfi were an outgrowth or continuation of a society that stemmed from primitive Jacobinism.[61] Claude Desjoyaux has hinted that they arose out of a secession from the Illuminati of a left-wing republican group who rallied around Lucien Bonaparte and General Malet.[62] Federico Confalonieri maintained that Colonel Oudet founded the Adelfi and that General Malet and "most of those who fell with him belonged to it."[63] According to another tradition, Angeloni, Marquis Marie Joseph de Lafayette, and Servan established the society in 1804.[64] Both Francovich[65] and Arthur Lehning,[66] however, maintain that the Adelfi were a derivation from the Philadelphians, whom "they replaced in a certain sense even though the Philadelphians also continued to exist after the Adelfia was founded."[67] Various other historians, perhaps influenced among other things by Confalonieri's statement to this effect,[68] have expressed the opinion that Adelfia and Philadelphia were two different names for the same organization.[69]

Various present-day Italian historians are convinced that the Adelfi existed in the Kingdom of Italy and already had close ties

[60] Bersano, "Adelfi, Federati e Carbonari," p. 413; Gallavresi, "La franc-maçonnerie et la formation de l'unité italienne," 419; Renato Soriga, "Pavia e i moti del 1821," *La Lombardia nel Risorgimento italiano*, Vol. XII (July, 1928), p. 53 (also in Soriga, *Le Società segrete*, p. 210); Soriga, "Le società segrete e i moti del '21 in Piemonte," p. 112; Falcionelli, *Les Sociétés secrètes italiennes*, p. 19; Lemmi, *La restaurazione austriaca a Milano*, p. 294.

[61] In his "Le sette in Italia dopo la restaurazione del 1814," pp. 10–11.

[62] See his "Le général baron Perrone di San Martino," *Il Risorgimento Italiano*, Vol. IV (1911), pp. 982–983.

[63] Confalonieri, *Memorie e lettere*, Vol. I, p. 91; Alessandro d'Ancona, *Federico Confalonieri. Su documenti inediti di archivi pubblici e privati*, p. 50.

[64] Bersano, "Adelfi, Federati e Carbonari," p. 413.

[65] See his "Gli Illuminati di Weishaupt," p. 584 (also in his *Albori socialisti nel Risorgimento*, p. 27).

[66] See his "Buonarroti and His International Secret Societies," p. 121.

[67] Francovich, "Gli Illuminati di Weishaupt," p. 584 (also in his *Albori socialisti nel Risorgimento*, p. 27).

[68] Confalonieri, *Memorie e lettere*, Vol. I, p. 91.

[69] Marcolongo, "Le origini della Carboneria," p. 239; Rinieri, "Le sette in Italia dopo la restaurazione del 1814," p. 28; Leti, *Carboneria e Massoneria*, p. 135; Spadoni, *Il moto del 20 aprile*, p. 24; Lemmi, *La restaurazione austriaca a Milano*, p. 294; Helfert, *Kaiser Franz und die Stiftung des Lombardo-Venetianischen Königreichs*, p. 137; Bersano, *L'abate Francesco Bonardi e i suoi tempi*, p. 85–86.

with the Great Firmament in Paris by the spring of 1814.[70] During the past quarter of a century it has commonly been thought that the Adelfi played a role in the Milanese revolution of April 20[71] and that they had a hand in the May 19 Turin conspiracy[72] to make Napoleon head of a new Roman empire.[73] These assertions have largely been based on testimony given by the Trentine conspirator Gioacchino Prati, especially his allegation that the death of Finance Minister Giuseppe Prina, who was murdered during the April 20 revolution in Milan, had as early as 1812 "been determined by the secret tribunal of the Great Firmament."[74] Additional evidence that the Adelfi existed in Milan in 1814 was supplied to the Austrian police in 1817 by the piano teacher at the Milan conservatory Benedetto Negri, who informed them that he had been invited to join the Adelfia society in the summer of 1814.[75] Furthermore, even though Confalonieri wrote in his memoirs that he "jealously kept his secret" about the Adelfia society into which he had been initiated in Paris in the summer of 1814,[76] it seems plausible to assume that, bitter and courageous an opponent of Napoleonic despotism and Habsburg absolutism as he was, he might have joined or promoted an Adelfia society in Milan or at least told his numerous liberal friends about it.

The aim of the Adelfia society was not only to overthrow Napoleon and later to expel the Habsburgs from Italy but also to put an end to despotism and to work for the "regeneration of the people."

[70] See, for example, Bersano, "Adelfi, Federati e Carbonari," pp. 414 and 417–418; Bersano, *L'abate Francesco Bonardi e i suoi tempi*, p. 91; Spadoni, *Il moto del 20 aprile*, pp. 24 and 278; Luigi Ceria, *L'eccidio del Prina e gli ultimi giorni del regno italico* (*1814*), p. 184; and *Storia di Milano*, Vol. XIII: *L'età napoleonica*, p. 297. It should noted, however, that the special committee appointed to try Silvio Pellico, Piero Maroncelli, and their companions reported that the Austrian police in Italy first heard of the Adelfi in 1816 (Orefici to Sardagna, Milan, August 21, 1822, St. A. [Vienna], Staatskanzlei, Provinzen, 1816–1822, Fasz. XXXVI, No. 247, Fo. 214.

[71] See *post*, p. 238.

[72] See *ante*, pp. 183–185.

[73] Weil, *Murat*, Vol. I, p. 101; Rinieri, "Le sette in Italia dopo la restaurazione del 1814," pp. 9–10; Bersano, *L'abate Francesco Bonardi e i suoi tempi*, p. 92.

[74] Pietro Pedrotti, *Note autobiografiche del cospiratore trentino Gioacchino Prati, con annotazioni e commenti. Sulla base di documenti inediti d'archivio*, pp. 33–34.

[75] Pagani memoir on secret societies, 1818, Soriga, "Le società segrete e i moti del '21 in Piemonte," Appendix I, p. 125.

[76] Confalonieri, *Memorie e lettere*, Vol. I, pp. 91–92.

The Adelfi exerted themselves to spread the ideas of freedom among the peasants and other untutored classes and strove to win influence in all the cabinets of Italy and Europe. In addition, they made concerted efforts to penetrate other secret societies and to assume supreme direction of all of them.[77]

Probably another goal of the Adelfi might have been to proselytize left-wing Jacobin ideas in Italy and in Europe. According to information collected by the police in the Papal States, when an Adelfo met another member of the society the following questions and replies were heard: "Who are you?" "Emilio." "Where are you going?" "In the forest." "Who will liberate you?" "A fire."[78] Various defendants in the Carbonari trials in the early 1820's asserted that the catechism for the first grade was highly symbolical and dealt exclusively with the fire which was to liberate the adepts, who were called "Emilio," from the darkness which surrounded them.[79] The Lombard police official Pagani maintained that, at least in 1814, the word "Emilio" was nothing but "an allusion to the homonymous work of Rousseau [i.e., Emile], which figured in every Adelfi church as the gospel of the free man."[80] If that was actually the case, one of the goals of at least some of the Adelfi must also have been "to regenerate the people" by imbuing them with the egalitarian ideas of the French Revolution with which Jean Jacques Rousseau's name was so intimately connected.

Since the Adelfi, like so many other conspiratorial sects, stemmed at least indirectly either from the Freemasons or the Illuminati, which was a Masonic offshoot, and retained close ties with them, their rites, signs of recognition, and symbols assumed a strong Masonic coloration.[81] In fact, the links between the two organizations

[77] Ibid., p. 91; collection of documents on the secret societies known in Italy between 1800 and 1818, Pardi, "Nuove notizie sull'origine della Carboneria," p. 477; secret report of an initiate in Turin, enclosed in Metternich memoir, 1824, Rinieri, Della Vita e delle Opere di Silvio Pellico, Vol. II, p. 62; Bersano, "Adelfi, Federati e Carbonari," p. 415; Soriga, "Pavia e i moti del 1821," pp. 53–54.

[78] Excerpt from a report sent to the cardinal secretary of state, n.d. [1818], St. A. (Vienna), Diego Graf Guicciardi, Geheime Correspondenz, Fasz. 1 (1816–1820), Fo. 2.

[79] Orefici to Sardagna, Milan, August 21, 1822, St. A. (Vienna), Staatskanzlei, Provinzen, 1816–1822, Fasz. XXXVI, No. 247, Fo. 214.

[80] Pagani memoir on secret societies, 1818, Soriga, "Le società segrete e i moti del '21 in Piemonte," Appendix I, p. 125.

[81] See also Luzio, La Massoneria e il Risorgimento italiano, Vol. I, p. 157.

remained so close that a decree of the Great Firmament of the Perfect Sublime Masters expressly stipulated that every Adelfo who was not a Mason was to have the three symbolic grades of that order conferred upon him.[82] The police officials in the Papal States and Austria were of the opinion that until 1817 or 1818, when they changed their secret code, the Adelfi used Masonic ciphers for their clandestine communications.[83] They probably also had another symbolic language, unknown to the Masons, which they used for private conversations with each other within the Masonic lodges.[84] It is possible that in some places their mode of correspondence and symbolism were taken over "from the Illuminati sect of Germany."[85]

The fact that so much of the evidence about the Adelfi is identical with or very similar to that about the Philadelphians indicates either that the two might have been the same organization or that a very close relationship might have existed between them. It is true that the decree of the Great Firmament of the Perfect Sublime Masters of the year 5812[86] and information given in his memoirs by the intriguing international conspirator and later police informant Johannes Wit von Dörring,[87] who was well versed in European secret societies, would make one think that the two societies were separate and independent of each other. The Austrian judges in the Carbonari trials also saw no connection between the two sects.[88] Nevertheless, other

[82] Decree, Great Firmament, 22nd day of the 7th lunar month, Year 5812, enclosed in Metternich memoir, 1824, Rinieri, *Della Vita e delle Opere di Silvio Pellico*, Vol. II, pp. 43–44; Jean Witt [Wit von Dörring], *Les sociétés secrètes de France et d'Italie, ou Fragments de ma vie et de mon temps* (hereafter cited as Wit von Dörring, *Les sociétés secrètes*), p. 9.

[83] Sedlnitzky to Strassoldo, Vienna, March 27, 1818, St. A. (Milan), Presidenza di governo. Atti secreti, 1818, Cart. XXI, No. 83/geh.

[84] Secret report from Turin, n.d., Rinieri, *Della Vita e della Opere di Silvio Pellico*, Vol. II, p. 53.

[85] Collection of documents on secret societies known in Italy between 1800 and 1818, Pardi, "Nuove notizie sull'origine della Carboneria," p. 477.

[86] In this decree it was expressly stated that the "societies of the Philadelphians and of the Adelfi are incorporated into the Order" (decree dated the 22nd day of the 7th month of the Year 5812, Rinieri, *Della Vita e delle Opere di Silvio Pellico*, Vol. II, p. 43).

[87] Wit von Dörring stated that at least during the time of the Malet conspiracy the Adelfi and Philadelphians were separate organizations. See his *Les sociétés secrètes*, p. 8.

[88] From the testimony which the defendants gave during their interrogations, the Austrian judges concluded that after the fall of Napoleon the Philadelphia

information which we have about the Adelfi and the Philadelphians lends strong support to the theory that the two organizations were the same. Except for the assertion that the Adelfia society was of English origin, the surmises about its origins boil down to theories that it was started in France as a schism or reform of the Freemasons, that left-wing Jacobins played an important role in establishing the organization, that it rose as a secession of radical republicans from the Illuminati, that Colonel Oudet founded the group, and that General Malet and Angeloni played important roles in it. These statements are almost identical with the most generally accepted conjectures about the founding of the Philadelphians: that General Oudet founded the Philadelphia society and that Angeloni and Malet were among its most important leaders. They also fit neatly into Francovich's thesis that the Philadelphians were founded by Freemasons in the French army and Jacobin elements in the Illuminati, especially since it appears that one of the aims of the Adelfi was the same as that of the Illuminati: that of proselytizing Rousseau's egalitarian principles. It thus appears that Confalonieri might possibly have been right when he expressed the opinion that the Adelfi and Philadelphians were the same group[89]—at least in 1814.

Perhaps the clue to the conflicting testimonies about the Philadelphia and Adelfia societies can be found in the clandestine activities of the enigmatic professional revolutionist Filippo Michele Buonarroti,

---

society divided itself into two societies: the Carbonari and the Regenerated Franks (Francs Regenérés), and that soon thereafter a group of secessionists from the latter group founded a new society called the European Regeneration. See Orefici to Sardagna, Milan, August 21, 1822, St. A. (Vienna), Staatskanzlei, Provinzen, 1816–1822, Fasz. XXXVI, No. 247, Fo. 214; summary of the testimony and proof given in the acts of the Austrian investigation commission in Milan in regard to the origins, spread, connections, and activities of the revolutionary societies in Italy, Milan, August 30, 1822, *ibid.*, Fos. 25–26; revelations of various persons who had higher grades in European revolutionary societies, Milan, August 30, 1822, *ibid.*, Fo. 14.

[89] Confalonieri, *Memorie e lettere*, Vol. I, p. 91. It should be noted that Miss Eisenstein says that because "of conflicting evidence and a confusing terminology further compounded by varying French and Italian orthography, it is almost impossible to identify the separate roles played by" the Adelfi and the Philadelphians (see her *Buonarroti*, p. 41 n.). Saitta asserts that it is impossible to come to any definitive conclusions as to whether the Adelfi and Philadelphians "differed from each other only in name or also in doctrine or in the way they were constituted" (see his *Buonarroti*, Vol. I, p. 81).

whose name is always mentioned in connection with both the Philadelphians and the Adelfi, and the role played in the European conspiratorial world by his own organization, the Perfect Sublime Masters—a highly secret society which frequently changed names[90] and the members of which were strongly prohibited from putting anything about their organization in writing.[91] There are indications that, like the Philadelphians and the Adelfi, the Perfect Sublime Masters were very much influenced by the aims, practices, and form of organization of the Illuminati.[92]

Like the Illuminati, the Perfect Sublime Masters sought to control the other secret societies and to use them for their own political ends. In fact, they aspired to become the clandestine directing committee for all the European revolutionary movements.[93] Following a highly symbolic ritual quite reminiscent of that of the Freemasons,[94] they professed a belief in God as the grand architect of nature, the author of everything moral and just, and the protector of the social order.[95] Its members were instructed to be "free, modest, generous, moderate and imperturbable." They were to obey only their own inner sense of duty, to feel that they were superior to nobody else, to conserve only the barest necessities for themselves, to eat and drink sparingly, and to fear nothing except crime or vice. They were told that the aim of their order was "to destroy despotism, pride, luxury, and superstition." They cherished the belief that at some future time virtue would triumph and the human race would prosper.[96] They were im-

[90] Excerpts from the interrogations of Andryane (in French), Rinieri, "Le sette in Italia dopo la restaurazione del 1814," p. 29. An Italian copy is in Rinieri, *Della Vita e delle Opere di Silvio Pellico*, Vol. II, p. 49.

[91] Luzio, *La Massoneria e il Risorgimento italiano*, Vol. I, pp. 158–159.

[92] Eisenstein, *Buonarroti*, pp. 35–36.

[93] Johannes Wit von Dörring, *Fragmente aus meinem Leben und meiner Zeit*, p. 24.

[94] Eisenstein, *Buonarroti*, p. 44; Saitta, *Buonarroti*, Vol. I, pp. 88–91; decree, Great Firmament, July 22, 1822, Rinieri, *Della Vita e delle Opere di Silvio Pellico*, Vol. II, p. 43; paragraphs 14 and 15 of the statutes of the Perfect Sublime Masters, n.d., *ibid.*, p. 53; Pagani memoir on secret societies, 1818, Soriga, "Le società segrete e i moti del '21 in Piemonte," Appendix I, pp. 127–128; Bersano, *L'abate Francesco Bonardi e i suoi tempi*, pp. 97 and 100.

[95] Constitution of the Perfect Sublime Masters, n.d., enclosed in duke of Modena to Metternich, March 24, 1822, St. A. (Vienna), Staatskanzlei, Provinzen, 1816–1822, Fasz. XXXVI, Fo. 125.

[96] *Ibid.*, Fos. 127–129. See also Lombardo-Venetian senate to Emperor Francis, Verona, August 27, 1823, Augusto Sandonà, *Contributo alla storia dei*

bued with the idea that "any power originating from any other source than the will of the many must be condemned as a crime."[97]

The members of the second highest rank in the hierarchy, the Sublime Elect, were informed that the true aim of the order was to work for the realization of a republican form of government, in which "only the people are the rulers" and in which those who wielded the executive power should be elected by the populace.[98] Only the few leaders in the highest rank, the Areopagus, however, knew that the final aim of the society was to destroy the institution of private property and to make the republic the "sole Proprietor" so that "like a mother it will afford to each of its members equal education, food and labour."[99] The real goal of Buonarroti's Perfect Sublime Masters, like that of the Illuminati, was, thus, to realize the principles of Rousseau's *Social Contract*[100] or perhaps even those of the Babeuf conspiracy.[101] The Perfect Sublime Masters not only intended to establish republican governments in Europe but also to make radical changes in the existing social and economic order.

There were three hierarchic grades in the order. The highest was that of Areopagus, which, like the top rank of the Illuminati bearing

---

processi del ventuno e dello Spielberg. Dagli atti ufficiali segreti degli archivi di Stato di Vienna e dal carteggio dell'imperatore Francesco I co'suoi ministri e col presidente del Senato Lombardo-Veneto del Tribunale supremo di Giustizia (1821–1838), p. 185.

[97] From J. P. de Prati's translation into English from the original Latin text of the credo of the Perfect Sublime Masters, as quoted in Lehning, "Buonarroti and His International Secret Societies," p. 123.

[98] From Prati's translation of the credo of the Sublime Elect, as quoted in *ibid.* See also excerpts from the interrogation of Andryane, in Rinieri, "Le sette in Italia dopo la restaurazione del 1814," p. 29 (also in Rinieri, *Della Vita e delle Opere di Silvio Pellico*, Vol. II, p. 48); paragraph 55 of the Book of Statutes of the Sublime Elect, n.d., in Rinieri, *Della Vita e delle Opere di Silvio Pellico*, Vol. II, pp. 49–51; and Lombardo-Venetian senate to Emperor Francis, Verona, August 27, 1823, Sandonà, *Contributo alla storia dei processi del ventuno*, pp. 185–187.

[99] From Prati's translation of the credo of the Areopagus, as quoted in Lehning, "Buonarroti and His International Secret Societies," p. 124. It should be noted that even Andryane, whom Buonarroti had initiated only into the second order, the Sublime Elect, did not know the final aims of the society, the knowledge of which was revealed only to the members of the Areopagus.

[100] Eisenstein, *Buonarrotti*, pp. 36 and 39.

[101] Lehning, "Buonarroti and His International Secret Societies," pp. 124–125; Saitta, *Buonarroti*, Vol. I, p. 92.

the same name, was comprised of the chosen few who alone knew the real aims of the society. Next were the Sublime Elect (*Sublimes Elus*). Below them were the Perfect Sublime Masters. The whole order was directed by a secret center, the Great Firmament, the headquarters of which was either in Paris or in Switzerland. Under the Great Firmament mobile deacons passed the commands of the supreme center to the territorial deacons, who supervised the synods, composed as they were of the Sublime Elect, and the churches, the members of which were the Perfect Sublime Masters, in the regions in their charge. The presiding officers of both the churches and the synods were called "sages." Each of the hierarchical grades of the order was a unit unto itself. The lower grades were kept in complete ignorance of the nature, catechism, and ritual of the higher grades. When a person was initiated into a higher rank he was exposed to an entirely new and different part of the creed. To be admitted to the society a person had to be a Freemason. Adelfi or Philadelphians who were not Masons were automatically given the three lowest Masonic grades when they joined the Perfect Sublime Masters. In countries where Masonry was permitted the Perfect Sublime Masters established Masonic lodges which they secretly directed and used as a front to cover up their own subterranean activities.[102]

The origins of the Perfect Sublime Masters have usually been traced back to the Napoleonic period.[103] Luzio conjectured that they were a grade of Scotch rite Freemasonry.[104] Soriga believed that they

[102] Lehning, "Buonarroti and His International Secret Societies," pp. 121–123; Eisenstein, *Buonarroti*, pp. 44–48; Rinieri, "Le sette in Italia dopo la restaurazione del 1814," pp. 28–29; Soriga, "Le società segrete e i moti del '21 in Piemonte," pp. 115–117; decree, Great Firmament, 22nd day of the 7th month, Year 5812, Rinieri, *Della Vita e delle Opere di Silvio Pellico*, Vol. II, pp. 43–44; Orefici to Sardagna, Milan, August 21, 1822, St. A. (Vienna), Staatskanzlei, Provinzen, 1816–1822, No. 247, Fos. 205 and 215; Lombardo-Venetian senate of justice to Emperor Francis, Sandonà, *Contributo alla storia dei processi del ventuno*, pp. 181–183; Saitta, *Buonarroti*, Vol. I, pp. 88–89.

[103] It should be noted, however, that Sandonà, who drew heavily on the revelations given to the Austrian police by Wit von Dörring, maintains that their origins go back no further than 1821 or 1822 (Gallavresi, "La franc-maçonnerie et la formation de l'unité italienne," p. 421). See also Wit von Dörring, *Fragmente aus meinem Leben*, pp. 22–24. Bersano (see his "Adelfi, Federati e Carbonari," p. 414, and his *L'abate Francesco Bonardi e i suoi tempi*, pp. 97–98) and Francovich (see his "Gli Illuminati di Weishaupt," p. 584) believe that the order was established in 1818.

[104] See his *La Massoneria e il Risorgimento italiano*, Vol. I, p. 158.

were established as a reform or eighteenth century Freemasonry by several fanatical supporters of Rousseau's and Gabriel Bonnet de Mably's humanitarian ideology.[105] The Piedmontese conspirator Francesco Bonardi related that he joined the society when it became evident to him that Napoleon would never carry out reforms championed by left-wing Jacobins.[106]

Other persons have, rightly in my opinion, associated the origins of the Perfect Sublime Masters with the Philadelphians and/or the Adelfi and have connected the founding of the society with the name of Filippo Michele Buonarroti. Alessandro Andryane testified before the Austrian investigation commission in the early 1820's that the order had been in existence ever since the French Revolution and that Buonarroti had already been a member of it for fifteen years.[107] The Lombard police official Pagani, after making a careful study of all records which he was able to find about secret societies, maintained that the order was founded in 1809 or 1810.[108] Buonarroti himself gave 1808–1809 as the date of its founding. Documents have been found relating to the Perfect Sublime Masters which are dated 1811 and 1812.[109] Evidence such as this has led recent scholars like Lehning and Elizabeth Eisenstein to conclude that the Perfect Sublime Masters were founded in Geneva by Buonarroti between 1808 and 1811.[110]

It is highly probable that by 1814 all three of the sects that were strongly influenced by the Illuminati which we have thus far discussed—the Perfect Sublime Masters, the Adelfi, and the Philadelphians—were the same organization or were closely affiliated with each other. The Austrian Police Assessor Pagani, who was well informed about secret societies, was convinced that the Perfect Sublime Masters were formed through a merger of the Philadelphians

[105] See his "Le società segrete e i moti del '21 in Piemonte," p. 114.

[106] Delio Cantimori, "Nuovi contributi alla storia delle società segrete," *Nuova Rivista Storica*, Vol. XLI, Fasc. 2 (May–August, 1957), p. 482.

[107] Excerpts from the interrogation of Andryane, in Rinieri, "Le sette in Italia dopo la restaurazione del 1814," pp. 29–30. Also in Rinieri, *Della Vita e delle Opere di Silvio Pellico*, Vol. II, p. 49.

[108] Pagani memoir on secret societies, 1818, Soriga, "Le società segrete e i moti del '21 in Piemonte," Appendix I, p. 128.

[109] Lehning, "Buonarroti and His International Secret Societies," p. 121.

[110] *Ibid.*, pp. 120–121; Eisenstein, *Buonarroti*, pp. 35 and 40–41. See also Pagani memoir on secret societies, 1818, Soriga, "Le società segrete e i moti del '21 in Piemonte," Appendix I, p. 128.

and the Adelfi in 1810.[111] According to evidence collected by the Austrian investigation commission during the Carbonari trials, two Estenese Adelfi were told by members of the Piedmontese Adelfia society in Alessandria that "the society of the Adelfi had been abolished by order of the Great Firmament."[112] Wit von Dörring stated that the Philadelphians and Adelfi were united to the Perfect Sublime Masters by the oldest decree of the Great Firmament, which was dated the 22nd day of the 7th lunar month of the year 5812.[113] If we agree with Lehning[114] that the 22nd day of the 7th lunar month of the year 5812 was July 26, 1812, or with Augusto Sandonà that it was July 22, 1812, of the Christian calendar, rather than with Rinieri that it was July 22, 1822,[115] it seems logical to assume that about the time of the second Malet conspiracy the Adelfia and Philadelphia societies either merged with the Perfect Sublime Masters or became subordinate orders of the same. If such a merger actually took place in 1812, obviously the decree of the Great Firmament of the year 5812 and Wit von Dörring's testimony[116] indicate only that the Philadelphians and Adelfi were separate organizations before 1812. The information collected by the Austrian investigation commissions in the early 1820's tends to corroborate the view that at that time the Perfect Sublime Masters and the Adelfi (by that time the Philadelphians were very likely no longer mentioned) were probably one and the same.[117] The symbolism, rites, and organizational structure of the

[111] Pagani memoir on secret societies, 1818, Soriga, "Le società segrete e i moti del '21 in Piemonte," Appendix I, p. 128.

[112] Orefici to Sardagna, Milan, August 21, 1822, St. A. (Vienna), Staatskanzlei, Provinzen, 1816–1822, Fasz. XXXVI, No. 247, Fo. 215.

[113] Wit von Dörring, *Les sociétés secrètes*, p. 9. The same decree can also be found in Rinieri, *Della Vita e delle Opere di Silvio Pellico*, Vol. II, pp. 43–44.

[114] See his "Buonarroti and His International Secret Societies," p. 121.

[115] Rinieri, "Le sette in Italia dopo la restaurazione del 1814," p. 33; Rinieri, *Della Vita e delle Opere di Silvio Pellico*, Vol. II, pp. 43–44.

[116] See *ante*, p. 207.

[117] Report of the Lombardo-Venetian supreme justice senate, May 5, 1823, *Verwaltungsarchiv* (Vienna), Polizeihofstelle, 1823, No. 8560; Orefici to Sardagna, Milan, August 21, 1822, St. A. (Vienna), Staatskanzlei, Provinzen, 1816–1822, Fasz. XXXVI, No. 247, Fos. 203 and 205; Angelo de Rosmini to Antonio Mazzetti, Milan, December 26, 1822, Pietro Pedrotti, *I processi del '21 nel carteggio di Antonio Mazzetti* (Vol. II of *Documenti e Studi del Comitato Nazionale di Studi sui Prigionieri Politici Italiani dello Spielberg*), p. 190; Metternich to Sardagna, Vienna, July 22, 1822, Pietro Pedrotti, "La Missione segreta del Consigliere Aulico De Sardagna in Italia durante i processi dei Carbonari," *Il Risor-*

three groups bore an interesting resemblance. The occasional references to the Great Firmament in the reports about the Adelfi seem
to indicate that they were receiving directions from the Great Firmament of the Perfect Sublime Masters. For all these reasons, it appears
quite plausible that by 1814 either the Perfect Sublime Masters, the
Adelfi, and the Philadelphians constituted one and the same group
or, more likely, the last two were closely associated with or merely
subordinate divisions of the first.[118]

There are strong indications that the Perfect Sublime Masters were
active in Lombardy in 1814. Around 1810 or shortly before two dissentient Masonic leaders in Milan, Professors Salfi[119] and Romagnosi,[120] founded a new secret political society "to incite the Italian
youth" to exert themselves "to shake off the yoke of despots and
form Italy into a united and independent nation."[121] The South Tyrolese conspirator Prati, a very close friend of both Salfi and Romagnosi,[122] wrote in an article published in the British *Penny Satirist* in
1837 that in 1810 he was initiated in a secret society in Milan that
was "a masonry in masonry, unknown to the very grand-masters and
deputy-grand masters." From that moment, he asserted, he became

---

gimento Italiano, Vol. XXII (1929), pp. 169–170; excerpts from the interrogation
of Andryane, in Rinieri, "Le sette in Italia dopo la restaurazione del 1814," p. 29
(also in Rinieri, *Della Vita e delle Opere di Silvio Pellico*, Vol. II, p. 49).

118 Saitta feels that "the intrinsic difference between the Adelfia and the Perfect Sublime Masters is a rather convincing argument in favor of a definite distinction between the two societies" (see his *Buonarroti*, Vol. I, p. 84). Pia Onnis
Rosa maintains that it is highly improbable that the Perfect Sublime Masters had
any ties with the anti-Napoleonic Adelfi (see his "Propaganda e rapporti di società intorno al 1817 [Rey, Blanc, Buonarroti]," *Rassegna storica del Risorgimento*, Vol. LI, Fasc. 4 [October–December, 1964], p. 495).

119 For a good account of Salfi's life, see Nardi, "La vita di Francesco Saverio
Salfi," pp. 161–332.

120 For accounts of Romagnosi's life and influence, see Clemente Rèbora, "G.
D. Romagnosi nel pensiero del risorgimento," *Rivista d'Italia, Lettere, Scienza ed
Arti*, Vol. XIV, Fasc. 11 (November, 1911), pp. 808–839; Antonio Monti, "G. D.
Romagnosi. Contributo biografico," *Nuova Antologia. Rivista di Lettere, Scienze
ed Arti*, 6th ser., Vol. CXCV, Fasc. 1111 (May, 1918), pp. 41–50; and S. F.,
"Giandomenico Romagnosi e la congiura milanese del 1814," *Bollettino Storico
Piacentino*, Vol. XXII, Fasc. 3 (July–September, 1927), pp. 120–123.

121 Pedrotti, *Note autobiografiche del cospiratore trentino Gioacchino Prati*, p.
31. See also Spadoni, *Il moto del 20 aprile*, pp. 23–24.

122 Pedrotti, *Note autobiografiche del cospiratore trentino Gioacchino Prati*, pp.
30–31.

associated with all the secret sects in Italy, France, and Germany. The Milan society, he wrote, was "a section of that 'directing committee,' which afterwards caused so much uneasiness to Napoleon, the Holy Alliance and to Louis-Philippe."[123]

It is at least likely that the secret society into which Prati was initiated was the same one which Salfi and Romagnosi established in Milan and that this society was a branch of the Perfect Sublime Masters. Certainly, its aims and mode of operation, as described by Prati, are the same as those of Buonarroti's organization. It seems at least probable that, although in order to deceive the Napoleonic police the Milan branch may still have paraded under the name of Adelfia, "the secret tribunal of the Great Firmament" which Prati asserted had determined that Finance Minister Prina was to be murdered[124] was none other than the central directing committee of the Perfect Sublime Masters. It is also quite plausible to assume that the society which Confalonieri joined in Paris in 1814 at the instigation of either Buonarroti[125] or Angeloni[126] was really the Perfect Sublime Masters rather than the Adelfi.[127] The conspirator Luigi Manfredini told the Austrian investigating committee in 1823 that Confalonieri was the head of the Milan church of the Perfect Sublime Masters.[128] Is it not possible that Buonarroti might have initiated him into his conspiratorial organization, the Perfect Sublime Masters, in 1814 for the express purpose of having him head a branch of the society in Lombardy?

It is a high tribute to the effectiveness of the Perfect Sublime Masters in safeguarding the secrets of their society that no mention was made either of them or the Adelfi and Philadelphians by the Austrian police in 1814. In their reports the Habsburg police referred only to

---

[123] As quoted in Lehning, "Buonarroti and His International Secret Societies," p. 118. See also Francovich, "Gli Illuminati di Weishaupt," p. 578 (also in his *Albori socialisti nel Risorgimento*, p. 22).

[124] See *ante*, p. 205.

[125] Confalonieri, *Memorie e lettere*, Vol. I, pp. 87–90; D'Ancona, *Federico Confalonieri*, p. 53; Castro, *Milano e le cospirazioni lombarde*, p. 91.

[126] Domenico Spadoni, "L'unione guelfa in Roma," *Roma. Rivista di studi e di vita romana*, Vol. XVI, No. 4 (April, 1938), p. 155; Leti, *Carboneria e Massoneria*, p. 135.

[127] See *ante*, p. 205.

[128] Eighteenth interrogation of Luigi Manfredini, Milan, June 30, 1823, Francesco Salata and Achille Giussani (eds.), *I costituti di Federico Confalonieri*, Vol. III, p. 243.

the Independists, the Liberals, the Raggi, and the Centri, especially to the last. The first of these societies was allegedly founded at Ancona, supposedly had Masonic connections, and was said to resemble the German Tugendbund.[129] The Liberals supposedly had aims which were similar to those of the Carbonari. They aspired to establish a republic, a federal state, or an Italian monarchy with its capital in Rome. The Austrians strongly suspected that they were supported by agents of the English opposition party who were traveling in Italy.[130] In all probability the Austrian police were confusing the Independists and the Liberals with other sects or parties. The Society of Italian Independence (*i.e.*, the Independists), of which the Brescian-Milanese conspirator Antonio Maria Caprotti admitted that he was a member, had the same passwords late in 1814[131] as the Centri. Obviously, it was nothing but a "front" for some other clandestine society. As for the Liberals, it is entirely possible that, with their phobia about both secret societies and liberalism, some of the Habsburg police could have mistakenly assumed that Italian partisans of liberalism constituted a dangerous clandestine sect by that name. If not, the Liberals could have been Guelfs or Carbonari in disguise. At least, the reports which the Austrian police made about the Liberals could fit either of these two secret societies.

The Raggi were apparently founded in 1798 in Milan and soon established themselves in Bologna. From these two centers they spread rapidly through Italy. Their goal was to work for the liberation of all Italy from foreign domination.[132] The sect, which was also referred to as the Platonic Astronomy Society, was divided into a solar circle, which was subdivided into two hemispheres, one of them at Milan and the other at Bologna. Each circle was divided into

[129] Note to Hager, Vienna, October 17, 1814, Weil, *Les dessous du Congrès de Vienne*, Vol. I, p. 314; Pingaud, "La Lombardie en 1814," p. 463.

[130] Hager reports, March 31 and May 12, 1815, St. A. (Vienna), Kabinets-Akten, 1815, No. 777 and ad No. 777; Hager to Goëss, Vienna, April 7, 1815, A. S. (Venice), Presidio di governo, 1815, No. 210/v.b.p.

[131] Spadoni, *Il moto del 20 aprile*, p. 275 n.

[132] Renato Soriga, "La ristampa milanese della 'Lira focese' di Antonio Ierocades," *Rassegna storica del Risorgimento*, Vol. V, Fasc. 4 (October–December, 1918), pp. 728–730; Domenico Spadoni, *Sette, cospirazioni e cospiratori nello stato pontificio all'indomani della restaurazione. L'occupazione napoletana; la restaurazione e le sette*, pp. cxxii–cxxiii n.; Pieri, *Le società segrete ed i moti degli anni 1820–21 e 1831*, p. 58; Marcologno, "Le origini della Carboneria," pp. 236–238.

segments, the segments into radii (*raggi*), and the radii into lines. The members of the society never communicated with each other in writing.[133] It has been asserted that around 1804 the Raggi had twenty thousand,[134] thirty thousand,[135] or even fifty thousand[136] members.

On October 18, 1814, Police President von Hager wrote Bellegarde that he had been informed that, under the pretext of performing charitable work, the Raggi sect was collecting money and spreading pernicious propaganda in Milan. According to Von Hager, distinguished persons, including members of the government, had been mentioned as belonging to the society.[137] Apparently this time the usually well informed Habsburg police were wrong. Shortly before or after the Austrians occupied Lombardy in 1814 the Raggi either disappeared or changed their name to Centri in order to prevent detection.[138]

Several references were made to the Centri in the correspondence of various Habsburg officials in 1814–1815. On October 19, 1814, Reuss-Plauen reported to Bellegarde the discovery of a sect which had the same signs of recognition and the same passwords which the Centri had.[139] In December Venetian Police Director Raab specifically mentioned the Centri by name. Drawing his information largely from an anonymous denunciation sent to him from Verona,[140] he reported that, under the name of Centri, the Carbonari were ordering all their members to provide themselves with guns.[141] Governor

133 Ottolini, *La Carboneria*, pp. 19–20.

134 Marcolongo, "Le origini della Carboneria," p. 238.

135 Ottolini, *La Carboneria*, p. 20.

136 Soriga, "La ristampa milanese della 'Lira focense'," p. 731; *Leti, Carboneria e Massoneria*, p. 81.

137 In a letter sent from Vienna, A. S. (Milan), Presidenza di governo. Atti secreti, 1814, Cart. V, No. 668/P.R.

138 The following historians believe that they changed their name to Centri: Angelo Ottolini ("Nel mondo settario: i Raggi e i Centri," *Rassegna storica del Risorgimento*, Vol. IV, Fasc. 6 [November–December, 1917], pp. 697–698); Ottolini (*La Carboneria*, p. 23); and Oreste Dito (*Massoneria, carboneria ed altre società segrete nella storia del Risorgimento italiano, con appendice ed illustrazioni*, p. 313).

139 A copy of the letter is in Lemmi, *La restaurazione austriaca a Milano*, Appendix XL, pp. 449–450.

140 Enclosed in Raab to Reuss-Plauen, Venice, December 9, 1814, A. S. (Venice), Presidio di governo, 1815–1819, Polizia, Fasc. II 13/4, No. 3, ad No. 621/P.R.

141 Raab to Reuss-Plauen, Venice, December 9, 1814, *ibid.*; Raab to Hager,

Reuss-Plauen wrote Hager that the Centri were circulating small circulars in various cities on which was written "The Italians demand their independence from the Allied Powers."[142] Six months later Raab notified the Habsburg police president that the Centri were again actively at work.[143]

Various Italians involved in the Brescian-Milanese conspiracy also mentioned the Centri in the testimony which they gave to the special commissions appointed to investigate those who were implicated in the plot. During interrogations on December 31, 1814, and on January 9 and 20 and March 30, 1815, Gian Bernardo Soveri Latuada related that he had been a member of the philosophical section of the Centri since 1812.[144] The society had both literary and political branches. The heads of these sections were Cavalier Pietro Custodi,

Venice, December 9, 1814, Lemmi, *La restaurazione austriaca a Milano*, Appendix LII, pp. 469–470.

[142] Reuss-Plauen to Hager, Venice, December 13, 1814, A. S. (Venice), Presidio di governo, 1814, No. 2241. See also Reuss-Plauen to Bellegarde, Venice, December 13, 1814, *ibid.*; and anonymous letter from Verona enclosed in Raab to Reuss-Plauen, Venice, December 9, 1814, A. S. (Venice), Presidio di governo, 1815–1819, *Polizia*, Fasc. II 13/4, No. 3, ad No. 621/P.R.

[143] Raab to Hager, Venice, June 3, 1815, Helfert, *Kaiser Franz und die Stiftung des Lombardo-Venetianischen Königreichs*, Appendix XII, pp. 567–568 (an Italian translation can be found in Lemmi, *La restaurazione austriaca a Milano*, Appendix LXXVI, pp. 502–503); Hager to Rosetti, Vienna, June 11, 1815, A. S. (Milan), Presidenza di governo. Atti secreti, 1815, Cart. IX, No. 16/g.p.

[144] Interrogation of Latuada on December 31, 1814, as cited in Domenico Spadoni, *Milano e la congiura militare nel 1814 per l'indipendenza italiana: La congiura militare e il suo processo* (hereafter cited as Spadoni, *La congiura militare*), p. 218; and as quoted in Domenico Spadoni, "Il processo per la congiura bresciano-milanese del 1814," *Atti del XIII Congresso Nazionale tenutosi in Genova nei giorni 26–28 ottobre 1925*, pp. 91–92; and in Renato Soriga, "Pietro Custodi cospiratore," in Soriga, *Le Società segrete*, pp. 141–142. The official records of the interrogations of the Brescian-Milanese conspirators by the special investigation and Mantua commissions were first discovered in the *Archivio di Stato* of Milan by Domenico Spadoni. When, at the request of this writer, officials of the *Archivio di Stato* made a careful search for them in 1957 they were unable to find them. In all probability they were among the many valuable documents destroyed during World War II. Fortunately, Spadoni made extensive and lengthy citations and quotations from these documents and organized nearly all of his material chronologically rather than topically in his *La congiura militare* and his *Milano e la congiura militare nel 1814 per l'indipendenza italiana: I giudizi di Mantova e la sorte dei congiurati* (hereafter cited as Spadoni, *I giudizi di Mantova*). As a consequence, Spadoni's summaries of the trial records constitute a good and reliable substitute for the original records.

former secretary general of the ministry of finance, and Antonio Smancini, former prefect of the Adige department. The political section included women among its members.[145] Of the other arrested conspirators, Colonel Gian Paolo Olini and Colonel Antonio Gasparinetti revealed that Latuada had told them that many persons of distinction belonged to the Centri.[146] Squadron Commander Cesare Ragani[147] and Colonel Gasparinetti[148] admitted that they belonged to the society. Other persons implicated in the Brescian-Milanese conspiracy were also accused of being members, but they denied it when questioned by the Austrian authorities.

Although Latuada indicated to the Austrian investigation commission on December 31, 1814, that the aim of the Centri was to work for the moral and civil regeneration of the Italian people,[149] and although a secret correspondent who denounced the society to the Austrian police in the fall of 1814 was of the opinion that its aim was "to defend Italian honor,"[150] both the Habsburg officials in Italy and at least some of the Brescian-Milanese conspirators were convinced that the real purpose of the Centri was to work for independence.[151] They believed that the principal center of the sect was Mantua, but they felt certain that it had adherents in all parts of Lombardy, Venetia, and Emilia. The society adopted a decentralized form of or-

[145] Interrogation of Latuada on January 9 and 20, 1815, as cited in Spadoni, *La congiura militare*, pp. 235 and 270; and in Spadoni, "Il processo per la congiura bresciano-milanese," p. 92.

[146] Interrogation of Olini on December 29, 1814, and January 1, 1815, as cited in Spadoni, *La congiura militare*, pp. 23 and 221; interrogation of Gasparinetti on February 13, 1815, as cited in Spadoni, *I giudizi di Mantova*, p. 53.

[147] Interrogation of Ragani on February 5, 1815, as cited in Spadoni, *La congiura militare*, p. 27; interrogation of Ragani on March 29, 1815, as cited in Spadoni, *I giudizi di Mantova*, p. 80.

[148] Interrogation of Gasparinetti on March 30, 1815, as cited in Spadoni, *I giudizi di Mantova*, p. 83.

[149] Interrogation of Latuada on December 31, 1814, as cited in Spadoni, *La congiura militare*, p. 218.

[150] Anonymous letter from Verona enclosed in Raab to Reuss-Plauen, Venice, December 9, 1814, A. S. (Venice), Presidio di governo, 1815–1819, Polizia, Fasc. II 13/4, No. 3, ad No. 621/P.R.

[151] Raab to Reuss-Plauen, Venice, December 9, 1814, *ibid.*; Reuss-Plauen to Hager, Venice, December 13, 1814, A. S. (Venice), Presidio di governo, 1814, No. 2241; interrogation of Ragani on February 5, 1815, as cited in Spadoni, *La congiura militare*, p. 27; interrogation of Latuada on March 28, 1815, as cited in Spadoni, *I giudizi di Mantova*, p. 68.

ganization which insured almost complete secrecy among the rank
and file. Five persons constituted a separate center. Each of the five
was charged with forming a center of his own, and each of these
with creating still another, and so on ad infinitum. Thus the chain
could be extended indefinitely. Since each member was sworn to complete secrecy and since nothing was placed in writing, each member
theoretically knew the names of only the other four members of his
own center and that of the person outside his own particular unit
who had recruited him.[152]

The Centri had signs of recognition and passwords which, to escape detection and betrayal, were changed from time to time. When
the Austrian police first learned of their existence in the fall of 1814
they apparently wore on their chests medallions with a sleeping lion
impressed upon them. When one Centro showed his medallion to
another the latter slowly raised his right fist towards his own body;
whereupon the member exposing the medallion raised his right hand
over his right eye and uttered the word "Help." The other added:
"To the unfortunate!" Then the first man exclaimed "Honor!" and the
second, "To Italy!"[153] In December, 1814, the secret reporter from
Verona described signs of recognition which differed somewhat from
the above. He wrote that when one Centro met another he touched
the bottom of the right sleeve of his coat. After he had done this the
second man lightly touched his forehead with his right hand. Then
the first man pressed the middle finger of the other man's right hand
three times with the thumb of his right hand. The second man responded in kind. After these actions had been completed, the first
man uttered "Help" and the other added the phrase, "To the unfortunate."[154] When interrogated by the Austrian authorities, the Brescian-Milanese conspirators Bartolomeo Cavedoni, Santino Gerosa, and

---

[152] Raab to Reuss-Plauen, Venice, December 9, 1814, A. S. (Venice), Presidio
di governo, 1815–1819, Polizia, Fasc. II 13/4, No. 3, ad No. 621/P.R.; anonymous letter from Verona enclosed in the above, *ibid.*; interrogation of Latuada
on December 31, 1814, as quoted in Spadoni, *Il moto del 20 aprile*, p. 275 n.,
and in Spadoni, "Il processo per la congiura bresciano-milanese," p. 92; Castro
Il mondo secreto, Vol. VIII, p. 102; Ottolini, "I Raggi e i Centri," pp. 700 and
702; Ottolini, *La Carboneria*, pp. 94 and 96.

[153] Reuss-Plauen to Bellegarde, Venice, October 19, 1814, Lemmi, *La restaurazione austriaca a Milano*, Appendix XL, pp. 449–450.

[154] Anonymous letter from Verona enclosed in Raab to Reuss-Plauen, Venice,
December 9, 1814, A. S. (Venice), Presidio di governo, 1815–1819, Polizia,
Fasc. II 13/4, No. 3, ad No. 621/P.R.

Latuada recounted signs of recognition and passwords which, with minor variations, were substantially the same as the above.[155] By the late spring of 1815 the signs and words of recognition had apparently again been altered.[156]

In all likelihood, the Centri were not a distinct, separate organization but only a "front" for some other secret society. But which one? We can immediately dismiss as untenable the surmise of Governor Reuss-Plauen[157] and the Brescian-Milanese conspirator Olini[158] that the Centri were a pro-British organization. There is also not too much evidence to support the conjecture that they were nothing but the Guelfs in disguise, which is largely based on Austrian Judge Antonio Salvotti's assertion in his prosecution charges against Silvio Pellico, Piero Maroncelli, and their co-defendants that "the *Guelfs*, under the name of *Society of the Centri*, were particularly diffused in Lombardy and in Milan in 1814."[159] This isolated piece of evidence, plus the fact that there were certain similarities between the organization and symbols of the Centri and those of the Guelfs, has aroused speculation about whether the Centri could possibly have been an affiliate of or a name taken at this time by the Guelf society.[160]

Much more credible is the hypothesis that the Centri society was connected with the Adelfi; or, if the theory that the Adelfi and Perfect Sublime Masters were the same in 1814 is correct, that it was a "front" for the Perfect Sublime Masters. In his memoir on secret societies, written in 1818, Pagani came to the conclusion that the Car-

---

155 See Spadoni, *Il moto del 20 aprile*, pp. 274–275 n.

156 Hager to Rosetti, Vienna, June 11, 1815, A. S. (Milan), Presidenza di governo. Atti secreti, 1815, Cart. IX, No. 16/g.p.; Raab to Hager, Venice, June 3, 1815, Helfert, *Kaiser Franz und die Stiftung des Lombardo-Venetianischen Königreichs*, Appendix XII, p. 567. An Italian copy of the last letter is in Lemmi, *La restaurazione austriaca a Milano*, Appendix LXXVI, pp. 502–503.

157 Reuss-Plauen to Bellegarde, Venice, October 19, 1814, Lemmi, *La restaurazione austriaca a Milano*, Appendix XL, p. 449; Reuss-Plauen to Hager, Venice, December 13, 1814, A. S. (Venice), Presidio di governo, 1814, No. 2241.

158 Interrogation of Olini on December 29, 1814, and January 1, 1815, as cited in Spadoni, *La congiura militare*, pp. 23–24.

159 Salvotti's prosecution charges against Maroncelli, etc., Venice, August 9–10, 1821, Alessandro Luzio, *Il Processo Pellico-Maroncelli secondo gli atti ufficiali segreti*, p. 445. The italics are in the original.

160 See especially Spadoni, *Sette, cospirazioni, e cospiratori nello stato pontificio*, pp. cxxi-cxxii n.; Spadoni, *Il moto del 20 aprile*, p. 278; and Ottolini, "I Raggi e i Centri," p. 700.

bonari and the Philadelphians, "who are easily identifiable with the *Centri* or *Raggi* and the 'Aid to the Unfortunate' [societies] functioned as preliminary grades of the Adelfia."[161] In June, 1815, the Austrian police in Italy expressed the opinion that the chiefs of the Centri were "in Switzerland, from where all orders are being sent to Piedmont, Italy, and the Tyrol."[162] Since the supreme directory of the Perfect Sublime Masters at this time was probably located in Switzerland, if the Adelfi had already been absorbed into the Perfect Sublime Masters by 1814 it does not seem too illogical to assume that the Centri were in some way or another connected with Buonarroti's far-flung, though small, conspiratorial organization. Spadoni believed that the various secret societies in Italy at that time were under some form of superior direction.[163] And Arturo Bersano has suggested that all the secret societies of northern Italy, including the Carbonari, were only sectarian tools of Buonarroti.[164]

Most historians, however, have been inclined to believe that the Centri were a variety of the Carbonari or that "Society of the Centri" was the name adopted by the Carbonari in northern Italy at that time.[165] Besides a few similarities between the organizational structure and symbols of the two societies, various assertions by Habs-

---

[161] As published in Soriga, "Le società segrete e i moti del '21 in Piemonte," Appendix I, p. 125.

[162] Raab to Hager, Venice, June 3, 1815, Helfert, *Kaiser Franz und die Stiftung des Lombardo-Venetianischen Königreichs*, Appendix XII, p. 567 (an Italian translation is in Lemmi, *La restaurazione austriaca a Milano*, Appendix LXXVI, p. 502); Hager to Rosetti, Vienna, June 11, 1815, A. S. (Milan), Presidenza di governo. Atti secreti, 1815, Cart. IX, No. 16/g.p.

[163] He wrote: "We are inclined to think, however, as we have already had occasion to declare, that the adoption of the clubbist method of organization and operation (adopted and necessary to be able better to preserve secrecy in the face of the prohibitions and rigors of the Restoration) was imposed on affiliated societies, like the Carbonari, by a superior directing society, which either the Platonic Union (Society of the Raggi or Centri) or, better, the Adelfia could have been at that time." See his *Il moto del 20 aprile*, p. 278.

[164] See his *L'abate Francesco Bonardi e i suoi tempi*, pp. 90–91.

[165] See, for example, Ottolini, "I Raggi e i Centri," pp. 700, 701, and 704–705; Ottolini, *La Carboneria*, pp. 94 and 95–96; Cantù, *Della indipendenza italiana cronistoria*, Vol. II, p. 1244; Castro, *Il mondo secreto*, Vol. VIII, p. 102; V. Tonni-Bazza, "La congiura militare bresciano del 1814," *Nel Cinquantenario delle X Giornate*, p. 46; Lemmi, *La restaurazione austriaca a Milano*, p. 328; Helfert, *La caduta della dominazione francese*, p. 197; and Weil, *Murat*, Vol. II, p. 55. It should be noted, however, that Domenico Spadoni has been inclined to doubt this theory (see his *Il moto del 20 aprile*, pp. 25 and 277–278).

burg police authorities in Italy in 1814, to the effect that the Carbonari had taken the name of Centri, support this theory.[166] Furthermore, during the Austrian processes against the Carbonari in Emilia in 1820–1821 it was asserted that in 1814 Carbonari affiliates assumed the name of Centri and Raggi.[167] Testimony was also given during the Confalonieri trials in the 1820's that in 1814 many Carbonari existed in Lombardy "under the form of the so-called society of the Centri."[168]

Although most Carbonari traditions[169] associate the beginnings of the society either with the patron saint of the order, the legendary eleventh century St. Theobald,[170] or with the Good Cousins who originated in France during either the middle ages or the sixteenth century,[171] most historians have connected the order with the Illuminati or the Freemasons. Because of a similiarity between the means

[166] See Raab to Reuss-Plauen, Venice, December 9, 1814, A. S. (Venice), Presidio di governo, 1815–1819, Polizia, Fasc. II 13/4, No. 3, ad No. 621/P.R.; Raab to Hager, Venice, December 9, 1814, Lemmi, *La restaurazione austriaca a Milano*, Appendix LII, p. 469; Reuss-Plauen to Hager, Venice, December 13, 1814, A. S. (Venice), Presidio di governo, 1814, No. 2241.

[167] Spadoni, *Il moto del 20 aprile*, p. 25.

[168] Orefici to Sardagna, Milan, August 21, 1822, St. A. (Vienna), Staatskanzlei, Provinzen, 1816–1822, Fasz. XXXVI, No. 247, Fo. 205.

[169] For a more detailed discussion of the origins of the Carbonari, see my "The Carbonari: Their Origins, Initiation Rites, and Aims," *The American Historical Review*, Vol. LXIX, No. 2 (January, 1964), pp. 353–356.

[170] *Memoirs of the Secret Societies of the South of Italy, particularly the Carbonari* (hereafter cited as *Memoirs of the Carbonari*), pp. 6–7; Giuseppe de Ninno, *La Setta dei Carbonari in Bari nel 1820–21. Ricordi storici seguiti da note biografiche dei deputati della Provincia di Terra di Bari al Parlamento Napoletano in detta epoca*, pp. 9–10; Marcolongo, "Le origini della Carboneria," p. 280.

[171] Castro, *Il mondo secreto*, Vol. VIII, pp. 27–28; Ettore Fabietti, *I Carbonari*, pp. 41–43; M. Saint-Edme [E. T. Bourg], *Constitution et organisation des Carbonari, ou documens exacts sur tout ce qui concerne l'existence, l'origine et le but de cette société secrète*, p. 5; letter from Rome, July 12, 1819, *ibid.*, pp. 192–195; Clavel, *Histoire de la franc-maçonnerie*, p. 379; G. Rossetti memoir, June 15, 1814, Renato Soriga, "Gl'inizi della Carboneria in Italia secondo un rapporto segreto del generale Giuseppe Rossetti," *Il Risorgimento Italiano*, Vol. XXI, Fasc. 1 (January–March, 1928), p. 78 (also in Soriga, *Le Società segrete*, p. 71); Albert Mathiez, "L'origine franc-comtoise de la Charbonnerie italienne," *Annales historiques de la Révolution française*, Vol. V, No. 6 (November–December, 1928), pp. 551–561; Jacques Godechot, "I francesi e l'unità italiana sotto il direttorio," *Rivista Storica Italiana*, Vol. LXIV, Fasc. 4 (1952), pp. 578–579; anonymous report, n.p., June 30, 1817, St. A. (Vienna), *Staatskanzlei, Provinzen, Lombardei-Venedig*, Fasz. XL, Kon. 1, Fo. 190.

of correspondence employed in Germany by the Illuminati and those used by the Carbonari, as well as other likenesses between the two associations, some recent scholars like Francovich[172] and Lehning[173] have argued that the Carbonari were founded by the Illuminati.[174] The best-substantiated hypothesis, however, is that the Carbonari emanated from the Freemasons. Considerable resemblance between the symbols, form of organization, and practices of the Carbonari and the Freemasons or such Masonic offshoots as the Tugendbund and the Illuminati[175] has led perhaps a majority of Italian historians to deduce that the Carbonari were either a branch or reform of or a schism from the Freemasons.[176] In other words, the Carbo-

---

[172] See his "Gli Illuminati di Weishaupt," pp. 580–583. Also in his *Albori socialisti nel Risorgimento*, pp. 24–27.

[173] See his "Buonarroti and His International Secret Societies," p. 121.

[174] Pietro Dolce, a spy in Habsburg pay, asserted positively that the Carbonari were founded in southern Italy during or immediately after Napoleon's Russian campaign, "by the Illuminati of Naples, directed by the Illuminati of London as well as by all the English Masonic lodges" (see his report to Saurau, November, 1815, Luzio, *La Massoneria e il Risorgimento italiano*, Vol. I, p. 117). Dolce's reliability as an expert on secret societies, however, is not too good (see my "La costituzione guelfa e i servizi segreti austriaci," pp. 368–369). For other sources supporting the theory, see Rossetti memoir, June 15, 1814, Soriga, "Gl'inizi della Carboneria in Italia," p. 79 (also in Soriga, *Le Società segrete*, p. 72); and Cesare D'Azeglio to Sardinian government, June 16 and 26, 1814, Luzio, *La Massoneria e il Risorgimento italiano*, Vol. I, pp. 123 and 124.

[175] See especially Ulisse Bacci to Gino Bandini, Rome, February 4, 1914, Luzio, *La Massoneria e il Risorgimento italiano*, Vol. II. p. 245; letter from Senator Dandolo of Ancona enclosed in Fontanelli to Luini, November 29, 1813, *ibid.*, p. 165 (the original MS is in A. S. [Milan], Presidenza di governo. Atti secreti, 1817, Cart. XV, Rub. ad No. 131/geh., No. 142/geh.); P. Ilario Rinieri, *I costituti del Conte Confalonieri e il Principe di Carignano*, pp. 8–16; Rossetti memoir, June 15, 1814, Soriga, "Gl'inizi della Carboneria in Italia," p. 79 (also in Soriga, *Le Società segrete*, p. 72); Marcolongo, "Le origini della Carboneria," p. 301; Mariutti, *Organismo ed azione delle società segrete del veneto*, p. 37; and Saint-Edme, *Constitution et organisation des Carbonari*, pp. 7–8.

[176] See especially Spadoni, *Sette, cospirazioni e cospiratori nello stato pontificio*, pp. civ–cv; anonymous memoir on the Carbonari in Orloff, *Mémoires sur le royaume de Naples*, Vol. II, p. 421; *The Fate of the Carbonari. Memoirs of Felice Foresti*, translated by Howard R. Marraro, p. 1; Wit von Dörring, *Fragmente aus meinem Leben*, p. 31; Dito, *Massoneria, carboneria ed altre società segrete*, pp. 69–71; "L'origine e lo scopo della Carboneria secondo i costituti de'primi Carbonari e Guelfi," *La Civiltà Cattolica*, Vol. LXVI (June 19, 1915), p. 654; Marcolongo, "Le origini della Carbonaria," pp. 284–285, 289, 299, and 301–302; Luzio, *La Massoneria e il Risorgimento italiano*, Vol. I, pp. 169–170; Pieri, *Le*

nari[177] were a "popular" Freemasonry established by liberal anti-Napoleon Masons to serve as a vehicle to arouse the uneducated masses in southern Italy against the French.[178]

The society spread rapidly during the last years of Napoleonic domination. By 1813 estimates of their total membership in the Kingdom of Naples ranged between 4,000[179] and 80,000.[180] In the Neapolitan capital and its environs alone it was reported that there were 24,000 Carbonari.[181] From Naples the sect expanded quickly in southern and central Italy and apparently soon won adherents in Lombardy-Venetia. During the trials in the Marches in 1817 a certain Cesare Giacomini of Ascoli affirmed that he knew of the existence of the Carbonari in Milan as early as 1811 and confessed that he had been initiated into the society in that city in the presence of between 150 and 200 Good Cousins.[182] In his memoirs, Giacomo Breganze tells us that, to the great perturbation of Prince Eugene, the name of the Carbonari was reported in all quarters between the Adige and Po rivers.[183] And the ex-conspirator Dolce informed the Austrian police that by the spring of 1814 all "Milan was Carbonarized and Carbonarism was being propagandized in all the Lombard provinces."[184]

---

società segrete ed i moti degli anni 1820–1821 e 1831, pp. 58–60; Rinieri, *Della Vita e delle Opere di Silvio Pellico*, Vol. II, p. 2; Cantù, *Della indipendenza italiana cronistoria*, Vol. I, p. 808; Filippo Montalbano Nobile, *Le società segrete nella rigenerazione politica d'Italia*, p. 12; Leti, *Carboneria e Massoneria*, pp. 69–71; and Gallavresi, "La franc-maçonnerie et la formation de l'unité italienne," p. 419.

177 For the initiation rites and doctrines of the Carbonari, see my "The Carbonari: Their Origins, Initiation Rites, and Aims," pp. 356–369.

178 See also Giuseppe de Ninno, *Filadelfi e Carbonari in Carbonara di Bari negli albori del Risorgimento italiano* (*1816–1821*), p. 14.

179 Anonymous report, n.d. [1813], annexed to General Police Director Luini to Prince Eugene, n.d. [1813], A.S. (Milan), Presidenza di governo. Atti secreti, 1817, Cart. XV, Rub. ad No. 131/geh., No. 142/geh.

180 Senator Dandolo's report, Ancona, August 25, 1813, annexed to War Minister Fontanelli to Luini, Milan, November 29, 1813, *ibid.*

181 Prefect of the department of Tronto to Luini, Fermo, September 6, 1813, *ibid.*

182 Ottolini, *La Carboneria*, pp. 75–76; Spadoni, *Il moto del 20 aprile*, pp. 25–26.

183 As quoted in Ottolini, *La Carboneria*, p. 76.

184 Dolce report, Milan, June 30, 1816, A. S. (Milan), Presidenza di governo. Atti secreti, 1816, Cart. XI, Rub. 669/geh. (Reisenden Dolce), Pezza 224. A

Since Dolce was known to be a very unreliable observer,[185] his assertion about the size of the Carbonari in Lombardy in 1814 was very likely greatly exaggerated. The testimony given to the Austrian investigating authorities by the Brescian-Milanese conspirators leaves no doubt, however, that the Carbonari actually existed in Lombardy at that time. It is true that General Giacomo Filippo de Meester,[186] Professor Giovanni Rasori,[187] and Colonel Gasparinetti[188] denied all knowledge of the Carbonari society, while Squadron Commander Ragani stated that he had heard of the society only in Naples.[189] Others of the conspirators, however, were not so circumspect. Colonel Silvio Moretti admitted that the Carbonari had been mentioned to him,[190] while Antonio Maria Caprotti conceded that he had enrolled a certain Cesare Carini, who he believed was a Milanese, in the society.[191] Assistant Commander Cavedoni confessed that he had first learned of the Carbonari towards the end of May, 1814, when he was at Montechiari visiting General Antonio Bonfanti. Somewhat later De Meester affiliated him in the society at Brescia and confided to him that the Carbonari were working for Italian independence. Cavedoni himself enrolled other members. He intimated that the society furnished money to maintain fifty soldiers recently returned from Corfu—whom the conspirators intended to use—and that the Brescian-Milanese conspiracy was known and supported by the Car-

---

copy is also in Luzio, *La Massoneria sotto il Regno Italico e la restaurazione austriaca*, p. 308.

[185] After interviewing Dolce in 1817, the Austrian governor of Lombardy, Count Franz Saurau, wrote Police President Sedlnitzky that his conference with him "again confirms the remark which I made to you in my earlier report about the way this otherwise not untalented observer has collected every declaration which has been thrown at him and accepted it without doubt" (A. S. [Milan], Presidenza di governo. Atti secreti, 1816–1817, Cart. XIII, No. 43/geh.).

[186] In his interrogation on December 31, 1814, as cited in Spadoni, *La congiura militare*, p. 216.

[187] In his interrogation on January 15, 1815, as cited in *ibid.*, p. 249.

[188] In his interrogation on February 13, 1815, as cited in Spadoni, *I giudizi di Mantova*, p. 53.

[189] Interrogations of Ragani on February 3 and 6, 1815, as cited in *ibid.*, pp. 25 and 33, and on February 5, 1815, as cited in Spadoni, *La congiura militare*, p. 31.

[190] In his interrogation on February 2, 1815, as cited in Spadoni, *I giudizi di Mantova*, p. 23.

[191] Interrogation of Caprotti on February 9, 1815, as cited in *ibid.*, p. 42.

bonari at Bologna and in the Romagna.[192] Latuada admitted that the Carbonari were numerous in the Romagna and that some affiliates were in Milan. The heads of the society in Milan, he maintained, were Senator Sebastiano Bologna; Antonio Smancini, former prefect of Adige department; and Secretary Custodi, former secretary general of the ministry of finance. The Carbonari were under orders always to keep guns at their houses.[193]

It was Gerosa, however, who provided the investigating officials with the most enlightening details about the society. Not only did he confess that he had joined the sect late in October or early in November, 1814, but he indicated that the Caffè dei Servi served as the meeting place of the society in Milan. There he conversed with various Carbonari about the details of the conspiracy. He told his Austrian interrogators that many people belonged to the organization and gave them a long list of names of persons who he believed were members. Among them were Senator Paradisi, Colonel Erculei, Senator Mocenigo, Prefect Smancini, General Pera or Peri (General Pino's former aide), Foscolo, and Ministers Antonio Aldini and Vaccari.[194]

With this testimony about the existence of the Carbonari in Lombardy-Venetia in 1814, it is surprising that, even though they were fully aware of the dangers of Carbonari intrigues in other parts of the peninsula,[195] the Habsburg authorities did not appear to be especially worried about Carbonari activities in Lombardy-Venetia.[196] In fact, as late as 1817 Habsburg officials in Italy were still sending bland assurances to Vienna that the Carbonari had never gained a foothold in the Lombardo-Venetian provinces.[197] Only a handful of

[192] Interrogations of Cavedoni on December 30 and 31, 1814, and January 23, 1815, as cited in Spadoni, *La congiura militare*, pp. 209–210, 213, 214, and 274.

[193] Interrogations of Latuada on December 31, 1814, and January 9 and 20, 1815, as cited in *ibid.*, pp. 218, 235, and 270.

[194] Interrogations of Gerosa on January 5, 6, 7, and 8, 1815, as cited in *ibid.*, pp. 224, 226, 230, and 232–233.

[195] See especially Hager report, July 5, 1814, St. A. (Vienna), Conferenz Akten, Ser. b, 1814, No. 1356; and Hager to Bellegarde, Vienna, July 5, 1814, Lemmi, *La restaurazione austriaca a Milano*, Appendix XXIV, p. 431.

[196] Mariutti, *Organismo ed azione delle società segrete del veneto*, p. 38.

[197] See, for example, Saurau to Sedlnitzky, Milan, May 6, 1814, A. S. (Milan), Presidenza di governo. Atti secreti, 1817, Cart. XV, Rub. ad No. 131/geh., No. 142/geh.; Saurau to Sedlnitzky, Milan, March 18 and April 3, 1817, *ibid.*, No. 228/geh.; Saurau to Kaunitz, Milan, August 3, 1817, *ibid.*, Cart. XVI, No. 772/

officials who had occasion to read the actual trial records of the Brescian-Milanese conspirators seemed to be aware that the Carbonari had actually made proselytes in Austria's provinces by 1814. In 1818 the writer of a report to the Venetian governor Count Goëss stated that the Carbonari "sent emissaries to Romagna and some of them also penetrated Lombardy to make proselytes." In the summer of 1814, he continued, the spirit of unrest which they helped to foment incited some of the dismissed Italian soldiers to plot a conspiracy[198] (*i.e.*, the Brescian-Milanese conspiracy). The special committee appointed to try Pellico and Maroncelli and their confederates pointed out to the Habsburg emperor that the Mantua process, at which the Brescian-Milanese conspirators were tried, definitely proved that a nationalist revolutionary spirit was being fomented in Lombardy in 1814 by both the Centri and the Carbonari.[199]

That the Austrian police took no particular notice of the Carbonari at that time perhaps demonstrates (a) that the Carbonari were extremely circumspect in keeping their presence in Lombardy secret, (b) that they were probably not very numerous in Lombardy in 1814, and (c) that they quickly retreated after the Brescian-Milanese conspirators were arrested. The judges of the special Austrian committee to try the Carbonari conspirators were probably right when they came to the conclusion in 1822 that the arrest and trial of the Brescian-Milanese conspirators and the vigilance of the police prevented the further spread of the Carbonari in Lombardy-Venetia[200] until 1817 when Carbonari lodges were instituted in the Polesine.

Another secret sect mentioned among those existing in Lombardy-Venetia in 1814 was the Guelf society. Ever since 1917, when Luzio published excerpts from the supposed October, 1813, Guelf consti-

---

geh.; Goëss to Archduke Rainer, Venice, May 25, 1818, St. A. (Vienna), Kabinets-Akten, 1818, ad. No. 453.

[198] The report is enclosed in Goëss to Archduke Rainer, Venice, May 25, 1818, St. A. (Vienna), Kabinets-Akten, 1818, ad No. 453.

[199] Orefici to Sardagna, Milan, August 21, 1822, St. A. (Vienna), Staatskanzlei, Provinzen, 1816–1822, Fasz. XXXVI, No. 247, Fos. 188–189; Inbegrif der Erhebungen und Anzeigen aus den Akten der Österr. Unters. Com. in Mailand über der Ursprung, die Ausbreitung, die Verbindungen, und die Umtriebe der revoluzionäre Gesellschaften in Italien, Milan, August 30, 1822, *ibid.*, Fo. 2; Governo Austriaco, *I Carbonari, ecc.*, pp. 1–2.

[200] Orefici to Sardagna, Milan, August 21, 1822, St. A. (Vienna), Staatskanzlei, Provinzen, 1816–1822, Fasz. XXXVI, No. 247, Fo. 189.

tution,[201] and particularly since 1924, when Spadoni published the complete text of it,[202] this constitution has been relied on by numerous historians as one of the principal sources for the early history of the Guelf society.

Basing their conclusions on this constitution, recent writers naturally attributed an extremely important role in the founding of the Guelf society to British agents, since Article 3[203] asserts that the Guelfs were placing themselves "under the most valorous protection" of England. Article 4 promises that as soon as the British agreed to protect them a member of the society would be in constant contact with "H. E. L. W. B. [His Excellency Lord William Bentinck], commander of the naval forces of H.B.M. [His Britannic Majesty] in the Mediterranean, to come to an agreement with him on the way to restore Italian independence." In another article[204] Lord "Bentinck is declared protector of the G. [Guelf] Order." A subsequent article[205] reveals that as soon as the revolution was carried to a successful conclusion "the votes of the G. [Guelfs] to obtain a prince" from the English dynasty, "in case the circumstances of the time did not permit the establishment of a republic," would be manifested "to H. E. L. W. [His Excellency Lord William] Bentinck." If it proved impossible to procure a British ruler, the crown could be offered to the son of Maria Louisa and Napoleon, the king of Rome; however,

---

[201] In his *La Massoneria sotto il Regno Italico e la restaurazione austriaca*, pp. 314–317.

[202] In his "Gli Statuti della Guelfia in possesso della Polizia austriaca nel 1816," *Rassegna storica del Risorgimento*, Vol. XI, Fasc. 3 (July–September, 1924), pp. 715–731. The handwritten copy which Spadoni in all probability printed in this article is in A. S. (Milan), Presidenza di governo. Atti secreti, 1816, Cart. XI, Rub. 531/geh. (Relation des Reisenden Frizzi), No. 531/geh. The present writer has in his possession a microfilm copy of still another text of this constitution, the original of which is appended as All. A to Appony to Guicciardi, Rome, July 1, 1816, St. A. (Vienna), Diego Graf Guicciardi, Geheime Correspondenz, Fasz. 1 (1816–1820), No. 6, All. A, Fos. 1–17. It should be noted that whereas the copy in Luzio bears the date of October 14, 1813, all other copies seen by this writer are dated October 15, 1813.

[203] Since citing the appropriate article will make it possible for interested persons easily to find the proper section in all three of the above copies, no other reference will be given to this constitution.

[204] Art. 43 in the text in the *Archivio di Stato* and in Spadoni; Art. 41 in the copy in the *Haus-, Hof-, und Staatsarchiv*.

[205] Art. 51 in the *Archivio di Stato* text copied by Spadoni; Art. 49 in the copy in the *Haus-, Hof-, und Staatsarchiv*.

all other members of the Bonaparte family were perpetually excluded from the Italian throne.[206] "If England wishes to retain Sicily and Malta as compensation for its favor," according to the Guelf constitution,[207] "the laws which are to determine the destinies of Italy" should also be extended to the inhabitants of these two places. "As for the exclusive commerce which the English hope to have in Italy, it is agreed that it ought to be reconciled with reciprocal advantages relative to national honor."[208]

The most significant sentence in the constitution and the one which has aroused perhaps the greatest interest among historians is Article 42 of the text of the constitution in the *Archivio di Stato*, which was published by Spadoni, and Article 40 of the copy in the *Haus-, Hof-, und Staatsarchiv*. In a sinister tone it threatens: "Prina, nefarious Minister of Finance of the Kingdom of Italy, who dissuaded Napoleon from separating Italy from France, is abandoned to the G. [Guelf] vendetta."[209]

The October 15, 1813, Guelf constitution was mentioned in the reports of two Austrian spies: Pietro Dolce, a Florentine who had once been a soldier in Murat's army; and Francesco Frizzi, who had formerly served under Bentinck. Both of them maintained that the British, and particularly their commander-in-chief in the Mediterranean Lord Bentinck were mainly responsible for founding the Guelf society. More important, they asserted that many articles of the Guelf constitution were written by Bentinck and others by Lord Holland.[210] Foscolo allegedly traveled to London with a letter to the prince regent entreating him to intercede in favor of the Italian

[206] Arts. 90 and 91 of the copy in the *Archivio di Stato* and in Spadoni; Arts. 88 and 89 of the copy in Vienna.

[207] Art. 73 in the *Archivio di Stato* text copied by Spadoni; Art. 71 in the one in Vienna.

[208] Art. 74 in the copy in Milan; Art. 72 of the text in the Viennese archives.

[209] It should also be noted that in his report on November 15, 1816, Dolce wrote that in Article 42 of the above constitution "the massacre of Minister Prina was determined." See Luzio, *La Massoneria sotto ill Regno Italico e la restaurazione austriaca*, pp. 324–325. The original is in A. S. (Milan), Presidenza di governo. Atti secreti, 1816, Cart. XI, Rub. 669/geh. (Reisenden Dolce), ad No. 669/geh.

[210] Pietro Dolce report, Milan, November 15, 1816, A. S. (Milan), Presidenza di governo. Atti secreti, 1816, Cart. XI, Rub. 669/geh. (Reisenden Dolce) ad No. 669/geh.; Frizzi memoir, *ibid.*, Rub. 531/geh. (Relation des Reisenden Frizzi), ad No. 531/geh. For an account of Frizzi's service with Bentinck, see Rosselli, "Il progetto italiano di Lord William Bentinck, 1811–1815," pp. 379–383.

cause[211] as championed by the Guelfs, and in 1814 a deputation of the Milanese provisional government went to London to offer the Italian crown to the duke of Sussex.[212]

Although Giuseppe Leti[213] uttered a few cautious reservations about the 1813 Guelf constitution immediately after it was published, and although in the latter part of his life Spadoni expressed very serious doubts about its authenticity,[214] during the past forty years various historians, including the present writer,[215] have made use of this constitution as though it were an authentic and reliable source, not only for the history of secret societies during the latter part of the Napoleonic era, but also for the events which led to Minister Prina's assassination on April 20, 1814.[216] However, as documents now housed in the *Haus-, Hof-, und Staatsarchiv* in Vienna prove, we have all erred in accepting this constitution as authentic. In 1816 the Austrians themselves substantiated beyond the shadow of a doubt that the 1813 Guelf constitution was an out-and-out forgery!

The constitution was actually drafted in 1816 for the deliberate purpose of lending support to a cock-and-bull story fabricated to extort money from the Austrians.[217] The main characters in the maneuver were a certain duke of Brindisi, an unscrupulous adventurer who had once served in Murat's police force and who more frequently went under the name of Filipetti and sometimes under that

---

[211] Frizzi memoir on the Guelf faction, October, 1816, A. S. (Milan), Presidenza di governo. Atti secreti, 1816, Cart. XI, Rub. 531/geh. (Relation des Reisenden Frizzi), ad No. 531/geh.

[212] Domenico Spadoni, "Il sogno unitario e wilsoniano d'un patriota nel 1814–15," *Rassegna storica del Risorgimento*, Vol. XIII, Fasc. 2 (April–June, 1926), p. 353 n.

[213] In his *Carboneria e Massoneria*, p. 83.

[214] See his "L'unione guelfa in Roma," pp. 155–163.

[215] See my *Fall of the Napoleonic Kingdom of Italy*, pp. 39–40.

[216] See, for example, *Storia di Milano*, Vol. XIII; *L'età napoleonica*, p. 327; Ceria, *L'eccidio del Prina*, p. 185; Ottolini, *La Carboneria*, p. 121; Capograssi, "L'unità d'Italia nel pensiero di Lord William Bentinck," p. 247; Capograssi, *Gl'inglesi in Italia durante le campagne napoleoniche*, pp. 191–193; Spadoni, "Il sogno unitario e wilsoniano d'un patriota nel 1814–15," p. 353; Spadoni, "Federazione e Re d'Italia mancati nel 1814–15," pp. 421–422; Spadoni, *Il moto del 20 aprile*, pp. 26–27; and Soriga, "Ugo Foscolo e il suo amico anglo-italo Augusto Bozzi Granville," p. 125.

[217] For the full story, see my "La costituzione guelfa e i servizi segreti austriaci." Here I am giving only the bare essentials of the plot.

of Ancirotta; and his confederate Enegildo Frediani, a Tuscan by birth who had been an officer in Murat's army and who in 1816 was working on a job in Rome which was highly displeasing to him.

The story began in Rome on March 10, 1816, when the duke of Brindisi sent a communication to the Russian minister General Thuyll pretending that he knew about a vast conspiracy that was soon to break out in Italy. A few days later he went to Florence to see Count Anton Appony, who was then Austrian minister plenipotentiary to Tuscany, to demand money and a carriage to use in personally delivering extremely important communications to the Austrian emperor and Metternich. In a number of lengthy conferences, first in Florence and then in Rome, Brindisi informed Appony and Count Felix Mier, the former Austrian ambassador to Naples, who was then in Rome, that a vast conspiracy was afoot to overthrow all existing governments in Italy. When asked to furnish proof, he took recourse in long delaying tactics, frequently changed his story, and finally handed Mier a Guelf catechism, some Guelf cipher codes, and a list of conspirators, all of which the Austrians immediately spotted as spurious. When further written evidence of the machination was demanded of him, he told the Habsburg diplomat that he first had to procure it from a Mr. Frediani. When he revealed to his interrogators that a central committee was meeting in Milan to direct the revolution, the Austrians dispatched him to the Lombard capital to collect all necessary proof that this committee actually existed.[218]

After the duke of Brindisi's departure for Lombardy, Appony got in touch with Frediani and won his confidence. Frediani gave him the exact text of the supposed Guelf constitution of October 15, 1813,[219] a copy of which the Habsburg diplomat immediately dispatched to Counts Ferdinand Bubna and Diego Guicciardi, who were in the meantime cross-examining Brindisi in Milan.

Before the copy arrived in the Lombard capital Bubna and Guicciardi had already become highly suspicious that the duke of Brindisi was a petty swindler; hence, they decided to use the constitution

218 Summary of Brindisi's conduct, [July, 1816], St. A. (Vienna), Diego Graf Guicciardi, Geheime Correspondenz, Fasz. I, Primo protocollo degli allegati, No. L, Fos. 55–58.

219 Ibid., Fo. 58; Appony to Daiser, Rome, June 15, 1816, ibid., Fasz. I (1816–1820), No. 4, All. A; Appony to Guicciardi, Rome, June 24 and July 1, 1816, ibid., No. 6, All. B, Fos. 1–4; summary of Lebzeltern's reports in regard to Italian secret societies, [1816]), ibid., No. 3, All. C.

to trap him in his prevarications. Questioning him about the details of the Guelf constitution, they found, not to their surprise, that he gave information about this document which differed considerably from the copy which had been sent to them from Rome. Upon his request, they allowed Brindisi to get in touch with a correspondent in Rome, only to confirm what they had already suspected when they examined the letter which he wrote: that Brindisi was warning Frediani, who up to now had been in perfect accord with him in the plot, not to give a version of the constitution to the Habsburg authorities in Rome different from the one which he had inadvertently mentioned in Milan.[220]

Frediani, however, either did not receive the warning or decided to betray his fellow conspirator. When confronted with the news of the duke of Brindisi's blundering statements in Milan, he confessed everything and readily admitted that he had himself forged the Guelf constitution.[221]

It was from Frediani that Dolce and Frizzi procured all their information about the constitution and the founding of the Guelfs. Dolce made this clear in his frequently cited November 15, 1816, report,[222] and Frizzi freely admitted the same when he was questioned by Habsburg authorities in Milan on November 20, 1816.[223] The reports of Dolce and Frizzi about the Guelfs looked so unreliable to the governor of Lombardy, Count Franz Joseph Saurau,[224] who was

[220] Summary of Brindisi's conduct, [July, 1816], *ibid.*, Fasz. I, Primo protocollo degli allegati, No. L, Fos. 58–63; Guicciardi to Metternich, Milan, July 26, 1816, *ibid.*, No. M, Fos. 63–65; Guicciardi to Appony, Milan, August 28, 1816, *ibid.*, No. O, Fos. 67–69; Bubna to Metternich, Milan, July 25, 1816, St. A. (Vienna), F. M. Lt. Graf Bubna, Geheime Correspondenz, Fasz. I (Jahrgang 1816 u. 1817), No. 5/3.

[221] Guicciardi to Metternich, Milan, September 30, 1816, St. A. (Vienna), Diego Graf Guicciardi, Geheime Correspondenz, Fasz. I, primo protocollo degli allegati, No. R, Fo. 77; Metternich to Bubna, Vienna, October 3, 1816, St. A. (Vienna), F. M. Lt. Graf Bubna, Geheime Correspondenz, Fasz. I (Jahrgang 1816 u. 1817), No. 16.

[222] A. S. (Milan), Presidenza di governo. Atti secreti, 1816, Cart. XI, Rub. 669/geh. (Reisenden Dolce), ad No. 669/geh.; and Luzio, *La Massoneria sotto il Regno italico e la restaurazione austriaca*, p. 324.

[223] Reply to questions asked of Frizzi, Milan, November 20, 1816, A. S. (Milan), Presidenza di governo. Atti secreti, 1816, Cart. XI, Rub. 531/geh. (Relation des Reisenden Frizzi), ad No. 531/geh.

[224] Count Franz Joseph Saurau (1760–1832) was appointed governor of Lombardy on February 22, 1815. After his initial appointment in the Austrian civil

kept in complete ignorance about Guicciardi and Bubna's clandestine intelligence activities,[225] that he expressed grave doubt about their validity and made arrangements to have the two intriguers closely watched. [226] Then, since it might have compromised their secret spy network in Italy had they dismissed them outright,[227] the Habsburg authorities sought to render them innocuous by ordering Dolce to go to Brescia as an ordinary correspondent and by sending Frizzi to Naples to serve in the same capacity under General Nugent's supervision.[228]

After exposing the duke of Brindisi's and Frediani's double-dealings, the Habsburg authorities who were familiar with the case were of the opinion that there was no Guelf society in Italy,[229] or at least that, if it existed at all, it was innocuous.[230] Had it not been for the fact that the conspirator Angeloni, whose name was on the list of prominent Guelfs handed to Count Appony by Brindisi, had just avowed to the French police that he was in close relations with malcontents in Italy,[231] the Austrians would have laughed off the whole idea of a Guelf society as a mere hoax.

Notwithstanding their skepticism, there is too much other evidence

---

service in 1789, in the capacity of *Stadthauptmann* in Vienna, he had advanced rapidly until he was made finance minister in 1797. Having resigned from that office in 1801, he was sent to St. Petersburg as Austrian ambassador. In 1805 he was appointed imperial commissioner to Styria. Five years later he became president of the Lower Austrian government, which post he left in 1814 to assume the position of imperial commissioner for the re-organization of the Illyrian provinces. In 1817 he left Lombardy to become chief chancellor of the new ministry of interior—a post which he held until shortly before his death.

225 See, for example, Metternich to Bubna, Vienna, July 7, 1816, St. A. (Vienna), F. M. Lt. Graf Bubna, Geheime Correspondenz, Fasz. 1 (Jahrgang 1816 u. 1817), No. 4a, Fo. 2.

226 Saura to Sedlnitzky, Milan, December 3, 1816, A. S. (Milan), Presidenza di governo. Atti secreti, 1816, Cart. XI, Rub. 669/geh. (Reisenden Dolce), No. 669/geh.

227 Sedlnitzky to Saurau, Vienna, January 28, 1817, *ibid.*, 1817, Cart. XV, No. 127/geh.

228 Saurau to Sedlnitzky, Milan, February 22, 1817, *ibid.*

229 Guicciardi to Appony, Milan, August 28, 1816, St. A. (Vienna), Diego Graf Guicciardi, Geheime Correspondenz, Fasz. I, Primo protocollo degli allegati, No. O, Fo. 68.

230 Metternich to Bubna, Vienna, October 3, 1816, St. A. (Vienna), F. M. Lt. Graf Bubna, Geheime Correspondenz, Fasz. I (Jahrgang 1816 u. 1817), No. 16, Fo. 4.

231 Metternich to Bubna, Vienna, September 8, 1816, *ibid.*, No. 11, Fos. 1–2.

pointing to the actual existence of the society in Italy and in Lombardy-Venetia to permit us to believe that the Guelfs were nothing but the figment of a common forger's imagination. The anonymous author of the report on Italian societies in the Tuscan archives related that the Guelfs were brought to Sicily about the time the British wanted to give the Sicilians a new constitution. From there they spread within a short time to the Marches, Romagna, Genoa, Lombardy, Venetia, and Piedmont.[232] The Romagnol conspirator Tommasi told Cardinal Tommaso Arezzo that in 1814 people began to speak of the Guelfs both in the Papal States and in Lombardy.[233] The Polesine Carbonaro Giambattista Canonici indicated that the Guelf society was well established before the Treaty of Vienna was signed in June, 1815.[234] He stated that his fellow Carbonaro Antonio Solera had brought a copy of the Guelf constitution from Milan around 1814 or 1815.[235] The Habsburg police president Count Josef Sedlnitzky believed that the order was brought to Italy in 1814.[236] Salvotti, the well known judge during the Carbonari trials, felt that the Guelf society had numerous adherents in Lombardy and in Milan in 1814,[237] while the Habsburg investigating committee during the Pellico-Maroncelli trials reported that the sect spread especially rapidly during the time of Murat's war for independence in the spring of 1815.[238] Confalonieri listed the Guelfs among the three principal secret societies in Italy in 1814 and admitted that during the time of the Brescian-Milanese conspiracy he had "frequent contacts with several members" of the order.[239] At his trial in 1822 he told the Austrian judges that the Guelfs originated during the last of the Napoleonic period "and more particularly in Italy at the time of the last war sustained by the Kingdom of Italy." One of their "principal centers" was located "in Bologna," and there was "another rather considerable one in Milan." After Murat's 1815 campaign "they successively

---

[232] Collection of documents on secret societies known in Italy between 1800 and 1818, Pardi, "Nuove notizie sull'origini della Carboneria," p. 475.

[233] "L'origine e lo scopo della Carboneria," p. 647.

[234] Giambattista Canonici, *Della mia vita. Narrazione apologetica,* pp. 16–22.

[235] Spadoni, *Sette, cospirazioni e cospiratori nello stato pontificio,* p. cxx.

[236] In a letter to Strassoldo, Vienna, March 27, 1818, A. S. (Milan), Presidenza di governo. Atti secreti, 1818, Cart. XXI, No. 83/geh.

[237] Dito, *Massoneria, carboneria ed altre società segrete,* p. 293.

[238] Orefici to Sardagna, Milan, August 21, 1822, St. A. (Vienna), Staatskanzlei, Provinzen, 1816–1822, Fasz. XXXVI, No. 247, Fo. 189.

[239] Confalonieri, *Memorie e lettere,* Vol. I, pp. 91–92.

dissolved or changed themselves and formed themselves again under other names into new societies which arose in their place"[240]

Thus there can be no question that the Guelf society actually existed in Lombardy-Venetia in 1814. The exposure of the efforts of the duke of Brindisi and Frediani to defraud the Habsburgs proves only that the alleged October 15, 1813, Guelf constitution and some other basic primary sources which various historians, including this writer, have used for the past four decades for some of their theories about the Guelf society must be either rejected or seriously questioned.

It is quite likely that the British had a hand in establishing the society and bringing it to Italy.[241] It is true that some writers have maintained that the Guelf society was an offshoot of the Freemasons,[242] and others have associated the Guelfs with either the Carbonari[243] or the Adelfi.[244] However, most of the evidence which this writer has examined definitely connects the beginnings of the society in Italy with the English. Apart from the spurious Guelf constitution and the unreliable reports of the gullible informers Dolce and Frizzi, various reliable sources attest that the British played a role in im-

[240] Thirty-third interrogation of Confalonieri, Milan, September 14, 1822, Salata and Giussani, *I costituti di Federico Confalonieri*, Vol. II, p. 74.

[241] Largely on the basis of British documents, Rosselli minimizes the role which the British played in Italian secret societies during the last years of the Napoleonic regime (see his "Il progetto italiano di Lord William Bentinck, 1811–1815," pp. 384–390). The present writer, however, still believes that there is so much evidence connecting the Guelfs with the British that it is quite likely that the British played at least some kind of role in bringing the society to Italy.

[242] See Dito, *Massoneria, carboneria ed altre società segrete*, p. 295. It should also be noted that Placido Sarti related to the papal inquisitors that the British, finding the Masons too subservient to the French, created a new society called Guelf to which only the best individual Freemasons were admitted (Spadoni, *Sette, cospirazioni e cospiratori nello stato pontificio*, p. cxvii).

[243] At one time Sedlnitzky believed that all the chiefs and most of the distinguished members of the Carbonari were affiliated with the Guelfs (Sedlnitzky to Strassoldo, Vienna, March 27, 1818, A. S. [Milan], Presidenza di governo. Atti secreti, 1818, Cart. XXI, No. 83/geh.), while Foresti expressed the opinion that the Guelfs "constituted the moral part of the Carbonari" (Interrogation of Foresti at Venice on March 20, 1820, Gino Bandini, "Carboneria e Guelfismo nei Costituti dei Carbonari del Polesine," *Rivista d'Italia, Lettere, Scienze ed Arti*, Vol. IX, Fasc. 9 [September, 1906], p. 496).

[244] See, for instance, Rinieri, "Le sette in Italia dopo la restaurazione del 1814," p. 11; Soriga, "Le società segrete e i moti del '21 in Piemonte," pp. 113–114; and Leti, *Carboneria e Massoneria*, p. 82.

planting the sect in the Apennine peninsula. The Austrian diplomat Richard Weiss von Starkenfels wrote that the Guelfs always had close ties with England.[245] The writer of the memoir in the Tuscan archives definitely asserted that the British brought the society to Italy.[246] Several prisoners implicated in the Macerata conspiracy— like Michele Manlio[247] and Placido Sarti[248]—attributed the introduction of the Guelfs in Italy to Lord William Bentinck. Also, Tommasi testified that the society was promoted and protected by England and proselytized by Lord William Bentinck and Sir Robert Wilson,[249] while the Polesine Carbonaro Costantino Munari told his interrogators that the Guelfs were instituted and promoted by Bentinck.[250] Furthermore, Austrian officials like Guicciardi,[251] the writer of a Venetian police report dated September 16, 1817,[252] Sedlnitzky,[253] and Orefici[254] all attributed to the British the bringing of the Guelfs to Italy.

We also know that the Guelfs exerted themselves to attain liberty, independence, and constitutional government for the Italian people. They also aspired to unite the various parts of the Apennine peninsula into a single national state in which there was to be freedom of the press and religion and in which all laws, money, and weights and measures were to be equal.[255]

---

[245] In his "Pio IX," in Antonio Filipuzzi, *Pio IX e la politica austriaca in Italia dal 1815 al 1848 nella relazione di Riccardo Weiss di Starkenfels* (Vol. XXXVI of *Studi e documenti di storia del Risorgimento*), p. 85.

[246] Collection of documents on secret societies known in Italy between 1800 and 1818, Pardi, "Nuove notizie sull'origini della Carboneria," p. 475.

[247] Rinieri, "Le sette in Italia dopo la restaurazione del 1814," p. 18.

[248] Spadoni, *Sette, cospirazioni e cospiratori nello stato pontificio*, pp. cxvii-cxviii.

[249] "L'origine e lo scopo della Carboneria," p. 647.

[250] Costantino Munari's interrogation by Commissioner Lancetti, March 10, 1819, Bandini, "Carboneria e Guelfismo," p. 503.

[251] Guicciardi to Metternich, [1816], St. A. (Vienna), Diego Graf Guicciardi, Geheime Correspondenz, Fasz. I (1816–1820), No. 3, Fos. 3–4.

[252] *Carte segrete della polizia austriaca in Italia*, Vol. I, p. 86.

[253] In a letter to Strassoldo, Vienna, March 27, 1818, A. S. (Milan), Presidenza di governo. Atti secreti, 1818, Cart. XXI, No. 83/geh.

[254] In a letter to Sardagna, Milan, August 21, 1822, St. A. (Vienna), Staatskanzlei, Provinzen, 1816–1822, Fasz. XXXVI, No. 247, Fo. 189.

[255] Guelf constitution drawn up by the Guelf directory of Milan, n.d., *Carte segrete della polizia austriaca in Italia*, Vol. I, p. 116; interrogation of Foresti in Venice on March 20, 1820, Bandini, "Carboneria e Guelfismo," p. 496; Salvotti

A detailed study of the available evidence thus makes it clear that Italian historians have not been wrong in pointing out during the past half century that in the summer of 1814 several secret societies existed in Lombardy-Venetia: the Freemasons, much dreaded by the Austrians but actually rent with schisms and badly disorganized; the Perfect Sublime Masters, and perhaps the Adelfi, but only as a subordinate affiliate of the former; the Carbonari, perhaps masked under the name of Centri; and the Guelfs. They have, however, overemphasized the role of these sects in the liberal anti-Habsburg movement at that time, particularly in the Milanese revolution of April 20, 1814, which opened the door for the Habsburgs to come to Milan to assume control of the government of Lombardy.

No mention was made about the participation of secret societies in this revolution in older accounts like those by Princess Cristina Belgiojoso-Trivulzio,[256] Massimo Fabi,[257] Francesco Cusani,[258] Giovanni de Castro,[259] Joseph Helfert,[260] and Francesco Lemmi.[261] It is true that Lemmi related that in the winter of 1813–1814 the Masons and other secret societies supported Murat's aspirations to become king of a united Italy,[262] but he also pointed out that in April, 1814, the Freemasons were no longer really active and no longer had any influence on the lower classes.[263]

The Habsburg officials in Italy who made a special study of clandestine conspiratorial sects in 1814 believed that the secret societies participated in no way in the April 20 revolution. This writer has seen only one Austrian report which specifically connected any secret sect with the April 20 revolt and then only by indirect implication. On June 5, 1816, Count Diego Guicciardi, who had been sent to Milan to help organize a highly secret intelligence network for Italy, wrote Metternich from Milan that just before April 20 there existed in Lom-

---

report, July 18, 1821, C. Cantù "Il Conciliatore. Episodio del liberalismo lombardo," *Archivio storico italiano*, 3rd ser., Vol. XXIII (1876), p. 486.

256 See her *Étude sur l'histoire de la Lombardie.*

257 See his *Milano e il ministro Prina. Narrazione storica del Regno d'Italia (aprile 1814). Tratta da documenti editi ed inediti.*

258 See his *Storia di Milano.*

259 See his *Principio di secolo: storia della caduta del regno italico.*

260 See his *La caduta della dominazione francese.*

261 See his *La restaurazione austriaca a Milano.*

262 *Ibid.*, p. 106.

263 *Ibid.*, p. 296.

bardy a Jacobin party "composed of a small number of officers and several Masons discontented with Eugene . . . who had republican views and who had relations with the Neapolitan army."[264] Guicciardi, however, denied that there was anything resembling a secret conspiracy in Lombardy in 1814.[265] Moreover, after making a thorough investigation of all the Milanese listed by Dolce as emissaries of secret societies in the spring of 1814, Governor Saurau insisted that, except for Confalonieri and Bossi, who might be members of the Carbonari, none of Dolce's accusations were true.[266]

Since the publication of Dolce's reports by Luzio, the Guelf constitution by Luzio and Spadoni, Prati's memoirs by Pedrotti, and articles and books largely based on the trial records of the Brescian-Milanese conspirators by Spadoni, however, there has been an increasing tendency to hold the secret societies at least partly responsible for plotting the April 20 uprising in Milan.[267] During the past forty or fifty years nearly all historians who have written on the subject have intimated that the Freemasons, Carbonari, Guelfs, or Adelfi, either together or singly, were implicated in some way or another in the revolution. They have taken at face value Dolce's assertion that the Masons detested Napoleon's "despotism and his inordinate pride" and felt that his downfall was necessary for the good of humanity.[268] More important, they have accepted as true the statement which Latuada, the good friend and secret agent of General Pino, made to the

---

[264] St. A. (Vienna), Diego Graf Guicciardi, Geheime Correspondenz, Fasz. I, Primo protocollo degli allegati, No. C, Fo. 43.

[265] *Ibid.*, Fos. 42–44.

[266] Saurau to Sedlnitzky, Milan, February 8, 1817, A. S. (Milan), Presidenza di governo. Atti secreti, 1816–1817, Cart. XIII, No. 43/geh.

[267] See, for example, Spadoni, "Le società segrete nella rivoluzione milanese dell'aprile 1814," pp. 197–211; Spadoni, "Il processo per la congiura bresciano-milanese," pp. 86–88; Spadoni, *Il moto del 20 aprile*, pp. 21–34; 51–53, 64–65, and 75–77; Soriga, *Il primo Grande Oriente d'Italia*, pp. 18–20; Soriga, "La ristampa milanese della 'Lira focense'," pp. 736–738; Ceria, *L'eccidio del Prina*, pp. 182–186; *Storia di Milano*, Vol. XIII: *L'età napoleonica*, pp. 297–298, 302–303, and 326–327; Ottolini, *La Carboneria*, pp. 81–85; and my *Fall of the Napoleonic Kingdom of Italy*, pp. 104–107 and 109.

[268] Dolce to Saurau, November, 1815, Luzio, *La Massoneria e il Risorgimento italiano*, Vol. I, Appendix VI, p. 117. This statement was first printed in German in 1884 and in Italian by Cipolla in 1885 as the statement of an anonymous reporter (see Cipolla, "Un Documento austriaco sui Massoni e sui Carbonari," p. 483), who was later identified by Luzio as Pietro Dolce (first in 1917 in his "La Massoneria sotto il Regno italico e la restaurazione austriaca," p. 320).

Austrian investigating authorities on December 10, 1814: that "all the projects made around the 20th of April and immediately before and after to assure the independence of Italy were concocted under the Masonic secret."[269]

As far as the participation of the Carbonari in the plot is concerned, stress has been placed on Dolce's declaration that by the spring of 1814 "all Milan was Carbonarized."[270] His bland averment that the "formation of the regency" immediately after the April 20 revolution, "its first acts, its first decrees, its proclamations," and "the convocation of the electoral colleges have all been Carbonari operations"[271] has also been used to support the theory that the Carbonari played a role in the events that led to Minister Prina's death. So also has Breganze's allegation in his memoirs that various Carbonari officers, "in agreement with the society in Milan," were in opposition to the majority of army officers, who wanted Prince Eugene made viceroy of an independent Kingdom of Italy.[272]

The only evidence for the conjecture that the Guelfs had a hand in Minister Prina's assassination which has found its way into the various accounts is the article in the supposed October 15, 1813, Guelf constitution stating that Prina "is abandoned to the G. [Guelf] vendetta" and a sentence in Dolce's much cited November, 1816, report alluding to the above article.[273] As for the thesis that the Adelfi, or, more likely, the Perfect Sublime Masters, may have participated in the affair, the sole primary source to support the contention is Prati's statement that the secret tribunal of the Great Firmament, or directing council of the Perfect Sublime Masters and/or Adelfia society, ordered Minister Prina's death.[274]

However, from what the Habsburgs discovered about the forgery of the 1813 Guelf constitution and the unreliability of Dolce's reports about secret societies it is clear that most of the primary sources upon which the theory that the secret societies were at least partly responsible for plotting the April 20 revolution are spurious or of such

[269] As quoted in Spadoni, "Le società segrete nella rivoluzione milanese dell'aprile 1814," pp. 200–201. See also Spadoni, *La congiura militare*, p. 154; and Spadoni, "Il processo per la congiura bresciano-milanese," p. 86.

[270] See *ante*, p. 225.

[271] Dolce to Saurau, November, 1815, Luzio, *La Massoneria e il Risorgimento italiano*, Vol. I, Appendix VI, p. 121.

[272] As quoted in Ottolini, *La Carboneria*, p. 82.

[273] See *ante*, p. 230.

[274] See *ante*, pp. 205 and 215.

doubtful value that they must be used with extreme caution. It becomes obvious at once that the conjecture that the Guelfs had a hand in Prina's murder has no valid basis whatsoever since it is based only on a statement in a constitution which is an out-and-out forgery and on a sentence in one of Dolce's reports alluding to that constitution. Since the gullible Dolce picked up much of his information about secret societies in an indiscriminate manner from forgers, intriguers, and other questionable characters,[275] his remarks about the constitution, as well as his statement that the Freemasons felt that Napoleon's downfall was necessary for the good of humanity, must also be subjected to careful scrutiny. This is true, too, with the most important basic documents cited to buttress the argument that the Carbonari participated in the revolution, since all but one of them consist of nothing but statements made by the undependable Dolce. After we discard the 1813 constitution and Dolce's evidence as questionable, to say the least, the only primary sources left to support the contention that the secret societies had a direct hand in plotting the April 20 revolution are Prati's assertion connecting Prina's assassination with the Great Firmament (and this comprises just a single sentence in a single memoir) Breganze's allegation about the sentiments of various Carbonari officers (and it requires much imagination to read the actual plotting of the revolution into his statement), and the testimony which just one of the Brescian-Milanese conspirators gave about the involvement of the Freemasons in everything that happened around April 20. Certainly more and better evidence is needed before we can state with finality that the April 20 revolution was actually plotted by the secret societies. The whole subject needs to be carefully re-examined and new evidence must be brought to light before the theory can be proved—or, for that matter, definitely disproved!

Nonetheless, we do possess ample evidence to substantiate the thesis that various secret societies had by 1814 definitely obtained a foothold in Lombardy and to a lesser extent in Venetia.[276] Although they differed from each other in ritual, aims, and organization, these sects worked together "to free Italy from the influence of foreign

[275] See especially Saurau to Sedlnitzky, February 8, 1817, A. S. (Milan), Presidenza di governo. Atti secreti, 1816–1817, Cart. XIII, No. 43/geh.

[276] See Reuss-Plauen to Hager, Venice, December 13, 1814, Weil, *Murat*, Vol. II, Appendix X, p. 517 n.; and *ante*, pp. 197, 199, 204–205, 214–215, 217–220, 225–228, and 235–236.

powers and to establish an independent Italian kingdom by amalga-
mating all states now existing there."[277] While it cannot be positively
stated that these societies organized or directed the Brescian-Milanese conspiracy—the sole organized effort of a group of Italians to
revolt against the Habsburgs in 1814—as the Austrians asserted in
1824,[278] it is clear that many of the conspirators were affiliated with
the sects.[279]

No doubt the sects played some kind of a role in fanning the embers of discontent against Habsburg rule in the summer of 1814; yet
their importance should not be overemphasized. They constituted
only one, and a very small one at that, of several groups who incited
an anti-Austrian spirit among the populace—dissentient officials of
the former Kingdom of Italy, malcontented intellectuals and businessmen, British and Neapolitan agents, emissaries from Emperor
Napoleon, and, above all, disgruntled and embittered officers of the
former Italian army. After all, one does not need to belong to an ex-
tremist clandestine sect to be unhappy about a political regime or to
organize a rebellion against it.

[277] Hager report, July 5, 1814, St. A. (Vienna), Conferenz Akten, Ser. b, 1814,
No. 1356. See also Hager to Bellegarde, Vienna, July 5, 1814, Lemmi, *La res-
taurazione austriaca a Milano*, Appendix XXIV, p. 431 (the original is in A. S.
[Milan], Presidenza di governo. Atti secreti, 1814, Cart. I, No. 65/P.R.); and
Inbegrif der Erhebungen und Anzeigen aus den Akten der österr. Unters. Com.
in Mailand über der Ursprung, die Ausbreitung, die Verbindungen, und die Um-
treibe der revoluzionäre Gesellschaften in Italien, Milan, August 30, 1822, St. A.
(Vienna), Staatskanzlei, Provinzen, 1816–1822, Fasz. XXXVI, Fo. 2.

[278] Governo Austriaco, *I Carbonari*, p. 1.

[279] See also Pieri, *Le società segrete ed i moti degli anni 1820–21 e 1831*, p.
64.

Chapter 6

THE BRESCIAN-MILANESE CONSPIRACY

Since many of the officers of the Italian army were pervaded with a violent anti-Austrian spirit; since various malcontents were turning to the British, to Napoleon, and to Joachim Murat for help in realizing their dreams of establishing some kind of constitutional regime; and since various secret societies were plotting to turn Italy into a united kingdom with a liberal government, it was only natural that numerous stories of anti-Habsburg demonstrations and various rumors about revolutionary conspiracies that were supposedly ready to break out at any moment in Lombardy-Venetia reached the Austrian police. It was reported to them that on the morning of July 25 unknown malevolents substituted the arms of the Kingdom of Italy for those of the Habsburgs on all the official notices posted on the municipal palace at Brescia.[1] Early in August the Austrian police announced the discovery of a large quantity of guns and ammunition at a house belonging to a certain Soresi in Milan,[2] and there were notices that weapons and gunpowder were found at the home of a merchant at Brescia.[3] Secret informers warned the Habsburg authorities that suspicious-looking persons were going around with stilettos hidden in their canes and shoes[4] and that a plot was being concocted to murder all Germans in Italy on July 10.[5] A couple of months later

[1] Sormani to Bellegarde, Milan, July 30, 1814, Lemmi, *La restaurazione austriaca a Milano*, Appendix XXVII, pp. 434–435.

[2] Police report, Milan, August 9, 1814, *Kriegs-Archiv* (Vienna), Feld Akten (Italien), 1814, Fasz. VIII, No. 34.

[3] Police report, Milan, September 14, 1814, *ibid.*, Fasz. IX, No. 42.

[4] Hager to Reuss-Plauen, Vienna, July 8, 1814, A. S. (Venice), Presidio di governo, 1814, ad No. 830.

[5] Hager report, July 18, 1814, St. A. (Vienna), Conferenz Akten, Ser. b, 1814, No. 1423.

other talebearers sent in information that seventeen employees in the
government chancellery in Milan were plotting to arrest various Austrian officials and then overthrow the government.[6] Disturbing messages were handed in about the dangerous public spirit in such
varied places as Bologna, Brescia, Bergamo, Milan, Pavia, Verona,
and Udine.[7] There were alarming reports that subscription lists were
supposedly being circulated in Italy inciting people to pledge arms
and money to support an anti-Austrian conspiracy.[8] Disquieting news
was noised about that the English were plotting a revolution in Genoa that was to spread through Italy.[9]

In Vienna Police President Baron von Hager was deeply perturbed
over the communications from Italy about the numerous manifestations of Austrophobia. On the emperor's orders, he instructed the
governors of both Lombardy and Venetia to keep an eagle eye on
public opinion. They were carefully to observe the progress of any
possible conspiracies[10] and to publish orders prohibiting private citizens from carrying weapons.[11] They were at all costs to ferret out
and arrest the emissaries who were inviting the populace to support
revolutionary enterprises and to keep a close watch on persons who
were manufacturing or selling stilettos and other weapons.[12] Further-

[6] Police report, Milan, September 14, 1814, *Kriegs-Archiv* (Vienna), Feld Akten (Italien), 1814, Fasz. IX, ad No. 41.

[7] Raab to Hager, Padua, June 25, 1814, A. S. (Milan), Presidenza di governo.
Atti secreti, 1814, Cart. I, No. 65/P.R.; Hager report, July 8, 1814, St. A. (Vienna), Conferenz Akten, Ser. b, 1814, No. 1335.

[8] Raab to Hager, Padua, June 25, 1814, A. S. (Milan), Presidenza di governo.
Atti secreti, 1814, Cart. I, No. 65/P.R.; Hager to Bellegarde, Vienna, July 8,
1814, *ibid.*, No. 46/P.R.; Reuss-Plauen to Bellegarde, Padua, July 21, 1814, *ibid.*,
Cart. II, No. 105/P.R.; Hager report, July 8, 1814, St. A. (Vienna), Conferenz
Akten, Ser. b, 1814, No. 1335.

[9] Anonymous report to Hager, Milan, August 10, 1814, A. S. (Milan), Presi-
denza di governo. Atti secreti, 1814, Cart. III, No. 273/P.R.; police report, Milan,
September 24, 1814, *Kriegs-Archiv* (Vienna), Feld Akten (Italien), 1814, Fasz.
IX, No. 86.

[10] Hager to Reuss-Plauen, Vienna, July 17, 1814, A. S. (Venice), Presidio di
governo, 1814, ad No. 830; Hager to Bellegarde, A. S. (Milan), Presidenza di
governo. Atti secreti, 1814, Cart. II, No. 120/P.R.

[11] Hager to Bellegarde, Vienna, July 15, 1814, A. S. (Milan), Presidenza di
governo. Atti secreti, 1814, Cart. I, No. 90/P.R.

[12] Hager to Bellegarde, Vienna, July 8, 1814, *ibid.*, No. 46/P.R.; Hager to
Reuss-Plauen, Vienna, July 8, 1814, A. S. (Venice), Presidio di governo, 1814,
ad No. 830; Torresani to Raab, Padua, July 18, 1814, *ibid.*

more, they were asked carefully to investigate the reports that the British were fomenting a revolution in Genoa.[13]

Although Emperor Francis and Police President von Hager were uneasy over the possibility that the Habsburg monarch's recently reacquired Italian subjects were being indoctrinated with pernicious revolutionary ideas, the Habsburg officials in Italy on the whole had little faith in the reports of an impending revolution. While he admitted that there was considerable dissatisfaction in the Italian army, the Venetian Police Director Raab insisted that there was nothing to fear from either the disaffected military or anyone else.[14] Bellegarde also assured Von Hager that his apprehensions over an imminent revolt in Italy were unjustified. It is true that, since some of the populace, particularly the military, were discontented with their new regime, he had asked the Lombard police to redouble their watch over suspected persons, but these were merely precautionary measures. Above all, he wrote Von Hager, no credence should be given to the excited missives about the double subscription lists. While it was evident that such lists had been passed around, they were the same lists which had been circulated during the last days of the Kingdom of Italy for the purpose of demanding a meeting of the electoral colleges and attempting to influence the Allied Powers to grant independence to the Kingdom of Italy.[15]

Raab and Bellegarde's soothing assurances that there was no reason to expect trouble in Lombardy-Venetia might have quieted the jittery nerves in Vienna had Metternich not received information about an approaching rebellion from another source: the imperial commissioner at the French court, Count Louis Bombelles. On July 15, Esquiron de St. Agnan, a self-styled man of letters, who affirmed that he had been granted a medal from Emperor Francis in 1808 for a book which he had presented to him and who stated that in the spring of 1814 he had handed the emperor another work entitled *God, Nature, and the Laws,* told Bombelles of a revolutionary plot

---

[13] Hager to Bellegarde, Vienna, August 19, 1814, A. S. (Milan), Presidenza di governo. Atti secreti, 1814, Cart. III, No. 273/P.R.

[14] Raab to Hager, Padua, August 13, 1814, Lemmi, *La restaurazione austriaca a Milano,* Appendix XXIX, p. 436.

[15] Bellegarde to Hager, Milan, July 19 and 20, 1814, A. S. (Milan), Presidenza di governo. Atti secreti, 1814, Cart. I, Nos. 45/P.R. and 46/P.R. A copy of the latter letter is in Lemmi, *La restaurazione austriaca a Milano,* Appendix XXVI, pp. 433–434.

about which a certain Count Comelli had recently given him information in London.[16]

Count Comelli, the son of a Habsburg official, was a notorious double-dealing adventurer who used the name of Count Carlo Francesco Comelli de Stuckenfeld. He was a former Austrian army officer who had deserted the imperial army in 1799 to take up service with the French military forces, where he was supposedly promoted to the rank of colonel, according to his story. In 1809 he acted for a time as a spy for Archduke John in Italy. Then he returned to France, only to be imprisoned. After his release, completely disgusted with both the French and the Austrians, he consorted with various conspirators, including the redoubtable Angeloni. Finally he went to London, where he posed as head of the so-called "Independists."[17]

In London Comelli and his radical companions drew up a fantastic plan of action for the 1814 campaign in Italy. The British navy was to transport to Italy Italian refugees in Spain, Portugal, and France. Once disembarked on Italian soil, they were to proclaim a national war of liberation against the French. After the campaign ended a Roman empire was to be established in the Apennine peninsula, with Rome as the capital. Comelli vainly attempted to interest the prince regent in his absurd scheme, but he was unable to see any British official of higher rank than Undersecretary of State Lord Hamilton, who extracted from him a promise that he would reveal his project to no other person. Hamilton apparently kept such close surveillance on the intriguing count that Comelli complained that he was held virtually a prisoner until Napoleon was overthrown. In spite of Comelli's assurances to Hamilton and the strict watch over him, however, he apparently managed to get in touch with an agent of Louis XVIII, with the Russian ambassador, and with Count d'Agliè, the London representative of the king of Sardinia. He probably talked with them about his scheme to create a Roman empire.[18]

Towards the middle of June, while he was still in London, Comelli met St. Agnan, who was then apparently acting as a French agent. The scheming count had become acquainted with the self-styled lit-

[16] Bombelles to Metternich, Paris, July 16, 1814, Helfert, *La caduta della dominazione francese*, Appendix III, p. 236. The full text of this letter is also given in Weil, *Murat*, Vol. I, pp. 236–241.

[17] Helfert, *La caduta della dominazione francese*, pp. 174–179; Lemmi, *La restaurazione austriaca a Milano*, pp. 337–339.

[18] Spadoni, "Carlo Comelli de Stuckenfeld," pp. 606–629.

térateur three years earlier in Paris. Comelli talked to St. Agnan about his vast dreams to establish a Roman empire ruled by three consuls and an emperor, who was to assume the name of "caesar." He informed him that he hoped to put his scheme into execution early in October. Neither Napoleon nor Prince Eugene knew of the project, but Comelli counted on the assistance of most of the higher officers of Napoleon's army, several generals of the Italian army, two officers who were in the Habsburg emperor's entourage, some important families in Rome and Milan, and various leaders of the party in the Italian Tyrol.[19]

Probably introduced to the group by Comelli, St. Agnan took part in a meeting of the conspirators at London towards the end of June, which was attended by about thirty persons. Four of them were English; the rest were Italians. According to Comelli's statement to St. Agnan, he was leaving London on July 1 for Holland, the Tyrol, and finally Milan, where a meeting of the chief conspirators of the plot was to be held on August 5.

Returning to Paris, St. Agnan presented himself to Bombelles to expose what Comelli had revealed to him in London about the revolutionary project in Italy. At the same time, he handed him three documents—one of them the design for a provisional government; the second, the plan to be followed in executing the plot; and the third, a proclamation for the inhabitants of the Roman empire. The proclamation, St. Agnan intimated, had been drafted by Comelli himself. St. Agnan warned the Austrian imperial commissioner that the conspirators hated Austria. He offered to go to Milan to meet with the machinators on August 5 and to procure enough evidence to enable the Habsburgs to unravel all the threads of the plot.[20]

St. Agnan created an unusually favorable impression upon the easily duped imperial commissioner to the French court. Count Bombelles, in fact, believed that the information which the French agent had disclosed to him was so highly significant that he immediately sent his brother, who had been present during the conversations, to Vienna to tell Metternich the details of St. Agnan's incredible story in person. His brother was enjoined to return posthaste to Paris with

---

[19] Bombelles to Metternich, Paris, July 16, 1814, Helfert, *La caduta della dominazione francese*, Appendix III, pp. 237–239.

[20] *Ibid.*, pp. 238–241. See also *ibid.*, pp. 181–182; Lemmi, *La restaurazione austriaca a Milano*, pp. 340–342; and Spadoni, "Carlo Comelli de Stuckenfeld," pp. 629–630.

instructions from the Austrian chancellor as to whether St. Agnan should be allowed to go to Milan in time to attend the meeting of the conspirators on August 5.[21] Bombelles also dispatched two letters to Metternich in which he related further details about the plot and implored him to let him know whether he should permit St. Agnan to travel to Italy.[22]

Metternich was inclined to attach much less importance to St. Agnan's implausible disclosures than Bombelles, particularly after he learned that August 5 had passed in Milan without incident. With some misgivings, he finally granted Bombelles permission to deal with the French intriguer; however, apparently at his suggestion, the government in Vienna did not inform Bellegarde before August 31 about St. Agnan's proposed trip to the Lombard capital.[23] When the Austrian chancellor learned that St. Agnan had attempted to wheedle Bombelles into giving him a considerable sum of money on the pretext that he was so heavily in debt that he could not possibly leave Paris before receiving an advance of 8,000 francs and, furthermore, that he had intimated to the imperial commissioner that his immediate presence in Milan was not urgent since the conspirators could not begin their revolt before October at the very earliest,[24] both he and Police President von Hager became highly suspicious of St. Agnan's intentions. However, in case there might be a semblance of truth in St. Agnan's revelations, they decided to abide by their previous plans. Nonetheless, Von Hager instructed Governors Bellegarde and Reuss-Plauen on September 13 and 15, respectively, secretly and carefully to observe Comelli's comings and goings in case he actually did turn up in Italy.[25] On September 15 Hager also warned that, in addition to St. Agnan, another person, Giovanni Rasori, who

---

[21] Bombelles to Metternich, Paris, July 16, 1814, Helfert, *La caduta della dominazione francese*, Appendix III, pp. 236 and 240–241.

[22] Weil, *Murat*, Vol. I, pp. 242–243.

[23] Council of war to Bellegarde, Baden, August 31, 1814, St. A. (Vienna), Staatskanzlei, Provinzen, Lombardei-Venedig, Fasz. III, Kon. 2, Fos. 70–71.

[24] Bombelles to Metternich, Paris, September 1, 1814, Helfert, *La caduta della dominazione francese*, Appendix V, pp. 242–243.

[25] Hager to Bellegarde, Vienna, September 13, 1814, A. S. (Milan), Presidenza di governo. Atti secreti, 1814, Cart. III, No. 399/P.R. (an Italian translation of this letter is in Lemmi, *La restaurazione austriaca a Milano*, Appendix XXXII, p. 440); Hager to Reuss-Plauen, Vienna, September 15, 1814, A. S. (Venice), Presidio di governo, 1814, No. 1305.

was well known for his pro-French sympathies and his bitter antipathy to the Habsburg regime, needed to be closely watched.[26]

Bellegarde was even less inclined to believe St. Agnan's strange tale than his superiors in Vienna. On September 22 he wrote Metternich that, although he had made a thorough investigation, he could find nothing to indicate that Count Comelli was in Italy or that there was any truth in St. Agnan's disclosure to Bombelles in Paris. He admitted that there was discontent in Italy. The malcontents could be divided into two classes: (1) the proponents of Italian independence, who were protected by the British; and (2) "adventurous intriguers who have connections with the king of Naples." These two groups could become dangerous only if the English joined forces with the king of Naples—a move which, he assured the Habsburg chancellor, was most unlikely on account of Lord Bentinck's strong aversion to Murat. All agitation in Italy, the Lombard governor insisted, would be wholly ineffectual "if our administrative and political conduct is such as to reconcile public opinion to us." Nonetheless, the Austrians could expect trouble if they did "not deal carefully with the national spirit in Italy," if they wished to institute in their Italian provinces "laws and institutions which are not suited to the different localities of the country and the customs of the inhabitants," and if they favored "the commerce and industry of our German provinces too much at the expense of our Italian provinces." The landowners, the great mass of the population, and persons with religious convictions were decidedly pro-Austrian, Bellegarde informed Metternich. "If we know how to hold and to cultivate their affection, we have nothing to fear from a small number of intriguers who are without strength today."[27]

After receiving these soothing reassurances from their commissioner plenipotentiary in Lombardy the Austrian authorities in Vienna might have forgotten the whole matter had not Anton Leopold von Roschmann-Hörburg, the imperial commissioner in the Tyrol, discovered another plot—one supporting Prince Eugene.[28] On his own authority he ordered the ex-mayor of Trent Luigi Cheluzzi to Milan

[26] Hager report, September 15, 1814, St. A. (Vienna), Conferenz Akten, Ser. b, 1814, No. 1695.

[27] Bellegarde to Metternich, Milan, September 22, 1814, St. A. (Vienna), Staatskanzlei, Provinzen, Lombardei-Venedig, Fasz. III, Kon. 4, Fos. 105–106.

[28] Weil, *Murat*, Vol. I, pp. 367–368.

to investigate the progress of the machination and uncover the conspirators.[29]

Roschmann's suspicions that some kind of conspiracy was afoot in Lombardy-Venetia were well founded. Various liberal groups still hoped to obtain independence and liberal political institutions. Among a small hard core of convinced opponents of Habsburg rule there remained a lingering expectation that in some way or another, whether by outside intervention, a popular uprising, or an insurrection of the former Italian army, their longings for freedom from foreign domination would finally be satisfied.

In the summer and fall of 1814 the prospect of foreign aid seemed hopeless to all but a handful of misty-eyed dreamers. The possibility of a successful mass revolt appeared to be even more improbable. The likelihood that disgruntled officers of the former Italian army might concoct a conspiracy which could become dangerous to Habsburg rule in Italy, however, became a frightening reality when the Austrians put into effect their reorganization scheme for the Italian army on July 31.[30] Many a proud and sensitive Italian officer, even among those accepted for service in the imperial army with the same rank which they had previously enjoyed, resented being placed under the command of Austrian officers, and many of those who were put on half-pay because no place could be found for them in the new table of organization were bitter and angry.[31]

Some of the more hotheaded and venturesome officers in this fractious group plotted an audacious, though foolhardy, cabal to chase the Austrians out of Lombardy-Venetia—the Brescian-Milanese conspiracy. The initiators of the machination were Colonel Silvio Moretti, a native of Zavallo and an ardent republican, who was then sta-

---

[29] Hager to Emperor Francis, Vienna, October 21, 1814, Helfert, La caduta della dominazione francese, Appendix VI, pp. 245–246. Emperor Francis was displeased with Roschmann for taking this step before consulting his superiors in Vienna; however, he approved allotting Cheluzzi enough money to carry out his mission provided that he remained in Italy no longer than was absolutely necessary (imperial resolution, November 14, 1814, ibid., p. 247.)

[30] See ante, pp. 167–168.

[31] See also Giuseppe Solitro, Un martire dello Spielberg (il colonnello Silvio Moretti) su documenti inediti degli Archivi di Milano e di Brünn (hereafter cited as Solitri, Il colonnello Silvio Moretti), p. 3; Pingaud, "La Lombardie en 1814," p. 459; and Della Porta report, Milan, January 26, 1815, Luzio, La Massoneria e il Risorgimento italiano, Vol. I, Appendix V, pp. 98–99.

tioned at Montechiari; and Colonel Gian Paolo Olini,[32] of Pinzano, in Friuli. The two colonels, who had received commissions in the imperial army, were irritated because the command of their regiments had been taken away from them. While sitting together in a theater in Brescia, they first talked about the possibility of organizing an insurrection towards the end of August or during the first days of September.[33] The two colonels informed Colonel Pietro Pavoni, who was also disconsolate over losing control of his military unit, about their plans. Since the number of Habsburg soldiers in Italy was relatively small and since they were widely scattered throughout Lombardy, Venetia, Piedmont, the Duchies, and the Legations, the three plotters believed that it would not be too difficult to rout the Austrian troops. They agreed that they should initiate the revolt by surprising Peschiera, near which Italian troops were stationed, in order to seize the arms and supplies stored there.[34]

Fully aware that the success of their project depended on finding a high-ranking officer with a distinguished reputation to lead it, Pavoni went to Milan to speak to Generals Achille Fontanelli and Carlo Zucchi. Fontanelli, a Modenese by birth, had been minister of war in the Kingdom of Italy, while Zucchi was commandant at Mantua during the last days of the French regime.

Pavoni first called on General Zucchi. Then the two went together to see Fontanelli, who, according to what Pavoni later told Olini, not only "consented to second their enterprise" but also agreed "to become the head of it." When he learned that Olini and Moretti were the chief instigators of the complot, he invited them to see him.[35]

---

[32] For a more complete account of Olini's activities, see Pietro Bastari, "Paolo Olini," in *Nel Cinquantenario delle X Giornate*, pp. 47–50.

[33] In older accounts the date of this encounter is usually given as around the middle of September (see, for example, Helfert, *La caduta della dominazione francese*, p. 195; Lemmi, *La restaurazione austriaca a Milano*, p. 345; Castro, *Milano e le cospirazioni lombarde*, p. 120; and Solitro, *Il colonnello Silvio Moretti*, p. 3). Spadoni, however, maintains that this meeting took place either during the last of August or in the very early part of September (see his *La congiura militare*, p. 8). Since Spadoni based his information on the actual testimony which Olini and Moretti gave to the Habsburg investigating authorities, and since, to my knowledge, Spadoni is the only historian who has made a careful examination of the official trial records of the Brescian-Milanese conspiracy, his information is more likely to be correct than that given by the other historians.

[34] Weil, *Murat*, Vol. II, pp. 51–52; Spadoni, *La congiura militare*, pp. 8–9.

[35] Conclusions of the special military commission in regard to Generals Fon-

Zucchi then left for Reggio after Pavoni promised to keep him posted about the further progress of the conspiracy, and Pavoni returned to Brescia to communicate the results of his interviews to Olini and Moretti. The last two went to Fontanelli a few days later to speak to him at length about their insurrectionary project. They informed him of their scheme to occupy Peschiera, which he fully approved, and talked with him about the troops that could be relied upon to carry out the enterprise. Fontanelli clearly intimated that when the time came to rout the Austrians from the Apennine peninsula they could count on him to lead the Italian troops. He even gave them permission to print proclamations in his name. He told them, however, that he did not wish openly to associate himself with the machination before the day of actual fighting.[36]

While on their visit to Milan Olini and Moretti made a short trip to Monza to see their friend Innocenzo Ugo Brunetti, a native of Lodi, former inspector of the French imperial guard, and a close friend of Foscolo, to enlist him in the venture. Brunetti enthusiastically assured them that they could count on his full support.[37]

---

tanelli and Zucchi, Mantua, February 17, 1815, Weil, *Murat*, Vol. II, Appendix III, p. 485. See also Spadoni, *La congiura militare*, p. 9.

[36] Conclusions of the special military commission in regard to Generals Fontanelli and Zucchi, Mantua, February 17, 1815, Weil, *Murat*, Vol. II, Appendix III, pp. 484–486; Della Porta report, Milan, January 26, 1815, Luzio, *La Massoneria e il Risorgimento italiano*, Vol. I, Appendix V, p. 100; Spadoni, *La congiura militare*, pp. 9–18. It should be noted that before Spadoni wrote his monumental accounts of the Brescian-Milanese conspiracy on the basis of the actual trial records, historians were inclined to believe that Fontanelli rejected the conspirators' invitation to head the rebellion (see, for example, Helfert, *La caduta della dominazione francese*, p. 196; Lemmi, *La restaurazione austriaca a Milano*, p. 347; Weil, *Murat*, Vol. II, pp. 53–54; Castro, *Milano e le cospirazioni lombarde*, pp. 121–122; and Solitro, *Il colonnello Silvio Moretti*, pp. 4–5), even though Gualterio and Princess Belgiojoso-Trivulzio wrote that Fontanelli at first promised to cooperate with the plotters (See F[ilippo] A[ntonio]) Gualterio, *Gli ultimi rivolgimenti italiani. Memorie storiche, con documenti inediti*, Vol. I, Pt. 1, p. 406; and [Belgiojoso-Trivulzio], *Étude sur l'histoire de la Lombardie*, pp. 107–108). Given the fact that all available primary sources—the summary of the testimony against the two generals by the Austrian court reporter and the evidence given by Olini, Moretti, Latuada, and Teodoro Lechi at their trial—clearly indicate that Fontanelli agreed to head the revolt when Pavoni, Olini, and Moretti first asked him to do so, it is clear that the older accounts are in error on this point.

[37] Weil, *Murat*, Vol. II, p. 53; Tonni-Bazza, "La congiura militare bresciano," p. 46.

Moretti also had two conferences with General Teodoro Lechi, a Brescian who fought with the French during most of the Napoleonic era and was a former grand master of the Grand Orient Masonic lodge of Italy. He informed the general that the enterprise was supported by Generals Gaspare Bellotti, Fontanelli, Carlo Ballabio, Palombini, Domenico Pino, Antonio Bonfanti, and Pietro San Andrea, a group of prominent Milanese, and a large number of malcontents in the Lombard capital. General Zucchi and Prince Astorre Ercolani, a former officer in the French army, a leading Freemason, and a prominent member of the Guelfs, had already readied plans for a revolt by troops stationed in Parma and Modena. Preparations were being made to provoke a general insurrection of all the Italian regiments in Lombardy-Venetia. Peschiera was to be surprised, after which contingents from Crema, Bergamo, and Brescia were to march to Milan and capture it, with the assistance of a popular revolution which was being planned in the capital city.[38]

Although it was obvious that Moretti was greatly exaggerating the assistance on which he could depend to carry out the conspiracy, General Lechi readily declared his willingness to join it. So did General Bellotti, a native of Turin and a thirty-eight-year-old brigadier general; Squadron Leader Cesare Ragani, of Bologna, who had been discharged by the Austrians because he was a foreigner and who had recently been granted a commission in the Neapolitan army; Colonel Filippo Bonfanti, a Milanese and a distinguished officer in the former French-Italian army; and Giacomo Filippo de Meester,[39] a Milanese who was director of the college for military orphans at San Luca.

Through De Meester's influence, Gian Bernardo Soveri Latuada, a young liberal lawyer barely twenty-five years old, who was eventually to become one of the most influential leaders of the cabal, was attracted to the complot. Latuada, an intimate friend of General Pino and an influential Freemason, had played a prominent role in the

[38] General Teodoro Lechi's confession to the Habsburg investigating authorities on December 29, 1814, as summarized in Spadoni, "Il processo per la congiura bresciano-milanese," pp. 94–95; and in his *La congiura militare*, pp. 15–18. For a full account of General Teodoro Lechi's life, see Alberto Lumbroso, "Conte Teodoro Lechi da Brescia (1778–1866) e la sua famiglia," *Rivista storica del Risorgimento italiano*, Vol. III, Fasc. 4 (1898), pp. 349–373.

[39] For a good account of De Meester's life and activities, see Domenico Spadoni, "Il gen. bar. Giacomo Filippo de Meester," *Rassegna storica del Risorgimento*, Vol. XVI, Fasc. 4 (October–December, 1929), pp. 849–882.

April 20 revolution in Milan. A week later he presented to Lord
Bentinck letters demanding independence for the Kingdom of Italy
from General Pino, the Milanese communal council, and over three
hundred other distinguished Milanese. With the aid of Professors
Salfi and Romagnosi,[40] both of whom were founders of the Royal
Josephine Lodge of Milan, he drew up, on behalf of that lodge, a
constitution for an independent Kingdom of Italy. It was dated April
24, 1814. This constitution was later to serve as the model for the government which the Brescian-Milanese conspirators hoped to establish.[41]

Upon De Meester's advice, Latuada went to Pompiano, where
Olini was stationed, either at the end of September or the beginning
of October. The young lawyer intimated to Olini that many partisans
of independence in Milan could be relied on to support the insurrection. In addition, the machinators could count on the civic guard for
assistance in executing the project. They could also use the guns and
ammunition stored in the national guard arsenal, as well as weapons
in the possession of a certain Barisoni. More important, Latuada
promised Olini the powerful support of the Centri society, to which,
he said, many persons of distinction and a large number of advocates
of freedom belonged. Since the Centri had the same aims as the Carbonari, the plotters could also expect aid from them, with their extensive membership in southern Italy. Through them perhaps even
Murat might be prevailed upon to enter the conspiracy.[42]

Particularly after Latuada joined the movement the number of
adherents increased day by day. Included among them were prominent Carbonari like Antonio Maria Caprotti, an employee of the military bookkeeping office in Milan; Santino Gerosa, of Luco, a bailiff
at the court of appeals; and Bartolomeo Cavedoni, of Modena, who
had once been General Giuseppe Lechi's aide. There were such well
known military men as Battalion Chief Luigi Delfini, from Piedmont;

[40] It should be emphasized, however, that Romagnosi did not take part in the
Brescian-Milanese conspiracy (see S. F., "Giandomenico Romagnosi," p. 121).
Neither did Salfi.

[41] See my *Fall of the Napoleonic Kingdom of Italy*, pp. 105, 131–132 n., and
160–161.

[42] Testimony given by Latuada on December 11, 1814, and by Olini on December 29, 1814, and January 1, 1815, as summarized in Spadoni, *La congiura
militare*, pp. 21–24; Helfert, *La caduta della dominazione francese*, pp. 198–199;
Lemmi, *La restaurazione austriaca a Milano*, p. 348; Weil, *Murat*, Vol. II, pp.
55–56; Castro, *Milano e le cospirazioni lombarde*, p. 124.

Commissioner of War Francesco Mancini; and the Milanese Colonel Pietro Varese. The most influential machinators who associated themselves with the venture around this time, however, were Colonel Antonio Gasparinetti, a Venetian, an ardent republican, a man of letters, and one of Foscolo's friends; and Giovanni Rasori, a distinguished scientist and doctor of medicine, who was unhappy over losing his position at the major hospital in Milan.[43] Apparently the last of the important leaders to enter the undertaking was Giovanni Battista Marchal, a native of Lorena who had left the army to open a store in Milan.[44]

As time went on the number of conferences among the directors of the cabal multiplied. De Meester, Latuada, Bellotti, Cavedoni, and Delfini saw each other almost daily, and Lechi and Moretti met frequently. Numerous meetings took place at Brunetti's residence and the home of Countess Favetti, and the plotters often conversed with each other in the Caffè dei Servi. As October progressed, Latuada, the most active of the ringleaders by then, who traveled endlessly between Brescia and Milan, was serving as the chief liaison man among the various conspirators everywhere. At the same time, he was carrying on a fervid correspondence with persons in London and Naples in the vain hope of receiving pledges of support from those quarters.[45]

In order to probe the sentiment in Naples, Ragani went there furnished with letters of recommendation from Latuada and De Meester to Professor Salfi. On behalf of the insurrectionists he agreed to inform Murat that if the Congress of Vienna tried to force him to abdicate he could rest assured that the large pro-independence party in northern Italy would support his cause.[46]

While Ragani was on his way to Naples, Pavoni traveled to Reggio

[43] For details about Rasori's life, see Carlo Frati, "Ricordi di Prigionia. Memorie autobiografiche e frammenti poetici di Giovanni Rasori," *Biblioteca di Storia Italiana Recente* (*1800–1870*), Vol. IX, pp. 1–132.

[44] Lemmi, *La restaurazione austriaca a Milano*, pp. 349–351; Helfert, *La caduta della dominazione francese*, pp. 199–200; Castro, *Milano e le cospirazioni lombarde*, pp. 124–125; Weil, *Murat*, Vol. II, pp. 56–57; Cusani, *Storia di Milano*, Vol. VII, pp. 203–205.

[45] Della Porta report, Milan, January 26, 1815, Luzio, *La Massoneria e il Risorgimento italiano*, Vol. I, Appendix V, p. 99; Weil, *Murat*, Vol. I, p. 59; Helfert, *La caduta della dominazione francese*, p. 202.

[46] Testimony given by Ragani on February 6, 1815, and by Latuada on December 13, 1814, as summarized in Spadoni, *La congiura militare*, pp. 27–28.

to ascertain whether the managers of the enterprise could still count on General Zucchi. Although the general had already been assigned to active duty in the German provinces of the monarchy, he told his visitor that he would pass through Brescia on his way north. While in that city he wanted to meet with some of the ringleaders to learn how the complot was progressing. At Brescia he promised the machinators, either in late October or early November, that he would assist them in whatever way he could if the revolt broke out before he left Italy. He told them that he would journey slowly through the peninsula in order to give them time to ready their strategies for the rebellion.[47]

Meanwhile, an entirely new factor had to be considered. Towards the end of October came rumors that the Italian troops were to be sent to Germany in the very near future. It was now impossible to temporize any longer. Even though innumerable conferences had been held during the past seven or eight weeks, no precise arrangements had yet been agreed upon that would insure the successful staging of the rebellion. Some of the plotters became nervous and edgy. The officers stationed at Brescia and Pompiano began to lose patience with their co-conspirators in Milan and loudly clamored for decisive actions from them.

If the conspiracy were to continue, the leaders in Brescia and Milan needed to devise explicit plans. For that purpose Moretti and Olini left Brescia for Milan for a meeting held on the evening of November 3 in Brunetti's home. Besides the two colonels from Brescia, Latuada, Lechi, and Cavedoni were present at this conference. De Meester, who was also invited, did not appear.

On November 3 and at subsequent meetings during the next few days,[48] in which all or some of the leaders of the cabal participated,

---

[47] Conclusions of the special military commission in regard to Generals Fontanelli and Zucchi, Mantua, February 17, 1815, Weil, *Murat*, Vol. II, Appendix III, pp. 488–489; testimony given by Olini on December 28 and 29, 1814, by Latuada on December 13, 1814, and by Moretti on February 11, 1815, as summarized in Spadoni, *La congiura militare*, pp. 34–36.

[48] Helfert, *La caduta della dominazione francese*, pp. 202–204; Weil, *Murat*, Vol. II, pp. 60–61; Castro, *I congiurati lombardi del 1814*, p. 14; Lemmi, *La restaurazione austriaca a Milano*, pp. 353–354; and Tonni-Bazza, "La congiura militare bresciano," p. 46, all relate that the plan of action described in this and the next two paragraphs was agreed upon on the evening of November 3. From the lengthy, though often confusing and contradictory, testimony given by various conspirators themselves and summarized in Spadoni, *La congiura militare*, pp.

the conspirators agreed that at a given moment, which was later fixed
as the night of November 19–20, the Italian regiments stationed at
Cremona, Bergamo, and Brescia were to lead the inhabitants of these
cities to revolt. At the same time, other contingents were to surprise
Peschiera and seize the arms stored there, while still others were to
capture Rocca d'Anfo and the artillery park at Verona from the feeble Austrian garrisons which held them. Troops quartered at Cas-
tiglione delle Stiviere, assisted by the Centri, were to take possession
of the citadel at Mantua. Even Modena was to be attacked, its duke
taken captive, and the ducal treasury appropriated.

After at least some of these maneuvers had been carried out, the
military forces at Peschiera, Bergamo, and Crema were to march on
Milan, where at the outbreak of the rebellion the populace was to be
called to arms by the ringing of all the clocks in the city. Italian veterans were to hurry through the streets shouting "Constitution! Liberty! Independence!" During the confusion the weak Habsburg
garrisons in the Lombard capital were to be attacked and forced either to surrender or to withdraw from the city. Fifty officers commanded by Cavedoni and a sizable detachment of enlisted men
were to apprehend Bellegarde and the other important Austrian
military and civil officers in the capital. Then the ringleaders were to
declare the re-establishment of the Italian kingdom and announce
that a provisional regency was temporarily to be in charge of the
government. If the plot failed, the conspirators were to retreat to
Tuscany.[49]

Thus during the first half of November the main directors of the
machination at last came to final agreement on all the details necessary to execute the rebellion. However, they still needed a "distinguished general" to head the uprising. Apparently General Zucchi

---

38–40 and 64–72, it is clear, however, that the details of the plan were drawn
up piecemeal, not only on November 3, but also at several other conferences that
went on for several days afterwards.

[49] Della Porta report, Milan, January 26, 1815, Luzio, *La Massoneria e il Risorgimento italiano*, Vol. I, Appendix V, pp. 103–105; *Biblioteca Ambrosiana*
(Milan), "Atto d'accusa contro Giovanni Soveri Latuada, Teodoro Conte Lechi,
Gaspare Bellotti, ecc. ecc." (MSS in a bound MSS volume entitled "Autografi
del Prof. Rasori e del Conte P. Latta"), Fos. 49–50; Castro, *I congiurati lombardi del 1814*, p. 14; Spadoni, *La congiura militare*, pp. 38–40 and 64–72;
Weil, *Murat*, Vol. II, pp. 60–61; Helfert, *La caduta della dominazione francese*,
pp. 202–204.

was already on his way to Germany and was no longer available.[50] Although Fontanelli had promised the leaders of the cabal in September that he would command the armed forces when the rebellion actually commenced, the testimony of various conspirators at their trial makes it clear that by early November the chief architects of the venture seriously doubted whether they could still count on him. Perhaps by then the general was beset by doubts. At any rate, he was no longer on speaking terms with General Pino, who was a close personal friend of several of the plotters. The ringleaders made a concerted effort to patch up the differences between the two generals and at a meeting on November 4 commissioned Latuada and Bellotti to visit both men. The two envoys returned from their mission confident that they had succeeded in reconciling the generals and that they could rely on each of them to take a leading role in executing the plot. However, they were deluded on both counts. When Latuada and Varese visited Fontanelli a couple of weeks later to entreat him to lead the insurrection, he positively refused to participate in it in any way, saying that because of the imminent departure of the Italian troops for Germany there was no longer sufficient time to carry out a successful rebellion. Advising the plotters that their machination was only a fantastic dream, General Pino also turned down their invitation to take part in it.[51]

The ringleaders of the complot were just as unsuccessful in their efforts to procure foreign aid as they were in their attempts to influence a well known general to lead the rebellion. Ragani reported from Naples that, although the higher officers of the Neapolitan army were inclined to look with favor on the project, the king would give no help whatever since he was now on excellent terms with the Austrian emperor. Furthermore, nothing could be counted on from

[50] At the conferences held early in November General Zucchi was no longer mentioned as a possible leader.

[51] Della Porta report, Milan, January 26, 1815, Luzio, *La Massoneria e il Risorgimento italiano*, Vol. I, Appendix V, pp. 100–101; conclusions of the special military commission in regard to Generals Fontanelli and Zucchi, Mantua, February 17, 1815, Weil, *Murat*, Vol. II, Appendix III, pp. 486–487 and 490; Spadoni, *La congiura militare*, pp. 45–49, 61, 77–78, and 80–83. Princess Belgiojoso-Trivulzio states that after Fontanelli refused to head the enterprise the plotters tried to induce General Lechi to command it. Modest as he was, she relates, Lechi turned down the invitation, saying that his name was not lustrous enough and that his character was too mild for him to be a successful leader of the rebellion ([Belgiojoso-Trivulzio], *Étude sur l'histoire de la Lombardie*, p. 109).

Switzerland, the British, or the Italian officers in English pay who were stationed at Novi.[52]

Even though the outlook should by now have been discouraging to anyone but a dreamer, thus far everything seemed to progress smoothly for the conspirators. However, in the early days of November they took a false step which led to the denunciation of the conspiracy to Field Marshal Bellegarde. In an effort to obtain outside aid, they sent the Piedmontese Michele Cimba, a former doctor in the royal guard, to Turin to enlist dissentients in the Sardinian capital in their undertaking. When Cimba arrived at Vercelli on November 6 he met General Alessandro Gifflenga, who advised him that his mission was useless and that he should return to Milan. A few days later Gifflenga himself visited the Lombard capital, where, on the 10th, he met with the conspirators. After Latuada outlined the details of the project, Gifflenga commented that the whole plan was so ill-conceived and absurd that it could succeed only if the king of Sardinia were invited to take charge of the government after the revolution was over. This the leaders in Milan refused to do. After telling the plotters that he wanted to have nothing whatsoever to do with their enterprise, Gifflenga departed for Piedmont the next day. When he returned to Vercelli he wrote his friend Bellotti asking him to send him notices about the progress of the machination.[53]

On November 6—the very day on which he first heard of it—Gifflenga gave Count Avogadro della Motta, the syndic of Vercelli, the details of the cabal which Cimba had revealed to him. The syndic immediately dispatched this information to the Sardinian minister of foreign affairs Count Antonio de Vallesa[54] who, on receiving the communication on November 8, sent it by confidential messenger the same day to Count Bellegarde.[55] Also on the 8th Count de Vallesa

---

[52] Della Porta report, Milan, January 26, 1815, Luzio, *La Massoneria e il Risorgimento italiano*, Vol. I, Appendix V, pp. 101–102 and 103; *Biblioteca Ambrosiana* (Milan), "Atto d'accusa contro Giovanni Soveri Latuada, ecc.," Fo. 50; Spadoni, *La congiura militare*, pp. 60–61.

[53] Spadoni, "Il processo per la congiura bresciano-milanese," pp. 96–97; testimony given by Latuada on December 21, 1814, as summarized in Spadoni, *La congiura militare*, pp. 53–56.

[54] Avogadro della Motta to Count de Vallesa, Vercelli, November 6, 1814, Domenico Perrero, "Il generale conte Alessandro di Gifflenga e la congiura militare lombarda del 1814," *Rivista storica del Risorgimento italiano*, Vol. I (1895), p. 298. Also in Spadoni, *La congiura militare*, p. 52.

[55] See Perrero, "Il generale conte Alessandro di Gifflenga e la congiura mili-

instructed Count della Motta to give Gifflenga a passport to go to Milan as soon as possible to collect more information about the conspiracy.[56] As soon as Gifflenga returned from the Lombard capital to Vercelli on November 12 he hastened to write Vallesa,[57] apparently to apprise him of his conversations with the Milanese machinators. On the 15th Vallesa transmitted to Bellegarde the new information from Gifflenga.[58]

Even before the field marshal received the warning from the Sardinian minister of foreign affairs that a rebellion was under way in Lombardy-Venetia, he had gotten other vague reports that some kind of insurrection was being concocted. The governor, however, considered these rumors the inventions of overzealous confidants. In Venetia Police Director Raab also dismissed information that reached him about secret machinations in Bergamo, Brescia, and Mantua as amounting to nothing more than attempts of enemies of the Habsburg regime to stir up trouble. Even Baron von Hager was inclined to take little stock in the reports.[59]

When the commissioner plenipotentiary received the communication from Vallesa in Turin, however, he suddenly became aware that

---

tare," pp. 298–299. On November 11, 1814, Bellegarde wrote Emperor Francis to inform him of the need to leave at least three regiments of the Austrian army in Italy. After giving several reasons why he thought that this was necessary, he wrote: "In order to give Your Majesty new proof that continuous caution and intelligence are necessary, I am humbly submitting in the enclosures a report which I have received from the Sardinian government" (*Kriegs-Archiv* [Vienna], Feld Akten (Italien), 1814, Fasz. XI, No. 14½). In Hager's report of November 27, 1814, he wrote among other things: "The concern over such disturbances [when the Italian troops would leave Italy] rests on secret notices which F. M. Count Bellegarde has received and which are supposed to have been confirmed by a ministerial work from Turin" (St. A. [Vienna], Kabinets-Akten, 1814, No. 883).

56 Count Vallesa to Avogadro della Motta, Turin, November 8, 1814, Perrero, "Il generale conte Alessandro di Gifflenga e la congiura militare," p. 299.

57 Vallesa to Gifflenga, Turin, November 14, 1814, *ibid.*, p. 300. See also Spadoni, *La congiura militare*, p. 56.

58 Vallesa to Bellegarde, Turin, November 15, 1814, Perrero, "Il generale conte Alessandro di Gifflenga e la congiura militare," p. 301.

59 Bellegarde to Emperor Francis, Milan, November 11, 1814, *Kriegs-Archiv* (Vienna), Feld Akten (Italien), 1814, Fasz. XI, No. 14½, Hager report, November 27, 1814, St. A. (Vienna), Kabinets-Akten, 1814, No. 883; Raab to Reuss-Plauen, Venice, November 18 and 19, 1814, A. S. (Venice), Presidio di governo, 1814, Nos. 1980 and 1981.

a real conspiracy was afoot, especially since around the same time news about a dangerous machination also came to him from other sources. On November 16 a police confidant avowed that a pensioned Italian officer had been urged to join a complot against the government, the participants of which were largely Italian soldiers. On the 18th a government employee reported that he "very clearly overheard two unknown persons walking ahead of him" say that "tomorrow, on the 19th, in the evening, a riot against the government is to break out."[60]

With the subsequent hearty endorsement of the authorities in Vienna,[61] Bellegarde moved rapidly to nip any possible conspiracy in the bud. Custodians of all bell towers in Milan were ordered to ring bells only for religious purposes and to indicate the hour of day. The guard was strengthened for the nights of November 19–20 and 20–21. Cavalry and infantry patrols made the rounds of the city, and detailed instructions were drawn up for the Milanese garrison in case of an actual uprising.[62] Governor Reuss-Plauen also took appropriate security measures in Venetia.[63] Perhaps these energetic actions convinced the plotters that they should abandon their plans for the time being; perhaps their inability to induce Fontanelli or Pino to head the movement also influenced the ringleaders to suspend the execution of the plot.[64] Be that as it may, although there were some minor disturbances among the Italian soldiers in Brescia,[65] the night of November 19–20 passed quietly in Milan.

[60] Bellegarde to Hager, Milan, November 22, 1814, Lemmi, *La restaurazione austriaca a Milano*, Appendix XLIII, p. 453. The complete text of the letter can also be found in Weil, *Murat*, Vol. II, Appendix IV, pp. 491–492.

[61] Hager to Bellegarde, Vienna, December 3, 1814, A. S. (Milan), Presidenza di governo. Atti secreti, 1814, Cart. VII, No. 910/P.R.

[62] Bellegarde to Hager, Milan, November 22, 1814, Lemmi, *La restaurazione austriaca a Milano*, Appendix XLIII, pp. 453–454 (also in Weil, *Murat*, Vol. II, Appendix IV, p. 492); entries of November 20 and 21, 1814, *Biblioteca Ambrosiana* (Milan), Mantovani, "Diario di Milano," Vol. V, pp. 324–325; Bellegarde project No. LXVIII, dated November 23, 1814, *Kriegs-Archiv* (Vienna), Feld Akten (Italien), 1814, Fasz. XI, No. 42; Helfert, *La caduta della dominazione francese*, pp. 220–221.

[63] Hager report, November 27, 1814, St. A. (Vienna), Kabinets-Akten, 1814, No. 883.

[64] See, for instance, Gerosa's testimony on January 5, 1815, as summarized in Spadoni, *La congiura militare*, pp. 76–77.

[65] General police directory bulletin, Milan, November 19, 1814, A. S. (Milan), Presidenza di governo. Atti secreti, 1814, Cart. VI, No. 775/P.R.

Bellegarde also ordered the Italian regiments to march from Italy to other parts of the Habsburg empire as quickly as possible.[66] After hearing that officers at Brescia were scheming to incite disorders among the Italian troops when they left the Apennine peninsula,[67] Police Director Raab went to Verona personally to cooperate with the Austrian military commander in arranging stringent security measures that would insure the maintenance of public tranquillity.[68] As it turned out, these precautionary steps were unnecessary. Although both officers and enlisted men complained loudly over having to leave their native country,[69] when they actually began their march shortly after November 20[70] their conduct was exemplary all the way to Germany.[71]

With the departure of the Italian troops from the Apennine peninsula, it was obvious to the Brescian-Milanese conspirators that their plans were no longer feasible. Nevertheless, the Austrian authorities still did not have the necessary legal proof to arrest and try the ringleaders of the machination. Up to that time the police had supplied them with nothing tangible about the complot. Roschmann's agent Cheluzzi, who arrived in Milan on the evening of November 19, actually discovered more about the cabal in a single day than the vaunted Milanese police had managed to find out during the whole two months when the conspirators were busily plotting under their

[66] Bellegarde to Emperor Francis, Milan, November 11, 1814, *Kriegs-Archiv* (Vienna), Feld Akten (Italien), 1814, Fasz. XI, No. 14½; order, Brigadier General Suden, Brescia, November 21, 1814, *Giornale di Venezia*, No. 163 (December 3, 1814), pp. 3–4; Cusani, *Storia di Milano*, Vol. VII, p. 216.

[67] Torriceri to Bellegarde, Brescia, November 24, 1814, A. S. (Milan), Presidenza di governo. Atti secreti, 1814, Cart. VI, No. 812/P.R. (also in Lemmi, *La restaurazione austriaca a Milano*, Appendix XLIV, pp. 455–456.

[68] Reuss-Plauen to Raab, Venice, November 20, 1814, A. S. (Venice), Presidio di governo, 1814, Nos. 1980 and 1981.

[69] Secret report, Venice, November 28, 1814, Lemmi, *La restaurazione austriaca a Milano*, Appendix XLV, pp. 457–458.

[70] The Italian soldiers stationed at Brescia left for Germany on November 23 (see Torriceri to Bellegarde, Brescia, November 24, 1814, A. S. [Milan], Presidenza di governo. Atti secreti, 1814, Cart. VI, No. 812/P.R. [also in Lemmi, *La restaurazione austriaca a Milano*, Appendix XLIV, p. 456]). Other troops passed through Verona on November 22 and 23 (see Reuss-Plauen to Hager, Venice, November 24, 1814, A. S. [Venice], Presidio di governo, 1814, No. 2022 e 2023.

[71] Reuss-Plauen to Hager, Venice, November 24, 26, 28, and 29, and December 17 and 23, 1814, A. S. (Venice), Presidio di governo, 1814, Nos. 2022 e 2023, 2050, 2066, 2086–2087–2088–2089, 2315, and 2366.

very noses! Before the end of November 20 Cheluzzi learned that a real conspiracy existed and that its ringleaders had plans to start something the moment the Italian troops departed for Germany. He knew the secret signs with which the plotters recognized each other and was aware that two of the leaders had visited Generals Fontanelli and Filippo Severoli to solicit their participation in the enterprise. Furthermore, he had heard that the machinators had their own treasury, which contained funds furnished by various merchants, and their own supply of arms.[72]

Still, this was not enough evidence to justify the arrest of the conspirators. The incriminating papers which the Austrians needed to imprison the leaders were supplied by neither Cheluzzi nor the Lombard police. They were presented to Bellegarde by St. Agnan. Though highly suspicious of the French agent's intentions, the government in Vienna was aware that the self-styled littérateur had definite information about conspiratorial activities in Italy. Finally, the Viennese authorities instructed Bombelles to dispatch St. Agnan to Milan. By the time he received these orders, however, Bombelles had become so distrustful of the wily spy that he believed it would be highly imprudent to allow him to go alone to the Lombard capital. For this reason, Bombelles sent the archivist Carlo Altieri, a trusted Austrophile, to Milan under the pretext of doing necessary work concerning the restitution of the Milanese archives.[73] Actually he was to deliver a confidential letter to Bellegarde and keep a close watch on St. Agnan.[74]

Altieri left Paris on November 1[75] and arrived in Milan on the 11th.[76] St. Agnan departed from the French capital on November 2[77]

---

[72] Cheluzzi to Roschmann, Milan, November 21, 1814, Lemmi, *La restaurazione austriaca a Milano*, Appendix XLII, pp. 451–452.

[73] Riccardo Blaas, "Carlo Altieri, un confidente di Metternich," *Rassegna storica del Risorgimento*, Vol. XLIV, Fasc. 4 (October–December, 1957), p. 616.

[74] Excerpt from a report of Count Bombelles dated Paris, November 2, 1814, Helfert, *La caduta della dominazione francese*, Appendix VII, pp. 248–249; Bombelles to Altieri, Paris, November 1, 1814, Weil, *Murat*, Vol. II, Appendix VI, pp. 494–495.

[75] Excerpt from a report of Count Bombelles dated Paris, November 2, 1814, Helfert, *La caduta della dominazione francese*, Appendix VII, p. 249.

[76] Bellegarde to Emperor Francis, Milan, November 11, 1814, *Kriegs-Archiv* (Vienna), Feld Akten (Italien), 1814, Fasz. XI, No. 14½.

[77] Excerpt from a report of Count Bombelles dated Paris, November 2, 1814, Helfert, *La caduta della dominazione francese*, Appendix VII, p. 249.

and entered the Lombard capital a week later than Altieri, on November 18.[78] After arranging for suitable lodgings, he presented himself to Bellegarde, upon whom he made a most unfavorable impression.[79]

According to the older accounts, like those by Princess Belgiojoso-
Trivulzio,[80] Cusani,[81] Castro,[82] Helfert,[83] Maurice Henri Weil,[84] and
Lemmi,[85] on his way from Turin to Milan St. Agnan confided to Marchal, one of the chief affiliates of the plot whom he had met earlier
in London and who was journeying in his company, that he was coming to Italy on a secret mission to ascertain whether there was enough
dissatisfaction to enable Louis XVIII to take the lead in forming an
independent Italy under the rule of his nephew, the duke of Berry.[86]

As Spadoni has rightly pointed out, however, the above account
is not substantiated by the facts given by the conspirators during
their investigation and trial.[87] Marchal, who certainly had no reason
to deny the truth on this point, told his interrogators that "after seeing him in London," he did not meet St. Agnan again until he ran
across him "in Milan eight days before his arrest."[88] In his summary
of the evidence presented during the preliminary investigation of the
conspirators, Francesco della Porta wrote that during the past July,
while he was in London, St. Agnan "came to know the other French-

[78] Provisional police prefecture of Olona department report, Milan, November
18, 1814, A. S. (Milan), Presidenza di governo. Atti secreti, 1814, Cart. VI, No.
776/P.R.

[79] See Bellegarde to Hager, Milan, November 22, 1814, Helfert, *La caduta
della dominazione francese*, Appendix VIII, p. 250.

[80] See her *Étude sur l'histoire de la Lombardie*, p. 110.

[81] See his *Storia di Milano*, Vol. VII, p. 217.

[82] See his *I congiurati lombardi del 1814*, p. 20; and his *Milano e le cospirazioni lombarde*, p. 146.

[83] See his *La caduta della dominazione francese*, pp. 221–222.

[84] See his *Murat*, Vol. II, pp. 84–86.

[85] See his *La restaurazione austriaca a Milano*, p. 367.

[86] It should be noted that I also believed this version of the story to be correct
when I wrote "The Habsburgs and Public Opinion in Lombardy-Venetia, 1814–
1815," in Edward Mead Earle (ed.), *Nationalism and Internationalism: Essays
Inscribed to Carlton J. H. Hayes* (see p. 328).

[87] See his "I documenti della congiura milanese carpiti da Sᵗ Agnan nel 1814,"
Il Risorgimento italiano, Vol. XIX, Fasc. 3 (July–September, 1926), pp. 302–
304; and his *La congiura militare*, pp. 91–96.

[88] Spadoni, *La congiura militare*, p. 94; Spadoni, "I documenti della congiura
milanese carpiti da Sᵗ Agnan," p. 303.

man Marchal, who had been domiciled there for two years. Betaking himself to Milan this past November, St. Aignan [*sic*] addressed himself to Marchal, through whom he made Dr. Rasori's acquaintance."[89]

From the above testimony it is clear that, except for a brief accidental meeting with him in London, St. Agnan did not actually see Marchal until four or five days after he arrived in Milan.[90] Furthermore, it is obvious that when St. Agnan first came to the Lombard capital he knew very little about an actual conspiracy. In fact, when he originally talked to Bellegarde he could provide him with the names of only two suspects: Rasori and Latuada.[91] Anxious as he may have been to procure for the Austrians precise and detailed information about some kind of a plot, St. Agnan may perchance have thought of the Frenchman whom he had met in London the past July and decided to call on him under the pretext of handing him some books.

During the course of his conversation with Marchal, St. Agnan learned that Marchal's wife was ill and under the care of Professor Rasori. Immediately he expressed a lively interest in meeting the famous doctor.[92] On the same day Marchal introduced the French agent to Rasori as a man whom he had met in London, who was a devoted subject of Louis XVIII and a member of one of the first families of France. After a few preliminary remarks St. Agnan confessed to Rasori that he was traveling to Naples and Rome, where he expected to meet Count Comelli de Stuckenfeld. He admitted to the professor that he had come to Italy as an emissary of the French government to ascertain whether that great love for independence about

[89] Della Porta report, Milan, January 26, 1815, Luzio, *La Massoneria e il Risorgimento italiano*, Vol. I, Appendix V, p. 106.

[90] Marchal was arrested on the night of December 3–4. Eight days before his arrest would be around November 26. In his summary of the testimony, Della Porta, however, plainly indicated that the first meeting between St. Agnan, Rasori, Latuada, and Gasparinetti took place on either November 22 or 23 (see Luzio, *La Massoneria e il Risorgimento italiano*, Vol. I, Appendix V, p. 107). If this was actually the case, in all probability St. Agnan visited Marchal on either the 22nd or the 23rd.

[91] Bellegarde to Hager, Milan, December 14, 1814, A. S. (Milan), Presidenza di governo. Atti secreti, 1814, Cart. III, ad No. 305/P.R.; Hager to Bellegarde, Vienna, December 6, 1814, *ibid.*

[92] Spadoni, *La congiura militare*, p. 95; Spadoni, "I documenti della congiura milanese carpiti da St Agnan," p. 303.

which the French and English papers were writing actually existed. Furthermore, he was commissioned by his government to assure the Italians that France was very much interested in seeing Italy free and independent.[93]

Since St. Agnan expressed such a great interest in becoming acquainted with other persons animated by the same pro-independence sentiments as the illustrious professor, Rasori naively invited Latuada and Gasparinetti to his house to meet him that very night. At this conference St. Agnan divulged more of the French sovereign's alleged plans for Italy. He maintained that Louis XVIII was prepared to send both money and an army to invade Savoy. Although the prince regent of England was supporting the undertaking, of the British ministers only Sir William Drake and the Marquis of Wellesley knew about it. The enterprise was being promoted in England by a certain Count Comelli. After the project was successfully concluded the duke of Berry was to become king of Italy. At this moment St. Agnan needed to know what kind of constitution the Italians wanted for their country. When Latuada voiced the opinion that Italy should have a republican form of government, the French agent exclaimed: "Very well, I will give you a republic."

The participants at the conference agreed that they would get together again in Rasori's house on the evening of November 26. Before this second meeting Rasori promised to draft both a proclamation and a manifesto informing the populace about the French monarch's pro-Italian sentiments. They were to serve as a model for the commander of the invading French army to use. Gasparinetti engaged himself to write a proclamation voicing the strong yearnings of the Italians for independence, while Latuada said that he would draft plans for the provisional government that was to be instituted after the venture succeeded.[94]

---

[93] Bellegarde to Metternich, Milan, December 5, 1814, St. A. (Vienna), Staatskanzlei, Provinzen, Lombardei-Venedig, Fasz. III, Kon. 4, Fo. 193; Della Porta report, Milan, January 26, 1815, Luzio, *La Massoneria e il Risorgimento italiano*, Vol. I, Appendix V, pp. 106–107; testimony given by Rasori on January 15, 1815, as summarized in Spadoni, *La congiura militare*, pp. 95–96; Spadoni, "I documenti della congiura milanese carpiti da St Agnan," pp. 303–304; [Belgiojoso-Trivulzio], *Étude sur l'histoire de la Lombardie*, pp. 111–112.

[94] Della Porta report, Milan, January 26, 1815, Luzio, *La Massoneria e il Risorgimento italiano*, Vol. I, Appendix V, p. 107; Spadoni, *La congiura militare*, pp. 98–101; Spadoni, "I documenti della congiura milanese carpiti da St Agnan,"

Innocently, Rasori, Gasparinetti, and Latuada brought their promised writings to the meeting on the evening of November 26. Rasori had three proclamations with him. The first was one for the commander of the invading French army to publish as soon as he reached Italy. It strongly denounced Austrian misdeeds in Italy and promised that Louis XVIII would come to the Apennine peninsula to proclaim independence, a kingdom, and a constitution.[95] The second, which was shorter, was directed to the Italians. It exhorted them to rise and cast off the shackles with which the Austrians had bound them.[96] The third, addressed to the Italian people, the soldiers, and the national guard, was in the same tenor.[97]

In his contribution, Gasparinetti developed the thesis that, through their egregious mistakes and by their abuse of the Italian people, the Austrians themselves had aided powerfully in nurturing a spirit of independence in Italy. With the welcome aid of France, the Italians would now be delivered from the Habsburg yoke, a French prince would be placed on the throne, and a new independent Italian kingdom would be established which would include, not only Lombardy and Venetia, but also Piedmont, Genoa, Parma and Piacenza, the Papal Legations and Marches, Tuscany, the Italian Tyrol, and even part of Switzerland.[98]

Latuada brought with him the plans for both a provisional and a permanent government which he had already drawn up on April 24.[99] The provisional government was to be headed by a regency of from three to five members selected by an electoral committee from per-

---

pp. 304–308; [Belgiojoso-Trivulzio], *Étude sur l'histoire de la Lombardie*, pp. 112–113.

[95] The full text of this proclamation can be found in Spadoni, "I documenti della congiura militare carpiti da St Agnan," pp. 316–317; and in Spadoni, *La congiura militare*, Appendix IA, pp. 277–278.

[96] See Spadoni, *La congiura militare*, Appendix I, pp. 279 n–280 n.; and Della Porta report, Milan, January 26, 1815, Luzio, *La Massoneria e il Risorgimento italiano*, Vol. I, Appendix V, pp. 107–108.

[97] For the text, see Spadoni, "I documenti della congiura militare carpiti da St Agnan," pp. 317–318; and Spadoni, *La congiura militare*, Appendix IB, pp. 278–279.

[98] For the text, see Spadoni, *La congiura militare*, Appendix II, pp. 280–281; and Spadoni, "I documenti della congiura militare carpiti da St Agnan," pp. 320–321. See also Della Porta report, Milan, January 26, 1815, Luzio, *La Massoneria e il Risorgimento italiano*, Vol. I, Appendix V, pp. 107–108.

[99] See *ante*, p. 254.

sons nominated by the "armed citizens" of the country. The regency was to name "directors" to head the judicial, financial, and internal administrations, the police, the treasury, and the army. There was also to be a national council composed of between fifteen and thirty members, which was to have a deliberative voice in running the government.[100] The second of the documents carried to the meeting by the imaginative young lawyer was an abstract discourse on the principles of sound, constitutional government.[101]

When the conference began in Rasori's study on the evening of November 26 St. Agnan hurriedly perused the documents which had been prepared for him and put them in his portfolio. During the course of the discussions about the projected invasion of Italy, Latuada, who was somewhat suspicious of the pseudo-French agent, questioned him sharply about whether help could be expected from the British. Also, he insisted that the ringleaders of the conspiracy should have some kind of personal assurance that Louis XVIII really approved the complot. Latuada suggested that either he or another one of the plotters should talk to the king. St. Agnan protested that such a personal visit was impossible. Latuada's presence was badly needed in Milan. Rasori should go to London, and Marchal ought to make a trip to Naples. Furthermore, no one was permitted to see the French king unless St. Agnan presented the person. When Latuada continued to voice doubts about the whole venture, the French agent pulled a pistol out of his pocket, exclaimed, with feigned agitation, that no one in his family had ever been disloyal, and threatened to shoot himself if Latuada thought he was a traitor.

Meanwhile, Rasori, who had been called outside, returned to inform St. Agnan that he feared that the house was being watched. He urged him to depart at once and to leave the papers in the house so that there would be no danger of compromising anyone; whereupon the French littérateur, avowing that he had no fears, flourished his pistol and hurriedly withdrew, taking all the incriminating evidence with him.[102]

---

[100] For the text, see Spadoni, *La congiura militare*, Appendix IIIA, pp. 281–284; and Spadoni, "I documenti della congiura militare carpiti da St Agnan," pp. 321–324.

[101] For a copy of the complete text, see Spadoni, *La congiura militare*, Appendix IIIB, pp. 384–386; and Spadoni, "I documenti della congiura militare carpiti da St Agnan," pp. 324–326.

[102] Spadoni, *La congiura militare*, pp. 109–112; Spadoni, "I documenti della

The papers which the credulous conspirators had foolishly prepared for him St. Agnan handed to Bellegarde.[103] The governor paid him 2,800 francs to cover the expenses of his sojourn in the Lombard capital and his trip from and to Paris.[104] With ready cash in hand, the pseudo-French spy now disappeared from Milan just as quietly and mysteriously as he had come.

The Habsburgs, however, were still not finished with the enterprising Frenchman. When he passed through Turin on his return to Paris St. Agnan managed to extort money from Count Bubna, on the pretext that he needed it to continue his journey to Paris.[105] While at the Sardinian capital, he also visited the Sardinian minister of foreign affairs to warn him that a close relationship existed between malcontents in Italy and certain radicals in the French capital and to offer to keep a close eye on the Sardinian troublemakers and their cohorts in Paris.[106] Now that he had still more money in his pocket, instead of resuming his trip to the French capital by the shortest route, the wily St. Agnan traveled to Sempsal, Switzerland, from where he dispatched an incredible letter to Bellegarde in which he accused Lord Bentinck, the duke of Buckingham, and other members of the opposition party in England, who were "in open war against the peace of nations," of plotting a revolution in Italy.[107]

After seeking to convince both the Sardinian foreign minister and the Austrian commissioner plenipotentiary in Lombardy that he could still render invaluable services to their two governments, St. Agnan resumed his journey to Paris. Soon after his arrival he again wrote Bellegarde stressing the inestimable value of his assistance in

congiura militare carpiti da St Agnan," pp. 308–311; [Belgiojoso–Trivulzio], *Étude sur l'histoire de la Lombardie*, pp. 113–114.

[103] Bellegarde to Hager, Milan, December 6, 1814, Lemmi, *La restaurazione austriaca a Milano*, Appendix XLVIII, p. 463; Bellegarde to Hager, Milan, December 14, 1814, A. S. (Milan), Presidenza di governo. Atti Secreti, 1814, Cart. III, ad No. 305; Bellegarde to Hager, Milan, December 27, 1814, St. A. (Vienna), Staatskanzlei, Provinzen, Lombardei-Venedig, Fasz. III, Kon. 4, Fo. 218.

[104] Bellegarde to Metternich, Milan, December 5, 1814, St. A. (Vienna), Staatskanzlei, Provinzen, Lombardei-Venedig, Fasz. III, Kon. 4, Fo. 195.

[105] Weil, *Murat*, Vol. II, p. 89.

[106] Count de Vallesa to Alfieri, Turin, December 12, 1814, *ibid.*, Vol. II, Appendix VIII, p. 511.

[107] St. Agnan to Bellegarde, Sempsal, Switzerland, December 4, 1814, St. A. (Vienna), Staatskanzlei, Provinzen, Lombardei-Venedig, Fasz. III, Kon. 4, Fos. 207–208. Also in Weil, *Murat*, Vol. II, pp. 502–503.

exposing a perilous conspiracy. He boldly asserted that Bubna and General Karl Ludwig Ficquelmont had already assured him of a magnificent reward for his fine work and, with a characteristic avarice, demanded that the Austrian sovereign grant him a title of nobility and a small piece of territory in Germany.[108] Audacious as he was, St. Agnan even wrote directly to Metternich on January 1, 1815, requesting permission to come to Vienna to bring an important communication and to collect a sum of 12,000 francs for the work which he was performing.[109]

The unscrupulous and avaricious adventurer was playing for too high stakes. He returned shortly from France to Switzerland, ostensibly because Comelli de Stuckenfeld was momentarily expected there but actually in the hope that he could wheedle still more money out of the Austrians and Sardinians. From Bern he wrote Vallesa in Turin that dangerous intriguers had sent emissaries working with Prince Eugene to Sardinia to revolutionize that country. Murat, he added, was also in league with the plotters.[110]

In his efforts to procure an exorbitant reward for his espionage, St. Agnan overshot his mark. On December 27 Bellegarde had assured Metternich that the French agent had rendered valuable assistance which merited equitable recompense.[111] However, after he learned about the communication which the crafty rogue had dispatched to Vallesa from Bern he admonished the Austrian chancellor that St. Agnan was a wily intriguer who was peddling his services to the highest bidder.[112] Count Bombelles also warned Metternich that St. Agnan was an indiscreet petty adventurer and double agent.[113] So did Ghisilieri.[114]

Notwithstanding these unflattering reports about St. Agnan, the Austrian emperor actually did reward him for his work in Milan. However, instead of granting him the title of nobility and territory

---

[108] St. Agnan to Bellegarde, Paris, December 10, 1814, St. A. (Vienna), Staatskanzlei, Provinzen, Lombardei-Venedig, Fasz. III, Kon. 4, Fos. 219–220.

[109] Weil, *Murat*, Vol. II, Appendix VII, p. 502; Spadoni, *La congiura militare*, p. 128.

[110] St. Agnan to Count de Vallesa, Bern, January 4 and 5, 1815, St. A. (Vienna), Staatskanzlei, Provinzen, Lombardei-Venedig, Fasz. IV, Kon. 4, Fos. 2–5.

[111] Bellegarde to Metternich, Milan, December 27, 1814, *ibid.*, Fo. 218.

[112] Bellegarde to Metternich, Milan, January 19, 1815, *ibid.*, Fo. 1.

[113] Bombelles to Metternich, Paris, December 23, 1814, Weil, *Murat*, Vol. II, Appendix VII, pp. 503–505.

[114] Ghisilieri to Hager, Milan, January 7, 1815, *ibid.*, p. 506.

in Germany which he solicited, he gave him only 4,000 francs. At the same time, he instructed his authorities in Italy to make certain that the notorious schemer never again set foot in Italy.[115] St. Agnan protested bitterly over receiving such a paltry sum for his dangerous and important services and in an insulting manner inquired whether the 4,000 francs represented the first portion of an annual or quarterly pension.[116]

With the definite proof of a conspiracy which had been furnished him by St. Agnan in his hands, Bellegarde ordered the arrest of the chief plotters. On the night of December 3–4 the police seized all the papers which they could find in Rasori's residence and took Rasori, Gasparinetti, Latuada, and Marchal—the naive victims of the mendacious French agent's own espionage plot—into custody.[117] On the basis of information which these four gave to the police during their preliminary investigation, Teodoro Lechi, Bellotti, and De Meester were arrested on the night of December 10–11.[118] Their detention

[115] Imperial resolution, December 19, 1814, St. A. (Vienna), Kabinets-Akten, 1814, No. 916; council of war to Bellegarde, Vienna, January 11, 1815, St. A. (Vienna), Staatskanzlei, Provinzen, Lombardei-Venedig, Fasz. IV, Kon. 1, Fo. 4.

[116] St. Agnan to Metternich, Paris, February 2, 1815, Weil, *Murat*, Vol. II, p. 508. It should be noted that during the hundred days Napoleon arrested St. Agnan as an Austrian spy (Spadoni, *La congiura militare*, p. 130). The French agent's woes did not end with Napoleon's defeat at Waterloo. The restored government of Louis XVIII imprisoned him on suspicion that he had been on the Isle of Elba during his trip to Milan. On November 25, 1815, St. Agnan wrote Bellegarde a tear-jerking letter from a Paris prison entreating him to beseech the Habsburg emperor to intervene on his behalf (St. A. [Vienna], Staatskanzlei, Provinzen, Lombardei-Venedig, Fasz. IV, Kon. 4, Fos. 25–26).

[117] Bellegarde to Metternich, Milan, December 5, 1814, St. A. (Vienna), Staatskanzlei, Provinzen, Lombardei-Venedig, Fasz. III, Kon. 4, Fo. 193 (a copy of this letter is also in Lemmi, *La restaurazione austriaca a Milano*, Appendix XLVIII, pp. 463–465); Cheluzzi to Roschmann, Milan, December 5, 1814, Lemmi, *La restaurazione austriaca a Milano*, Appendix XLVII, pp. 460–462; Carrer to Hager, Milan, December 5, 1814, Helfert, *La caduta della dominazione francese*, Appendix IX, pp. 251–252 (also in Weil, *Murat*, Vol. II, Appendix IX, pp. 512–513); entry of December 4, 1814, *Biblioteca Ambrosiana*, (Milan), Mantovani, "Diario di Milano," Vol. V, p. 327.

[118] Bellegarde to Metternich, Milan, December 12, 1814, St. A. (Vienna), Staatskanzlei, Provinzen, Lombardei-Venedig, Fasz. III, Kon. 4, Fo. 206; Ghisilieri to Hager, Milan, December 8, 9, 10, and 11, 1814, Weil, *Murat*, Vol. II, Appendix X, pp. 518–519; Carrer to Hager, Milan, December 14, 1814, Lemmi, *La restaurazione austriaca a Milano*, Appendix LVIII, p. 475; Bartolomeo Benincasa to Vincenzo Dandolo, Milan, December 9, 1814, C. A. Vianello, "Sulla

was followed on the night of the 12th–13th by that of Gerosa[119] and two nights later by that of Olini in Brescia.[120] Upon Bellegarde's request,[121] Cavedoni was apprehended in Modena on the night of December 17–18[122] and returned to Milan under guard sometime shortly before the 24th.[123] Early in January further arrests were made. Varese was taken on the night of the 5th–6th, Caprotti on the 7th, and Brunetti on the 9th.[124] About the same time Colonel Mazzuchelli and Generals Mazzuchelli and Zucchi were also seized.[125] Moretti and Pavoni were taken into custody in Graz,[126] and Ragani was finally captured in Bologna on February 1.[127] A few of the other ringleaders of the Brescian-Milanese conspiracy managed to flee or escape.

As for Comelli de Stuckenfeld, whose revelations to St. Agnan about his revolutionary schemes first set in motion the chain of events which eventually led the Austrians to uncover the Brescian-Milanese conspiracy, there are only vague references to him after 1814. No mention was made of him in the testimony of the imprisoned Brescian-Milanese conspirators. Bellegarde heard rumors that he might be in Rome and hastened to ask the Austrian minister to

---

caduta del Regno Italico. Note ad illustrazioni di un carteggio Dandolo-Benincasa (1814)," *Il Risorgimento*, Vol. VIII, Fasc. 3 (October, 1956), p. 144.

[119] Ghisilieri to Hager, Milan, December 12, 1814, Weil, *Murat*, Vol. II, Appendix X, p. 520; interrogation of Gerosa on December 18, 1814, as summarized in Spadoni, *La congiura militare*, p. 182.

[120] Hager to Emperor Francis, Vienna, December 27, 1814, Weil, *Murat*, Vol. II, Appendix X, p. 520; Monti, *Rasori*, p. 78.

[121] Bellegarde to Steffanini, Milan, December 11, 1814, A. S. (Milan), Presidenza di governo. Atti secreti, 1814, Cart. VII, No. 1011/P.R.

[122] Munarini to Bellegarde, Modena, December 18, 1814, Weil, *Murat*, Vol. II, Appendix X, pp. 520–521 (also in Lemmi, *La restaurazione austriaca a Milano*, Appendix LVII, p. 474).

[123] Carrer to Hager, Milan, December 24, 1814, Weil, *Murat*, Vol. II, Appendix X, p. 523.

[124] Helfert, *La caduta della dominazione francese*, pp. 229–230; Weil, *Murat*, Vol. II, pp. 93–96; Castro, *Milano e le cospirazioni lombarde*, pp. 152–153.

[125] Entry of January 14, 1815, *Biblioteca Ambrosiana* (Milan), Mantovani, "Diario di Milano," Vol. V, p. 327.

[126] Monti, *Rasori*, p. 78.

[127] Bellegarde to Metternich, Milan, February 3, 1815, St. A. (Vienna), Staatskanzlei, Provinzen, Lombardei-Venedig, Fasz. IV, Kon. 2, Fo. 18; entry of February 2, 1815, *Biblioteca Ambrosiana* (Milan), Mantovani, "Diario di Milano," Vol. V, p. 339.

the Papal States to have him carefully watched.[128] Ludwig von Leb-zeltern was unable to find any trace of him, however, and Bellegarde was never able positively to verify whether or not Comelli ever came to Italy.[129] Where he actually was in 1814 and 1815 has not been definitely ascertained. In November, 1814, he went to the Habsburg ambassador in London to demand a pass to travel to Vienna—a request which was refused.[130] There were reports that he talked about leaving Europe, perhaps to go to Africa or the Orient. If he actually did intend to travel to another continent he must have changed his mind, for in May, 1815, he sent a letter to Foscolo from "the western Alps" and in July news reached Metternich that he was then in southern Switzerland.[131] Early the next year the Austrian chancellor heard that Comelli was in Italy and instructed Lebzeltern to arrest him if he set foot in the Papal capital.[132] If Comelli actually showed up in the Apennine peninsula in 1816 it was probably only for a brief interval on his way to the Ottoman empire, for on October 8, 1816, Metternich was able to send Bubna the happy news that Comelli de Stuckenfeld had died in the Dardanelles while on his way to Constantinople "to hatch new intrigues against us and against the social order."[133]

[128] Bellegarde to Lebzeltern, Milan, December 10, 1814, A. S. (Milan), Presidenza di governo. Atti secreti, 1814, Cart. III, No. 1008/P.R.; Bellegarde to Hager, December 14, 1814, *ibid.*, ad No. 305/P.R.

[129] Protocol of the December 31, 1814, session of the Lombard Presidenza di governo, *ibid.*, Cart. VII, No. 1020/P.R.

[130] Hager to Hingenau, Vienna, March 14, 1815, A. S. (Venice), Presidio di governo, 1815–1819, Polizia, Fasz II 11/17, No. 1065/P.P.

[131] Spadoni, "Carlo Comelli de Stuckenfeld," pp. 638–641.

[132] Saurau to Lebzeltern, Milan, March 19, 1816, A. S. (Milan), Presidenza di governo. Atti secreti, 1816, Cart. X, No. 67/g.p.

[133] Metternich to Bubna, Vienna, October 8, 1816, St. A. (Vienna), F. M. Graf Bubna, Geheime Correspondenz, Fasz. I (Jahrgang 1816–1817), No. 16, Fos. 10–11.

Chapter 7

THE MANTUA PROCESS

Immediately after their arrest the first four of the apprehended conspirators—Rasori, Gasparinetti, Latuada, and Marchal—were carefully questioned, in the presence of Lieutenant Colonel Gedeone Maretich, by Giulio Pagani, the head of the Milan police force and previously secretary of the police prefecture of the Kingdom of Italy.[1] Field Marshal Bellegarde also participated in some of the interrogations.

The violently anti-Austrian Princess Belgiojoso-Trivulzio, in an account later copied by Cusani[2] and bandied about by Italian nationalists, accused Pagani of employing diabolical deceit and unspeakable treachery in wringing a confession from the innocent Gasparinetti during these preliminary inquisitions. When Gasparinetti was first "questioned by an Austrian major, assisted by Mr. Pagano [sic]," he denied everything, she asserted. However, one morning when the major was momentarily absent, the wily police chief, avowing that Gasparinetti's accomplices had already confessed everything, chided him for denying the existence of a complot. Then he added: "Why do you not have more confidence in me? Am I not an Italian like you?' " Believing that the guileful Pagani was a trusted friend who was trying to save him, the unsophisticated Gasparinetti informed the major, upon his return, about the details of the machination, re-

[1] Bellegarde to Hager, Milan, December 6, 1814, A. S. (Milan), Presidenza di governo. Atti secreti, 1814, Cart. VII, No. 1019/P.R. The full text of this letter can also be found in Lemmi, *La restaurazione austriaca a Milano*, Appendix XLVIII, pp. 463–465; and in Weil, *Murat*, Vol. II, Appendix IX, pp. 513–516. It should be noted, however, that Spadoni, the only historian who has made a careful study of the trial records, maintains that Bellegarde misinformed Hager on this point. See his *La congiura militare*, pp. 137–138.

[2] See his *Storia di Milano*, Vol. VII, pp. 219–220.

vealed to him the names of all the conspirators, and even bared his innermost thoughts and hopes to him.[3] Princess Belgiojoso-Trivulzio's accusation was partly confirmed by Teodoro Lechi, who wrote in his memoirs: "Gasparinetti, deceived by Under Director Pagani, not only told everything that he knew but also what he thought."[4]

Princess Belgiojoso-Trivulzio's strong indictment of Habsburg police investigation practices makes interesting reading, but it is not borne out by actual facts. The only scholar who has made a careful investigation of the trial records of the Brescian-Milanese conspirators Spadoni has expressed strong doubts about the accuracy of the princess's story.[5] Certainly the trial records which Spadoni so painstakingly summarized do not indicate that Pagani employed tactics different from those normally used by police investigators.

In the first place, one of the prisoners, Professor Rasori, had already given damaging evidence to Count Bellegarde very shortly after his incarceration.[6] Panicky when the field marshal showed him the proclamations which he had brought to the meeting with St. Agnan on November 26, Rasori, apparently without any real effort to parry the commissioner plenipotentiary's questions, immediately confessed that he had written them. Then he related to Bellegarde how Marchal had introduced him to St. Agnan and how the latter had announced that he had come as an emissary of the French government to ascertain whether the Italians were imbued with a spirit of independence. He told his interrogator of St. Agnan's assertion that his government had charged him with assuring the Italians that the French wanted to see Italy free and independent and had promised him that the Italians would obtain their freedom if they offered the crown to a French prince.[7]

Since Rasori had apprised the Austrians of the above facts, it was certainly not necessary for Pagani to utilize dishonest artifices to persuade the guileless Gasparinetti to divulge what he knew about St. Agnan's actions in Milan, which is all that Gasparinetti revealed on

---

[3] [Belgiojoso-Trivulzio], *Étude sur l'histoire de la Lombardie*, pp. 116–117.

[4] As quoted in Spadoni, *La congiura militare*, p. 137 n.

[5] See *ibid.*, p. 138.

[6] *Ibid.*, p. 131.

[7] Bellegarde to Metternich, Milan, December 5, 1814, St. A. (Vienna) Staatskanzlei, Provinzen, Lombardei-Venedig, Fasz. III, Kon. 4, Fo. 193. Spadoni, who writes that there was no mention in the trial records or anywhere else of what actually took place during Rasori's conference with Bellegarde (see his *La congiura militare*, p. 131), apparently never saw the above letter.

December 4. Pagani needed only to show him the official record of what Rasori had already disclosed to Bellegarde.

When he was questioned on December 4, Gasparinetti half-heartedly attempted to evade giving incriminating responses to Pagani's initial questions. However, when the police commissioner asked him whether he knew St. Agnan, he at once spoke without hesitation about the French agent's journey to the Lombard capital. Suspecting that his companions had betrayed him, he readily related all he knew about the meetings with the Gallic intriguer. He went on to mention that many officials and members of the first families of Milan, including Cavedoni, De Meester, Visconti, and Varese, were making concerted efforts to procure an independent prince for their country. He admitted that St. Agnan had told Marchal that he was to command five hundred soldiers when Savoy was invaded and that Ragani had been sent on some mission.[8]

When he was examined the next day, Latuada talked just as freely as Gasparinetti. He informed the police about the meetings with the Frenchman in Rasori's house and about the constitution which he and Salfi had drafted on behalf of the Freemasons in April, and admitted that he had handed it to St. Agnan. He confessed that Gasparinetti, Rasori, and he were all Freemasons. He told his interrogators that he was acquainted with Cavedoni, Ragani, De Meester, Ludovico Peyri, and Varese; however, he insisted that he could not recollect whether or not he had conversed with them about political matters.[9]

Of the four conspirators arrested on the night of December 3–4 Marchal alone failed to supply his questioners with damaging information. When he was interrogated in the office of the police prefecture of the department of Olona on December 4, he refused to divulge anything more than a few innocuous details about St. Agnan's activities. All he admitted was that he had met St. Agnan in London, that St. Agnan had brought him some books which he had personally taken to the Brera Library, that he had seen him three times, and that he had introduced him to Rasori. Steadfastly, he in-

<hr>

[8] Interrogation of Gasparinetti on December 4, 1814, as summarized in Spadoni, *La congiura militare*, pp. 133–136.

[9] Interrogation of Latuada on December 5, 1814, as summarized in *ibid.*, pp. 138–142.

sisted that when he was together with St. Agnan and Rasori they talked only about literature and St. Agnan's ailing stomach.[10]

Nonetheless, in spite of Marchal's obduracy, the Habsburg police managed to extract vital facts from the other three prisoners during the first two days following their arrest.[11] At this time, however, their revelations dealt only with the pseudo-plot contrived by St. Agnan to trick the machinators into presenting him with written documents which he could pass on to Count Bellegarde. Their testimony, which enabled the Habsburgs to unravel the threads of the conspiracy, was heard by a special commission appointed by the commissioner plenipotentiary on December 6 to collect legal evidence which could be presented at a formal trial. To head this commission he nominated a former judge of the court of appeals at Venice Francesco della Porta. As the other civilian member he selected Aulic Counselor Filippo Ghisilieri. General Raban Spiegel and Major Franz Weiss von Rettemberg represented the military on the commission.[12]

The commission began its sessions the very next day in the Castello Sforzeso. It first questioned each prisoner and gave him an opportuni-

---

[10] Interrogation of Marchal on December 4, 1814, as summarized in *ibid.*, pp. 132–133. In his brief allusions to the above interrogation, Bellegarde wrote that Marchal denied everything. See Bellegarde to Metternich, Milan, December 5, 1814, St. A. (Vienna), Staatskanzlei, Provinzen, Lombardei-Venedig, Fasz. III, Kon. 4, Fo. 193; Bellegarde to Hager, Milan, December 6, 1814, Lemmi, *La restaurazione austriaca a Milano*, Appendix XLVIII, p. 464 (the original text is in A. S. [Milan], Presidenza di governo. Atti secreti, 1814, Cart. VII, No. 1019/P.R.).

[11] On December 5, 1814, Bellegarde wrote Metternich: "All [of the arrested conspirators] have avowed their interviews with Mr. St. Agnan and have recognized the pieces which they delivered to him as coming from them. Only Marechal [sic], who wrote nothing, is entrenching himself in a system of absolute denial, but the statements of the others ought to convince him" (St. A. [Vienna], Staatskanzlei, Provinzen, Lombardei-Venedig, Fasz. III, Kon. 4, Fo. 193). The next day Bellegarde wrote Hager: "Yesterday and today [sic] Mr. Pagani, in the presence of Lieutenant-Colonel Maretich, made the first examinations of Lattuada [sic], Gasparinetti, and Marechal [sic], and, except for the last, who constantly denied having had the least knowledge of Rasori's plans, all the others have avowed their crime" (see Lemmi, *La restaurazione austriaca a Milano*, Appendix XLVIII, p. 464).

[12] Bellegarde to Hager, Milan, December 6, 1814, Lemmi, *La restaurazione austriaca a Milano*, Appendix XLVIII, p. 465; Ghisilieri to Pagani, Milan, December 7, 1814, *ibid.*, Appendix XLIX, p. 466; Della Porta report, Milan, January 26, 1815, Luzio, *La Massoneria e il Risorgimento italiano*, Vol. I, Appendix V, p. 96.

ty to relate everything which he knew about the conspiracy. It also allowed him to refute any specific delations which his co-conspirators might have made about him. If he denied the charges, the commission named the person or persons who had given the incriminating testimony about him. If he still insisted that the denunciations were false, he was confronted by his accusers.[13]

Rasori, Gasparinetti, and Latuada talked just as unhesitatingly to the special commission about their dealings with St. Agnan as they had earlier to Count Bellegarde and the Milanese police. What is more important, they now revealed important details about the real Brescian-Milanese conspiracy and freely gave the names of its ringleaders.

Although Rasori, who was questioned on December 7, limited most of his testimony to the conferences with St. Agnan, he disclosed the existence of a "Benevolent Society" which, he said, was working for Italian independence. He also admitted that Latuada had confided to him that Gasparinetti, De Meester, and Romagnosi belonged to it.[14] In thus divulging the existence of a "dangerous" society, Rasori inadvertently furnished the commission with essential information which it could subsequently draw on to induce some of the other machinators to betray actual details of the complot.

Although Rasori's initial testimony proved to be extremely damaging, it was Gasparinetti and Latuada who blurted out the most incriminating particulars about the real machination. When questioned on December 8, 9, and 10, Gasparinetti, hoping to win the commission's indulgence, freely bared some of the innermost secrets of the plotters. He talked without hesitation about his conversations with Latuada and the futile efforts to induce Generals Zucchi, Pino, and Fontanelli to lead the rebellion. He revealed the various schemes to use the Italian troops and the plans to seize the fortresses of Peschiera and Mantua. Teodoro Lechi, he intimated, was the officer around whom all the military projects were centered. Other officers,

13 Bellegarde to Emperor Francis, marked "expedited on January 8, 1815," A. S. (Milan), Presidenza di governo. Atti secreti, 1814, Cart. VII, No. 1009/P.R. This document is printed as an undated letter in Lemmi, La restaurazione austriaca a Milano, Appendix LXXII, pp. 494–498.

14 Interrogation of Rasori on December 7, 1814, as summarized in Spadoni, La congiura militare, pp. 145–148. See also Ghisilieri to Hager, Milan, December 7, 1814, Weil, Murat, Vol. II, Appendix IX, p. 516 (also in Lemmi, La restaurazione austriaca a Milano, Appendix L, pp. 466–467).

including Olini, Bellotti, Cavedoni, Delfini, and Moretti, were also among the chief plotters. So were De Meester and Romagnosi. Furthermore, Murat was fully aware of the intrigues of the conspirators.[15]

After Gasparinetti's admissions his fellow-prisoners found themselves overwhelmingly implicated. As Della Porta wrote, the confessions which Gasparinetti so willingly and so spontaneously made opened "to the commission the road to useful and interesting discoveries."[16] His testimony and the information which Latuada readily divulged paved the way "for a more extended inquisition thanks to which it [the commission] came to know the different threads and the means conceived by the conspirators to succeed in their criminal designs."[17]

Thus Gasparinetti provided the Habsburgs with important details about the real conspiracy. Latuada, the lawyer, supplied most of the remaining particulars. Although his legal training should have warned him of the foolhardiness of his scheme, Latuada, believing that his best defense lay in pretending that he had participated in the conspiracy to use his influence to suppress it,[18] readily told about the role which the other ringleaders played in the plot. He frankly admitted his own associations with the Freemasons and freely discussed the constitutional projects which he, Salfi and Benedetto Giuseppe Solustri had written in April.[19] He mentioned his contacts with Professor Romagnosi, although he insisted that the illustrious jurist knew nothing about the machination. He exposed the genesis of the plot among the officers stationed at Brescia and the participation of Olini, Pavoni, Moretti, De Meester, Lechi, Bellotti, Bonfanti, Zucchi, Varese, Cavedoni, and Delfini. Endlessly he stressed his repeated attempts to dissuade them from the undertaking. He talked about Ragani's trip to Naples and General Michele Carascosa's willingness to aid the plotters with Neapolitan troops even if Murat refused to

[15] Interrogations of Gasparinetti on December 8, 9, and 10, 1814, as summarized in Spadoni, *La congiura militare*, pp. 148–153; Ghisilieri to Hager, December 8, 1814, Lemmi, *La restaurazione austriaca a Milano*, Appendix LI, pp. 467–468.

[16] Della Porta report, Milan, January 26, 1815, Luzio, *La Massoneria e il Risorgimento italiano*, Vol. I, Appendix V, pp. 109–110.

[17] *Ibid.*, p. 97.

[18] *Ibid.*, p. 110.

[19] Interrogation of Latuada on December 10, 1814, as summarized in Spadoni, *La congiura militare*, pp. 154–155.

have anything to do with them. He mentioned the conference in Brunetti's house, the efforts to patch up the quarrel between Generals
Pino and Fontanelli, the attempts to gain the support of the civic and
national guards,[20] and Gifflenga's trip to Milan.[21]

When they were interrogated by the special investigation commission, Rasori, Gasparinetti, and Latuada thus proved themselves less
than heroic. In actual fact, of the four plotters arrested on the night
of December 3–4 only Marchal displayed any real courage and strove
to protect his co-conspirators from implication in the complot.
Throughout his interrogation he steadfastly refused to give more
than a few inconsequential facts about his meetings with St. Agnan
and Rasori.[22] Even after he was informed that Gasparinetti had affirmed that he knew all about the plot and the conversations with St.
Agnan in Rasori's house,[23] Marchal courageously refrained from relating anything that was incriminating.[24]

At the outset the three leaders of the machination who were arrested on the night of December 10–11 as a consequence of the
depositions made by Gasparinetti and Latuada—Lechi, Bellotti, and
De Meester—repulsed the efforts of their inquisitors to persuade
them to make inculpatory statements. However, in the end Lechi
and Bellotti's resistance collapsed as completely as that of Gasparinetti and Latuada. Only De Meester showed as much fortitude as
Marchal in denying everything.

In his first two interrogations on December 11 and 22, Lechi made
only simple and evasive replies to the questions directed at him. He
admitted that he knew Latuada, Olini, Moretti, and Zucchi, but he
avowed that his relations with them were simply those of a good
friend. He denied that he had made any efforts to reconcile Generals
Pino and Fontanelli, although he conceded that he had heard rumors that such attempts had been made. He acknowledged that
various Italian officers had frequently visited him, but he insisted

[20] Interrogations of Latuada on December 13, 14, and 15, 1814, and January
18, 1815, as summarized in *ibid.*, pp. 166–173 and 257–260.

[21] Interrogation of Latuada on December 21, 1814, as summarized in *ibid.*, pp.
183–184.

[22] Interrogation of Marchal on December 17, 1814, as summarized in *ibid.*, pp.
176–178.

[23] Interrogation of Gasparinetti on December 18, 1814, as summarized in *ibid.*,
p. 179.

[24] Della Porta report, Milan, January 26, 1815, Luzio, *La Massoneria e il
Risorgimento italiano*, Vol. I, Appendix V, p. 110.

that at these meetings the conversations were limited strictly to military matters. He pretended complete ignorance of everything resembling a conspiracy. He even went so far as to assert that he had never heard anyone speak of one.[25]

Then, after his refusal to utter any incriminating evidence during his first two interrogations, Lechi, deciding that other prisoners had already revealed so much that it was useless to refrain from telling what he knew,[26] confessed his own guilt on December 29 and gave information which was highly damaging to some of his accomplices. Declaring that for his own peace of mind he could no longer continue to lie to the commission, he discussed what had taken place during his meetings with Moretti and Pavoni in September and early October, the conferences in Brunetti's house, the plans to incite a rebellion in the Lombard capital, and Ragani's journey to Naples.[27]

Bellotti's resistance vanished even more quickly than Lechi's. When he was first questioned on December 12 he denied everything and even declared that no one had ever spoken to him about a project to attain Italian independence.[28] At his next encounter with the commission on December 24, however, he changed his tactics and talked frankly about his conversations in regard to the conspiracy with Olini, De Meester, Lechi, and Latuada.[29]

Then, after this partial confession, Bellotti, remorseful at the very thought of having betrayed his companions, retracted the testimony

---

[25] Interrogations of Lechi on December 11 and 22, 1814, as summarized in Spadoni, *La congiura militare*, pp. 158–160 and 186–187. See also Ghisilieri to Hager, Milan, December 23, 1814, Lemmi, *La restaurazione austriaca a Milano*, Appendix LXVI, p. 482.

[26] Lechi later wrote in his memoirs: "I was led before and was interrogated three times by this Commission. The first two times I was able to maintain a wholly negative stand, but the third time I had to admit that it would have been useless to continue to deny those things, because they were proved and established as fact by the depositions of the other prisoners, which they made me read and which were verified by their signatures" (as quoted in Spadoni, *La congiura militare*, p. 207 n.).

[27] Interrogation of Lechi on December 29, 1814, as summarized in *ibid.*, pp. 207–208.

[28] Interrogation of Bellotti on December 12, 1814, as summarized in *ibid.*, pp. 161–162.

[29] Interrogation of Bellotti on December 24, 1814, as summarized in *ibid.*, pp. 193–194; Ghisilieri to Hager, Milan, December 24, 1814, Weil, *Murat*, Vol. II, Appendix X, p. 522 (also in Lemmi, *La restaurazione austriaca a Milano*, Appendix XLVII, p. 483).

which he previously rendered when he met with the commission a third time on December 26. In the face of repeated admonitions to tell the truth, he made only evasive or negative replies to the numerous incisive questions which were asked of him during a long day of tiresome interrogation.[30]

When examined again on January 11, 13, and 15 Bellotti once more decided to be truthful and made a full confession. Apparently because he believed that it was Latuada who had betrayed him and his fellow-conspirators, he talked at length about the plans for the revolt which Latuada had confided to him, Olini, Moretti, Lechi, and De Meester. He informed the commission about the projects to capture Peschiera and Mantua, force the Habsburg troops to withdraw from Milan, and enlist the aid of the national guard. He revealed the efforts of the ringleaders to induce Pino or Fontanelli to head the rebellion, the active correspondence carried on with Bologna and London, and the missions sent to Bentinck and Murat. He admitted that Pavoni, Varese, Cavedoni, and Delfini had participated in the plot and testified freely about the provisional government that was to be organized after the successful conclusion of the revolt.[31]

Of the three conspirators arrested on the night of December 10–11, De Meester alone managed, in spite of the incriminating evidence given by his accomplices, to defend himself to the very end with vague and deceptive replies.[32] When he was interrogated on December 12 he denied all knowledge of any machination and pretended that he knew nothing whatever about a secret society called the Carbonari.[33] When questioned again on the 22nd, he persisted in giving negative, evasive, or non-incriminating responses to the queries fired at him.[34] Even when it was pointed out to him on December 31 that Cavedoni, Lechi, Bellotti, and Latuada had already disclosed his role in the conspiracy, De Meester still remained obdurate. Heatedly denying that he ever belonged to the Carbonari, he controverted the

[30] Interrogation of Bellotti on December 26, 1814, as summarized in Spadoni, *La congiura militare*, pp. 195–199.

[31] Interrogations of Bellotti on January 11, 13, and 15, 1815, as summarized in *ibid.*, pp. 239–242, 243–244, and 253.

[32] Della Porta report, Milan, January 26, 1815, Luzio, *La Massoneria e il Risorgimento italiano*, Vol. I, Appendix V, p. 110.

[33] Interrogation of De Meester on December 12, 1814, as summarized in Spadoni, *La congiura militare*, pp. 162–164.

[34] Interrogation of De Meester on December 22, 1814, as summarized in *ibid.*, pp. 185–186; Spadoni, "Il gen. bar. Giacomo Filippo de Meester," p. 859.

accusations which his co-conspirators had made about his participation in the complot by repeatedly asserting that he knew nothing whatsoever about a conspiracy. He admitted that he had visited Lechi, Bellotti, and Latuada, and that he had seen General Gifflenga, but he maintained that the conversations with them were entirely non-political in nature.[35] Determined never to confess no matter what circumstances might arise, De Meester handed the commission a memoir on January 13 in which he flatly denied all the charges against him and boldly asseverated that he had never had a hand in any intrigues or conspiracy against the Habsburg monarch.[36]

The other three leaders of the Brescian-Milanese conspiracy who were arrested before the end of December—Olini, Gerosa, and Cavedoni—comported themselves before the special commission in a manner remarkably similar to that of Lechi and Bellotti. The first of the three, Olini, resisted, confessed, and then recanted, only to confess again; the other two made only a slight effort to hold out and then readily confessed what they knew about the plot.

When interrogated on December 16, Olini gave either negative or evasive replies to all questions, although he did not deny that he was personally acquainted with several of the leaders.[37] During his second examination two days later he admitted certain specific details about the complot. He acknowleged that he had talked with Latuada about a project to win Italian independence; that Latuada had informed him that Lechi, Bellotti, De Meester, Melzi, Pino, Bonfanti, Gasparinetti, Fontanelli, and other persons approved of the conspiracy; that General Carascosa had promised to cooperate in the rebellion; and that Ragani had been sent to Naples.[38]

When called before the commission a third time on December 28, however, Olini was stricken with remorse over betraying various friends and repudiated the incriminating testimony recorded in the

[35] Interrogation of De Meester on December 31, 1814, as summarized in Spadoni, *La congiura militare*, pp. 215–218; and Spadoni, "Il gen. bar. Giacomo Filippo de Meester," pp. 859–860.

[36] Spadoni, *La congiura militare*, pp. 244–247; Spadoni, "Il gen. bar. Giacomo Filippo de Meester," p. 860.

[37] Interrogation of Olini on December 16, 1814, as summarized in Spadoni, *La congiura militare*, pp. 173–176.

[38] Interrogation of Olini on December 16, 1814, as summarized in *ibid.*, pp. 179–181; Ghisilieri to Hager, Milan, December 23, 1814, Weil, *Murat*, Vol. II, Appendix X, p. 521 (also in Lemmi, *La restaurazione austriaca a Milano*, Appendix LXVI, p. 482).

protocol of his second interrogation. When the commission apprised him of the fact that he could not retract evidence which he had already given, he argued that he had rendered the testimony which he did on the 18th only because on that day he was of unsound mind. Then, finding this ruse totally ineffectual, he resorted to repeatedly denying everything that was asked of him. However, when Bellotti's denunciations of him and his companions were read to him and when the commission assured him that everything he said would be held as a carefully guarded secret, Olini ended his resistance. Abandoning himself to the clemency of the Austrian emperor, he now exposed everything that he knew: the efforts to win over Fontanelli and Pino; Moretti, Varese, and Zucchi's roles in the plot; Visconti's efforts to procure the cooperation of the civic guard; the meetings in Brunetti's house; the plans to incite a rebellion in Milan and to surprise Mantua; the deposits of arms that were assembled by the conspirators; and the correspondence with Ragani.[39]

Gerosa also disavowed everything when he was first examined on December 18 and January 1.[40] After he was convinced that he would be punished only for failing to reveal to the proper authorities what he knew about a conspiracy, however, he agreed to testify.[41] Assured of immunity from punishment for actually conspiring against the constituted authorities, Gerosa talked freely on January 5, 6, 7, and 8 about particulars already related by the other prisoners and matters still not fully known by the Habsburg officials. Among other things, he informed them about the meetings of the Carbonari in the Caffè dei Servi in Milan and handed the commission a long list of names of persons who allegedly belonged to the society. He conversed at length about Mancini, Varese, and Caprotti's part in the machination; about the arms, munitions, and money which the plotters expected to receive from England; about the plans for the November 19 rebellion; and about the provisional regency which was to be created. He stated that the revolution was to extend all the way from Paris to Naples and asserted that, with the exception of Sormani and the head of the

[39] Interrogations of Olini on December 28 and 29, 1814, and January 1, 1815, as summarized in Spadoni, *La congiura militare*, pp. 200–207 and 221.

[40] Interrogations of Gerosa on December 18, 1814, and January 1, 1815, as summarized in *ibid.*, pp. 182 and 219.

[41] Della Porta report, Milan, January 26, 1815, Luzio, *La Massoneria e il Risorgimento italiano*, Vol. I, Appendix V, pp. 110–111; Spadoni, *La congiura militare*, pp. 222–223.

gendarmes, the entire Lombard police force and all the gendarmes, as well as the Italian troops stationed at Pompieri, were implicated in the plot.[42]

Cavedoni furnished information to the special commission which was every bit as incriminating as that which Gerosa had obligingly related. After a faint-hearted effort to avoid giving incriminating evidence,[43] he abandoned himself to the clemency of the emperor and willingly recounted all that he knew. He told how De Meester had enrolled him in the Carbonari and how he himself had recruited other members, including Delfini. He warned his interrogators that their revolutionary goals made the Carbonari an extremely perilous society. Although he gave no names, he maintained that the Carbonari had a large membership in Milan. Turning specifically to the Brescian-Milanese conspiracy, Cavedoni talked at considerable length about different meetings of a directing committee, which, he asserted, had close relations with various countries of Italy and planned to expel the German troops from Italy. He confessed that at the outbreak of the rebellion, with a detachment of four hundred men under his personal command, he was to seize Field Marshal Bellegarde and all the other Austrian generals in Milan. He added that at a meeting with Latuada and Delfini a suggestion was even made that all the commanding officers of the Habsburg army should be killed.[44]

Of the four plotters arrested in January who were actually questioned by the special commission, Bonfanti, who had played a relatively minor role in the machination, was interrogated only once. When the Austrians informed him that Olini and Latuada had already avowed everything he willingly answered the few questions addressed to him.[45] Caprotti responded vaguely and evasively on first being interrogated. When he was confronted with Gerosa, he still refused to admit his complicity in the conspiracy. The ensuing day, however, his resistance broke down and he made a full confession.[46]

---

[42] Interrogations of Gerosa on January 5, 6, 7, and 8, 1815, as summarized in Spadoni, *La congiura militare*, pp. 224–228, 229–230, and 232–233.

[43] Interrogation of Cavedoni on December 23, 1814, as summarized in *ibid.*, pp. 187–188.

[44] Interrogations of Cavedoni on December 30 and 31, 1814, as summarized in *ibid.*, pp. 209–215.

[45] Interrogation of Bonfanti on January 2, 1815, as summarized in *ibid.*, pp. 221–222.

[46] Interrogations of Caprotti on January 7, 17, and 18, 1815, as summarized in

Varese stubbornly defended himself against all charges during his three interrogations.[47] Brunetti admitted that Olini, Moretti, Latuada, Lechi, and Cavedoni had been in his house on the night of November 2–3, but he steadfastly insisted that this meeting was merely a fortuitous encounter of friends and acquaintances.[48]

Thus nine of the arrested conspirators—Gasparinetti, Latuada, Rasori, Lechi, Bellotti, Olini, Cavedoni, Caprotti, and Gerosa—after a faint show of resistance in certain instances, confessed their roles in the plot and gave incriminating details about their co-conspirators. During their interrogations by the special commission only four—De Meester, Marchal, Brunetti, and Varese—managed to deny all complicity and to protect their friends from inculpation.[49]

Why did the majority of the defendants talk so freely to the Austrian inquisitors? Nineteenth century nationalist historians have tended to exculpate the Italian prisoners by asserting that the Habsburg interrogators used nefarious tactics to wring information from righteous patriots. In their opinion the chief villain of the piece was Aulic Counselor Ghisilieri, who, they asserted, resorted to the most opprobrious chicanery to extort confessions from the credulous ringleaders of the Brescian-Milanese conspiracy. Believing that of all the defendants Lechi could give the commission the most important details of the machination, Ghisilieri, according to Princess Belgiojoso-Trivulzio, spent considerable time chatting with him in his prison cell in order subtly to plan how he could influence him to betray his fellow prisoners. Learning that the general was greatly devoted to his mother, and feigning friendship for his unfortunate victim, the astute judge talked to him one morning in such heart-rending terms about his innocent mother's anguish over his fate that tears flowed down the cheeks of the devoted general. Taking advantage of Lechi's momen-

---

ibid., pp. 231, 255–256, and 260–263; Della Porta report, Milan, January 26, 1815, Luzio, *La Massoneria e il Risorgimento italiano*, Vol. I, Appendix V, p. 111.

[47] Interrogations of Varese on January 6, 16, and 19, 1815, as summarized in Spadoni, *La congiura militare*, pp. 228–229, 255–256, and 263–268; Della Porta report, Milan, January 26, 1815, Luzio, *La Massoneria e il Risorgimento italiano*, Vol. I, Appendix V, p. 111.

[48] Interrogations of Brunetti on January 10 and 15, 1815, as summarized in Spadoni, *La congiura militare*, pp. 237–238 and 253–254; Della Porta report, Milan, January 26, 1815, Luzio, *La Massoneria e il Risorgimento italiano*, Vol. I, Appendix V, p. 111.

[49] See also Della Porta report, Milan, January 26, 1815, Luzio, *La Massoneria e il Risorgimento italiano*, Vol. I, Appendix V, pp. 97–98 and 109–111.

tary state of emotion, he insinuated that the general would be free again to embrace his beloved mother the moment he would, for her sake, reveal what he knew of the conspiracy. Only then did the dutiful son confess.[50] This tale, which is based in part on what Lechi himself wrote in his memoirs,[51] as well as on other stories of Ghisilieri's supposed trickery and deceit, was accepted by such nationalist historians as Cusani[52] and Castro[53] and soon became one of the standard legends of the Risorgimento.

Of course, it is impossible to know exactly what took place when Ghisilieri exchanged pleasantries with various prisoners in their cells. It is easy for an ambitious investigator to overstep the bounds of propriety in his zeal to procure the facts of a case. We know that the authorities in Vienna gave Ghisilieri full credit for playing the most important part among the officials in Milan in obtaining information from the defendants.[54] Yet, the harsh denunciations of Ghisilieri by nationalist historians hardly warrant belief, for they sound all too much like the vituperations vociferated against Metternich during the revolution of 1848[55] or like the savage criticism of other public officials who were suddenly turned into objects for anathema. More important, they resemble the attacks upon Salvotti, the zealous but able Austrian judge during the Carbonari trials of the early 1820's, that have been disproved by Luzio.[56] Until better evidence is discovered than that provided by the bitter adversary of the Habsburgs Princess Belgiojoso-Trivulzio, one must remain skeptical of the validity of the charges against Ghisilieri.

It is true that various statements in Lechi's memoirs and De Meester's account of the trial[57] tend to bear out the accusations against

[50] See [Belgiojoso-Trivulzio], *Étude sur l'histoire de la Lombardie*, pp. 121–122.

[51] Quoted in Spadoni, *La congiura militare*, p. 192.

[52] See his *Storia di Milano*, Vol. VII, p. 221.

[53] See his *Milano e le cospirazioni lombarde*, p. 160; and his "La restaurazione austriaca a Milano," p. 642. See also Gualterio, *Gli ultimi rivolgimenti italiani*, Vol. I, Pt. 1, pp. 408–409.

[54] See especially Hager to Ghisilieri, Vienna, December 15, 1814, Lemmi, *La restaurazione austriaca a Milano*, Appendix LIX, pp. 475–476.

[55] For examples, see my *The Viennese Revolution of 1848* (Austin, Texas: University of Texas Press, 1957), pp. 114–117.

[56] See especially his *Il Processo Pellico-Maroncelli*; his *Antonio Salvotti e i processi del ventuno* (No. 1–2 of *Biblioteca storia del risorgimento italiano*, 3rd ser.); and his *Nuovi documenti sul processo Confalonieri*.

[57] See Spadoni, *La congiura militare*, p. 208 n.

Ghisilieri. Nonetheless, historians cognizant of the unreliability of allegations made in the memoirs of controversial persons about matters in which they had a deep emotional involvement should hesitate to accept them as prima facie evidence. In this particular instance, the writings of the principal figures in the trial should be scrutinized with especial care, for the prisoners in later life were under pressure by violent enemies of the Austrians to explain why they had confessed so readily in 1814 and 1815.

Certainly the transcript of the day by day interrogations so carefully recorded by Spadoni makes it clear that, at least during its formal sessions, the special commission employed only tactics customarily used at that time in criminal investigations. It pointed out disparities in testimony and the accusations of other conspirators to the prisoner and repeatedly exhorted him to tell the truth. Occasionally it confronted him with other defendants who had made charges against him. These practices were similar to those used by the Habsburg and other European courts or investigating committees in the early part of the nineteenth century. Moreover, after the revelations of Gasparinetti and Latuada during their first examinations what was to be gained by refusing to admit that which was common knowledge? This writer does not wish to imply that the imprisoned Brescian-Milanese conspirators were abject betrayers of their Italian co-conspirators or the Italian cause. They were just not heroes. As ordinary human beings they ceased resisting when it became obvious that stubborn denial was futile.

Regardless of whether or not the tactics used by the investigating officials were reprehensible, historians must at least agree that the testimony given by the defendants convinced the Habsburg officials beyond the shadow of a doubt that they had discovered the existence of a definite plot "to procure the independence of Italy, chiefly with the aid of Italian troops."[58] When, on January 26, 1815, the special commission reported on the results of its investigation, it advised the government that, even though it had not interrogated Moretti, Pavoni, Delfini, and Mancini, whose arrest it had ordered as a consequence of the confessions made by the prisoners, it had procured legal proof that all the prisoners were guilty of actively participating

---

[58] Bellegarde to Emperor Francis, marked "expedited on January 8, 1815," A.S. (Milan), Presidenza di governo. Atti secreti, 1814, Cart. VII, No. 1009/P.R. Also in Lemmi, *La restaurazione austriaca a Milano*, Appendix LXXII, p. 495.

in a conspiracy against the government or of failing to denounce to the proper authorities what they knew about the existence of such a plot.[59]

When he learned about the first confessions of the prisoners Emperor Francis immediately began deciding how they were to be formally tried. On December 19 he instructed Baron von Hager to ask Bellegarde to advise him as quickly as possible on the following points: (1) According to the laws which were in force in Lombardy, what authorities were available to try crimes of the nature of the Brescian-Milanese conspiracy? (2) Could these authorities be trusted in all instances? (3) If so, would it be advisable to appoint Austrian commissioners to control and supervise them? (4) If it were not possible to have the ordinary judicial authorities examine and judge the prisoners, what kind of extraordinary commission should be created to handle the trial according to existing laws? (5) Was it wise to conduct the trial in Milan or should the prisoners be transported to some other place like Mantua or Palmanova?[60]

The very next day Von Hager dispatched a special military courier, Lieutenant Maykirt, to Milan with a letter requesting Bellegarde's answer to the points raised in the emperor's note.[61] A week later the commissioner plenipotentiary sent his reply to the Habsburg capital. Through Von Hager he informed Emperor Francis that, according to the Italian code, the imperial prosecutor drew up the charges against the defendants. Accused persons were tried in open court where witnesses were heard and both sides presented their cases in public. Then the court rendered its verdict.

The Lombard prosecutor was staunchly pro-Austrian, and there were "very distinguished individuals among the judges"; nevertheless, the judges in office would be placed "in too delicate a position" to make it advisable to try the prisoners in the regular courts existing in Lombardy, since "in a process of this nature their integrity would

59 Della Porta report, Milan, January 26, 1815, Luzio, *La Massoneria e il Risorgimento italiano*, Vol. I, Appendix V, pp. 96–97 and 109. According to Article 55 of the Austrian penal code, people who failed to denounce to the proper authorities persons they knew to be guilty of high treason were punishable with life imprisonment (see *Codice penale universale austriaco coll'appendice delle più recenti norme generali*, p. 24).

60 Emperor Francis to Hager, December 19, 1814, St. A. (Vienna), Kabinets-Akten, 1814, No. 916.

61 Hager to Bellegarde, December 20, 1814, A. S. (Milan), Presidenza di governo. Atti secreti, 1814, Cart. VII, No. 1018/P.R.

be subjected to too harsh a test, on account of the many connections which the accused have here and even on account of the nature of their offense, which has its source in the folly of Italian independence, with which all the employees of the former Kingdom of Italy are more or less permeated."[62]

Because of the prevailing Italian judicial practices, it was also inappropriate to appoint a commissioner to work with the court. For these reasons, Bellegarde recommended that a special commission, comprised in part of military officers, should be created to try the prisoners. Since the conspirators were to be tried according to the Napoleonic code, great care should be taken to appoint to this commission only judges well versed in French law who had a good command of Italian. Because of his qualifications on both of these scores and his loyalty to the Habsburgs, Luca Valeri, the imperial prosecutor at the court of justice at Venice, was well qualified to serve as imperial prosecutor for this commission. So also was General Prosecutor Counselor Fortis. For judges Bellegarde recommended Sardoni, Draghi, Cattanei, Bonacina, and Pace. As to where the trial should be held, Bellegarde thought that it should take place in some city other than Milan and suggested that Mantua might be a suitable location.[63]

Except for not believing that all the accused should be tried by the same commission, Emperor Francis accepted most of Bellegarde's recommendations. In an imperial resolution dated January 8, 1815, he stipulated that those defendants who belonged to the Austrian army were to be tried by a special court-martial which was to follow the procedures prescribed by the Austrian legal code. The rest were to be prosecuted, in accordance with the laws still in effect in Italy, by a special commission, which was to sit at Mantua and which was to be composed of a president, six counselors, and an imperial prosecutor. As president the emperor named the vice-president of the Venetian court of appeals, Baron Girolamo Trevisan. Bellegarde's nominee Luca Valeri was made imperial prosecutor. Guglielmo Gardani (misspelled as Sardoni in Bellegarde's letter), Girolamo Cat-

[62] Bellegarde to Hager, Milan, December 27, 1814, *ibid.*, No. 1009/P.R. Also in Lemmi, *La restaurazione austriaca a Milano*, Appendix LXX, p. 487; and in Weil, *Murat*, Vol. II, Appendix XI, p. 525.

[63] Bellegarde to Hager, Milan, December 27, 1814, A. S. (Milan), Presidenza di governo. Atti secreti, 1814, Cart. VII, No. 1009/P.R. Also in Lemmi, *La restaurazione austriaca a Milano*, Appendix LXX, pp. 486–491; and in Weil, *Murat*, Vol. II, Appendix XI, pp. 524–527.

taneo (whose name was also misspelled by the commissioner plenipotentiary), Giuseppe Maria Draghi, and Francesco Bonacina, all of
whom Bellegarde had suggested, were appointed counselors. After
consulting Rosetti and Fratnich, Bellegarde himself was to select the
rest of the commission's personnel. With the exception that the trial
was not held in public, the laws which were in effect in Lombardy-
Venetia (*i.e.*, the Napoleonic code) were to be punctiliously followed
in regard both to procedure and to the verdict rendered. After reaching a decision, the commission was to send its verdict, together with
the acts of the process, directly to the emperor. Under no circumstances was the public to be informed of the judgment decided by the
court.[64]

A few days later, on January 13, the emperor appointed the members of the special military court which was to try De Meester, Olini,
and Moretti. Lieutenant Field Marshal Annibale Sommariva was
chosen as president of this body, and Joseph Bührent was made reporter and charged with preparing the case. The selection of the other
officials was left to Bellegarde. The military court was instructed to
keep in close touch with the special commission which was being established to try the civilian conspirators. It was to reach a verdict as
soon as possible and send it, along with all documents appertaining
to the case, to the aulic war council and then to the emperor for final
judgment.[65]

The prisoners were taken from the Castello in Milan sometime between January 29 and February 5[66] and transported in thirteen car-
riages to Mantua, where they probably arrived at 3:00 A.M. on the
following day.[67] Even before their arrival in Mantua, Bellegarde, in
line with the practice followed by the previous French-Italian gov-

[64] Imperial resolution, January 8, 1815, St. A. (Vienna), Kabinets-Akten, 1815, No. 339.

[65] Imperial resolution, Vienna, January 13, 1815, *ibid.*, ad No. 336.

[66] Mantovani recorded in his diary that they left Milan on January 29. The Sardinian consul in the Lombard capital wrote that they departed on January 31. In his memoirs, Lechi indicated that they were taken from there early in Feb-ruary. In a letter to Hager on February 1, 1815, Bellegarde related that they left at 3:00 A.M. on January 30 (see Spadoni, *I giudizi di Mantova*, pp. 14–15 and 14–15 n.). An anonymous report, dated Milan, February 5, 1815, stated, how-ever, that they left on the night of February 4–5 (Lemmi, *La restaurazione au-striaca a Milano*, Appendix LXXIII, p. 499).

[67] Bellegarde to Hager, February 1, 1815, as quoted in Spadoni, *I giudizi di Mantova*, pp. 15–16.

ernment always to have a minimum of eight judges on every investigating body, had increased the number of judges on the special commission from six to eight. To make up the full complement of judges, he chose Giovanni Gognetti, Gaetano Astolfi, and Girolamo Freganeschi as counselors. At the same time, he selected Della Porta, who had been chairman of the commission which had interrogated the prisoners in Milan in December and January, to investigate and draw up the charges against the defendants.[68] His instructions to the commission were the same as those issued by the emperor in his imperial resolution of January 8.[69]

Before all the members of this commission arrived in Mantua, another group, composed of General Joseph Lauer, Colonel Wilhelm Dressery, Major Weiss, and Della Porta, which had also been appointed by Bellegarde, had already begun interrogating those conspirators who had been arrested at too late a date to be examined by the special investigating committee at Milan.[70]

The first of this group of prisoners to be questioned by the Lauer investigating committee was Moretti. During his initial examination on February 2 Moretti denied everything which could have implicated him in the conspiracy, although he admitted his acquaintanceship with Olini, Varese, Pavoni, Fontanelli, Lechi, Bellotti, De Meester, Brunetti, Cavedoni, Zucchi, and Latuada. When pressed, however, he acknowledged the fact that he had been in Brunetti's house early in November even though he stated that he had gone there only for personal business.[71] Two days later Moretti proved equally obdurate in resisting the repeated efforts of his questioners to shake him by telling him about the incriminating evidence given by

---

[68] *Ibid.*, pp. 16 and 17 n. With her customary careless disregard for exactness, Princess Belgiojoso-Trivulzio wrote inaccurately that the commission "was composed of Count Cardani, president; of Messrs. Freganeschi, Bonacina, Borghi, and Gianni, judges; and of Mr. Draghi, royal prosecutor. All were already celebrated for the ferocious hatred which they had given evidence of during the events of 1799" (see her *Étude sur l'histoire de la Lombardie*, p. 121).

[69] *Biblioteca Ambrosiana* (Milan), "Atto d'accusa contro Giovanni Soveri Latuada ecc.," Fo. 48.

[70] Spadoni, *I giudizi di Mantova*, p. 17. It should be noted that Spadoni has misspelled Lauer and Dressery's names as Laver and Dessery.

[71] Interrogation of Moretti on February 2, 1815, as summarized in *ibid.*, pp. 18–23.

other conspirators.[72] Finally, during his third examination on February 11, Moretti announced that he wanted to confess. However, even then he talked only in vague terms about matters which he believed that the other conspirators had already revealed.[73]

Ragani, the second of the ringleaders who had been arrested too late to be interrogated in Milan, was not so tight-lipped. After a feeble but genuine effort to restrain himself from telling too much when he was first questioned on February 3, he dropped his guard when he was again examined on the 5th and 6th and chatted freely about his connection with many of the plotters, as well as about his mission to Naples.[74] Of the three Italian officers who were examined in Mantua early in February, 1815, only Pavoni managed, in spite of the repeated efforts of the Austrian inquisitors to break his resistance, to remain steadfast in his determination to give merely negative, evasive, or wholly non-incriminating responses.[75]

In addition to Moretti, Ragani, and Pavoni, the Lauer committee thought it advisable to interrogate again four prisoners who had already been questioned in Milan—Caprotti, Olini, Gasparinetti, and Varese—before drawing up the formal charges against the defendants. Caprotti was asked about the persons he had enrolled in the Carbonari and his conversations with Mancini, Delfini, and Varese.[76] Olini was questioned in detail about his relations with Pavoni, Zucchi, and Fontanelli and about Ragani's trip to Naples;[77] and Gasparinetti was queried about Ragani's journey to the Neapolitan capital and his visit with Carascosa at Ancona.[78] Three of the prisoners gave their interrogators information that was of some value; Varese,

[72] Interrogation of Moretti on February 4, 1815, as summarized in *ibid.*, pp. 25–29.

[73] Interrogation of Moretti on February 11 and 12, 1815, as summarized in *ibid.*, pp. 46–52.

[74] See interrogations of Ragani on February 3, 5, and 6, 1815, as summarized in *ibid.*, 24–25, 29–31, and 32–35.

[75] See interrogations of Pavoni on February 7, 9, and 14, 1815, as summarized in *ibid.*, pp. 35–42 and 54–58.

[76] Interrogation of Caprotti on February 9, 1815, as summarized in *ibid.*, pp. 42–43.

[77] Interrogation of Olini on February 10, 1815, as summarized in *ibid.*, pp. 43–44.

[78] Interrogation of Gasparinetti on February 13, 1815, as summarized in *ibid.*, pp. 52–53.

however, remained as stubbornly on the defensive as he had in January and continued to deny all knowledge about the projected insurrection.[79]

When these examinations were concluded, the committee headed by General Lauer handed the protocol of its interrogations of the civilian prisoners to the imperial procurator. The next day (February 16) it turned over the documents dealing with the prisoners on active duty in the Habsburg army to the reporter assigned to the military court that was to try them.[80]

A day later, on the 17th the Lauer committee, after a careful study of the testimony, sent a detailed report to Bellegarde on the "conclusions" which it had reached in regard to General Fontanelli's and General Zucchi's alleged involvement in the plot.[81] The committee expressed the opinion that there was enough legal proof to warrant trying the two generals for the crime of failing to notify the proper authorities of the existence of a conspiracy against the Habsburg government, of which they were fully cognizant. What was more important, the two generals had expressed their full approval of the plot, had encouraged Olini and Moretti to further it, and had actively participated in it themselves. In fact, they had promised the machinators that they would take leading roles in the enterprise when the favorable moment arrived. Although he did not want to appear before he could be certain that the conspiracy was likely to succeed, Fontanelli had actually offered to direct the insurrection. Zucchi had assured Moretti and Olini that he would cooperate in the rebellion and had delayed his trip to Germany in the hope that it would break out before his departure from Italy. Since the evidence clearly showed that Fontanelli and Zucchi were gravely implicated in the machination, the committee strongly urged the commissioner plenipotentiary to issue orders to have the two generals arrested.[82]

The transmittal of this report to Bellegarde was the last official action of the Lauer committee. Henceforth the fate of the prisoners was to be in the hands of the two commissions which the emperor had

[79] Interrogation of Varese on February 10, 1815, as summarized in *ibid.*, pp. 44–45.

[80] Spadoni, *I giudizi di Mantova*, p. 58.

[81] The full text of this document, which is entitled "Conclusions against Fontanelli and Zucchi" and dated Mantua, February 17, 1815, is published in Weil, *Murat*, Vol. II, Appendix III, pp. 483–491.

[82] *Ibid.*, pp. 489–491.

appointed to deal with them. According to the original plans, the commission which was to try the civilian defendants was to begin its work on February 10. However, various unexpected delays made it impossible for the commission actually to commence hearing the trial arguments until a month and a half later. First of all, the commission could not function until the Lauer committee concluded its interrogations on February 14. Four days later the commission held its first meeting. However, several weeks elapsed before the prosecutor drew up the formal act of accusation against the defendants, which was required by French law, and each prisoner selected a lawyer to defend him.[83]

The official act of accusation preferred against Latuada, Lechi, Bellotti, Cavedoni, Brunetti, Gasparinetti, Rasori, Ragani, Gerosa, Caprotti, and Marchal was finally completed by Valeri, the imperial prosecutor, on March 2 and handed to the prisoners on the 6th. In it Latuada was charged with conspiring to overthrow the existing government and inciting "the inhabitants to arm themselves against the legitimate authority of their sovereign." In addition, he was accused of actively engaging in machinations and of "having relations with what he supposed was an agent of a foreign power" in order to provoke that country "to undertake war against the state." Lechi, Bellotti, Cavedoni, and Brunetti were arraigned for participating in a plot "to destroy the actual government" and urging the populace to take up arms against their ruler. Gasparinetti and Rasori were accused of dealing with the purported representative of another country for the purpose of influencing its ruler to commit hostilities against Austria and for failure to denounce the conspiracy to the proper authorities. Marchal was indicted for non-revelation of the complot and having relations with the presumed emissary of another ruler. Ragani, Gerosa, and Caprotti were cited only for not fulfilling their obligation to inform the Habsburg authorities of the existence of a dangerous conspiracy of which they were fully cognizant.[84]

After the charges were drawn up against the Brescian-Milanese conspirators, either the defendants themselves or the commission chose lawyers to represent them at their trial. Lodovico Dalonio was selected to defend Latuada. The Mantuan lawyer Agostino Zanelli

---

[83] Spadoni, *I giudizi di Mantova*, pp. 62–64.

[84] *Biblioteca Ambrosiana* (Milan), "Atto d'accusa contro Giovanni Soveri Latuada ecc.," Fos. 48–56, especially Fos. 55–56.

represented Brunetti and Rasori. Giovanni Predaval championed the interests of Gasparinetti, Ragani, and Caprotti; and Giuseppe Dagni took over Gerosa's cause. Insisting that the commission could not try him since he was a military officer, Lechi at first refused to allow anyone to argue his case;[85] however, after the commission rejected this argument, he asked the Brescian lawyer Luigi Gerardi to be his counsel. So did Bellotti. Agostino Ruggeri was deputized by the court to defend Cavedoni and Marchal.[86]

President Trevisan set March 28 as the date on which the prisoners and their attorneys were to begin pleading their cases in the presence of the other defendants. During the first three days the accused themselves were heard. Using the same curious defense which he had employed when he was interrogated by the investigating commission in Milan, Latuada talked long about how he had participated in the conspiracy solely to exert his personal influence to prevent it from breaking out. As before, he managed to spin a tight web around practically every other plotter before concluding. While they discussed most of the details of the machination, Lechi, Bellotti, and Cavedoni denied Latuada's specific charges against them and asseverated that Latuada himself had been the most active and ardent of the ringleaders and had drawn up nearly all the plans to carry out the revolt. Brunetti held to the same story which he had told in his defense in January and, in spite of Latuada's assertions to the contrary, still pretended that only innocent and innocuous conversations had taken place at his house during the oft-mentioned meeting early in November. Besides repeating the particulars about his trip to Naples, Ragani added a word or two about his enrollment in the Centri society and gave information about the complot which was especially damaging to Latuada, Bellotti, Lechi, and De Meester. Caprotti spoke unreservedly about the Carbonari and revealed what little he knew of the various schemes to effectuate the conspiracy. As he had in December, Gasparinetti willingly told all of which he was aware. Rasori, on the other hand, proved even more recalcitrant than during his initial interrogations in Milan. While he talked freely about the conferences with St. Agnan, he denied all knowledge of any real con-

---

[85] Police report, February 22, 1815, St. A. (Vienna), Kabinets-Akten, 1815, ad No. 339.

[86] Spadoni, *I giudizi di Mantova*, pp. 82, 91, 92, 96, and 97.

spiracy. Marchal limited his presentation to his associations with St. Agnan and the conferences with him at Rasori's house.[87]

The imperial prosecutor Valeri presented his case on March 31. He demanded the death penalty for Latuada, Bellotti, Brunetti, Lechi, Gasparinetti, Cavedoni, and Rasori. As for Caprotti, Ragani, and Marchal, he insisted that they be punished with three years' imprisonment and a fine of 1,000 lire. Gerosa, he said, had fulfilled his obligations to gain the impunity promised him before he made his confession; however, the government was still entitled to penalize him for violating the August 26, 1814, decree prohibiting membership in secret societies.[88]

The lawyers for the defense presented their arguments later on the same day and on April 1. Dalonio spoke first. With self-assurance, he maintained that Latuada could not possibly be guilty of plotting to overthrow the government because the only conspiracy which actually existed was the one manufactured by St. Agnan for the express purpose of producing evidence to turn over to the government. Ingeniously, he argued that, since the Allied Powers had still not determined the future destiny of the country, it was impossible for anyone to conspire against a legitimate sovereign in Lombardy-Venetia. Gerardi attempted to exonerate his clients, Lechi and Bellotti, by emphasizing the vagueness of the accusations which the other prisoners had made against them and the nebulousness of the projects in which they had supposedly participated. The insurrection, he asserted, was never actually prepared or executed. Nothing was ever agreed upon, and no overt action was taken. Zanelli presented similar arguments on behalf of Brunetti and joined Dalonio in scoffing at the very idea that his protégé's actions could possibly be construed as conspiratorial in nature. As for Rasori, he called attention to the professor's international repute as a scientist and laughed at the charge that his relations with St. Agnan were of a criminal nature. The next attorney to speak Ruggeri described Cavedoni's behavior as very natural for a recently discharged military man who was imbued with a sincere longing for Italian independence. As for Marchal, Ruggeri pleaded that, ignorant as he was of the Italian language, he was never really aware of what actually transpired at the meetings with St. Ag-

[87] For an excellent summary of the arguments presented by the defendants on March 28, 29, and 30, 1815, which is based on a careful analysis of the actual trial records, see *ibid.*, pp. 68–87.

[88] *Ibid.*, pp. 87–88.

nan. Predaval rested his plea for Gasparinetti, Ragani, and Caprotti mainly on the contention that the defendants would never have been arrested had not a thoroughly discredited and reprehensible adventurer, imposter, and spy turned questionable writings over to the government. The last defense lawyer to participate in the debate Dagni limited his statements to reminding the commission that his client, Gerosa, had honorably fulfilled every condition imposed upon him by Bellegarde to gain impunity.[89]

The commission was given until April 4 to look over the testimony and reach a verdict. Its main task was to decide whether or not the defendants had actually participated in a conspiracy against the existing government, as defined in Articles 87 and 89 of the French penal code,[90] or were guilty of the crime of machination described in Article 76[91] or of failing to denounce the above transgressions as required by Articles 76, 87, 89, 103, and 105.[92]

The commission came to a decision within the allotted interval. As

[89] See *ibid.*, pp. 88–99; and Helfert, *Kaiser Franz und die Stiftung des Lombardo-Venetianischen Königreichs*, p. 200.

[90] According to Article 87 of the Napoleonic penal code, persons who conspired against the person of the emperor, or plotted to take the life of a member of the imperial family, "to destroy or change the government or the order of succession to the throne," or "to incite the citizens or inhabitants to arm themselves against the imperial authority" were "to be punished with the death penalty and with confiscation of their property." Article 89 read: "A conspiracy exists as soon as the resolution to act is planned and decided upon between two or more conspirators, even though an *attentat* is not actually committed" (*Codice penale, ossia dei delitti e delle pene* [Vol. XXXV of *Raccolta delle leggi, provvidenze, manifesti ec. pubblicati sotto l'attuale R. Governo. Cominciando dalli 26. maggio 1799 in poi*], p. 34).

[91] Article 76 provided that anyone who "participated in machinations or had relations with foreign powers or with their agents for the purpose of engaging them to commit hostilities or to undertake war against France or to procure the means for them [to do so] will be punished with death and his goods will be confiscated" (*ibid.*, pp. 28–30).

[92] Article 103 required all persons "having knowledge of any complots or crimes against the internal or external security of the state" to denounce them to the proper authorities within twenty-four hours after they first became aware of the existence of such a conspiracy or crime. If they failed to do so, they were to be punished for "non-revelation," even though it was proved that they were "exempt from all complicity." According to Article 105, persons guilty of violating the prescriptions of the above article were to be punished with from two to five years of imprisonment and with fines ranging from 500 to 1,000 francs (*ibid.*, p. 42).

for Latuada, Cavedoni, Lechi, Bellotti, and Brunetti, who were charged in the act of accusation with conspiring against the government, it concluded that, although much of the testimony presented at the trial showed that they had participated in such a crime, it was not definite enough to prove beyond the shadow of a doubt that they were guilty of conspiring in the manner stipulated by Articles 87 and 89 of the French penal code. All the judges were convinced that Latuada had resolved to organize a conspiracy; nevertheless, since no witness had sworn that he had come to an agreement on a precise course of action with two or more of his accomplices, they were of the opinion that there was not sufficient legal proof of the existence of a bona fide conspiracy to justify condemning him to death as provided by law. The commission arrived at the same conclusion in regard to Cavedoni. Although the evidence plainly showed that he belonged to the Carbonari, that he had participated in several conferences at which various methods to carry out the plot were discussed, and that he had offered to lead the detachment that was to imprison Field Marshal Bellegarde, there was no proof that he and the other plotters had resolved to execute these plans. Lechi and Bellotti were present at various meetings where the details of the complot were threshed out, but they had promised to take part in the enterprise only if Generals Pino and Fontanelli joined it, and they had refused to play an active role in leading the uprising in Milan; hence they could not be deemed guilty of conspiring against the government. Neither could Brunetti. However, all three of them, as well as Caprotti, Gasparinetti, Rasori, and Ragani, were clearly guilty of failing to reveal to the proper authorities the existence of a dangerous plot about which they were fully informed. Gerosa would also have been liable to punishment on this count had he not merited impunity by his confession.

As for the charge that the defendants had actually take part in a machination and had dealings with the agent of a foreign power, which was preferred only against Latuada, Gasparinetti, and Rasori, the commission declared that sufficient evidence was at hand to prove the three conspirators guilty of conversing with St. Agnan, the agent of another country, about procuring French aid for a war against Austria. Nevertheless, their culpability was mitigated by the fact that the trial records did not definitely prove that St. Agnan was actually a bona fide agent of that foreign power.

According to the commission, because Latuada and Cavedoni were the two major offenders, they merited the most severe punishment the law allowed. On the other hand, it declared that there was insufficient evidence to convict Marchal of any crime at all.[93] With these considerations in mind, the commission sentenced Latuada and Cavedoni to exile for ten years; Bellotti, Gasparinetti, Lechi, and Rasori each to five years' imprisonment and a fine of 2,000 lire; Ragani, to three years in prison and a 1,000 lire fine; Caprotti, to a 500 lire fine and three years' incarceration; and finally, Brunetti, to two years in jail and a fine of 1,000 lire. At the same time, the commission declared that Marchal and Gerosa should be set free.[94]

In compliance with Emperor Francis' instructions, the special commission did not inform the defendants or the public about its verdict but sent it directly to Bellegarde. On the authorization of the commission, the commissioner plenipotentiary ordered Gerosa's release from prison. He also transmitted to Vienna the commission's report, together with the official records of the trial and a special letter from Imperial Prosecutor Valeri. In view of the valuable information which Gasparinetti had given the Habsburg authorities, Valeri wrote that the Mantua commission was proposing entirely too harsh a penalty for the conspirator.[95]

On May 26 the emperor handed these documents to the president of the supreme court of justice and requested him to appoint a special committee composed of several justices in his court to review the work of the Mantua commission. Also, he was to propose a sentence for the emperor to give in way of grace.[96] This committee advised the supreme court early in October, 1815, that Marchal should not have been exonerated and that the sentence for the rest of the prisoners was too severe. It recommended that the emperor reduce Latuada and Cavedoni's sentence to five years' imprisonment; Bellotti, Gasparinetti, Lechi, and Rasori's to two years; and Brunetti, Ragani,

[93] Trevisan to Bellegarde, Mantua, April 6, 1815, Spadoni, *I giudizi di Mantova*, Appendix, pp. 257–264.

[94] Police report, April 20, 1815, St. A. (Vienna), Kabinets-Akten, 1815, ad No. 339; Spadoni, *I giudizi di Mantova*, p. 103.

[95] Spadoni, *I giudizi di Mantova*, pp. 104–108; Spadoni, "Il processo per la congiura bresciano-milanese," p. 97.

[96] Emperor Francis to Oettingen, Vienna, May 26, 1815, St. A. (Vienna), Kabinets-Akten, 1815, ad No. 339 (also quoted in full in Spadoni, *I giudizi di Mantova*, pp. 123–124). See also Helfert, *Kaiser Franz und die Stiftung des Lombardo-Venetianischen Königreichs*, pp. 249 and 395.

and Caprotti's to one year. Also, Marchal should be incarcerated for one year.[97]

Several members of the committee found serious fault with the way the trial had been conducted by the special commission. They deplored the fact that the verdict of the Mantua commission did not answer the charges in the act of accusation point by point, as required by prevailing French-Italian practices. Furthermore, they maintained that the commission had erred by not having the sentence read to the prisoners, as stipulated by the laws then in effect in Lombardy-Venetia. Also, it had failed to establish procedures by which the defendants could appeal their case in the manner prescribed by the Napoleonic penal code. For these reasons, the special committee recommended that the verdict of the Mantua commission should be quashed and the case retried by another body.[98]

The supreme court of justice also expressed its disapprobation of the way the trial had been handled at Mantua and on October 11 counseled the emperor to reopen the case. First of all, it suggested that the more than sixty persons implicated in the conspiracy who had still not been interrogated[99] should be questioned and where necessary charges preferred. Furthermore, unless the Austrian code provided for milder penalties for the offenses with which they were charged, the defendants, including those already examined at Mantua, should be tried by the criminal court at Venice according to the provisions of the existing Italian penal code. Before the sentence was

[97] Protocol of the sessions of October 7–10, 1815, of the supreme court of justice, as quoted in Spadoni, *I giudizi di Mantova*, pp. 124–125.

[98] Spadoni, *I giudizi di Mantova*, pp. 125–127.

[99] In a chart which Metternich sent to Bubna from Vienna on December 10, 1816, the following persons against whom no inquisition had been instituted were listed among those implicated in the conspiracy in some way or another: Mancini, Delfini, Fontanelli, Zucchi, Pino, Zecchi, Romagnosi, Locatelli, Morlo, Bazzoni, Comelli, Agucchi, Ercolani, Cimba, Gifflenga, Lonati, General Bonfanti, Colonel Bonfanti, St. Andrea, Ballabio, Salfi, Irene Favetti, Giacinto Bossi, Counselor of State Luigi Bossi, Bonafous, Carta, Viglezzi, Malacarne, Vincenzo Ferrari, Giovanni Battista Ferrari, ex-Major Vittorio Ferrari, Baldalassi, Mauro, Casallini, Villata, Montallegri, Martinengo, Martinez, Paradisi, Molini, Montebruni, Comerio, Zoboli, Lancetti, Melzi, Visconti, Lampati, Valentini, Bertoletti, Radaeli, Antoni, Violino, Cortesi, Crovi, Grandi, Rezia, Viganoni, Fontana, Turati, and Robiati. The charges made against each of these individuals and the name of the person or persons who made them are also given in the chart (see St. A. (Vienna), F. M. Graf Bubna, Geheime Correspondenz, Fasz. I (Jahrgang 1816 u. 1817), No. 20b, Fos. 1–2).

published the trial documents were to be carefully reviewed by the court of appeals at Venice and the supreme court of justice in Vienna, which was to submit its verdict directly to the emperor.[100]

After reading these criticisms, Emperor Francis instructed the president of the supreme court to ask the imperial council of war for an explanation of why several of the prisoners who were pensioned military officers had been tried by the civil commission in Mantua rather than by a military court. Also, after consulting Count Saurau, the new governor of Lombardy, Fratnich, the vice-president of the court of appeals, and Valeri and Della Porta, of the former Mantua commission, Bellegarde was to confer with the president about the wisdom of holding a new trial for the arrested conspirators and other persons denounced for participating in the plot. After hearing from the council of war and Bellegarde the supreme court was to advise the emperor as to what actions he should take.[101]

In reply to the president's inquiry, the aulic council of war explained that the pensioned military officers had been turned over to the civil commission for trial on the express orders of the emperor himself. Furthermore, since the former army officers could not receive a lighter sentence from a court-martial than the one given by the Mantua civil commission, they would gain no advantage from such a trial. Bellegarde wrote the supreme court that Saurau, Fratnich, Valeri, Della Porta, and he himself were unanimously agreed that it would be highly inadvisable to reopen the process or to examine those persons whose names had been mentioned in the trial who had not yet been arrested.[102]

After receiving these reports the supreme court advised the emperor on May 20, 1816, that it would be unwise to retry the prisoners or to prosecute persons inculpated in the conspiracy against whom no formal charges had yet been made. However, it expressed the opinion that as a matter of justice the sentence proposed in October, 1815, for Latuada and Cavedoni should be reduced from five to three years' imprisonment and for Brunetti from one year to six months. Marchal should be immediately freed and sent to France rather than incarcerated for one year, as the supreme court had recommended in 1815.

[100] Spadoni, *I giudizi di Mantova*, pp. 127–128; Spadoni, "Il processo per la congiura bresciano-milanese," pp. 98–99.

[101] Emperor Francis to Oettingen, Venice, November 24, 1815, as quoted in Spadoni, *I giudizi di Mantova*, pp. 129–130.

[102] Spadoni, *I giudizi di Mantova*, pp. 131–137.

Bellotti, Gasparinetti, Lechi, Rasori, Ragani, and Caprotti's punishment should remain as originally fixed: two years of imprisonment for the first four and one year for the last two.[103]

Exactly one month later, on June 20, 1816, the emperor announced what punishment should be meted out to the prisoners who had been tried by the civil commission at Mantua. Over and above the time which they had already spent in jail, the prisoners were, by way of grace, to be sentenced as follows: Latuada and Cavedoni were to be confined in a fortress for two years. Lechi, Bellotti, Gasparinetti, and Rasori were to be held under simple arrest for eighteen more months; Ragani and Caprotti, for a year; and Brunetti, for another six months. Marchal was to be deported from Austrian territory. The prisoners were to pay no fines; nor were they to be charged for the costs of the process, as stipulated by law. After serving his full sentence, Cavedoni was to be turned over to the government of Modena, and Bellotti and Ragani were to be deported. The fate of Latuada and Rasori was to be decided when they were released from prison. Neither the prisoners nor other persons incriminated by their testimony were to be subjected to further inquisitions.[104]

For some reason or other the bureaucratic wheels in Vienna ground so slowly that the emperor's verdict did not reach the supreme court of justice before August 1. On the 12th this body decreed that the sovereign resolution was to be communicated immediately to Police President von Hager, the governor of Lombardy, and the court of appeals at Milan. On August 26 the court of appeals transmitted the emperor's decision to Gognetti, the president of the court of justice at Mantua,[105] who finally read the sentence to the prisoners on September 17, 1816.[106]

[103] *Ibid.*, pp. 137–140.

[104] Imperial resolution, Vienna, June 20, 1816, *Kriegs-Archiv* (Vienna), Hof Kriegs-Rath–Präsidial Akten, Fasz. VIII, No. 35. The text is printed in full in Spadoni, *I giudizi di Mantova*, pp. 141–142.

[105] Spadoni, *I giudizi di Mantova*, pp. 142–143. It should be noted that well-informed Milanese like Mantovani apparently knew what the emperor's decision was as early as August 22. See entry of August 22, 1816, *Biblioteca Ambrosiana* (Milan), Mantovani, "Diario di Milano," Vol. VI, pp. 67–68.

[106] For the official text of the sentence read to the prisoners on September 17, 1816, by Giovanni Gognetti, president of the court of justice of Mantua, see Weil, *Murat*, Vol. II, Appendix XII, p. 529. In this communiqué the date of the emperor's resolution is erroneously given as August 12, 1816. The reader's attention should also be called to the fact that at least some of the prisoners knew

Thus the Brescian-Milanese conspirators tried by the civil commission at Mantua languished in prison for one year and eight months before they, officially at least, heard the verdict pronounced against them. The five who were adjudged by the military court—De Meester, Moretti, Olini, Pavoni, and Varese—had to wait even longer before they learned their fate.

In addition to Sommariva and Bührent, whom the emperor had assigned to the military court on January 13, 1815, in the capacity of president and reporter,[107] Bellegarde appointed the following other military personnel to serve on this tribunal: Generals Albert de Best and Lauer, Colonels Dressery and Eberl, Majors Clemens Landenberg and Karl Amade Gyurtsak, First Lieutenants Ludwig von Perremans, Mazetti, Johann Thomann, and Michele Sartorio, and Grenadier Leaders Joseph von Klesheim and Alexander Nefzern. Although all the above-mentioned persons were instructed to be at Mantua before February 10,[108] the court did not begin its sessions before March 1.

The procedures followed by the military tribunal differed considerably from those of the civilian commission at Mantua. In the first place, in accord with the customary practices at court-martial hearings, the prisoners were tried by military law—in this case by Austrian military law—rather than by the Napoleonic penal code, as the civilian defendants were. Furthermore, unlike the civilian conspirators, the military prisoners had no lawyers to defend them. Then, too, although the civil commission rendered its verdict a few days after the questioning of the prisoners and the conclusion of the debates between the imperial prosecutor and the attorneys for the defense, the military court did not reach a decision until eight months after the interrogation of the prisoners ended.

The military commission began by questioning the defendants and confronting them with other prisoners who had presented incriminating evidence against them. During these proceedings, De Meester again denied everything incriminatory that was imputed to him, as

---

what the sentence was several days before it was officially communicated to them. See, for instance, the joint letter (the recipient is not given) of Cavedoni and Latuada dated Mantua, September 12, 1816, in Lemmi, *La restaurazione austriaca a Milano*, Appendix LXXX, pp. 509–510.

107 See *ante*, p. 291.

108 Bellegarde to Schwarzenberg, Milan, February 14, 1815, *Kriegs-Archiv* (Vienna), Hof Kriegs-Rath–Präsidial Akten, Fasz. VII, No. 12.

he had in December and January. While De Meester admitted that he had talked about political matters with Cavedoni and Bellotti, he remained adamant in denying that he had engaged in any conspiratorial undertaking. Pavoni and Moretti also assumed negative attitudes. Declaring that the confession which he had made in February[109] had been extracted from him at a moment when he was not in full control of himself, Moretti asseverated his innocence.[110]

After the interrogation of the prisoners there was a long delay in the proceedings while Emperor Francis decided whether or not Generals Zucchi and Fontanelli should be arrested on account of the grave charges which the civil commission had drawn up against them.[111] Both Bellegarde and Von Hager urged the emperor not to have them taken into custody since such a course of action would have an adverse effect upon public opinion. Instead, he was advised to have the two generals carefully watched and privately questioned about what knowledge they had of the complot. The Habsburg sovereign followed their advice.

Thus in spite of all the incriminating evidence against them, Generals Zucchi and Fontanelli endured nothing more humiliating than the unpleasantness of a rather gentle interrogation by Habsburg officers.[112] Another Italian general whose name was frequently mentioned by the prisoners, Pino, was not even questioned.[113]

[109] See *ante*, pp. 292–293.

[110] Spadoni, *I giudizi di Mantova*, pp. 109–112; Spadoni, "Il gen. bar. Giacomo Filippo de Meester," p. 862.

[111] See *ante*, p. 294.

[112] When they were actually questioned both generals emphatically denied the validity of all the charges which various prisoners had made against them (Helfert, *Kaiser Franz und die Stiftung des Lombardo-Venetianischen Königreichs*, pp. 148–149, 249, and 359–396; Spadoni, *I giudizi di Mantova*, pp. 112–125).

[113] Spadoni, *I giudizi di Mantova*, p. 115. Albert Pingaud has maintained that Pino was not questioned or arrested by the Habsburgs because he was one of their secret informers (see *ibid.*, pp. 115–116). He based his accusations against the popular Italian general largely on a letter which General Pino sent to the police directory on July 18, 1816, in which he warned the Austrian police that "several Neapolitan and Roman individuals, egged on by the English party, are traveling through Italy to organize a new insurrection. You will not ignore the fact that under other circumstances when a storm was brewing I did not fail to inform you as well" (as quoted in *ibid.*, p. 116 n.). This writer has not seen the above letter, but he has found another one which Count Bubna sent to Metternich from Milan on July 25, 1816, in which Bubna related that General Pino had

The protracted correspondence and reports about Zucchi and Fontanelli prolonged the proceedings considerably. Then, too, there was another long interruption because some of the officers assigned to the court were called up for active military duty during the 1815 campaign against Napoleon and Murat. Finally, there was another delay while a decision was made as to whether Mancini and Delfini should be arrested and questioned about their connections with foreign powers.[114]

come to him on July 16 to inform him that he had been approached by a stranger, a Neapolitan duke who called himself Brindisi who pretended that he was traveling around the peninsula proselytizing patriots for the cause of Italian independence. Pino told Bubna that the Neapolitan duke's conduct was so suspicious that he felt that he should immediately warn the Austrian military commander in Lombardy that the "duke" was an extremely dangerous man (St. A. [Vienna], F. M. Graf Bubna, Geheime Correspondenz, Fasz. I [Jahrgang 1816 u. 1817], No. 5/3, Fos. 3–4). In the hope of extorting money from them, the duke of Brindisi had come to the Habsburg authorities in Florence and Rome with a "cock-and-bull" story about a vast conspiracy financed by the British and directed by Lord Bentinck which was to break out at any minute in Italy (see my "La costituzione guelfa e i servizi segreti austriaci"). Pino must have given Bubna the same information on July 16 which he sent to the police two days later. Given the circumstances under which Pino made this report to the Habsburg authorities, the fact that he told them that agents were traveling through Italy to organize an insurrection does not necessarily prove that General Pino had been an informer in 1814. The next sentence in his letter to the police ("You will not ignore the fact that under other circumstances when a storm was brewing I did not fail to inform you well"), however, can be looked upon as more incriminating especially in the light of other information which Bubna gave to Metternich in a letter which he sent him from Milan on December 11, 1818. In this dispatch he wrote the Austrian chancellor about two letters which General Pino had sent him. In the first, the general informed Bubna about intrigues in London in which Sigismondo Trecchi, Foscolo, and Confalonieri were involved. In the second, Pino wrote Bubna, among other things, that "Latuada, Rasori, and their consorts had not reformed themselves" (see St. A. [Vienna], F. M. Graf Bubna, Geheime Correspondenz, Fasz. II [Jahrgang 1818 u. 1819], No. 27/30). Is it illogical to suspect that a man who gave damaging information to Count Bubna about Confalonieri, Trecchi, Foscolo, Latuada, and Rasori in 1818 might *possibly* also have acted in the capacity of secret informer in 1814 or 1815 or even denounced the Brescian-Milanese conspiracy to the Austrians? There is, of course, no positive proof that he did. However, Pino's behavior in 1816 and 1818 shows that at least on certain occasions a few years after 1814 he had no compunction about giving damaging information to the Austrian authorities about the Milanese conspirators.

[114] Helfert, *Kaiser Franz und die Stiftung des Lombardo-Venetianischen Königreichs*, pp. 249 and 394.

Partly as a consequence of these interruptions, the military court was unable to complete its work before November, 1815. After ending its long drawn out investigation, the court, upon the recommendations of Bührent, the reporter who drew up the case against the prisoners, declared that Pavoni and Varese should be released from prison since there was not enough legal evidence to prove their participation in any conference at which methods to carry out the conspiracy were discussed and decided upon. As for Moretti, Olini, and De Meester, the other officers on trial, the proof that they had taken an active part in a dangerous conspiracy to overthrow the legally constituted government was sufficient to warrant punishing them. It was true that there were extenuating circumstances in favor of all three offenders. Olini had willingly confessed what he knew about the undertaking, and Moretti had been in the German provinces of the monarchy when the machinators completed the last details of the plot. Then, too, the conspiracy had never matured and no disorders had actually broken out. Nevertheless, it was evident that all three were ringleaders of a plot which was to be executed with assistance from two foreign powers—Naples and France. Olini and Moretti were clearly guilty of high treason. Therefore, in accord with the provisions of the Austrian military code, after being deprived of their military rank and their property, they should be hanged. De Meester was also guilty of high treason. He should be deprived of his rank, dismissed from his position at the military orphanage, have his property confiscated, and be condemned to the harshest kind of life imprisonment.[115]

[115] Spadoni, *I giudizi di Mantova*, pp. 118–123; Spadoni, "Il gen. bar. Giacomo Filippo de Meester," pp. 862–863; Helfert, *Kaiser Franz und die Stiftung des Lombardo-Venetianischen Königreichs*, pp. 396–397. The Austrian penal code provided for three categories of imprisonment: (1) ordinary imprisonment, (2) harsh imprisonment, and (3) the harshest type of imprisonment. Persons sentenced to the first kind of imprisonment were not put in irons. They were fed a regular diet and could have visitors in the presence of the custodian of the prison. Those condemned to harsh imprisonment wore iron bands around their feet. They were fed only hot soup without meat, slept on a bare plank bed, and were not allowed to have visitors. Those given the harshest degree of imprisonment were locked up in isolated cells and prevented from conversing with anyone. They were forced to wear heavy iron bands around both arms and both feet. In addition, they wore a heavy iron band around their waist, to which a chain was always attached when they were not working. They were given hot soup without meat every second day. The rest of the time they were fed only bread and water (Arts. 11–14 of the Austrian *Codice penale*, pp. 10–11).

On December 11, 1815, the verdict of the military court at Mantua and the trial records were transmitted to the general military court of appeals, which sent them to the aulic council, together with its own recommendations. From there the case was referred to the emperor for final decision. Emperor Francis found the sentence too severe and requested that a lighter one be submitted to him. Finally, after the requested verdict was drawn up, the emperor issued a resolution on November 9, 1816, in which he pronounced his own judicial judgment. Varese and Pavoni were absolved from all punishment. Moretti, Olini, and De Meester were sentenced to eight years' harsh imprisonment in a fortress and deprived of all military honors. After the prisoners served half of their sentence a new recommendation was made to the emperor about reducing their terms of incarceration.[116]

Naturally various nationalist littérateurs have taken the Habsburgs severely to task for allegedly violating all civilized judicial procedures when trying the Brescian-Milanese conspirators. Princess Belgiojoso-Trivulzio excoriated the Mantua commission for condemning the prisoners' failure to denounce a conspiracy which the court itself admitted never existed. She upbraided the Austrians for their cynical cruelty in keeping the prisoners in jail three whole years before sentencing them. Also, she chided Emperor Francis for condemning the prisoners to eighteen months of imprisonment in addition to the three years which they had already spent in confinement.[117]

Filippo Antonio Gualterio was even harsher in his strictures. He censured the Austrians for using unfair and tricky methods to extort testimony from the defendants. In his words,

The conduct of the prosecutors was iniquitous; that of the judges, weak; that of the government, hypocritical. They had no confessions except vague ones, procured by means of surprising ethical tactics. . . . Lacking real proof of the conspiracy, the judges hesitated; and the government announced its mild intentions to them antecedently [to the time when they made their decision] for the purpose of quieting their remorse and to prepare for themselves a beautiful occasion to make a display of compassion.

---

[116] Spadoni, *I giudizi di Mantova*, pp. 143–146; Spadoni, "Il gen. bar. Giacomo Filippo de Meester," p. 863; Bastari, "Paolo Olini, p. 49; V. Tonni-Bazza, "Silvio Moretti (1772–1823)," *Nel Cinquantenario delle X Giornate*, p. 14.

[117] See [Belgiojoso-Trivulzio], *Étude sur l'histoire de la Lombardie*, pp. 123–126.

. . . The sentence was communicated to the prisoners only after three years.[118]

Cusani repeated the legend initiated by Lechi's unreliable memoirs[119] and spread by Princess Belgiojoso-Trivulzio[120] that as the trial was about to end Bellegarde prompted the judges to pronounce a harsh verdict by informing them that the emperor intended giving the prisoners an easy sentence as a special act of grace. Castro combined the foregoing legends with others in a vitriolic indictment of the whole Mantua process. He castigated the members of the Mantua commission for their rabid reactionary views. He censured such actions as showing the prisoners forged signatures and making them believe that their companions had already revealed everything to extort false confessions from them. He condemned the death penalty which was inflicted after Bellegarde had asked the commission "to be as severe as the law would permit so that the sovereign clemency will be more lustrous."[121]

Today, a quarter of a century after Spadoni published his painstaking summaries and trenchant analyses of the Mantua process, it is difficult to accept the validity and accuracy of Princess Belgiojoso-Trivulzio, Gualterio, and Castro's condemnations of the Mantua process, which became part of the accepted national mythology of numerous Italian patriots. As the account of the day-to-day proceedings so carefully described in Spadoni's monumental study clearly shows, the assertion that the prisoners made "no confessions except vague ones" extorted from them by questionable methods is untrue. As for the asseveration that the judges were rabid reactionaries, it should be noted that the president of the Mantua civilian commission Trevisan had been a trusted official of the French-Italian regime and a devoted follower of Napoleon. In regard to the charge that Bellegarde attempted to influence the commission to inflict a severe sentence against the defendants, Spadoni, after an exhaustive search of all available records, could find no evidence that the governor ever sent such a communication.[122] It is a plain misrepresentation of the

[118] Gualterio, *Gli ultimi rivolgimenti italiani,* Vol. I, Pt. 1, p. 409.

[119] See Spadoni, *I giudizi di Mantova,* p. 99.

[120] See her *Étude sur l'histoire de la Lombardie,* p. 123.

[121] See Castro, *I congiurati lombardi del 1814,* p. 26; his *Milano e le cospirazioni lombarde,* pp. 157–162 and 281–294; and his "La restaurazione austriaca in Milano," p. 642.

[122] See Spadoni, *I giudizi di Mantova,* p. 99 n.

facts to declare, as Castro did, that the punishments recommended
for the conspirators by the Mantua commission, which ranged from
ten years' exile to two years' imprisonment for the civilian prisoners
and from the death penalty to complete exoneration for the officers
tried by court-martial, amounted to the death sentence. Furthermore,
the prisoners languished in prison between nineteen and twenty
months and not for three long years before they heard their sentences. And the Austrians did not make them wait that long in a deliberate effort to torture them!

It should not be forgotten that the majority of prisoners were accused of high treason—a crime usually punishable by the death penalty. Article 89 of the Napoleonic penal code, under which the civilian
prisoners were tried, interpreted the crime of high treason broadly
enough to include planning and deciding upon a conspiratorial
course of action, whether or not the plot was actually carried out. It
seems to this writer that the details which so many of the defendants
revealed about the projects to surprise various fortresses, to incite an
open rebellion in Milan, and to seize the governor and various Habsburg generals might have influenced a group of "reactionary judges"
intent on severe punishment to pronounce the death sentences
against Latuada, Cavedoni, Lechi, Bellotti, and Brunetti, the civilian
prisoners charged with high treason. Imperial Prosecutor Valeri per-
suaded himself that the testimony of the prisoners was damaging
enough to convict them for that crime.[123] Nevertheless, the Mantua
civil commission concluded that the evidence was too ambiguous to
prove beyond every shadow of a doubt that the accused had actually
participated in a conspiracy to overthrow the government and consequently convicted them merely of violating Articles 103 and 105 of
the French code—i.e., of failing to reveal to the proper authorities
the known existence of a crime against the internal or external security of the state.

Princess Belgiojoso-Trivulzio's argument that it was unlawful to
find the prisoners guilty of failure to report the plot since the commission could not find enough evidence to punish them for conspiracy is specious, to say the least. Article 103 of the French code clearly
obligated everyone who knew of any plot or crime affecting the security of the state to denounce it within twenty-four hours. Certainly

---

[123] See Valeri to Ghisilieri, Mantua, April 6, 1815, as quoted in *ibid.*, pp. 104–
105.

the defendants were aware that someone (in this case they themselves) was plotting to overthrow the government! As for the princess' castigation of the emperor for condemning the prisoners to eighteen months of imprisonment in addition to the time they had already served, the sentences for the civilian defendants to which she was probably referring actually varied between six months and two years. More important, in 1816 the prisoners themselves apparently did not agree with their latter-day champion, for they wrote effusive letters expressing their deep gratitude for the light penalties inflicted by Emperor Francis.[124]

Had the Habsburgs been as reprehensible in dealing with the Brescian-Milanese conspirators as some nineteenth century liberal and nationalist writers have asserted, they would very likely have arrested or at least interrogated everyone in the conspiracy whom they could manage to seize. In actual fact, of the seventy-eight persons implicated in the conspiracy by the testimony of the prisoners, the Habsburgs tried only sixteen. A few others like Mancini, Delfini, and Ignazio Bonafous would probably have been arrested if the Austrians had been able to lay hands on them. Generals Zucchi and Fontanelli, so often mentioned by the defendants, got off with gentle, quiet interrogations. General Pino was not even questioned. Some of the others mentioned who were not visited or examined by the police were Romagnosi, who was alluded to in Gasparinetti, Rasori and Latuada's depositions; Annibale Locatelli, who was denounced by Gasparinetti, Latuada, and Lechi; Giovanni Bazzoni, who was inculpated by Latuada, Lechi, and Gasparinetti; Count Alessandro Agucchi, whose part was made known by Gasparinetti, Lechi, and Latuada; Ercolani, whose complicity was pointed out by Gasparinetti, Lechi, and Latuada; Ballabio, who was mentioned by Lechi and Gerosa; Irene Favetti, whose name came out in statements made by Bellotti, Cavedoni, and Latuada; and Baldalassi, who was involved by Lechi and Gerosa.[125] Although they were by no means always so

---

[124] See the two letters, one dated Mantua, September 19, 1816, and signed by Lechi, Bellotti, Brunetti, Rasori, Gasparinetti, and Caprotti, and the other signed by Cavedoni and Latuada and dated Mantua, September 12, 1816, printed in Lemmi, *La restaurazione austriaca a Milano*, Appendices LXXIX and LXXX, pp. 508–510.

[125] See the chart listing the persons implicated in the Brescian-Milanese conspiracy enclosed in Metternich to Bubna, Vienna, December 10, 1816, St. A. (Vienna), F. M. Graf Bubna, Geheime Correspondenz, Fasz. I (Jahrgang 1816 u. 1817), No. 20b, Fos. 1–2.

astute, in this particular instance the Austrians were wise enough to foresee the deleterious effects on Italian public opinion of an intensive, all-embracing investigation.

That is not to say that the Mantua process and the interrogations which preceded it were above reproach. We must certainly agree with Italian nationalist writers that Bellegarde was wrong in allowing a notorious adventurer like St. Agnan to conjure up a fake conspiracy to trick Latuada, Rasori, and Gasparinetti into giving him writings to turn over to the governor as legal evidence to justify their arrest. Furthermore, Bellegarde should not have promised Gerosa immunity for tattling on his fellow-prisoners and revealing all that he knew about the plot.

The commissioner plenipotentiary's errors of judgment, however, were not as serious as those of the Mantua civil commission. The pensioned Italian officers should have been tried by court-martial, as they had every right to be according to existing practice, rather than by a civil commission. Furthermore, it was unfair to indict Latuada, Gasparinetti, and Rasori for having relations with an agent of another country, for this accusation was based on nothing more substantial than their conversations with St. Agnan. Even though the Mantua commission refused to convict them on this charge, the imperial prosecutor should never have arraigned them for this crime in the first place.

More important, although the non-military prisoners were tried according to the French law which still prevailed in Italy, several procedures spelled out in the Napoleonic code were clearly violated. In the first place, on account of Emperor Francis' great aversion for open court hearings, the trial was held in secret rather than in public, as stipulated by the French code. Secondly, the verdict rendered by the Mantua commission did not answer the charges in the act of accusation point by point. Thirdly, the sentence was not read to the prisoners immediately after it was agreed upon; and, last of all, no provision was made for the accused to appeal the case in the manner prescribed by the French regulations. While it is true that the Austrians could rightly argue that a Napoleonic decree of March 21, 1808, which was still in effect gave them a legal right to dispense with the safeguard of popular liberties specified in the French code and that the French themselves had done so on various occasions, nonetheless, the Habsburgs' failure to follow the procedures of the Napoleonic code in their entirety was reminiscent of the despotic, not the more humanitarian, practices of the Napoleonic government.

Probably even more censurable than the violation of certain procedures in the Napoleonic code was the fact that the Austrians held the defendants in prison for approximately twenty months before informing them of their punishment. While this delay was due no doubt to the unwieldiness of the administrative and judicial machinery, and not to cynical brutality, in well-administered states prisoners do not wait more than a year and a half before learning the verdict of a court.

In short, there were many shortcomings in the Mantua process, but they stemmed from Bellegarde's faulty advice to the monarch, the emperor's phobia about public trials, and clumsy bureaucratic procedures rather than from wilful tyranny. The nationalist and liberal writers were correct in criticizing the Mantua process; they were wrong in censuring it for the wrong things.

Since the Habsburg sovereign was so alarmed by secret societies, it is surprising that the Austrians did not turn the Mantua process into a veritable "witch hunt" for everyone denounced by various defendants as a member of a clandestine sect. Although immediately after the first conspirators were arrested Bellegarde was of the opinion that secret societies had nothing whatever to do with the Brescian-Milanese conspiracy,[126] he quickly changed his mind when the prisoners began to talk at length about the complot.[127] During their preliminary interrogations in December and January various prisoners named approximately fifty persons who were supposedly members of the Carbonari or Centri societies.[128] Among them were six of the sixteen defendants in the Mantua process—Caprotti, Cavedoni, De Meester, Gerosa, Latuada, and Ragani—and two other conspira-

---

[126] Bellegarde to Metternich, Milan, December 5, 1814, St. A. (Vienna), Staatskanzlei, Provinzen, Lombardei-Venedig, Fasz. III, Kon. 4, Fo. 194.

[127] See Bellegarde to Lebzeltern, Milan, December 10, 1814, Weil, *Murat*, Vol. II, Appendix X, p. 517 n.

[128] Forty-six names were included in the list of persons named by Gerosa, Cavedoni, and Caprotti as belonging to the Carbonari which was enclosed as All. B in a letter which Metternich sent to Bubna from Vienna on December 10, 1816 (St. A. [Vienna], F. M. Graf Bubna, Geheime Correspondenz, Fasz. I [Jahrgang 1816 u. 1817], No. 20b, Fos. 1–2). In a list of Carbonari and Centri members based on testimony given by the arrested Brescian-Milanese conspirators which was drawn up on September 2, 1817, fifty-three persons are listed (A. S. [Milan], Presidenza di governo. Atti secreti, 1817, Cart. XVI, No. 893/geh.).

tors—Delfini and Mancini—who managed to escape arrest.[129] In addition, the prisoners designated Favetti, Foscolo, ten army officers, thirteen officials of the former Kingdom of Italy, and various and sundry other persons as members. The defendants talked about the existence of a "Society for Italian Independence" and another group called "Aid to the Unfortunates"—names obviously adopted by the Centri and the Carbonari at that time as camouflage. Cavedoni informed his interrogators on December 30, 1814, that Delfini and Latuada had spoken to him of a directing committee with ties with various countries of Italy (obviously a reference to Buonarroti's Perfect Sublime Masters). On the very next day, however, Latuada denied that such a committee existed.[130]

Yet, though their participation is obvious, the actual role of clandestine sects in the Brescian-Milanese conspiracy should not be exaggerated. Although various defendants admitted their own membership in secret societies and freely supplied the names of other persons who belonged, they furnished the Austrians with surprisingly little precise information about these sects. They revealed to their examiners that the aim of the Centri and the Carbonari was to work for Italian independence. They gave vague descriptions of the organizational structure of these two organizations and magnified their strength.[131] However, they told very little about what the secret societies actually did in the Brescian-Milanese conspiracy itself. That plans were made to support fifty soldiers coming from Corfu with money paid by the Carbonari; that certain officers who were to direct the uprising in Milan were financed by the Carbonari treasury; that Ercolani, the prominent Romagnol leader of several secret societies, attended a few meetings of the Brescian-Milanese conspirators; and that Latuada presented the same constitution to St. Agnan in late November, 1814, which he had written "under the Masonic secret" on April 24 are about the only facts that can be gleaned from the testimony of the defendants which in any way connect the clandestine sects with the conspiracy.[132]

---

[129] All eight of these persons were named in both of the above lists.

[130] See Spadoni, *La congiura militare*, pp. 210–211 and 218.

[131] On January 5, 1815, for example, Gerosa stated that the Carbonari had 360,000 members and extended from Paris to Naples (*ibid.*, p. 225.)

[132] Hager report, January 16, 1815, St. A. (Vienna), Kabinets-Akten, 1815, ad No. 339; Della Porta report, Milan, January 26, 1815, Luzio, *La Massoneria e il Risorgimento italiano*, Vol. I, Appendix V, pp. 98–111; *Biblioteca Ambrosiana*

Since the prisoners talked so freely about other details of the conspiracy, it seems logical to suspect that the main reason why they gave so little definite information about the part played by the clandestine sects is that at the most it was a very minor one. Certainly the Habsburg court official who wrote in 1824 that the secret societies plotted the Brescian-Milanese conspiracy[133] was guilty of gross exaggeration. It is also very difficult for anyone who has read the trial records to accept Alessandro Luzio's thesis that the conspiracy "was of a specifically Masonic character."[134] This writer believes that Piero Pieri has come the closest to the truth when he wrote: "These first conspiracies did not emanate from the occult direction of a sect, but almost all of the conspirators belonged to sects" and "used the sectarian secret."[135] While some of the ringleaders undoubtedly belonged to the Centri, the Carbonari, the Freemasons, and perhaps even the Perfect Sublime Masters, officially at least these organizations took no actual part in directing the enterprise. Whatever aid, if any, which they may have given the plotters was certainly insignificant. In short, the Brescian-Milanese conspiracy was little more than a plot of discontented officers, aided and abetted by a sprinkling of dissatisfied citizens.

(Milan), "Atto d'accusa contro Giovanni Soveri Latuada ecc." Fos. 48, 50, and 52–55; Trevisan to Bellegarde, Mantua, April 6, 1815, Spadoni, *I giudizi di Mantova*, Appendix, pp. 259–260; testimony given by Cavedoni on December 20, 1814; by Rasori on January 15, 1815; by Gerosa on January 5 and 8, 1815; and by Latuada on January 10, 1815, as summarized in Spadoni, *La congiura militare*, pp. 21, 95–96, 224–225, 232–233, and 235; testimony given by Gasparinetti on February 13, 1815; and by Cavedoni and Ragani on March 25, 1815, as summarized in Spadoni, *I giudizi di Mantova*, pp. 53, 77, and 80.

133 Governo Austriaco, *I Carbonari*, p. 1.
134 Luzio, *La Massoneria e il Risorgimento italiano*, Vol. I, Appendix V, p. 95.
135 Pieri, *Le società segrete ed i moti degli anni 1820–21 e 1831*, p. 67.

Chapter 8

JOACHIM MURAT'S "WAR OF
ITALIAN INDEPENDENCE"

The news of the arrest of the Brescian-Milanese conspirators inspired fear in the ranks of anti-Austrian malcontents, particularly in Brescia and Milan.[1] The large majority of Lombards and Venetians, however, appeared unconcerned about the incarceration of the ringleaders of a plot which, if they mentioned it at all, they ascribed mainly "to the offended *amour-propre* of the generals, who heretofore had the most brilliant hopes, the most lucrative posts, and the largest fixed incomes," and who suddenly faced a sharply reduced style of living.[2] Many champions of peace and tranquillity—and this group constituted a large element, probably a substantial majority of the populace—were indignant that a machination had been plotted by a few disgruntled officers and expressed satisfaction that these troublesome disturbers of public security had been arrested and imprisoned.[3]

Even so, the winter of 1814–1815 found the Lombards and Venetians far from satisfied with Habsburg rule. Foreign observers from Prussia, the Papal States, Sardinia, and England were disturbed by the antipathy towards Austria and the pro-independence spirit in Habsburg-dominated Italy. From Berlin Barthold Georg Niebuhr, the distinguished historian of ancient Rome, wrote that Habsburg

[1] See anonymous report to Hager, Vienna, January 8, 1815, Weil, *Les dessous du Congrès de Vienne*, Vol. II, p. 19; Angelo Ottolini, "U. Foscolo e la risoluzione dell'esilio," *Archivio storico lombardo*, Vol. LV (1928), p. 173; [Belgiojoso-Trivulzio], *Étude sur l'histoire de la Lombardie*, p. 127.

[2] Hager to Metternich, Vienna, December 28, 1814, Lemmi, *La restaurazione austriaca a Milano*, Appendix LXXI, p. 493.

[3] Cheluzzi to Roschmann, Milan, December 5, 1814, *ibid.*, Appendix XLVII, p. 462.

misrule was forcing the Italians to take refuge in a spirit of revolt.[4] Baron Karl von Nostritz recorded that travelers from Italy nearly always spoke of the great aversion for the Austrians and "of the agitation and striving towards independence."[5] Cardinal Consalvi expressed his concern over the magnitude of the popular discontent with the existing government.[6] From London the Sardinian minister d'Agliè cautioned his superior in Turin that the "fermentation in Lombardy and in a great part of Italy ought to be a subject of worry for us, for where there is fire in the house one can not foresee where it will stop burning."[7] Burghersh wrote Castlereagh from Florence that "in Lombardy, at Milan, where the Austrians are pursuing a system of holding the people through intimidation and force rather than trying to attract and flatter them and to win them over, the idea of independence was almost general among all those who want to put an end to this regime."[8]

Habsburg officials in Italy also warned the government in Vienna "that the public in general is discontented."[9] Secret informers disclosed new plots. A certain Luigi Sprocani came to Police Director Raab with a tale about an ominous machination allegedly headed by former Minister of War Fontanelli and the ex-prefect of Verona Smancini to plunge all Lombardy and Venetia into a bloody revolution as soon as the Congress of Vienna ended.[10] From Paris the ever

---

[4] In letters sent from Berlin to Marcard on January 10, 1815, and to Dore Hensler on January 20, 1815, Dietrich Gerhard and William Norvin (eds.), *Die Briefe Barthold Georg Niebuhrs*, Vol. II, pp. 546–547 and 553.

[5] See the notes of Baron von Nostritz, January, 1815, Frederick Freksa, *A Peace Congress of Intrigue* (*A Vivid, Intimate Account of the Congress of Vienna Composed of the Personal Memoirs of Its Important Participants*), pp. 119–120.

[6] In a letter from Vienna to Cardinal Pacca on February 25, 1815, P. Ilario Rinieri, *Corrispondenza inedita dei cardinali Consalvi e Pacca nel tempo del Congresso di Vienna (1814–1815); ricavata dall'archivio secreto vaticano, corredata di sommarii e note. Preceduta da uno studio storico sugli stati d'Europa nel tempo dell'impero napoleonico, e sul nuovo assestamento europeo e da un diario inedito del Mse. di San Marzano*, pp. 293–319.

[7] In a letter which he sent to Saint-Marsan on January 27, 1815, Weil, *Les dessous du Congrès de Vienne*, Vol. II, p. 205.

[8] In a letter dated January 31, 1815, as quoted in Weil, *Murat*, Vol. II, p. 347.

[9] Raab to Hager, Venice, December 9, 1814, Lemmi, *La restaurazione austriaca a Milano*, Appendix LII, p. 469.

[10] Reuss-Plauen to Bellegarde, Venice, December 20, 1814, A. S. (Venice), Presidio di governo, 1814, No. 2307; Reuss-Plauen to Hager, Venice, December 20, 1814, *ibid.*

alert Bombelles revealed that the malcontents in France were in secret correspondence with those in Milan and other places in Italy.[11]
Other confidants avowed to Von Hager that a general revolt was
ready to break out in Italy at any minute.[12]

Even though most of the reports, whether those of foreign observers or those of secret informers, were very probably based on rumors,
hopes, or fears, there is no denying that considerable animadversion
was voiced against the Austrian provisional regime in Lombardy in
late 1814 and early 1815. The officers and soldiers of the former Italian army were bitterly anti-Austrian.[13] There was also considerable
dissatisfaction with Habsburg rule among the former French-Italian
government employees, the liberal nobility, and the middle class
business, commercial, and professional people in Lombardy. Some of
the government functionaries had lost their jobs, and those who remained at their posts looked with dismay at the Austrian pay scale
and promotion practices. The liberal nobility and the better educated
and more prosperous bourgeoisie, who had enjoyed the emoluments
of a favored class under the Napoleonic regime, looked with scorn at
the new favorites, the old nobility and the clergy, who understand-
ably demanded the immediate restoration of their former honors and
privileges. Even though during the last days of the Napoleonic Kingdom of Italy the business and commercial groups had loudly denounced the economic oppressions of their French masters, they
feared substantial financial losses now that Milan was a relatively
unimportant provincial capital. The intelligentsia abhorred the Habsburg censorship and deplored the introduction of the Austrian school
system. Those who had criticized the French officials for their harshness and inflexibility took offense at Vice-President Rosetti's abrupt-
ness in dealing with subordinate officials. Those who had admired
the efficiency of the French administration ridiculed the inefficiency
and unwieldiness of the Habsburg provisional administration; and
those who had disapproved of the arbitrariness and ruthlessness of
their former masters were disturbed by the continuance of police

[11] Council of war to Bellegarde, Vienna, January 11, 1815, St. A. (Vienna),
Staatskanzlei, Provinzen, Lombardei-Venedig, Fasz. IV, Kon. 1, Fos. 4 and 4a.
[12] See, for instance, anonymous to Hager, Vienna, November 20, 1814, Weil,
Les dessous du Congrès de Vienne, Vol. I, p. 567.
[13] Secret report, Venice, November 28, 1814, Lemmi, La restaurazione austriaca a Milano, Appendix XLV, pp. 457–458; police report, Milan, December 25,
1814, Kriegs-Archiv (Vienna), Feld Akten (Italien), 1814, Fasz. XII, No. 39.

regimentation and the seeming inability of the Habsburgs to check thievery and brigandage.[14]

Although these anti-Habsburg groups in Lombardy were unhappy in the winter of 1814–1815, after the miscarriage of the Brescian-Milanese military conspiracy they limited their expressions of displeasure against the Austrians to grumbling and malicious satires.[15] As long as they showed no inclination to engage in overt subversive actions, the Habsburgs had little to fear from them, since the working classes and the great mass of peasants, who constituted the large majority of the inhabitants, were either neutral or pro-Austrian and yearned for the preservation of peace and security.[16]

Even though they were much less prosperous than the Lombards, the Venetians were considerably more Austrophile than their compatriots west of the Mincio. Of course, some Venetians uttered anti-Austrian gibes in private conversations.[17] Furthermore, on at least one occasion the Habsburg police found a sign with the words "Long live our Emperor Napoleon" posted on the Piazza delle Erbe in Verona.[18] Also, they were rather perturbed over the ardent pro-French sentiments manifested by various public officials in Rovigo.[19] However, during the winter of 1814–1815 the grievances of the Venetians were only rarely political in nature; instead, they stemmed from the misery and near-starvation which ensued from disastrous crop failures and the existing commercial stagnation. The public opinion reports from

[14] See anonymous report to Hager, Vienna, January 7, 1815, Weil, *Les dessous du Congrès de Vienne*, Vol. II, p. 20; Raab to Hager, Venice, December 9, 1814, Lemmi, *La restaurazione austriaca a Milano*, Appendix LII, p. 469; Cheluzzi to Roschmann, Milan, December 3, 1814, Weil, *Murat*, Vol. II, p. 500 (also in Lemmi, *La restaurazione austriaca a Milano*, Appendix XLVI, p. 459); and Cusani, *Storia di Milano*, Vol. VII, p. 250.

[15] For an example, see Hager to Bellegarde, Vienna, December 20, 1814, A. S. (Milan), Presidenza di governo. Atti secreti, 1814, Cart. VII, No. 1005/P.R.

[16] Cheluzzi was right when he wrote Roschmann from Milan on December 5, 1814, that "the *large majority of Milanese* not only disapprove of every project for a rebellion, but *would in every case be ready to risk their lives to maintain the existing system*" (as published in Lemmi, *La restaurazione austriaca a Milano*, Appendix XLVII, p. 462). The italics are in the copy in Lemmi.

[17] See, for example, the entry of January 23, 1815, in *Museo* (Venice), "Diario di Cicogna," p. 2081.

[18] Raab to Reuss-Plauen, Venice, January 19, 1815, A. S. (Venice), Presidio di governo, 1815–1819, Polizia, Fasz. II 5/13, No. 61.

[19] Reuss-Plauen to Hager, Venice, December 12, 1814, A. S. (Venice), Presidio di governo, 1814, No. 1903–2026–2028–2049/P.P.

the various departments of Venetia were full of complaints about the lack of jobs, the desperate poverty and squalor of the inhabitants of numerous towns and villages, the high prices of foodstuffs, the rapaciousness of speculators, the onerous tax burden, and the pitilessness of the authorities in sequestering the personal goods of impoverished wretches who were delinquent in their tax payments. Although warning voices were raised that the "pro-independence party" could easily take advantage of the desperation of the inhabitants to stir them up against their new rulers, the writers of the reports emphasized that, in spite of their hopeless plight, the Venetians were on the whole surprisingly pro-Austrian and loyal to their Habsburg sovereign.[20]

Although the large majority of Lombards and Venetians were undoubtedly still pro-Austrian, there was enough inflammable material in these provinces to attract impetuous and self-seeking adventurers to seek to light the fuse. Chief among them was the restless and scheming king of Naples. Since Murat's inordinate ambitions, mercurial temperament, and penchant for intrigue were well known by all cabinets of Europe, various high-ranking figures assumed that the Neapolitan sovereign had in some way been connected with the Brescian-Milanese conspiracy. Malicious gossipers in Vienna circulated an unfounded rumor that, in order to curry favor with the Habsburgs for the purpose of insuring his continuance on the throne of Naples, Murat himself had denounced the conspiracy to the Austrians.[21] Others argued that Murat must have been fully cognizant

[20] Brenta department political report for December, 1814, Ottolenghi, *Padova e il Dipartimento del Brenta*, Appendix XXIX, p. 454; political report for the departments of Padua, Vicenza, Treviso, Belluno, and Udine for October, 1814, A. S. (Venice), Presidio di governo, 1814, No. 2477; political reports for the Venetian provinces for December, 1814, and for January and February, 1815, A. S. (Venice), Presidio di governo, 1815–1819, Polizia, Fasc. II 10/1, Nos. 94/P.R., 136/P.R., and 221/P.R.; Raab to Reuss-Plauen, Venice, January 19, 1815, *ibid.*, Fasc. II 5/13, No. 61; Hager reports, January 22 and February 25, 1815, St. A. (Vienna), Kabinets-Akten, 1815, Nos. 361 and 427; anonymous report dated Venice, January 30, 1815, *Carte segrete della polizia austriaca in Italia*, Vol. I, p. 33; secret report, Venice, February 22, 1815, Helfert, *Kaiser Franz und die Stiftung des Lombardo-Venetianischen Königreichs*, Appendix IV, p. 551.

[21] Anonymous report to Hager, [Vienna,] December 25, 1814, Lemmi, *La restaurazione austriaca a Milano*, Appendix LXIX, p. 486 (also in Weil, *Murat*, Vol. II, p. 102); Hager to Metternich, Vienna, December 28, 1814, Lemmi, *La restaurazione austriaca a Milano*, Appendix LXXI, p. 493; anonymous reports to Hager, Vienna, December 30, 1814, and February 26, 1815, Weil, *Les dessous du Congrès de Vienne*, Vol. I, pp. 761–762, and Vol. II, p. 256; police report, Milan,

of the plans of the conspirators and must have given his full consent for his own generals to participate in the intrigue. Some went so far as to maintain that he had concocted the plot.[22]

There is no doubt that Murat was aware that discontented officers were conspiring against the Habsburg government in Lombardy-Venetia. However, it is a plain misstatement of fact baldly to asseverate that he personally assisted or encouraged the machinators. The king of Naples still counted on the Austrians to convince the Allied Powers that he should be allowed to retain the Neapolitan crown. He instructed his foreign minister on November 26—three weeks after Gifflenga had first exposed the Brescian-Milanese conspiracy and eleven days after the Sardinian foreign minister had sent Bellegarde an account of the general's conversations with the plotters in Milan— to warn the Austrian minister in Naples that trouble was brewing. Specifically, he stated that, to Murat's great displeasure and without his prior knowledge, a conspiracy was afoot to circulate proclamations in favor of Italian independence in which the king of Naples was referred to "as the only chief who was capable of directing and making such a project succeed."[23] A few days earlier Murat had instructed General Carascosa to inform Bellegarde that the troops under his command at Ancona had been ordered to cooperate with him in case any unforeseen emergency arose which would make such assistance useful to the Habsburg commander-in-chief.[24] After learning of this offer, Bellegarde was convinced that Murat definitely knew that trouble was brewing in Lombardy, although he strongly suspected that his proffer of help was only a ruse to save himself in

December 3, 1814, *Kriegs-Archiv* (Vienna), Feld Akten (Italien), 1814, Fasz. XII, No. 5; Weil, *Murat*, Vol. II, pp. 97–98 and 104–105.

[22] Anonymous report to Hager, [Vienna,] December 25, 1814, Lemmi, *La restaurazione austriaca a Milano*, Appendix LXIX, p. 486 (also in Weil, *Murat*, Vol. II, p. 102); Hager to Metternich, Vienna, December 28, 1814, Lemmi, *La restaurazione austriaca a Milano*, Appendix LXX, p. 493; Bellegarde to Metternich, Milan, December 5, 1814, St. A. (Vienna), Staatskanzlei, Provinzen, Lombardei-Venedig, Fasz. III, Kon. 4, Fos. 194–195 (also in Weil, *Murat*, Vol. II, Appendix VII, p. 498); police report, Milan, December 3, 1814, *Kriegs-Archiv* (Vienna), Feld Akten (Italien), 1814, Fasz. XII, No. 5.

[23] Murat to Duke de Gallo, San Leucio, November 26, 1814, Weil, *Murat*, Vol. II, p. 100.

[24] Carascosa to Bellegarde, Ancona, November 25, 1814, *ibid.*, Appendix XIII, pp. 530–531.

case the Congress of Vienna decided not to leave him on the throne of Naples.[25]

The testimony of the Brescian-Milanese conspirators confirms the validity of the field marshal's conclusions. The confessions of the ringleaders of the plot indicate that Murat knew about the conspiracy. Nonetheless, the crafty king of Naples rejected the pleas of the machinators for assistance, though not so emphatically that he could not change his mind later if unexpected circumstances developed which might make it beneficial for him to aid the plotters. Furthermore, it appears that some of his military officers like General Carascosa convinced the conspirators that they would personally support the enterprise regardless of what their king ordered.[26]

The wily Murat refused to encourage the Brescian-Milanese conspirators to rebel against the Habsburgs only because he felt that their plot was ill-conceived and foolhardy.[27] In actual fact, Napoleon's double-dealing former marshal had been fishing in troubled waters in Italy for some time before the Brescian-Milanese conspirators concocted their own project for revolt.[28] The Habsburg police had long suspected that some of the unusually large number of Neapolitan travelers in Lombardy had been instructed to go there by their king for the deliberate purpose of intriguing against the Austrians.[29]

[25] Bellegarde to Metternich, Milan, December 5, 1814, St. A. (Vienna), Staatskanzlei, Provinzen, Lombardei-Venedig, Fasz. III, Kon. 4, Fos. 194–195 (also in Weil, *Murat*, Vol. II, Appendix VII, p. 498).

[26] Della Porta report, Milan, January 26, 1815, Luzio, *La Massoneria e il Risorgimento italiano*, Vol. I, Appendix V, pp. 101–102; *Biblioteca Ambrosiana* (Milan), "Atto d'accusa contro Giovanni Soveri Latuada ecc.," Fo. 50; testimony given by Lechi on December 29, 1814, as summarized in Spadoni, *La congiura militare*, p. 61; testimony given by Gasparinetti on February 13, 1815, and by Ragani and Latuada on March 29, 1815, as summarized in Spadoni, *I giudizi di Mantova*, pp. 52–53 and 81; Ghisilieri to Hager, Milan, December 7 and 8, 1814, Lemmi, *La restaurazione austriaca a Milano*, Appendix L, p. 467, and Appendix LI, pp. 467–468; Raab to Hager, Venice, December 9, 1814, *ibid.*, Appendix LII, p. 469.

[27] Domenico Spadoni, "Nel centenario del proclama di Rimini," *Rassegna storica del Risorgimento*, Vol. II, Fasc. 2 (March–April, 1915), p. 349.

[28] See *ante*, p. 188.

[29] Police report, Milan, October 24, 1814, *Kriegs-Archiv* (Vienna), Feld Akten (Italien), 1814, Fasz. X, No. 58; Bellegarde to Hager, Milan, November 22, 1814, Lemmi, *La restaurazione austriaca a Milano*, Appendix XLIII, pp. 454–455; secret report, Venice, February 22, 1815, Helfert, *Kaiser Franz und die*

Murat's propaganda activities in behalf of national independence inevitably had some influence on malcontents in Italy, including Lombardy-Venetia. When the Austrians first assumed control of Lombardy-Venetia the majority of partisans of liberalism were willing to settle for a wide degree of autonomy within the Habsburg monarchy. As time went on a small group of extremists among them objected to remaining under Habsburg rule in any form. By early fall it was apparent that the most bitter Austrophobes were divided into two camps: a minority who wanted independence under British protection and a larger number who responded favorably to the strident liberalism and nationalism championed by Murat.[30] From the confidential reports collected by the Habsburg police, it would appear that by the winter of 1814–1815 most of the enemies of Austria were in the pro-Murat camp. These included a sprinkling of dreamers, a number of honest liberals who were disillusioned with Habsburg policies and practices, a handful of government officials, former admirers of Napoleon, the members of the secret societies, and practically all the officers and soldiers of the former Italian army.[31]

Often transmitted by gullible and sometimes avaricious informers whose chief aim in many cases was to ingratiate themselves with the Austrians, these secret reports were probably grossly exaggerated. Nonetheless, warnings of serious unrest and of Murat's dangerous intrigues arrived in Von Hager's office frequently enough to alarm the Habsburgs. They feared that if an opportune moment arrived, the king of Naples might launch a campaign to entice all malcontents in the Apennine peninsula to join his cause. Their uneasiness over the intentions of the cunning Neapolitan king changed to extreme anxiety as they received more and more messages that he was openly

---

Stiftung des Lombardo-Venetianischen Königreichs, Appendix IV, pp. 551–552; Castro, *Milano e le cospirizioni lombarde*, p. 169; Castro, "La restaurazione austriaca a Milano," p. 647; Francesco Lemmi, "Gioacchino Murat e le aspirazioni unitarie nel 1815," *Archivio storico per le province napoletane*, Vol. XXVI (1901), p. 181; Wiedemann-Warnhelm, *Die Wiederherstellung der österreichischen Vorherrschaft in Italien*, p. 61.

[30] Bellegarde to Metternich, September 22, 1814, as quoted in Weil, *Murat*, Vol. I, p. 381. See also Pingaud, "La Lombardie en 1814," p. 462.

[31] Secret report, Venice, February 22, 1815, Helfert, *Kaiser Franz und die Stiftung des Lombardo-Venetianischen Königreichs*, Appendix IV, pp. 551–552; Freddi to Hager, Vienna, December 25, 1814, Weil, *Les dessous du Congrès de Vienne*, Vol. I, p. 732; note to Hager, Vienna, March 3, 1815, *ibid.*, Vol. II, p. 278; Weil, *Murat*, Vol. I, p. 439; Pingaud "La Lombardie en 1814," p. 462.

talking about waging a war of independence and making himself king of a united Italy.[32] The reports that he was inviting an increasing number of Italian soldiers from Lombardy-Venetia and elsewhere to enlist in his own army,[33] that he was seeking to win the British over to his side,[34] and that he was making elaborate preparations for war[35] increased their perturbation.

The Austrians were particularly disturbed over the stories that arms were being transported to the Kingdom of Naples from Habsburg territory. News reached Bellegarde that in July twenty-seven thousand guns from Trieste destined for the king of Naples had arrived in Rimini.[36] The next month Sub-Intendant Benicky, of Rimini, wrote that a large consignment of weapons from Venice had been shipped through that city to Naples.[37] Early in 1815 the Austrians received information that a load of twenty thousand guns was being conveyed from Milan to Ancona for the Neapolitan army.[38]

In all probability some of these shipments consisted of weapons procured for Murat's army by Peccheneda, the Neapolitan consul in Venice. During the spring of 1814, while the city of Venice was blockaded by the Habsburg army and the British navy, Peccheneda, alleging that as an occupying power his government was entitled to

[32] Police report, November 16, 1814, *Kriegs-Archiv* (Vienna), Feld Akten (Italien), 1814, Fasz. XI, No. 27; anonymous report, December 25, 1814, Lemmi, *La restaurazione austriaca a Milano*, Appendix LXIX, pp. 485–486; secret report, Venice, February 22, 1815, Helfert, *Kaiser Franz und die Stiftung des Lombardo-Venetianischen Königreichs*, Appendix IV, pp. 550–551; Lemmi, "Gioacchino Murat e le aspirazioni unitarie," p. 181; Helfert, *La caduta della dominazione francese*, p. 212.

[33] Reuss-Plauen to general governments of Illyria and Trieste, Venice, January 3, 1815, A. S. (Venice), Presidio di governo, 1814, No. 2417; Weil, *Murat*, Vol. I, p. 439; Wiedemann-Warnhelm, *Die Wiederherstellung der österreichischen Vorherrschaft in Italien*, p. 61.

[34] Police report, November 16, 1814, *Kriegs-Archiv* (Vienna), Feld Akten (Italien), 1814, Fasz. XI, No. 27; Weil, *Murat*, Vol. I, pp. 203–209.

[35] Hager to Reuss-Plauen, Vienna, September 10, 1814, A. S. (Venice), Presidio di governo, 1814, No. 1239; Reuss-Plauen to Raab, Venice, December 2, 1814, *ibid.*, No. 2114; Weil, *Murat*, Vol. I, pp. 207–208, 366, and 497; Helfert, *La caduta della dominazione francese*, p. 213.

[36] General police directory report to Bellegarde, Milan, August 3, 1814, A. S. (Milan), Presidenza di governo. Atti secreti, 1814, Cart. II, No. 160/P.R.

[37] Bellegarde to Reuss-Plauen, Milan, September 23, 1814, A. S. (Venice), Presidio di governo, 1815–1819, Polizia, Fasz. II 4/1, No. 1982.

[38] Torresani to presidency of the military government, Venice, March 27, 1815, *ibid.*, No. 1115/P.P.

a substantial quantity of arms and ammunition, traveled around the Venetian countryside demanding that thousands of weapons of various kinds be turned over to him. When the Austrians protested such actions, the Neapolitan consul resorted to purchasing what he could lay his hands on. Finally, after the Austrian authorities forbade him to buy arms and issued a decree prohibiting the export of military weapons, Peccheneda gave solemn assurances that he would no longer purchase guns. Nonetheless, in spite of the consul's protestations of future correct behavior, the Austrian police were still collecting evidence that he was continuing secretly to purchase arms and smuggle them out of the country. As a result the government in Vienna issued a formal protest to the Neapolitan foreign minister.[39]

With alarming reports about Murat's hostile intentions and his intrigues with the Carbonari and other secret societies coming to Vienna, the Habsburg government became more and more nervous over the prospect of eventual involvement in an armed conflict with the wily and ambitious king. Highly suspicious that Napoleon's betrayer might turn against Austria at any moment, the cabinet in Vienna readied measures to deal with such a contingency. The Habsburg court instructed the authorities in Venetia to prepare a detailed report on the actual strength of Murat's army and the extent of his war preparations.[40] Also it requested them to compile a list of all persons who had recently journeyed to Ancona, presumably to go on from there to Naples, or who had expressed any intention of traveling there.[41] Then, estimating that Murat had an army of sixty thousand men at his disposal, of whom twenty thousand were located in the March of Ancona, in contrast to the fewer than thirty-five thousand troops which the Habsburgs had stationed in Italy, the Austrian gov-

---

[39] Marchal to Reuss-Plauen, Venice, August 21, 1814, *ibid.*, No. 500/P.P.; Bellegarde to Reuss-Plauen, Milan, September 23, 1814, *ibid.*, No. 1361/P.P.; Guicciardi to Reuss-Plauen, Vienna, January 27, 1815, *ibid.*, No. 500/P.P.; Raab to presidency of the Venetian government, Venice, March 17, 1815, *ibid.*, No. 983/P.P.; Torresani to presidency of the military government, Venice, March 27, 1815, *ibid.*, No. 1115/P.P.; Raab to Reuss-Plauen, Venice, August 25, 1814, A. S. (Venice), Presidio di governo, 1814, No. 994/P.R.; Barbaro to Reuss-Plauen, Venice, October 6, 1814, *ibid.*, No. 1466; minutes of the presidency of the Venetian government, October 9, 1814, *ibid.*, No. 1500/P.R.; Reuss-Plauen to Lazanzky, Venice, October 16, 1814, *ibid.*, No. 1474.

[40] Hager to Reuss-Plauen, Vienna, September 10, 1814, A. S. (Venice), Presidio di governo, 1814, No. 1239.

[41] Castro, *Milano e le cospirazioni lombarde*, p. 170.

ernment, on February 23, 1815, ordered a number of its regiments to Italy to reinforce the troops already there.[42]

What troubled Austria and the other Allied Powers most about Murat's intentions was their growing apprehension that he had a covert understanding that Napoleon would aid him in conquering the whole Apennine peninsula when the propitious moment arrived for the former French emperor to escape from Elba.[43] They were fully aware that Napoleon was in touch with various Italian and French malcontents[44] and strongly suspected that shortly after he was enthroned in Elba he had patched up his quarrel with the king of Naples.[45] During the winter of 1814–1815 as the reports about Napoleon and Murat's clandestine contacts multiplied[46] and the rumors increased that Napoleon would soon make a concerted effort to conquer Italy with the help of the king of Naples, the secret societies, and others, Austrian misgivings grew. The pseudo-oil merchant—the confidant in the pay of the French consul at Leghorn who was consorting with Napoleon's intimates at Elba—notified his emperor that preparations had been readied for the ex-emperor to proclaim himself king of Italy and perhaps also to wage war against the restored Bourbons of France. The officers for this enterprise had already been selected, and detailed plans had been agreed upon to precipitate a revolution in Italy as assistance to Napoleon's troops when they invaded the peninsula. The revolution, the oil merchant cautioned, was scheduled to break out in March at the latest.[47] The Florentine police and others who pretended to have inside information were also warning that Napoleon, in league with Murat and numerous Italian revolutionaries, was preparing to incite a spirit of revolt and to wage a war in Italy at the first opportune moment.[48]

The writers of these reports were correct in predicting that Napoleon was planning to leave his island retreat; they were wrong in surmising that he intended to exchange the crown of Elba for that of

[42] Weil, Murat, Vol. II, pp. 350, 412, 415, and 416–417.

[43] See also Helfert, Joachim Murat, pp. 33–34.

[44] See ante, pp. 180–187.

[45] See also Pellet, Napoléon à l'île d'Elbe, pp. 60 and 62.

[46] Journal of the oil merchant, January 6, 1815, ibid., Appendix VII, p. 147; Livi, Napoleone all'isola d'Elba, pp. 142, 155, 175, and 179.

[47] Journal of the oil merchant, December 27 and 31, 1814, and January 6, 1815, Pellet, Napoléon à l'île d'Elbe, Appendix VII, pp. 136, 142, and 146–148.

[48] Livi, Napoleone all'isola d'Elba, pp. 141–142, 175–177, and 179; Houssaye, 1815, p. 180.

Italy. Although he had encouraged Italian sympathizers to believe that they could reckon on his assistance, Napoleon cherished the dream, not of subjugating Italy, but of conquering France.[49] In working out last minute details to obtain much needed succor from his erstwhile marshal, he greatly increased his correspondence with Naples during the busy weeks preceding his departure from his inhospitable prison. Between February 17 and 22 alone the fake oil merchant mentioned five different messengers who had gone to or arrived from the Neapolitan capital.[50] What Napoleon had in mind was not a joint French-Neapolitan offensive in Italy, from which the king of Naples could draw rich benefits, but an attack on France itself. When he sent Colonna d'Istria to Naples to inform Murat of his resolution to leave Elba for France he instructed him to counsel the ambitious Neapolitan king not to commence an all-out attack on the Habsburg army in the Apennine peninsula. Instead, as soon as he heard of Napoleon's departure, he was to place his army of sixty thousand troops in readiness to immobilize as many Austrian divisions as possible in Italy, to dispatch a confidential agent to Vienna to assure Emperor Francis' government of his peaceful intentions, and patiently to await the outcome of Napoleon's own ambitious venture.[51]

Murat did carry out the second of Napoleon's requests. When he learned on March 4 that Napoleon had escaped from Elba on the night of February 26–27 he reaffirmed his loyalty to the Austrians, regardless of the outcome of the former French emperor's undertaking. He was too impetuous, however, to heed his former mentor's sagacious advice not to advance across the frontiers of his own kingdom but merely to hold his troops in readiness near the border and wait to see what would happen. Having no positive guarantees that the Allied Powers at the Congress of Vienna would allow him to remain on the throne of Naples, mistakenly fancying that Napoleon would again make himself the arbiter of Europe, deluding himself into believing that the discontent against the restored monarchs of Italy was so widespread that legions of malcontents would follow him if he became their champion, and completely overestimating the

---

[49] See *ante*, p. 186; and Houssaye, *1815*, pp. 179–180.

[50] Journal of the oil merchant, February 17, 18, 19, 20, 21, and 22, Pellet, *Napoléon à l'île d'Elbe*, Appendix VII, pp. 152, 152–153, 156, 158, and 160.

[51] Napoleon I, "L'île d'Elbe et les cent-jours," p. 40; *Mémoires de Marchand*, Vol. I, p. 86.

strength and discipline of his own army, Murat decided on March 18 —against the advice of his queen, most of his ministers, friends, and advisers—to order part of his troops to march in two columns through the Papal States and Tuscany towards the Po.[52]

After these forces were well on their way, he issued a decree, an order of the day, and a proclamation at Rimini on March 30 in which he flung down the gauntlet at Austria. In the decree he declared the annexation of the Marches and the districts of Pesaro, Urbino, and Gubbio to the Kingdom of Naples.[53] In the order of the day he exhorted the soldiers of his army to wage a holy national war against the oppressor of Italian provinces the inhabitants of which "are calling loudly for arms to avenge the honor of the Italian name." They were to be delivered "from the forever detested yoke of Austria," a faithless and perfidious enemy "which has violated the sacred faith of treaties" and "turned its armies against us in order to support our eternal and implacable enemies."[54] The proclamation was addressed to the Italian people. Announcing to them that the hour had struck when "Providence is at last calling upon you to be an independent nation," Murat appealed to the Italians to join the eighty thousand Neapolitan soldiers commanded by a king who had vowed not to stop fighting until all Italy, from the Alps to the seas, was liberated and to take up arms to free their beautiful fatherland from foreign yoke and establish "a government of our choice, a truly national representation," and "a constitution worthy of the century and of

[52] Colletta, *Storia del reame di Napoli*, Vol. II, pp. 182–186; Lemmi. "Gioacchino Murat e le aspirazioni unitarie," pp. 182–191; Helfert, *Joachim Murat*, pp. 35–48; Weil, *Murat*, Vol. III, pp. 26–34, 41–66, 106–121, 128–144, 181–183, and 188–196; Pompilio Schiarini, "La prima impresa per l'indipendenza italiana e la battaglia di Tolentino," *Atti e memorie della R. Deputazione di Storia Patria per le Marche*, new ser., Vol. X, Fasc. 2 (May-December, 1915), pp. 228 and 237–238; Spadoni, "Nel centenario del proclama di Rimini," pp. 346, 350–352, and 354; Orloff, *Mémoires sur le royaume de Naples*, Vol. II, pp. 262–263; Bruto Amante, *I napoletani nel 1815. La prima guerra per l'unità d'Italia*, pp. 24–25; Colletta to Murat, Naples, March 11, 1815, F. Palermo, "Pietro Colletta, uomo di stato e scrittore," *Archivio storico italiano*, new ser., Vol. III, Pt. 1 (1856), pp. 63–64.

[53] Colletta, *Storia del reame di Napoli*, Vol. II, p. 186; Helfert, *Joachim Murat*, p. 49.

[54] Murat, order of the day to his army, Rimini, March 30, 1815, Weil, *Murat*, Vol. III, Appendix XXI, pp. 506–507.

you."[55] Within the next few days a number of Murat's officials issued similar appeals to such diverse groups as the inhabitants of the departments of Reno, Rubicone, Basso Po, and Panaro; the citizens of Rimini, Faenza, Forlì, Cesena, and Bologna; and the students of the Universities of Bologna and Modena entreating them to join the Neapolitan monarch in his holy battle for national redemption.[56]

Murat's war preparations, of which the Austrians were fully aware, deeply worried Habsburg officials in Italy. Having gradually withdrawn their troops and much equipment from the Apennine peninsula during the past six months, they estimated that there were only between eight and twenty thousand soldiers and seventy-eight cannon available to oppose the king of Naples, and all possible reinforcements were a considerable distance away.[57] To get ready for the eventuality of a war against the impetuous Neapolitan sovereign, the supreme war council hurriedly ordered reinforcements from neighboring areas to march to Italy and commanded Lieutenant Field Marshal Friedrich Bianchi to hasten there to make a thorough investigation of all available military forces and fortifications in the area. Lieutenant Field Marshal Nugent was called upon to direct special operations in Tuscany, and General Johann Frimont was ordered to assume supreme command of all Austrian troops in the Apennine

[55] Murat, proclamation to the Italians, Rimini, March 30, 1815, St. A. (Vienna), Staatskanzlei, Provinzen, Lombardei-Venedig, Fasz. IV, Kon. 2, Fos. 131–132. Copies of the complete text of the proclamation can also be found in Gualterio, *Gli ultimi rivolgimenti italiani*, Vol. I, *Documenti*, pp. 127–129; Weil, *Murat*, Vol. III, Appendix XX, pp. 504–506; and Amante, *I napoletani nel 1815*, pp. 25–27. The actual authorship of this stirring proclamation has been attributed by various writers to such different persons as Salfi, Poerio, Manzi, Carascosa, and Pellegrino Rossi. See Leti, *Carbonaria e Massoneria*, p. 63; and Spadoni, "Nel centenario del proclama di Rimini," pp. 356–359.

[56] See Rossi, proclamation, Bologna, April 4, 1815, Domenico Spadoni, *Per la prima guerra d'indipendenza italiana nel 1815. Proclami, decreti, appelli, ed inni*, p. 94; Lemmi, "Gioacchino Murat et le aspirazioni unitarie," pp. 191–194; Amante, *I napoletani nel 1815*, pp. 27–28; and Albano Sorbelli, "Gli studenti bolognesi per Gioacchino Murat e per l'indipendenza italiana nel 1815," *L'Archiginnasio. Bollettino della Biblioteca comunale di Bologna*, Vol. XI (1916), pp. 203 and 206–208.

[57] Reports to Hager, March 4 and 8, 1815, Weil, *Les dessous du Congrès de Vienne*, Vol. II, pp. 283–284 and 300; Bellegarde to Metternich, Milan, March 17, 1815, St. A. (Vienna), Staatskanzlei, Provinzen, Lombardei-Venedig, Fasz. IV, Kon. 2, Fo. 65; Weil, *Murat*, Vol. III, pp. 96 and 125–127.

peninsula. Bellegarde was instructed as quickly as possible to prepare defensive positions along the Po River and in the citadel of Ferrara. Italian officers not in active service, including Generals Bonfanti, Peyri, Severoli, Ballabio, and Livio Galimberti, were given posts at the ranks which they had previously held. In case Murat began hostilities, General Airone Joseph Steffanini, who was stationed at Bologna, was instructed to withdraw his troops to the Po as slowly as possible. If war broke out, the Austrians planned to make a stand at Ferrara and on the Po River until enough reinforcements could be brought in from the interior of the monarchy to begin an effective counteroffensive.[58]

When the fighting began the Habsburgs had a total of sixty-nine thousand troops stationed in Italy, but they were scattered in such widely separated places as the Valtelline, Milan, Piacenza, Parma, Mantua, Verona, Udine, Venice, Turin, Bologna, Lucca, and Piombino. Probably only between eighteen and twenty thousand men were immediately available to fight the king of Naples.

The paper strength of Murat's army amounted to almost eighty-two thousand men. However, when he began to mobilize his troops against the Austrians he could muster no more than fifty-two thousand soldiers, of whom only about twenty-four thousand were actually available at the beginning of his military operations.[59]

In line with the Austrian campaign plan, General Steffanini ordered the detachments under his command to retreat before the oncoming Neapolitans without allowing themselves to be lured into open battle. When General Carascosa attacked Cesena on March 30, the twenty-five hundred Austrians stationed there retreated to Forlì and then, when again pressed, to Faenza, Imola, and Bologna. When General Guglielmo Pepe approached Bologna on April 2, General Bianchi, who had taken over command shortly before, quietly sent the Habsburg troops in and around that city to Cento and Modena. It was not until General Carascosa got ready to cross the Panaro River on April 4 to capture Modena that Bianchi decided to resist

[58] Allgemeine Zeitung. Mit allerhöchsten Privilegien, Nos. 102 and 103 (April 12 and 13, 1815), pp. 411 and 415; Helfert, Kaiser Franz und die Stiftung des Lombardo-Venetianischen Königreichs, pp. 177–178; Oreste Dito, La campagna murattiana della indipendenza d'Italia secondo i rapporti del Ministro di Polizia Napoletana ed altri documenti ufficiali. Con un'appendice sulla morte del Murat a Pizzo, pp. 22–23; Weil, Murat, Vol. III, pp. 8–10, 36–41, 95–99, and 126–127.
[59] Weil, Murat, Vol. III, pp. 92 and 100.

the advancing enemy troops. After a show of determined resistance in the face of a furious Neapolitan onslaught at Spilimberto, the Austrians again withdrew in the direction of the Po. In the meantime, other Neapolitan troops occupied Cento and then advanced to Ferrara on April 4. Acting under orders, the Habsburg troops who occupied the citadel refused to yield or retreat. Without waiting until they could be forced to surrender, Murat hurriedly pressed on to fight his way across the Po at Occhiobello. Here the Austrians, in what turned out to be the most decisive battle of the campaign, made an all-out stand on April 7 and 8, finally halted the Neapolitan advance, and kept Murat's forces from crossing the river into Habsburg territory.[60]

Although his troops had managed to march rapidly to the Po, things were going rather badly for Murat's guard detachments under Generals Livron and Strongoli Pignatelli in Tuscany, harassed as they were by a small but highly mobile unit of three thousand men, half of them Tuscans, under General Nugent. Worse, still, while he was at Occhiobello Murat received the jolting news that the British had decided to join the Austrians in their war against him and were threatening to invade his kingdom from Sicily.[61]

Most important of all, the king of Naples learned to his surprise and discouragement that there was very little likelihood of his receiving the strong support from the Italian populace which was vital to the success of his enterprise. Even though his agents continued to issue proclamations in a vain effort to persuade the Italian populace that "the Austrians are the falsest of people,"[62] and although they exhorted them to aid their sovereign in his struggle for their redemption,[63] only a Liliputian minority of implacable Austrophobes

---

[60] Colletta, *Storia del reame di Napoli*, Vol. II, pp. 187–189; Dito, *La campagna murattiana*, pp. 26–29; Orloff, *Mémoires sur le royaume de Naples*, Vol. II, pp. 265–266; Helfert, *Joachim Murat*, pp. 49–51; Weil, *Murat*, Vol. III, pp. 203–204, 248–254, 263–283, 286–289, 293–301, 306–319, 322–329, 334–336, and 345–366; R. M. Johnston, *The Napoleonic Empire in Southern Italy and the Rise of the Secret Societies*, Vol. I, pp. 355–359.

[61] Colletta, *Storia del reame di Napoli*, Vol. II, pp. 189–191; Helfert, *Joachim Murat*, pp. 50–51; Dito, *La campagna murattiana*, p. 31; Weil, *Murat*, Vol. III, pp. 224–225, 254–258, 364, and 388; Amante, *I napoletani nel 1815*, p. 29.

[62] Cook to Stewart, Rome, April 15, 1815, Vane, *Memoirs and Correspondence of Viscount Castlereagh*, Vol. X, p. 311.

[63] Weil, *Murat*, Vol. III, pp. 289–290, 333, and 334.

and enthusiastic nationalists answered Murat's fervent appeals for volunteers.[64]

Murat made glowing promises to officers and soldiers of the army of the former Kingdom of Italy who would fight under his banner. To recruit volunteers among the youth, he established a special commission at Bologna. He ordered his officers and municipal officials in the occupied areas to make a concerted effort to enroll "patriots" in his army by promising jobs to all of them at the end of the war and special rewards if they distinguished themselves during the campaign.[65]

A markedly small number of Italians responded to Murat's exhortations to associate themselves with his "holy cause." There were hardly four hundred according to writers like Pietro Colletta, Pepe,[66] and Helfert;[67] fewer than one thousand according to Giuseppe la Farina;[68] and perhaps a total of between fifteen hundred and two thousand according to Spadoni,[69] who has made the highest estimate which this writer has seen. The Italian people were weary from the long years of fighting under Napoleon and, on the whole, too content with their restored monarchs to second the efforts of a foreign king momentarily ruling the Neapolitans, for whom many of them had little love or respect. Many believed that absorption by the Kingdom of Naples, not the independence of Italy, was at stake. Furthermore, Murat's vague, ill-defined proclamations of independence and liberty reminded even those who were dissatisfied with their own rulers of

64 *Ibid.*, pp. 304, 333, 387, and 405–406; Helfert, *Joachim Murat*, pp. 51–52; Santorre di Santarosa, *Delle speranze degli Italiani. Opera edita per la prima volta con prefazione e documenti inediti da Adolfo Colombo*, p. 38; Schiarini, "La prima impresa per l'indipendenza italiana," p. 232; Orloff, *Mémoires sur le royaume de Naples*, Vol. II, p. 264; Colletta, *Storia del reame di Napoli*, Vol. II, p. 191.

65 Helfert, *Joachim Murat*, p. 51; Murat, decree, Bologna, April 9, 1815, Weil, *Murat*, Vol. III, Appendix XXXII, pp. 532–533; Weil, *Murat*, Vol. III, pp. 301, 333–334, 376, and 385–386; Domenico Spadoni, "I volontari per l'indipendenza italiana nel 1815," *Atti e memorie della R. Deputazione di Storia Patria per le Marche*, new ser., Vol. X, Fasc. 2 (May–December, 1915), pp. 302–307; Sorbelli, "Gli studenti bolognesi per Gioacchino Murat," pp. 206–207; Domenico Spadoni, "Bologna e Pellegrino Rossi per l'indipendenza d'Italia nel 1815," *Rassegna storica del Risorgimento*, Vol. III, Fasc. 1–2 (January–April, 1916), p. 108.

66 Spadoni, "I volontari per l'indipendenza italiana," p. 297.

67 See his *Joachim Murat*, p. 52.

68 Spadoni, "I volontari per l'indipendenza italiana," pp. 297–298.

69 *Ibid.*, p. 310.

similar promises made by the French. Some laughed at the fact that a call for national unity came from an ambitious Frenchman. The overwhelming majority of the populace remained indifferent to Murat's appeals.[70]

Fully aware that it would be foolhardy to continue advancing without the assistance of the guard detachments in Tuscany, with the British on the point of invading his kingdom, and with little prospect of tangible aid from the Italian populace, the king of Naples decided, after his repulse at Occhiobello, to abandon the offensive and retreat. At the same time, the Habsburg commander, who had now received the first of the expected reinforcements from the interior of the monarchy, changed his delaying, rear-guard tactics to a strategy of steady attack.

Two days after the battle of Occhiobello General Bianchi advanced against the Neapolitans at Carpi and forced them to evacuate that place, to withdraw from Modena and Reggio, and to retire behind the Panaro. On April 12 other troops stationed around the bridgehead at Occhiobello assumed the offensive and forced the Neapolitans to give up the siege of the citadel and evacuate Ferrara, which the Austrians entered the next day. On the evening of the 14th, Bianchi launched a surprise attack at Spilimberto and compelled the Neapolitans to retreat from the Panaro in such haste that they left their arms and supplies and fled in great disorder to Bologna, which they were obliged to evacuate on the 16th.

The Austrians now had several armies pushing forward south of the Po. After the Neapolitans were driven out of Bologna, General Frimont decided to divide the main Habsburg military force into two units to continue the pursuit. One army, commanded by General Neipperg, was ordered to follow the king in his retreat through Emilia and along the Adriatic littoral with the seventeen thousand troops at his disposal. General Bianchi, with fourteen thousand, was instructed to march southwestward, through Florence and Umbria, to strike at the enemy's communication lines from the rear and to try to turn the flank of the Neapolitan army near Ancona. Meanwhile, General Nugent was to march quickly towards Rome with his small

[70] See also Schiarini, "La prima impresa per l'indipendenza italiana," pp. 228–232; Santorre di Santarosa, *Delle speranze degli Italiani*, pp. 39–40; Spadoni, "I volontari per l'indipendenza italiana," pp. 298–301; Helfert, *Joachim Murat*, p. 52; Weil, *Murat*, Vol. III, pp. 304 and 387; and Orloff, *Mémoires sur le royaume de Naples*, Vol. II, pp. 264–265.

force operating in Tuscany and then onward to the Neapolitan frontier.

Pursued by Neipperg, Murat, who now was plagued by desertion, lack of discipline, and insubordination in the ranks of his army, found himself constrained to evacuate Imola, Faenza, and Forlì. On April 21 his army was defeated in a battle on the Ronco River near Forlimpopoli. Two days later Murat was back at Rimini. Then, learning about Bianchi's plans to attack him from the rear, he abandoned Rimini and retreated to Pesaro, near which the Austrians inflicted another defeat on the Neapolitans. Leaving his subordinates in charge of his troops, the disconsolate king of Naples went to Ancona on April 29 and then to Macerata the next day. At Macerata he decided to attack Bianchi's army at nearby Tolentino before it could join Neipperg's troops, who were still at Metauro, a four-days' march away. A bloody battle was waged in and around Tolentino between May 2 and 5. For a long time the outcome of the bitter fighting was in doubt. However, when Murat received the unexpected and shocking news during the midst of combat on the third day that General Nugent had just reached Aquila, within the frontiers of his own kingdom, he ordered his troops immediately to fall back on Macerata and proceed in the direction of Naples as rapidly as possible.

The end came quickly after Tolentino. Murat's commissariat had already broken down, the number of deserters was growing daily, the troops were completely demoralized, and various officers and enlisted men were becoming increasingly insubordinate. The king of Naples saw his army veritably disintegrating before his eyes as the Austrians pressed his forces relentlessly. A couple of days after Tolentino the Neapolitan army was in full retreat towards Fondi and then Chieti. On the 14th Murat's troops were on the Volturno, where they were surprised and defeated by the Austrians at Mignano on the night of May 16–17. By that time they numbered fewer than nine thousand.

On the 18th Murat handed over the command of what remained of his army to General Carascosa and hurried to Naples in a desperate effort to save his crown. When he reached his destination he found that to all intents and purposes he was already dethroned. British naval units had appeared in the Gulf of Naples on May 13 and threatened to bombard the city if the forts and arsenal were not immediately turned over to them. On the same day the Neapolitan government had surrendered its fleet to the English. In the capital people had been threatening "Death to Joachim!" for some time before the disconsolate monarch returned, weary and haggard, late on the 18th. In the hope of retrieving the situation, he issued a proclamation granting the inhabitants a constitution. His disgusted subjects ignored it. The next day the downcast and bewildered king rode out of Naples for the last time towards Ischia, from where he intended going to France. He left, an utterly defeated man rejected by a bitter and hostile populace. The Austrians refused to deal with him or his minister the duke of Gallo, who was still loyal to him, about ending hostilities. Instead, when they signed an armistice on May 20 it was with Generals Carascosa and Colletta. Two days later the Austrian army and Prince Leopold, the son of King Ferdinand of the Two Silicies, entered the Neapolitan capital while the capricious inhabitants jubilated. King Ferdinand made a formal entrance into the city on June 7.[71]

In such a reckless manner did Joachim Murat throw away his crown. Had he a year earlier granted the constitution which he announced to his people at the last moment of desperation[72] and had he followed Napoleon's counsel to hold his army in readiness within his own kingdom and patiently await events, he might have remained king of Naples. At least he would have been in a strong position to negotiate with Austria and the other Allied Powers about continuing on the Neapolitan throne in return for positive assurances that he would not support the former French emperor.[73] Instead, the ambitious, impetuous, and foolish Murat threw everything away to follow the dream of becoming king of a united Italy—a dream which no foreigner, certainly not a Frenchman, could ever have hoped to realize.

The king of Naples could not even win over to his national inde-

---

[71] Helfert, *Joachim Murat*, pp. 52–75; Dito, *La campagna murattiana*, pp. 31–78; Amante, *I napoletani nel 1815*, pp. 29–31; Weil, *Murat*, Vol. III, pp. 390–463, Vol. IV, pp. 3–420, and Vol. V, pp. 1–237; Schiarini, "La prima impresa per l'indipendenza italiana," pp. 242–256; Johnston, *The Napoleonic Empire in Southern Italy*, pp. 361–385; Colletta, *Storia del reame di Napoli*, Vol. II, pp. 192–216; *Giornale di Venezia*, No. 103 (April 14, 1815), p. 3, No. 107 (April 18, 1815), pp. 3–4, No. 108 (April 19, 1815), p. 4, No. 110 (April 21, 1815), p. 4, No. 114 (April 25, 1815), p. 4, No. 117 (April 28, 1815), pp. 3–4, No. 118 (April 29, 1815), pp. 3–4, No. 121 (May 2, 1815), pp. 3–4, and No. 131 (May 12, 1815), p. 3.

[72] See Lemmi, "Gioacchino Murat e le aspirazioni unitarie," pp. 169–170.

[73] See also *Mémoires de Marchand*, Vol. I, pp. 155–156.

pendence project the Carbonari, who had a much larger following in Naples and the Papal States than anywhere else in Italy. After originally protecting and favoring them, he came to fear them and began persecuting them, only to find himself confronted with a number of attempted Carbonari revolts against him in the spring of 1814, which prompted him to issue a decree prohibiting the society in his kingdom. Naturally, the Carbonari remained suspicious and aloof when he courted their support during his "war of Italian independence" in the spring of 1815. There is evidence that they even sided with the enemy during his ill-fated campaign. At least, it was rumored that the Carbonari in the Abruzzi sent the Bourbon king of Sicily a substantial sum of money after the war broke out to demonstrate that their sympathies were with him and not with the actual king of Naples. Stories were also current that the Carbonari strove to induce various soldiers to desert the Neapolitan monarch's army.[74]

Disregarding the disputed question of whether Murat's war was a genuine war of Italian independence,[75] one can at least affirm that the king of Naples hoped to utilize the discontented elements and pro-independence and nationalist sentiment in the peninsula to further

[74] Report on the Carbonari by the Prussian consul in Italy, Jacob Solomon Bartoldy, annexed to Saurau to Sedlnitzky, Milan, September 1, 1814, A. S. (Milan), Presidenza di governo. Atti secreti, 1817, Cart. XVI, ad No. 890/geh.; anonymous report enclosed in Goëss to Rainer, Venice, May 25, 1818, St. A. (Vienna), Kabinets-Akten, 1818, ad No. 453; anonymous report, June 30, 1817, St. A. (Vienna), Staatskanzlei, Provinzen, Lombardei-Venedig, Fasz. XL, Kon. 1, Fos. 191–193; Thomas Frost, *The Secret Societies of the European Revolution, 1776–1876*, Vol. I, pp. 224–226; Pieri, *Le società segrete ed i moti degli anni 1820–21 e 1831*, pp. 61–62; *Memoirs of the Carbonari*, pp. 16–17; Fabietti, *I Carbonari*, pp. 66–67.

[75] In 1927, at the Macerata Congress of the National Society for the History of the Italian Risorgimento, Domenico Spadoni argued that Murat's war of 1815 and not the 1848–1849 revolutionary movement was the first war for Italian independence (see his "Quella del 1815 fu veramente la prima guerra per l'indipendenza italiana?" *Atti del XV Congresso Nazionale della Società nazionale per la storia del Risorgimento italiano, tenutosi in Macerata nei giorni 1–2–3 settembre 1927, pp. 121–134*). Bruto Amante has championed the same thesis (see his *I napoletani nel 1815*, p. 10). Antonio Monti, however, maintains that Spadoni and Amante were wrong, for in 1815, he insists, the majority of Italians wanted neither unity nor independence but either were content to be under foreign control or accepted it with resignation (see his "L'impresa di Gioacchino Murat nel 1815 e la prima guerra di indipendenza," *Rendiconti del Reale Istituto lombardo di Scienze e Lettere*, 2nd ser., Vol. LXIII, Fasc. 2 [1930], pp. 191–200).

his own designs. In the words of Richard Weiss von Starkenfels, the Austrian minister at Turin from 1823–1827 and at Rome from 1827–1848,

Murat nurtured . . . the project [of the Carbonari and other secret societies for unification and independence] for the purpose of extending his dominion over all Italy. For this reason and for his own purpose, he voiced the pro-independence ideas and aspirations of the Italians to escape [the charge of] abuse of power by an authoritarian ruler.[76]

Realizing the king of Naples' overweening ambitions but overestimating his appeal to the Italian populace, the Austrians prepared for a long war, readied elaborate arrangements to defend the city of Venice in case Murat's troops attacked it,[77] and took concerted steps to crush revolts which, according to rumors reaching the police, were scheduled to break out in Brescia, Bergamo, Milan, Verona, Mantua, Peschiera, and Legnago.[78] In the hope of counteracting any anti-Austrian feeling which might have been stirred up by Murat's Rimini proclamation, Field Marshal Bellegarde issued a proclamation on April 5, which was posted in all communes in Lombardy-Venetia,[79] in which he scornfully castigated Murat as a foreigner who, for the purpose of realizing his own vainglorious ambitions, tried to plunge Italy into war at a time when the Allied Powers in Vienna were on the point of establishing "the bases for a long peace." Not only that, the Lombard commissioner plenipotentiary continued, but the king of Naples was attempting "to light the devastating fire of revolution everywhere with the help of the vain image of Italian independence, which has already" made it easier for him "to rise from the status of a private to that of sovereign." In his consuming desire to plunge the

[76] Filipuzzi, *Pio IX e la politica austriaca in Italia,* p. 85.

[77] Ottolenghi, *Padova e il Dipartimento del Brenta,* pp. 264–265; Wiedemann-Warnhelm, *Die Wiederherstellung der österreichischen Vorherrschaft in Italien,* pp. 62–63; Torresani to Hager, Venice, March 26, 1815, A. S. (Venice), Presidio di governo, 1815–1819, Polizia, Fasc. II 5/19, No. 1112/P.P.

[78] Hager report, April 5, 1815, St. A. (Vienna), Kabinets-Akten, 1815, No. 854; Torresani to Hager, Venice, March 25 and 26, 1815, A. S. (Venice), Presidio di governo, 1815–1819, Polizia, Fasc. II 5/19, Nos. 1100/P.P. and 1112/P.P.; Marziani to imperial military government, Verona, March 24, 1815, *Kriegs-Archiv* (Vienna), Feld Akten (Frimont in Italien), 1815, Fasz. III, No. 88a.

[79] See, for example, provisional prefect of the Adige department to presidency of the Venetian government, Verona, April 8, 1815, A. S. (Venice), Presidio di governo, 1815–1819, Oggetti politici di stato, Fasc. X 2/6, No. 146/P.R.

Apennine peninsula into a maelstrom of chaos and destruction so that he could attain his aims, he,

as much a total stranger in Italy as a newcomer among rulers, is ostentatiously cultivating a language with the Italians which an Alexander Farnese, an Andrea Doria, and a Trivulzio the Great could hardly have used with them, and is proclaiming himself head of an Italian nation which itself possesses dynasties which have reigned for centuries, and which has seen born in its own beautiful countries that august family which governs so many nations with its restraining paternalism. He, king of the most distant part of Italy, would, with the specious idea of natural boundaries, delude the Italians with the phantasmagoria of a kingdom for which it would be difficult even to determine its capital precisely because nature, with its limitations, has prescribed particular governments for the various parts of Italy and has taught us that, not territorial extent, not the number of people, not the armed forces, but good laws, the preservation of old customs, and an economical administration bring happiness to a people. It is for this reason that the immortal names of Maria Theresa, Joseph, and Leopold are still remembered with admiration and gratitude in Lombardy and in Tuscany.[80]

Even before Bellegarde issued this proclamation the Austrians had instructed the Venetian police to observe closely the Neapolitan consul in Venice.[81] After fighting commenced the Habsburg government broke all diplomatic relations with Naples and ordered the Neapolitan diplomatic and consular personnel, as well as the agents of Murat's government and officers of his army, immediately to leave Austrian territory.[82] All Lombards and Venetians who were serving in the Neapolitan army were enjoined to return home on pain of los-

[80] The writer has found handwritten copies of this proclamation in St. A. (Vienna), Staatskanzlei, Provinzen, Lombardei-Venedig, Fasz. IV, Kon. 2, Fo. 133; and in A. S. (Venice), Presidio di governo, 1815–1819, Oggetti politici di stato, Fasc. X 2/6, No. 1461/P.R. The complete Italian text can also be found in Atti del governo lombardo, 1815, Vol. I, pp. 35–38. A good French translation is in Weil, Murat, Vol. III, Appendix XXVIII, pp. 519–521. The copy printed in Gualterio, Gli ultimi rivolgimenti italiani, Vol. I, Documenti, pp. 129–131, should be used with caution, since in various places it differs substantially from the three Italian texts cited above which this writer has found in the Viennese, Venetian, and Milanese archives.

[81] Torresani to Hager, Venice, March 18, 1815, A. S. (Venice), Presidio di governo, 1815–1819, Polizia, Fasc. II 4/1, No. 983/P.P.

[82] Hager to Goëss, Vienna, April 12, 1815, A. S. (Venice), Presidio di governo, 1815, No. 195/v.b.p.

ing their property or their right to inherit it if they failed to do so.[83] The Austrians cut off communications between Lombardy-Venetia and the areas occupied by Neapolitan troops,[84] forbade entrance into Habsburg territory to visitors from France, Naples, or Neapolitan-held regions, and directed Austrian officials in Italy to refuse passes to persons who wished to travel to France or the Neapolitan states and to keep a close surveillance on all individuals who expressed a desire to go there.[85] French *émigrés* fleeing from their homeland in fear of the newly restored Napoleonic regime were to be granted refuge on Austrian territory only if "their mode of thinking and their past conduct" justified it and then only upon the approval of both the aulic police directory and the aulic chancellery in Vienna.[86] The police were also instructed carefully to observe the actions and behavior of all foreigners and travelers in Lombardy-Venetia, regardless of what country they came from.[87]

Thus, the Austrians took various precautionary steps to keep potential enemy spies and agents out of Lombardy-Venetia. They also initiated extraordinary measures to protect the populace against subversion by hostile native agitators. At the emperor's orders, the police force in Lombardy-Venetia was doubled and the authorities were urged to work quickly and circumspectly to control subversive and revolutionary agitation, uncover any possible machinations, and swiftly repress any tumults that might break out.[88] Special patrols

---

[83] Bellegarde, proclamation, Milan, May 3, 1815, *Atti del governo lombardo*, 1815, Vol. I, pp. 93–94; proclamation, Venice, May 3, 1815, *Collezione di leggi venete*, 1815, Vol. I, pp. 164–165.

[84] Lattermann to Marquis von Chasteler, Padua, April 24, 1815, A. S. (Venice), Presidio di governo, 1815–1819, *Oggetti politici di stato*, Fasc. X ⅔, no number given.

[85] Hager to Goëss, Vienna, March 31, 1815, A. S. (Venice), Presidio di governo, 1815, No. 111/v.b.p.

[86] Goëss to Raab, Venice, May 19, 1815, *Carte segrete della polizia austriaca in Italia*, Vol. I, pp. 209–211. A French translation of this letter can be found in E. Rodocanachi, "La police secrète autrichienne et les français dans les provinces lombardo-vénitiennes de 1815 à 1819," *Revue historique*, Vol. CXXVIII (May–August, 1918), pp. 86–87.

[87] Hager to Hingenau, Vienna, April 7 and 21, 1815, A. S. (Venice), Presidio di governo, 1815–1819, Polizia, Fasc. II 1/1, No. 1574/P.P., and Fasc. II 11/28, No. 1844/P.P.

[88] Imperial resolution, April 9, 1815, St. A. (Vienna), Kabinets-Akten, 1815, No. 854; Hager to Goëss, Vienna, April 11, 1815, A. S. (Venice), Presidio di governo, 1815, No. 194/v.b.p. See also Hager to Hingenau, Vienna, March 15,

were put on duty in the streets and at the gates of various cities.[89]

The police and other local authorities were instructed to follow public opinion closely and to keep the populace tranquil and pro-Austrian.[90] To aid them, the authorities proscribed the circulation of all books, pamphlets, and other writings which dealt favorably with Napoleon, his government, his generals, or his family.[91] The police were ordered to watch persons who were spreading false rumors or circulating news prejudicial to the Habsburg cause. They were "especially to take strong measures against those who pronounce themselves openly and loudly in favor of Napoleon and his revolutionary system."[92] People who disturbed the public peace or participated in imprudent political conversations in taverns, cafés, or similar public places were to be punished.[93]

More important, the authorities were instructed to draw up lists of persons who had once served in Murat's army or who, because of their attachment to the previous French government, their immoral or revolutionary attitudes, their membership in the Freemasons, or their personal interests, hatreds, or passions, might be looked upon as likely to cooperate with the enemy or disturb the public peace.[94] They were exhorted to enforce existing decrees prohibiting secret societies,[95] to investigate known French and Neapolitan sympathiz-

---

1815, A. S. (Venice), Presidio di governo, 1815–1819, Oggetti politici di stato, Fasc. X 2/6, no number given.

[89] See entry of April 3, 1815, *Biblioteca Ambrosiana* (Milan), Mantovani, "Diario di Milano," Vol. V, p. 351; and Wiedemann-Warnhelm, *Die Wiederherstellung der österreichischen Vorherrschaft in Italien*, p. 63.

[90] Bellegarde to Metternich, Milan, April 14, 1815, St. A. (Vienna), Staatskanzlei, Provinzen, Lombardei-Venedig, Fasz. IV, Kon. 2, Fo. 138; A. S. (Venice), Presidio di governo, 1815–1819, Oggetti politici di stato, Fasc. X 2/6, no number given; Torresani to Hager, Venice, March 16, 1815, *ibid.*, Fasc. X 2/1, No. 925/P.P.; Ottolenghi, *Padova e il Dipartimento del Brenta*, pp. 257–258.

[91] Malamani, *L'Austria e i Bonapartisti*, p. 16.

[92] Torresani to Hager, Venice, April 10, 1815, A. S. (Venice), Presidio di governo, 1815–1819, Oggetti politici di stato, Fasc. X 2/6, No. 1326 e 1391.

[93] Decree, Strassoldo, Milan, April 3, 1815, *Notizie del mondo*, No. 97 (April 10, 1815), p. 3; Hager report, April 15, 1815, St. A. (Vienna), Kabinets-Akten, 1815, No. 545.

[94] Ottolenghi, *Padova e il Dipartimento del Brenta*, p. 271; Hager to Goëss, Vienna, April 11, 1815, A. S. (Venice), Presidio di governo, 1815, No. 196/v.b.p.; Malamani, *L'Austria e i Bonapartisti*, pp. 11–12.

[95] Hager to Hingenau, Vienna, April 9, 1815, A. S. (Venice), Presidio di governo, 1815–1819, Polizia, Fasc. II 13/1, No. 1596.

ers,[96] and rigorously to prosecute those who openly demonstrated a spirit of hostility towards the Austrians or the Habsburg military forces.[97] To provide for the speedy trial of suspected enemies of the state and disturbers of public tranquillity, a special extraordinary court, composed of five judges from various courts of appeal and three military officers selected by Bellegarde, was instituted in Milan on March 31.[98] In addition, Emperor Francis decreed that all persons whose presence in Italy was regarded as inimical to the preservation of public peace or dangerous to the security of the state were to be transported to the interior provinces of the monarchy, where they were to be placed under careful supervision.[99]

Of all suspected groups in Lombardy-Venetia the former officers of the Kingdom of Italy who had not been accepted for active duty in the Habsburg army or who had been retired at half-pay gave the Austrians the greatest cause for anxiety. Soon after hostilities commenced, in order to make effective use of their talents in the war against Murat or at least to neutralize them as a potentially hostile force, they were recalled to active duty at the same ranks which they had held in the French-Italian army. Whether or not they joined the

[96] Torresani to Hager, Venice, April 9, 1815, A. S. (Venice), Presidio di governo, 1815–1819, Oggetti politici di stato, Fasc. X 2/5, No. 1349/P.R.; Ottolenghi, *Padova e il Dipartimento del Brenta*, p. 270.

[97] Bellegarde to Emperor Francis, Milan, June 15, 1815, St. A. (Vienna), Kabinets-Akten, 1815, ad No. 885.

[98] Decree, Bellegarde, Milan, March 31, 1815, *Notizie del mondo*, No. 92 (April 4, 1815), p. 4. Also in *Giornale di Venezia*, No. 93 (April 4, 1815), p. 4. See also Hager report, April 15, 1815, St. A. (Vienna), Kabinets-Akten, 1815, No. 545.

[99] Hager to Hingenau, Vienna, April 5, 1815, A. S. (Venice), Presidio di governo, 1815–1819, Polizia, Fasc. II 1/1, No. 1459/P.P. There is no way of knowing exactly how many persons were arrested or transported to the German provinces, but there is ample evidence to indicate that various suspects were at least imprisoned. For instance, Mantovani recorded in his diary that several persons were arrested (presumably in Milan) on the night of March 7–8. See entry of March 8, 1815, *Biblioteca Ambrosiana* (Milan), Mantovani, "Diario di Milano," Vol. V, p. 345. On April 3 he noted: "During the last two nights many arrests were made" (*ibid.*, p. 351). On April 5, 1815, Torresani wrote Hager from Venice that several disturbers of the peace and troublemakers were under arrest (A. S. [Venice], Presidio di governo, 1815–1819, Oggetti politici di stato, Fasc. X 2/5, No. 1349/P.R.). On April 10 he again wrote him: "The General Police Directory has already arrested various [persons] who expressed themselves maliciously in regard to events in France and the war with Naples" (*ibid.*, Fasc. X 2/6, No. 1329 e 1391).

Habsburg military forces, all such officers who resided in Lombardy were ordered to take a special oath of allegiance to the Habsburg emperor before April 15. Those who lived in Venetia were required to do so before the 30th. Officers who refused were to lose their pay and pensions. They were no longer allowed to wear military insignia and under no circumstances were to be re-admitted into the service.[100] Also, they could be sent to the German provinces of the monarchy any time the authorities deemed it wise.[101]

In addition to a concerted effort to recruit former French-Italian officers for the Habsburg army, the Austrians also encouraged enlisted men to offer their service in the war against the king of Naples. Deserters from the army of the former Kingdom of Naples were promised full pardon if they enrolled in the Habsburg military forces. In addition, the supreme war council in Vienna instructed the communal officials in Lombardy-Venetia to do all they possibly could to engage volunteers for the Austrian army. If necessary to meet the quotas established for their communes, they were empowered to draft young men for military duty.[102]

The government also imposed forced loans upon various groups in Lombardy and Venetia. To meet the extraordinary expenses of the war Bellegarde imposed a forced loan of 1,100,000 lire upon Lombard businessmen on March 25. The loan, which was to be procured before April 10 and which was to bear 6 per cent interest, was to be repaid within a year out of sums collected by a special tax of 1.5 centesimi for every scudo of assessed value levied on all property-owners.[103] The government in Vienna instructed the Venetian governor on April 24 to impose a similar forced loan of 600,000 lire upon the Venetians to pay for provisioning the fortresses located in that province, but apparently the war ended before it was collected and it was rescinded at the beginning of June.[104]

100 Bellegarde order, April 1, 1815, *Giornale di Venezia*, No. 103 (April 14, 1815), p. 4; Weil, *Murat*, Vol. III, pp. 184 and 321; Cusani, *Storia di Milano*, Vol. VII, pp. 252–253.

101 Hager to Hingenau, Vienna, April 8, 1815, A. S. (Venice), Presidio di governo, 1815–1819, Oggetti politici di stato, Fasc. X 2/5, no number given.

102 Hofkriegsrat report, May 7, 1815, St. A. (Vienna), Staats-Rath Akten, 1815, No. 3260.

103 Notice, Bellegarde, Milan, March 25, 1815, *Giornale di Venezia*, No. 86 (March 28, 1815), p. 4. Cusani erroneously writes that the above loan amounted to 1,200,000 lire (see his *Storia di Milano*, Vol. VII, p. 252).

104 Stadion to Goëss, Vienna, June 2, 1815, A. S. (Venice), Presidio di gover-

The practical measures enacted by the Habsburgs in Lombardy-Venetia during the course of the war were designed to aid them in repressing espionage and subversion, in strengthening the morale of a populace confronted by Murat's liberal and nationalist proclamations, and in procuring additional men and financial resources. The Habsburgs also promulgated an important constitutional decree during Murat's "war of independence" which they hoped would exert a powerful influence on public opinion. On April 7, 1815, Emperor Francis issued a patent outlining the fundamental bases of the permanent government which the Habsburgs intended to institute in Lombardy-Venetia.

Several days earlier, on March 28, Bellegarde had written Metternich about the urgent need for the emperor to take a dramatic step to counter the deleterious effects of Murat's liberal and nationalist appeals to a proud, though uneasy, populace which was still uninformed about its future destiny. "Everyone who is capable of bearing arms in Italy," he admonished, "is re-knitting ties with France, if he is a *Napoleonist*, or with Murat, if he is a *partisan of Italian independence*."[105] The emperor should seek to change this spirit, which was so dangerous to Habsburg interests in the Apennine peninsula, Bellegarde insisted, by immediately assuming "the title of king of Lombardy."[106] After the emperor satisfied this urgent longing of the Lombards and Venetians, "we can confidently hope that Italy will unite her efforts with ours to defend herself against an invasion by France and that it will resist the seductions of the king of Naples."[107]

Long before Bellegarde's admonitory missive arrived in Vienna the central government had been drawing up plans for the permanent government of Lombardy-Venetia. The aulic central organization commission, set up by the emperor on July 31, 1814, to reorganize the governments of the newly acquired provinces so that they would fit into the administrative structure of the Habsburg

---

no, 1815–1819, Censo, Fasc. VIII 3/15, No. 2488/P.P.; Goëss to Stadion, Venice, June 15, 1815, *ibid.*, No. 2648/P.P.

[105] As quoted in Weil, *Murat*, Vol. III, p. 233.

[106] As quoted in *ibid.*, p. 234; and in Wiedemann-Warnhelm, *Die Wiederherstellung der österreichischen Vorherrschaft in Italien*, p. 64.

[107] As quoted in Weil, *Murat*, Vol. III, pp. 234–235.

monarchy,[108] had made detailed recommendations to Emperor Francis on January 3, 1815, about the political and administrative machinery to be established in Lombardy-Venetia.[109] The emperor approved most of the commission's proposals in an imperial resolution dated February 22.[110] For some time he was undecided as to the name for the Italian provinces, but on April 1 he finally resolved that they were to be called the Lombardo-Venetian kingdom.[111]

Obviously neither the war against Murat nor Bellegarde's urgent injunctions of March 28 exerted any significant influence on determining the nature of the permanent government in Lombardy-Venetia outlined in the imperial patent on April 7, 1815. However, both probably hastened the date on which the patent was issued.[112] Cer-

---

[108] See Emperor Francis' letters to Ugarte and Lazanzky, Schönbrunn, July 31, 1814, St. A. (Vienna), Staats-Rath Akten, 1814, No. 2050.

[109] A copy of this report is in St. A. (Vienna), Kaiser Franz Akten, Fasz. XV, Kon. 1, Pt. 2, Fos. 77–89; and Helfert, *Zur Geschichte des Lombardo-Venezianischen Königreichs*, Appendix IV, pp. 316–319.

[110] For this resolution, see St. A. (Vienna), Kaiser Franz Akten, Fasz. XV, Kon. 1, Pt. 2, Fos. 87–90; and Helfert, *Zur Geschichte des Lombardo-Venezianischen Königreichs*, Appendix I, pp. 260–314.

[111] Emperor Francis to Metternich, April 1, 1815, as quoted in Helfert, *Kaiser Franz und die Stiftung des Lombardo-Venetianischen Königreichs*, p. 207.

[112] There is still some confusion in regard to the date on which the April 7, 1815, patent was first proclaimed in Milan. Princess Belgiojoso-Trivulzio says that Bellegarde announced it on April 16 (see her *Étude sur l'histoire de la Lombardie*, p. 113). Cusani relates that the patent was published in Milan on April 20 (see his *Storia di Milano*, Vol. VII, p. 253). Helfert merely states that it was printed in the *Wiener Zeitung* on April 14 and in the *Oesterreichischer Beobachter* on the 15th (see his *Kaiser Franz und die Stiftung des Lombardo-Venetianischen Königreichs*, p. 208). As for contemporary records, Bellegarde announced in his proclamation of April 16 that the emperor had created a Lombardo-Venetian kingdom, that he was going to appoint a viceroy to represent him in this kingdom, and that he had named Bellegarde as lieutenant of the viceroy (see Bellegarde proclamation, Milan, April 16, 1815, A. S. [Milan]), Presidenza di governo. Atti secreti, 1815, Cart. VIII, No. 43/Aff.[i] Dip.[a]). On April 12, 1815, Mantovani noted in his diary: "Two decrees of our emperor have given consoling news to our populace: The formation of a Lombardo-Venetian Kingdom and the promise of a viceroy in Milan. The addition of the Valtelline to this kingdom" (*Biblioteca Ambrosiana* [Milan], Mantovani, "Diario di Milano," Vol. V, pp. 354–355). On April 21 he wrote: "An imperial dispatch which turns all the territory of the former so-called Kingdom of Italy into a Lombardo-Venetian kingdom in which a viceroy will reside was published yesterday" (*ibid.*, p. 356). An article in the *Allgemeine Zeitung* stated that the April 7 patent was proclaimed in Milan on May 17 (see No. 151 [May 31, 1815], pp. 611–612). The data given in the *All-*

tainly it was not a hastily devised war measure proclaimed for the express purpose of keeping the Italian populace from falling under the spell of Murat and Napoleon!

As specified in the imperial patent, the newly acquired Italian areas were to be organized into a Lombardo-Venetian kingdom, with its own court and court officials and with a viceroy to represent the emperor. The coat of arms of the kingdom was to be incorporated in that of the Austrian empire, and the emperor's new royal title was to be added to his other titles. The ancient crown of iron was to be conserved as the crown of the Lombardo-Venetian kingdom, and all the successors of the Habsburg monarch were to be crowned king of the Lombardo-Venetian kingdom when they acceded to the imperial throne. For administrative purposes, Lombardy and Venetia were to have their own governments, each headed by a governor and a government council. Both were to be under the direct supervision of the aulic departments in Vienna. Each government was to be divided into provinces governed by royal delegations. The provinces were to be split into districts, in each of which there was to be a tax registrar (*cancelliere del censo*); and the districts into communes. For the time being the prevailing division of the communes into three classes and the existing municipal administrations were to be preserved. In order better to know the wishes and needs of the inhabitants and to profit from the counsels of representatives of the inhabitants, the emperor would establish a central congregation in each of the two governments. Furthermore, each province was to have a provincial congregation, and the existing communal councils were for the time being to be retained.[113]

---

gemeine *Zeitung* is obviously erroneous. From the information given in these contemporary sources, it would appear that, although the creation of the Lombardo-Venetian kingdom and the emperor's promise to appoint a viceroy were known in Milan by April 12 and officially announced by Bellegarde on the 16th, Cusani was probably right when he wrote that the patent itself was not published in Milan before April 20.

[113]Imperial patent, Vienna, April 7, 1815, *Atti del governo lombardo*, 1815, Vol. I, pp. 47–51; Lazanzky to Goëss, Vienna, April 7, 1815, A. S. (Venice), Presidio di governo, 1815, No. 136/v.b.p. Complete texts of this patent can also be found in Sandonà, *Il Regno Lombardo Veneto*, pp. 77–80; Amyot, *Recueil des traités, conventions et actes diplomatiques concernant l'Autriche et l'Italie*, pp. 162–164; Comte D'Angeberg [Jacob Leonard Chodźko], *Le Congrès de Vienne et les traités de 1815*, Vol. II, Pt. 4, pp. 1045–1047; and Geo. Fréd. and Charles Martens, *Nouveau recueil de traités d'alliance, de paix, de trève, de*

In the spring of 1815 Bellegarde anticipated in large measure the criticisms which Italian liberals eventually made of the most important concessions in the imperial patent—the establishment of the Lombardo-Venetian kingdom and the appointment of a viceroy to represent the emperor in that kingdom.[114] On April 13, after he had learned that a viceroy was to be appointed but before he had seen the patent itself, he revealed his apprehensions to Metternich. He wrote:

What could do great damage to the results promised by the new measure which H[is] M[ajesty] is going to take in turning this country into a kingdom is a prolonged delay in the nomination of the Prince whom He destines to be the Viceroy. Those with bad intentions will not fail to circulate [reports] that all this is only a bait which has been offered to amuse them, to tranquilize them by cherishing their favorite idea. [They will say] that, under a *changed name*, everything will continue nearly the same as before, that we will not have a court which will give luster to the capital, that all the inconveniences of a distant bureaucracy will continue to exist, that the Italian nation will no longer constitute a national body as it did before, and that false hopes will be the only harvest which they [the Italians] will reap from the prestige of the kingdom with which their vanity and their credulity are being lulled.[115]

In the years to come Bellegarde's forebodings proved remarkably correct, both in regard to the way the Habsburgs conducted their administration in Lombardy-Venetia and the impression which the Austrian regime made on a large number of politically minded intellectual and business groups in Italy. However, this was not immediately apparent in the spring and summer of 1815. Right after the April 7 patent was issued it was generally greeted with considerable enthusiasm in all parts of Lombardy-Venetia.[116]

---

neutralité, de commerce, de limites, d'échange, etc. et de plusieurs autres actes servant à la connaissance des rélations étrangères des puissances et états de l'Europe, Vol. V, pp. 55–58.

[114] For these criticisms, see my "L'amministrazione austriaca nel Lombardo Veneto (1814–1821)," *Archivio economico dell'unificazione italiana*, Vol. IX, Fasc. 1 (1959), p. 18; and Dolce report, Milan, June 30, 1816, A. S. (Milan), Presidenza di governo. Atti secreti, 1816, Cart. XI, Rub. 669/geh. (*Reisenden Dolce*), Pezza 224.

[115] In a letter sent from Milan, St. A. (Vienna), Staatskanzlei, Provinzen, Lombardei-Venedig, Fasz. IV, Kon. 4, Fo. 16.

[116] Hager report, September 20, 1815, St. A. (Vienna), Kabinets-Akten, 1815, No. 814; Raab to presidency of the Venetian government, Venice, May 23, 1815,

The note of pessimism expressed by Bellegarde in his letter to Metternich on April 13 merely reflected the general concern of numerous other Habsburg officials in Italy over the state of public opinion in Lombardy-Venetia in the spring of 1815. Troubled by the sizable number of Italians who were still permeated with the liberal and pro-independence predilections instilled in them by the French; worried that the depressed business conditions, the commercial stagnation, the unemployment, and the famine which prevailed in many parts of Emperor Francis' Italian domains might incline unhappy or impoverished wretches to lend a ready ear to demagogues with enticing promises for a change; possessed by a horrifying thought that the Carbonari and other secret societies might attempt to revolutionize Italy to aid Murat's efforts to drive the Habsburgs out of the Apennine peninsula; disturbed by the belief that the Piedmontese army might join the French and the Neapolitans at any moment; distressed by the relatively small size of their own military forces in Italy, many Austrian officials feared that the Habsburgs would be faced with a long and dangerous war in the Apennine peninsula.[117]

Fortunately for the Habsburg causes in Italy, they were needlessly alarmed. When the news of Napoleon's flight from Elba reached Milan on March 6[118] and other parts of Lombardy-Venetia shortly thereafter it immediately became the chief topic of conversation among an excited populace. The wildest conjectures about the reasons for Napoleon's escape were noised about. Amateur political experts maintained that, egged on by the Russians, the king of Naples had enticed Napoleon again to take up the cudgel. Others insisted that the British were back of the move. Possessed by an all-consuming

A. S. (Venice), Presidio di governo, 1815–1819, Polizia, Fasc. II 10/1, No. 2278/P.P.; Raab to Goëss, Venice, June 28, 1815, *ibid.*, No. 738/P.R.

117 Strassoldo to Metternich, Milan, April 16, 1815, St. A. (Vienna), Staatskanzlei, Provinzen, 1792–1844, Fasz. XXXII, Fos. 102–104; Reuss-Plauen to Bellegarde, Venice, March 25, 1815, *Kriegs-Archiv* (Vienna), Feld Akten (Frimont in Italien), 1815, Fasz. III, No. 88; Hager report, April 5, 1815, St. A. (Vienna), Kabinets-Akten, 1815, No. 854; anonymous report to Hager, April 7, 1815, A. S. (Venice), Presidio di governo, 1815, No. 241/v.b.p.; anonymous report, April 7, 1815, Lemmi, *La restaurazione austriaca a Milano*, Appendix LXXV, pp. 500–502; *Allgemeine Zeitung*, No. 195 (July 14, 1815), p. 786; secret report, Venice, February 22, 1815, Helfert, *Kaiser Franz und die Stiftung des Lombardo-Venetianischen Königreichs*, Appendix IV, pp. 550–554.

118 Entry of March 6, 1815, *Biblioteca Ambrosiana* (Milan), Mantovani, "Diario di Milano," Vol. V, p. 344.

ambition to turn Italy into a liberal, constitutional country that would be tributary to England, they had, with typical Albion perfidy, incited the ex-emperor again to embark upon a military career and then allowed him to escape from captivity to wage a war from which only the British could emerge victorious. A handful of self-styled experts looked upon the former French sovereign's wife Maria Louisa as the real villain of the piece, while a much larger number asserted that, after consulting Murat, Napoleon had made the decision himself.[119]

If more than a small minority of Lombards and Venetians were enthusiastic about the possibility of Napoleon's chasing out the Habsburgs and again making himself master of their country, they remained hidden from the eyes of the watchful police. A few embittered Italian army officers and other malcontents, a comparatively small number of French partisans and ardent admirers of the former emperor, and a handful of sanguine protagonists of independence like Foscolo and Confalonieri openly expressed their eagerness, hoped that Napoleon would be successful, occasionally shouted encomiums to the French emperor, and here and there surreptitiously posted in public places a few sonnets or other writings praising Napoleon. Nevertheless, in spite of these manifestations of pro-Napoleonic sentiment, the police and other public officials agreed that the overwhelming majority of the populace, including some well-known partisans of independence, were either apathetic about Napoleon's battle to regain power or downright angry over the very thought that the ex-emperor was again forcing Europe into a war which might involve them.[120]

[119] Livi, *Napoleone all'isola d'Elba*, pp. 211–212; Torresani to Hager, Venice, March 16, 1815, A. S. (Venice), Presidio di governo, 1815–1819, Oggetti politici di stato, Fasc. X 2/1, No. 925/P.P.

[120] Hager report, March 14, 1815, St. A. (Vienna), Kabinets–Akten, 1815, No. 471; police report, April 14, 1815, *ibid.*, No. 821; political commissioner of San Paolo to the general police director in Venetia, Venice, March 15, 1815, *Carte segrete della polizia austriaca in Italia*, Vol. I, p. 40; Bellegarde to Metternich, Milan, March 17, 1815, St. A. (Vienna), Staatskanzlei, Provinzen, Lombardei-Venedig, Fasz. IV, Kon. 2, Fo. 65; Ficquelmont to Frimont, Milan, March 17, 1815, *Kriegs-Archiv* (Vienna), Feld Akten (Frimont in Italien), 1815, Fasz. III, No. 33¼; Torresani to Hager, Venice, March 16 and April 9, 1815, A. S. (Venice), Presidio di governo, 1815–1819, Oggetti politici di stato, Fasc. X 2/1, No. 925/P.P., and Fasc. X 2/5, No. 1349/P.R.; Torresani to Hager, Venice, March 19 and 24, and April 4, 1815, A. S. (Venice), Presidio di governo, 1815–1819, Polizia, Fasc. II 5/13, Nos. 1000/P.R. and 1070/P.P., and Fasc. II 5/19, No.

Murat's Rimini proclamation and the manner in which he deliberately plunged Italy into war elicited even less show of approval in Lombardy-Venetia than Napoleon's escape from Elba. Generally the Lombards and Venetians were openly contemptuous of his audacious pretentions, for they looked upon him as a greedy foreigner who was arrogating to himself a right to proclaim Italian independence which was not his. In their eyes he was nothing more than a reckless adventurer totally uninterested in the welfare of the Italian people and exclusively devoted to the furthering of his own inordinate ambitions. Even ardent supporters of Napoleon looked askance at the king of Naples, for they regarded him as a fickle, selfish, and treacherous friend who had abandoned his command during the Russian campaign and then betrayed Napoleon in January, 1814, by joining the Allied Powers in warring against his friend and benefactor. Thus the impetuous king of Naples was either ignored or denounced by everyone except a few malcontents. Although Murat had counted on attracting a large number of volunteers in Lombardy-Venetia, not one came. In vain, he tried to induce the former members of the dissolved Italian army to join forces with him. Although a few Italian officers like Foscolo left for Switzerland rather than take the required oath of allegiance to the Habsburg emperor,[121] none of them enlisted in Murat's army, and many a distinguished Italian officer took up service in the Austrian military against him.[122]

The intense aversion of the Lombards and Venetians for Murat's "war of independence" should not have surprised the Habsburg au-

---

1271/P.P.; Raab to presidency of the Venetian government, March 29, 1815 (two different letters), *ibid.*, Fasc. II 5/22, No. 1201/P.P., and Fasc. II 5/19, No. 1178/P.P.; political commissioner of San Paolo to Venetian general police director, Venice, March 19, 1815, Rodocanachi, "La police secrète autrichienne," pp. 85–86; Raab to police commissioner of San Paolo, April 7, 1815, *ibid.*, p. 86; Ottolini, "U. Foscolo e la risoluzione dell'esilio," p. 176; Ottolenghi, *Padova e il Dipartimento del Brenta*, pp. 247–248, 266, and 279–280.

121 See Strassoldo to Metternich, Milan, April 16, 1815, St. A. (Vienna), Staatskanzlei, Provinzen, 1792–1844, Fasz. XXXII, Fo. 104; and Silvio Pellico to his brother Luigi (Milan), April 25, 1815, Rinieri, *Della Vita e delle Opere di Silvio Pellico*, Vol. I, p. 109.

122 See Lemmi, "Gioacchino Murat e le aspirazioni unitarie," p. 195; Cusani, *Storia di Milano*, Vol. VII, p. 259; police report, April 15, 1815, St. A. (Vienna), Kabinets-Akten, 1815, No. 811; Torresani to Hager, Venice, April 13, 1815, A. S. (Venice), Presidio di governo, 1815–1819, Oggetti politici di stato, Fasc. X 2/6, No. 1461/P.R.; and Torresani to Hager, Venice, April 26, 1815; A. S. (Venice), Presidio di governo, 1815–1819, Polizia, Fasc. II 10/1, No. 1071/P.P.

thorities in Italy. The Lombards and Venetians, like most other Italians and Europeans in 1815, were still permeated with a great longing for peace—peace at almost any price. To them Murat and Napoleon were not liberators but esurient gamblers who wished to rob them of that tranquillity which they so ardently desired. Furthermore, although many Lombards and Venetians grumbled loudly about various policies and practices of the Habsburgs, in 1815 the Austrian regime had not become unpopular enough for anyone except a few virulent Austrophobes to wish to see it overthrown by a reckless adventurer who was king of the hated Neapolitans. In actual fact, a large majority of the populace were still rather well satisfied with Habsburg rule. The bad impression made upon them by various unpopular measures was canceled by the mildness of various officials like Bellegarde and by their conscientious efforts to deal fairly with the people. Even the inefficiency and slowness of their new masters provided a pleasant contrast to the nervous and sometimes ruthless energy of the previous French officials. Then, too, those Lombards and Venetians who wished to have the Habsburgs out of Italy realized the futility of fighting the Austrians. Furthermore, the arrest and trial of the Brescian-Milanese conspirators had served as a jolting reminder of the need for caution in conspiring against their new rulers.[123]

Of course, there was some discontent with Habsburg rule in Lombardy and Venetia, and not everyone was overjoyed with the Austrian victory over Murat and the Allied triumph over Napoleon. There was just not enough dissatisfaction or bitterness to drive the inhabitants to revolt or to take up arms to help Murat and Napoleon in the spring of 1815.

Even though their feeling of hostility was not strong enough to cause them to rebel, the public opinion reports prepared by the Lombard general police director during the spring and summer of 1815, as well as various communications which Bellegarde sent to Vienna, indicate plainly enough that many Lombards found grounds for

[123] Police report, April 15, 1815, St. A. (Vienna), Kabinets-Akten, 1815, No. 811; Torresani to Hager, Venice, April 13, 1815, A. S. (Venice), Presidio di governo, 1815–1819, Oggetti politici di stato, Fasc. X 2/6, No. 1461/P.R.; *Allgemeine Zeitung*, No. 195 (July 14, 1815), pp. 786–787; Helfert, *Kaiser Franz und die Stiftung des lombardo-venetianischen Königreichs*, pp. 134 and 262; Lemmi, "Gioacchino Murat e le aspirazioni unitarie," p. 196; Lemmi, *La restaurazione austriaca a Milano*, pp. 384–385.

complaint about the Habsburg regime which had been instituted in their province just a year before. The French revolution and the Napoleonic regime, as the Habsburg police rightly noted, had wrought such a fundamental transformation in political opinions and aspirations in Italy, particularly in Milan and other Lombard cities, that large groups in Lombardy, even those who had just a year before vociferated in stentorian voices about the onerous exactions and oppressions of the French, were bound to look askance at a newly restored government which they suspected of intending to re-establish many trappings of the old pre-revolutionary system. What is equally important, during the Napoleonic period new classes of people had rapidly forged ahead to positions of economic, political, social, and intellectual pre-eminence. They saw their recently ac-quired status seriously threatened by a regime which was suspicious of many of the very revolutionary policies and practices which had enabled them to prosper.

Furthermore, Napoleon had stimulated a strong feeling of local patriotism among the Lombards, particularly the Milanese, by mak-ing Milan the capital of an extensive Kingdom of Italy and the cen-ter of a brilliant court life. The proud Lombard elite, especially the newly created nobility, the intelligentsia, and the professional classes, and even lowly workers and agriculturists, were aggrieved because Milan was now a mere provincial administrative center of a large multinational empire. Even the announcement in April, 1815, that Lombardy and Venetia were to be turned into a Lombardo-Venetian Kingdom, although greeted with considerable enthusiasm at the out-set, did little to assuage their feeling of humiliation over the vastly reduced standing of their capital. Although Napoleon had kept a tight reign on the government of the Kingdom of Italy and had al-lowed it to be little better than a colony to be exploited by the French, he had opened to many an Italian the prospect of a brilliant political future by appointing mostly natives to the highest admin-istrative offices in the kingdom. Although the Habsburgs retained many Italians in important posts in their own administration, the topmost positions were dominated either by Germans or by Italian-speaking Tyrolese.

Thus, the refusal of the Austrians to recognize the profound altera-tions in political aspirations wrought by the French revolution and their failure to cater adequately to the sensibilities of a proud and patriotic (though in the narrow Lombard rather than in the broad

Italian nationalist sense of the word) populace, as the Habsburg
police in Italy and as Count Bellegarde pointed out, accounted for
some of the anti-Austrian feeling of various Lombards in the spring
of 1815. So did the fact that many of them were disillusioned because
ardently desired changes which they expected the new regime immediately to make were not effectuated. Even though the Habsburgs had granted the Lombards substantial decreases in both indirect and direct taxes,[124] they had still not accorded them that drastic
reduction which property owners and other groups so ardently desired. The peasants and agricultural workers were provoked because
military conscription, so hated under the French regime, was re-introduced. The employees of the previous French-Italian government
who had been temporarily retained in office were worried because
they had still not been told whether they would continue in their
positions after the permanent administration was instituted. The depressed business conditions, the bad crops, and the rising prices of
foodstuffs sharply worsened the living conditions of practically all
classes of people. Then, too, many Lombards were deeply disturbed
when they learned that the Austrian legal codes and judicial system
were to be introduced in their province without modifications which
took into account the fact that the habits, character, conditions, and
language of the people differed greatly from those of the Germans.
They expressed their displeasure over some of the officials sent to
Lombardy from other provinces who did not have a command of the
Italian language and who were totally unfamiliar with the customs
of the inhabitants. Furthermore, the Lombards were unhappy because their government was still on a provisional basis, and they
longed to have a permanent regime instituted as quickly as possible.[125]

[124] See my "Economic Conditions in Lombardy and Venetia, 1813–1815, and
Their Effects on Public Opinion," *Journal of Central European Affairs*, Vol.
XXIII, No. 3 (October, 1963), pp. 273–275; and *ante*, pp. 105–107.

[125] For the above evaluation of Lombard public opinion by Austrian officials,
see Hager report of September 20, 1815, which includes the public opinion and
police administration report of the Milanese general police director Count Strassoldo for January 1–July 31, 1815, St. A. (Vienna), Kabinets-Akten, 1815, No.
814; Hager report of November 6, 1815, including the public opinion and police
administration report from Milan for August and September, 1815, *ibid.*, No.
816; and Bellegarde to Hager, Milan, August 10, 1815, Helfert, *Kaiser Franz und
die Stiftung des lombardo-venetianischen Königreichs*, Appendix XV, pp. 572–
579.

In Venetia the police reported the same complaints about conscription as did their counterparts in Lombardy. Unlike the Lombard police, however, they advised their superiors that if a military draft was unavoidable the Venetians preferred the mild Austrian system to the harsh French one which was still in use. As in Lombardy, the former French-Italian government employees were demoralized because they remained uncertain about their future. The Venetians voiced their displeasure over the high price of foodstuffs and other necessities and found fault with the prevailing high tax rate much more than the Lombards. In fact, the police expressed the opinion that oppressive taxes and the financial policies of the Austrians gave more grounds for dissatisfaction with Habsburg rule than anything else. Whereas in Lombardy the loudest grumbling was about the property tax, in Venetia the main object for aversion was the poll or capitation tax. In addition, the Venetians growled about the onerous registration tax, extortionate judicial taxes, and the high salt prices—accusations which were not referred to in the public opinion reports from Lombardy.

The Venetian police and departmental authorities also reported various other grievances not noted by the officials in Milan. Some Venetians deprecated the failure of the Habsburgs punctually to make the promised repayment of the forced loans which they had levied in the spring of 1814. Most of them were displeased because the postal administration was still charging the French tariff for letters rather than the cheaper Austrian rate. Landlords were discontented and jealous because they believed that the Austrians were favoring commerce to the disadvantage of Venetian agricultural interests. Other inhabitants of the former Republic of San Marco were unhappy over the customs line which had been established on the Mincio River, separating Venetia from Lombardy.

The longing of the Venetians to have a permanent government instituted as rapidly as possible was considerably stronger than that of the Lombards. Apparently much more than the Lombards, a large number of Venetians, probably a considerable majority, looked forward to being ruled by the Habsburgs, whom they regarded as mild and benevolent. To a much greater extent than those from Lombardy, the public opinion reports from Venetia emphasized the great displeasure of the populace over the retention of French-Italian laws and practices which they thoroughly abhorred. Everywhere in Venetia there were bitter complaints about the employees of the former

Kingdom of Italy who were still kept in public office, many of whom, it was asserted, remained fanatical supporters of the former Napoleonic regime.[126]

Thus it is apparent that during the spring and summer of 1815 in Venetia there was much more hostility towards the former French-Italian regime and considerably less antipathy towards Habsburg rule than in Lombardy. On the one hand, there was greater poverty and much more grumbling about taxation and financial policies in Venetia than in Lombardy; but, on the other, the Lombards, around whom the Kingdom of Italy had been centered, were embittered because Milan was no longer the capital of an important kingdom—a complaint which was more likely to gratify rather than to wound the sensibilities of the Venetians, who had never been overly fond of the Lombards and who themselves wanted to have Venice rather than Milan become the capital of the newly created Lombardo-Venetian kingdom.[127] Furthermore, although the Lombards were deeply perturbed over the Austrians' failure to take into consideration the special customs and habits of the people and local conditions in Lombardy and objected to the German officials sent to Milan to assume important offices in the administration, this writer could find no single word of complaint on this score in the Venetian public opinion reports.

All the evidence which this writer has seen clearly shows that

[126] Raab report, Venice, November 11, 1815, St. A. (Vienna), Hofreisen, Fasz. XLIII, Fos. 536–543; secret police report, Venice, November 7, 1815, *ibid.*, Fo. 534; Hager report, November 14, 1815, St. A. (Vienna), Kabinets-Akten, 1815, No. 817; Goëss to Hager, Belluno, April 28, 1815, A. S. (Venice), Presidio di governo, 1815, No. 189/v.b.p.; Onigo to presidency of the Venetian government, Belluno, August 18, 1815, *ibid.*, 1815–1819, Fasc. II 10/1, ad No. 6530/P.P.; prefect of Adige department to Goëss, Verona, October 22, 1815, *ibid.*; Raab to Goëss, Venice, June 28, 1815, A. S. (Venice), Presidio de governo, 1815–1819, Polizia, Fasc. II 10/1, No. 738/P.R.; provisional prefect of Adige department to presidency of the Venetian government, Verona, September 14, 1815, *ibid.*, Fasc. II 5/19pe2, No. 5385/P.P.; Porcia to presidency of the Venetian government, October 11, 1815, *ibid.*, Fasc. II 10/1, ad No. 6530/P.P.; political report for the Adriatico department for August, 1815, *Carte segrete della polizia austriaca in Italia*, Vol. I, pp. 33–39; political report for Brenta department for August, 1815, Ottolenghi, *Padova e il Dipartimento del Brenta*, Appendix XLII, pp. 518–519.

[127] See, for instance, entry of May 5, 1815, *Museo* (Venice), "Diario di Cicogna," p. 3018.

there was a great deal of anti-Habsburg feeeling in Lombardy in the spring and summer of 1815. Although Governor Franz Joseph Saurau, who replaced Bellegarde as the emperor's chief political representative[128] in Lombardy early in 1815,[129] pointed out to Baron von Hager that, in contrast to the great unrest in the Papal Legations, everything was peaceful in Lombardy,[130] and although Bellegarde later asserted, in a report to the emperor in which he summed up the results of his work as commissioner plenipotentiary of Lombardy, that he had succeeded "in creating a large majority [*überwiegende*] party" in favor of Austria,[131] in the summer of 1815 Bellegarde himself advised the Habsburg police director in Vienna that "a large party can be found which, though they differ among themselves in their views, is united in hating the present state of things and can be held in check only by force."[132] He went on to warn Von Hager that "the opposition in the provinces which have fallen to us is stronger than in nearly all other parts of Italy."[133] The police director in Milan Count Strassoldo wrote that, although "the general opinion" was "decidedly in favor of the person" of the emperor, it was "in no way manifested in favor of the principles of the government."[134] Finally, in the Milanese general police directory report on public opinion in Lombardy during the months of August and September, 1815, the following statement was made about public opinion in Lombardy: "In general public opinion is in no way bad in the sense that one must

128 It should be pointed out that, although Saurau was officially appointed governor, Bellegarde's official title had been commissioner plenipotentiary.

129 See imperial resolution, February 22, 1815, St. A. (Vienna), Kaiser Franz Akten, Fasz. XV, Kon. 1, Pt. 2, Fo. 88; and Lazanzky to Saurau, Vienna, February 28, 1815, *Verwaltungsarchiv* (Vienna), Hofkanzlei, Fasz. CCCLVII, III, A, 4, Lombardei-Venedig.

130 Saurau to Hager, Milan, September 29, 1815, A. S. (Milan), Presidenza di governo. Atti secreti, 1815, Cart. IX, No. 156/g.p.

131 Bellegarde to Emperor Francis, Milan, March 25, 1816, St. A. (Vienna), Kaiser Franz Akten, Fasz. XV, Kon. 2, Fo. 124.

132 Bellegarde to Hager, Milan, August 10, 1815, Helfert, *Kaiser Franz und die Stiftung des lombardo-venetianischen Königreichs*, Appendix XV, p. 572.

133 *Ibid.*, p. 578.

134 Strassoldo to Saurau, Milan, January 6, 1816, A. S. (Milan), Presidenza di governo. Atti secreti, 1816, Cart. X, Pt. 1 (Stimmungsberichte), No. 2/g.p. Another copy can also be found in St. A. (Vienna), *Hofreisen*, Fasz. XLIII, Fo. 458. See also Strassoldo to Saurau, Milan, January 26, 1816, A. S. (Milan), Presidenza di governo. Atti secreti, 1816, Cart. X, Pt. 1 (Stimmungsberichte), No. 19/g.p.

be apprehensive about conspiracies or revolutions, but it is not at all good and has, on the contrary, actually worsened."[135]

In sharp contrast to the admonitions about anti-Austrian feeling sent in from Lombardy, the police and departmental officials in Venetia were practically unanimous in maintaining that Venetian public opinion was strongly pro-Austrian. There were reports that a couple of posters containing the words "N. B. II" (Napoleon Bonaparte II) were found posted on the walls of two cafés in the commune of Montagnana, near Padua;[136] that a few University of Padua students had voiced pro-Napoleonic sentiments in the Pedrocchi café in Venice;[137] that a small number of Bonapartists and partisans of independence were openly agitating against the Austrian government in Verona;[138] and that in the departments of Passariano, Tagliamento, and Piave, where famine conditions were acute, public opinion was not as pro-Austrian as was desirable.[139] However, the number of Venetians who actively opposed Habsburg rule in Italy was small. As the Venetian police director reported, the Venetians were convinced that

after the loss of their aristocratic government no better fate could have befallen them than to come under the mild Austrian scepter. Of course, a party has existed which was dissatisfied with the present order of things. However, after the misfortune which befell their heroes [*i.e.*, Murat and Napoleon] it practically entirely disappeared. People want peace and are seeking to bring order into the existing chaotic property relationships.[140]

---

[135] Police report, November 6, 1815, St. A. (Vienna), Kabinets-Akten, 1815, No. 816.

[136] Pasqualigo to presidency of the Venetian government, Padua, August 2, 1815, A. S. (Venice), Presidio di governo, 1815–1819, Polizia, Fasc. II 5/36, No. 9370/p.p.

[137] Lancetti to Padua police director, Venice, September 6, 1815, *Carte segrete della polizia austriaca in Italia*, Vol. I, pp. 40–41. Also in Rodocanachi, "La police secrète autrichienne," pp. 88–89.

[138] Prefect of Adige department to Goëss, Verona, October 22, 1815, A. S. (Venice), Presidio di governo, 1815–1819, Fasc. II 10/1, ad No. 6530/P.P.; provisional prefect of Adige department to presidency of the Venetian government, Verona, September 14, 1815, A. S. (Venice), Presidio di governo, 1815–1819, Polizia, Fasc. II 5/19, No. 5385/P.P.

[139] Goëss to Hager, Belluno, April 28, 1815, A. S. (Venice), Presidio di governo, 1815, No. 189/v.b.p.

[140] Raab report, Venice, November 11, 1815, St. A. (Vienna), Hofreisen, Fasz. XLIII, Fos. 542–543.

Everywhere in Venetia, whether in the departments of Adriatico, Adige, Bacchiglione, Brenta, Passariano, Piave, or Tagliamento, the officials attested to the highly satisfactory state of public opinion from the Austrian point of view. Expressions of approval were numerous: "Public opinion is always satisfactory." "Public opinion continues to be very good." "The best possible public spirit has been manifested in this department." "Every report on the public spirit of this department is excellent." "Public opinion is the best possible and people everywhere look upon the wise and benevolent measures of the government with satisfaction and admiration." "The populace in general finds great satisfaction in being ruled by the August Austrian House." "The public is generally well disposed towards the August Austrian House, religion, and good order, and hostile to the French, to the former government, and to modern maxims." Endorsements of the Habsburgs like these were repeated in all the reports on public opinion in the various departments of Venetia during the spring and summer of 1815.[141]

How can this striking difference between Lombard and Venetian public opinion be explained? Economic conditions are not the answer. Had economic factors played a significant role in determining the attitude of the Lombards and Venetians towards their new rulers, the feelings of the inhabitants of the two areas would have been exactly opposite from what they were, for it was the Venetians and not the Lombards who were the most sorely afflicted by Austrian economic and fiscal practices. Not only were the Lombards exempt

[141] See Raab to presidency of the Venetian government, Venice, May 23 and July 18, 1815, A. S. (Venice), Presidio di governo, 1815–1819, Polizia, Fasc. II 10/1, Nos. 2278/P.P. and 973/P.R.; Raab to Goëss, Venice, June 28, 1815, *ibid.*, No. 738/P.R.; Onigo to presidency of the Venetian government, Belluno, August 18, 1815, *ibid.*, ad No. 6530/P.P.; Pasqualigo to presidency of the Venetian government, Padua, October 10, 1815, *ibid.*; Tornieri to presidency of the Venetian government, Vicenza, October 10, 1815, *ibid.*; provisional prefect of Adige department to Goëss, Verona, October 22, 1815, *ibid.*; provisional prefect of Adige department to presidency of the Venetian government, Verona, September 14, 1815, *ibid.*, Fasc. II 5/19pe2, No. 5385/P.P.; Goëss to Hager, Venice, July 26, 1815, A. S. (Venice), Presidio di governo, 1815–1819, Fasc. II 10/1, No. 3868/ P.P.; public opinion and administration report of the Venetian general police directory for October, 1815, St. A. (Vienna), Kabinets-Akten, 1815, No. 817; and Brenta department political reports for March, May, June, July, August, September, and October, 1815, Ottolenghi, *Padova e il Dipartimento del Brenta*, Appendices XXXVII, XXXIX, XL, XLI, XLII, XLIII, and XLIV, pp. 493–494, 504, 510, 514, 518–519, 524, and 528–529.

from most of the onerous military requisitions and compulsory levies inflicted on the Venetians by the Habsburgs during the spring of 1814, but, of equal importance, the Lombards benefited from a significant number of reductions in indirect taxes which the Venetians never received, and during the last half of 1814 land taxes were approximately 66⅔ per cent higher in Venetia than in Lombardy. Also, the Lombards were largely spared the famine and starvation which so grievously plagued the inhabitants of the mountainous areas of Venetia.[142]

The difference in public opinion between the two areas can not be accounted for by Austrian political and administrative practices even though the Lombards complained loudly about them. Because the Habsburgs confirmed the provisional regency which they found on their arrival in Milan and allowed it to supervise the administration of the country until January 2, 1816, the Lombards enjoyed at least a slight measure of self-administration which was largely denied the Venetians. Furthermore, Lombardy was much more efficiently governed in 1814–1815 than Venetia. It is true that the Lombards grumbled over the many Germans who were given posts in their administration, but Germans were also assigned to the most important positions in the Venetian government. The Lombards were annoyed by the crude and haughty behavior of the Austrian soldiers and some of the German administrative officials, but so were the Venetians. Some Lombards were angered because so many employees of the previous French government were left at their posts and because the hated French laws and judicial and administrative practices were kept intact,[143] but French personnel, laws, and practices were also retained in Venetia.[144]

Neither can it be argued that the Lombards were more Austrophobe than their compatriots east of the Mincio because the Habsburgs oppressed them more than the Venetians. It is true that

---

[142] See my "Economic Conditions in Lombardy and Venetia, 1813–1815."

[143] See especially confidential reports from Milan, June 9 and 23, 1814, A. S. (Milan), Presidenza di governo. Atti secreti, 1814, Cart. I, No. 89/P.R.; Hager to Bellegarde, Vienna, July 17, 1814, ibid., Cart. II, No. 124/P.R.; Pirelli di Varena to Bellegarde, Varena, July 15, 1814, ibid., Cart. I, No. 57/P.R.; Hager reports, June 25 and 29, 1814, St. A. (Vienna), Conferenz Akten, Ser. b, 1814, Nos. 1262 and 1276; and entries of August 1, 1814, and June 27, 1815, Bibloteca Ambrosiana (Milan), Mantovani, "Diario di Milano," Vol. V, pp. 296–297 and 370.

[144] See ante, pp. 353–354.

Emperor Francis and various Habsburg officials had a phobia about liberalism and secret societies, but so did the rulers of many other states during the immediate post-Napoleonic period. Then, too, in 1814–1815 the Austrian police and censorship restrictions were no more onerous than those in many other Italian and European states, and they were less oppressive than those of the Napoleonic regime. In Venetia the Austrians pursued the same police and censorship practices as in Lombardy. Of course, a number of Lombard conspirators who had plotted to overthrow the Austrian government in Italy were arrested in December, 1814, and January, 1815; however, the vast majority of Lombards, as well as Venetians, were unaffected by the arrest of the ringleaders of the Brescian-Milanese conspiracy and indignant over the very idea that a handful of disgruntled officers were machinating to disturb the tranquillity of their country.

Then why did considerable hostility develop towards the Habsburgs in the province which was relatively well treated by them? In the province which was subjected to oppressive economic policies and where the administration was disorganized and inefficient the majority of the inhabitants remained loyal. To find the real clue one must look not to economic and political but to ideological, psychological, and sociological factors. Part of the answer lies in the fact that the Lombards had been much more favored by Napoleon than the Venetians. The French emperor had flattered the ego of the Lombards, particularly the Milanese, by making Milan the center of a brilliant court life. Their pride was wounded when Milan became the capital of a mere province. The Venetians, on the other hand, who had never been favored by the French, had not been particularly happy with the Kingdom of Italy. Also, they scorned and distrusted the Lombards, whom they accused of willingly cooperating with the French to reduce Venice to the status of an impoverished second-class city.

Then, too, a much larger number of persons who had suddenly risen to power and influence during the Napoleonic period—the bourgeois intellectuals and professional people, government officials and army officers, traders and businessmen—lived in Lombardy than in Venetia. As Bellegarde wrote Baron von Hager on August 10, 1815,[145] the political, economic, and social power and privileges of

145 In a letter sent from Milan and published in Helfert, *Kaiser Franz und die Stiftung des lombardo-venetianischen Königreichs*, Appendix XV, pp. 572–579.

this newly risen middle class were dependent on the "liberal" revolutionary system which the French emperor had inaugurated in Italy. Seeing their newly gained power and affluence threatened by the Habsburg regime, and longing for a "liberal" government in which they would play the dominant role, the bourgeoisie, with some of the liberal nobility who had been created and flattered by Napoleon, and a number of clergy who had cooperated with the Napoleonic government, quite naturally constituted an element that was extremely hostile to Austrian rule in Lombardy in 1814–1815.[146]

In Venetia, where the middle class, which had never been favored by the French, was considerably smaller than in Lombardy, the great majority of the inhabitants, according to the prefectural and police reports, were content with Habsburg rule. The nobility and clergy on the whole were strongly pro-Austrian and unalterably opposed to the principles of the French Revolution and the Napoleonic government. With rare exceptions, the urban workers and the great mass of peasants and agricultural workers were inimical to the previous French government, friendly to the Austrian regime, and devoted to the Habsburg sovereign. Although most of the professional classes, especially the lawyers, students, physicians, and other "intelligentia," were still enamored of revolutionary ideas and as a consequence hostile to Habsburg interests, and although some of the mercantile and business groups were pro-French and "liberal" in attitude, apparently a fairly substantial majority of the bourgeoisie were pro-Austrian. If not, they were uninterested in political matters.[147]

The sharp difference between Lombard and Venetian public opinion must be taken into account when evaluating the successes and failures of the Austrian provisional government in Lombardy-Venetia in 1814–1815. It can not be denied that the Austrian administration was lamentably inefficient and that the financial and taxation policies of the Habsburgs were oppressive in one of their newly reacquired Italian provinces. Also, in both areas the Habsburgs were dominated by a phobia about secret societies which prompted them to maintain an excessively careful watch over potentially dangerous subversive groups. Nonetheless, it is significant that it was the Venetians, who suffered the most from Habsburg administrative and

146 *Ibid.*, pp. 472–477.
147 See, for example, prefect of Adige department to Goëss, Verona, October 22, 1815, A. S. (Venice), Presidio di governo, 1815–1819, Fasc. II 10/1, ad No. 6830/P.P.

financial practices, who were pro-Austrian, and that it was the Lombards, who were comparatively well off, who were the most critical of the Habsburgs. Had Austrian political, financial, and economic practices been as shortsighted and harsh as various nationalist historians have maintained, surely the Venetians would have been equally as anti-Habsburg as the Lombards. Although one might assume that economic and political conditions should have been most important in determining Lombardo-Venetian public opinion in 1814 and 1815, evidence seems to point to the fact that they were over-balanced by the pro-liberal convictions of the bourgeoisie, who were much more numerous in Lombardy than in Venetia; the resentment of the Lombards over losing the privileged positions accorded them by the French; and the fears of the Lombard middle class that the Habsburgs were a real threat to their newly gained power and influence. The Habsburgs can be charged with lack of wisdom for not dealing more effectively with these ideological, psychological, and sociological factors; however, this does not necessarily mean that their government in Lombardy-Venetia was tyrannical or oppressive in 1814–1815.

BIBLIOGRAPHY

ARCHIVAL MATERIAL

VIENNA

Haus-, Hof-, und Staatsarchiv (cited as St. A.[Vienna])
Conferenz Akten, Ser. a and b, 1813–1815. An invaluable source, investigated by the author in 1937–1938, which was unfortunately totally destroyed during World War II.
F. M. Lt. Graf Bubna, Geheime Correspondenz, 1816–1819
Diego Graf Guicciardi, Geheime Correspondenz, 1816–1820
Hofreisen
Kabinets-Akten, 1813–1818. Contains summaries of many of the police reports destroyed during the July, 1927, burning of the Ministry of Justice Palace.
Kaiser Franz Akten
Staatskanzlei Akten
Staatskanzlei, 1815, An Bellegarde
Staatskanzlei, Bello Severoli
Staatskanzlei, Provinzen
Staatskanzlei, Provinzen, Lombardei-Venedig
Staatskanzlei, Vorträge
Staats-Rath Akten, 1814–1815. Examined in 1937–1938. Destroyed during World War II.

Hofkammer Archiv
Central-Organisirungs-Hof-Commission Akten, 1814–1815
Central-Organisirungs-Hof-Commission Akten, Rinna
Kredit Akten, 1813–1815

Kriegs-Archiv
Feld Akten (Italien), 1814
Feld Akten (Frimont in Italien), 1815
Hof Kriegs-Rath—Präsidial Akten, Italien, 1814–1815.
Kriegs-Ministerium Akten, 1813–1815

Verwaltungsarchiv

Hofkanzlei Akten. It should be noted that most of this material was destroyed in the 1927 burning of the Ministry of Justice building.

Hofkanzlei, Lombardei-Venedig
Hofräte, Lombardei-Venedig
Polizeihofstelle

Unterrichtsarchiv

Studienhofcommission Akten, 1814–1815

MILAN

Archivio di Stato (cited as A. S. [Milan])

Commissario Plenipotenziario I. R. Lomb. Veneto. Presidenza di governo. Atti secreti, 1814–1818 (cited as Presidenza di governo. Atti secreti)

Commissione Plenipotenziaria presieduta dal Conte di Bellegarde. Nearly all the valuable documents in this archive were destroyed during World War II. What is left is now together in a single *busta*. The writer took a few excerpts from these documents for the year 1814 in 1938.

Uffici e Tribunali Regi, Parte moderne, Cart. LI (Tribunali. Governo Reggenza. Provvid. gener. 1814–1815); Cart. LII (Governo Reggenza. Impiegati, 1814–1815); Cart. LIII (Appuntamenti 1814); Cart. LIV (Appuntamenti 1815); Cart. LV (Governo. Uffici diversi); Cart. LVI–LVII–LVIII (Governo, Registro Generale del Regno d'Italia e della Reggenza Austriaca, 2 gennaio al luglio 1814); Cart. LIX–LX–LXI; and Cart. LXII

Biblioteca Ambrosiana

"Atto d'accusa contro Giovanni Soveri Latuada, Teodoro Conte Lechi, Gaspare Bellotti, ecc. ecc." Handwritten text in bound MSS volume entitled "Autografi del Prof. Rasori e del Conte P. Latta."

Mantovani, Luigi, "Diario politico-ecclesiastico di Milano. Estratti dal Diario Politico-Ecclesiastico di Milano del Canonico Mantovani." Manuscript given to the Ambrosiana Library on February 12, 1889, by Dr. Carlo Casati.

Biblioteca di Brera

"Protocolli originali della reggenza provvisoria del Regno d'Italia nel 1814" (filed under the name De Pagave)

Museo del Risorgimento italiano

Carte del Giacomo Beccaria. Copious notes were taken from these valuable papers in 1938. Unfortunately the papers themselves were destroyed during World War II.

VENICE

Archivio di Stato (cited as A. S. [Venice])

Governo veneto, 1814–1821
Atti Hiller, 1813
Dazi consumo, 1814
Finanza, 1813–1814

Imposta, 1814
Oggetti di polizia, 1814
Organizzazione, 1813–1814
Polizia, 1813–1814
Pubblico politico, 1813

Presidenza di governo, 1813–1848
Presidio di governo, 1814
Presidio di governo, 1815
Presidio di governo, 1815–1819
Presidio di governo, 1815–1819, Censo
Presidio di governo, 1815–1819, Finanza
Presidio di governo, 1815–1819, Oggetti politici di stato
Presidio di governo, 1815–1819, Polizia

Museo del Risorgimento italiano

"Il diario di Emanuele Cicogna"

PRINTED CONTEMPORARY RECORDS

Allgemeine Zeitung. Mit allerhöchsten Privilegien, 1813–1815.

Amyot. *Recueil des traités, conventions et actes diplomatiques concernant l'Autriche et l'Italie.* Paris: Lahure et Cie., 1859.

The Annual Register, or a View of the History, Politics, and Literature, for the Year 1814. London: Baldwin, Cradock, and Joy, 1815.

*Appello ad Alessandro, Imperatore e Autocrate di tutte le Russie, sul destino dell'Italia. Scritto nelle tre lingue dall'editore dell'*Italico [Bozzi Granville]. London: Ricardo and Taylor, 1814.

Arese, Franco, and Achille Giussani (eds.). *Carteggio di Federico e Teresa Confalonieri. Aggiunte al Carteggio del Conte Federico Confalonieri, pubblicato da Giuseppe Gallavresi.* Milan: Museo del Risorgimento e Raccolte Storiche del Comune di Milano, 1956.

[Belgiojoso-Trivulzio, Principessa Cristina]. *Étude sur l'histoire de la Lombardie dans les trente dernières années, ou des causes du défaut d'énergie chez les Lombards. Manuscrit d'un Italien, publié par H. Lézat de Pons.* Paris: Jules Laisné, 1846. In 1847 an anonymous Italian edition of the same work was published in Paris under the title: *Studi intorno alla storia della Lombardia negli ultimi trent'anni e delle cagioni del difetto d'energia dei Lombardi. Manoscritto in francese di un Lombardo, voltato in italiano da un Francese.*

Bollettino delle leggi della Repubblica Italiana e del Regno d'Italia. 27 vols. Milan: n.p., 1802–1814.

Borda, Andrea. See Gallavresi

Bossi, Giuseppe. See "Memorie inedite di Giuseppe Bossi"

Canonici, Giambattista. *Della mia vita. Narrazione apologetica.* Bologna: Volpe, 1848.

Carte segrete ed atti ufficiali della polizia austriaca in Italia dal 4 giugno 1814 al 22 marzo 1848. 3 vols. Turin: Tipografia Elvetica, 1851–1852.

Casati, Gabrio (ed.). *Federico Confalonieri, Memorie e lettere.* 2 vols. Milan: Ulrico Hoepli, 1889–1890. Cited as Confalonieri, *Memorie e lettere.*

Castlereagh, Viscount. See Vane

Cauchard-D'Hermilly, G. F. *Des Carbonari et des fendeurs Charbonniers.* Paris: Chez L'Huillier, 1822.

Codice civile de'francesi. Vol. XII of *Raccolta delle leggi, provvidenze, manifesti ec. pubblicati sotto l'attuale R. Governo. Cominciando dalli 26. maggio 1799 in poi.* 43 vols. Turin: Dalla Stamperia Davico e Picco, [1799]–1814.

Codice civile generale austriaco. 2nd official ed. Milan: Della cesarea regia stamperia, 1815.

Codice di procedura civile. Vol. XXII of *Raccolta delle leggi, provvidenze, manifesti ec.*

Codice penale, ossia dei delitti e delle pene. Vol. XXXV of *Raccolta delle leggi, provvidenze, manifesti ec.*

Codice penale universale austriaco coll'appendice delle più recenti norme generali. 2nd official ed. Milan: Dall'imp. regia stamperia, 1815.

Collezione di leggi e regolamenti pubblicati dall'imp. regio governo delle provincie venete, 1813–1815. Venice: Andreola, 1814–1816.

Confalonieri, Federico. See Arese; Casati; Gallavresi

Confalonieri, Teresa. See Arese

Correspondance de Napoléon Ier: publiée par ordre de l'empereur Napoléon III. 32 vols. Paris: H. Plon, J. Dumaine, 1858–1870.

D'Angeberg, Comte [Chodźko, Jacob Leonard]. *Le Congrès de Vienne et les traités de 1815.* 2 vols. Paris: Ch. Lahure, 1864.

Dernière campagne de l'armée franco-italienne, sous les ordres d'Eugène-Beauharnais, en 1813 et 1814, suivie de mémoires secrets sur la révolution de Milan, du 20 avril 1814, et les deux conjurations du 25 avril 1815; la campagne des Autrichiens contre Murat; sa mort tragique, et la situation politique actuelle des divers états d'Italie, par le chevalier S. J°°°, témoin oculaire. Paris: J. G. Dentu, 1817.

Fabi, Massimo. *Milano e il ministro Prina. Narrazione storica del Regno d'Italia (aprile 1814). Tratta da documenti editi ed inediti.* Novara: Agostino Pedroli, 1860.

The Fate of the Carbonari. Memoirs of Felice Foresti. Translated by Howard R. Marraro. New York: Italian Historical Society, 1932.

Filipuzzi, Angelo. *Pio IX e la politica austriaca in Italia dal 1815 al 1848 nella relazione di Riccardo Weiss di Starkenfels. Prefazione di Roberto Cessi.* Vol. XXXVI of *Studi e documenti di storia del Risorgimento.* Florence: Felice le Monnier, 1958.

Filos, Francesco. *Autobiografia. Memorie e confessioni di me stesso. Con note a cura di Bruno Emmert.* Rovereto: Ugo Grandi, 1924.

Foresti, Felice. See *The Fate of the Carbonari.*

Foscolo, Ugo. *Opere complete.* 2 vols. Naples: n.p., 1860.

———. "Epistolario," *Opere complete,* Vol. II, pp. 1–365.

———. "Prose politiche," *Opere complete,* Vol. I, pp. 545–715.

Francis II (I). *Politische Gesetze und Verordnungen für die Oesterreichischen, Böhmischen und Galizischen Erbländer. Auf allerhöchsten Befehl, und unter Aufsicht des Directorii herausgegeben.* Vols. I–XVI (1792–1801) published, Vienna: k. k. Hof- und Staats- Aerarial-Druckerey, 1815–1817; Vols. XVII–LXIII (1802–1835) published, Vienna: k. k. Hof- und Staats-Druckerey, 1806–1837.

Freska, Frederick. *A Peace Congress of Intrigue (A Vivid, Intimate Account of the Congress of Vienna Composed of the Personal Memoirs of Its Important Participants).* Translated by Harry Hansen. New York: Century, 1919.

Gallavresi, Giuseppe (ed.). *Carteggio del conte Federico Confalonieri ed altri documenti spettanti alla sua biografia; con annotazioni storiche.* 3 vols. Milan: Ripalta, 1910–1913.

——— (ed.). *Il carteggio intimo di Andrea Borda.* Estratto dall'Archivio storico lombardo, Vol. XLVII (1920). Milan: Tipogr. Pont. ed Arcio S. Giuseppe, 1921.

———. "I ricordi ed il carteggio del conte Ludovico Giovio," *Periodico della Società storica della Provincia e antica Diocesi di Como,* Vol. XVII–XVIII (1906–1908), pp. 221–250.

———. "Testimonianze tratte dalle carte Giovio per la storia dei fatti del 1814," *Bollettino ufficiale del primo congresso storico del Risorgimento italiano* (1906), pp. 131–137.

Gebhardt, Bruno (ed.). *Wilhelm von Humboldt's politische Denkschriften.* 2 vols. Berlin: Behr, 1903.

Gerhard, Dietrich, and William Norvin (eds.). *Die Briefe Barthold Georg Niebuhrs.* 2 vols. Berlin: Walter de Gruyter & Co., 1929.

Gesetzbuch der Grossen Freymaurer-Loge Royale York zur Freundschaft oder des unter Constitution und zu dem System der Grossen Mutterloge R. Y. z. F. vereinigten Logenbundes. Berlin: Orient von Berlin, 1806.

Giornale dipartimentale dell'Adriatico, 1814.

Giornale di Venezia, 1814–1815.

Giornale italiano, 1814–1815.

Giovio, Ludovico. See Gallavresi.

Governo Austriaco. *I Carbonari, ecc.* Milan: Dall'imp. regia stamperia, 1824.

Granville, Paulina B. (ed.). *Autobiography of A[ugustus] B[ozzi] Granville, M.D., F.R.S.—being eighty-eight years of the life of a physician who practised his profession in Italy, Greece, Turkey, Spain, Portugal, the West Indies, Russia, Germany, France, and England.* 2 vols. London: Henry S. King & Co., 1874.

Hansard, T. C. *The Parliamentary Debates from the Year 1803 to the Present Time.* London: Hansard, 1804—.

Huegel, Baron von. See Lemmi

Humboldt, Wilhelm von. See Gebhardt

Journal historique sur la campagne du Prince Eugène, en Italie, pendant les années 1813 et 1814, par L. D****, capitaine attaché à l'état-major du Prince, et chevalier de la légion d'honneur. Paris: Plancher, Delaunay, et Guibert, 1814.

Klüber, Johann Ludwig. *Acten des Wiener Congresses in den Jahren 1814 und 1815.* 8 vols. Erlangen: J. J. Palm and Ernst Enke, 1815–1819.

Koch, Christophe G. de, and Friedrich Schoell. *Histoire abrégé des traités de paix, entre les puissances de l'Europe, depuis la paix de Westphalie.* 15 vols. Paris: Gide, 1817–1818.

Kropatschek, Joseph. *Oestreichs Staatsverfassung vereinbart mit den zusammengezogenen bestehenden Gesetzen, zum Gebrauche der Staatsbeamten, Advokaten, Oekonomen, Obrigkeiten, Magistraten, Geistlichen, Bürger und Bauern, zum Unterrichte, für angehende Geschäftsmänner.* 8 vols. and 1 supplement. Vienna: Johann Georg Edlen von Mössle, [1794–1804].

Lemmi, Francesco (ed.). *La restaurazione in Italia nel 1814 nel diario del barone von Huegel (9 decembre 1813–25 mai 1814).* Milan: Albrighi, Segati e C., 1910.

Luzio, Alessandro. *Nuovi documenti sul processo Confalonieri.* Milan: Albrighi, Segati e C., 1908.

———. *Il Processo Pellico-Maroncelli secondo gli atti ufficiali segreti.* Milan: L. F. Cogliati, 1903.

M***, *Des projets de l'Autriche sur l'Italie.* Paris: P. Mongie, 1821.

Manuel maçonnique, ou Tuileur de tous les rites de maçonnerie pratiques en France; dans lequel on trouve l'Étymologie et l'Interprétation des Mots et des Noms mystérieux de tous les Grades qui composent les différens Rites. Par un vétéran de la maçonnerie. Paris: Hubert et Brun, 1820.

Marchand. See *Mémoires de Marchand.*

Martens, Geo. Fréd., and Charles. *Nouveau recueil de traités d'alliance, de paix, de trève, de neutralité, de commerce, de limites, d'échange, etc. et de plusieurs autres actes servant à la connaissance des rélations étran-*

gères des puissances et états de l'Europe. 16 vols. and supplement. Göttingen: Dietrich, 1817–1842.

Melzi d'Eril, Francesco, Duca di Lodi. *Memorie-documenti e lettere inedite di Napoleone I. e Beauharnais. Raccolte e ordinate per cura di Giovanni Melzi.* 2 vols. Milan: Gaetano Brigola, 1865.

Mémoires de Marchand, premier valet de chambre et exécuteur testamentaire de l'empereur, publiés d'après le manuscrit original par Jean Bourguignon. Vol. I: *L'île d'Elbe—les cent-jours.* Paris: Plon, 1952.

Memoirs of the Secret Societies of the South of Italy, Particularly the Carbonari. Translated from the original manuscript. London: Murray, 1821.

"Memorie inedite di Giuseppe Bossi," *Archivio storico lombardo,* Vol. V (1878), pp. 275–307.

Napoleon I. "L'île d'Elbe et les cent-jours," *Correspondance de Napoléon Ier, publiée par ordre de l'empereur Napoléon III,* Vol. XXXI, pp. 1–158.

————. See also *Correspondance de Napoléon Ier*; Melzi d'Eril.

Niebuhr, Barthold Georg. See Gerhard and Norvin

Notizie del mondo, 1814–1815.

Oesterreichischer Beobachter, 1814–1815.

Oesterreichisch-Kaiserliche privilegirte Wiener Zeitung nebst Amtsblatt, 1814–1815. Cited as *Wiener Zeitung.*

Orloff, Grégoire. *Mémoires historiques, politiques et littéraires sur le royaume de Naples.* 5 vols. Paris: Chasseriau et Hécart, 1819–1821.

Pedrotti, Pietro. *Note autobiografiche del cospiratore trentino Gioacchino Prati, con annotazioni e commenti. Sulla base di documenti inediti d'archivio.* Rovereto: Ugo Grandi, 1926.

Philo's [Adolf Kniegge's] endliche Erklärung und Antwort, auf verschiedene Anforderungen und Fragen, die an ihn ergangen, seine Verbindung mit dem Orden der Illuminaten betreffend. Hanover: Schmidtschen Buchhandlung, 1788.

Pilot, A. "Venezia nel blocco del 1813–14. Da noterelle inedite del Cicogna," *Nuovo Archivio Veneto,* Vol. XIV (1914), pp. 191–227.

Prati, Gioacchino. See Pedrotti

Précis historique des opérations militaires de l'armée d'Italie, en 1813 et 1814, par le chef de l'état-major-général de cette armée. Paris: Barrois, 1817.

Quadri, Antonio. *Prospetto statistico delle provincie venete.* Venice: Francesco Andreola, 1826.

Raccolta degli atti del governo e delle disposizioni generali emanate dalle diverse autorità in oggetti sì amministrativi che giudiziarj, 1814–1815. Milan: Imp. regia stamperia, 1816–1817. Cited as *Atti del governo lombardo.*

Raccolta delle leggi, provvidenze, manifesti ec. pubblicati sotto l'attuale R. Governo. Cominciando dalli 26. maggio 1799 in poi. 43 vols. Turin: Dalla Stamperia Davico e Picco, [1799]–1814.

"Ricordi di Felice Foresti sui Carbonari, sui processi del Veneto nel 1821, e sulle vittime dello Spielbergo," in Atto Vanucci, *I martiri della libertà italiana. Dal 1794 al 1848.* 3rd ed. Florence: Felice le Monnier, 1860. Pp. 605–639.

Rinieri, P. Ilario. *Corrispondenza inedita dei cardinali Consalvi e Pacca nel tempo del Congresso di Vienna (1814–1815); ricavata dall'archivio secreto vaticano, corredata di sommarii e note. Preceduta da uno studio storico sugli stati d'Europa nel tempo dell'impero napoleonico, e sul nuovo assestamento europeo e da un diario inedito del Mse. di San Marzano.* Rome: Unione Tipografico, 1903.

————. *I costituti del Conte Confalonieri e il Principe di Carignano.* Turin: Renzo Streglio e C., 1902.

Saint-Edme, M. [E. T. Bourg]. *Constitution et organisation des Carbonari, ou documens exacts sur tout ce qui concerne l'existence, l'origine et le but de cette société secrète.* Paris: Corby, Peytieux, Delaunay, Pelicier, 1821.

Salata, Francesco, and Achille Giussani (eds.). *I costituti di Federico Confalonieri.* Vols. I–III edited by Francesco Salata and published, Bologna: Nicola Zanichelli, 1940–1941; Vol. IV edited by Achille Giussani and published, Rome: Istituto Storico Italiano per l'Età Moderna e Contemporanea, 1956.

Sandonà, Augusto. *Contributo alla storia dei processi del ventuno e dello Spielberg. Dagli atti ufficiali segreti degli archivi di Stato di Vienna e dal carteggio dell'imperatore Francesco I co'suoi ministri e col presidente del Senato Lombardo-Veneto del Tribunale supremo di Giustizia (1821–1838).* Turin: Bocca, 1911.

Santorre di Santarosa. *Delle speranze degli Italiani. Opera edita per la prima volta con prefazione e documenti inediti da Adolfo Colombo.* Milan: Casa editrice Risorgimento R. Caddeo & Co., 1920.

Spadoni, Domenico. *Per la prima guerra d'indipendenza italiana nel 1815. Proclami, decreti, appelli ed inni.* Pavia: Istituto pavese di arti grafiche, 1929.

Statuti generali della Società dei Liberi Muratori. Del Rito Scozzese antico ed accettato, stampati a cura del F ∴ V ∴ della M ∴ L ∴ LA SEBEZIA OR ∴ DI NAPOLI. 2nd ed. Naples: Fibreno, 1863.

The Times (London), 1814–1815.

Vane, Charles, Marquis of Londonderry (ed.). *Memoirs and Correspondence of Viscount Castlereagh, Second Marquess of Londonderry.* Vols. I–IV published, London: Colburn, 1848–1849. Vols. V–XII published under the title of *Correspondence, Despatches, and other Papers of Vis-*

count Castlereagh, Second Marquess of Londonderry. London: Shoberl, 1851–1853.

La vérité sur les cent jours, principalement par rapport à la renaissance projetée de l'empire romain; par un citoyen de la Corse. Brussels: H. Tarlier, 1825. In 1829 an Italian edition was published under the title, *Delle cause italiane nell'evasione dell'imperatore Napoleone da l'Elba.*

Webster, Charles K. *British Diplomacy, 1813–1815 (Select Documents dealing with the Reconstruction of Europe).* London: Bell and Sons, 1921.

Weil, M[aurice] H[enri]. *Les dessous de Congrès de Vienne, d'après les documents originaux des archives du ministère impérial et royal de l'intérieur à Vienne.* 2 vols. Paris: Payot, 1917.

Wilson, Robert. *Private Diary of Travels, Personal Services, and Public Events, during Mission and Employment with the European Armies in the Campaigns of 1812, 1813, 1814.* 2 vols. London: Murray, 1861.

Wit von Dörring, Johannes. *Fragmente aus meinem Leben und meiner Zeit.* Brunswick: Friedrich Bieweg, 1827. French edition published under the following title: Witt, Jean, *Les sociétés secrètes de France et d'Italie, ou Fragments de ma vie et de mon temps.* Paris: Levasseur, 1830.

SPECIAL ARTICLES AND REPRINTS

Arese, Franco. "La Lombardia e la politica dell'Austria: un colloquio inedite del Metternich nel 1832," *Archivio storico lombardo,* Vol. LXXVII (1950), pp. 5–57.

Aretin, Karl Otmar von. "Eugene Beauharnais' Königreich Italien beim Übergang zur österreichischen Herrschaft im April 1814. Aus den nachgelassenen Papieren des k. k. Feldzeugmeisters Ludwig Frhr. v. Welden," *Mitteilungen des Österreichischen Staatsarchivs,* Vol. XII (1959), pp. 257–288.

Avena, Antonio. "La censura delle stampe in Verona durante la dominazione austriaca (1814–1866)," *Il Risorgimento Italiano,* Vol. II (1909), pp. 952–1035.

Bandini, Gino. "Carboneria e Guelfismo nei Costituti dei Carbonari del Polesine," *Rivista d'Italia, Lettere, Scienza ed Arti,* Vol. IX, Fasc. 9 (September, 1906), pp. 489–506.

Barazzoni, Marga. "Le società segrete germaniche ed i loro rapporti con i cospiratori lombardi del 1821," *Rassegna storica del Risorgimento,* Vol. XIX, Fasc. 1 (January–March, 1932), pp. 89–138.

Barbiera, Raffaello. "La polizia austriaca e le spie a Milano," *Nuova Antologia. Rivista di Lettere, Scienze ed Arti,* 6th ser., Vol. CXCIII, Fasc. 1103 (January, 1918), pp. 33–42.

Bastari, Pietro. "Paolo Olini," *Nel Cinquantenario delle X Giornate.* Brescia: L'Istituto Sociale d'Istruzione, 1899. Pp. 47–50.

Berger, Wilhelm von, "Freimaurerei und französische Revolution," *Die Freimaurerei Österreich-Ungarns. Zwölf Vorträge am 30. und 31. März und 1. April 1897 zu Wien gehalten.* Vienna: B. Herder Verlag, 1897. Pp. 163–199.

Bersano, Arturo, "Adelfi, Federati e Carbonari. Contributo alla Storia delle Società segrete," *Atti della Reale Accademia delle Scienze di Torino,* pubblicati dagli accademici segretari delle due classi, Vol. XLV (1909–1910), pp. 409–430.

Biandrà Trecchi, Dario. *Milano e gli inglese nel 1814.* Estratto dal *Rassegna storica del Risorgimento,* Vol. XIII (1926), pp. 521–554.

Blaas, Riccardo. "Carlo Altieri, un confidente di Metternich," *Rassegna storica del Risorgimento,* Vol. XLIV, Fasc. 4 (October–December, 1957), pp. 611–635.

Bonfadini, R. "Federico Confalonieri," *Nuova Antologia. Rivista di Lettere, Scienze ed Arti,* 4th ser., Vol. LXXII, Fasc. 24 (December, 1897), pp. 671–687.

Boyer, Ferdinand. "Pierre Lagarde, policier de Napoléon à Venise en 1806," *Rassegna storica del Risorgimento,* Vol. XLIV, Fasc. 1 (January–March, 1957), pp. 88–95.

Briguglio, Letterio. "Aspetti della politica ecclesiastica austriaca nell'opera dei censori veneti (1798–1805)," *Rassegna storica del Risorgimento,* Vol. XLIV, Fasc. 4 (October–December, 1957), pp. 644–653.

Brusatti, Alois. "Graf Philipp Stadion als Finanzminister," *Österreich und Europa. Festgabe für Hugo Hantsch zum 70. Geburtstag.* Graz: Verlag Styria, 1965. Pp. 281–294.

Buccella, M. R. "La congiura e l'offerta dell'impero romano a Napoleone all'isola d'Elba," *Nuova Antologia. Rivista di Lettere, Scienze ed Arti,* Anno LXV, Fasc. 1393 (April, 1930), pp. 352–362.

Buquoy, Ferdinand. "Von Kaisers Franz Logenverbot bis 1848," *Die Freimaurerei Österreich-Ungarns,* pp. 234–259.

Cantimori, Delio. "Nuovi contributi alla storia della società segrete," *Nuova Rivista Storica,* Vol. XLI, Fasc. 2 (May–August, 1957), pp. 480–486.

Cantù, C. "Il Conciliatore. Episodio del liberalismo lombardo," *Archivio storico italiano,* 3rd ser., Vol. XXIII (1876), pp. 80–114, 272–296, and 469–488; Vol. XXIV (1876), pp. 90–114, 270–290, and 452–468; and Vol. XXV (1877), pp. 65–83.

Capograssi, Antonio. "L'unità d'Italia nel pensiero di Lord William Bentinck," *Rassegna storica del Risorgimento,* Vol. XXI, Fasc. 2 (March–April, 1934), pp. 227–257.

Castelnuovo, Enrico. *A Venezia, un secolo fa. Discorso letto nell'adu-*

nanza solenne del 25 maggio. Estratto d'*Atti del Reale Istituto Veneto di Scienza, Lettere ed Arti* (1912–1913). Venice: C. Ferrari, 1913.

Castro, Giovanni de. "La restaurazione austriaca in Milano (1814–1817). Notizie desunte da diarj e testimonianze contemporanee," *Archivio storico lombardo,* Vol. XV (1888), pp. 591–658 and 905–979.

――――. "I ricordi autobiografici inediti del marchese Benigno Bossi," *Archivio storico lombardo,* Vol. XVII (1890), pp. 894–937.

Cessi, Roberto. "Il Veneto nel Risorgimento," *Rassegna storica del Risorgimento,* Vol. XLIV, Fasc. 4 (October–December, 1957), pp. 569–601.

Chiattone, Domenico. "Nuovi documenti su Federico Confalonieri per le sue relazioni intime e patriottiche prima del processo," *Archivio storico lombardo,* Vol. XXXIII (1906), pp. 47–114.

Cipolla, C. "Un Documento austriaco sui Massoni e sui Carbonari," *Rassegna Nazionale,* Vol. VII (1885), pp. 478–500.

Comandini, Alfredo. "Un Milanese per l'Italia a Londra nel 1814," *Il Secolo,* April 10, 1919, no pp. given.

Demarco, Domenico. "L'economia degli stati italiani prima dell'unità," *Rassegna storica del Risorgimento,* Vol. XLIV, Fasc. 2–3 (April–September, 1957) pp. 191–258.

Desjoyaux, Claude. "Le général baron Perrone di San Martino," *Il Risorgimento Italiano,* Vol. IV (1911), pp. 973–1009.

Favaro, Antonio, "La università di Padova un secolo fa," *Atti e memorie della R. Accademia di Scienze, Lettere ed Arti in Padova,* Anno CCCLXXV (1915–1916), new ser., Vol. XXXII (1916), pp. 107–117.

Fraenkel, Hans. "Politische Gedanken und Strömungen in der Burschenschaft um 1821–1824," *Quellen und Darstellungen zur Geschichte der Burschenschaft und der deutschen Einheitsbewegung, herausgegeben von Herman Haupt,* Vol. III. Heidelberg: Carl Winter's Universitätsbuchhandlung, 1912. Pp. 241–326.

Francovich, Carlo. "Gli Illuminati di Weishaupt e l'idea egualitaria in alcune società segrete del Risorgimento," *Movimento operaio. Rivista di storia e bibliografia,* new ser., Vol. IV (July–August, 1952), pp. 553–597.

Frati, Carlo. "Ricordi di Prigionia. Memorie autobiografiche e frammenti poetici di Giovanni Rasori," *"Biblioteca di Storia Italiana Recente (1800–1870),* Vol. IX. Turin: Bocca, 1921. Pp. 1–132.

Fulin, R. "E. A. Cicogna. Discorso letto nell'aula del R. Liceo Marco Polo nell'occasione della festa letteraria XVII marzo MDCCCLXXII," *Archivio Veneto,* Vol. III, Pt. 2 (1872), pp. 211–240.

Furlani, Silvio. "Augusto Bozzi Granville e l'Austria," *Rassegna storica del Risorgimento,* Vol. XXXIV, Fasc. 1–2 (January–June, 1947), pp. 65–73.

Gallavresi, Giuseppe. "La franc-maçonnerie e la formation de l'unité italienne," *Revue des questions historiques*, Vol. XCVII, No. 2 (October, 1922), pp. 415–437.

————. "Per una futura biografia di F. Confalonieri," *Archivio storico lombardo*, Vol. XXXIV (1907), pp. 428–470.

————. "Ricerche intorno alla rivoluzione milanese del 1814," *Rendiconti del Reale Istituto lombardo di Scienze e Lettere*, 2nd ser., Vol. XL, Fasc. 7 (1907), pp. 403–415.

————. "La rivoluzione lombarda del 1814 e la politica inglese secondo nuovi documenti," *Archivio storico lombardo*, Vol. XXXVI (1909), pp. 97–166.

Ghisalberti, Carlo. "Sulle amministrazioni locali in Italia nel periodo napoleonico," *Rassegna storica del Risorgimento*, Vol. XLVII, Fasc. 1 (January–March, 1960), pp. 33–54.

Godechot, Jacques. "Démographie et économie dans les origines du Risorgimento," *Rassegna storica del Risorgimento*, Vol. XLIV, Fasc. 2–3 (April–September, 1957), pp. 382–389.

————. "I francesi e l'unità italiana sotto il direttorio," *Rivista Storica Italiana*, Vol. LXIV, Fasc. 4 (1952), pp. 548–580.

Haas, Arthur G. "Kaiser Franz, Metternich und die Stellung Illyriens," *Mitteilungen des Österreichischen Staatsarchivs*, Vol. XI (1958), pp. 373–398.

Helfert, Joseph Alexander. "Die Anfänge der Freimaurerei in den habsburgischen Erblanden unter Karl VI. und Maria Theresia," *Die Freimaurerei Österreich-Ungarns*, pp. 38–77.

Johnston, R. M. "Lord William Bentinck and Murat," *The English Historical Review*, Vol. XIX (1904), pp. 263–280.

K[armin], O. "L'esprit public en Italie, en juin 1814, d'après un diplomate autrichien," *Revue historique de la révolution française et de l'empire*, Vol. XI (January–June, 1917), p. 322.

Lehning, Arthur. "Buonarroti and His International Secret Societies," *International Review of Social History*, Vol. I, Pt. 1 (1956), pp. 112–140.

Lemmi, Francesco. "La fine di Gioacchino Murat," *Archivio storico italiano*, 5th ser., Vol. XXVI (1900), pp. 250–294.

————. "Gioacchino Murat e le aspirazioni unitarie nel 1815," *Archivio storico per le province napoletane*, Vol. XXVI (1901), pp. 169–211.

Lumbroso, Alberto. "Conte Teodoro Lechi da Brescia (1778–1866) e la sua famiglia," *Rivista storica del Risorgimento italiano*, Vol. III, Fasc. 4 (1898), pp. 349–373.

Luzio, Alessandro, "La Massoneria sotto il Regno italico e la restaurazione austriaca," *Archivio storico lombardo*, Vol. XLIV (1917–1918), pp. 241–362. A separate reprint of this article was published in Milan by Cogliati in 1918. Another reprint was published in Milan by the *Archivio storico lombardo* in 1921.

Maddalena, A. de. "I prezzi dei generi commestibili e dei prodotti agricoli sul mercato di Milano dal 1800 al 1890." Fasc. 3 of *Archivi economico dell'unificazione italiano*, Vol. V (1957).

Malamani, Vittorio. *L'Austria e i Bonapartisti (1815–1848). Studi fatti negli archivi del governo austriaco nel Lombardo-Veneto.* Estratto dalla *Rivista Storica Italiana*, Vol. VII, Fasc. 2 (1890). Turin: Bocca, 1890.

————. "La censura austriaca delle stampe nelle provincie venete," *Rivista storica del Risorgimento italiano*, Vol. I, Fasc. 5–6 (1896), pp. 489–521; Vol. II, Fasc. 7–8 (1897), pp. 692–726; and *Il Risorgimento Italiano*, Vol. II (1909), pp. 491–541.

Manfra, Modestino Remigio. "Melchiorre Gioia Economista. Ambiente politico e ambiente culturale del Gioia," *Nuova Rivista Storica*, Vol. XXXII, Fasc. 1–3 (January–June, 1948), pp. 50–68.

Mangini, Nicola. "La politica scolastica dell'Austria nel Veneto dal 1814 al 1848," *Rassegna storica del Risorgimento*, Vol. XLIV, Fasc. 4 (October–December, 1957), pp. 769–783.

Marcolongo, Bianca. "La massoneria nel secolo XVIII," *Studi Storici*, Vol. XIX (1910), pp. 407–477.

————. "Le origini della Carboneria e le Società segrete nell'Italia Meridionale dal 1810 al 1820," *Studi Storici*, Vol. XX (1912), pp. 233–348.

Marx, Julius. "Die amtlichen Verbotslisten. Neue Beiträge zur Geschichte der österreichischen Zensur im Vormärz," *Mitteilungen des Österreichischen Staatsarchivs*, Vol. XI (1958), pp. 412–466.

Mathiez, Albert. "L'origine franc-comtoise de la Charbonnerie italienne," *Annales historiques de la Révolution française*, Vol. V, No. 6 (November–December, 1928), pp. 551–561.

Mazziotti, M. "L'offerta del trono d'Italia a Napoleone I esule all'Elba," *Rassegna storica del Risorgimento*, Vol. VII, Fasc. 1 (January–March, 1920), pp. 1–18.

Miani-Calabrese, Donato. "Politica economica e politica sociale nel pensiero di Melchiorre Gioia," *Rivista di Politica Economica*, Vol. XLV, Fasc. 1–2 (January–February, 1955), pp. 34–45.

Monti, Antonio. "G. D. Romagnosi. Contributo biografico," *Nuova Antologia. Rivista di Lettere, Scienze ed Arti*, 6th ser., Vol. CXCV, Fasc. 1111 (May, 1918), pp. 41–50.

————. "L'impresa di Gioacchino Murat nel 1815 e la prima guerra di indipendenza," *Rendiconti del Reale Istituto lombardo di Scienze e Lettere*, 2nd ser., Vol. LXIII, Fasc. 2 (1930), pp. 191–200.

Nardi, Carlo. "La vita di Francesco Saverio Salfi (1759–1832)," *Rassegna storica del Risorgimento*, Vol. VII, Fasc. 2 (April–September, 1920), pp. 161–332.

"L'origine e lo scopo della Carboneria secondo i costituti de'primi Carbonari e Guelfi," *La Civiltà Cattolica,* Vol. LXVI (June, 1915), pp. 641–661.

Ottolini, Angelo, "Nel mondo settario: i Raggi e i Centri," *Rassegna storica del Risorgimento,* Vol. IV, Fasc. 6 (November–December, 1917), pp. 693–705.

———. "Noterelle Foscoliane," *La Lombardia nel Risorgimento italiano,* Vol. III (1916), pp. 27–45.

———. "U. Foscolo e la risoluzione dell'esilio," *Archivio storico lombardo,* Vol. LV (1928), pp. 168–180.

Palermo, F. "Pietro Colletta, uomo di stato e scrittore," *Archivio storico italiano,* new ser., Vol. III, Pt. 1 (1856), pp. 61–78.

Pardi, Giuseppe. "Nuove notizie sull'origine della Carboneria e di qualche altra Società segreta," *Nuova Rivista Storica,* Vol. X, Fasc. 6 (November–December, 1926), pp. 469–477.

Patetta, Federico. "La congiura torinese del 1814 per la rinascita dell'Impero Romano e per l'offerta del trono a Napoleone," *Atti della Reale Accademia delle Scienze di Torino,* Vol. LXXII (1936), pp. 276–327.

Pedrotti, Pietro. "Governatori austriaci durante i primi anni del restaurazione," *Rassegna storica del Risorgimento,* Vol. XXXIV, Fasc. 1–2 (January–June, 1947), pp. 58–64.

———. "La Missione segreta del Consigliere Aulico De Sardagna in Italia durante i processi dei Carbonari," *Il Risorgimento Italiano,* Vol. XXII (1929), pp. 161–224.

——— and Antonio Zieger. "Giovanni Wit von Doerring e le sue memorie," *Rassegna storica del Risorgimento,* Vol. XIX, Fasc. 4 (October–December, 1932), pp. 311–314.

Perrero, Domenico. "Il generale conte Alessandro di Gifflenga e la congiura militare lombarda del 1814," *Rivista storica del Risorgimento italiano,* Vol. I (1895), pp. 295–304.

Pesci, Ugo. "La principessa Belgioioso," *La Rassegna Nazionale,* Vol. XXIV (July, 1902), pp. 330–340.

Pingaud, Albert. "La Lombardie en 1814," *Revue d'histoire diplomatique,* Vol. XLI (1927), pp. 434–467.

Quilici, Nello. "Felix Austria in Lombardia," *Nuovi problemi di politica, storia ed economia,* Vol. II, Fasc. 3–4 (March–April, 1931), pp. 129–180.

Raich, Johann Michael. "Freimaurerische Principien und Logensysteme," *Die Freimaurerei Österreich-Ungarns,* pp. 1–37.

Rath, R. John. "L'amministrazione austriaca nel Lombardo Veneto (1814–1821)." Fasc. 1 of *Archivio economico dell'unificazione italiana,* Vol. IX (1959).

———. "The Austrian Provisional Government in Lombardy-Venetia, 1814–1815," *Journal of Central European Affairs,* Vol. II, No. 3 (October, 1942), pp. 249–266.

————. "The *Carbonari*: Their Origins, Initiation Rites, and Aims," *The American Historical Review*, Vol. LXIX, No. 2 (January, 1964), pp. 353–370.

————. "La costituzione guelfa e i servizi segreti austriaci," *Rassegna storica del Risorgimento*, Vol. L, Fasc. 3 (July–September, 1963), pp. 343–376.

————. "Economic Conditions in Lombardy and Venetia, 1813–1815, and their Effects on Public Opinion," *Journal of Central European Affairs*, Vol. XXIII, No. 3 (October, 1963), pp. 267–281.

————. "The Habsburgs and the Great Depression in Lombardy-Venetia, 1814–18," *The Journal of Modern History*, Vol. XIII, No. 3 (September, 1941), pp. 305–320.

————. "The Habsburgs and Public Opinion in Lombardy-Venetia, 1814–1815," in Edward Mead Earle (ed.). *Nationalism and Internationalism: Essays Inscribed to Carlton J. H. Hayes*. New York: Columbia University Press, 1950. Pp. 303–335.

————. "Training for Citizenship in the Austrian Elementary Schools during the Reign of Francis I," *Journal of Central European Affairs*, Vol. IV, No. 2 (July, 1944), pp. 147–164.

Rèbora, Clemente. "G. D. Romagnosi nel pensiero del risorgimento," *Rivista d'Italia, Lettere, Scienza ed Arti*, Vol. XIV, Fasc. II (November, 1911), pp. 808–839.

Rinieri, P. Ilario. "Le sette in Italia dopo la restaurazione del 1814. La congiura di Macerata (1817)," *Il Risorgimento Italiano*, Vol. XIX, Fasc. 1–2 (January–June, 1926), pp. 1–76.

Rodocanachi, E. "La police secrète autrichienne et les français dans les provinces lombardo-vénitiennes de 1815 à 1819," *Revue historique*, Vol. CXXVIII (May–August, 1918), pp. 85–91.

Rosa, Pia Onnis. "Propaganda e rapporti di società intorno al 1817 (Rey, Blanc, Buonarroti)," *Rassegna storica del Risorgimento*, Vol. LI, Fasc. 4 (October–December, 1964), pp. 481–504.

Rosselli, John. "Il progetto italiano di Lord William Bentinck, 1811–1815," *Rivista Storica Italiana*, Vol. LXXIX, Fasc. 2 (1967), pp. 355–404.

S. F. "Giandomenico Romagnosi e la congiura milanese del 1814," *Bollettino Storico Piacentino*, Vol. XXII, Fasc. 3 (July–September, 1927), pp. 120–123.

Salvisenti, Bernardo. "La missione Porro presso le Alte Potenze nel 1814," *La Lombardia nel Risorgimento italiano*, Vols. I–II (June, 1914), pp. 33–45 (two vols. in one).

Schiarini, Pompilio. "La prima impresa per l'indipendenza italiana e la battaglia di Tolentino," *Atti e memorie della R. Deputazione di Storia Patria per le Marche*, new ser., Vol. X, Fasc. 2 (May–December, 1915), pp. 219–257.

Solitro, Giuseppe. "Maestri e scolari dell'università di Padova nell'ultima dominazione austriaca (1813–1866)," *L'Archivio Veneto-Tridentino,* Vol. I (1922), pp. 109–193.

Solmi, Arrigo. "L'idea dell'unità italiana nell'età napoleonica," *Rassegna storica del Risorgimento,* Vol. XX, Fasc. 1 (January–March, 1933), pp. 1–19.

Sorbelli, Albano. "Gli studenti bolognesi per Gioacchino Murat e per l'indipendenza italiana nel 1815," *L'Archiginnasio. Bollettino della Biblioteca comunale di Bologna,* Vol. XI (1916), pp. 203–212.

Soriga, Renato. "Augusto Bozzi Granville e la Rivista 'L'Italico'," *Bollettino della Società pavese di storia patria,* Vol. XIV (1914), pp. 265–301.

———. "Bagliori unitari in Lombardia avanti la restaurazione austriaca (1814)," *Bollettino della Società pavese di storia patria,* Vol. XV, Fasc. 1–2 (January–June, 1915), pp. 3–18.

———. "Gl'inizi della Carboneria in Italia secondo un rapporto segreto del generale Giuseppe Rossetti," *Il Risorgimento Italiano,* Vol. XXI, Fasc. 1 (January–March, 1928), pp. 72–80.

———. "Pavia e i moti del 1821," *La Lombardia nel Risorgimento italiano,* Vol. XIII (July, 1928), pp. 47–68.

———. "Pietro Custodi cospiratore," in Renato Soriga, *Le Società segrete, l'emigrazione politica e i primi moti per l'indipendenza. Scritti raccolti e ordinati da Silio Manfredi* (Vol. XXIX of *Collezione storica del Risorgimento italiano*). Modena: Società tipografica modenese, 1942. Pp. 137–145.

———. "Il primo Grande Oriente d'Italia," *Bollettino della Società pavese di storia patria,* Vol. XVII, Fasc. 1–4 (January–December, 1917), pp. 94–115. A reprint was published in Pavia in 1917 by Premiata Tipografia Successori Fratelli Fusi.

———. "La ristampa milanese della 'Lira focense' di Antonio Ierocades," *Rassegna storica del Risorgimento,* Vol. V, Fasc. 4 (October–December, 1918), pp. 727–738.

———. "Settecento massonizzante e massonismo napoleonico nel primo risorgimento italiano," *Bollettino della Società pavese di storia patria,* Vol. XIX, Fasc. 1–4 (January–December, 1919), pp. 23–85. Also printed in Soriga, *Le Società segrete,* pp. 1–60.

———. "Le società segrete e i moti del '21 in Piemonte," in Soriga, *Le Società segrete,* pp. 107–136.

———. "Le società segrete e i moti del 1820 a Napoli," *Rassegna storica del Risorgimento,* Vol. VIII, Centennial Fasc. (1921), pp. 147–178.

———. "Ugo Foscolo e il suo amico anglo-italo Augusto Bozzi Granville," *La Lombardia nel Risorgimento italiano,* Vol. XIII (January, 1928), pp. 121–140.

Spadoni, Domenico. "Aspirazioni unitarie d'un austriacante nel 1814,"

La Lombardia nel Risorgimento italiano, Vol. XVIII (July, 1933), pp. 71–80.

―――. "Bologna e Pellegrino Rossi per l'indipendenza d'Italia nel 1815," *Rassegna storica del Risorgimento,* Vol. III, Fasc. 1–2 (January–April, 1916), pp. 103–145.

―――. "Carlo Comelli de Stuckenfeld e il trono de'Cesari offerto a Casa Savoja nel 1814," *Rassegna storica del Risorgimento,* Vol. XIV, Fasc. 4 (October–December, 1927), pp. 593–656.

―――. "Nel centenario del proclama di Rimini," *Rassegna storica del Risorgimento,* Vol. II, Fasc. 2 (March–April, 1915), pp. 329–363.

―――. "I documenti della congiura milanese carpita da St Agnan nel 1814," *Il Risorgimento Italiano,* Vol. XIX, Fasc. 3 (July–September, 1926), pp. 299–326.

―――. "Federazione e Re d'Italia mancati nel 1814–15," *Nuova Rivista Storica,* Vol. XV, Fasc. 5–6 (September–December, 1931), pp. 398–433.

―――. "Il Foscolo cospiratore nel 1813–14," *Studi su Ugo Foscolo, editi a cura della R. Università di Pavia nel primo centenario della morte del poeta.* Turin: Giovanni Chiantore, 1927. Pp. 555–600.

―――. "Il gen. bar. Giacomo Filippo de Meester," *Rassegna storica del Risorgimento,* Vol. XVI, Fasc. 4 (October–December, 1929), pp. 847–896.

―――. "Un poeta estemporaneo carbonaro (Leopoldo Fidanza)," *La Lombardia nel Risorgimento italiano,* Vol. XIII (July, 1928), pp. 31–45.

―――. "Il processo per la congiura bresciano-milanese del 1814," *Atti del XIII Congresso Nazionale tenutosi in Genova nei giorni 26–28 ottobre 1925.* Genoa: G. B. Marsano, 1926. Pp. 81–99.

―――. "Quella del 1815 fu veramente la prima guerra per l'indipendenza italiana?" *Atti del XV Congresso Nazionale della Società nazionale per la storia del Risorgimento italiano, tenutosi in Macerata nei giorni 1–2–3 settembre 1927,* pp. 121–134.

―――. "Le società segrete nella rivoluzione milanese dell'aprile 1814," *Nuova Antologia. Rivista di Lettere, Scienze ed Arti,* 7th ser., Vol. CCLXV (May, 1929), pp. 197–211.

―――. "Il sogno unitario e wilsoniano d'un patriota nel 1814–15," *Rassegna storica del Risorgimento,* Vol. XIII, Fasc. 2 (April–June, 1926), pp. 341–355.

―――. "Gli Statuti della Guelfia in possesso della Polizia austriaca nel 1816," *Rassegna storica del Risorgimento,* Vol. XI, Fasc. 3 (July–September, 1924), pp. 704–738.

―――. "L'unione guelfa in Roma," *Roma. Rivista di studi e di vita romana,* Vol. XVI, No. 4 (April, 1938), pp. 154–163.

―――. "I volontari per l'indipendenza italiana nel 1815," *Atti e memo-*

rie della R. Deputazione di Storia Patria per le Marche, new ser., Vol. X, Fasc. 2 (May–December, 1915), pp. 297–330.

Tonni-Bazza, V. "La congiura militare bresciana del 1814," *Nel Cinquantenario delle X Giornate,* pp. 45–47.

———. "Silvio Moretti (1772–1832)," *Nel Cinquantenario delle X Giornate,* pp. 13–15.

Trecchi, Dario Biandrà. "Milano e gli Inglesi nel 1814. La missione del barone Trecchi," *Rassegna storica del Risorgimento,* Vol. XXIV, Fasc. 2 (March–April, 1937), pp. 521–554.

Tucci, U. "Le monete del regno lombardo-veneto dal 1815 al 1866." Fasc. 3 of *Archivio economico dell'unificazione italiana,* Vol. II (1956).

Verga, Ettore, "La deputazione dei collegi elettorali del regno d'Italia a Parigi nel 1814," *Archivio storico lombardo,* Vol. XXXI (1904), pp. 303–333.

Vianello, C. A. "Sulla caduta del Regno Italico. Note ad illustrazione di un carteggio Dandolo-Benincasa (1814)," *Il Risorgimento,* Vol. VIII, Fasc. 3 (October, 1956), pp. 133–158.

Zieger, Antonio, "I primi risultati delle ricerche austriache sui massoni lombardi nel 1814 e 1815," *La Lombardia nel Risorgimento italiano,* Vol. XIII (July, 1928), pp. 5–29.

SPECIAL WORKS

Amante, Bruto. *I napoletani nel 1815. La prima guerra per l'unità d'Italia.* Campobasso: Cav. Giovanni Colitti e figlio, 1916.

Arneth, Alfred Ritter von. *Johann Freiherr von Wessenberg, ein österreichischer Staatsmann des neunzehnten Jahrhunderts.* 2 vols. in 1. Vienna: Braumüller, 1898.

Bandini, Gino. *Giornali e scritti politici clandestini della Carboneria romagnola (1819–1821).* No. 8 of *Biblioteca Storica del Risorgimento Italiano,* 8th ser. Rome: Società editrice Dante Alighieri di Albrighi, Segati e C., 1908.

Beer, Adolf. *Die Finanzen Österreichs im XIX. Jahrhundert. Nach archivalischen Quellen.* Prague: F. Tempsky, 1877.

Beidtel, Ignaz. *Geschichte der österreichischen Staatsverwaltung, 1740–1848.* 2 vols. Innsbruck: Wagner'schen Universitäts-Buchhandlung, 1896–1898.

Bersano, Arturo. *L'abate Francesco Bonardi e i suoi tempi. Contributo alla storia delle società segrete.* Turin: Deputazione subalpina di storia patria, 1957.

Biadego, Giuseppe. *La dominazione austriaca e il sentimento pubblico a Verona dal 1814 al 1847.* Rome: Società editrice Dante Alighieri, 1899.

Bianchi, Matteo. *Geografia politica dell'Italia*. Florence: Società Editrice Fiorentina, 1845.

Blesch, Josephine. *Studien über Johannes Wit, genannt v. Dörring und seine Denkwürdigkeiten nebst einem Exkurs über die liberalen Strömungen von 1815–1819*. Heft 63 of *Abhandlungen zur Mittleren und Neueren Geschichte*. Berlin: Verlagsbuchhandlung Dr. Walter Rothschild, 1917.

Bonfadini, R[omualdo]. *Mezzo secolo di patriotismo. Saggi storici*. 2nd ed. Milan: Fratelli Treves, 1886.

Boni, Filippo de. *Lo straniero in Lombardia*. Milan: Carlo Turati, 1848.

Caemmerer, Rudolf von. *Die Befreiungskriege, 1813–1815. Ein strategischer Überblick*. Berlin: Ernst Siegfried Mittler und Sohn, 1907.

Cantù, Cesare. *Il Conciliatore e i Carbonari*. Milan: Fratelli Treves, 1878.

————. *Della indipendenza italiana cronistoria*. 3 vols. Turin: Unione Tipografico, 1872–1877.

Capograssi, Antonio. *Gl'inglesi in Italia durante le campagne napoleoniche: Lord W. Bentinck*. Bari: Gius. Laterza e Figli, 1949.

Castro, Giovanni de. *I congiurati lombardi del 1814. Conferenza tenuta al Circolo Filologico di Milano l'8 aprile 1894*. Milan: Max Kantorowicz, 1894.

————. *Milano e le cospirazioni lombarde (1814–1820) giusta le poesie, le caricature, i diari e altre testimonianze dei tempi*. Milan: Fratelli Dumolard, 1892.

————. *Il mondo secreto*. 9 vols. Milan: G. Daelli & C., 1864.

————. *Principio di secolo: storia della caduta del regno italico*. 2nd ed. Milan: Treves, 1897.

Ceria, Luigi. *L'eccidio del Prina e gli ultimi giorni del regno italico (1814)*. Milan: Mondadori, 1937.

Clavel, F. T. B. *Histoire pittoresque de la franc-maçonnerie et des sociétés secrètes anciennes et modernes*. 3rd ed. Paris: Pagnerre, 1844.

Colletta, Pietro. *Storia del reame di Napoli dal 1734 sino al 1825*. 2 vols. Florence: Felice le Monnier, 1848.

Cutolo, Alessandro. *Il duca di Brindisi*. Milan: Aldo Martello, n.d.

D'Ancona, Alessandro. *Federico Confalonieri. Su documenti inediti di archivj pubblici e privati*. 2nd ed. Milan: Treves, 1898.

Deschamps, N. *Les sociétés secrètes et la société ou philosophie de l'histoire contemporaine*. 6th ed. 2 vols. Paris: Oudin, 1882.

Dito, Oreste. *La campagna murattiana della indipendenza d'Italia secondo i rapporti del Ministro di Polizia Napoletana ed altri documenti ufficiali. Con un'appendice sulla morte del Murat a Pizzo*. Milan: Società editrice Dante Alighieri di Albrighi, Segati & C., 1911.

————. *Massoneria, carboneria ed altre società segrete nella storia del*

Risorgimento italiano, con appendice ed illustrazioni. Turin: Roux e Viarengo, 1905.

Eisenstein, Elizabeth L. *The First Professional Revolutionist: Filippo Michele Buonarroti (1761–1837). A Biographical Essay.* Cambridge, Massachusetts: Harvard University Press, 1959.

Fabietti, Ettore. *I Carbonari.* Milan: Istituto per gli studi di politica internazionale, 1942.

Falcionelli, Albert. *Les sociétés secrètes italiennes. Les Carbonari.—La Camorra. La Mafia.* Paris: Payot, 1936.

Ferrieri, Pio. *Dalla via del Monte di Pietà allo Spielberg.* Milan: Fratelli Dumolard, 1889.

Findel, J. G. *Geschichte der Freimaurerei von der Zeit ihres Entstehens bis auf die Gegenwart.* 2 vols. Leipzig: Hermann Luppe, 1861.

Francovich, Carlo. *Albori socialisti nel Risorgimento. Contributo allo studio delle società segrete (1776–1835).* Florence: Felice le Monnier, 1962.

Frost, Thomas. *The Secret Societies of the European Revolution, 1776–1876.* 2 vols. London: Tinsley Brothers, 1876.

Greenfield, Kent Roberts. *Economics and Liberalism in the Risorgimento: A Study of Nationalism in Lombardy, 1814–1848.* Baltimore: The Johns Hopkins Press, 1934.

Gualterio, F[ilippo] A[ntonio]. *Gli ultimi rivolgimenti italiani. Memorie storiche, con documenti inediti.* 4 vols. Florence: Felice le Monnier, 1850–1851.

Haas, Arthur G. *Metternich, Reorganization and Nationality 1813–1818: A Story of Foresight and Frustration in the Rebuilding of the Austrian Empire.* Wiesbaden: Franz Steiner Verlag, 1963.

Helfert, Joseph Alexander. *La caduta della dominazione francese nell'alta Italia e la congiura militare bresciano-milanese nel 1814.* Bologna: Zanichelli, 1894. An Italian translation of the author's *Ausgang der französischen Herrschaft in Ober-Italien und Brescia-Miländer Militär-Verschwörung,* which was first published in 1890 in Vol. LXXVII, No. 2, of *Archiv für österreichische Geschichte.* Vienna: Alfred Hölder, 1890.

———. *Joachim Murat. Seine letzten Kämpfe und sein Ende. Mit Benützung von Schriftstücken des k. k. Haus- Hof- und Staats-Archivs.* Vienna: Manz'sche k. k. Hof- Verlags- und Universitäts-Buchhandlung, 1878.

———. *Kaiser Franz I. von Österreich und die Stiftung des Lombardo-Venetianischen Königreichs. Im Zusammenhang mit den gleichzeitigen allgemeinen Ereignissen und Zuständen Italiens.* Vol. VII of *Quellen und Forschungen zur Geschichte, Litteratur und Sprache Österreichs und seiner Kronländer.* Innsbruck: Wagner'schen Universitäts-Buchhandlung, 1901.

———. *Zur Geschichte des Lombardo-Venezianischen Königreichs.*

Vol. XCVIII of *Archiv für österreichische Geschichte*. Vienna: Alfred Hölder, 1908.

Hoch, Carl, and Herm. Ign. Bidermann. *Der österreichische Staatsrath (1760–1848)*. Vienna: Wilhelm Braumüller, 1879.

Holtz, Georg von. *Die innerösterreichische Armee 1813 und 1814*. Vol. IV of Alois Veltzé (ed.), *1813–1815: Österreich in den Befreiungskriegen*. Vienna: Edlinger, 1912.

Horneffer, August. *Die Freimaurerei*. 3rd ed. Stuttgart: Reclam Verlag, 1948.

Houssave, Henry. *1815: la première restauration—le retour de l'île d'Elbe—les cent jours*. 66th ed. Paris: Perrin et Cie, 1920.

Italy. Ministero della guerra, commando del corpo di stato maggiore— ufficio storico. *Gli Italiani in Illiria e nella Venezia (1813–1814)*. Rome: Libreria dello Stato, 1930.

Johnston, R. M. *The Napoleonic Empire in Southern Italy and the Rise of the Secret Societies*. 2 vols. London: MacMillan, 1904.

Knoop, Douglas, and G. P. Jones. *An Introduction to Freemasonry*. Manchester: Manchester University Press, 1937.

Lemmi, Francesco. *La restaurazione austriaca a Milano nel 1814 (con appendice di documenti tratti dagli archivi di Vienna, Londra, Milano, ecc.)*. Bologna: Zanichelli, 1902.

Leti, Giuseppe. *Carboneria e Massoneria nel Risorgimento italiano. Saggio di critica storica*. Genoa: Libreria Editrice Moderna, 1925.

Livi, Giovanni. *Napoleone all'isola d'Elba secondo le carte di un archivio segreto ed altre, edite ed inedite*. Milan: Treves, 1888.

Lombroso, Giacomo. *Complicazioni promosse dall'Austria dal Congresso di Vienna sino all'esaltazione di Pio IX per conservare la Lombardia*. n.p.: n.p., [1848].

Lorenzoni, Antonio. *Istituzioni del diritto pubblico interno pel regno lombardo-veneto*. 4 vols. Padua: Minerva, 1835–1836.

Luzio, Alessandro. *Antonio Salvotti e i processi del ventuno*. No. 1–2 of *Biblioteca Storica del Risorgimento Italiano*, 3rd ser. Rome: Società editrice Dante Alighieri, 1901.

————. *La Massoneria e il Risorgimento italiano. Saggio storico-critico. Con illustrazioni e molti documenti inediti*. 2 vols. Bologna: Nicola Zanichelli, [1925].

Maass, Ferdinand. *Der Josephinismus. Quellen zu seiner Geschichte in Österreich 1760–1850. Amtliche Dokumente aus dem Haus-, Hof-, und Staatsarchiv und dem Allgemeinen Verwaltungsarchiv in Wien*, Vol. IV: *Der Spätjosephinismus 1790–1820*. Vienna: Herold, 1957.

Mariutti, Angela. *Organismo ed azione delle società segrete del veneto durante la seconda dominazione austriaca (1814–1847)*. Vol. III of *Miscellanea di storia veneta*. Venice: La R. Deputazione, 1930.

Martire, Egilberto. *La massoneria italiana. A proposito di una massoneria filo-cattolica.* Milan: Edizioni tramontana, 1953.

Marx, Julius. *Die österreichische Zensur im Vormärz.* Vienna: Verlag für Geschichte und Politik, 1959.

Meynert, Hermann. *Kaiser Franz I. Zur Geschichte seiner Regierung und seiner Zeit. Nach Original Mittheilungen und ungedruckten Quellen.* Vienna: Hölder, 1872.

Monti, Achille. *Giovanni Rasori nella storia della scienza e dell'idea nazionale.* In *Corsi autunnali per Italiani e stranieri tenuti nella R. Università di Pavia. Lezione e conferenze dell'anno 1928.* Pavia: Istituto pavese di arti grafiche, 1929.

Mutinelli, Fabio. *Annali delle province venete dall'anno 1801 al 1840.* Venice: G. B. Merlo, 1843.

Natali, Giovanni. *L'Italia durante il regime napoleonico: Lezioni tenute alla Facoltà di Lettere dell'Università di Bologna durante l'Anno Accademico 1954–55.* Bologna: Riccardo Patron, [1955].

Ninno, Giuseppe de. *Filadelfi e Carbonari in Carbonara di Bari negli albori del Risorgimento italiano (1816–1821).* Bari: Giuseppe Pansini & Figlio Saverio, 1922.

———. *La Setta dei Carbonari in Bari nel 1820–21. Ricordi storici seguiti da note biografiche dei deputati della Provincia di Terra di Bari al Parlamento Napoletano in detta epoca.* Bari: Prem. Stab. Tip. "Alighieri" Lella & Casini, 1911.

Nobile, Filippo Montalbano. *Le società segrete nella rigenerazione politica d'Italia.* Catania: Cav. S. di Mattei & C., 1921.

Ottolenghi, Lelio. *Padova e il Dipartimento del Brenta dal 1813 al 1815,* Padua: A. Draghi di G. B. Randi e F°., 1909.

Ottolini, Angelo. *La Carboneria dalle origini ai primi tentativi insurrezionali (1797–1817).* Vol. XVI of *Collezione storica del Risorgimento italiano.* Modena: Società tipografica modenese, 1936.

Pedrotti, Pietro. *I processi del '21 nel carteggio di Antonio Mazzetti.* Vol. II of *Documenti e Studi del Comitato Nazionale di Studi sui Prigionieri Politici Italiani dello Spielberg.* Rome: G. Bardi, 1939.

Pellet, Marcellin. *Napoléon à l'île d'Elbe—Mélanges historiques.* Paris: G. Charpentier et Cⁱᵉ, 1888.

Pieri, Piero. *Le società segrete ed i moti degli anni 1820–21 e 1831. Con 159 illustrazioni e tavole fuori testo.* 2nd ed. Milan: Francesco Vallardi, 1948.

Rath, R. John. *The Fall of the Napoleonic Kingdom of Italy (1814).* No. 484 of *Studies in History, Economics and Public Law.* New York: Columbia University Press, 1941.

Redding, Moses W. *The Illustrated History of Free Masonry.* New York: Redding & Co., 1907.

Rinieri, P. Ilario. *Della Vita e delle Opere di Silvio Pellico. Da lettere e documenti inediti.* 3 vols. Turin: Roux di Renzo Streglio, 1898–1901.

Roberti, Melchiorre. *Milano capitale napoleonica: la formazione di uno stato moderno 1796–1814.* 3 vols. Milan: Fondazione Treccani degli Alfieri per la storia di Milano, 1946–1947.

Romani, Mario. *L'agricoltura in Lombardia dal periodo delle riforme al 1859: struttura, organizzazione sociale e tecnica.* Milan: Società editrice "Vita e Pensiero," 1957.

Rosselli, John. *Lord William Bentinck and the British Occupation of Sicily 1811–14.* Cambridge: Cambridge University Press, 1956.

Rossler, Hellmuth. *Graf Johann Philipp Stadion, Napoleons deutscher Gegenspieler.* 2 vols. Vienna: Verlag Herold, 1966.

Saitta, Armando. *Filippo Buonarroti. Contributi alla storia della sua vita e del suo pensiero,* Vol. I. In *Storia ed economia. Studi, testi, documenti, quaderni.* Rome: Edizioni di "Storia e Letteratura," 1950.

Sandonà, Augusto. *Il Regno Lombardo Veneto 1814–1859, la costituzione e l'amministrazione. Studi di storia e di diritto; con la scorta degli atti ufficiali dei dicasteri centrali di Vienna.* Milan: L. F. Cogliati, 1912.

Simonyi, Ludwig von. *Geschichte des Lombardisch Venezianischen Königreich: Charakteristisch-Artistisch-Topographisch-Statistisch- und Historisch.* 2 vols. Milan: Joseph Redaeilli, 1844–1846.

Smola, Karl Freiherrn von. *Das Leben des Feldmarschalls Heinrich Grafen von Bellegarde.* Vienna: J. G. Heubner, 1837.

Solitro, Giuseppe. *Un martire dello Spielberg (il colonnello Silvio Moretti) su documenti inediti degli Archivi di Milano e di Brünn.* Padua: Fratelli Drucker, 1910.

Soriga, Renato. *Le Società segrete, l'emigrazione politica e i primi moti per l'indipendenza. Scritti raccolti e ordinati da Silio Manfredi.* Vol. XXIX of *Collezione storica del Risorgimento italiano.* Modena: Società tipografica modenese, 1942.

Spadoni, Domenico. *Milano e la congiura militare nel 1814 per l'indipendenza italiana: Il moto del 20 aprile e l'occupazione austriaca.* Modena: Società tipografica modenese, 1936.

———. *Milano e la congiura militare nel 1814 per l'indipendenza italiana: La congiura militare e il suo processo.* Modena: Società tipografica modenese, 1937.

———. *Milano e la congiura militare nel 1814 per l'independenza italiana: I giudizi di Mantova e la sorte dei congiurati.* Modena: Società tipografica modenese, 1937.

———. *Sette, cospirazioni e cospiratori nello stato pontificio all'indomani della restaurazione. L'occupazione napoletana; la restaurazione e le sette.* Rome: Roux e Viarengo, 1904.

Srbik, Heinrich Ritter von. *Metternich, der Staatsmann und der Mensch.* 3 vols. Munich: F. Bruckmann, 1925, 1954.

Tarlé, Eugène. *Le Blocus continental et le Royaume d'Italie. La Situation économique de l'Italie sous Napoléon Ier d'après des documents inédits.* Paris: Félix Alcan, 1928.

Valente, Angela. *Gioacchino Murat e l'Italia meridionale.* Turin: Giulio Einaudi, 1941.

Walter, Friedrich. *Die Zeit Franz' II. (I.) und Ferdinands I. (1792–1848).* Vol. I of *Die österreichische Zentralverwaltung,* Pt. II: *Von der Vereinigung der österreichischen und böhmischen Hofkanzlei bis zur Einrichtung der Ministerialverfassung (1749–1848).* Vienna: Adolf Holzhausens Nachfolger, 1956.

Wangermann, Ernst. *From Joseph II to the Jacobin Trials: Government Policy and Public Opinion in the Habsburg Dominions in the Period of the French Revolution.* London: Oxford University Press, 1959.

Weil, M[aurice] H[enri]. *Joachim Murat, roi de Naples. La dernière année de règne (mai 1814–mai 1815).* 5 vols. Paris: Albert Fontemoing, 1909–1910.

———. *Le prince Eugène et Murat 1813–1814; opérations militaires, négociations diplomatiques.* 5 vols. Paris: Albert Fontemoing, 1902.

Welden, Ludwig von. *Der Krieg der Österreicher in Italien gegen die Franzosen in den Jahren 1813 und 1814.* Graz: Damian u. Sorges' Universitäts-Buchhandlung, 1853.

Wiedemann-Warnhelm, Adolf von. *Die Wiederherstellung der österreichischen Vorherrschaft in Italien (1813–1815).* Vienna: Adolf Holzhausen, 1912.

Zanoli, Alessandro. *Sulla milizia cisalpino-italiana. Cenni storico-statistici dal 1796 al 1814.* 2 vols. Milan: Borroni e Scotti, 1845.

GENERAL HISTORIES AND REFERENCES

Balbo, Cesare. *Della storia d'Italia dalle origini fino ai nostri giorni; sommario, a cura di Fausto Nicolini.* 2 vols. Bari: G. Laterza & figli, 1913–14.

Benedikt, Heinrich, *Kaiseradler über dem Apennin. Die Österreicher in Italien 1700 bis 1866.* Vienna: Verlag Herold, 1964.

Berkeley, G. F. H. *Italy in the Making 1815 to 1846.* Cambridge: Cambridge University Press, 1932.

Bermann, Moriz. *Oesterreich-Ungarn im neunzehnten Jahrhundert. Mit besonderer Berücksichtigung aller wichtigen Vorfälle in der Geschichte,*

Wissenschaft, Kunst, Industrie und dem Volksleben. Vienna: Hugo Engel, 1884.

Bianchi, Nicomede. *Storia della politica austriaca rispetto ai sovrani ed ai governi italiani dall'anno 1791 al maggio del 1857.* Savona: Luigi Sambolino, 1857.

Bibl, Viktor. *Der Zerfall Österreichs: Kaiser Franz und Sein Erbe.* Vienna: Rikola Verlag, 1922.

Botta, Carlo. *History of Italy during the Consulate and Empire of Napoleon Buonaparte.* 2 vols. London: Baldwin & Cradock, 1828.

Cusani, Francesco. *Storia di Milano dall'origine ai nostri giorni e cenni storico-statistici sulle città e province lombarde.* 8 vols. Milan: Pirotta, 1861–1884.

Ferrari, Giuseppe. *La rivoluzione e i rivoluzionari in Italia (dal 1796 al 1844).* Palermo: Remo Sandron, 1901.

Ghisalberti, Alberto M. *Gli albori del Risorgimento italiano (1700–1815).* Rome: Paolo Cremonese, 1931.

―――. *Introduzione alla storia del Risorgimento.* Rome: Edizioni cremonese della S. A. editrice Perrella, 1942.

Hantsch, Hugo. *Die Geschichte Österreichs,* Vol. II: *1648–1918.* Graz: Styria Steirische Verlagsanstalt, n.d.

King, Bolton. *A History of Italian Unity, Being a Political History of Italy from 1814 to 1871.* 2 vols. New York: Scribner's, 1899.

Lemmi, Francesco. *Le origini del Risorgimento italiano (1748–1815).* 2nd ed. Milan: Ulrico Hoepli, 1924.

Leo, Heinrich. *Geschichte der italienischen Staaten.* 5 vols. Hamburg: Perthes, 1829–1837.

Peverelli, P[ietro], *Storia di Venezia dal 1798 sino al nostri tempi.* 2 vols. in 1. Turin: Castellazzo e Deguadenzi, 1852.

Reuchlin, Hermann. *Geschichte Italiens von der Gründung der regierenden Dynastien bis zur Gegenwart.* 4 vols. Leipzig: Hirzel, 1859–1873.

Spellanzon, Cesare. *Storia del Risorgimento e dell'unità d'Italia,*Vol. I. Milan: Rizzoli & C., 1933.

Springer, Anton. *Geschichte Österreichs seit dem Wiener Frieden 1809.* 2 vols. Leipzig: Hirzel, 1863–1865.

Storia di Milano, Vol. XIII: *L'età napoleonica (1796–1814).* Milan: Fondazione Treccani degli Alfieri per la storia di Milano, 1959.

Tivaroni, Carlo. *L'Italia prima della rivoluzione francese (1735–1789).* Vol. I of *Storia critica del Risorgimento italiano.* Turin: Roux e C., 1888.

―――. *L'Italia durante il dominio francese (1789–1815).* Vols. II–III of *Storia critica del Risorgimento italiano.* 2 vols. Turin: L. Roux e C., 1889. Cited in the footnotes, Tivaroni, *L'Italia durante il dominio francese (1789–1815),* Vols. I and II.

Vannucci, Atto. *I martiri della libertà italiana. Dal 1794 al 1848*. 3rd ed. Florence: Felice le Monnier, 1860.

Wurzbach, Constant von. *Biographisches Lexikon des Kaiserthums Österreich, enthaltend die Lebensskizzen derjenigen Personen, welche seit 1750 in den österreichischen Kronländern gelebt und gewirkt haben*. 60 vols. Vienna: Universitäts-Buchdruckerei von Zamarski, 1856–1891.

INDEX

396